CONSTRUCTION
MATERIALS
AND
PROCESSES

CONSTRUCTION MATERIALS AND PROCESSES

DON A. WATSON, AIA, FCSI
Member of the American Institute of Architects
Fellow of the Construction Specifications Institute
Assistant Professor of Architecture, Pasadena City College

McGRAW-HILL BOOK COMPANY
New York   San Francisco   St. Louis
Düsseldorf   Johannesburg   Kuala Lumpur
London   Mexico   Montreal
New Delhi   Panama   Rio de Janeiro
Singapore   Sydney   Toronto

This book was set in Melior by Applied Typographic Systems and printed and bound by Levison McNally Company. The designer was Janet Bollow. The editors were Cary F. Baker, Jr., and Marge Woodhurst. Charles A. Goehring supervised production.

**CONSTRUCTION
MATERIALS
AND
PROCESSES**

Printed in the United States of America.

Library of Congress catalog card number: 72–38622

67890 HAHA 79876

07–068467–7

CONTENTS

The material in this book has been selected and organized for students in architecture, architectural drafting, specifications writing, building construction, materials, or related lower-division courses in universities, technical institutes, community colleges, and trade schools. Although the book is intended primarily as a text, some materials and construction processes are covered in more depth than would be necessary for classroom purposes. Thus it also serves as a reference for those in the design professions and the construction industry.

Students and those in the architectural and construction fields who have not yet gained a knowledge of the mechanical and electrical trades through experience will be able to see the relation of these specialized materials and assemblies to construction as a whole. Electrical and mechanical engineers, whose experience usually does not include the construction of buildings, require some knowledge of the materials and processes that relate to their own work. Of course, the engineering calculations necessary for the proper exploitation of many materials and structural systems are not covered in detail, since an exhaustive study of individual materials is beyond the scope of this book.

As a guide to more detailed information on particular materials or processes, a list of references for further study is included at the end of each chapter. In addition, a list of trade associations, with their current addresses, is included as an appendix. Although not all associations concerned with construction materials are included, and such associations form, dissolve, and relocate with alarming frequency, this list does provide a starting point for gathering up-to-date, authoritative information on materials and processes.

With the advent of new materials and the prefabricated or integrated assemblies produced for systems construction, it is no longer possible to study only the basic raw materials of construction. Those assemblies are discussed which would be of value to the designer, draftsman, or specifications writer in preparing a set of working drawings or specifications. Particular attention is given to definitions of terms. Since building codes, trade practices, and terms vary greatly throughout the United States, the coverage is of necessity general. Where there are wide variances in usage or nomenclature, common regional trade practices are discussed.

The manufacture of materials and the basis of selection among alternative materials are covered briefly. Materials testing is discussed only where such tests are usually conducted by supervisors or inspectors on the job site. Laboratory testing and physical or chemical composition are discussed only as necessary to clarify the properties of the finished product.

It would be impossible to list all sources of the information in this book. Many technical books devoted to one aspect or another of the material covered were frequently consulted. Manufacturers' and association literature provided information available nowhere else. I thank those who furnished the data and copy for the hundreds of

photographs, tables, and drawings. Wherever possible, credits have been given either with illustrations or tables.

My special thanks to the following experts who reviewed portions of the manuscript and brought me up to date on the latest materials and processes: George Lavenberg, FCSI, of the Ceramic Tile Institute; Ralph Lane, FCSI, of PPG Industries; R. Redmond Coghlan, AIA, FCSI, of Powell, Morgridge, Richards and Coghlan; Clyde Barnes of the Sheet Metal Industry Fund of Los Angeles; Allen Bears of Dunn-Edward Paint Company; Archie McMullan of Sinclair Paint Company; James Klein of Southwest Portland Cement Company; and my many friends in the Construction Specifications Institute who gave freely of their time to keep me informed on new materials and their correct usage. Last, but not least, I thank my wife, Evelyn, who typed and retyped manuscript, read proof, and gave encouragement at all times.

DON A. WATSON

CONSTRUCTION
MATERIALS
AND
PROCESSES

MATERIALS EVALUATION

The evaluation and selection of materials becomes more difficult with each passing year. At one time it was possible to select a basic material, such as brick, stone, wood, or iron, and leave its assembly to the craftsman on the job. The designer must now contend with hundreds of new materials each year. Old materials are being put to new uses or are being combined with new materials to form new prefabricated or preassembled products. The processes of construction can no longer be separated from the materials themselves. Building systems that contain many basic materials must be evaluated as a whole, and not in terms of the individual components. Prefabrication is becoming more widely accepted by building-trade groups, although many of the newer building processes such as curtain-wall systems, lift-slab and tilt-up techniques of concrete construction, and integrated ceiling systems cross traditional trade jurisdictions. Building codes and zoning ordinances are also being modified to accept new materials and subassemblies of materials.

Materials and processes can be divided into several broad classifications:

Products manufactured on the job site: This group includes basic raw materials that are mixed or processed on the job site, such as concrete, mortar, plaster, and carpentry work.

Products assembled on the job site: This group consists of the assembly of manufactured products that require the assembly on the job to become a functioning system, such as masonry units, plumbing piping and fixtures, electrical wiring and devices, and roofing.

Factory-manufactured assemblies: These are products that are manufactured and assembled into units in the factory and delivered to the job site for final positioning and anchorage, such as prefabricated metal shower stalls, steel doors and frames, windows and frames, and integrated ceiling units that include lighting, air distribution, soundproofing, and insulation.

REFERENCES

There are many reference works, in both book and periodical form, to help the designer select materials and methods for assembly on the job site. Most basic materials are manufactured to rigid standards which specify their chemical and physical properties. Trade magazines present many useful articles by experts in various fields. Trade associations publish literature on new techniques and construction methods and discuss the problems that may arise in the use of specific materials.

Evaluation of factory-manufactured products that have proprietary formulations is more difficult. Virtually the only information available is that provided by the manufacturer's own literature, which often contains more sales promotion than factual data. Even though manufacturers seldom dwell on the limitations of their products, few issue literature that is deliberately misleading. The designer must learn to evaluate products on the basis of their use in a particular project.

It is not enough to evaluate a product on its merits alone. It must be compatible with adjacent products and structural systems. The designer must also determine whether it conforms to standards and building codes governing construction in the particular area in which it is to be used.

Building Codes

The materials to be selected for incorporation in a building project are governed to a great extent by local building codes. These codes have been established for the purpose of providing minimum standards to safeguard life, health, property, and public welfare by regulating and controlling the design, construction, quality of materials, use and occupancy, location, and maintenance of all structures within a given political jurisdiction. For most projects the designer must consider these local codes his primary reference source in selecting materials and construction methods. He must determine which code or codes he will be working under and thoroughly familiarize himself with their requirements. He must then keep copies of all applicable codes close at hand for constant reference.

The first known building code was prepared by Hammurabi, king of ancient Babylon, in 2250 B.C. This code was written on a black tablet discovered about 70 years ago. It consists of six short sentences, the first of which stipulates the wage the builder was to receive. Converted into today's costs and wages, this would amount to approximately 10 cents a square foot. The remaining five sentences spell out the penalties that were to be imposed if the building collapsed. If the owner of the building was killed, the architect (builder) was to be put to death. If the son of the owner was killed, the son of the architect was to be put to death. From this clear-cut performance code we have progressed to an estimated 18,000 local jurisdictions in the United States alone, which can and do promulgate their own building, electrical, and plumbing codes, some of which vary widely from each other and from standard national trade practices.

MODEL BUILDING CODES   At the present time there are four model building codes, sponsored by four different organizations:

"Basic Building Code" (BOCA), Building Officials Conference of America, Inc., 1313 East 60th Street, Chicago, Ill., 60637.

"National Building Code," American Insurance Association, 85 John Street, New York, N.Y., 10038.

"Southern Standard Building Code," Southern Building Code Congress, 116 Brown-Marx Building, Birmingham, Ala., 35203.

"Uniform Building Code" (UBC), International Conference of Building Officials, 50 South Los Robles, Pasadena, Calif., 91101.

None of these national and regional codes has any authority until it is adopted through legislative action by a municipality, county, or state. When a city has passed an ordinance adopting one of the codes, by reference, this becomes the local code. In most instances a particular edition of the code is adopted, and this edition remains the official code until a new resolution is passed adopting a later edition. As a result, one city may be operating under, say, the 1967 edition of a particular model code while an adjacent city is operating under the 1947 edition of the same code. Many cities and counties adopt the basic code with modifications that they feel are necessary in their locality. Thus, to be sure that the materials and construction techniques he selects will comply with all relevant codes and regulations, the designer must determine which basic code is in effect, which edition of that code is in effect, what modifications are in effect in that particular area, and what other agencies will be concerned with the project.

SPECIALIZED CODES   Most city and regional building codes do not cover electrical and mechanical work. Cities may adopt separate codes for these sections such as "The Uniform Plumbing Code," published by the International Association of Plumbing and Mechanical Officials, "The Uniform Mechanical Code," published jointly by the International Association of Plumbing and Mechanical Officials and the International Conference of Building Officials, or the "National Electrical Code," published by the National Fire Protection Association.

Most states have also established safety codes that apply to construction. These codes cover a wide range of subjects, such as fire protection, wall openings, scaffoldings, lifts, electrical hazards, and protection of the public. The designer must be sure that his building conforms to the requirements of the safety codes in force in that particular area.

Certain local agencies, bureaus, commissions, or committees may have a say in the design and materials used for a particular project. City planning committees, art commissions, air-pollution control districts, water-pollution control boards, fire departments, public-health departments, the Department of Health, Education and Welfare (HEW), the Department of Housing and Urban Development (HUD), and many others may have to be consulted.

UNIFORMITY OF CODES Because of the number of codes in use and their varying requirements, specifications are often confusing and inconsistent. It is difficult to understand why a particular type and grade of wood will support 1800 psi in one location but will support only 1600 psi on the other side of a political boundary. Some progress in unifying codes is being made by the National Conference of Building Officials, a coalition of officials from all 50 states working under the auspices of the National Bureau of Standards. This committee is attempting to reduce the hundreds of codes that may exist within a state to one broad standard, so that designers and builders working anywhere within the state will know what is approved and where to go for information, appeals, and testing.

Manufacturers' Literature

Literature that is provided by manufacturers must be evaluated carefully. The advertising that appears in both general publications and trade magazines tends to present products in terms of eye-catching photographs of a pretty girl holding a cast-iron sewer pipe or admiring a can of roofing compound, with catchy wording intended to influence the general public. A great deal of this type of promotional literature arrives daily on the architects' desk and goes directly into the wastebasket. However, well-done, colorful promotional literature of a nontechnical nature can be useful. Clients may have to be sold on a product when they cannot visualize how it will look in finished form. Photographic examples of buildings usually cite the architects and engineers, who can be contacted for further information.

Most large manufacturers also distribute to architects and engineers catalogs which give information on all their products. These may be bound in a hard cover and indexed so that any product manufactured by the company can be located easily. As the material becomes outdated or products are superseded by new items, the catalogs are replaced. Some manufacturers distribute hardback ring binders which their architectural representatives keep up-to-date continually.

SWEET'S CATALOG SERVICE "Sweet's Catalog File," a large collection of manufacturers' literature, published annually, is a good reference for the designer. The 1970 edition of the "Architect's Library" contains approximately 150,000 pages of information on the products of some 1800 manu-

Fig. 1-1 A Spec-Data sheet. NOTE: Right-hand side is keyed for filing. (*By permission of the Construction Specifications Institute.*)

facturers. A smaller set, limited to residential or light construction, is also published. "Sweet's Catalog File" does not solve all design problems. It contains literature from companies throughout the United States. However, the fact that an item does not appear in the file does not mean that it is not available. Many companies, both large and small, employ other forms of advertising, and so their products are not listed here. A second caution is that many of the products that are listed are not readily available in all parts of the country. The designer must make sure there is a local distributor or representative before specifying an item. Most manufacturers list their distributors on the last page of their literature. If there is no distributor nearby, it is necessary to proceed with caution and to find out beforehand whether the product can be furnished when it will be needed for construction.

These catalogs are available from Sweet's Catalog Service, F. W. Dodge Company, a division of McGraw-Hill, Inc., 330 West 42d Street, New York, N.Y., 10036. There is no charge for the catalogs. However, since they are published and distributed on the basis of contracts with the manufacturers, they are available only to those doing a given volume of business. The F. W. Dodge Company will send applications on request, which the architect or engineer must return requesting the catalog service.

A-E-C WESTERN CATALOG & REFERENCE FILE   This catalog and reference file presents building materials and products from Western manufacturers and only those products of Eastern manufacturers which are readily available from Western distribution centers. It is available free of charge to architects, engineers, designers, specifiers, and contractors throughout the fourteen Western states. Further informa-

tion on this service may be obtained from A-E-C Western Catalog & Reference File Company, 5909 West Third Street, Los Angeles, Calif., 90036.

This publication is particularly valuable because, in addition to manufacturers' literature, each issue includes reference material on a wide variety of materials and processes. The catalog also has a complete conversion sched-

Fig. 1-2 A Spec-Data II product selector. (*Information Handling Services, Inc.*)

```
08-11-02-02            *                                                              **********
                       *                     PRODUCT SELECTOR GRID                    * SPEC-D *
DOORS, WINDOWS, & GLASS *                    VSMF BUILDING PRODUCT FILE               *   A   *
WOOD DOORS             *                     ---------------------------             * II T *
    FLUSH             *                                                              *   A   *
       SOLID CORE     *                                                              **********
    ----------------* *INDICATES OTHER CUSTOM VARIATIONS AVAILABLE
*****************************************************************************************************
                       * BOURNE MFG CO.            BRADLEY PLYWOOD CORP      W. D. CROOKS & SONS
MANUFACTURER           * 7321 GRATIOT AVE          PO BOX 1428              PO BOX 908
                       * DETROIT, MI 48213         SAVANNAH, GA 31402       WILLIAMSPORT, PA 17701
                       *
    -----------------* * ----------------------    ----------------------    ----------------------
    SPEC DATA...CART/FRAME *  SPEC DATA....          SPEC DATA....            SPEC DATA....
    -----------------* * ----------------------    ----------------------    ----------------------
    CATALOG.....CART/FRAME *  CATALOG......2027/0753  CATALOG......2028/0292   CATALOG......2026/1194
    -----------------* * ----------------------    ----------------------    ----------------------
    MARKET AREAS      * NATIONAL                  SE, S,                   NATIONAL
****************************************************************************************************
BRAND NAMES           * CHEMCLAD                  CENTURY
SPECS/STANDARDS       * UNDERWRITERS LABEL        CS 171-35
    -----------------* * ----------------------    ----------------------    ----------------------
DIMENSIONS--HEIGHT    * TO 7'2"                   TO 16'
(MAXIMUM  --WIDTH     * TO 4'0"                   TO 4'
OR RANGE) --THICKNESS *                           1-3/8",1-3/4" TO 2-1/4"  1-3/8" TO 2-1/4"
    -----------------* * ----------------------    ----------------------    ----------------------
VARIATIONS--PLAIN     * PLAIN                     PLAIN                    PLAIN
       --SASH/LITE    * SASH/LITE                 SASH/LITE                VARIOUS LITE DESIGNS
       --LOUVERED     * LOUVERED
       --DECORATOR    *                                                    TO ARCHITECT'S REQ'MTS.
       --STORM        *
       --SCREEN       *
       --COMBINATION  *
       --FLUSH        * FLUSH                     FLUSH                    FLUSH
       --PANELED      *
    -----------------* * ----------------------    ----------------------    ----------------------
CORE CONSTRUCTION     * CHEMCORE OR SOLID WOOD    STAVED WOOD/CROSSBANDING
   --HOLLOW CORE      *
   --SOLID CORE       * SOLID CORE                SOLID CORE               BUILT-UP, FRAMED/DOWELED
   --MINERAL CORE     *
    -----------------* * ----------------------    ----------------------    ----------------------
MATERIALS--CORE       * WOOD                      LOW DENSITY WOOD BLOCKS  WHITE PINE
       --FACING       * LAMINATED PLASTIC         SELECTION OF HARDWOODS   CHOICE OF SAWN VENEERS
       --EDGES        * LAMINATED PLASTIC FACED                            SAME SPECIES AS VENEER
       --STILES/RAILS *
       --PANELS       *
****************************************************************************************************
COLOR/FINISH          * CHOICE--COLORS/PATTERNS
   PREFINISHED        * SATIN FINISH
   UNFINISHED         *
   SANDED             *                                                    SANDED
   SEALED/PRIMED      *
   PLASTIC-LAMINATE FACED * PLASTIC-LAMINATE FACED
   COATED             *
    -----------------* * ----------------------    ----------------------    ----------------------
SOUND TRANSMISSION    *
FIRE RATING           *
WEATHERSTRIPPED       *
RECOMMENDED USE       *                           INTERIOR OR EXTERIOR     INTERIOR OR EXTERIOR
    -----------------* * ----------------------    ----------------------    ----------------------
UNIQUE/SPECIAL FEATURES * CUSTOM MORTISED & PRE-   5/100 YEAR GUARANTEE     SINGLE-PLY 1/4" VENEER
                       * FITTED TO SPECIFICATION                            FACES FOR HEAVIER DOORS
****************************************************************************************************
                                          L771
```

ule of the old AIA filing system to the new 16-division format. All information in the catalog is organized in accordance with the Uniform System.

SPEC-DATA The Construction Specifications Institute (CSI) has developed a program that offers specifications writers and designers specific information on materials in a standard format. This program, called *Spec-Data*, was originally set up by the Producers' Council and was later taken over by CSI. Manufacturers subscribing to this service present information on their products in a form that enables the designer or specifications writer to evaluate any product quickly and easily. The standard format includes the product name, manufacturer, product description, limitations and advantages of the product, sizes and colors available, and other technical data necessary for proper installation.

The advantage of the Spec-Data program is that all the information is presented in a concise, orderly, and uniform system. Thus the designer can compare one product with another without spending hours trying to find the necessary information in advertising material.

SPEC-DATA II CSI's Spec-Data program is now being expanded to a data-retrieval system called Spec-Data II. Materials information obtained from manufacturers is put into a standard form, stored in computer memory banks, and reproduced on microfilm. In 1970 the catalog section contained over 450,000 pages of manufacturers' literature. This system includes a unique product-selector feature, listing the primary product characteristics, as extracted from manufacturers' literature. Products having similar characteristics can quickly be identified, and specific catalog pages can be quickly located for more detailed information. The user can make a dry print, in six seconds, of any manufacturers' catalog page. The products are indexed by manufacturer, by brand name, by catalog, and according to the computer-generated Product Selector, which is arranged in the 16-division CSI format. Further information is available from Information Handling Services, Division of Indian Head, Inc., Department B, 5500 South Valentia Way, Denver Technological Center, Englewood, Colo., 80110.

TRADE ASSOCIATIONS

There are many groups of manufacturers, applicators, or contractors formed for joint promotion of the correct use of their products or services. These groups may call themselves associations, bureaus, institutes, councils, societies, or producers. Some such organizations are formed to promote a particular product or trade; however, most are concerned with improving quality, setting standards, establishing stock sizes, and promoting higher standards of workmanship.

A designer or specifications writer can usually obtain information on products or methods of application from

Fig. 1-3 A personal data station. (*Information Handling Services, Inc.*)

one of these associations. A partial list of the hundreds of such groups is given in the Appendix. Some are nationwide, and some are local only. Many of the associations listed as national organizations have local chapters or representatives. Many of them publish literature of general interest regarding their services or products. Information published by reputable trade associations is undoubtedly some of the best available. The data are usually reliable as to quality, since most trade associations are formed to improve or protect an image. Others furnish technical help, reference material, and suggested standard specifications. Many of these organizations are commonly identified by their acronyms. For example, the American Society of Heating, Refrigerating and Air-conditioning Engineers, Inc., is known as ASHRAE, Underwriters' Laboratory as UL, and the Ceramic Tile Institute as CTI.

Self-policing of Construction Trades

Many quality-control agencies have been set up that will stamp and certify the quality of a material; however, these standards are valueless if the material is installed incorrectly. What is needed is a trade inspection team that can certify the entire operation from design to installation. If such a team is to operate successfully, it must include all factions of the trade, such as engineers, manufacturers, contractors, union officials, and inspectors. For example, the Ceramic Tile Institute, which operates in southern California, one of the largest and fastest-growing construction areas in the world, has set up a non-profit organization called Bonded Tile Installations (BTI), which provides an unbiased professional consulting service, inspection, and bonding for architectural firms and their clients.

Fig. 1-4 Certificate of bonded tile installation. (*Ceramic Tile Institute.*)

Another such organization, also in southern California, is Roofing Inspection and Consulting Services (RICS). Their services consist of prejob consultations, tests of roofing installations, job site inspections while work is in progress, and final certificates of approval or rejection. The Woodwork Institute of California (WIC) has had a quality-control system in effect for the past 10 years. This organization publishes a regularly revised "Manual of Millwork" for use by designers and manufacturers, setting forth grades and qualities of millwork. Most of their inspection is done in the factory and not on the job site, although they will reinspect on the job site by request.

Many other trade groups throughout the United States are setting up similar trade inspection teams. The designer or specifier would be wise to encourage more of this type of activity. It is often difficult to obtain a true evaluation of materials and installation methods from individual manufacturers.

The Construction Specifications Institute

The Construction Specifications Institute (CSI) is an organization of specifications writers, architects, engineers, manufacturers' representatives, contractors, building officials, and others interested in the preparation and utilization of specifications in the construction industry. Its members also conduct studies and technical research to "improve and implement the science of communications in construction technology through service, education and research." The results of their research are published as technical studies or monographs in the CSI's national monthly magazine, *The Construction Specifier.* These studies on many materials and construction processes are prepared by committees from local chapters, composed of members from industry and professional members of the CSI, and are valuable reference sources on various phases of manufacture, supply, installation, and use of building products. The monthly magazine also contains interesting articles on materials and installation methods.

The CSI has over 10,000 members in more than 100 chapters throughout the United States. Valuable information on new materials and new and improved construction techniques is presented to members by panels of experts from industry at monthly chapter meetings. Regional and national conventions and conferences allow interchange of ideas and give the members an opportunity to hear outstanding authorities in the construction industry. In 1970 the first student chapter of the CSI was formed at California State Polytechnical College in San Luis Obispo. Materials, construction information, and literature are provided for architectural and engineering students. Panels of experts from the entire state travel to the college to help the students in their study of materials, processes, and the preparation of construction documents.

Information on CSI publications and activities is available from The Construction Specifications Institute, Suite 300, 1150 17th Street, N.W., Washington, D.C., 20036.

THE CSI FORMAT FOR CONSTRUCTION SPECIFICATIONS   In 1963 the CSI, as the result of extensive meetings throughout the United States and comments and criticism by members of the construction industry, adopted "The CSI Format for Building Specifications." This document was revised and enlarged in 1965 and published as "The CSI Format for Construction Specifications." This format arranges the information to be included in a set of construction specifications into 16 basic divisions, with general and specific sections in each division. The division headings and numbers are identical for every set of specifications. The work of a single trade, the work done under a single contract, or a basic unit of work is grouped in a technical section or a trade section. Several trade sections are grouped in each division.

THE UNIFORM SYSTEM   For several years the CSI participated in a Joint Industry Conference devoted to the development of a data-filing and -retrieval system that would meet the pressing needs for a better and faster method of classifying, filing, and identifying technical data. It was agreed that a data-filing system based on the specifications would be the most adaptable to the rapidly multiplying new materials and techniques in construction. This system was further expanded to include a specifications outline and a contractors' cost-accounting guide. The resulting "Uniform System for Construction Specifications, Data Filing & Cost Accounting," based on the CSI 16-division format, was published jointly by the American Institute of Architects, the Associated General Contractors of America, the Construction Specifications Institute, and the Council of Mechanical Specialty Contracting Industries. Many other associations, as well as municipal and governmental agencies, have adopted this system, and most manufacturers identify their products on this basis for ease of filing and retrieval.

TABLE 1-1 Uniform filing system

DIVISION	DESCRIPTION
1. General requirements	Encompasses certain aspects of the job which are the general contractors' responsibility and are often included in the contract under general conditions or special conditions
2. Site work	Includes Work performed on the site, such as clearing, grading, excavating, underpinning, drainage, site utilities, roads and walks, and lawns and planting
3. Concrete	Concrete formwork, reinforcing, and precast and cast-in-place concrete
4. Masonry	Mortar, unit masonry, stone, and masonry restoration
5. Metals	Structural steel, open-web joists, metal stud-and-joist systems, miscellaneous metal items manufactured to standard details and sizes, ornamental wrought metal or die-cast nonferrous metalwork such as grilles and louvers (sheet-metal work is usually included in division 7)
6. Carpentry	Wood and wood framing materials, rough and finish carpentry (excluding cabinetwork)
7. Moisture protections	Waterproofing, dampproofing, thermal insulation, roofing materials, sheet metal and flashing, skylights, caulking, and sealants
8. Doors, windows, and glass	Doors, windows, finish hardware, weatherstripping, glass and glazing, curtain walls, window walls, storefront systems

TABLE 1-1 Uniform filing system (*Continued*)

DIVISION	DESCRIPTION
9. Finishes	Lath and plaster, tile, terrazzo, acoustical surfacing materials, flooring, wall coverings, painting
10. Specialties	Prefabricated products and proprietary devices such as chalkboards, demountable and movable partitions, firefighting devices, fireplace equipment, flagpoles, signs, lockers, sun-control devices, toilet and bath accessories
11. Equipment	Bank, ecclesiastical, commercial, educational, laboratory, medical, food service, and restaurant equipment; residential equipment, including all kitchen cabinetwork, countertops and splashes of plastic laminates; bath lavatories and cabinets (excluding medicine cabinets); built-in range tops, ovens, refrigerators, dishwashers, garbage disposals; and prefabricated range and oven exhaust systems
12. Furnishings	Artwork, prefabricated cabinets and fixtures, blinds, shades, drapery, carpeting, furniture, and seating
13. Special construction	Special-purpose rooms, integrated ceilings, prefabricated structures, storage vaults, and swimming pools
14. Conveying systems	Dumbwaiters, elevators, moving stairs, lifts, hoists, cranes, materials-handling systems
15. Mechanical	Plumbing systems, heating systems, fire-extinguishing systems, air-conditioning systems, and refrigeration
16. Electrical	Electrical services and distribution systems, lighting fixtures, communications systems, electrical power equipment, electrical heating or cooling systems

The Uniform System provides for product literature and related material to be filed under one of the 16 divisions shown in Table 1-1.

This is only a partial listing of the items that are included under each division. A complete listing, along with a keyword index that can be used to locate the proper grouping of particular products, is given in "The Uniform System for Construction Specifications, Data Filing & Cost Accounting," Document 001a, or "The CSI Format for Construction Specifications," Document 001, available from the Construction Specifications Institute, Inc., Suite 300, 1150 17th Street, N.W., Washington, D.C., 20036.

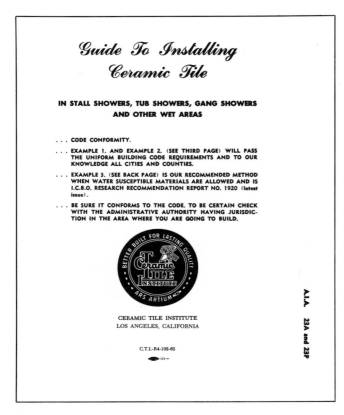

Fig. 1-5 An association standard. (*Ceramic Tile Institute.*)

REFERENCE STANDARDS

Many organizations write standards that can be included in specifications by reference. They may also be included in building codes by reference. In order to reduce the bulk of a building code, many cities have set up standards or use established standards to which they refer in their regularly published codes. These standards are published in a separate volume. For example, the 1967 edition of the "Uniform Building Code," published by the Pacific Coast Building Officials Conference, in referring to the quality of portland cement, states that "Portland cement shall conform to UBC standard number 26-1-67." Volume II of the "Uniform Building Code" gives this standard in full. The standard is identical to ASTM standard C150-67, which can be found in "ASTM Standards in Building Codes," published annually by the American Society for Testing and Materials.

Association Standards

Trade-association standards and specifications are produced by member companies or individuals within the trade. These standards are formulated by experts in the particular field and are constantly updated to keep abreast of the latest materials and techniques in their field. When the trade-association standards are included in specifications by reference, firms that do not belong to the association are not excluded from furnishing the product, as long as the product conforms to the standards set up by the association. Copies of association standards can be obtained without cost from most associations. Examples of trade-association standard specifications are "Aluminum Prime Windows: Double-hung (and Single-hung) Windows, for Residential-type Buildings," Specification DH-B1, published by the Architectural Aluminum Manufacturers' Association, and "Standard Specifications for Installation of Ceramic Tile with Water Resistant Organic Adhesives," published by the Ceramic Tile Institute.

THE AMERICAN SOCIETY FOR TESTING AND MATERIALS (ASTM) This organization was formed in 1902 for the "promotion of knowledge of materials of Engineering, and the standardization of specifications and the method of testing." It now has over 20,000 members and has published more than 4100 standards. The ASTM membership consists of both producers, and consumers. Publications are issued

Fig. 1-6 An Association Standard. (*Architectural Aluminum Manufacturers' Association.*)

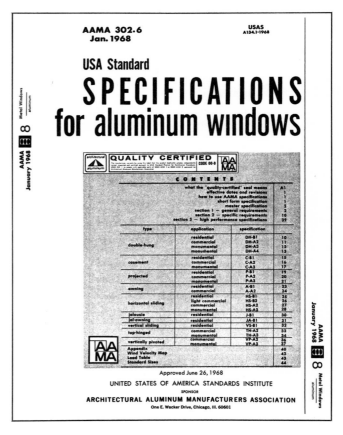

by committees of producers and consumers formed to establish joint standards for the industry. Committees are constantly studying new materials, new applications of old materials, and new testing methods for the use of industry. The ASTM publishes an annual "Index to Standards," which lists all available standards. The title page of this index states that "single copies will be sent on request to those indicating a need for it in construction design . . . and related activities in the materials field."

The ASTM books of standards consist of 32 separate parts, each of which covers a specific field of interest. The 1969 edition consisted of 29,000 pages of standards which apply to design, manufacturing, construction, and maintenance. Most large architectural or engineering offices purchase complete sets of these standards as they are published. Every office should have a copy of the current edition of "ASTM Standards in Building Codes." This book contains all standards that have been adopted by reference in the major nationally recognized building codes. The ASTM also sells, at nominal prices, copies

Fig. 1-7 ASTM standard. (*American Society for Testing and Materials.*)

Fig. 1-8 ANSI standard. (*American National Standards Institute.*)

of separate standards for individual materials or testing methods. The annual index of standards is very convenient for locating information on materials or testing procedures. Single copies are available without charge from the American Society for Testing and Materials, 1916 Race Street, Philadelphia, Pa., 19103.

AMERICAN NATIONAL STANDARDS INSTITUTE (ANSI) This organization, founded in 1918 as the American Engineer Standards Committee, was later expanded to include standards of all types, and in 1928 it was reorganized as the American Standards Association (ASA). In 1966 it became the United States of America Standards Institute (USASI), and on October 6, 1969, it was again reorganized as the present American National Standards Institute. The institute represents industry, consumers, and government agencies. It does not issue its own standards, but acts as a national coordinating institution "through which interested organizations may cooperate in establishing, recognizing, and improving voluntary standards of the United States of America."

ANSI includes more than 160 technical, professional, and trade organizations and 1000 companies. Standards developed by member associations, such as AAMA or

---

AMERICAN SOCIETY FOR TESTING AND MATERIALS

1916 Race St., Philadelphia, Pa., 19103

Reprinted from the Annual Book of ASTM Standards, Copyright ASTM

Standard Specification for

STRUCTURAL STEEL[1]

ASTM Designation: A 36 – 70

This Standard of the American Society for Testing and Materials is issued under the fixed designation A 36; the number immediately following the designation indicates the year of original adoption or, in the case of revision, the year of last revision. A number in parentheses indicates the year of last reapproval.

Scope

1. (*a*) This specification[2] covers carbon steel shapes, plates, and bars of structural quality for use in riveted, bolted, or welded construction of bridges and buildings, and for general structural purposes. When the steel is used in welded construction, welding procedure shall be suitable for the steel and the intended service.

(*b*) Supplemental Requirements are provided where improved notch toughness is important. These shall apply only when specified by the purchaser in the order.

Appurtenant Materials

2. Unless otherwise provided in the order, the current edition of the specifications of the American Society for Testing and Materials listed in Table I shall govern the delivery of otherwise unspecified appurtenant materials when

included with material purchased under this Specification for Structural Steel (ASTM Designation: A 36).[3] Unless otherwise specified, all plain and threaded bars used for anchorage purposes shall be subjected to mechanical tests and shall conform to the tensile requirements of Section 7; headed bolts used for anchorage purposes, and all nuts, shall conform to the requirements of the Specification for Low-Carbon Steel Externally and Internally Threaded Standard Fasteners (ASTM Designation: A 307).[3]

General Requirements for Delivery

3. Material furnished under this specification shall conform to the applicable requirements of the current edition of the Specification for General Requirements for Delivery of Rolled Steel Plates, Shapes, Sheet Piling, and Bars for Structural Use (ASTM Designation: A 6).[3]

Bearing Plates

4. (*a*) Unless otherwise specified, plates used as bearing plates for bridges shall be subjected to mechanical tests and shall conform to the tensile requirements of Section 7.

[1] Under the standardization procedure of the Society, this specification is under the jurisdiction of the ASTM Committee A-1 on Steel and is the direct responsibility of Subcommittee II on Structural Steel. A list of committee members may be found in the ASTM Year Book.
Current edition effective April 13, 1970. Originally issued 1960. Replaces A 36 – 69.
[2] For ASME Boiler and Pressure Vessel Code applications see related Specification SA-36 in Section II of that Code.
[3] Annual Book of ASTM Standards, Part 4.

32

5–72

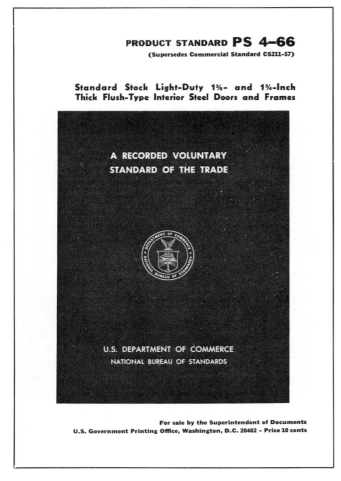

Fig. 1-9 A product standard. (*National Bureau of Standards.*)

ASTM, may be submitted for approval as an ANSI standard. A committee that represents all interested groups, including manufacturers, users, government agencies, and the general public, will review the standard to determine that it has been developed in accordance with the procedures of the institute, which include agreement among all interested and affected parties. Completely new standards may also be developed and submitted by committees of ANSI.

ANSI also serves as representative of United States industry on the technical committees of the International Organization for Standardization, International Electrotechnical Commission, whose purpose is to develop standards that have worldwide acceptance.

The institute publishes an annual catalog listing all ANSI standards by letters and numbers. Each entry designates other associations that also issue the standard. The ANSI standards can be purchased individually or as a set, either to fit into ring binders, or as microfiche, which consists of many individual pages reproduced on a 4 × 6 film.

Commodity Standards

The U.S. Department of Commerce issues two series of standards, "Commercial Standards," and "Simplified Practice Recommendations." The commercial standards were set up to establish definite quality levels for certain commercial products as a means of promoting sound commercial practices in their manufacture, marketing, and application. They give technical requirements for materials, construction, dimensions, tolerances, testing, grading, marking, and other details. Uniform methods and practices are established for achieving and determining compliance. The simplified practice recommendations are essentially lists of stock or staple items in greatest demand. They make possible a choice, in accordance with generally recognized trade practices, between standard items that are widely available from distributors' stocks, and special items, which may require factory orders and entail more costly production and handling methods. Some specifications give standards for methods, such as packaging (see Figure 1-9).

Federal Specifications

In 1949 an act of Congress set up a procedure to authorize the General Services Administration (GSA) to prescribe standard specifications for purchases made by federal government agencies. One of the GSA's functions is to establish standards and procedures that will result in maximum value received for public funds expended. Many state, county, and municipal governments and some institutional and educational bodies stipulate these standards (usually referred to as Fed. Specs.) in their construction specifications, and manufacturers are, for the most part, familiar with their requirements. In some instances the materials producer is required to have his material pretested in order to qualify it for purchase by government agencies. If the material meets or conforms to a federal specification, the designer has some assurance that the product has certain characteristics. It should be noted, however, that federal standards are usually only the minimum requirements for many products.

TESTING LABORATORIES

Certain materials that are to be installed on a project must be tested before, during, or after construction. These tests may be made by an independent testing laboratory. Such laboratories should meet the requirements of ASTM E329-67T, "Tentative Standard of Recommended Practice for Inspection and Testing Agencies for Concrete and Steel Used in Construction." They should employ the latest equipment for the storage and testing of materials and should be staffed with experts in the field. They may process samples brought to the laboratory or send inspectors into the field to inspect and test materials for conformance with the specifications.

Independent Laboratories

An independent testing laboratory is employed to protect the interests of the owner and to furnish such technical knowledge as may be of benefit to the project. It is usually selected and paid by the owner, through his architect or engineer. The laboratory does not accept or reject material, but merely certifies its compliance or noncompliance with the contract documents. Independent testing laboratories are also used by manufacturers to test their products. These laboratory reports are presented in the manufacturer's literature as unbiased reports on the quality or uses of a particular material or method of production. However, it should be recognized that in this case the laboratory has been employed by the manufacturer, and unless it is a

laboratory that is known to be impartial, the reports may require careful evaluation.

Underwriters' Laboratories

Underwriters' Laboratories (UL) is a nonprofit corporation organized "to establish, maintain, and operate laboratories for the investigation of materials, devices, products, equipment, constructions methods, and systems with respect to hazards affecting life and property." Offices and testing stations are located in Chicago and Northbrook, Illinois; Nelville, New York; Westwood, New Jersey; and Santa Clara, California. A producer wishing to secure an investigation and listing of his product, may, for a fee, have it tested by the laboratories. If the product comes up to UL

Fig. 1-10 Testing a floor assembly. A 50-ton remote-controlled crane is positioning a floor panel onto the UL floor furnace preparatory to a fire test of the entire assembly. The assembly, which has been cured for a specific period of time, contains a reinforced-concrete floor to which is attached an acoustical tile ceiling. The temperature is raised to 1000°F in the first 5 min, 1700°F the first hour, 1850°F the second hour, 1925°F the third hour, and 2000°F the fourth hour. (*By permission of Underwriters' Laboratories, Inc.*)

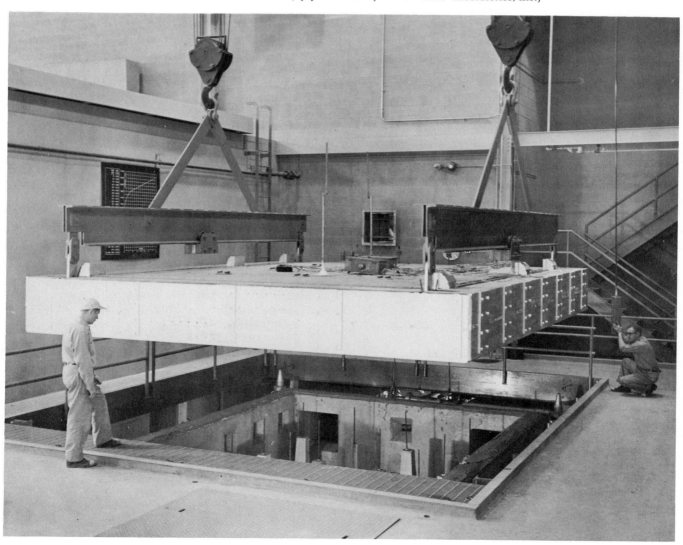

standards, it is included on UL's annual approved-materials lists, and the producer is authorized to attach a UL seal of approval to the product. UL reserves the right to reinspect the product during manufacture and after it has been placed on the market. If the product fails at any time to meet the standards, it is removed from UL's lists, and the UL label is withdrawn until it is brought up to standard.

UL publishes a set of standards and specifications for the construction and performance under test and in actual use of systems, devices, materials, and appliances of numerous classes submitted to the laboratories. It also undertakes research projects in numerous areas of safety and has issued over 50 research bulletins. Further information and a "Directory of Research Bulletins" are available from Underwriters' Laboratories, Inc., 207 East Ohio Street, Chicago, Ill., 60611.

QUESTIONS

1. Give three examples of products manufactured on the job site.

2. What is the purpose of building codes?

3. What are model building codes and how are they used?

4. What is a specialized building code?

5. What factors must be considered in evaluating manufacturers' literature?

6. What are the limitations of "Sweet's Catalog File"?

7. What is the Spec-Data program and what are its advantages?

8. Describe Spec-Data II.

9. Why is trade-association literature sometimes more valuable than manufacturers' literature?

10. Why are associations in the construction industry formed?

11. What is the CSI and what are the advantages of belonging to this organization?

12. Describe the CSI Format.

13. How does the Uniform System differ from the CSI Format?

14. Under what division of the Uniform System would you find information on cranes, dishwashers, kitchen cabinets, painting?

15. Explain how reference standards are used.

16. Why are associations interested in developing standards?

17. Describe the activities of the ASTM.

18. How does the ASTM differ from ANSI?

19. Who develops commodity standards and who publishes them?

20. When are federal specifications used?

21. Who usually pays an independent testing laboratory for the services of an inspector sent to a job site?

22. How do manufacturers utilize the services of a testing laboratory?

23. What is UL?

24. What agency of the federal government is concerned with setting up standards?

25. What is the full name of the following organizations: AAMA, ASHRAE, CSI, AIA?

REFERENCES FOR FURTHER STUDY

Aikman, W. F.: Building Codes Past and Present, *The Construction Specifier*, June 1969.

American National Standards Institute: 1430 Broadway, New York, N.Y., 10018. "What Is the National Standards Institute?" 1970. "ANS Institute Catalog," published yearly.

American Society for Testing and Materials: 1916 Race Street, Philadelphia, Pa., 18103. "Index to Standards," published yearly.

Building Research Institute: 2101 Constitution Avenue, N.W., Washington, D.C., 20418. "The Building Science Directory," 1970.

Construction Specifications Institute: Suite 300, 1150 17th Street, N.W., Washington, D.C., 20036. "The Use of Reference Standards," 1965. "The CSI Format for Construction Specifications," Document 001, 1967. "The Uniform System," Document 001a, 1966.

General Services Administration: Washington, D.C., 20402. "Index of Federal Specifications and Standards," published yearly. "Guide to Specifications and Standards of the Federal Government," 1962. "Doing Business with the Federal Government," 1961.

Lavenberg, George: Self-policing of Construction Trades, *The Construction Specifier*, January 1969.

National Referral Center for Science and Technology: U.S. Government Printing Office, Washington, D.C., 20402. "A Directory of Information Resources in the United States," 1970.

Rosen, Harold J.: Materials Failure Responsibility, *The Construction Specifier*, March 1969, p. 65.

Underwriters' Laboratory, Inc.: 207 East Ohio Street, Chicago, Ill., 60611. "Testing for Public Safety," 1969. "Building Materials Lists." "Electrical Appliance and Utilization Equipment List." "Electrical Construction Materials." "Gas and Oil Equipment." All published yearly.

U.S. Business and Defense Services Administration, Office of Technical Services: Washington, D.C., 20034. "Commodity Standards."

Vansant, Robert E.: Materials Evaluation, *The Construction Specifier*, March 1969, p. 55.

Watson, D. A.: "Specifications Writing for Architects and Engineers," McGraw-Hill, New York, 1964.

SOIL CLASSIFICATION

The study of soils and soil engineering is a very exact science. However, the architect and builder must have at least a basic knowledge of soils and their reactions under load. In designing foundations and footings for structures, the nature of the material on which these foundations will rest is an important consideration. Building codes identify soils and specify the maximum loads that can be superimposed on each type. Geologists and soils engineers make investigations of soil conditions on particular building sites and report on what they have found. The designer must be able to interpret their reports and design his foundation structures accordingly.

Soils are the product of mechanical and chemical weathering of rock, and they are found in a wide range of particle size, shape, and composition. Although there are several methods of classifying soils, the method most commonly used by engineers in the field and referred to in building codes is the classification of soil types by texture and structure on the basis of visual inspection.

Bedrock

The earth's surface consists of rock, called *bedrock*, overlaid by an unconsolidated layer called *soil*, derived from rock and organic materials. Bedrock may be exposed on the surface, or it may be covered by several hundred feet of soil. It is not solid over large areas, but is broken into relatively small units by faults, joints, bedding planes, and other structural weaknesses. These faults may lie in horizontal, vertical, or sloping planes. Layers of rock may be separated by layers of slippery clay that will allow the rock to move or slip when it is disturbed, either by man or by nature, as in the case of earthquakes.

Rock is not always satisfactory as a foundation bed. Weathering can weaken certain rock formations. Some disintegrate in the presence of water. The firmness of a rock sample may be a poor criterion of the strength of the entire formation under a load. For example, the limestone rock in the vicinity of Mammoth Caves in Kentucky has a high compressive strength, but its capacity to support construction projects is modified by the presence of large underground caverns. The true bearing capacity of rock can be determined only by a detailed geological study of the inclinations, trends, and precise locations of rock strata and structures in the construction area.

Texture and Structure of Soils

The grouping of soils shown in Table 2-1 is similar to that found in several building codes.

TABLE 2-1 Texture and structure of soils

TYPE OF SOIL	DESCRIPTION
Compact coarse sand	This soil consists of coarse particles, ¼ in. or less in diameter, predominately quartz with no binder, which have been compacted by the weight of overburden or weather. The grains are generally spherical or angular in shape, depending on the extent of weathering or decomposition. Coarse sand is little affected by water or frost, as the particles fit closely together.
Compact fine sand	When confined, whether wet or dry, this material will bear heavy loads. Water will make fine sand flow more readily than coarse sand. Fine sand has a lower bearing value than coarse sand, since the fine particles can be rearranged and tend to squeeze together.
Loose sand	Loose sand, either fine or coarse, will flow under the action of water. The finer particles move more readily, leaving voids in the soil. Loose sand tends to flow under a load unless it is confined.
Clay	Clay consists mainly of the mineral feldspar and various impurities. The particles in clay are much finer than those in sand. They consist of submicroscopic needle- or disk-shaped grains whose surfaces are large in proportion to their volume. The physical properties of clays are greatly altered by water. Compact dry clay will support heavy loads, whereas wet clay becomes slippery and unstable. Clay will also expand and contract in relation to the amount of water present, so that its volume may vary from 10 to 20 percent.
Sandy clay	This type of soil is sandy with enough clay to act as a binder. Thus it exhibits many of the properties of sandy soils without the movement of loose sand and without the slipping qualities of clays.
Silt	Silt is the very fine, soft material deposited by rivers or on the bottom of lakes that have receded. It may consist

TABLE 2-1 Texture and structure of soils (*Continued*)

TYPE OF SOIL	DESCRIPTION
	of the finer portions of mineral or inorganic sand, sometimes with fine amounts of decomposed organic materials. The grains are microscopic in size and have little or no plasticity. Loose silts are usually unsuitable for bearing. However, plastic silts can be treated as clays. Some nonplastic silts have characteristics similar to those of fine sand.
Loam	A friable (easily crumbled or pulverized) mixture of relatively even proportions of sand, silt, and clay, usually with some organic matter.
Sandy loam	A sandy soil containing enough clay and silt to render it cohesive (to make it stick together).
Silt loam	A soil having a moderate amount of clay and sand, in which over 50 percent of the sand is extremely fine particles.
Clay loam	A mixture of sand, clay, and silt having a large percentage of clay.
Hardpan	A sedimentary formation ranging from clay to gravel. This term denotes the degree of hardness and cementation of highly consolidated clay mixed with sand, gravel, or boulders, rather than a specific soil composition.
Shale	An intermediate stage between clay and slate, highly consolidated by pressure. Shale may be reduced to a plastic state by moderate grinding and the addition of water.

SOIL BEHAVIOR

Soils may be solid, viscous, plastic, or fluid in consistency. These characteristics must be considered in designing the foundation of a building or a road.

Solid soils have constant density and internal resistance that is little affected by temperature changes, moisture variations, or vibration. These basic characteristics remain, however, only if the soil is not disturbed. Excavation, moving water, and extreme temperature changes in exposed solid soils may alter their characteristics. All soils are compressible, and their compressibility and consequent reduction in volume can be determined by testing procedures and laboratory analysis.

Viscous, plastic, and *fluid soils* have the common property of resisting changes in volume, (liquid that is contained in a vessel is almost incompressible). However, such soils constantly change shape. Viscous, plastic, and fluid soils vary only in the amount of force required to start them moving. A plastic soil will cease moving when the force is removed. Viscous and fluid soils will continue to move until a counteracting force intervenes. (In water-bearing soils, if movement, change in chemical composition, or loss of water can be prevented, volume change or settlement can be avoided.)

Soil Water

Water may be present in soils in several forms. *Capillary water* is contained in minute pores of individual soil particles and binds them together. Water that flows through the soil and can be removed by pumping is classified as *gravitational water. Film water* may surround the individual soil grains; this water can be removed by oven drying. *Absorbed water* clings to the surfaces of soil particles and cannot be removed by drying.

The *groundwater level*, or *water table*, is the level of gravitational water in the soil. This water flows, just like surface water. Thus the groundwater level is not constant. It varies with the amount of rainfall, the pumping of water from wells, and the construction of sewers, drains, and other underground works.

Water may be pulled above the level of the water table by *capillary rise*. When a thin tube is inserted in a container of water, the surface tension and the affinity of the water for the surface of the tube draws water up the tube. The distance depends on the diameter of the tube. Similarly, the capillary rise in soil depends on the size of the pores between the particles. In sand the grain size, and thus the pores between grains is relatively large, so that there is very little capillary action. In contrast, the capillary rise in fine-grained clays is considerable. The pores of clay are usually filled with water many feet above the groundwater level. This capillary water cannot be removed from the soil by any system of drainage.

The density (weight per cubic foot), of soil that is compacted, as in fills, depends on the amount of water it contains. Water films around individual grains act as a lubricant to the soil during compaction. For a given size and weight of tamper and given number of tamps, on a given area of soil deposited in a given thickness, there is a moisture content that will produce a fill of the greatest density. This is called the *optimum moisture content*. The optimum moisture content differs for each type of soil and must be determined by laboratory tests.

Swelling and Shrinkage

Clay soils tend to change in volume as the moisture content changes. Some will swell like a sponge even when

Fig. 2-1 Earth-moving equipment at work. (*Shepherd Machinery Company.*)

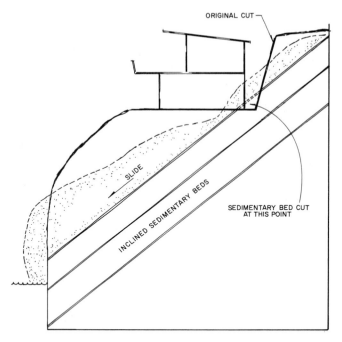

Fig. 2-2 Cross section of slippage along fault lines. Slide was caused by cutting inclined sedimentary beds.

they appear to be hard and dry. These clays are termed *expansive clays*. If water is drained or removed from wet clays, the drying soil will shrink from 10 to 20 percent in volume and will break up into small fragments. For clay soils to serve as a satisfactory base for building foundations, their water content must be kept constant. Water penetrating expansive clays around the outside of a building can cause the soil to expand, thereby raising the perimeter footings. The protected clay under the building will then dry and shrink, removing the support under interior foundations.

Bearing Capacities of Soils

Building codes usually specify the allowable bearing pressure for various types of soils. As shown in Table 2-2, this allowable pressure is stated as the maximum number of pounds that can be supported by one square foot of soil without excessive settlement or rupture of the foundation material. Note that the allowable pressure increases as the depth of the foundation is increased. For example, in medium-stiff clay or sandy clay, if the bottom of a foundation excavation is 1 ft below the surface of the ground, a foundation 1 ft square will support 2000 lb. For each additional foot that the excavation is carried below this mini-

TABLE 2-2 Allowable soil pressure per square foot for footings below adjacent virgin ground

MATERIAL	MIN. DEPTH	PERMISSIBLE VALUE, LB/SQ FT	INCREASE IN VALUE PER FT ADDITIONAL DEPTH	MAX. VALUE
Rock	0′	20% of ultimate crushing strength	0	20% of ultimate crushing strength
Compact coarse sand	1′	1500*	300*	8000
Compact fine sand	1′	1000*	200*	8000
Loose sand	2′	500*	100*	3000
Hard clay or sandy clay	1′	4000	800	8000
Medium-stiff clay or sandy clay	1′	2000	200	6000
Expansive soils	1′-6″	1000†	50	—
Soft sandy clay or clay	2′	1000	50	2000
Compact inorganic sand-and-silt mixtures	1′	1000	200	4000
Loose inorganic sand-and-silt mixtures	2′	500	100	1000
Loose organic sand-and-silt mixtures and muck or bay mud	0′	0	0	0

* These values are for footings 1 ft in width and may be increased in direct proportion to the width of the footing, to a maximum of three times the designated value.
† For depths greater than 8 ft use values given for clay of comparable consistency.

By permission of the ICBO.

mum depth, an additional 200 lb/sq ft may be placed on the foundation, up to a maximum of 6000 lb/sq ft.

In construction areas subject to freezing, the depth of the foundation is determined by the *frost line*, the maximum depth to which the ground freezes. This varies with the locality. In some parts of the country the frost line may be deeper than 6 ft; in other parts the ground may never freeze.

Tables of allowable soil pressures seldom take into account the compressibility of soils or the presence of water. Soils are both complex and highly variable. Building-code tables can be used for light structures, such as one- and two-story frame residences or small commercial buildings, since they usually contain a high factor of safety. For a larger project, however, an accurate determination should be made of soil properties.

Fig. 2-3 Movement of expansion soils: (*a*) soil settlement; (*b*) soil heave.

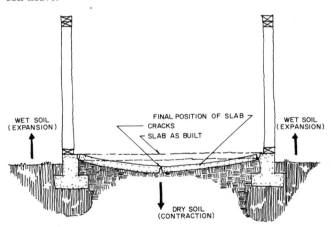

EXPANSIVE SOIL SETTLEMENT

(*a*)

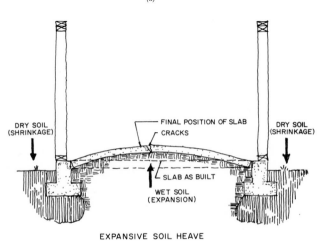

EXPANSIVE SOIL HEAVE

(*b*)

Fig. 2-4 Leaning tower of Pisa.

Subsidence

When a load is applied, soil tends to react in three different ways: (1) there is elastic compression (as in a rubber mat when it is stepped on), (2) the soil is consolidated as water and air are squeezed out, and (3) there is plastic creep or flow of the soil particles.

All footings settle when they are loaded. The settlement of a rigid structure resting on a uniform soil and subsurface of bedrock can be determined, and if it is within the design limitations, it is not serious. However, if the underlying strata vary throughout the site, the consequences of settling can be quite serious. The elastic compression of a soil depends on the weight above it, and if a heavier portion of a building settles unevenly, the building will tilt. If the composition of the soil varies in its resistance to compression, it will also settle unevenly and cause the building to tilt. Of course, this does not always result in a failure. The leaning bell tower of Pisa attracts tourists from all over the world even though the baptistry and the cathedral, which form the rest of this structure, are much more interesting artistically and architecturally.

When water is pumped from the ground near a structure or the water table is lowered through lack of rain, the entire building may settle. The Palace of Fine Arts in Mexico City has settled nearly 6 ft. A deep excavation next to an existing building may allow soil to flow from under the foundations, causing collapse.

Landslides

Certain areas, such as the coastal region of California, are made up of layers of sedimentary rock. This rock originally formed in horizontal layers which were later pushed into positions resembling a tilted deck of cards. When such strata are exposed to water and weather, the edges are left with no support, and an entire hillside may slide into the sea. This exposure may be the result of unwise grading, too much weight on the top strata, or cuts made through a number of layers for roads or utilities.

Seismic Forces

Seismic forces are those that pertain to or are caused by earthquakes. An earthquake has been described as a vibration or shaking of the ground by some natural phenomenon within the earth. The vibrations start at one point,

called the *epicenter*, and proceed in waves in all directions. The resulting ground motions affect buildings and structures in varying degrees, depending not only on their distance from the epicenter, but on the type of soil on which they rest. Buildings on marshy or filled land are more affected than those on underlying rock.

Predicting earthquakes is a very inexact science. However, there are certain known geological faults in the earth's crust along which major earthquakes are more likely to occur. One of the most noted of these is the San Andreas fault, which runs the length of California. Major earthquakes have also occurred in other parts of the country. Several organizations have set up maps of the United States indicating the seismic probability or defining the zones that are most likely to experience a major earthquake.

Construction projects in areas that have a high earthquake probability require special precautions regarding soil structures and foundations. Buildings in an earthquake zone must be designed to resist lateral, or sideways, force, as well as the vertical forces exerted by the weight of the building. Earthquake engineers are becoming increasingly concerned with the effects of soil conditions on the intensity of vibrations set up in a building during an earthquake. It has been shown that the damaging forces acting on a

Fig. 2-5   Center of earthquake at Anchorage, Alaska, 1964. (*Masonry Research.*)

Fig. 2-6 Earthquake damage at Olive View Sanitarium, Sylmar, California, 1971.

building may vary by as much as 100 percent, depending on the soil conditions at the site.

SOIL INVESTIGATION

A construction site can be divided into two distinct areas of concern—the portion above grade and the portion below grade. That portion which is above grade is the responsibility of the architect and the structural engineer. That portion below grade is the responsibility of the geologist and the soils engineer, who must conduct a number of tests to determine the physical characteristics of the soil, its trends, and the precise locations of rock strata. Their reports must satisfy public agencies and lending institutions, which issue permits or make commitments on the basis of such reports.

Geological Investigations

The geologist investigates the geological history of the area. He determines what effects development of the site will have on future construction and whether there is a possibility of seismic disturbances in the area. He must also evaluate the economic and population factors that might lead to a lowering of the water table.

Aerological investigation is a recently developed tool of the geologist. Aerial photographs of the site and surrounding terrain enable him to determine drainage patterns, slopes, and vegetation. This information, along with geological reconnaissance, provides general knowledge of subsurface conditions. Further geological information can be obtained from *seismic-refraction surveys*. Seismic-refraction surveys measure the time required for a shock wave to travel a known distance from an explosion point to the ground surface. The velocity of the waves indicate the characteristics of underlying strata.

Subsurface Exploration

The simplest method of subsurface exploration is to dig a pit by hand. Frequently this is combined with some stage of construction, such as excavation for a cesspool. A more precise method consists of boring a test hole and making core-sample tests.

Coring tests, properly made, will indicate the depth, thickness, and texture of each layer. An auger is turned into the ground for a given distance, and a $1\frac{1}{2}$- to 2-in.

Fig. 2-8 Operating a Soiltest R-117 seismic timer. Designed for quick and accurate subsurface exploration to obtain such information as depth of soil over burden, profiles of rock, soil types, and the elastic qualities of surface and subsurface materials. (*Soiltest, Inc.*)

sampling tube, called a *Shelby tube*, is lowered into the hole. The Shelby tube is forced into the undisturbed earth at the bottom of the hole by blows of a hammer of a given weight. Thus the resistance of the earth at that depth can be determined by the number of blows necessary to sink the Shelby tube a given distance. The sample of earth removed with the tube will show the undisturbed condition of the soil at that point. Where the soil investigation is particularly critical, as for tall buildings, 5-in.-diameter samples may be taken.

Another method of making test holes is *wash boring*. This method can be used in sampling rock as well as unconsolidated soils. A bit is mounted at the bottom of a pipe, called a *drill rod*. The drill rod is turned slowly as it is worked up and down in the hole. Water is forced down the pipe as a lubricant and to wash away the waste material. A sampling tube is then lowered in the same manner as with a bore hole, and samples are taken at various depths. The sampling tube is sealed at both ends, marked with the depth and location, and transported to the laboratory for testing.

Determining the proper number and depth of borings requires judgment and experience. The number of borings needed depends on the reason for the soil investigation.

Fig. 2-7 Map of the United States showing zones of approximately equal seismic probability. (*By permission of the International Conference of Building Officials.*)

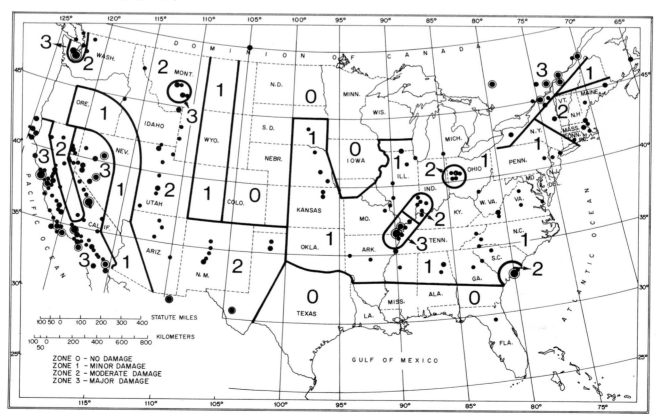

Preliminary borings on a large site may be limited to one per acre. Borings within the proposed limits of a building may be needed at each corner and every 100 ft. within the perimeter, or one for every 2,500 sq ft of building area. Further borings may be needed after the foundation engineer has determined the exact type and placement of foundation structures.

Laboratory Soils Tests

Laboratory soils tests have limited usefulness, since the samples that are taken represent only a small portion of soil which must support the structure. Their primary value is confirmation of the findings of the expert who is handling the boring equipment. Most laboratory tests require undisturbed soils samples.

Table 2-3 describes tests normally requested by a soils engineer:

TABLE 2-3 Laboratory soil tests

TEST	PURPOSE
Grain-size analysis	Important in determining the admixes needed to bring fill material to required bearing strength.
Plasticity index of soils	To determine the quality of silty or clayey soils and predict their behavior.
Consolidation tests	Calculation of the actual settlement that will occur in the field.
Direct shear test	Measurement of the relationships between compression and shear strength of a soil at several pressures.
Field density test	To determine the dry weight per cubic foot and moisture content of the soil sample.
Moisture-density relations of soils	A series of consolidation tests on samples of soils with varying amounts of water added, to obtain the maximum soil weight or *optimum density*. If a sample of soil in a fill, for example, weighs 95 lb/cu ft and its maximum density is determined in the laboratory to be 100 lb/cu ft, the compacted fill in the field would be described as 95 percent compacted.

SOIL MODIFICATION

Soil differs from other natural materials, such as stone, in that it can be modified to conform to certain desired characteristics. Proper drainage may improve the characteristics of some soils. Some soils can be compacted to provide a base for a structure. Various materials may be mixed with the soil to provide a denser subbase. The solution of foundation problems requires application of the soil and foundation engineer's experience and judgment, based on the results of field and laboratory studies.

Fig. 2-9 Operating a refraction seismograph. Shock waves shown on the oscilloscope enable the operator to determine the subsurface conditions over a wide area. (*Soiltest, Inc.*)

Dewatering

When a foundation is to be carried below the groundwater level, as for a basement, it is possible to control the flow of subterranean water by means of open-joist drain tiles. These drain tiles are placed just above the footing to lead away free water before it can move or soften the bearing stratum. Groundwater can be controlled temporarily by means of sumps and pumps. Well points driven into the soil can be used to remove unwanted water. Sheetpiling driven into the site before excavation is begun will reduce unbalanced water pressures and control soil strength.

Compaction

The primary objective of compacting soils is to achieve a soil density that will carry the specified loads without undue settlement. The work necessary and the method to be used, determined by tests at the site, depend on soil types, moisture content, weather conditions, and equipment available.

Soil settles under a load for two reasons: air and water are expelled through compression, and soil is forced outside the site into the surrounding areas. Soil compaction is intended to accomplish these things artificially so that most settlement will take place before construction. The most common method of compacting soil is by using sheep's-foot rollers, flat-wheel rollers, pneumatic-tired units, or tampers to remove the water and air in the soil. Compaction by heavy rubber-tired vehicles will produce

(a)

(b)

Fig. 2-10 Soil core samples: (a) drilling a test hole; (b) removing a soil sample from a split spoon. (*Soiltest, Inc.*)

a change in density as deep as 4 ft. Sheep's-foot rollers, which are large weighted drums studded with 6-in. projections, do an efficient job of compacting fills. Sheep's-foot rollers weigh as much as 15 tons and will compact a 10-ft strip to a depth of 6 in. below the surface. Hand or mechanical tampers are used in less accessible areas.

For proper compression and compaction, the earth must be placed in layers sufficiently thin to permit water and air to be expelled easily. The depth of the layers depends on the type of soil being compacted. Clays must be placed in thin layers, while most sandy soils may be satisfactorily placed in thick layers. Sheep's-foot rollers do not compact the top layer of the soil. This must be finished with smooth-surfaced steel rollers or by blading off with the steel blade of a grader. The compaction of soil requires movement and rearrangement of the individual particles, in order to fit them together and to fill voids. For this movement to take place, friction must be overcome. Friction can be reduced by the proper amount of moisture. If too much moisture is present, some of it must be expelled. If too little is present, there will not be adequate lubrication of the soil particles. For each soil type and condition there is an optimum moisture content. The optimum moisture content is based on the laboratory tests for moisture-density relations of soils, as described in Table 2-3.

Fills are seldom compacted beyond 95 percent of optimum density.

The supporting characteristics of compressible soils can sometimes be improved by *surcharging*, or placing a temporary fill on the site as a load. The weight of this temporary fill compresses the subsoils. When the subsoil is sufficiently compressed, the surcharge is removed, and the building construction can begin.

Another method of compacting soils is a process called *vibroflotation*. This is particularly effective for loose granular soils. The granular material is vibrated to a greater density while sand and water are pumped into the voids created. Explosive shock waves can also be used to increase density in loose granular material.

Slope Stability and Retaining Structures

A *retaining wall* is a structure whose primary purpose is to prevent the flow or lateral movement of soil. Basement walls of a residence may act as retaining walls. In this instance they must not only prevent the flow of soil, but support a load as well. There are several types of retaining walls. The type chosen for a particular job depends on the soil conditions, construction conditions, economics, and function. The stability of a retaining wall must be investigated for tendencies to slide horizontally on its base, to overturn at the toe, and to crush or settle at the toe or outer edge.

Soil Stabilization

Loose soils can be densified by pulverizing the natural soil, mixing it with lime, cement, or salt, and compacting the mixture. This stabilized soil has increased strength and bearing qualities. It also has decreased water sensitivity, which diminishes the amount of volume change in expansive clays. Soil stabilization is used to provide a firm base under paved areas and floor slabs and to increase the bearing qualities of soils in the bottom of foundation excavations.

STABILIZING SOILS WITH LIME   Lime is an especially good stabilizing agent for expansive clays. Expansive clays can crack concrete floor slabs or create rough joints as the slabs heave and then settle during wet and dry cycles. Lime alleviates this problem in two ways: (1) by reducing the soil's expansive qualities and (2) by forming a moisture barrier which prevents water from reaching the expansive soil. Stabilization with lime eliminates the need to remove unsatisfactory soil from the site and bringing in soil with better bearing qualities. The pronounced drying action when lime is mixed with soil also expedites construction during wet weather. Wet sticky soils can be

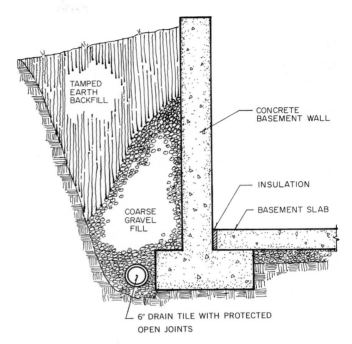

Fig. 2-12 Open-joint drain tile at a basement wall.

Fig. 2-11 Soils test report. Data are for estimating purposes only, and their accuracy is not guaranteed by the owner.

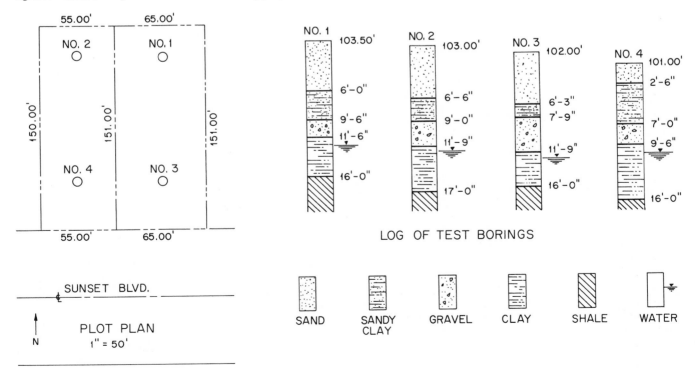

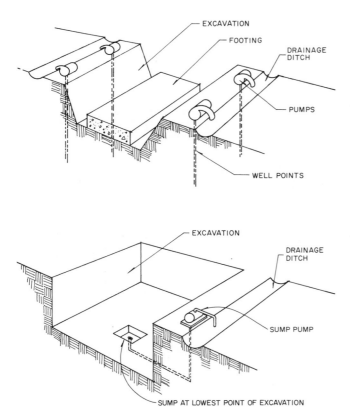

dried to the point necessary for compaction in a matter of hours after treatment.

The most common procedure in lime stabilization of base soil involves spreading sack hydrated lime or quick-lime over the soil and mixing it with the base material by machine. Water is added to the mixture if the moisture content is below the optimum moisture content. Preliminary mixing is usually accomplished by a rotary mixer to a depth of 12 to 18 in., which is later reduced to 6 in. by compaction. Final curing for 3 to 6 days is necessary to allow the soil to harden.

Lime may be introduced into the soil by drilling, pressure injection, or irrigation trenches. After the lime is placed in the soil, it gradually spreads. However, its effect on the soil decreases rapidly with distance from the source. In the pressure-injection method, lime, mixed with water to form a *slurry*, is forced into the soil at pressures of 150 to 660 psi. The lime moves out through the soil, following the path of least resistance to form sheetlike layers that are impervious to water.

STABILIZING SOILS WITH SALT   Salt is often used in stabilizing base courses for roads or parking areas. Common coarse-crushed rocksalt is mixed with well-graded clay or loamy soil having some limestone fines. Silt and sand are not suitable binders. Salt and water act as a binder for the soil particles, forming a mass of maximum stability. Salt may be added to soil either in dry form or as a brine. The amount

Fig. 2-13 Methods of dewatering a site. The excavation is kept dry by pumps until the footing is poured and has set.

Fig. 2-14 Compacting a fill with a sheep's-foot roller. (*Shepherd Machinery Company.*)

of salt depends on the nature of the soil and the bearing strength desired. The stabilized layer is seldom more than 12 in. thick.

The salt and soil may be mixed on the site or in a stationary plant. It is important that the site be well drained to remove excess water before the mixture is placed. For on-site mixing the soil is *scarified* (pulverizing and mixing of surface soils) to the correct depth. Salt and water are added and mixed. The stabilized layer is compacted and graded, and the surface is watered and rolled. The salt-and-water mixture coats the soil particles, aiding in compaction. The compaction process forces a salt-soil mortar to the surface to provide a very smooth finish. After compaction the soil must be allowed to cure for a period of 10 to 14 days, depending on the weather.

STABILIZING SOILS WITH CEMENT   All soils can be stabilized with portland cement, provided enough cement is added. The higher the clay content of the soil, the more cement must be added for proper stabilization. The cement and water form a chemical bond between the soil grains. As a secondary effect, when lime is formed during setting of the cement, the silica and alumina in the soil produce a cementitious material.

The steps for placement, compaction, and curing of cement-stabilized soils are the same whether the materials are plant mixed or site mixed. If the cement-treated base is to be no more than 6 in. thick, it is placed and compacted in one layer. If the thickness exceeds 6 in., the compacted base is placed in two layers. Compaction of the base must be completed within 2 hr after water is added to the mix. Final compaction is usually accomplished with pneumatic-tire rollers, which provide a kneading action. Immediately after final compaction, a bituminous curing seal is applied uniformly to the surface, and the soil is left to cure for a period of three to seven days.

Fig. 2-15 Operating a pneumatic tamper. (*Kelley Industrial Company.*)

Soil Poisoning

The termite is a very determined character. He will chew through plastics, asphalt-impregnated building paper, and even metals such as lead and tin to reach the cellulose

Fig. 2-16 Types of retaining walls.

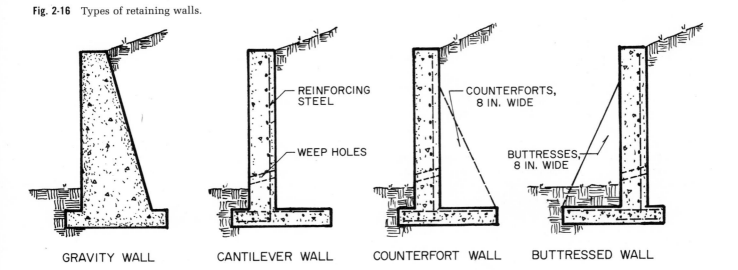

GRAVITY WALL   CANTILEVER WALL   COUNTERFORT WALL   BUTTRESSED WALL

REINFORCING STEEL

WEEP HOLES

COUNTERFORTS, 8 IN. WIDE

BUTTRESSES, 8 IN. WIDE

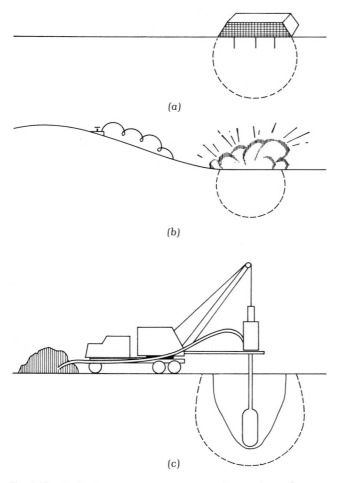

Fig. 2-17 Methods of compaction: (*a*) Surcharge; (*b*) explosives; (*c*) vibroflotation.

materials which it must have to live. The probability of termite attack on buildings depends on environmental conditions. If the termite is sufficiently well fed, it may not touch manmade structures. If it cannot find sufficient water, it will die of thirst. If air is allowed to circulate around its abode, it will die of the cold. There is a mistaken belief that a steel or concrete building is safe from termite damage. Termites need cellulose to survive; however, wood is not the only form of cellulose. It is also present in furnishings provided by the occupants of the building. Valuable records, books, mattresses, paper, and even the paper covering of gypsum wallboard beneath a painted surface may be food for hungry termites.

It is true that termites cannot eat through concrete. However, they can and do enter through construction joints, expansion joints, small fissures around plumbing pipes, electrical conduits, and small shrinkage cracks. A concrete slab on grade actually provides ideal conditions

for termites. The subbase is quite likely to be somewhat moist, with no circulation to dry out the underside of the slab. Subterranean termites must always be in contact with the earth, and the underside of the slab is in contact at all times. For this reason soil poisoning has proved to be one of the most effective methods of controlling termites.

The U.S. Department of Agriculture has done extensive testing of soil-poisoning agents. The official publication of the Federal Housing Administration, "Minimum Property Standards," lists acceptable soil poisons that have withstood minimum exposure in U.S. Forest Service tests without failure. These formulations are identified by their chemical composition rather than by trade name. Recommended toxicants that are generally available as water emulsions are Aldrin, Chlordane, Dieldrin, Heptachlor. Of course, the list does not include all toxicants that have been used or that may prove useful at some later time. Brand-name formulations should be evaluated on the basis of their chemical ingredients and test reports from independent or government laboratories.

Fuel oil is commonly used as a dilutant for toxicants; however, it should not be used under concrete slabs on grade. Its slow rate of evaporation can create objectionable and perhaps toxic odors for a long period of time. Only the water-emulsion type of toxicants should be used under floor slabs. The toxicants are usually spread at the rate of 1 gal per 10 sq ft. The most economical time to apply them is on the rough grade, before any rock fill is placed.

FOUNDATIONS AND PILES

Foundations

That part of a building below the surface of the ground is called the *foundation*. The foundation may represent only a small portion of the cost of a project, but it must provide a stable base for the entire structure. The foundation must distribute the weight of the building and its supports, as well as all live loads, over an area of subgrade large enough to prevent uneven settling or collapse. Before a particular type or size of foundation can be selected, the types of soil present under the entire site must be determined. The total load that the foundation is to support must be calculated to include the weight of all occupants, furniture, machinery, and stored goods. The allowable foundation types, and the bearing pressure permitted for each type of soil must be determined from the local building codes.

Basically, any type of foundation consists of three parts: the *foundation bed*, the rock or soil on which the building rests; the *footing*, that section of the foundation, normally widened, which rests on the foundation bed; and the *foundation wall*, the portion of the foundation rising from the footing to a point above the ground.

This last portion may be a column or pedestal instead of a wall. If it is a wall, it forms what is called a *continuous foundation*.

Fig. 2-18 Lime stabilization. (*National Lime Association.*)

Fig. 2-19 Mixing soil cement. (*Portland Cement Association.*)

CONTINUOUS FOUNDATIONS   This type of foundation is the one most commonly used for residences or small buildings. The design calls for a foundation wall extending above a footing slab. The building load it must transmit to earth depends on the vertical loads imposed by the unsupported length and the height of the walls to be placed on it. The size of the footing and the thickness of the foundation wall are specified by local building codes on the basis of the type of soil at the site. Most building codes require that the bottom of the footing be horizontal and that any slopes on the building site be compensated for by stepping the bottom of the footing.

GRADE-BEAM FOUNDATIONS   These are widely used for residential construction, where permitted by local code, especially where basements are not required. A grade beam is a reinforced concrete beam at ground level around the entire perimeter of the building. It is supported by a series of concrete piers extending down into undisturbed soil. The grade beam supports the load of the building, and the piers distribute this load to the foundation bed. This type of foundation is frequently used on sloping sites or in areas subject to earth slippage.

SPREAD FOUNDATIONS   When girders or roof trusses are supported at intervals along a wall, the continuous footing may be widened at those points to compensate for the additional weight. In this instance the walls above the footing

are thickened to form buttresses. Spread footings under walls or isolated footings under columns distribute the load so that the load per square foot will not exceed the bearing capacity of the soil at the foundation bed. Spread footings are usually reinforced with steel to resist the shear and bending moments exerted by the columns. The footings may be flat, stepped, or sloped.

MAT FOUNDATIONS   A mat or raft foundation consists of a heavily reinforced concrete slab under the entire building. The slab spreads the total load of the building over the entire site and is especially useful when the subsoil is uneven. On uneven subsoil, if the columns rest on individual footings, and some footings settle more than others, serious cracking and strains can develop in the building. However, a properly designed mat foundation acts as a unit, and so minimizes the problems of unequal settlement. This type of foundation is sometimes called a *floating foundation*.

PIERS   Concrete piers are used when rock or suitable load-bearing soil lies some distance below the surface. Shafts, with or without wood or steel casings, are sunk to the desired depth and filled with concrete. If the shaft is carried through water or water-bearing soil, it may be necessary to use a caisson. This is a watertight chamber, usually of wood or steel, that is carried down the shaft with the excavation. For excavations too deep for controlling the water with an ordinary caisson, a pneumatic caisson is

Fig. 2-20 Spreading soil cement. (*Portland Cement Association.*)

used. The top of the pneumatic caisson is sealed, and the work is done under compressed air to counterbalance the hydrostatic pressure of the water in the soil. Entrance to the working chamber is through double-gated locks.

Bell-shaped enlargements are sometimes made at the bottom of excavations for piers. These bells distribute the weight of the pier when it is not resting on bedrock. The pier is then used as a column base, and the structural column is placed on top.

Piles

A pile is a slender structural unit introduced into the ground in order to transmit loads to underground strata. Piles transfer load to surrounding strata by resistance along their surface or by direct bearing on the compressed soil at and near the bottom.

The amount of load that can be transferred by friction to surrounding soil formations has specific limits. The frictional resistance along the surface of the pile can be determined by formula, test loadings, or on the basis of the energy necessary to force the pile into the ground.

WOOD PILES If wood piles are kept continuously wet, they will last for centuries. For example, the large, heavy stone buildings that were erected in Venice in the fourteenth and fifteenth centuries rest on thousands of wood piles. The piles were driven through some 54 low swampy islands in the Adriatic Sea, where they were continuously wet. It is only in the past 50 years that they have shown much evidence of deterioration. This deterioration has not resulted from continual submersion in water, but has been caused by the power boats that now throng the canals between the buildings. The wakes of these boats have been

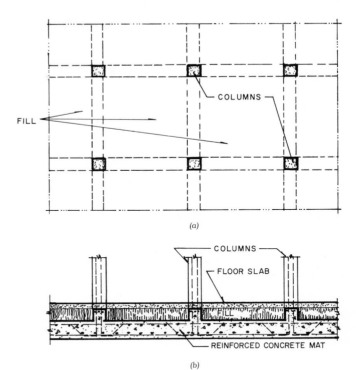

(a)

(b)

Fig. 2-22 Mat, or raft, foundations: (a) plan; (b) section.

washing away the wet earth between the pilings, allowing the wood to be alternately wet and dry. As a result the Rennaissance city of Venice is slowly sinking as the wood piles deteriorate.

Wood piles are usually tree trunks with the limbs and bark trimmed off. Except in special cases, the piles are driven into the ground with the smaller end first. This end of the pile may be fitted with a steel point if rocks are likely to be encountered. Cedar and cyprus, because of their resistance to decay, are commonly used for piles. Douglas fir and southern pine piles take the shock of driving very well and will accept decay-resistant preservatives.

The diameter of wood piles depends on the load to be placed upon them. The minimum diameter of the driving point is 6 in. The diameter of the butt end is seldom less than 12 in.

STEEL H PILES Rolled-steel wide-flange structural sections are used where driving is impeded by boulders, thin strata of hardpan, or rock that is underlain by a soil of lower bearing qualities. Steel piles are usually used for driving to bedrock. When the H section is driven into the ground, the earth is usually gripped between the flanges of the section. The soil resistance must therefore be calculated on the rectangular section of the H, and not on the total surface area. Structural-steel H sections have been driven in lengths of 200 ft. An advantage of steel piles is that they can extend above the water table and act as columns.

Fig. 2-21 Wall and column foundations.

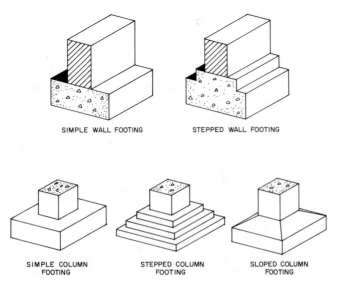

SIMPLE WALL FOOTING   STEPPED WALL FOOTING

SIMPLE COLUMN   STEPPED COLUMN   SLOPED COLUMN
FOOTING   FOOTING   FOOTING

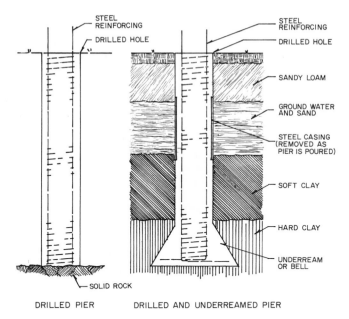

STEEL
REINFORCING
DRILLED HOLE

STEEL
REINFORCING
DRILLED HOLE
SANDY LOAM
GROUND WATER
AND SAND
STEEL CASING
(REMOVED AS
PIER IS POURED)
SOFT CLAY
HARD CLAY
UNDERREAM
OR BELL
SOLID ROCK

DRILLED PIER   DRILLED AND UNDERREAMED PIER

Fig. 2-23 Excavating for piers.

Where steel piles are adjacent to seawater, their unprotected life will vary with conditions of exposure. Available methods of protection include cathode protection, a flame-sprayed aluminum coating, organic and inorganic coatings, and concrete jacketing. Special rolled-steel H piles are available in standard A36 steel or in high-strength low-alloy steels.

PRECAST CONCRETE PILES   Piles of reinforced concrete are widely used. These piles may be cylindrical, square, or octagonal. If they are to be driven into soft or mucky earth, they are usually tapered. Those used in sand, gravel, clay, or hardpan are usually cylindrical. Piles driven into plastic soils are square ended, whereas those that must penetrate hard strata have long tapered points.

Precast concrete piles must be heavily reinforced to withstand handling, with especially heavy reinforcement toward the top to withstand the impact of driving. The fact that exact lengths must be determined before driving and the added cost of cutoff make precast concrete piles somewhat more expensive than cast-in-place piles.

CAST-IN-PLACE CONCRETE PILES   Piles that are cast on the job site may be classified generally as shell, or cased, piles, and shell-less, or uncased, piles. A *shell pile* is formed by driving a hollow steel tube, or shell with a closed end into the ground and filling it with concrete. Several types of

Fig. 2-24 Buildings resting on wood piles installed during the fourteenth and fifteenth centuries A.D. Venice, Italy.

shells are used for this purpose. They may be of fluted steel sheet to withstand driving forces. When the piles have been driven to the proper depth, the shell is cut off at the surface and filled with concrete.

Tapered shells of relatively thin sheet steel are driven with a split mandrel inside the casing. After driving the mandrel is removed and the casing is filled with concrete.

A *shell-less* pile is formed by driving a casing and a core with a piledriver to the required depth. The core is removed and the casing is filled with concrete. The casing is then removed, leaving the concrete in contact with the earth. The fluid pressure of the concrete forces the plastic concrete against the sides of the earth, increasing the frictional resistance.

A *pedestal pile* is formed by driving a casing and core into the ground, removing the core, and then raising the casing a few feet above the bottom of the hole. The casing is then partially filled with concrete, and the concrete is rammed to form a bulge or pedestal at the bottom of the hole. The remainder of the hole is then filled as the casing is withdrawn. This type of pile can only be used where there is not enough pressure to force the earth up into the casing when the core is being lifted.

Pipe piles consist of heavy steel pipe driven and filled with concrete. Smaller sizes are driven with closed ends, and the larger sizes are driven with the ends open. Compressed air is used to remove the soil inside the pipe as it is being driven. With larger sizes of pipe piles the earth may be removed by augers or small orange-peel buckets. When the pipe pile has been driven to the proper depth, all earth is removed from the inside, and concrete is poured into the pipe.

COMPOSITE PILES   There are also combination piles of wood and cast-in-place concrete. A wood pile is driven its full length into the ground. A permanent reinforced-steel shell with a core is then placed on top of this, and the combination is driven. The core is removed, and the steel shell is filled with concrete. At the completion of driving the wood portion of the combination pile should be entirely below the permanent groundwater level.

SHEET PILING   One method of confining earth for deep excavations or to protect foundations of adjacent buildings is by means of sheet piling. Sheet piling may be wood or steel. Wood sheet piling consists of planks driven into the soil side by side; in some cases they may have tongue-and-groove joints to hold them in alignment.

Sheet piling is driven around the site before excavation is begun. If the driving is easy, the sheet piling may be driven to its entire depth at this point. Otherwise it can be driven in stages, as long as it is always kept below the bottom of the excavation. As the excavation is carried down, the piling must be braced against the lateral pressure of the retained earth.

Fig. 2-25   Pile driver in action. (*Raymond International, Inc.*)

Pile Driving

The equipment and methods necessary to drive piles vary with the size of piles and the type of soil. The simplest type of pile driver is a *drop hammer*. This is a hammer in a vertical frame between two guides. The hammer, which may weigh from 500 to 2000 lb, is raised to the top of the frame and dropped onto the pile.

This type of pile driver has, for the most part, been replaced by the *steam hammer*. Steam hammers may be either single acting or double acting. The single-acting steam hammer consists of a heavy ram or hammer enclosed in a cylinder. Steam is allowed to enter the cylinder, where it raises the hammer a distance of 2 to 4 ft. When the steam pressure is released, the hammer falls of its own weight. The hammer is placed on top of the pile by a pile driver or is suspended from the boom of a crane. In a double-acting steam hammer the ram or hammer is raised by steam pressure from 4 to 20 ft. Instead of being allowed just to fall, the ram is forced down by steam entering the top of the cylinder. Steam hammers can be operated by air pressure as well as steam.

Piles may also be set with the aid of a water jet. When they are being driven in sand, a water pipe is lowered beside the pile, and a jet of water is forced through the pipe. The water washes away the sandy soil below the pile and acts as a lubricant during driving. Some concrete piles are precast with pipes in the center. Water is forced down this pipe to wash away the sand beneath the pile. The pile is then usually driven the last 3 ft without the use of water.

PAVING AND SURFACING MATERIALS

The term *paving* is used primarily to refer to a rigid surface, such as concrete, stone, or brick; the term *surfacing* generally refers to the more flexible asphalt, tar, and waterbound surfaces. However, the two terms are often used interchangeably. Both asphalts and tars are bitumens, solid or semisolid hydrocarbons. Asphalts may be naturally formed native asphalts, or they may be the products of petroleum refining. Most tar is a by-product of the distillation or carbonization of coal. Partial distillation of coal produces the material commonly called *coal-tar pitch*. Coal-tar pitch stands up well under moderate heat, water, and cold; however, its instability under extremely hot sun limits its usefulness as a surfacing material or paving material.

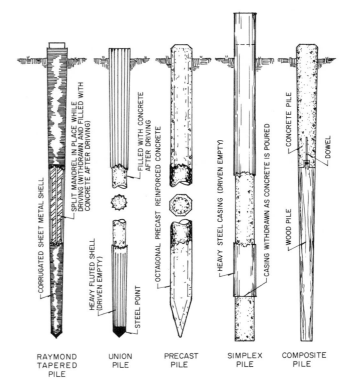

Fig. 2-27 Types of concrete piles.

Fig. 2-26 Driving wood piles with a steam hammer. (*American Wood Preservers' Institute.*)

Bases and Subbases

Early methods of watering the soil and grading the natural soil to provide drainage were replaced by hand laying of rocks and blocks to make hard surfaces. These methods were replaced in turn by *waterbound macadam*, which consists of layers of broken stone compacted by rolling and adding water and stone dust or clay to bind the material into a firm, stable surface. When bituminous materials came into use, water was replaced by oil to settle dust.

The subbase of a paving project consists of materials selected to improve the foundation for surfacing. The use of a subbase reduces the amount of more expensive base material required. Subbases should be constructed of materials that will compact well. Some materials, such as those containing clay, may be satisfactory for subbases even though they have characteristics that make them unsuitable for bases. The success or failure of a paving project depends largely on whether the foundation provides continuous, firm, and uniformly distributed support. The subbase must have sufficient bearing strength and stability to carry the load of the base courses and traffic. Gravel subbases may be necessary where the subgrade soils have low bearing strength or poor drainage.

The structural design of the pavement depends on the thickness of the subbase, base, and surfacing materials to be placed over natural soils. The layers of material, with the best at the top and the poorest at the bottom, should be designed to derive the maximum benefit from each. Subbase materials may be improved by the addition of cement, salt, or lime, as described under densification of soils. Relatively dry soils usually give adequate support for paving; however, some soils soften and deform with excessive moisture. Areas surfaced with bituminous materials must have a minimum slope of $\frac{1}{8}$ in/ft for proper drainage. Drainage ditches adjacent to the surfaced area must be deep enough to drain both the subbase and the base courses. If subsurface water is within 4 to 6 ft of the surface paving, the surfacing can be damaged by water rising through capillary action.

Subsurface water can be intercepted and diverted by the use of subsoil drains. These drains may be constructed of open-joint clay pipe, concrete pipe, or perforated steel pipe. The pipes are laid in ditches below the seepage zone and are covered to the level of the subbase with clean

INSTALLATION PROCEDURE

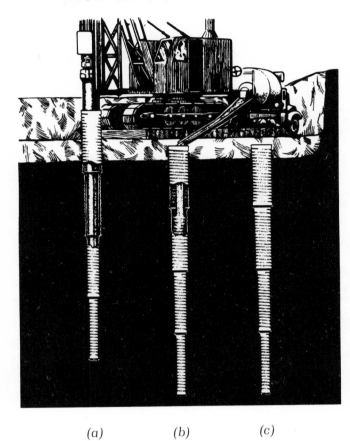

(a)   *(b)*   *(c)*

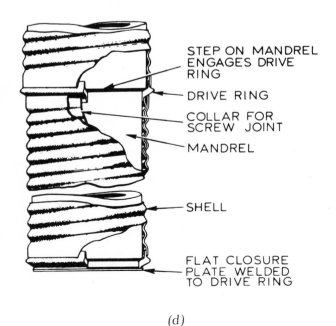

STEP ON MANDREL ENGAGES DRIVE RING

DRIVE RING

COLLAR FOR SCREW JOINT

MANDREL

SHELL

FLAT CLOSURE PLATE WELDED TO DRIVE RING

(d)

Fig. 2-28 Driving Raymond step-taper piles. (a) A steel shell is placed over a rugged steel core or mandrel extending to the pile tip, and the core and shell are driven to the required bearing. The heavy rigid core permits driving to high resistance with minimum loss of hammer energy. (b) When the core is removed, the shell remains in the ground to maintain driving resistance and protect the poured concrete filling. The shell is internally inspected and filled with concrete. (c) Excess shell is removed to show the completed pile. (d) Detail showing joint of two sections of pile shell, the closure plate on the pile tip, and engagement of the mandrel within the shell. (*Raymond International, Inc.*)

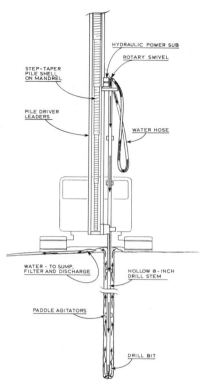

STEP-TAPER PILE SHELL ON MANDREL

HYDRAULIC POWER SUB

ROTARY SWIVEL

PILE DRIVER LEADERS

WATER HOSE

WATER - TO SUMP, FILTER AND DISCHARGE

HOLLOW 8-INCH DRILL STEM

PADDLE AGITATORS

DRILL BIT

Fig. 2-29 Wet rotary preexcavation for piles. Wavy arrows indicate flow of water in the preexcavation system. (*Raymond International, Inc.*)

gravel or crushed rock uniformly graded from ½ to 2 in. The top of the subdrain backfill should be an impervious material in order to keep the surface water out of the drain.

Types of Asphalt

Asphalts are dark-brown to black, solid or semisolid, cementitious materials which gradually liquefy when heated. The main components are bitumens. Native asphalts may occur as *lake asphalt*, surface deposits in depressions in the earth; as *rock asphalt*, porous rock impregnated with asphalt; or *gilsonite*, an exceptionally pure, brittle form found in veins similar to coal.

Native asphalt was used as a waterproof coating for canoes 5000 years ago by the Sumerians who inhabited the Tigris and Euphrates Valley, now a part of Iraq. Modern Iraqi still use this material to cover their boats. Asphalt was used as a mortar for the beautifully glazed bricks of Babylonian architecture in 1700 B.C. The use of asphalt as a paving material dates back to 1800 A.D., when it was employed in France as a surfacing for bridges, walks, and floors. The first asphalt-surfaced street in the United States was laid in Washington, D.C., in 1876. With the discovery that asphalt could be produced from crude oil or petroleum, and with the growth of automotive and air transportation, the manufacture of asphalt paving ma-

terial continues to be one of the most rapidly expanding industries in the world.

The asphalts and related materials most commonly used for paving or surfacing are shown in Table 2-4.

TABLE 2-4 Asphalts used for paving and surfacing

MATERIAL	USE
Air-refined asphalts	Used for blending with other kinds of asphalts, as subsurface sealers under concrete pavements, and to waterproof structures both above and below grade. Air-refined asphalts are not susceptible to temperature change and have a higher melting point than most steam-refined asphalts.
Steam-refined asphalts	Residual materials of petroleum distillation, refined by steam. They are used as binders in various types of bituminous surfacing, in the preparation of emulsified asphalts, and as paving asphalts.
Paving Asphalts	Solids or semisolids whose consistency changes with temperature. Paving asphalts are viscous and will adhere to most aggregates. They are classified by their resistance to penetration in tenths of millimeters of a standard needle at 77°C (as defined by ASTM D978) and range from consistencies of 40 to 300 (the higher the number, the softer the asphalt). Paving asphalts are usually the binding ingredient in asphalt concrete and plant-mixed surfacing.
Liquid asphalts	Blends of asphalt and some solvent, to make them fluid for ease of application. Steam-refined asphalts may be liquefied with naptha, kerosene, light oils, or some other petroleum product. These carriers may be either volatile or nonvolatile. Asphalt may also be combined with water to form an emulsion. By means of different carrying agents, the consistency can be varied from a light, oily liquid to a heavy, sticky paste (softer than a rating of 300). Liquid asphalts are used as a soft binder for cold-layed pavements.
Slow-curing asphalts	Asphalts which have a slow volatization rate. This form is used when it is necessary to stockpile asphaltic materials until they are needed. They are also used where frequent reworking of the surface is needed. *Medium-curing asphalts*, which have been cut back with some volatile solvent (usually kerosene), are used where workability is required. The final surfacing then sets hard as the solvent evaporates.

TABLE 2-4 Asphalts used for paving and surfacing (*Continued*)

MATERIAL	USE
Rapid-curing asphalts	Asphalts that have been cut back with gasoline or naptha, solvents which evaporate rapidly. They are used where quick setting is desirable, generally to impart tensile strength to mixtures that contain clean, fine sands.
Asphalt emulsions	Asphalt materials mixed with water. These may be penetration-type or mixing-type emulsions, depending on their stability, or the ease with which the bituminous material and the water separates. The water in penetration-type emulsions separates from the bituminous materials soon after application, and the asphalt cannot then be mixed. The use of penetration emulsions is limited to surface treatments and sealers. The mixing types can be used in construction processes that require mixing on the job site.
Dust palliatives	Bituminous products of relatively low viscosity which will penetrate or be absorbed into a surface. They are used to reduce dust nuisances, waterproof the surface of subgrade materials, and form a priming base for future surfacing operations.
Prime coats	Similar to dust palliatives. They are used on untreated compacted surfaces to form an adhesive film which will bond with subsequent surfacing materials. The prime coat penetrates the sub-base, sealing the pores and plugging the capillary voids.
Tack coats	Very viscous liquid-asphalt emulsions or rapid-cure asphalts. They are used to form an adhesive film between a slick surface and new surfacing. The new surfacing is placed while the tack coat is still sticky.
Seal coats	May be either bituminous or other materials. They are applied to the surface of the paving to keep out moisture or air, to rejuvenate dry or weathered surfaces, to prevent damage by petroleum products, and generally to protect the load-bearing materials.
Armor coats	Similar to seal coats. They are applied in thicknesses of 1 in. or less to protect the surfacing against abrasion, impact, or action of the elements. The armor coat is simply a wearing surface and adds little to the structural strength of the paving. Armor coats are usually applied in two layers, each layer compacted with a steel-tired roller.

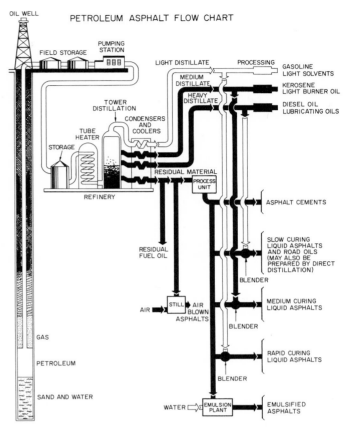

Fig. 2-30 Flow chart showing recovery and refining of petroleum asphaltic materials. (*Asphalt Institute.*)

Asphalt Construction Methods

Bituminous materials are combined with mineral aggregates in several ways. They may be road mixed or plant mixed. The surfacing material may be hot mixed or cold mixed.

ROAD-MIXED SURFACING   When facilities for plant mixing are not economically available, a grader may be used to mix native or imported aggregate with either hot or cold asphalts on the job. There is no accurate method of determining the results of this type of surfacing. If hot asphalt is applied over unheated aggregate, the spreading and compaction time can vary enough to produce uneven results. If a traveling mixer is used, there is a somewhat more even distribution of materials, and consequently more control of the spreading process. If liquid asphalt of the penetrating type is used in the cold-asphalt process, the results are usually better.

PLANT-MIXED SURFACING   Stationary mixing plants can turn out large quantities of high quality hot-mix surfacing materials. In a well-organized hot-mix plant an aggregate drier is used to reduce the water content of the aggregate to the point at which it will combine most readily with the bituminous materials. There are heating devices, screens and storage bins for separating and storing the hot aggregate, asphalt heating and storage tanks, measuring devices for accurate proportioning of ingredients, and a mechanical mixer with temperature gauges and other attachments for positive control and efficient operation.

ASPHALT MACADAM   Surfacing can be prepared by the penetration method. Coarse crushed stone, coarse gravel, or blast-furnace slag is placed on a prepared subbed. It is then compacted with steel rollers or tampers to a smooth surface. A penetration-type asphalt emulsion or hot asphalt is sprayed over the compacted rock bed. The layer of coarse aggregate is then covered with finer aggregates, and the surface is again rolled to force the fines into the voids in the coarse aggregate. The surfacing may then be given a seal coat to form a final bond for the surface.

ASPHALT CONCRETE   Asphalt concrete or asphaltic concrete is a combination of dense, carefully graded aggregate, mixed hot with paving asphalt at a central plant. There are more fines (usually limestone dust or cement) in the aggregate than in the standard hot mix. Paving asphalts of the lower-penetration type are used as the binder.

The hot-mixed material is carried to the job site in dump trucks, where it is spread with mechanical spreaders or bladed into place. The materials are spread in such a manner that they form compacted horizontal layers not over 2 in. thick. The major portion of the compaction is done by rolling with a steel-tired roller, starting at the outer edge and working toward the center. The outside edges of the surfacing, which are not accessible to the roller, must be compacted by hand. The usual thickness

for residential driveways, parking areas, and walks is about 2 in.

Surface Sealers

Gasoline and oil drippings can cause asphalt drives and parking areas to soften and crumble. The hot sun can cause asphalt binders to evaporate. Water penetrating the surface of asphalt surfacing can cause deterioration. Many chemicals used for deicing cause the surface to pit and crumble. These problems of asphalt surfacing can be minimized by the use of an effective sealer.

Pavement sealers fall into three basic groups: native-asphalt base materials, coal-tar bases, and vinyl-base coatings. Gilsonite ore, a native asphalt, liquefied by the addition of a volatile carrier, is used as a sealer to reactivate the binder in old pavement and improve the binder in new pavement. It is said to make the pavement stay cleaner because voids are filled. This sealer, however, is subject to damage by oil and gasoline spillage.

Coal-tar pitch offers complete protection from spillage of gasoline, oil, hydraulic fluid, and all types of petroleum products. Coal-tar-pitch emulsions provide a continuous adhesive coating. Alternate rain and sunlight exposure has a destructive effect on asphalt and ultimately penetrates and breaks down the binder. Such deterioration is greatly aggravated during cold weather by freezing and thawing. The coal-tar sealer forms an impermeable barrier between the pavement and rain or snow because it resists penetration or displacement by water.

A new development in coal-tar sealers is latex (rubberized) tar emulsions. These compounds have a tensile strength two to three times that of regular coal-tar sealers. Coal-tar–latex compounds are also used for sealing expansion joints and cracks in asphalt surfaces.

Fig. 2-31   Applying asphaltic concrete. (*Flint Asphalt and Paving Company.*)

Several sealers based on vinyl and epoxy resins overcome the color limitations of coal-tar sealers. These highly durable vinyl emulsions come in several colors and form an opaque protective coating over black asphalt. They are tough and weather resistant, stop oxidation and frost damage, increase pavement life, and provide colorful surfacing for tennis courts, play yards, and residential and commercial drives.

Headers

Temporary or permanent edges of driveways, walks, and paved areas must be finished with substantial wood or concrete headers. Wood headers are usually 1″ × 3″ redwood strips anchored into the ground with 1″ × 3″ redwood stakes at 6 ft on center. The redwood headers can be bent to follow the contour of the paved area. A concrete curb may also be used to confine the surfacing. Although concrete is more expensive, it is more permanent.

Concrete Paving

Portland cement concrete paving for roads and highways is usually placed by a traveling plant, which moves along with the construction. After the subgrade is placed and compacted, side forms are placed to serve as guides as well as forms for the plastic concrete. The side forms also serve as riding rails for the mechanical spreader and finishing machine.

The thickness and the cross-section design of the concrete pavement depend on the location and type of joints used. The *expansion joint* is made by pouring concrete against the form or expansion-joint filler, to allow for expansion and contraction of the slabs with temperature changes; the *construction joint* is formed by pouring against an existing concrete slab; and the *contraction joint* is created by the natural shrinkage of continuously placed concrete.

Modern practices of laying continuous ribbons of concrete paving have shown that controlled contraction joints every 15 to 25 ft completely eliminate the need for expansion joints under most climatic conditions. The original shrinkage of the concrete during setting is enough to provide space for future expansion with temperature changes.

The finishing of concrete paving depends on the type of service expected. Rough textures may be used to reduce skidding in wet weather. Smooth-troweled surfaces are needed for athletic courts. Various decorative surfaces may be used for landscaping and walkways. Finishes for concrete slabs and paving are discussed in detail in Chapter 3.

Stone Paving

Many types of decorative stone pavings can be used in landscaping the home or commercial building projects. The use of stone as a surfacing material dates back to the Roman roads of Pompeii. The Romans paved their roads with carefully cut stones set on well-graded bases of gravel in a matrix of concrete. Many of these roads, which once covered the Roman Empire, are still in existence. Brick and cobblestone streets are still in service in some parts of the United States, and cobblestones, round or square stones set in beds of sand, are still being installed in major European cities.

Paving materials used in landscaping, walks, terraces, or patios may be set on and bonded to concrete slabs. In areas that are not subject to frost a well-drained coarse of 1- to 3-in. gravel, crushed rock, or slag should be placed under the concrete slab, and the slab must be reinforced to counteract the shrinking and swelling due to freezing and thawing cycles.

Most paving materials can also be set directly on well-tamped beds of sand. Those with squared edges, such as

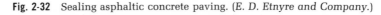

Fig. 2-32 Sealing asphaltic concrete paving. (*E. D. Etnyre and Company.*)

Fig. 2-33 Roman paving in Pompeii.

Fig. 2-34 Marble cobblestones ready for placement on a sand cushion, Munich, Germany.

brick, precast concrete units, and quarry tile, may be set with tight joints in a variety of patterns. Flagstone, slate, bluestone, and other irregularly shaped paving materials may be placed on sand beds with mortar in the spaces between them. With precast concrete rounds, sections of logs, and stepping stones the spaces may be filled with white or colored gravel, crushed stone, or rounded beach stones.

QUESTIONS

1. Why is it necessary for an architect to have some knowledge of soils and soil structure?

2. What are four characteristics of rock that may make it unsatisfactory as a foundation bed?

3. Describe clay soil and list its advantages and disadvantages as a foundation material.

4. What is the groundwater lever?

5. What is the required size for a spread footing 1 ft deep, resting on compact coarse sand, to support a load of 6000 lb?

6. What is the required width for a continuous footing resting on compacted fine sand, to support a uniform load of 2000 lb per linear foot of wall?

7. How does soil react under a load?

8. Discuss the geologic features that can lead to landslides.

9. What kind of forces must buildings in earthquake zones be designed to resist?

10. How can the designer determine the probability of an earthquake in a given location?

11. Describe the process of taking a test boring.

12. What are the limitations of test borings?

13. Describe three methods of increasing the bearing capacity of soils.

14. What physical changes take place in a soil when it is compacted?

15. What is meant by 95 percent of *optimum density* of a fill?

16. What are the three criteria for the stability of a retaining wall?

17. Describe the process of soil densification through the use of materials other than those at the site.

18. How can termites attack a concrete or steel building?

19. Why is it unwise to use oil-emulsion poisons under a concrete slab?

20. What are the three basic parts of a building foundation?

21. Describe the two most common types of foundation used in residential construction.

22. What is a caisson, and where is it used?

23. Are the tops of wood piles above or below groundwater level?

24. Describe the process of placing a cast-in-place concrete pile.

25. What is the most common use of sheet piles?

26. How can the operator of a pile driver determine the underground conditions when he is driving piles?

27. Define the following terms: bitumens, tar, coal-tar pitch, asphalts.

28. Describe a method of preventing subsurface water from entering a basement.

29. How are paving asphalts classified?

30. What is a cut-back asphalt?

31. Describe three types of seal coats, and give the advantage of each.

32. What are some of the difficulties encountered in laying road-mixed surfacing?

33. Describe three types of joints used in concrete paving.

34. What materials are used for asphalt concrete, and how is it laid?

35. Describe four types of decorative pavings that could be used for terraces or patios.

REFERENCES FOR FURTHER STUDY

Ambe, T. W.: "Soil Testing for Engineers," Wiley, New York, 1951.

American Institute of Architects: 1785 Massachusetts Avenue, N.W., Washington, D.C., 20036. How to Design Against Earthquakes, *AIA Journal*, 1965.

The Asphalt Institute: Asphalt Institute Building, University of Maryland, College Park, Md. "Asphalt Handbook," 1961.

Construction Specifications Institute: Suite 300, 1150 17th Street, N.W., Washington, D.C., 20036. Soils, *Construction Specifier*, May, June, July 1968. "A Report on Paving and Related Work," fall 1958.

Field, Jacob: "Failures in Foundations," Soiltest, Inc., 2205 Lee Street, Evanston, Ill., 60202, 1965.

Merritt, Frederick S.: "Building Construction Handbook," McGraw-Hill, New York, 1958.

National Research Council, Building Research Advisory Board: 2101 Constitution Avenue, Washington, D.C., 20025. "Protection against Decay and Termites in Residential Construction," Publ. 448, 1959.

Parking and Highway Improvement Contractors Association: 5107 West First Street, Los Angeles, Calif., 90004. "Parking Design Manual," 1969.

Scott, Roland F.: "Principles of Soil Mechanics," Addison-Wesley, Reading, Pa., 1963.

Tomlinson, M. J.: "Foundation Design and Construction," Wiley, New York, 1969.

U.S. Agricultural Research Service: Washington, D.C., 20025. "Soil Treatment: An Aid in Termite Control," leaflet 324, rev. 1961. "Eastern Subterranean Termite Forest Pest," leaflet 68, April 1962.

CONCRETE

3

CEMENT

The characteristics of concrete vary widely, depending on the composition of the aggregates and the chemical and physical properties of the cement paste. The term *cement*, in its broader meaning, applies to any material that will bind two or more nonadhesive substances together. The cements to be considered here are those which have a limestone, oyster-shell, coquina shell, or similar lime base and are used to form concrete.

Types of Cement

ROMAN CEMENT   Concrete has been used as a construction material for centuries. Before 100 B.C. the Romans had developed an excellent concrete which enabled them to erect vast structures and works of engineering.

On the slopes of Mt. Vesuvius and in extinct volcanic areas near Rome they found a light, porous volcanic rock. Its rough surface formed a good bond for cementitious material (a substance capable of acting as a cement), or mortar. The cement was prepared from a mixture of lime and a volcanic ash called *pozzolana*, named after the village of Pozzuoli near Mt. Vesuvius. When the pozzolana was mixed with limestone and burned, the resulting material, ground and mixed with water, gave a cement of unprecedented strength. Roman cement was a *hydraulic cement*, one that will harden underwater. This cement, mixed with small pieces of volcanic rock, formed a lasting concrete.

As the Roman Empire expanded, the knowledge of concrete spread throughout Europe and Asia. The quality of the concrete had to be determined by extensive trial and error and varied from area to area, depending on the purity and composition of the available raw materials.

NATURAL CEMENT   Certain natural rocks, when quarried, crushed, and processed, will produce a natural cement. If enough heat is applied to drive off gases, a hydraulic cement results, but it has very low strength. Lime and natural rock were the only sources of cementitious materials for many centuries. Because the strength and other physical properties of natural cements vary greatly, very few building codes allow its use in concrete.

PORTLAND CEMENT   In 1824 Joseph Aspdin in England developed and patented a hydraulic cement that was superior to the natural cement of the time. He called this cement *portland cement*, because of its resemblance to a grayish limestone mined on the Isle of Portland. Portland cement was first manufactured in the United States, in Pennsylvania, in 1872. It was discovered that if a carefully controlled mixture of limestone and clay was burned at a much higher heat than had been used before, the resulting cement had better hydraulic qualities. At this higher heat the clay and limestone fused into hard, marble-sized clinkers composed of the two original materials in a new form. These clinkers, when ground, produced portland cement as we know it now.

Portland cement has the following basic composition:

Lime	60–65%
Silica	10–25%
Iron Oxide	2–4%
Alumina	5–10%

Most of the ingredients in portland cement are found in nature, but they cannot always be used in their natural form. Limestone, shale, slate, clay, chalk, marl, oyster shells, cement rock, silica sand, iron ore, and blast-furnace slag may be used as raw materials. Each cement plant may use a different combination of raw materials, which, when ground, blended, and tested under rigid control, produce a cement that is uniform in strength and quality.

Manufacture of Portland Cement

Portland cement is manufactured by two basic processes: the wet process and the dry process. In the wet process proper proportions of raw materials are mixed with enough water to form a *slurry*, which is 30 to 35 percent water. In this form the materials are further proportioned, mixed, ground, and pulverized and then pumped to a furnace called a *kiln*. The dry process is similar, except that the materials are proportioned, stored, ground, mixed, pulverized, and fed into the kiln in a dry state. Quality control of materials is critical, and throughout the manufacturing process samples are continually taken for laboratory analysis.

Portland cement is fired continuously in horizontal revolving kilns. These kilns are steel cylinders up to 20 ft in diameter and 300 to 700 ft long, lined with refractory fire brick. The raw materials are fed in one end, and fuel, which may be oil, powdered coal, or gas, is ignited and blown in the other. As raw material rolls from one end of the slightly sloping, rotating cylinder to the other, it

Fig. 3-1   Rotating kiln. (*Portland Cement Association.*)

slowly fuses into marble-sized greenish-black clinkers, which have specific physical and chemical characteristics. A predetermined percentage of gypsum is added to regulate the setting time that will be required for a particular cement. The clinkers and gypsum are mixed and ground so fine that more than 90 percent of the powdered mixture will pass through a sieve that has 105.625 (325 mesh) openings per square inch.

The finished portland cement is then conveyed or blown into large storage bins. Most of it is shipped from the plant in bulk; bulk shipments constitute about 90 percent of the total cement movement in the United States. The cement is pumped or conveyed directly into hopper cars, trucks, or ships for delivery to large construction sites, ready-mixed-concrete plants, and products manufacturers. The remainder is packed in paper sacks for delivery to building-materials dealers. A standard sack contains 94 lb, or approximately a cubic foot, of loose cement.

Types of Portland Cement

For most construction purposes a standard type of portland cement is used. However, special types are manufactured for specific uses. When cement is mixed with water, a chemical reaction takes place. This chemical reaction produces heat, and in large masses of concrete, such as dams, the heat generated by the hardening con-

crete can be a problem. Certain soils and waters contain sulfates or alkalies that can disintegrate concrete. There are times when it is necessary or desirable to have a concrete which will set quickly and develop a large part of its ultimate strength at an early stage. Special types of portland cement have been developed to cope with all these problems.

The five types of portland cement normally available in most parts of the United States are shown in Table 3-1. If no specific instructions are given when the cement is ordered, Type I will usually be furnished.

AIR-ENTRAINING PORTLAND CEMENT   When certain chemical *air-entraining agents* are added to portland cement during manufacture, the resulting concrete will contain billions of microscopic bubbles. The bubbles hold solid particles of the concrete mixture in place and reduce segregation. Less water is needed to produce a workable concrete mix. Air-entraining portland cement has better resistance to freezing and thawing. Air-entraining cements with properties similar to Types I, II, and III are designated IA, IIA, and IIIA, respectively.

WHITE PORTLAND CEMENT   A very-light-colored portland cement is produced by a careful selection of raw materials. White cement is used principally for architectural effects. It makes a good base for light-colored pigments in colored concrete. White portland cement has the same basic physi-

Fig. 3-2 Steps in the manufacture of portland cement. (*Portland Cement Association.*)

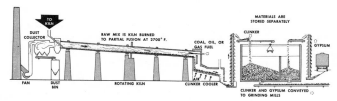

1 Stone is first reduced to 5-in. size, then ¾ in., and stored

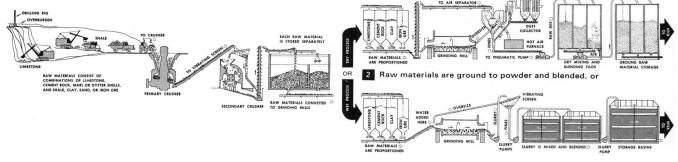

2 Raw materials are ground, mixed with water to form slurry, and blended

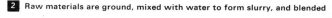

3 Burning changes raw mix chemically into cement clinker

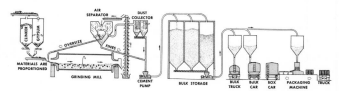

4 Clinker with gypsum added is ground into portland cement and shipped

TABLE 3-1 Types of portland cement

TYPE	USE
I. Normal portland cement	This is standard portland cement for general construction. It is generally a grayish color.
II. Modified portland cement	This cement has a lower heat of hydration than Type I and generally sets more slowly. It also has better resistance to the action of sulfates. It is used in drainage structures, foundations, and floors slabs where the soil contains a moderate amount of sulfates.
III. High-early-strength portland cement	This type develops approximately 190 percent of the strength of Type I at three days and 90 to 130 percent at 28 days. It develops considerable heat during setting. Type III cement is used when it is desired to remove forms at an early stage to speed up construction and to shorten the time the concrete must be protected against freezing while it sets.
IV. Low-heat portland cement	Concrete made with this type of cement sets very slowly and generates little heat. Low-heat portland cement was first developed for use in the construction of Hoover Dam. Its slow setting time is an advantage in large structures, where solid one-piece construction is desired.
V. Sulfate-resistant portland cement	A special cement intended for use in structures exposed to severe sulfate action of soils or waters with a high alkali content. It has a slower rate of hardening than Type I.

cal characteristics as normal portland cement and develops the same strength.

SPECIAL CEMENTS   Mixtures of portland cement and pozzolanic materials, ground together during manufacture, are produced for special purposes. Plastic cements containing admixtures give the performance necessary for stucco, plastering, and masonry applications.

Setting and Hardening

When portland cement is mixed with a sufficient amount of water and left undisturbed, the paste loses its plasticity and becomes a solid. Cement does not harden by drying. It hardens because of a chemical reaction; the water and the cement combine chemically to form a new compound. This process is called *setting*. Initial setting may take a few minutes or several hours. When the cement paste has been combined with aggregates and has set, it will then continue to harden, or gain strength, for months and years.

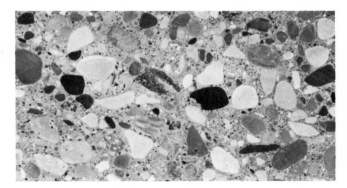

Fig. 3-3 Sections through concrete showing good distribution of aggregate. (*Portland Cement Association.*)

If insufficient water is used in the mix, some particles of cement will not be chemically changed. If too much water is used, the excess water may be trapped in the cement paste. In either case, the resulting concrete will be weakened. The temperature of the materials and the moisture in the air affect the exact amount of water to be added to the mixture. It is usually impossible or impractical to add exactly the amount of water needed for the chemical reaction. Additional water is needed to make a plastic mixture that can be handled. This additional water, which is not part of the chemical process, must escape from the paste.

AGGREGATE

Aggregates, which do not react chemically with cement and water, make up approximately 66 to 78 percent of the volume of concrete. Aggregates range from fine sand to rocks 1½ in. in diameter or larger. The quality of the concrete is affected in several ways by the aggregate. The strength of the aggregate limits the strength of the concrete; concrete is a combination of several materials and is only as strong as its weakest element. The surface of the grains affects the plasticity of a concrete mix. Rounded grains will move more easily as the concrete is placed. Long, thin, or striated aggregate will weaken concrete.

Standard-weight Aggregate

The aggregates used in concrete may be *natural aggregates*, such as sand and gravel taken directly from river banks or gravel deposits, or they may be by-products of an industrial process. Natural aggregates frequently are mixed with dirt or other foreign substances which must be removed before they can be used.

By-products aggregates are inert materials such as blast-furnace slag or cinders. Blast-furnace slag, air cooled and crushed, is quite hard and sometimes has considerable strength. The surface is very porous and affords a good

Fig. 3-4 Vermiculite. (*W. R. Grace and Company.*)

bond with cement. Its use in structural concrete is somewhat limited, however, because of the high sulfur content in most slag. Cinders resulting from the burning of anthracite coal or coke are also occasionally used for concrete. Cinder concrete has a low strength and is not suitable for structural concrete.

Lightweight Aggregate

Certain materials can be processed by heat to produce a *lightweight aggregate*. During the heating process the gas that forms inside the material expands it to a lightweight, porous form. This material is crushed and graded to size, either before or after expansion, for use in lightweight structural concrete.

VERMICULITE AND PERLITE *Vermiculite*, a type of mica, may expand to 20 times its original volume when it is heated. In its expanded form it weighs only 6 to 20 lb/cu ft, in contrast to its weight as natural stone, 135 to 160 lb/cu ft. Vermiculite will form a nonstructural fill concrete that weighs 20 to 40 lb/cu ft instead of the 150 lb/cu ft of standard concrete. *Perlite*, a type of volcanic rock, can also be expanded by heating. The crude perlite, as it is mined, contains quite a bit of water, and when it is heated, the resulting steam forces the material into a light, fluffy form. Perlite weighs approximately 85 lb/cu ft before expansion and 6 to 12 lb/cu ft after expansion.

Concrete made with perlite or vermiculite aggregate has excellent insulating properties and is easy to place

and work. However, because of their low strength, these materials are not suitable for structural concrete.

EXPANDED SLAG If the molten slag from a blast furnace is sprayed with a limited amount of water as it is removed from the furnace, it will be expanded or *foamed*. Expanded slag contains minute air cells that reduce its weight. This grayish-brown material is sometimes used as an aggregate in lightweight concrete.

Grading of Aggregate

Most concrete aggregates are natural-mineral aggregates, either bank-run gravel or crushed rock. The two materials have somewhat different properties, but their uses in standard concrete are similar. The important points are the strength, shape, and size of the particles.

Aggregates are generally designated as fine or coarse. Although there is no exact line of demarcation between the classes, fine aggregate generally called sand, consists of particles that are ¼ in. or less in diameter. Particles that are ⅜ in. or larger are classed as coarse aggregate.

To secure a dense, strong concrete that is impervious to water each particle of aggregate must be completely coated with cement paste. In that cement is relatively expensive and aggregate is relatively inexpensive, the less cement required to accomplish this, the more economical the concrete, up to a point. For best results it is necessary to grade or proportion the aggregate from large to fine to obtain a mixture that will provide the desired working qualities and strength. Aggregates are graded by a process called *sieve analysis*. A sample of aggregate is poured through a stack, or nest, of vibrating sieves, which have square holes of decreasing size. The particles retained in each sieve are then weighed and tabulated. A sample of aggregate can thus be graded according to the percentage of small, medium, and large particles it contains.

Each sieve is numbered according to the size of openings in the screen. A No. 40 sieve has 40 openings per linear inch; a No. 4 sieve has 4 openings per linear inch. For openings larger than No. 4 the sizes are given in inches— ⅜″, ¾″, and so on. A standard set of sieves used for grading fine and coarse aggregates might consist of numbers 100, 50, 30, 16, 8, 4, ⅜″, ¾″, 1½″, and 2″.

FINE AGGREGATE To provide the proper characteristics for good, workable concrete, sand should contain both coarse and fine particles. Generally, the fine aggregates will be graded as follows:

SIEVE NO.	PERCENTAGE RETAINED
4	2
8	15
16	35
30	55
50	79
100	97

Well-graded sand of these proportions will produce an economical and strong concrete mix. The finer particles will fill in the voids between the larger ones, and the cement paste can bind the aggregate together to form strong concrete. If the sand contains too many extremely fine particles, or *fines*, there is too much surface area for the cement to coat each grain.

COARSE AGGREGATE   Coarse aggregates are graded in sizes corresponding to fractions of an inch. Coarse aggregate with rock particles up to 6 in. in diameter may be used on massive structures such as dams, but aggregate is usually no larger than 1½ in. The maximum size is generally governed by the thickness of the section to be constructed.

Coarse aggregate may vary over a wide range without effect on the cement requirement of the concrete if workability is retained through proper amounts of fine aggregate. Generally, the larger the maximum size of coarse aggregate, the less cement paste will be required to produce concrete of a given strength.

Fig. 3-5   Grading aggregate: (a) pouring an aggregate sample into a nest of sieves;

Mixing and Sampling Aggregate

When concrete is mixed on the job, the storage, handling, and measurement of aggregate to produce uniform mixes is difficult. On small jobs the number of shovelsfull of fine and coarse aggregate may be used as a measure. Scales may be installed to weigh the materials. The actual quantity of materials will vary with the amount of water mixed with or absorbed into aggregate. Wet sand may contain ¼ to 1 gal of water per 100 lb of sand.

Aggregate at the job site or the mixing site must be sampled carefully for testing. It is critical to obtain samples that are truly representative. Large quantities of both fine and coarse aggregate are usually reduced by the *quartering method*. Samples are taken from several places in the pile and mixed together. The mixture is then spread out in a layer 3 to 4 in. thick and divided into four pie-shaped wedges. The two opposite wedges are discarded, and the rest is mixed and divided again. This process is repeated until the sample is small enough for testing. The sample may then be graded by sieve analysis.

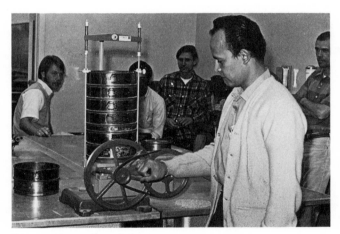

(b) operating a sieve shaker;

ADMIXTURES

Any material other than water, cement, or aggregate added to concrete immediately before or during mixing is considered an *admixture*. Admixtures are used to modify the properties of a concrete mix. They may be employed to speed or retard setting and hardening, to entrain air, to improve workability, or to reduce segregation of aggregate. A stiff concrete mix may be made more plastic without the addition of water through the use of an admixture. Resistance to freezing and thawing or to abrasion may be improved.

(c) weighing aggregate samples.

Fig. 3-6 A sample of well-graded aggregate. (*Portland Cement Association.*)

Fig. 3-7 Taking aggregate samples by quartering.

AIR-ENTRAINING ADMIXTURES Air-entraining materials are foaming agents. When they are included in a concrete mix, they entrap millions of stable, closely spaced, microscopic air bubbles. It is possible to obtain portland cement containing air-entraining admixtures that have been interground with the cement clinkers during the manufacturing process. There are also air-entraining admixtures that can be added to concrete at the mixer.

Air-entrained concrete was originally used for highway construction subject to freezing and thawing. The advantages, such as greater workability with less water, have made its use in all types of construction accepted. Air entrainment may reduce the strength of a given mix of concrete. However, since less water is needed for workability, and the strength of concrete is increased as the amount of water used in the mix is decreased, there is the possibility of increased strength in air-entraining concrete.

WATER REDUCERS Certain chemicals, when added to freshly mixed concrete, reduce the amount of water necessary for workability. These substances may also retard or accelerate setting. This is an advantage for hot-weather placement of concrete but can cause too great a delay in setting during cold weather.

The correct use of a water-reducing admixture can often increase the strength of a given mix. However, the performance of the admixture must be checked carefully, as concrete made with some admixtures have shown excessive shrinkage during curing.

RETARDERS A set-retarding admixture is used to delay the initial setting time of concrete. Some water-reducing admixtures are also set-retarding agents. Retarders are used in concrete to offset the accelerating effect of hot weather on the setting of concrete or to delay the set of concrete during difficult or unusual placing conditions. There is generally some reduction in the strength of the concrete during the early hardening period when retarders are used. It is difficult to predict the effects of retarders on various types of cements and aggregates. Before retarders

Fig. 3-8 Microphoto of air-entrained concrete. (*Portland Cement Association.*)

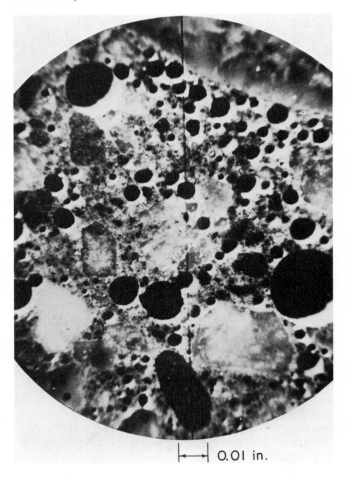

$\longmapsto$ 0.01 in.

are used, tests should be made with the actual job materials at the anticipated temperature.

ACCELERATORS   The use of an accelerator can often speed up construction. It will increase the strength of concrete at ages of 1 to 7 days with no decrease in the ultimate strength of concrete. This permits earlier removal of forms and a consequent speed up in production.

DAMPPROOFING AGENTS   Certain stearic acids and asphalt emulsions may reduce the *capillary action*, or the ability of concrete to absorb and pass water. Waterproofing admixtures do not make concrete waterproof, but they do minimize its absorption of water. Although the strength of the concrete is reduced, other desirable properties are developed in concrete containing such admixtures.

SURFACE HARDENERS   Several hardeners may be applied to the top of concrete slabs. Most of these surface agents consist, in the main, of particles which are more ductile or malleable than stone aggregate. Thus the surface will give with the traffic and last longer. These surface hardeners are floated on the fresh concrete to form a wearing surface. Certain abrasive substances may be used as admixtures or surface toppings for better traction.

POZZOLANIC MATERIALS   Pozzolans are sometimes used as admixtures in place of a portion of the portland cement. The pozzolanic materials most commonly used as admixtures are pumice, tuffa, volcanic ash, diatomaceous earth, and calcined clays. The use of pozzolans will reduce the heat generated in setting and may reduce the strength. Certain aggregates, classed as *reactive aggregates*, react chemically with portland cement and expand. A proven pozzolan may be used to control this expansion.

COLOR PIGMENTS   Colored concrete floors can be obtained by introducing color pigments into the concrete mix. Color pigments may be included in the mix for the entire floor, or they may be only in the topping. The pigments are usually metallic oxides of a nonfading nature. If they constitute more than 10 percent of the mix by weight, the strength of the concrete may be seriously impaired. The inclusion of color pigments in concrete may require the addition of water and increase the tendency of concrete to crack.

WATER

Concrete consists of hardened water-cement paste that binds aggregate of various sizes and types into a conglomerate stonelike material. Provided that the aggregate is sound and each particle is completely surrounded by cement paste, the strength and durability of concrete will be governed by the strength of the cement paste.

Quality of Water

Attention is seldom given to the quality of water used in concrete. Often "water suitable for drinking" is specified.

The drinking water in most urban areas is relatively free of chemicals or materials that could harm concrete. However, not all water suitable for drinking is satisfactory for concrete. In some areas drinking water contains large amounts of sulfates. Water containing small amounts of sugar or citrate would be suitable for drinking. Some water that is unsuitable for drinking will produce excellent concrete. Water contaminated by certain industrial wastes may reduce the quality of concrete.

Heating and Cooling

The setting time of concrete is greatly affected by temperatures. If water freezes before the concrete has set, it will not be available to combine chemically with the cement paste. If it freezes during the setting process, the expansion during freezing will cause fractures. Aggregate can be heated by steampipes placed in storage piles or bins. If the aggregate is free of ice and snow, heating the water to a point just below boiling may warm the aggregate to a desired temperature of 80°F. If the water or aggregate is too hot when it comes in contact with the cement, the concrete may set prematurely. Cement should never be heated. The temperature of the concrete, as it is placed, should never be lower than 50°F except for certain mass pours. The best results are obtained when the temperature of materials is between 60 and 80°F.

Direct sun during hot weather can raise the temperature of aggregate or water to a point where the mixing of concrete can be difficult. Some of the water in the mix may evaporate. High temperatures can cause too rapid setting, which will lower the strength of the concrete and make it difficult to place. If stock-piled aggregate is soaked or sprinkled with water, the resulting evaporation will cool the material.

One of the most effective methods of reducing the temperature of the concrete when it is placed is by using crushed ice in place of some of the mixing water. Ice is incorporated directly into the mixer. It must, however, be crushed fine enough to melt completely before the mixing is finished.

Water/Cement Ratio

The quality of cement paste is determined by the proportion of water to cement. Too much water prevents proper setting; too little water prevents complete chemical combination. A 94-lb bag of cement requires 2½ to 3 gal of water for complete chemical combination of materials. However, the use of exactly the amount of water needed for chemical combination is not practical under field conditions. Usually 4 to 8 gal must be used for each sack of cement. The extra water serves as a lubricant to carry the cement paste into small pores of the aggregate. Excess water is also needed to wet the aggregate so that it will not absorb water needed by the cement.

The more water added to the mix, the more fluid and plastic it will be, and the weaker the concrete will be.

Too much water will cause the aggregate to segregate, resulting in concrete that is uneven in strength and workability. The excess water will float the fine, light particles of cement to the top of freshly placed concrete. This process is called *bleeding*. Some bleeding is not detrimental; in fact, it is necessary for proper finishing.

The amount of water to be mixed with a given quantity of cement is expressed as the number of gallons of water to each 94-lb bag of cement. The proportion of water to cement is referred to as the *water/cement ratio W/C*. Water may be measured either by volume or by weight. The tanks on modern concrete mixers are equipped with water gauges or meters that assure the proper amount of water for each batch. The amount of water in the aggregate must be determined so that the total amount of water in the design mix will be correct.

Strength of Concrete

With a given water/cement ratio, if a concrete mix is plastic enough to be workable and is properly cured, its strength will be the same, up to a point, regardless of the amount of aggregate used. The strength of concrete is usually measured at 3 days, 7 days, and 28 days after it has been cast. The compressive strength at various intervals for concrete with different water/cement ratios is shown in Table 3-2. These figures are the results of tests made with a series of $6'' \times 12''$ concrete cylinders of Type I portland cement mixed, cast, and moist cured under laboratory conditions at Pasadena City College.

TABLE 3-2 Average compressive strength of samples tested

WATER, GAL/SACK CEMENT	AVERAGE STRENGTH, LB/SQ IN.			
	7 DAYS	14 DAYS	28 DAYS	1 YEAR
5	3500	4200	5000	7800
6	2400	3200	5300	6200
7	1700	2200	2900	5000
8	1100	1600	2000	4000
9	900	1100	1600	3200

DESIGN OF MIX

The water/cement ratio of a given concrete determines its strength. However, to produce concrete that is economical as well as strong, the proper aggregate type, grading, and proportions must be selected. The durability, permeability, and ease of placement will be affected by this selection. The amount, type, and size of the various aggregates determine how the concrete will flow or react when it is placed in forms. Well-graded aggregate will produce dense, strong concrete.

The selection of the proper portions of the various sizes of aggregate can be determined by trial mixes, either in a laboratory or in the field. A concrete that has too large a percentage of coarse aggregate may contain excessive voids. There may not be enough cement paste to fill all the spaces between fine particles of aggregate. In a mixture

that contains excess sand, there may be too much surface area for the paste to coat each particle. Although a concrete with excess sand may be smooth and strong, it will not be economical.

Proportioning of Materials

In the past, but to a very limited degree at the present time, the proportions of cement, sand, and coarse aggregate were specified for concretes of various strengths. Little or no importance was placed on the water/cement ratio, which has been found to govern the strength of finished concrete. A 1:3:4 mix is one that contains, by volume, one part cement, three parts sand, and four parts rock. A 1:2½:3½ mix contains one part cement, 2½ parts sand, and 3½ parts rock. Enough water was added to this dry mix to make it plastic enough to flow into the forms. This method produced concrete having wide variances in physical properties.

Cement Factor

In addition to the water/cement ratio of concrete, the percentage of cement in a cubic yard of concrete is usually specified. This is called the *cement factor*. By adjusting the grading of aggregate, without changing the water/cement ratio, it is possible to change the stiffness of a mix. With a given water/cement ratio and a given gradation of aggregate, it is possible to determine the number of sacks of cement that will be needed to form a cubic yard of concrete. Stiff mixes require more labor in placing; however, they may be more economical in materials.

Fig. 3-9 Making a slump test.

Slump

The consistency of fresh concrete is measured in terms of its *slump*, the distance in inches of subsidence (slump) of a truncated (cut-off) cone of freshly mixed concrete released immediately after molding in a standard slump cone. The minimum slumps recommended for various types of work are as follows:

Mass concrete (not reinforced) and slabs on soil	2 to 5 in.
Reinforced concrete other than thin walls	3 to 6 in.
Thin reinforced concrete walls	3 to 6 in.

To test the slump of a concrete mix, samples are taken directly from the mixer or ready-mixed truck as the concrete is being discharged. These samples are placed in three layers in a slump cone 12 in. high, 8 in. round at the base, and 4 in. round at the top. Each layer is rodded 25 times with a 5/8 in. steel rod having a rounded end. The concrete is struck off even with the top of the cone. The cone is then removed, and the number of inches that the

Fig. 3-11   Capping a concrete test cylinder.

fresh concrete settles, or slumps, is measured. If the concrete sample does not have the specified slump, the mix must be redesigned. Water should never be added to produce the desired slump, since it will weaken the resulting concrete.

Design Strength

The design strength of concrete is based on the compressive strength developed by $6'' \times 12''$ cylinders of concrete after 28 days of curing under laboratory conditions. Cylinders are made on the job site by representatives of the engineer, architect, or an independent testing laboratory to ascertain whether the concrete comes up to the specified design strength. Representative samples of the concrete are taken as the concrete is being poured. These samples are combined and placed into 6 in.-diameter molds in three layers. Each layer is compacted with 25 strokes of a 5/8-in.-diameter steel rod with a rounded end. The top of the concrete is struck off flush with the top of the 12 in.-high mold, and the sample is capped tightly to prevent evaporation of water. Three to six cylinders are usually taken for each pour that is to be tested. The cylinders remain on the job site for 24 hr and are then transported to a testing laboratory. Newly made test cylinders must be handled with care and not jarred or moved during the first day of curing. The temperature of test cylinders at the job site must be maintained at 60 to 80°F. Improper handling

Fig. 3-10   Taking a concrete test cylinder.

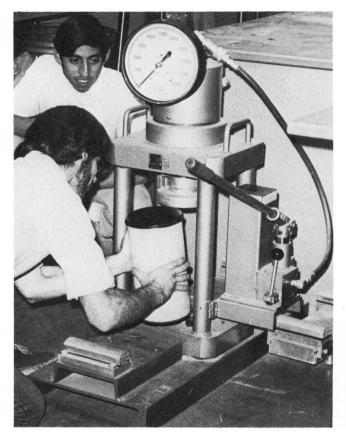

Fig. 3-12 Inserting a capped test cylinder into a compression-testing device.

or storage of test cylinders can result in false test reports of the cured concrete.

After curing in the laboratory for 7 days one to three cylinders are tested. After 28 days three other cylinders are tested. A load is applied continuously to the cylinder until it yields or breaks. The compressive strength of the concrete is calculated as the number of pounds per square inch resisted by the sample (see Table 3-2). The average strength of three cylinders is considered to be the compressive strength of the concrete at that time.

Core Tests

If tests indicate that concrete has not developed the strength anticipated at the end of 7 or 28 days, further tests may be required on concrete in place at the job site. Cylindrical core specimens are cut from the structure with a core drill and are taken to the laboratory for testing. If the core tests show that the concrete has not developed its design strength, the contractor may have to remove the concrete and replace it or otherwise strengthen the structure.

Mixing of Concrete

Another factor in the workability and strength of concrete is the method used to mix the ingredients. It is essential that all ingredients be thoroughly mixed to ensure uniformity. Prolonged mixing, however, can decrease the workability.

MIXING TIME   The mixing time required depends on the size and efficiency of the mixer. The time of mixing should not be less than 1 minute for concrete of medium consistency mixed in a 1-cu-yd or smaller mixer. Larger mixers require 15 sec additional mixing time for each yard of concrete. A harsh concrete mixture may require additional mixing time. The length of time a concrete mix will remain plastic during mixing is reduced during hot weather. The mixing time is calculated from the time all solid particles are in the mixer. All water should be added before one-fourth of the mixing time has elapsed.

Fig. 3-13 Compression testing of concrete cylinder.

Prolonged mixing will not affect the strength of the concrete as long as the mixture remains plastic and additional water is not added to increase the slump. The speed of the mixer is not as critical as the mixing time. The peripheral speed of the mixing drum and blades should be between 100 and 200 ft/min. Manufacturers of mixers specify the number of revolutions per minute the drum should turn to obtain these speeds. It is important that mixers not be loaded beyond their capacity.

JOB-MIXED CONCRETE Concrete materials may be mixed in a rotating-drum batch mixer at the job site. However, this is not recommended unless the job is of sufficient size to warrant proper devices for the measuring of materials or, on a small job, there are no ready-mix facilities. On small jobs materials are sometimes measured by shovelfuls. The measuring of materials by volume may be quite inaccurate. The moisture content of sand and coarse aggregate will vary and affect the water/cement ratio.

READY-MIXED CONCRETE In most areas concrete can be purchased from a central plant. These plants are equipped to furnish concrete, conforming to a given mix or guaranteed to meet a specified strength, ready-mixed to the job site.

Delivery of Concrete

Ready-mixed concrete is delivered by special trucks designed for the purpose. The initial mixing may be done at the central plant, with the remainder accomplished in the truck on the way to the job, or the entire mixing process may be done in transit. The materials are combined in the truck, and the mixing drum will rotate not less than 50 times nor more than 100 times. The truck manufacturer designates this mixing speed. Any additional mixing is done at *agitating speed*, which is 6 to 9 rpm. The concrete must be discharged in less than 1½ hr time after the water is added. In hot weather this maximum time may have to be reduced. Tests have shown that excessive grinding action and heat generation takes place after 100 revolutions of the drum.

Mixer trucks are equipped with devices that count the number of turns the drum has made since the load was introduced. Most trucks are also equipped with water tanks equipped with accurate automatic timing and locking water-measuring devices. Ready-mixed concrete is sometimes delivered to the job with less than the total water in the mixer, and the remainder of the water is added to the mix at the job site. After the water is added, the drum on the truck must be rotated at least 20 times at mixing speed before the concrete is discharged. If the specified time or number of revolutions is exceeded, concrete in the truck must be removed from the job site and dumped. Water should never be added at the job site if the amount would exceed the total water content prescribed by the mix design.

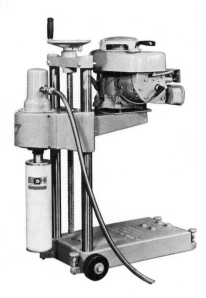

Fig. 3-14 A pavement coring machine. (*Soiltest, Inc.*)

PLACING CONCRETE

Quality concrete depends on proper placement, finishing, and curing. For uniform results these operations should be directed by an experienced foreman or supervisor. Several steps are necessary to achieve a strong, lasting, and finished surface for a concrete structure. The site and forms must be properly prepared. The concrete must be placed so that it is uniform throughout, and it must be finished so that the surface is compact and has the desired characteristics. It must then be allowed to cure so that a minimum number of cracks develop and the surface has a lasting finish, free of defects.

Site Preparation

The forms within which the concrete is to be placed and the soil on which it will be deposited should be properly moistened or protected with *form oils* or plastic liners so that they do not soak up necessary water from the concrete mix. All vegetable matter and loose material that could become mixed with the wet concrete should be removed. Muddy and soft spots should be compacted to provide a good base for the concrete as it is poured. For best results concrete should be placed on a base of sand or gravel.

Forms must be true to shape and tight enough to retain the water in the concrete. They must also be strong and well braced in order to withstand the pressure of the concrete and the vibration that may be necessary to consolidate it. Forms may be made of wood, either prefabricated or job built, hardboard, or metal. There are some recently developed special materials that serve as forms and are then left in place as a finish material. Plastic-coated wood forms are used to produce smooth finished surfaces on concrete. Reinforcing must be clean, free of rust, and securely anchored in place. Bolts, anchors, sleeves, and inserts which are to be cast in the concrete must be in place.

Methods of Placement

If the concrete cannot be placed directly where it is needed by the chute of the mixer, it must be conveyed as close as possible to the final location by pumping, belt conveyors, concrete buggies, or buckets moved by cranes.

Concrete should be placed in horizontal layers of 6 to 18 in. If it is piled in one spot and worked or allowed to flow to distant parts of the form, the coarse aggregate usually segregates. The lighter materials flow faster than the heavy aggregates, leaving pockets that are deficient in cement paste.

If concrete is allowed to fall freely for a distance of more than 3 or 4 ft, the aggregate also tends to segregate. The heavier particles are concentrated at the bottom of the pour, leaving the upper layer with an excess of fine aggregate. When concrete is to be cast into deep forms, *drop chutes* may be used. These chutes are lowered into the forms to reduce the free fall of the concrete. Windows may be built into the forms. The concrete is then placed through the side of the form to reduce the amount of free fall.

PUMPING   Pumping ready-mixed concrete through pipes is not a new development. However, until recently this method was limited to large-volume jobs using 6- or 8-in. fixed pipes. New types of pumps capable of pumping concrete through small-diameter flexible lines have greatly extended this technique. It is now possible to pump concrete 500 ft horizontally or 100 ft vertically. The pumps are either self-powered trailer units or units mounted on the body of the truck and operated by the truck engine. The concrete is received in a hopper from the ready-mix truck and is pumped through rigid pipe or flexible hose. The flexible hose allows the concrete to be placed exactly where it is needed with minimum labor.

A concrete mix that is to be pumped requires extremely careful design. Uniformity of aggregate is necessary for proper pumping. If the aggregate is not properly graded, the distance the concrete can be pumped is greatly reduced. Many pumps for use with 3- to 4-in. flexible lines are limited to a maximum coarse-aggregate size of ³/₈ in. This size of aggregate is commonly known as *pea gravel*. New pumps are now being produced that can handle aggre-

Fig. 3-15 Pumping concrete for a highway bridge. (*Royal Industries, Thomsen Division.*)

gate up to 1 in. in diameter. The slump of concrete to be pumped is usually 5 to 6 in.; it may be as low as 4 in. with air entrainment.

PNEUMATIC PLACEMENT Air pressure has been used for many years to place concrete. A dry mixture of cement and sand is blown through hoses, and water injected at the nozzle. This is called *gunite, pneumatically placed mortar,* or *sprayed concrete,* and is referred to as *shotcrete* by the American Concrete Institute. In the past this method has been limited to the repair of disintegrating or damaged structures, but many new uses are being found for shotcrete. In the original gunite process a mixture of cement, sand, and water was sprayed. Equipment has now been developed that will spray concrete with aggregate as large as ¾ in.

Recent construction of domes, concrete-shell structures, and swimming pools have shown the adaptability of pneumatically placed concrete. Instead of being placed in the forms, the concrete may be shot into two sides of metal lath to form the finished structure. Equipment manufacturers have developed compact mobile units that consist of a mixer, pump, and air tank necessary to place concrete.

Consolidation of Concrete

Several types of vibrators run by compressed air, electricity, or gasoline engines may be immersed directly in the concrete. Immersion vibrators consist of revolving eccentric elements, turning at 7000 rpm or more, enclosed in a watertight cylinder 1 to 4 in. in diameter and approximately 18 in. long. On deep-section concrete the vibrator is inserted vertically into the concrete at points 18 to 30 in. apart. The concrete is vibrated from 5 to 15 sec at each spot. In thin slabs the vibrator is inserted into the fresh concrete horizontally or at a very slight angle. Concrete that is to be vibrated can be placed when it has less than half the slump of concrete that is to be compacted by hand. The lower slump leads to a lower water/cement ratio and consequently a stronger concrete. Vibration and consolidation of concrete may also be accomplished by vibrating devices attached to the forms or applied to the surface of the concrete.

Laitance

In wet concrete mixes a soupy mixture of extremely fine sand, cement, and water will sometimes float, or bleed, to the surface of a pour. This is called *laitance.* Laitance will show up as a whitish scum on the surface of fresh concrete or as light streaks in finished concrete. These light streaks of poor-quality concrete are very susceptible to failure when exposed to freezing and thawing and must be removed before the next pour is made.

Laitance can be controlled by using stiffer mixes or an air-entraining admixture.

JOINTS

Construction Joints

When fresh concrete is poured against hardened concrete, it is usually necessary to produce a good bond and a watertight joint between the new and old concrete. Only a

Fig. 3-16 Pumping a concrete slab. (*Royal Industries, Thomsen Division.*)

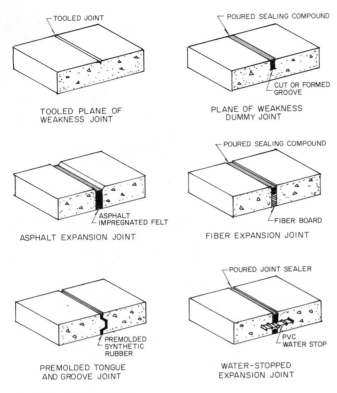

Fig. 3-17 Concrete joints.

limited quantity of concrete can be placed in one working day, so the concrete must be cast in sections. The design and location of these joints between hardened and fresh concrete, called *construction joints*, must be considered carefully.

Before fresh concrete can be placed, the surface of the hardened concrete must be roughened and cleaned. This may be done before or after the concrete has reached initial set. The concrete may be washed with a jet of water from 4 to 12 hr after it is placed in order to expose a clean surface of sound concrete. The surface of the freshly placed concrete may be brushed with a stiff broom or steel brush before initial set, to form a roughened surface ready to receive the new concrete. After hardening the concrete may be wet sandblasted and washed to provide the roughened clean surface necessary for good bond when new concrete is poured.

On deep-section concrete, when the new concrete is placed against hardened concrete it is necessary to provide a cushion of mortar. This mortar consists of a 1/2- to 1-in. layer of cement, sand, and water, with the same water/cement ratio as the concrete. This mortar must be applied immediately before the fresh concrete is poured and worked into the irregularities of the hardened concrete to ensure a good bond.

Relief Joints

Concrete expands and contracts with temperature changes. Although this expansion and contraction is only 55-millionths of an inch per degree of temperature, this amounts to over 1/2 in. in each 100 ft of structure for a 100° temperature change. Concrete shrinks when it dries and expands when it absorbs moisture. This contraction and expansion may be as great as that caused by temperature change. A combination of the two factors can double the expansion or contraction of a concrete structure. For this reason, properly designed *relief joints* must be included to prevent unsightly random cracking.

Relief joints may be constructed as built-in strips of elastic material, openings to be filled later with an elastic material, or false joints cut or molded in the concrete surface. In order to keep the two portions of the slab or wall in alignment, keyways may be cast in each section of the wall or slab to maintain proper alignment as the concrete moves or works. Steel dowels may be provided to bridge the joint for the same purpose. One side of the dowel is anchored firmly in the concrete; the other end is coated with a mastic or encased in a plastic tube so that it will not bond to the concrete, but will allow for movement while maintaining alignment.

BUILT-IN JOINTS   Preformed rubber or plastic shapes of many designs may be used to bridge expansion and contraction joints. These long flexible strips are cast into the concrete. The dumbbell-shaped or serrated edges of the strips are gripped by the freshly poured concrete. This type of joint can move but still remain watertight.

FILLED JOINTS   Joints left open for sealing at a later time can be filled with elastic materials that will allow movement. These joint sealants, classed as *formed-in-place sealants*, are generally vinyl foams, neoprene foams, or polyurethane foams. The materials are delivered to the job in liquid form and, when mixed properly and forced into the joint, provide an elastic, waterproof joint.

FALSE JOINTS   Relief joints may be formed in the concrete by the use of metal or wood strips fastened to the inside of forms. These strips are removed after the concrete has hardened. Weakened planes are thus formed where the strips have been removed, confining the cracks to that area. The weakened plane joints can be designed and detailed in such a manner as to become an architectural feature in the overall design of the structure. The strips can be located so that each pour of concrete will be stopped at these strips. By the use of this method, the irregular lines of construction joints on plain surfaces can be avoided. Relief joints may also be formed by sawing grooves in the concrete. This is usually done as soon as the concrete has set sufficiently to support the weight of the concrete saw. Relief joints must penetrate the slab for a distance of one-fifth the slab thickness to be effective.

FINISHING AND CURING CONCRETE

Leveling

When concrete has been placed and consolidated, it is brought to the proper level by means of *screeds*. Screeds are guides placed on both sides of the slab, and sometimes within the perimeter of large slabs, with their tops at the desired level of the finished concrete. A long 2 × 4 or a 2 × 6 is then rested on the screeds and pushed back and forth in a sawing motion to strike off excess concrete and show up any areas that are low. After the concrete has been brought to the proper level, any screeds within the slab are removed, and the depressions they have left are filled with fresh concrete.

After leveling, concrete is sometimes compacted with a *hand tamp*. This is an open metal mesh stretched over a frame, designed to push the coarse aggregate below the surface. The hand tamp should be used with extreme care. It should never be used on concrete that has more than 1 in. slump. Hand tamping brings excess fine aggregate and cement paste to the surface. This can result in a weak surface that tends to crack.

Floating

After the concrete has been brought to its final level, while it is still plastic, the surface is floated with a long-handled flat-surfaced wood tool called a *bull float*. There are machines with rotating wood blades that can be used for

Fig. 3-19 Using a vibrating screed to finish tilt-up panels. (*Kelly Industrial Company.*)

Fig. 3-18 Screeding concrete. (*Portland Cement Association.*)

Fig. 3-20 Using a bull float on a tilt-up panel.

floating and initial troweling. The proper use of the bull float, either manual or power, will bring the surface to true grade, fill the low spots, and eliminate the high spots. Overworking, however, will produce a weak surface susceptible to *dusting*. Dry cement should never be sprinkled on the surface. The concrete should be allowed to stiffen by itself to the point where all the surface water has evaporated and the concrete will withstand the weight of a

Fig. 3-21 Applying a steel-troweled finish. (*Portland Cement Association.*)

workman. The edges of construction joints and slabs are rounded at this time. Wood floats used in the floating operation can produce a rough-textured finish.

Final Finish

When the edges and joints have been rounded and the slab has lost its sheen, it is time to begin the final finishing. This may be 4 to 6 hr after placement, depending on the job and the weather conditions. Timing of the final finishing process is critical in producing a sound, defect-free surface. This operation should be delayed until fine particles and water are no longer brought to the surface by trowel testing. Many workmen tend to start the final finishing too soon. The finish desired will govern the number of times the slab is to be steel troweled. The oftener the surface is troweled, the smoother and denser it becomes.

If a nonslip finish is desired, the surface may be broomed after the floating operation. The coarseness and stiffness of the bristles in the broom and the length of time after floating will govern the final appearance of the slab. If a finer texture is desired, brooming may follow the first steel troweling.

Special Toppings and Finishes

Materials have been developed that can be troweled into the freshly floated concrete to densify the surface or produce a nonslip or decorative finish. These materials are usually sprinkled on the slab after the floating operation. Extremely hard nonmetallic, nonrusting abrasive granules are used as hardeners and for nonslip surfaces exposed to the weather or subject to heavy traffic. Products are avail-

able which both densify and decorate. They are sometimes used on walks, steps, and floors, where durable decorative finishes are desired.

Many special finishes may be given to concrete before or after it has completely set. When the concrete has partially set, the surface may be scrubbed with a stiff brush while a stream of water is played on it. This process exposes the aggregate by removing the cement paste and sand from the surface. The scrubbing and the washing must be done when the concrete has developed enough strength to hold the coarse aggregate in place, but before it has become so hard that the fine particles cannot be removed. This process may also be accomplished by spraying a set-retarding admixture on the surface while the concrete is still plastic. Aggregate having uniform size, shape, and color may be pressed or rolled into the plastic concrete while it is being finished. Removal of the cement paste when the concrete has partially hardened will expose the aggregate and present a decorative surface.

Curing

Proper curing of concrete is an important factor in achieving a satisfactory, waterproof, strong concrete free of surface defects. The watertightness and strength of concrete improves rapidly when it is first placed and continues to increase at a slower rate as long as conditions are favorable. Enough water must be retained in the concrete to allow complete chemical reaction. The temperature of the con-

Fig. 3-22 Edging concrete. (*Portland Cement Association.*)

crete must be maintained between certain limits to assure a proper chemical reaction. When temperatures are below 70°F, chemical action slows. It takes concrete twice as long to set up and gain strength at 50°F, and practically no chemical action takes place at 30°F or below.

If the water in the fresh concrete is allowed to freeze, the expansion can ruin the concrete. If enclosed spaces are heated to keep the concrete warm, wet heat must be used to keep the concrete moist. Open fires produce carbon dioxide, which can soften the surface of concrete in a

Fig. 3-23 Precast exposed-aggregate columns. (*Portland Cement Association.*)

Fig. 3-24 An exposed-aggregate concrete drive with redwood headers. (*Portland Cement Association.*)

tightly enclosed area. High temperatures cause the concrete to set too fast, resulting in excessive shrinkage, cracks, poor surfaces, and loss of strength. For best results the concrete should be kept at temperatures between 60 and 80°F. The most critical period is the first 7 days. Forms left in place will help retain moisture and protect the fresh concrete. Exposed concrete surfaces must be protected from weather changes and excessive evaporation.

WATER CURING   Covering a flat slab with a thin layer of water is one way to prevent the evaporation of moisture from concrete. The layer of water will also help to keep the concrete cool in hot weather. Earth dikes may be built around the slab during the curing period. This is an excellent method of curing concrete, although the cost of building and maintaining such dikes is usually quite high.

Sprinkling or fog nozzles can be installed to spray freshly placed concrete. If the sprinklers miss some portions of the concrete, however, the uneven curing will cause cracks and defects in the surface. Wind may also affect the coverage of sprinklers. The water must be controlled in such a way as to prevent alternate wetting and drying of concrete, which causes crazing or cracking.

BURLAP CURING   Wet burlap is often used to cover the concrete during curing. The burlap must cover all the concrete, including the sides of members, and must be kept moist at all times.

PAPER CURING   Waterproof paper can also be used as a cover to prevent evaporation. The paper must cover the concrete completely, with the edges and joints taped to make a continuous cover. A layer of wet sand placed on top of the waterproof paper will hold it in place and help to control temperature.

PLASTIC SHEETING   A lightweight plastic sheeting has been developed for curing concrete. This material is almost impermeable to moisture and is sufficiently flexible to seal in intricate shapes. It can be obtained in rolls up to 32 ft wide, in several thicknesses. The plastic sheet used for curing concrete is usually white or milky rather than clear. This helps to reflect the sun's rays, thereby lowering the temperature somewhat during hot weather. The edges of adjoining sheets can be sealed by heat or with special solvents to form a completely airtight and watertight cover.

CURING COMPOUNDS   Curing compounds, sprayed on freshly placed concrete with a hand or machine sprayer, will form a continuous membrane which assures proper curing. Some curing compounds dry very rapidly and develop a thin, tough membrane in a short time. These compounds may be clear or pigmented. The clear compounds are usually used where the appearance of the finished concrete is important. However, since it is difficult to apply a clear compound evenly, to assure complete coverage a dye which will fade in a few days is sometimes added. White pig-

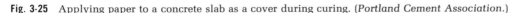

Fig. 3-25   Applying paper to a concrete slab as a cover during curing. (*Portland Cement Association.*)

ments added to clear compounds can produce a heat-reflecting membrane that will reduce internal temperatures of concrete approximately 15°F. Black compounds absorb heat and should not be used in hot weather, but they can be used advantageously during cold weather. Care must be taken in choosing a curing compound for a surface that is to receive a finish. Some compounds inhibit the bonding of paint to concrete. Others provide a poor base for the adhesives used to apply resilient floor coverings.

REINFORCED CONCRETE

Concrete has great compression strength. Each square inch of concrete can be designed to support loads of 10,000 lb or more. However, concrete has little tensile strength, or resistance to pulling action. The tensile strength of steel is 50,000 psi or more. In reinforced concrete, steel and concrete are combined to take advantage of the high compressive strength of concrete and the high tensile strength of

Fig. 3-26 Plastic sheeting used as a curing membrane. (*Portland Cement Association.*)

Fig. 3-27 Applying curing compound to a concrete road. (*Portland Cement Association.*)

steel. In a reinforced-concrete member the concrete is generally assumed to resist all compressive loads and the steel to resist all tensile loads. Sometimes, to reduce the size of the concrete members, steel may also be used to resist a portion of the compression.

Concrete is cast around reinforcing steel bars, and as it hardens, it grips the steel bars to form a bond with the steel. This bond becomes stronger as the concrete hardens. Steel and concrete expand and contract with temperature at rates so nearly equal (0.0000061 in./°F for steel and 0.0000059 in./°F for concrete) that the two work together as a unit under most conditions of temperature change.

Location of Reinforcement

A brief explanation of the mechanics of beam action will help show the importance of the location of reinforcing steel in reinforced-concrete structures.

When a vertical load is placed on any beam (or slab) that rests on supports, the beam tends to bend at points between the supports. This bending action places the top of the beam in *compression* near the center of the span; the bottom of the beam is then in *tension* at these points. Where the beam passes over the supports, which now exert an upward pressure, the action is reversed, and the top portion of the beam is in tension. The steel, which will resist this tension, must therefore be located near the bottom of the beam in the middle portion of the span and near the top at points over the supports.

In addition to the bending action of beams, a *shearing action* takes place near supports. This shearing action is resisted by reinforcing steel *stirrups*, hoops of steel which

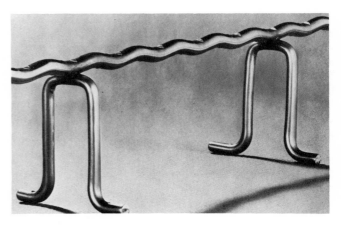

Fig. 3-29 Patented saddles to support reinforcing bars. (*Dayton Sure Grip and Shore Company.*)

are placed vertically in the beam near supports. Concrete expands and contracts with moisture as well as temperature changes, so horizontal reinforcing bars are placed in the top of the concrete member at right angles to the tension steel. This steel is called *temperature steel*.

Protection of Reinforcement

Steel reinforcing in structural members is tied firmly in place with 16-gauge soft wire so it cannot move when the concrete is poured around it, compacted, and vibrated. Saddles are also used to keep the steel in place. Devices called *chairs*, made of steel or concrete, are placed inside

Fig. 3-28 Placement of reinforcing in a typical concrete beam: (*a*) end span of continuous beam; (*b*) section.

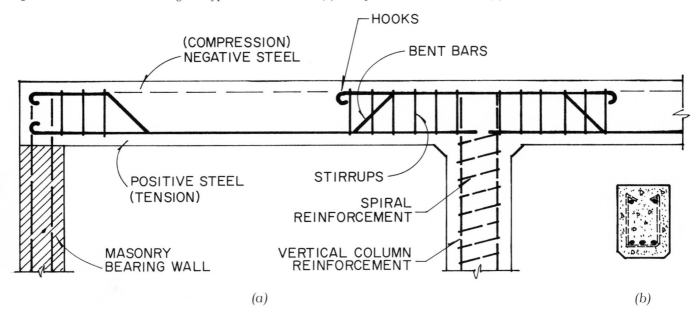

(*a*)   (*b*)

the forms to hold the steel a fixed distance from the outside surfaces of the concrete. Steel exposed to the elements soon deteriorates. It must also be protected from the heat of fire. Minimum thicknesses for concrete covering over reinforcement are shown in Table 3-3.

TABLE 3-3 Covering over reinforcement

TYPE OF STRUCTURE	MIN. CONCRETE THICKNESS, IN.
Footings and other principal structural members in which concrete is deposited against the ground	3 in. between steel and ground
Where concrete surfaces are exposed to weather or ground after removal of forms: bars $5/8$ in. or larger	2
Bars less than $5/8$ in.	$1\frac{1}{2}$
Where surfaces of slabs and walls are not directly exposed to weather or ground	1
Beams, girders, and tied columns	$1\frac{1}{2}$
Concrete joists	1

Types of Reinforcement

REINFORCING BARS Reinforcing steel is usually in the form of round bars. These bars may be smooth or deformed. *Deformed bars* are rolled with projections on the surface; the pattern of projections varies with each rolling mill. Deformed bars are used almost exclusively because of the added bond strength developed by the surface projections. Deformed bars are numbered from 3 to 8, according to their diameters in eighths of an inch. Thus a No. 3 bar is $3/8$ in. in diameter and a No. 7 bar $7/8$ in. in diameter. (A No. 2 round bar, $1/4$ in. in diameter, is available, but only with a smooth surface.) Deformed bars larger than 1 in. are numbered differently. A No. 9 bar is 1.128 in. in diameter; a No. 10 bar is 1.27 in.; a No. 11 bar is 1.41 in.

The bars may be bent or hooked at the ends to increase their anchorage, or resistance to pulling or slipping under a load.

WIRE MESH Several types of wire mesh are used as reinforcement in concrete slabs. The most common is a right-angle mesh, with the intersections electrically welded or mechanically locked. A triangular-mesh wire fabric has

Fig. 3-30 Placing wire mesh in a concrete slab. Workers carry into place a sheet of welded wire fabric for placement over protruding bars of column. The fabric is easy to fit over bars because of the spacing of the wires and furnishes in one or two pieces all the reinforcement required. Note that the workmen walk on previously laid wire fabric with no danger of displacing it, because all the members of the sheet are factory fused in place. (*Wire Reinforcement Institute.*)

Fig. 3-31 Erecting precast white concrete panels at California State College, Los Angeles, architects Honnold, Reibsamen, and Rex. (*Portland Cement Association.*)

also been developed as reinforcement. This is a series of parallel wires held in place by smaller wires twisted around them to form a triangular pattern. Wire mesh can be obtained in various sizes or gauges of wire with many different spacings. The spacing and size of the wire may be uniform in both directions, or it may form what is called a *one-way* mesh. A reinforcing wire mesh designated as 6×6 10/10 would indicate a square mesh having 10-gauge wire placed at 6 in. on center.

Spacing of Reinforcement

Before concrete is placed, the steel reinforcement must be cleaned of any loose mill scale, loose rust, and other coatings that may reduce the bond. The size of bars used in the member determines the spacing. Bars are usually spaced a distance equal to their minimum diameter, but no closer together than 1 in. Thus all bars less than 1 in. in diameter must be placed an inch apart. Larger bars must be more widely spaced. Spacing is important, in that the size of the coarsest aggregate in the concrete is limited by the opening.

PRECAST CONCRETE

The labor involved in building forms and the machinery or equipment needed to transport and place concrete in tall, thin walls are major cost factors for cast-in-place concrete. If wall slabs, floor slabs, roof slabs, and structural-concrete members can be cast flat on the ground and tilted or lifted into place after they have hardened, costs may be appreciably reduced. Work done at ground level is simpler and less expensive.

Fig. 3-32 Tilt-up wall forms with door and window frames in place, ready for pouring.

Job Precast Concrete

If the concrete is cast on a flat surface, such as the floor slab of the future building, the only forms necessary are those around the perimeter. One side of the slab may be finished with a trowel, eliminating the patching necessary when forms are removed. Production time is reduced, since it is not necessary to wait for the concrete floors or walls to gain their design strength before a second slab is poured directly on top of the previously poured slab. Complicated roof shapes can be poured over shaped earth or forms constructed at ground level and lifted into place without the expensive scaffolding and forming necessary if they were cast in place.

Yard Precast Concrete

Intricate shapes with various textures and colors may be yard or job cast in wood, metal, plastic, or plaster forms. The best quality control is normally achieved in a precast-concrete-manufacturing yard. These precast units, sometimes called *cast stone*, are then delivered to the job to be set by masons. Larger units may be incorporated in the structural system of the building or attached to the structural frame as a curtain wall or finish material.

Wood, steel, concrete, plastic, rubber, or a combination of these materials are used for molds to form panels or structural shapes with a decorative surface of exposed aggregate. After the form has been built, it is coated with a retarder to keep a thin outside layer of cement from setting. When the unit is removed from the mold, this thin layer is brushed away to expose the natural aggregate.

Tilt-up Construction

Concrete wall sections may be cast in horizontal position and then tilted into place after they have hardened. A flat, smooth, level casting bed is needed, with wood or metal forms around the edges. A waste slab, which will later be removed, may be cast near the final location of the member. If feasible, the finished first-floor slab is used as a casting bed. Forms can be placed where door or windows will be installed. The actual steel door or window frames may be placed within the outer forms and thus incorporated into the wall sections.

When one section has been finished, several more wall sections may be cast successively. After the concrete has developed sufficient strength, the sections are lifted by cranes into their final positions. Individual wall sections are generally joined by poured-in-place concrete pilasters or columns. Reinforcing steel projecting from adjacent precast wall panels is welded together when the wall sections are in place. The pilaster is then poured, making the wall a rigid structure.

Lift-slab Construction

This type of construction is similar to tilt-up construction. A succession of slabs are cast, one on top of another, to be

Fig. 3-33 Erecting precast-concrete floor and roof slabs. (*Portland Cement Company.*)

lifted up columns which are already in place. The first-floor slab is cast, and steel or reinforced-concrete columns are erected. A concrete slab, which will eventually become the second-floor slab, is cast on top of the first-floor slab. Several more slabs may be cast, each to become another floor. The final slab is the one which will become the roof.

Starting with the roof, the slabs are lifted vertically at a rate of 7 to 10 ft/hr by hydraulic jacks attached to the columns. The slabs must be handled very carefully. The controls are brought to a central control panel, where the force exerted by each jack is regulated. As each slab reaches its final location, it is welded or attached in place by devices that have been cast into the concrete. Buildings over 13 stories high have been constructed by the lift-slab method.

Bond-breaking Materials

In both tilt-up and lift-up construction, to ensure that cast concrete slabs will separate and not be bonded together, a *bond-breaking* or *parting agent* must be used between them. There are many such agents on the market. Some of them also contain materials that act as combination curing membranes and bond-breaking agents. Care must be taken in selecting parting and curing agents that will not affect the finish materials to be placed on the slabs later.

Fig. 3-34 Prestressed-beam principles. The greater the pressure, the more books can be lifted.

PRESTRESSED CONCRETE

A prestressed-concrete beam or structure is a combination of steel and concrete in which the steel is put in tension before or after the concrete is poured. After the concrete has set, the tension on the steel is released and is transferred through its bond to compression on the concrete.

The action of the prestressed beam is like that in lifting a row of books from a bookshelf. If we place one hand on each end of the row of books and press inward, the row can be lifted as a unit. The harder the pressure, the more weight or the more books we can lift. The row of books is now in compression and will act as a beam. A prestressed beam acts on exactly the same principal, except that it is being pulled into compression from the inside instead of being pressed from the outside. The concrete is stressed by strands of steel cable or rods capable of withstanding forces of 250,000 psi.

The American Concrete Institute (ACI) defines prestressed concrete as "concrete in which there has been introduced internal stresses of such magnitude and distribution that the stresses resulting from given external loadings are counteracted to a desired degree. In reinforced concrete, the prestress is commonly introduced by tensioning the steel reinforcement." Prestressed concrete may become one of the most important developments of the twentieth century. The first prestressed structure in the United States was completed in 1950. A prestressed structural member may be designed to use half the concrete and one-quarter the steel required for a conventional reinforced-concrete member. In addition to the saving in material, the saving in weight reduces the size of foundation needed. Thus the smaller size of the member, the

Fig. 3-35 Installing reinforcement in forms in preparation for pouring a prestressed concrete beam. (*Portland Cement Company.*)

longer spans possible, and the ease and speed of erection may result in an appreciable reduction in cost.

Prestressed structures may be either pretensioned or posttensioned.

PRETENSIONED CONCRETE   In pretensioning the wire strands are stretched the length of the forms and put in tension with jacks. The concrete is cast around them and allowed to harden to its design strength, usually about 3,500 psi. The tension of the steel strand is then released, putting the concrete in compression. In pretensioned concrete no permanent anchorage is necessary at the ends of the steel cables. The steel is kept in tension by the bond between the concrete and steel. Prestressed concrete beams can be cast in forms several hundred feet long and then cut into shorter beams.

POSTTENSIONED CONCRETE   In posttensioned beams, the steel strands or tendons are encased in light metal or paper tubes so that the concrete will not bond to the cable. After the concrete has hardened, the strands are put in tension by jacks and anchored at each end. The space between the tubes and the strand is then filled with grout. Posttensioning has several advantages. Heavy abutments do not have to be built in the forms to take the thrust of the powerful jacks used to put the steel cables in tension, since the concrete itself acts to resist the thrust of the jacks. The steel cables need not be straight, but can be threaded through tubes located at the bottom of the beam at midspan and at the top where beams will pass over supports. Pretensioning is more prevalent in the United States for individual members. Posttensioning is more often used in slabs.

Fig. 3-36 Installing prestressed concrete beams. (*Portland Cement Company.*)

QUESTIONS

1. What is a hydraulic cement?

2. Where did portland cement originate, and what are its principal characteristics?

3. What are the principal ingredients in portland cement and how is it produced?

4. Describe the five types of portland cement and give examples of a use of each.

5. What is air-entraining portland cement, and what is its use?

6. What makes cement paste set?

7. Why are aggregates needed in concrete?

8. Describe five types of aggregate.

9. Why is it desirable to have several sizes of aggregate in a sample of concrete?

10. What is meant by the water/cement ratio?

11. What is the cement factor?

12. Describe the process of making a sieve analysis.

13. Describe the process of making a slump test.

14. What are admixtures, and why are they sometimes used in concrete?

15. When and why are concrete test bores made?

16. What is slump? How is it tested, and why is it important?

17. In placing concrete, what four steps must be taken to assure a lasting surface free of defects?

18. What is the difference between pumped concrete and pneumatically placed concrete?

19. What is laitance?

20. Describe the finishing of concrete.

21. How does the fact that concrete expands and contracts affect the design of concrete structures?

22. What is a weakened-plane joint, and why is it used in concrete construction?

23. Describe five methods used in curing concrete.

24. Discuss the function of steel reinforcing in concrete structures.

25. Sketch the approximate placement of reinforcing steel in a simple beam supported at each end.

26. Discuss the theory of prestressed-concrete construction.

27. What is pretensioned concrete?

28. What is posttensioned concrete?

REFERENCES FOR FURTHER STUDY

American Concrete Institute: P.O. Box 4754, Bedford Station, Detroit, Mich., 48217. "ACI Standards," 1959. "Building Code Requirements for Reinforced Concrete Structures," 1959. "Formwork for Concrete," 1961. "Recommended Practice for Electing Proportions for Concrete," 1954. "Recommended Practice for Measuring, Mixing, and Placing Concrete," 1959. "Reinforced Concrete Design Handbook," 1955. "Admixtures for Concrete," 1954.

American Society for Testing and Materials: 1916 Race Street, Philadelphia, Pa., 19103. "Portland Cement Specifications," ASTM C150-60. "Specifications for Air-entraining Portland Cement," ASTM C175-53. "Specifications for Slag Cement," ASTM C358-58. "Specifications for Portland-Pozzolan Cement," ASTM C340-58T. "Concrete Aggregates," ASTM C33-59T. "Lightweight Aggregates for Insulating Concrete," ASTM C332-56T. "Sieve Analysis of Fine and Coarse Aggregates," ASTM C136-46. "Making and Curing Concrete Compression and Flexure Test Specifications in the Field," ASTM C39-59. "Securing, Preparing, and Testing Specimens from Hardened Concrete for Compressive and Flexural Strengths," ASTM C42-60.

American Society of Civil Engineers: 345 East 47th Street, New York, N.Y., 10017. "Tentative Recommendations for Prestressed Concrete," 1959.

Concrete Reinforcing Steel Institute: 228 North La Salle Street, Chicago, Ill., 60601. "Reinforced Concrete," 1955.

Hoadley, A. H., "Essentials of Structural Design," Wiley, New York, 1964.

Hornbostel, Caleb, "Materials for Architecture," Reinhold, New York, 1963.

Kaiser Cement and Gypsum Corporation: Permanente, Calif., "Concrete Topics," a series of technical bulletins. "Concrete Trends," a series of special reports.

Merrit, Frederick S., "Building Construction Handbook," McGraw-Hill, New York, 1958.

Parker, Harry, "Simplified Design of Reinforced Concrete," Wiley, New York, 1960.

Portland Cement Association: 33 West Grand Avenue, Chicago, Ill., 60610. "Design and Control of Concrete Mixtures." "Architectural Concrete Specifications." "Effect of Aggregate Characteristics on Quality of Concrete." "Proportioning, Mixing, Transporting and Placing Architectural Concrete." "Finishing Architectural Concrete." "Forms for Architectural Concrete." "Cement and Concrete Reference Book." "Concrete Technology."

Portland Cement Research and Development Laboratories: 5420 Old Orchard Road, Skokie, Ill. "Manufacture and Use of Lightweight Aggregates for Structural Concrete," 1962. "Journal of the PCA Research and Development Laboratories."

Prestressed Concrete Institute: 205 West Wacker Drive, Chicago, Ill., 60606. "Research Bibliographies," 1965.

Protex Industries, Inc.: 1331 West Evans Avenue, P.O. Box 9327 South Denver Station, Denver, Colo. "Facts on Air-Entrained Concrete," 1964. "Facts on Water Reducing Admixtures," 1964.

Short, Andrew, and William Kinniburgh, "Lightweight Concrete," Wiley, New York, 1963.

Troxell, G. F., et al., "Concrete," McGraw-Hill, New York, 1956.

U.S. Business and Defense Service Administration, Office of Technical Service: "Concrete Technology," OTR-107.

Wilson, G., "Exposed Concrete Finish," Wiley, New York, 1964, 2 vols.

Winter, George, et al., "Design of Concrete Structures," 7th ed., McGraw-Hill, New York, 1964.

MASONRY

4

STONE

The natural materials available for construction have generally determined the character of the architecture produced by any culture. Neither the massive buildings of ancient Egypt nor the exquisite temples of Greece would have been possible without an abundant supply of excellent building stone. Stone has been used as a structural material, as a finish material, and as roofing throughout the centuries. With the development of new materials and new methods of construction, it is now used almost entirely for its decorative value. The range of color, texture, and finish of stone is almost inexhaustible. While some types of stone are available only in limited quantities or areas, others are found all over the world.

Quarrying

Present-day methods of quarrying stone are similar to those used by the ancient Egyptians. The Egyptians drove wooden wedges into natural faults of the stone and then poured water onto them. The swelling of the wood wedges split the rock into sizes suitable for the mason to work into final shape with hand tools. Quarries begun by the Romans and the Greeks are still in use today.

Sandstone and limestone are stratified, which simplifies their removal from their natural beds. The size of stones will vary from quarry to quarry. In stratified rock a series of holes is drilled perpendicular to the stratification, and the material between the holes is removed. Stones are then split from the quarry along the lines of stratification. In rock that is not stratified, such as granite, holes must be drilled both horizontally and vertically into the bed.

In quarrying of softer stones, such as limestone, sandstone, and some marbles, channeling machines or wire saws may be used to remove the rough stones. The harder stones must still be removed by drilling and wedges. Light charges of powder may be used to form the channels or remove the stone. One of the newer methods of splitting stone from its natural bed is use of a flame drill to heat portions of the bed to a very high temperature. Then water is applied to the heated portion to disintegrate the rock.

Dressing

When the stones have been removed from the quarry, they are taken to a finishing mill for final dressing. Some stones may be used just as they come from the quarry, with the quarry face unchanged. Most stones are split and then cut to the size needed for final installation. Sometimes several building stones are cut at one time with gang saws. All saws use an abrasive agent in cutting the stone. One operation uses steel shot as an abrasive material between the saw and stone. This is called *shot sawing*.

Individual stones may be given several types of finish, depending on their use. A *chat-sawn* finish is produced by rough gang saws using an abrasive known as *chat*. Large planers may be used to give the stones a relatively smooth surface or to cut them into sizes and shapes for use as moldings. The surface may also be *plucked*. In this process, small particles are removed from the surface to form a texture. Stone may be given a *hand-split surface*, produced by various types of hand chisels. *Machine-tooled surfaces* are cut in one direction by machine-held chisels and are hand tooled in the opposite direction. The surface may be *pointed, peen-hammered, bush-hammered, rusticated,* or given several other types of textured surfaces. The surface may be *wet rubbed* for a smooth surface, *carborundum rubbed* for a smoother surface, or *honed* for a polished surface.

Stones may be cut to a specific size and finish to conform to requirements for a particular job. This type of stone is termed *dimension stone*. The designer must select the desired size, shape, and finish available from particular quarries or mills. The stones will be produced with each stone numbered and accompanied by shop drawings to show where it will fit in the finished building.

Classification of Stone

Stone is classified geologically as igneous, sedimentary, and metamorphic. The characteristics of each type have a definite bearing on their durability and use. *Igneous rock* is the product of heat and pressure, such as that caused by volcanic activity and pressure exerted by the shifting of the earth's surface. *Sedimentary rock* is made up of silt or the

skeletal remains of marine life that have been deposited by ancient seas. *Metamorphic rock* is formed by the gradual change in the character and structure of igneous and sedimentary rock. All types of stone are used in building, but the most important ones in the construction industry are granite, sandstone, slate, limestone, and marble.

GRANITE Granite is an igneous rock that has been formed and cooled beneath the earth's surface. It varies from a finely granulated form to one that is crystalline in nature. The color ranges from white to a deep bronze or black, depending on the quarry. The National Building Granite Quarries Association has divided granite into three groups, based on their use (see Table 4-1).

Granite can be obtained as dimension stones in finishes ranging from a polished mirror gloss that gives sharp reflections to a sawn surface scored $^3/_{32}$ in. deep. Stones are produced in random sizes from 6″ to 18″ long, 2″ to 18″ high, and $3^3/_4$″ to $4^1/_2$″ thick. They may be either square or angular, with the edges sawn parallel as surfaces for mortar joints.

Granite is suitable for use where strength or hardness is required. Steps, squared paving, and random paving of granite stand up well under heavy wear and abrasion. The highly durable, crystalline surface of polished granite makes a colorful lasting finish for building exteriors.

SANDSTONE Sandstone is a sedimentary rock composed of angular or rounded grains of sand held together by a cementitious material. Cementitious materials containing a high percentage of iron oxides give sandstone red to brown tones. This type of sandstone, sometimes called *brownstone* or *redstone*, is soft and easy to work, but it is not always durable. Certain sandstones, classed as *Ohio sandstone*, have been formed under extreme pressure and contain very little cementing material. These light-grey or buff stones are easy to work and are also hard and durable.

Sandstone with definite, close-spaced cleavage lines is widely used as flagstones or paving. A reddish sandstone, sometimes called *Arizona flagstone*, is prevalent throughout the West. *Bluestone*, produced in quarries in North Carolina, is a medium to dark bluish-grey stone used for paving, veneers, and as rough building stone.

SLATE Most slates are composed of high-silica clays laid down as silt in ancient sea bottoms. This clay has formed into rock that can be split into thin sheets with smooth regular faces along natural cleavage lines. The colors of slate are caused by small amounts of impurities such as iron, carbon, and chlorite. The colors may be *nonfading* or *weathering* (change color with exposure to the weather), depending on the nature of the coloring agent.

Slate can be split as thin as $^1/_4$ or $^3/_8$ in. for use as a roofing material. Slates as thick as 2 in. are used for exterior and interior veneers, platforms, walks, walls, and countertops. Slates used for paving or flagstones are produced in standard thicknesses of $^3/_8$″, $^1/_2$″, $^3/_4$″, $^7/_8$″, and

TABLE 4-1 Types of granite

TYPE	USE
Standard building granite	For buildings in which the exterior material is used structurally, either self-supporting or as bonded masonry
Granite veneer	For buildings in which the exterior facing serves as a decorative and protective veneer, rather than as a structural element
Masonry granite	For more rugged types of construction in which the exterior material is an integral part of the masonry, and massive strength and durability are the primary requirements

1″. They may be obtained with all four edges squared, with two edges parallel and the ends irregular, or as random irregular flagstones.

Slate is produced with several surface finishes. It may be *natural cleft*, with no surface finish except that obtained by natural cleavage, or *semirubbed*, with approximately 50 percent of the natural cleft face removed. It may be given a *hone finish*, similar to a sand-rubbed finish, but with a very smooth surface. The back of the slates may be *gauged* to produce cleftface slates of a more uniform thickness.

LIMESTONE Limestone is sedimentary rock that contains carbonate of lime, the remains of shells, or the skeletons of prehistoric animals, and certain other essential elements. It may be white, cream, buff, grey, or variegated patterns of these colors. Some limestones have an even, dense grain structure with no stratification. *Travertine* and *Mexican onyx* are types of limestone that owe their beauty to alternate layers showing many irregular cavities. Other limestones show fossilized fish shells, coral, and leaves preserved in the stone. Limestone is comparatively soft when it is taken from the ground; at this time

it can be worked with ease. However, with exposure to the air, limestone develops a hard, long-wearing surface.

Most limestone used as building stone in the United States is called *Bedford* or *Indiana limestone*. The grading of Indiana limestone is based on the allowable limits of texture and color. The rules established for the grading of Bedford or Indiana limestone are shown in Table 4-2.

MARBLE Marble is a metamorphic, crystalline limestone. In common usage any crystalline rock having interlocking or mosaic grains that is capable of taking a polish is considered marble. The ASTM defines and describes several building stones such as calcite marble and dolomite marble, which are not true marbles. Marble has a wide range of colors, textures, grains, working qualities, and finish properties. *Brecciated marbles* consist of round or angular particles of many colors embedded in a naturally colored cementitious material. Some marbles are not affected by exposure to the weather; others must be protected.

Although modern practice has confined the use of marble to interior and exterior veneers placed over structural frame, marble has been used through the centuries

Fig. 4-1 Translucent marble panels on Beineke Rare Book and Manuscript Library, Yale University, architects Skidmore, Owings, and Merrill. (*Marble Institute of America, Inc.*)

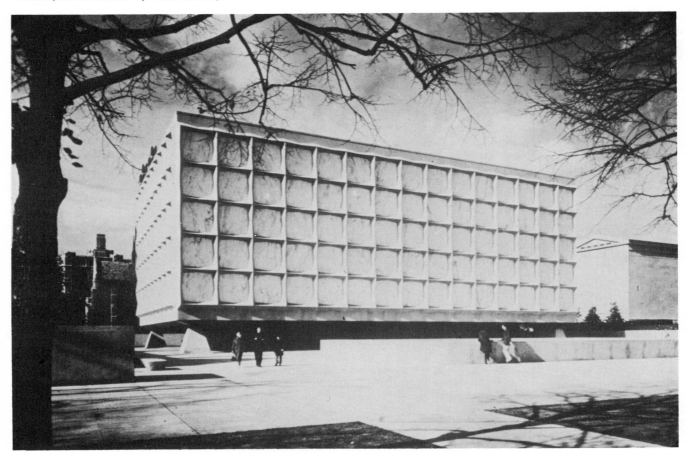

as a structural material. Quarries in the Aegean Islands have been operated continuously since 66 B.C. Marble is produced by more than 100 quarries in the United States, from Vermont to California. American marble ranges from creamy white to black. Imported varieties add hundreds of other colors and patterns. The limitations of size for individual marbles depend on the type of marble and the quarry. The standard thicknesses of interior and exterior marble are $7/8''$, $1 1/4''$, $1 1/2''$, and $2''$.

Marble is classified by the Marble Institute of America into four grades, as shown in Table 4-3. With proper methods of manufacture, all the marbles in each group are considered equivalent in performance, durability, and utility. Marbles vary greatly in their ability to withstand the elements. Some crumble under severe weather conditions or pollutants in the air. Certain very beautiful marbles will disintegrate in the presence of water and can

Fig. 4-2 Lowering marble panels for Beineke Rare Book and Manuscript Library. (*Marble Institute of America, Inc.*)

Fig. 4-3 Setting marble panels in Beineke Rare Book and Manuscript Library. (*Marble Institute of America, Inc.*)

TABLE 4-2 Limestone grades

GRADE	DESCRIPTION
Statuary	A very fine, uniform-grained buff limestone used for sculpture and fine carvings
Select	A dense, fine-grained stone with only minor variations of grain and texture and no pore spaces larger than $1/25$ in.
Standard	A less dense stone with more variation of grain and more and larger pore spaces
Rustic	Stones defined by color but not selected for uniformity of grain or texture
Old Gothic	Mixtures of buff and grey limestone with seams and other markings, ranging from a moderately uniform buff to stones having light and dark streaks and a wide variety of color
Variegated	Mixtures of buff and grey limestones which are unselected for grain and textures

TABLE 4-3   Marble grades

GRADE	DESCRIPTION
Group A	Sound marbles and stones with uniformly good working qualities
Group B	Marbles and stones similar in character to Group A, but with working qualities somewhat less favorable; limited amount of *waxing, sticking,* and *reinforcing* of occasional natural faults (Sticking, waxing, and reinforcing are manufacturers' terms for filling natural voids, lines of separation, and repairing faults in marble.)
Group C	Marbles and stones of uncertain variation in working qualities; frequent geological flaws, voids, veins, and lines of separation repaired by sticking, waxing, filling, and reinforcing
Group D	Marbles and stones similar to Group C and subject to the same methods of finishing and manufacture, but with maximum variation in working qualities and a larger portion of faults; includes many of the highly colored marbles prized for their decorative qualities

be used only for interiors. The Group A marbles are, in most instances, suitable for exterior use. Most of the others are not suitable for exterior use except in sheltered locations.

The most commonly used surface finishes for marble are given in Table 4-4. Polished marble tends to lose its polished surface and color on the exterior of buildings unless it is constantly maintained. The Marble Institute of America recommends sand-rubbed rather than honed or polished finishes for exterior marble.

STONE MASONRY

Stone masonry walls are classified according to shape and surface finish of the stone as *rubble, ashlar,* and *cut stone* or *dimension stone.* Within each of the classifications variations may be used to provide interest or to bring out the characteristics of a particular type of stone.

Types of Stonework

RUBBLE   Rubble masonry is composed of stones as they are either collected, called *fieldstone,* or stone as it comes

Fig. 4-4   Marble panels on American National Bank, Beaumont, Texas, architects Harrel and Hamilton. (*Marble Institute of America, Inc.;* *photo by Frank Lotz Miller.*)

TABLE 4-4 Marble finishes

FINISH	DESCRIPTION
Split face	Rough natural face of the stone, used for masonry stonework consisting of small, uneven, narrow stones
Natural finish	A moderately rough face produced by sawing with the use of sand as an abrasive
Sand finish	A finish produced by sand rubbing to a dull, smooth surface
Sand blown	A finish produced by sand blasting to a smooth, matte surface
Grit finish	A finish produced by rubbing the surface with abrasive grit to produce a dull, smooth surface that is somewhat smoother than a sand finish
Hone finish	A velvety smooth finish with little or no gloss produced by machine and hand rubbing with special abrasives
Polished	A mirrorlike glossy finish which brings out the full color of the marble; requires periodic maintenance

Fig. 4-5 Polished aresbacto marble floor in Midwestern United States Life Insurance Building, Fort Wayne, Indiana. (*Marble Institute of America, Inc.; photo by Wesley Pusey, Technika, Inc.*)

from the quarry. Thus the stones may have rounded natural faces or angular broken faces. *Random rubble* consists of fieldstones or quarry stones laid in an irregular pattern of sizes and shapes, with the large spaces between them filled with *spalls*, or broken bits of stone. A special type of rubble masonry, called *polygonal*, *mosaic*, or *mosaic web-wall*, is composed of random-shaped stones fitted together to expose a web of more or less uniform mortar joints. *Mosaic dry wall* is similar, but is laid close together with no mortar showing. *Coursed-rubble* or *strip-rubble walls* are constructed of stone that has been quarried in layers of uniform thickness or of roughly shaped stones laid in approximately level beds. The stones are split to length by the mason on the job.

Fig. 4-6 Common types of stonework.

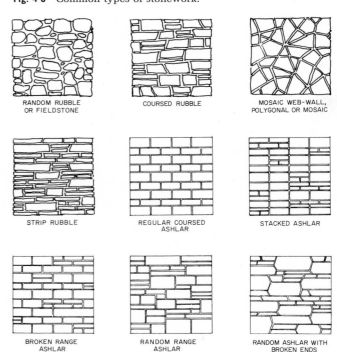

ASHLAR   Ashlar masonry is constructed of squared stones set in random or uniform courses. Uniform continuous courses of the same height are called *regular-course ashlar*. Walls of squared stones of different sizes set in random courses are classed as *random* or *broken-range ashlar*. A wall of squared stones that is not measured and cut according to shop drawings, but is set at the discretion of the mason, is considered an ashlar wall. The surface finish of ashlar walls may be quarry face, hand split, or a finish compatible to the stone used.

CUT STONE   *Cut stone*, sometimes called dimension stone, is defined here as stones which are wholly fabricated and finished at the mill ready to be set in the building in conformity to drawings and specifications. Each stone is numbered and located on shop drawings and setting diagrams.

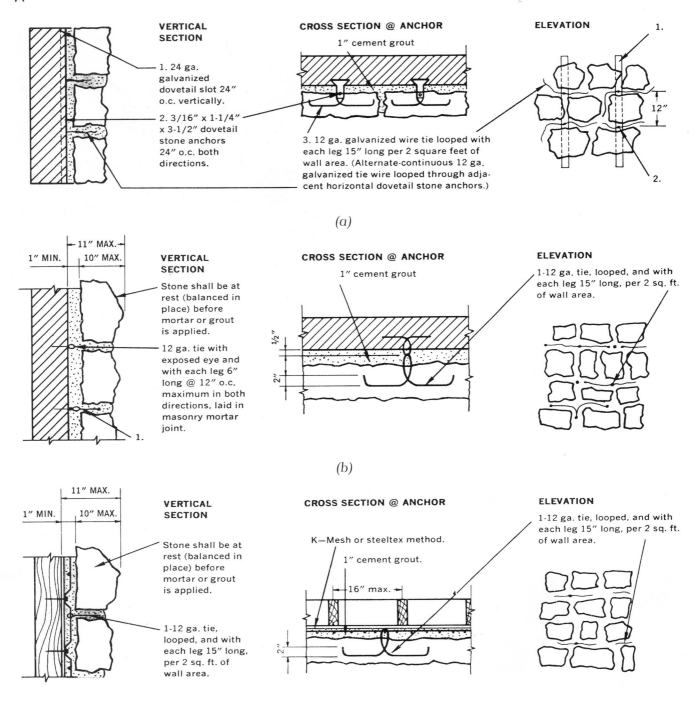

VERTICAL SECTION

1. 24 ga. galvanized dovetail slot 24" o.c. vertically.

2. 3/16" x 1-1/4" x 3-1/2" dovetail stone anchors 24" o.c. both directions.

CROSS SECTION @ ANCHOR

1" cement grout

3. 12 ga. galvanized wire tie looped with each leg 15" long per 2 square feet of wall area. (Alternate-continuous 12 ga. galvanized tie wire looped through adjacent horizontal dovetail stone anchors.)

ELEVATION

1.

12"

2.

(a)

VERTICAL SECTION

1" MIN.   11" MAX.   10" MAX.

Stone shall be at rest (balanced in place) before mortar or grout is applied.

12 ga. tie with exposed eye and with each leg 6" long @ 12" o.c. maximum in both directions, laid in masonry mortar joint.

1.

CROSS SECTION @ ANCHOR

1" cement grout

1/2"

2"

ELEVATION

1-12 ga. tie, looped, and with each leg 15" long, per 2 sq. ft. of wall area.

(b)

VERTICAL SECTION

1" MIN.   11" MAX.   10" MAX.

Stone shall be at rest (balanced in place) before mortar or grout is applied.

1-12 ga. tie, looped, and with each leg 15" long, per 2 sq. ft. of wall area.

CROSS SECTION @ ANCHOR

K—Mesh or steeltex method.

1" cement grout.

16" max.

2"

ELEVATION

1-12 ga. tie, looped, and with each leg 15" long, per 2 sq. ft. of wall area.

Thickness of different types may be from 3" to a maximum of 11".

(c)

Fig. 4-7 Methods of attaching natural-stone veneer: (a) on concrete backing; (b) on masonry backing; (c) on wood backing. (*Courtesy of the Los Angeles Chapter, Construction Specifications Institute.*)

Cut stones are seldom used as structural members. The most common use is as masonry veneer, which is attached to a backing with wire ties or nonrusting anchoring devices. The tie wires, corrugated metal straps, or anchoring devices are cast into or attached to the backing material and extend into the mortar joints between the stones. Anchors for cut-stone veneer may be cast into structural-concrete backing walls. Dovetail slots may be formed into the structural wall to receive special anchors. These special anchors of brass, medium-hard drawn copper, or stainless steel fit into holes or slots drilled or sawed into the cut stone. The cut stone is held away from the backing by the anchors. Continuous horizontal angles bolted into the backing may be used to support and hold the cut-stone veneer in place. The spaces between the cut stones may be maintained by aluminum or plastic spacers.

Stone columns may be made of one piece of stone turned on a lathe, or the base and cap may be turned separately. For large columns the stones may be formed into drums to be combined on the job. Sheet lead is sometimes placed in the joints between the drums to act as a cushion.

Stone Masonry Joints and Mortar

Ordinary cements used in concrete or mortar will stain stones such as limestone. A water barrier or dampproofing must therefore be used on the backing material, unless the facing is held away from the backing to maintain a 2 in. cavity. Marble and other thin stone veneers are usually set by spotting with plaster of paris. Corrosion-resistant ties, secured to the structural wall and extending into the joints, hold the stone veneer in place. A 1-in. air space is usually maintained between the structural wall and the back of the veneer. Some building codes require that this space be filled with grout. In this case nonstaining cement grout mixed with clear, white, washed sand is used.

Mortar and grout for stone masonry usually consists of white portland cement, hydrated lime, and sand. Trade associations recommend certain proportions for best results. However, local building codes set allowable limits of each material, and these must be followed. Mortar in the joints between the stone is usually *raked*, or cut back from the surface as the stone is set. This joint is later *pointed*, or filled, to make the finished joint. Pointing material may be the same as the mortar between the joints, or it may be a colored synthetic sealant. In most mortar joints the pointing compound is tooled with a concave tool to obtain a hard surface and to make the joints impervious to moisture.

BRICK

Building bricks are solid masonry units, usually $4 \times 4 \times 12$ in., composed of inorganic nonmetalic materials hardened or burned by heat or chemical action. Building brick may be solid or it may have cored openings not to exceed 25 percent of its volume. Bricks are produced in a wide variety of color, shape, and texture.

Fig. 4-8 Marble drum from an ancient Greek temple, Olympus, Greece.

Recent excavations in Egypt have shown that the ancient Egyptians used sun-dried and kiln-burned bricks for houses and palaces of nobility. In the Babylonian civilization (4000 B.C.), which developed in the valley of the Tigris and Euphrates Rivers, the thick mud and clay laid down by these rivers was well suited for brick, which thus became the usual building material of this civilization. Palaces and temples were constructed of sun-dried brick, faced with brilliant kiln-burned glazed brick.

The Romans also made wide use of brick, in conjunction with the very efficient mortar of volcanic tufa and lime. The Roman bricks were comparatively thin for their length. They were laid in thick beds of mortar in several patterns. After the fall of the Roman Empire the art of brickmaking was lost throughout Europe until the beginning of the fourteenth century. The first brick buildings on the North American continent were erected in 1633 on Manhattan Island with bricks imported from Holland and England. The first brick kilns were put into operation in the United States in about 1650.

Classes of Brick

Bricks are generally classified as *adobe*, made of natural sun-dried clays or earth and a binder; *kiln burned*, composed of clays or shales to which other materials may have been added and fired to hardness; *sand-lime*, mixtures of sand and lime hardened under steam pressure and heat; and *concrete*, solid or cored units composed of portland cement and aggregates.

ADOBE BRICK   Sun-dried brick formed of sandy clay found in the Southwestern United States has been used for centuries by the various Indian tribes of the area. Adobe brick is still used in this semiarid area, where its good insulating qualities can be used to advantage. Modern adobe brick is composed of soil that contains sufficient clay to bind the particles together but does not contain more than 0.2 percent of water-soluble salts. The soil is mixed with a stabilizing agent of emulsified asphalt to provide the required resistance to absorption. Adobe bricks are commonly 3″ to 6″ high, 8″ to 13″ wide, and from 12″ to 18″ long.

Adobe construction is usually limited to structures of one story. The adobe masonry is set on concrete foundations that extend 6 in. or more above ground. Adobe brick is set in standard masonry mortar, and in southern California it is heavily reinforced with steel set in concrete-bond beams to resist earthquake stresses. A normal bearing wall of adobe brick is usually 16 in. thick. Although the adobe brick is stabilized with an asphalt emulsion to resist water, walls are usually protected by water-resistant coatings and wide roof overhangs.

KILN-BURNED BRICK   The most widely used type of building brick is made of natural sand and clays or shale. These clays are composed of silicate or alumina and small percentages of other minerals. Clays with a large percentage of feldspar and iron oxide turn a salmon, red, or brown on firing. Clays with a large percentage of calcium carbonate burn to a yellowish color. Shale is a type of clay that has been solidified under pressure. It is not soluble in water in its solid form and must be ground or pulverized to be used in the manufacture of clay products.

SAND-LIME BRICK   Sand-lime brick is a pearl-grey brick formed much like dry-pressed burned-clay brick. Lime, in the form of dolomite lime or a high-calcium lime, is mixed with clean, washed sand and allowed to stand for several hours before it is delivered to a press. The brick is then allowed to harden in closed vessels under steam pressure. The grading and use of sand-lime brick is similar to that of hard-burned clay brick.

CONCRETE BRICK   Concrete (cement brick) is made of portland cement and a suitable aggregate. The materials are mixed together and formed in molds of the same size as burned brick. The brick may be cured by steam or by the dry process. Concrete brick is used where a particular texture or color is desired.

Manufacture of Brick

The clays used for kiln-burned brick are usually obtained by surface digging or quarrying. Some clays require very

Fig. 4-9   Modern brick building at Masonry Industry Center, Los Angeles, California, architects O'Leary and Terasawa. (*Masonry Research.*)

little preparation, while others require extensive grinding. The clay is delivered to a granulator, which breaks up the larger pieces with steel knives. It is then discharged onto large pans, where it is ground to a fine powder by steel rollers. After the clay is ground, it is tempered in a *pug mill*. *Tempering* is the process of reducing the clay to a homogenous plastic mass. At this point sand and water are added to produce the desired consistancy for molding. Bricks may be molded by a soft-mud, stiff-mud, or dry-press process.

The *soft-mud process* consists of mechanically forcing wet, soft clay into molds. The molding machine forces the wet clay into several molds under pressure, cuts off excess clay, and turns the molded bricks out onto a pallet or conveyor, to be carried away for drying. The inside of the mold may be sprayed or dipped in water to prevent the clay from sticking. These bricks are called *water-struck bricks*. *Sand-struck bricks* generally have sharper, cleaner edges than water-struck bricks.

In the *stiff-mud process* only enough water is used to form the clay into a cohesive mass, which is then forced or extruded in a column through dies in a brick-making machine. The column of clay is forced onto a wire cutting table, where it is cut into appropriate lengths by taut wires. This produces a *wire-cut* face. Brick may be *end cut* or *side cut*, depending on the size and shape of the die.

Dry-pressed brick is manufactured of relatively dry or nonplastic clays. The material is fed into the machine by hoppers, where it is compressed into molds under high pressure. Dry-pressed bricks are compact, strong, and well-formed. Many face bricks are formed by this process.

When the bricks come from the brick-making machine, they contain from 7 to 30 percent moisture, depending on the process used. They may be stacked in open sheds for periods of 7 days to 6 weeks for final drying. Most brick is now dried in mechanical driers under controlled conditions of heat, moisture, and air velocity for 2 to 4 days.

Brick Kilns

The earliest type of kiln used to fire brick consisted of a series of arches composed of the naturally dried brick. The remainder of the dried, or *green*, bricks were piled on top of the arches, and a fire was built under the arches. As the heat distribution in this type of kiln is very uneven, the bricks closest to the fire were burned to a vitrified, shiny surface that was almost black. These shiny, occasionally warped, dark bricks are sometimes used for special architectural effects. The bricks at the top of the pile were partially burned and were a light-pink or salmon color. Those between varied in color and hardness, depending on their location in the pile. While this type of kiln may still be used in some small brickyards, most brick are now burned in kilns having permanent enclosures, with the heat generated in ovens outside the wall. The heat may be furnished through grates under bricks piled in arches as before. These kilns are called *up-draft kilns*. If the heat enters near the top of the kiln and passes down through the piled

brick and out through openings in the floor to chimneys, the kiln is called a *down-draft kiln*.

Kilns may be either intermittent or continuous. In the *intermittent kiln*, the bricks must be fired, the fires extinguished, the bricks allowed to cool, the kiln dismantled, and the bricks removed before a new pile of green bricks are piled to be fired. The development of the *continuous kiln* greatly speeded up the process. The continuous kiln may consist of several compartments fired by a single oven. The heat is regulated in each section so that while the remaining water is being removed from the brick in one compartment, bricks are being fired in a second compartment and cooled in a third. The continuous *tunnel kiln* is now widely used. The tunnel kiln consists of either a straight or a curved tunnel, with several zones in which heat is carefully controlled. Bricks are loaded onto special cars and pulled through the preheating, firing, and cooling zones at a constant rate of speed. The tunnel kiln is very efficient and produces a more uniform product.

Brick Types and Sizes

Bricks are available in many different sizes and types, which vary greatly from area to area. For example, over 100 different clay-brick units are manufactured in southern California alone. Hence the designer of a brick-masonry structure must check carefully to ascertain whether a particular type, color, or texture is manufactured or stocked locally. The most generally used solid clay masonry units are common building brick, face brick, special brick, and custom brick.

COMMON BRICK Common brick is the most widely used building brick. This is the ordinary red brick used for walls, backing, and other structures where a special color, shape, or texture is not required. The color may vary from dark orange to a deep red color, depending on the composition of the local clay. Common brick can be obtained in some areas with rug-face, ruffle, scored, combed, roughened, smooth, wire-cut, bark-face, stone-face, and several other finishes. Grades of common brick are shown in Table 4-5. Common brick is manufactured in many sizes, depending on local practices. Some of the more common sizes are shown in Table 4-6.

MODULAR BRICK Bricks which can be laid to modular dimensions are available in some localities. These bricks are sized so that the brick plus the mortar joint will form a 4″,

TABLE 4-5 Common-brick grades

GRADE	USE
SW	For rigorous exposure conditions, such as heavy rain, snow, or continual freezing
MW	For average exposure to moisture and moderate freezing
NW	For exposure to minimal moisture and freezing

	Height	Width	Length
STANDARD BUILDING BRICK:	2½″	x 3⅞″	x 8¼″
OVERSIZE BUILDING BRICK:	3¼″	x 3¼″	x 10″
MODULAR BUILDING BRICK:	3⅜″	x 3″	x 11⅜″
STANDARD FACE BRICK:	2³⁄₁₆″	x 3½″	x 7½″
NORMAN FACE BRICK:	2³⁄₁₆″	x 3½″	x 11½″
CONTINENTAL FACE BRICK:	3⅜″	x 3″	x 11½″
ROMAN FACE BRICK:	1½″	x 3½″	x 11½″
IMPERIAL or ATLAS BRICK:	5⅜″	x 3″	x 15⅜″
PADRE BRICK:	4″	x 3″	x 15½″
	4″	x 3″	x 11½″
	4″	x 3″	x 7½″
"FOUR-16" BRICK:	3½″	x 3″	x 15⅜″
ROYALE (Ceramic Block):	7⅝″	x 5½″	x 15½″
	7⅝″	x 7½″	x 15½″
PAVING BRICK:	2³⁄₁₆″	x 3½″	x 7½″
PAVING TILE:	1¼″	x 3½″	x 7½″
	1¼″	x 3½″	x 11½″
BEL AIR PAVER:	2¼″	x 5½″	x 11½″
FIRE BRICK:	2½″	x 4½″	x 9″
FIRE BRICK SPLITS:	1¼″	x 4½″	x 9″

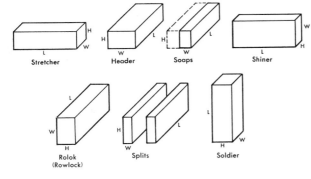

Fig. 4-10 Nomenclature and brick sizes and shapes. (*Masonry Research.*)

TABLE 4-6 Common-brick sizes

TYPE	SIZES
Standard	2½″ × 3⅞″ × 8¼″ or 2¼″ × 3¾″ × 8″
Oversize	3¼″ × 3¼″ × 10″ (often varies)
Modular	
For ¼ in. joints	2½″ × 3¾″ × 7¾″ or 11¾″ or 2⁵⁄₁₂″ × 3¾″ × 7¾″
For ½ in. joints	2¼″ × 3½″ × 7½″ or 11½″ or 2¹⁄₁₆″ × 3½″ × 7½″

8″, or 12″ increment, or module. Thus three bricks $2^5/_{12}″ \times 3^3/_4″ \times 7^3/_4″$ plus ¼-in. joints would form a $4″ \times 8″ \times 8″$ block.

FACE BRICK   Face brick is made under controlled conditions that produce close dimensional tolerances and high structural qualities. It is available in two grades, which conform to the same standards as SW and MW grades of common brick. The ASTM groups face brick into three basic appearance classifications, as shown in Table 4-7. Standard sizes of face brick are shown in Table 4-8.

TABLE 4-7 Face-brick grades

TYPE	USE
FBX	For general use in exposed exterior and interior masonry walls and partitions where a high degree of mechanical perfection, narrow color range, and minimum permissible variation in size is desired
FBS	For general use in exposed exterior and interior masonry walls and partitions where wide color ranges are desired and greater variation in size is permitted
FBA	Brick manufactured and selected to produce characteristic architectural effects resulting from nonconformity in size, color, and texture of the individual units

TABLE 4-8 Face-brick sizes

TYPE	SIZES
Standard	$2^1/_2″ \times 3^1/_2″ \times 11^1/_2″$
Norman	$2^3/_{16}″ \times 3^1/_2″ \times 11^1/_2″$ or $2^1/_4″ \times 3″ \times 11^{11}/_{16}″$
Roman	$1^1/_2″ \times 3^1/_2″ \times 11^1/_2″$

Fig. 4-11 Face-brick finishes.

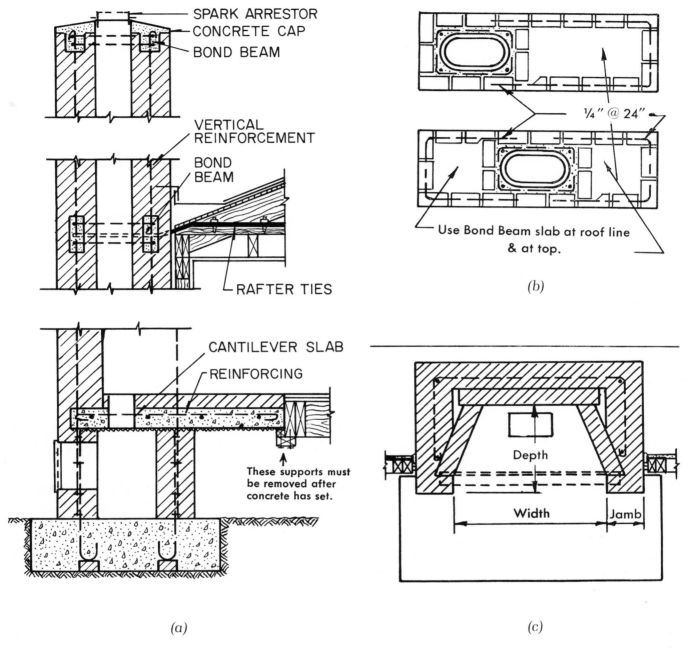

Fig. 4-12 Typical residential reinforced masonry fireplace: (a) unlined chimney section with details for fireplace and chimney; (b) details for wide chimneys (anchorage as required by local codes for standard-width chimneys); (c) fireplace and chimney details for plan at top of hearth.

GLAZED FACE BRICK Glazed brick is produced to the same close tolerances as other face brick, but it has been given a hard, impervious face with a dull, satin mottled, or glossy finish. The brick is sprayed with a ceramic glaze and is then fired to temperatures of nearly 2000°F to fuse the glaze to the brick. Many colors, textures, and finishes are produced in this manner. Glazed surfaces may be produced by applying metallic salts to the face of the brick before firing. This transparent *salt-glaze* allows the original brick color to show through the glaze.

FIRE BRICK Brick made of clays having a high percentage of alumina or silica, flint, and feldspar are used where masonry will be subject to extreme heat. Fire brick is used for the lining of fireplaces, incinerators, chimney stacks, and industrial fire boxes and smelting furnaces. Fire brick is softer than common brick and is light beige to brown in color. A fire brick is normally $2\frac{1}{2}'' \times 4\frac{1}{2}'' \times 9''$; fire-brick *splits* are $1\frac{1}{4}'' \times 4\frac{1}{2}'' \times 9''$.

CORED BRICK   Some building codes allow the use of unreinforced 6 in. walls. A type of brick with 10 vertical cores $1\frac{3}{8}$ in. in diameter was developed to satisfy the need for a masonry unit $5\frac{1}{5}'' \times 2\frac{1}{16}'' \times 11\frac{1}{2}''$, for use with a $\frac{1}{2}$ in. joint. The vertical cores through the unit reduce the weight. The SCR, produced by Structural Clay Research, is a brick of this type. A wall constructed of SCR brick looks like a wall laid up with Norman brick.

PAVING BRICK   Special hard-burned paving bricks, or *pavers*, are produced for installation where wear or abrasion is a factor. These pavers are burned at a high temperature to make them impervious to water and resistant to abrasion. They are usually obtainable in depths of $2\frac{1}{2}''$, $3''$, and $3\frac{1}{2}''$ with a $4'' \times 8\frac{1}{2}''$ face.

Special Brick

Brick is manufactured in special shapes for specific purposes. Caps, sill, lintels, and corners are manufactured and stocked by many producers. Bull-nose shaped bricks are manufactured for window and door trim. Interior and exterior rounded corners are sometimes available. The increased use of reinforced brickwork has led to the development of special shapes to allow either horizontal or vertical steel reinforcing to be placed in the brick wall. Many building codes in areas subject to wind or earthquake require reinforcement of masonry construction, and most companies now produce these special shapes in either standard or modular sizes.

Bricks made to order for special designs are also available from many brickmakers. These custom bricks may be made in special shapes, colors, and textures. One architect wanted a special long, thin unit to carry out the lines of his building. The owner of a chain of motels and restaurants wanted a unique brick to be used in all his buildings to establish a company image. The cost of custom brick may often be offset by the importance of such factors.

BRICKWORK

Appearance, strength, and weathering quality of brick masonry depend greatly on the quality of workmanship. Strength is generally the function of proper mortars, bond, and workmanship, rather than strength of the individual masonry units. Brickwork must be designed so that the

Fig. 4-13   Wall of custom masonry units. (*Masonry Research.*)

individual units are bonded into a structure that will act as a whole. Joints between individual units must be well formed and watertight. Each masonry unit must be set with full beds of mortar in both the horizontal and vertical joints.

Bonds

The bond is the arrangement of bricks in rows, or *courses*. Bonds are designed for appearance, to tie together a structural wall, or to tie an outer wall, or *wythe*, to an inner or back-up wall. A wythe, also called *withe* or *tier*, is a vertical section of wall one brick thick. The most universally used bonds are common bond, running bond, English bond, English cross bond, Flemish bond, and stacked bond.

Common bond consists of bricks placed end to end in a *stretcher course*, with the vertical joints of one course centered on the bricks in the next course. Every sixth or seventh course is made up of bricks turned 90° to extend into the wall. This is called a *header course*, and is used to tie the face wythe to the back wythe or backing. If header courses are not included in the wall, the bond is considered a *running bond*.

English bond consists of alternate courses of stretchers and headers. This provides one of the stongest types of bonds. The appearance is generally not as pleasing. However, English bond is sometimes used for special effects, with darker or lighter bricks for the header courses or shadow lines created by extending the header course out from the face of the wall. *English cross bond*, sometimes called *Dutch bond*, differs from the English bond in the position of the stretchers in alternate courses.

Flemish bond consists of alternate stretchers and headers in every course. Flemish bond is widely used because of its ease of laying and attractive appearance. A variation of this bond is the *double-stretcher Flemish bond*, in which two stretchers are placed tightly together as a *blind joint* and alternated with headers.

Brick may also be laid in herringbone, basketweave, or stacked-bond patterns. *Stacked bond* consists of stretchers layed directly above one another, with unbroken vertical mortar joints. Bricks set on end with the narrow side showing are called *soldiers*; bricks set on end with the wide side showing are called *sailors*. A course of brick set on edge with the end showing, or the end and one side, is called a *rowlock course*. If irregular, twisted, or warped brick are included in a wall, either in a pattern or with random placement, it is said to be *skintled brickwork*.

Used brick is sometimes salvaged from old buildings and used in new construction. It is more expensive than new brick in some locations but is widely sought after for its texture and interesting color variations.

Joints

The size, texture, and color of the joints affect not only the strength and water resistance of a brick wall, but its appearance as well. A wide mortar joint in a contrasting color

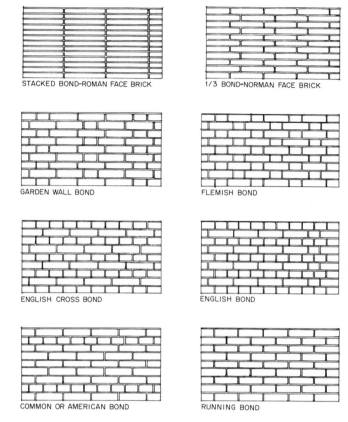

Fig. 4-14 Types of brick bonds.

may be used to create a pattern. A wide joint cut back from the surface can be used to create shadow lines. If the horizontal joints are *raked*, or cut back from the surface, and the vertical joints are *struck*, or left flush with the surface, a series of horizontal shadow lines are developed. Some types of joints provide a barrier to the passage of water, while others tend to be porous.

The size of joints depends on the desired effect and the type and size of the brick. The usual joint for common brick is ½ in. With a ½-in. joint, two headers plus one joint equal the length of one stretcher. Joints may range from ¼ in. to 1 in., but mortar joints over ½ in. are more difficult to lay and more expensive.

If a V-shaped or *beaded* joint is made with a trowel, the mortar is compressed, and the joint tends to be more watertight. Shoved, sacked, flush, struck, or rough-cut joints do not always provide a waterproof seal.

Mortar

Mortar consists of cementitious materials, sand, and water. Mortars vary greatly, depending on the properties of the materials and the ratios of these materials to sand and water. The dry materials are usually proportioned by volume, with the three most commonly used materials—portland cement, hydrated lime, and sand—given in that

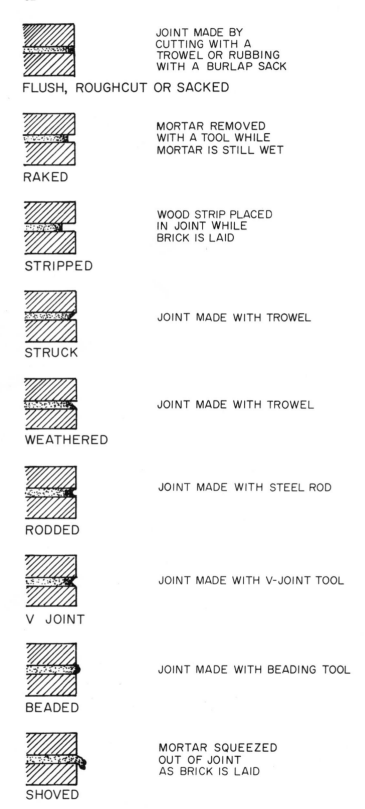

FLUSH, ROUGHCUT OR SACKED — JOINT MADE BY CUTTING WITH A TROWEL OR RUBBING WITH A BURLAP SACK

RAKED — MORTAR REMOVED WITH A TOOL WHILE MORTAR IS STILL WET

STRIPPED — WOOD STRIP PLACED IN JOINT WHILE BRICK IS LAID

STRUCK — JOINT MADE WITH TROWEL

WEATHERED — JOINT MADE WITH TROWEL

RODDED — JOINT MADE WITH STEEL ROD

V JOINT — JOINT MADE WITH V-JOINT TOOL

BEADED — JOINT MADE WITH BEADING TOOL

SHOVED — MORTAR SQUEEZED OUT OF JOINT AS BRICK IS LAID

Fig. 4-15 Joints in brickwork.

order. For example, a 1:$\frac{1}{4}$:3 mortar would contain 1 cu ft of portland cement, $\frac{1}{4}$ cu ft of lime, and 3 cu ft of sand.

The primary function of mortar is to develop a strong and durable bond with the brick masonry units. A good masonry mortar must remain workable long enough to permit the workmen to position the units. It must have relatively little shrinkage value, a high degree of resistance to moisture penetration, and the strength to resist the forces that may be applied to it. Masonry units vary in the rate at which they absorb water. If they absorb the water in the mortar too quickly, the mortar may stiffen prematurely and lose its adhesive qualities. Thus masonry units with high rates of absorption, or *suction*, may have to be wetted to provide a proper bond. The amount of wetting will depend on the rate of absorption of the brick at the time of laying. At temperatures below 40°F mortar will not set properly, causing poor bond and lowered strength of the brick wall. If the brick must be laid in cold weather, there must be suitable provisions to heat the masonry materials and protect the completed work for a minimum of 48 hr.

The type of mortar allowed by building codes varies widely throughout the country. Some of the most commonly used proportions are shown in Table 4-9.

TABLE 4-9 Masonry mortar types

TYPE	DESCRIPTION
Lime mortar	A 1:3 mixture of hydrated lime and sand; banned by most building codes and seldom used.
Lime-cement mortar	A 1:1:6 mixture of portland cement and hydrated lime or lime putty, used only above grade where small stresses exist.
Cement mortar	1:$\frac{1}{4}$:3 or 1:$\frac{1}{2}$:4$\frac{1}{2}$. Many codes describe and limit portland cement mortar as follows: "Damp, loose aggregate shall consist of not more than 3 times the sum volumes of the cement and lime used."
Masonry cement	Sometimes called *plastic cement* or *waterproof cement*; Types I and II portland cement with plasticizing agents added at the time of manufacture. Hydrated lime or lime putty may be added, but not in excess of one-tenth the volume of the cement.

Grout

Mortar of pouring consistency is classed as *grout*. Grout is placed or poured between the outer wythes, or faces, of a brick wall. It may enclose reinforcing located in the space between the outer wythes of the wall. The outer wythes are carried up three or four courses and the grout is poured. Masonry units may be placed, or *floated*, in the grout space as the grout is poured.

A method called *high-lift grouting* has recently been developed by Masonry Research of Los Angeles, and the Associated Brick Manufacturers of Southern California.

With high-lift grouting the two outside faces of a wall are built to full height without grouting, and the entire height of the wall is grouted at one time. This method has been tested with walls as high as 24 ft and with several types of brick and grouts of different moisture content and containing various admixtures.

Efflorescence

A soft white powder often appears on the face of brickwork, particularly after it has been exposed to water. This is caused by salts, such as sodium or magnesium, in the brick or mortar which have been brought to the surface by the action of the water. Efflorescence can be controlled to some extent by selecting materials with a minimum amount of water-soluble salts in their composition. Watertight joints and flashings that prevent the entry of water into the brickwork will help prevent the formation of efflorescence. Efflorescence can be removed from masonry surfaces with diluted muriatic acid, followed by a clearwater rinse.

Brick Walls

Masonry walls may be either bearing walls or non-bearing walls. A bearing wall is one that supports any vertical load other than itself. A *spandrel wall* is a non-bearing wall which is attached to structural floors on the outside of a building and usually spans from the head of a window to the windowsill of the floor above. A *curtain wall* is a non-bearing wall attached to structural members only as a curtain against the elements.

SOLID BRICK WALLS   Solid walls constructed of two or more wythes of solid masonry units may be bonded together in several ways. The thickness of solid brick walls may be from 8 to 24 in. The allowable ratio of height to thickness is governed by local building codes. The wythes may be held together by brick headers extending either entirely through the thickness of the wall or into the adjacent wythe. The wall may be bonded by means of noncorrosive metal ties inserted as the wall is built. These ties are placed in alternate courses with a spacing of 18 to 36 in., depending on building-code requirements.

CAVITY WALLS   In order to reduce cost and weight, and to produce hollow areas in walls for improved insulating value, *cavity walls* are used. Cavity walls are not allowed in areas subject to high earthquake probability. In cavity-wall construction the two outer wythes are spaced 2 in. apart and held together by 3/16-in. stiff metal ties embedded in horizontal mortar joints. The outer wythe is usually one brick thick; the inner wall may be 4, 8, or 12 in. The ties are usually bent at right angles or have long pins that fit into the vertical joints. These ties are placed 18 to 36 in. on center both horizontally and vertically. One advantage of the cavity wall is its resistance to exterior moisture as a

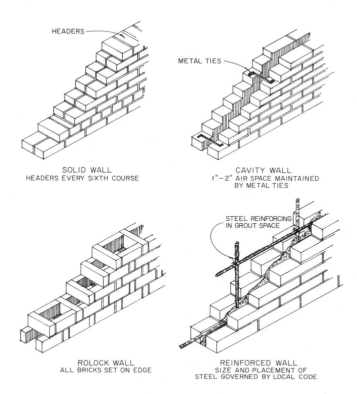

Fig. 4-16   Types of masonry wall construction.

result of the complete separation of inner and outer wythes. Care must be taken to remove any mortar bridges, which would allow the passage of moisture from the outside surface to the inner wall. The cavity may be filled with an insulating material. *Weep holes* are provided in the outer wythe to allow moisture to escape.

A hollow rowlock type of brick wall is constructed of brick wythes in which all or some of the bricks are set on edge. The 8- or 12½-in. walls are held together by headers set on edge spanning the hollow portion of the wall.

FACED WALLS   A faced wall consists of a facing of brick masonry units bonded to a backup wall of some other material. The two materials are so bonded that structurally they perform as a unit. A faced wall may consist of face brick with a backing of common brick. If the face brick is the same size as the backing brick, the wall can be bonded together with header courses so that the face brick acts as a unit with the backing.

The backing may be hollow structural clay-tile units or hollow concrete-block units. The size and thickness of the tile or block are varied to allow header courses of face brick to extend into the backing, and so bond the wall to act as a unit. Face brick may be bonded into a poured-concrete wall.

VENEERED WALLS   A wall in which the facing material, tied securely to a structural wall but is not structurally bonded to it, is a *veneered wall*. The facing material, whether it be

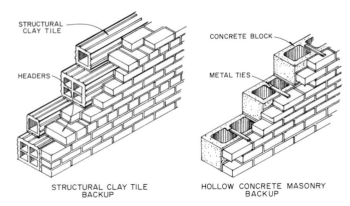

STRUCTURAL CLAY TILE

CONCRETE BLOCK

HEADERS

METAL TIES

STRUCTURAL CLAY TILE BACKUP

HOLLOW CONCRETE MASONRY BACKUP

Fig. 4-17 Faced walls.

stone, brick or other material, is held in place by cast-in or built-in anchors or tie wires.

In some parts of the country brick or stone veneer is commonly used over wood-frame construction. The wood studs are covered with solid sheathing and waterproof building paper, and the brick or stone veneer is spaced to leave a 1-in. space between the building paper and the veneer. Some codes require this to be air space and others require the space to be filled with grout. Noncorrosive ties are attached to the supporting wall and embedded in mortar joints. These ties may be of 6-gauge wire and usually are spaced so that each tie supports not more than 2 sq ft of veneer. The weight of masonry veneer attached to wood-frame walls must be supported entirely on footings. Veneer over openings such as doors and windows is supported on steel angles attached to the wood frame. In lieu of tie wires to hold the veneer in place, paper-backed reinforcement, of reinforcing wires attached to a waterproof paper, may be attached directly to the wood studs, with 1-in. grout space left between the paper-backed reinforcement and the veneer. As the veneer is laid up, the space is filled with mortar, and the veneer is bonded to the structure.

Reinforced Brick Masonry

The use of reinforcing steel with brick masonry has greatly increased in recent years. Certain sections of the country subject to earthquakes, extreme wind conditions, or tornados require that most brick masonry construction be steel reinforced. The steel reinforcing is placed either in the mortar joints between the courses or in grout spaces between the outer faces of the wall. The bricks are bound together by the reinforcing to increase the bending strength and the shear strength of the wall.

Prefabricated masonry joint reinforcement has several advantages over headers. Headers extending through a wall tend to produce points of weakness and create a shelf for the entry of water. One of the most commonly used joint reinforcements is a patented product that consists of two parallel deformed steel bars held apart by truss-shaped continuous steel rods. This joint reinforcing is manufactured in several widths to fit into walls of different thicknesses, with the parallel deformed bars usually

spaced 1 in. back from the face of the wall. The joint reinforcement is placed in the horizontal joints as the brick wall is laid up. The spacing of the reinforcing will depend on the load to be resisted and on local building-code requirements.

In reinforced grouted brick masonry vertical and horizontal steel bars are inserted in a grout space between the outer faces of brick walls, beams, or columns. The steel is completely surrounded by the portland cement grout and acts in the same manner as the reinforcing in concrete. Common or face brick may be used for reinforced masonry. Bond beams, beams over openings, piers, or pilasters are reinforced with bricks called *soaps*, which are half the width of normal brick.

Special brick sizes and shapes have been developed for use in reinforced brickwork. In some areas $3\frac{1}{4}'' \times 3\frac{1}{4}'' \times 10''$ bricks are produced, with the inner corners rounded or clipped to receive the reinforcing steel. A grouted wall of this brick could be $7\frac{3}{4}$ to $16\frac{3}{4}$ in. thick, depending on the design requirements. Special L-shaped bricks are manufactured for use where beams or piers occur.

STRUCTURAL CLAY TILE

Structural clay tiles are burned-clay building units, larger than bricks, with cored openings or parallel open cells. Structural tile has many uses in the construction industry. The hollow-celled units may be produced in load-bearing or non-load-bearing forms. They are used for load-bearing walls and partitions as structural units, as filler, or as back-up in faced walls. Structural clay tile may be used to fire-proof structural steel or as furring inside curtain walls.

Fig. 4-18 Brick veneer over wood studs.

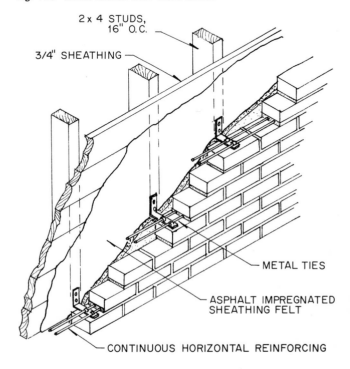

2 x 4 STUDS, 16" O.C.

3/4" SHEATHING

METAL TIES

ASPHALT IMPREGNATED SHEATHING FELT

CONTINUOUS HORIZONTAL REINFORCING

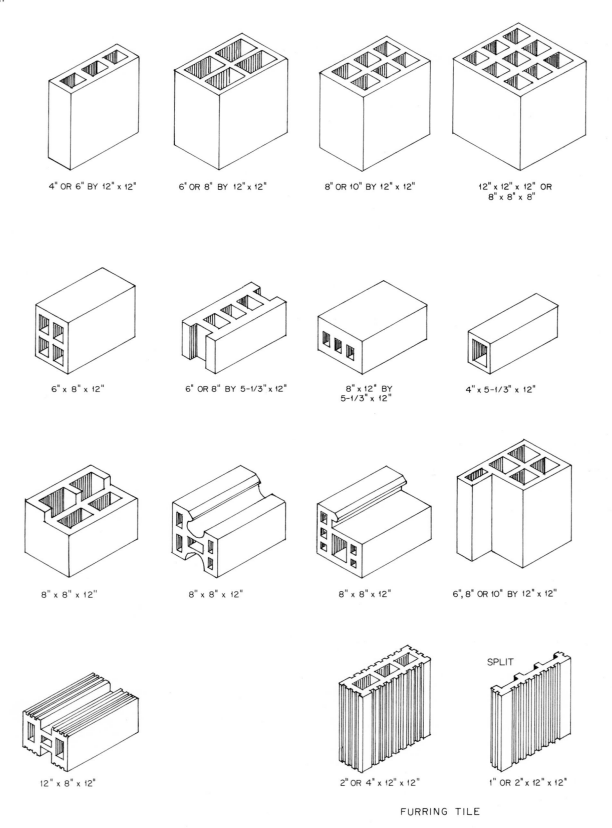

4" OR 6" BY 12" x 12"

6" OR 8" BY 12" x 12"

8" OR 10" BY 12" x 12"

12" x 12" x 12" OR 8" x 8" x 8"

6" x 8" x 12"

6" OR 8" BY 5-1/3" x 12"

8" x 12" BY 5-1/3" x 12"

4" x 5-1/3" x 12"

8" x 8" x 12"

8" x 8" x 12"

8" x 8" x 12"

6", 8" OR 10" BY 12" x 12"

12" x 8" x 12"

2" OR 4" x 12" x 12"

SPLIT

1" OR 2" x 12" x 12"

FURRING TILE

Fig. 4-19 Structural clay tile sizes and shapes. Tile may be set with cells vertical or horizontal.

Types of Structural Clay Tile

Structural clay tiles are classified as non-load-bearing, terra cotta, load-bearing, facing, and ceramic facing tiles.

STRUCTURAL CLAY NON-LOAD-BEARING TILE The materials used in the manufacture of all structural clay tile are similar to those used for brick. Non-load-bearing tile that is to be covered with another material is usually limited in its physical characteristics only by the rate at which it absorbs water. Non-load-bearing tile for fireproofing must meet additional requirements. The surface of non-load-bearing tile may have a *smooth finish*, a plain surface formed by a die during manufacture; a *scored* or a *combed finish*, a surface given a series of parallel cuts to provide a better bond to plaster or mortar; a *plaster-base finish*, intended for the direct application of plaster; or a *roughened finish*, with the face of the tile broken by wire cutting or brushing, for use when it is not to be covered with another material.

Non-load-bearing tile for partitions is usually produced in thicknesses of 2″ to 12″ with a 12″ × 12″ face. Tiles to be used as fireproofing around steel structural members can be obtained in various sizes. *Furring tile*, or *split tile*, is a non-load-bearing tile that has been split parallel to the openings in the tile to thicknesses of 1½″ and 2″ for use as insulation, furring, and as a water barrier on the interior of walls.

STRUCTURAL CLAY LOAD-BEARING TILE Structural clay load-bearing wall tile may be used as an unfaced bearing wall, a plastered bearing wall, or as the structural element of a faced wall. The two grades produced are designated by the ASTM as shown in Table 4-10. The tile surface finish may be smooth, plaster-base, combed, or roughened. Structural clay load-bearing wall tile is produced in thicknesses of 4″ to 12″, heights of 2⅔″ to 10⅔″, and lengths of 8″ or 12″.

TABLE 4-10 Structural clay load-bearing tile grades

GRADE	USE
LBX	Suitable for general use in masonry construction and adapted for use in masonry exposed to weathering, provided they are burned to the normal maturity of the clay. They may also be considered suitable for the direct application of stucco.
LB	Suitable for general use in masonry where not exposed to frost action, or for use in exposed masonry where protected with a facing of 3 in. or more of stone, brick, terra cotta, or masonry.

A special type of *structural clay floor tile* is produced for use in flat-arch or segmented-arch floor construction. These tiles may also be used in conjunction with concrete as fillers in ribbed floor construction. Finishes are the same as for wall tile.

STRUCTURAL CLAY FACING TILE Structural clay facing tile is designed for use as interior and exterior unplastered walls and partitions of buildings. It is classified as either standard or special duty, on the basis of thickness of the face shells and strength (see Table 4-11). Facing tile is produced with either one or two finish faces.

TABLE 4-11 Structural clay facing tile

GRADE	USE
FTX	Smooth-faced tile suitable for general use in exposed exterior and interior masonry walls and partitions. For use where a tile low in absorption, easily cleaned, and resistant to staining is required and where a high degree of mechanical perfection, narrow color range, and minimum variation in face dimensions are desired.
FTS	Smooth or rough-textured tile suitable for general use in exposed exterior and interior masonry walls and partitions. For use where tile of moderate absorption, moderate variation in face dimensions, and medium color range is desired and where minor defects in surface finish, including small handling chips, are not objectionable.

Structural clay facing tile can be obtained in many different sizes and shapes. Special tile is available for internal and external corners, sills, caps, wall ends, and coves and in other special shapes necessary for wall construction. The faces have natural finishes of the fired clay. Structural clay facing tile may have a smooth or a scored surface with a salt-glazed finish.

CERAMIC GLAZED STRUCTURAL CLAY FACING TILE Structural clay load-bearing facing tile is produced in the same sizes and shapes as unglazed tile. Glazed tile has either a transparent or an opaque vitreous surface that is glass-smooth and impervious to moisture. The transparent glazes will tone the natural clay body in several subdued, satin, or glossy finishes. Color glazes, fused to the body of the tile, come in a wide range of colors, in plain or mottled finishes.

TERRA COTTA *Terra cotta*, which means "baked earth" in Italian, is a non-load-bearing burned-clay unit similar in composition to brick. It has been used for centuries as a substitute for stone, as an ornamental element in buildings, for sculpture, and for pottery. Terra cotta may be formed by pressing tempered clay into molds by hand or by an extrusion process similar to that used in the stiff-mud process of brickmaking. Approximately 90 percent of the terra cotta made today is produced by machine extrusion. Terra cotta may be obtained for use as a veneer in solid-back, closed-back, or open-back form. Original sculptures can be reproduced in hand-made terra cotta for architectural effects. Terra cotta may be left in its natural red color or given a colored glazed finish.

Setting and Mortar

Structural clay tile may be designed to be set with the hollow cells either horizontal or vertical. If it is designed to be set with the hollow cells horizontal and to receive its principal stress at right angles to the axis of the cells, it is termed *side-construction tile*. If it is designed to receive its principal stress parallel to the axis of the cells, it is termed *end-construction tile*.

Mortar for structural clay tile is similar to that used in brickwork. Joints between units vary from ¼ in. for glazed face tile to ½ in. for structural wall and back-up tile. Special bonding shapes are produced for use in walls more than one unit thick. Metal ties or anchors may be used to bond the wall together. Prefabricated horizontal steel reinforcing may be placed in the joints, or steel bars may be placed in filled cells to produce reinforced walls where necessary.

Joints

The joints in a wall of structural clay facing tile are usually raked out to a depth of at least ³/₁₆ in. before the mortar has set. On completion of the wall the joints are filled with a mixture of white sand and white cement or with a commercial pointing compound. The process is called *grouting* or *pointing*. Excess pointing compound may be removed from the face of the tile with a clean, flat sponge to make a smooth flush joint. The mortar joints are tooled while the pointing compound is still workable. The ¼-in. joint is tooled with a round bar of at least 1 in. diameter to form a slightly concave joint which is dense and easy to keep clean.

CONCRETE BLOCK

Hollow masonry units of portland cement and sand, gravel, or other suitable aggregate are termed *concrete block*. Concrete block is used for interior and exterior bearing and nonbearing walls, partitions, and backing.

Precast concrete parts to be set by masons are sometimes called *artificial stone* or *cast stone*. As discussed above (see Precast Concrete), precast panels with exposed aggregate may be used as curtain walls or facings for buildings.

The weight, color, and texture of concrete block depends largely on the type of aggregate used in its manufacture. Block made with sand and gravel or crushed rock weighs from 40 to 45 lb per 8″ × 8″ × 16″ unit. These blocks are strong and durable, with a low absorption rate. Blocks made with lightweight aggregate may weigh 25 to 35 lb. Lightweight blocks are produced as non-load-bearing units, for use as back-up walls, or as load-bearing units, for use as the finished surface of both interior and exterior walls.

Standard concrete blocks have the typical light-grey color of concrete. Colored blocks may be made with naturally colored aggregates or by including inert mineral

Fig. 4-20 Patterned-concrete-block wall. (*Masonry Research; photo by Larry Harmon.*)

pigments in the concrete mix. Lightweight concrete blocks are available with colored surfaces produced by applying compounds of silica sand and color pigments. This type of block is used on interiors where a smooth, durable, washable, colorful surface is desired.

Lightweight concrete block is used where a lightweight material with good strength and high insulating or acoustical qualities is desired. Its use also simplifies the attachment of finish materials or accessories to a structural wall, in that common nails can be driven into the block.

Types and Sizes

Concrete block is manufactured in many sizes and shapes. The most commonly used block is designated as 8″ × 8″ × 16″. It is designed to be laid up in a single thickness to produce a wall which is actually 7⅝ in. thick with courses 8 in. high. For this reason the actual unit dimensions are

Fig. 4-21 Concrete-block-making machine. (*Columbia Machine Company.*)

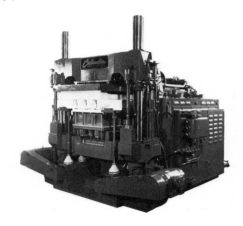

Fig. 4-22 Detailed concrete block.

usually $3/8$ in. smaller than the nominal sizes to allow for the thickness of mortar joints. For example, a standard 16″ unit is actually only $15^5/8$ in. long; with a $3/8$-in. mortar joint it will occupy 16 in. in the wall. Similarly, the $7^5/8$-in. height plus a $3/8$-in. mortar joint is exactly 8 in. This allowance for mortar joints makes all wall measurements work out to even modular dimensions. Blocks are produced for the construction of walls and partitions in nominal thicknesses of 4″, 6″, 8″, 10″, and 12″. Half-blocks are produced for use at the ends of walls laid in running bond. Blocks 4″ high are available in some areas.

The face shells and webs of concrete blocks vary in thickness from $1^1/4$ to 2 in., depending on the size of the block and the use for which it was designed. Some blocks are manufactured with closed cells at the ends, while others are open at one or both ends.

Many special shapes are produced for specific purposes. Bullnose blocks, used for rounded exterior corners, are available in most sizes. Specially shaped sill blocks are manufactured for windows. Blocks with vertical slots cast into one end are used in conjunction with the installation of metal windows or for the installation of wood bucks to which door casings can be nailed. Header and bond beam blocks are open-end blocks which have been hollowed out to allow the pouring of reinforced concrete beams over openings. Special shapes are produced for use where reinforced pilasters are to be included in a structural wall.

DETAILED BLOCK   Forms may be used in block-making machines to produce a block with a patterned face. Some block has vertical and horizontal grooves to simulate mortar joints. Blocks with triangular, or rectangular indented areas may be laid in different directions to create interesting shadow patterns. Surface textures resembling that

of rough adobe brick are produced in some areas. These textured blocks are called *slumped block*, termed Slumpstone by one manufacturer.

SCREEN UNITS   The use of concrete masonry units to form open grilles is an innovation that has had a great impact on building design, particularly in California. Screen-wall masonry units can be molded with an almost infinite variety of pierced openings. The manufacturing of screen units is similar to that of standard concrete blocks. Sizes and shapes of units vary with the patterns. The most common sizes are designed to make a screen wall that is 4 to 6 in. thick when the units are set on edge. Screen units are set with mortar in the same manner as standard blocks. The horizontal and vertical joints may be reinforced to provide resistance to wind and earthquake forces. Standard concrete block may be used to develop a screen by exposing the cored openings. Screen-wall masonry units may be used as a veneer attached to a structural wall to create deep shadow lines and texture. If the units are used as a veneer, they are supported on an extension of the wall footing and tied to the structural wall with steel angles or tie wires.

Reinforced Concrete Masonry

Concrete masonry structures in areas subject to earthquakes or severe windstorms must be reinforced in accordance with local building-code requirements. This is usually done by building reinforced-concrete beams and studs as an integral part of the concrete masonry wall. Vertical alignment of the hollow cores in the units permits reinforced concrete studs or columns to be built at regular intervals in the wall, as well as at the corners, and the use of special block facilitates the construction of beams.

Single-thickness structural concrete-block walls are usually erected on cast-in-place footings and foundation walls. Steel dowels are cast into the foundation walls at intervals corresponding to the open cells of the concrete blocks. The spacing of these dowels and the length they must extend above the foundation is governed by local building codes. The reinforcing is located to coincide with the dowels extending up from the foundation. Horizontal steel reinforcing bars are placed at mid-height, around openings, and as lintels or bond beams above openings. The masonry wall is usually built up to the first horizontal beam, and the vertical reinforcing steel is placed in the cells. At this point grout is poured in those cells that contain reinforcement to form a reinforced structural stud. To assure that the reinforcing is in place, and to clean out any mortar droppings, small openings or *cleanouts* are left at the bottom of all cells that are to be grouted.

As the structural wall is built up, bolts, anchors, electrical conduit, pipes for plumbing, heating ducts, and other devices to be embedded in the wall must be placed in position. All bolts placed in a concrete-block wall must be adequately anchored by hooking around reinforcing steel or by some other means to prevent the bolt from pulling out or failing under load. When a wood roof structure is to be connected, redwood plates are attached to the wall by means of bolts embedded in the bond beam at the top of the wall.

Bonded Walls

When hollow concrete masonry units are to be part of a faced masonry wall, provision must be made for bonding the facing material to the concrete-block backing. This may be accomplished by varying the thickness of the block backing to receive header courses of the brick or stone facing. Metal ties spanning a grout space may be used to tie the outer face of the wall to the back-up wall.

If structural concrete block is to form the exterior or interior finish, many patterns may be used to create texture. The simplest and most commonly used bond is the *running bond*, in which the blocks are laid in straight uniform courses, with the units in the courses above regularly breaking the joints with the courses below. This can be varied by raking the horizontal joints back from the face of the unit and cutting the vertical joints flush. Blocks may also be laid directly above each other in a stacked bond, with the vertical joints raked and the horizontal joints cut off flush. A block wall may be laid with some blocks extending out from or recessed into the surface of the wall. Blocks of various sizes may be combined in an ashlar pattern. Open-end units may be turned 90° in a wall to create pattern or texture. Detailed block may be combined in many ways to create distinctive designs.

Mortar and Joints

The physical characteristics of the mortar and the design of the joints is extremely critical in hollow concrete masonry construction, particularly in walls one unit thick which serve as both the exterior and interior finish surface. The strength of the wall depends substantially on the adhesive qualities of the mortar. A mortar with good adhesive bond to the masonry unit, even at the cost of compressive strength, has been shown to resist the forces of earthquakes. Most failures of masonry have been adhesion bond failures. The proportions of portland cement, sand, and an appropriate plasticizer are governed by local building codes.

Tight joints are essential to good masonry. Both the vertical and horizontal joints must be filled to the depth of the face shells. Three types of joints are recommended: *V-shaped, weathered,* and *concave.* Each of these joints provides a surface for the shedding of water. Also, their formation requires an amount of pressure sufficient to compress the mortar and create a firm bond between the mortar and the unit. Joints for concrete masonry units should be a uniform 3/8 in. to provide proper bedding for the units.

GYPSUM BLOCK

Gypsum masonry units, termed *gypsum partition tile* or *plaster block,* are solid or hollow units composed of gypsum and a binder or vegetable fiber, asbestos, or wood chips. Gypsum block is never used where it would be subjected to moisture. The most common use is for non-load-bearing, fire-resistant interior partitions and as a fireproofing material around structural steel beams and columns. The face of most gypsum block is scored to receive a plaster finish coat.

Gypsum blocks are produced with a face dimension of 12″ × 30″ and in thicknesses of 2″, 3″, 4″, and 6″. Solid 2″ gypsum blocks are used primarily as fireproofing around steel beams and columns. These blocks are sometimes used for partitions; however, the 3″, 4″, and 5″ hollow-core units are usually preferred because of their better acoustical and fire-retardant qualities.

Gyspum-block partitions are relatively inexpensive to install because of their light weight. Grounds and door casings can be nailed easily. Blocks over openings are supported on steel angles or by steel reinforcing inserted in the horizontal cells of gypsum mortar-filled blocks. Gypsum blocks are easily sawed by hand to fit into difficult corners or grooved to receive electrical conduit.

GLASS BLOCK

Glass block is formed by fusing together two glass shells that have been pressed to shape in forms creating a partial vacuum. This partial vacuum provides good insulating qualities and helps to reduce the problem of condensation on walls. The additional advantages of low maintenance and controlled daylight suggest that many problems can be solved by the use of glass block. Glass block may be used as windows, interior partitions, screens, or for entire curtain walls of buildings.

Types and Sizes

Glass block may be translucent or completely transparent. A fibrous glass screen may be fused in the center of the block to filter the light. In addition to softening the light, this screen divides the block into two dead air spaces for better insulation. The outer shells of the blocks may be cast with built-in prisms and corrugations to alter the path of light. A *light-directing block* bends the incoming light rays upward onto the ceiling plane. A *light-diffusing block* diffuses the transmitted light in all directions. Decorative block may give good visibility through a panel, partial privacy, or complete privacy, depending on the fluted or cast designs of the face shells. Colored glass blocks are made with a fired-on ceramic enamel coating on one face of a standard unit. Many colors are available, and special colors can be produced on order.

Glass blocks are produced in a nominal thickness of 4″. The actual thickness varies from 3½ to 3⅞ in., depending on the manufacturer. Glass-block faces are usually 6″, 8″ or

(a)

Fig. 4-23 Single-wall concrete-block masonry construction.

(b)

(c)

(d)

Fig. 4-24 Steel dowels and electrical conduit in place in concrete-block residence.

12″ square. Some blocks are available in sizes of 4″ × 12″ and 5″ × 8″. These face sizes are nominal dimensions; the actual sizes are ¼ in. smaller to allow for a ¼-in. mortar joint. Some building codes limit the size of unsupported glass-block panels for exterior walls to 144 sq ft, and not more than 15 ft in any dimension. For interior walls, glass-block panels usually do not exceed 250 sq ft of unsupported area nor more than 25 ft in any dimension.

Setting

Glass block is usually laid up in cement-lime mortar, of a consistency somewhat stiffer than that used for ordinary brickwork. The horizontal joints of the glass-block panel are reinforced with galvanized-steel double-wire mesh formed of two parallel 9-gauge wires 2 in. on center, with electrically welded cross wires at regular intervals. This reinforcing is embedded in the horizontal joints approximately 24 in. on center, and in joints immediately above and below all openings within panels.

The nonabsorptive surface of glass makes the mortar joints difficult to seal. Coatings of plastic, in which sand or other grit has been embedded, are applied to the edges of the glass block to increase the mechanical bond to mortar. Blocks must be laid with full mortar joints to prevent the penetration of water and to assure a good bond. Unless excellent workmanship is used on exterior glass-block walls, the joints will open and the wall exposed to weather will leak badly.

A glass-block panel or wall will expand from 1½ to 2 times as much as a masonry wall. This expansion must be anticipated and allowed for. Every glass-block panel should be provided with ½-in. expansion joints at the sides and top. These expansion joints should be entirely free of mortar and should be filled with a resilient material.

Fig. 4-25 Textured concrete-block wall. (*Masonry Research.*)

Fig. 4-26 Concrete-unit masonry screen. (*Masonry Research; photo by Martel-Howlatt Studios.*)

Fig. 4-27 Glass-block exterior wall. Granville County Library, Oxford, North Carolina, architects George Watts and Son. (*Pittsburgh-Corning Corporation.*)

QUESTIONS

1. Describe three geological classifications of rock commonly used in masonry construction.

2. Describe the quarrying and milling of limestone.

3. What is marble?

4. Describe the four basic types of brick.

5. What are the differences between common brick and face brick?

6. What are the three processes used in molding brick?

7. Describe three surfaces used for face brick.

8. What is the function of a header course in brickwork and stonework?

9. What is a wythe?

10. What is a soldier in masonry construction?

11. What are the characteristics of a good masonry mortar?

12. Define efflorescence.

13. What is the function of grout in an unreinforced masonry wall?

14. What are the advantages of cavity masonry walls?

15. What are the advantages of reinforced brick masonry construction?

16. Describe the differences between structural clay load-bearing and non-load-bearing tile.

17. Describe the surfaces available on structural clay facing tile.

18. What are the basic ingredients of a mortar designated as 1:¼:3?

19. Name and sketch three masonry joints that help increase the watertightness of a masonry wall.

20. What governs the weight, color, and texture of concrete block?

21. What is detailed concrete block?

22. Where are screen blocks used?

23. What is the composition of gypsum block, and where is it commonly used?

24. What are the advantages and disadvantages of glass block?

REFERENCES FOR FURTHER STUDY

AA Wire Products Company: 6100 South New England Avenue, Chicago, Ill., 60638. "Reinforcing Guide," 1968.

American Society for Testing and Materials: 1916 Race Street, Philadelphia, Pa., 19103. "Definitions of Terms Relating to Natural Building Stones," ASTM C119-50.

"Abrasion Resistance of Stone Subject to Foot Traffic," ASTM C241-51. "Specifications for Concrete Building Brick," ASTM C55-55. "Specifications for Structural Clay Load-bearing Wall Tile," ASTM C34-57. "Specifications for Hollow Load-bearing Concrete Masonry Units," ASTM C90-59. "Specifications for Sand-lime Building Brick," ASTM C73-51.

Associated Brick Manufacturers of Southern California: 553 South Western Avenue, Los Angeles, Calif., 90005. "Southern California Standard Specifications for Reinforced Grouted Brick Masonry, and Brick Veneer," 1960.

Building Stone Institute: 420 Lexington Avenue, New York, N.Y., 10017. "Stone Catalog," 1964, 1965.

Criswell, "Masonry," Drake, Skokie, Ill., 1958.

Dalzell, J. Ralph, "Simplified Masonry Planning and Building," McGraw-Hill, New York, 1955.

Dalzell, J. Ralph, and G. Townsend, American Technical Society, 848 East 58th Street, Chicago, Ill. "Masonry Simplified," 2 vols., 1957. "Bricklaying Skill and Practice," 1954. "Concrete Block Construction for the Home and Farm," 1957.

Dur-O-Wal National, Inc.: Box 150, Cedar Rapids, Iowa. "Comprehensive Data File on Masonry Wall Reinforcement," 1964.

Facing Tile Institute: 333 North Michigan Avenue, Chicago, Ill., 60601. "Structural Clay Facing Tile Handbook," 1959.

Gilluly, James, "Origin of Granite," Geological Society, Baltimore, Md., 1948.

Indiana Limestone Institute, Inc.: 702 H Street, N.W., Washington, D.C., 20001. "American Standard Specifications for Indiana Limestone," 1948.

Kraftile Company: Fremont, Calif. "Graphic Standards for Glazed Tile," 1964.

Marble Institute of America, Inc., Pennsylvania Building, Washington, D.C., 20004. "American Standard Specifications for the Support, Anchorage, and Protection of Exterior and Interior Marble Veneer," 1958. "Home Decorating with Marble," 1962.

Masonry Industry: 3055 Overland Avenue, Los Angeles, Calif., 90034. *Masonry Industry*, A monthly periodical.

Masonry Research: 2550 Beverly Boulevard, Los Angeles, Calif., 90057. "Specifying Natural Stone Veneer," 1965.

Pacific Clay Products: 1255 West Fourth Street, Los Angeles, Calif., 90017. "Face Brick Design Studies," 1966.

Portland Cement Association: 33 West Grand Avenue, Chicago, Ill., 60610. "Building Right with Concrete Masonry," 1953.

Stowell, "Limestone as a Raw Material for Industry," Oxford University Press, New York, 1963.

Structural Clay Products Institute: 1520 18th Street, N.W., Washington, D.C., 20036. "ASTM Specifications Structural Clay Masonry Units and Mortar," 1958.

CHARACTERISTICS OF WOOD

One of the first materials used by man in the construction of shelter was wood. At one time, when great stands of large trees covered most of the United States and Canada, it was possible for a builder to go into the forest and select a tall, straight tree for beams or structural members of almost any size. This now is seldom possible. The modern builder must adapt the wood that is still available to his requirements. Wood can be glued, laminated, and bonded to metal or plastics. Wood fibers can be mechanically or chemically separated and recombined to form new products.

The resistance of wood to the elements, to fire, and to insects can be improved by coatings. Chemicals may be forced entirely through individual members to increase their resistance to the destructive forces of nature. Wood products can be tailor-made to meet most structural or decorative needs.

The selection of the proper wood or wood product to do a particular job is very important. Over 600 varieties of trees grow in the United States, and hundreds of others are found throughout the world. Only a few of the thousands of species, however, are suitable for construction purposes, and fewer yet are available in sufficient quantities to be of commercial importance.

Hardwoods and Softwoods

Woods used in construction are generally classified broadly as *hardwoods* and *softwoods*. The terms are misleading in that there is no direct relationship between these designations and the hardness or softness of wood. South American Balsa, one of the softest woods known, is classed as a hardwood. The designations actually refer to certain growth and foliage characteristics. Softwoods come from trees classed as *evergreens* or *conifers*. These trees have needlelike leaves which are generally not shed at the end of each growing season. Hardwoods are obtained from trees classed as *deciduous*. Deciduous trees have broad leaves which are generally shed at the end of each growing season.

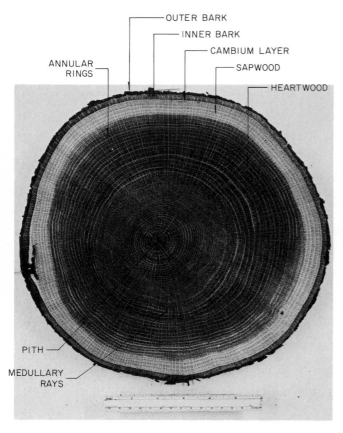

OUTER BARK
INNER BARK
CAMBIUM LAYER
SAPWOOD
HEARTWOOD
ANNULAR RINGS
PITH
MEDULLARY RAYS

Fig. 5-1 Section through a log. (*U.S. Forest Products Laboratory.*)

Growth of Wood

Both hardwoods and softwoods are *exogenous*; they are formed by the addition of a layer of new wood each year around a small central core called the *pith*. The *cambium* is a reproductive layer of cells under the bark which provides the new layers of wood. The *sapwood*, under the cambium, carries the sap, which has absorbed carbon from the air during the summer period of growth. The fast growth of the wood during the spring produces *springwood*, which is light-colored and rather porous. The slow growth during the summer produces *summerwood*, which is usually darker and denser. These alternate periods of growth produce concentric rings called *annular rings*. Since one pair of rings is produced during each year of the tree's growth, the age of a tree can be determined by counting the annular rings. Scientists have counted thousands of these rings on the giant redwoods of California, tracing their history back through the centuries.

The annular rings show not only the age of a tree, but the weather conditions that existed during each year's growth. In years of heavy rainfall, or years in which conditions are favorable to rapid growth, the rings will be spaced farther apart, while periods of drought will produce narrow

rings of springwood. Closely spaced bands of the denser summerwood will usually result in stronger lumber. The width and spacing of the annual growth rings determine, to a large extent, the characteristics of the lumber that will be cut from a particular species of tree. Some trees such as douglas fir and southern pine, show a marked difference between summerwood and springwood and are said to have a prominent grain. Others, such as ponderosa pine and eastern white pine, produce annular rings that are relatively inconspicuous.

Certain wood fibers in the growing tree arrange themselves in such a manner as to form lines of dense fibers that radiate out from the center of the tree and extend through the growth rings. These rays are called *medullary rays*. In some woods the medullary rays are quite prominent. Oak, cut to expose these rays (quarter-sawed oak), owes its beauty to the medullary rays.

As the tree continues to add annual growth rings, its inner portion becomes progressively less active. The portion of the tree which no longer carries sap is called the *heartwood*. Heartwood is usually darker than the outer portion, the sapwood. Heartwood is more resistant to the attack of insects, and as a rule it is more resistant to decay. The strength properties of heartwood and sapwood vary from species to species. The actual demarcation line of the heartwood and the sapwood is more clearly defined in some types of wood than in others.

DEFECTS IN WOOD

The growth of limbs or branches of a tree disturbs the symmetry of the annular rings. As the limb curves out from the tree and is surrounded by new growth, the grain of the wood is bent. The strength of finished lumber cut from the trees will be affected by the direction of the grain. When the grain of the wood turns more or less at right angles to the cut surface, it is called *cross grain*. A knot sawed lengthwise is called a *spike knot*.

As long as a limb is growing, its layers of wood form a continuation of the layers of wood in the main trunk of the tree. This intergrown limb in lumber is classed as an *intergrown knot*. As limbs die, and the trunk of the tree continues to grow and deposit layers of wood around a dead limb, an *encased knot* is formed. Considerable distortion of the grain will be present around an intergrown knot. This area of the wood will usually be denser than the surrounding fibers. Encased knots cause relatively less distortion of the surrounding grain. Knots may actually improve the strength, hardness, or appearance of a piece of wood. Knots which are so fixed in the wood structure that they will remain firmly in position are classed as *tight knots*. If the knot is free from decay, it is considered a *sound knot*.

While sound, tight knots may not materially reduce the usefulness of lumber, the nonuniform hardness produced by knots makes the lumber more difficult to machine and tends to increase warpage in boards. Knots may be accompanied by deposits of *pitch*, or hardened sap, which can cause problems when the wood is finished. Pitch pockets, filled with pitch or particles of bark, are sometimes found in the trunk of a tree, between the annular rings. Wood fiber may also have areas of *decay*, caused by certain insects or fungi. The decay may be barely perceptible spots or large soft areas. Decay in lumber is usually called *rot* or *dote*. *Stain* is a discoloration that penetrates the wood fiber, and may be of any color other than the natural color of the piece in which it is found. When a piece of lumber has been cut to include a portion of the bark along one or two edges, or a portion of one edge is missing, it is said to contain *wane*.

Holes in wood made by insects, fungi, or worms may reduce the strength of lumber. Certain douglas fir trees growing in the Pacific Northwest are infested with a fungus (Fomes pini) that leaves pockets filled with strands of white cellulose. As in most infestations of this type, there is no further growth of the fungi after the lumber has been cut. This defect, called *white pocket*, reduces the strength of lumber by a very small amount.

Cracks in wood are classified according to the direction in which they run. A *shake* is a separation along the grain between the annual growth rings. A crack running completely through a piece of lumber from face to face is called a *through shake*. A *check* is a separation of wood across the rings of annual growth. Checks usually occur during the seasoning process as a result of shrinking. Lumber will *warp*, *bow*, *cup*, and *twist*. Each of these defects may affect its strength or usability.

PREPARATION OF LUMBER

The growth of wood takes place in the presence of moisture. From 35 to 55 percent of the weight of a growing tree consists of water. Before wood is used for construction purposes, its moisture content should be reduced below 19 percent. Moisture content is the weight of *water* expressed as a percentage of the weight of *oven-dry wood*. A piece of wood will give off or take on moisture from the surrounding atmosphere. This process will continue until the wood has reached a point of equilibrium, or has come to a balance with the moisture in the atmosphere. As wood loses moisture, it becomes lighter in weight and shrinks. As the wood loses moisture and shrinks during drying, it gains strength.

Wood shrinks both across the grain and in the direction of the grain (lengthwise). The amount of shrinkage will vary from species to species. Some woods will shrink only 2 percent from green to oven-dry stages, while others will shrink as much as 14 percent. Wood shrinks more in the direction of the annual growth rings and less across the rings.

As wood shrinks, defects develop that tend to overcome the strength difference between green lumber and dry lumber. Summerwood shrinks more than springwood. The varying degrees of shrinkage in different directions set up patterns of stress in the wood. Unequal drying

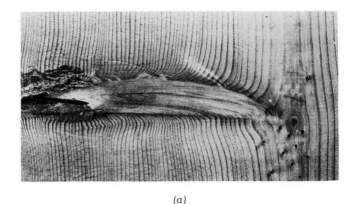

(a)

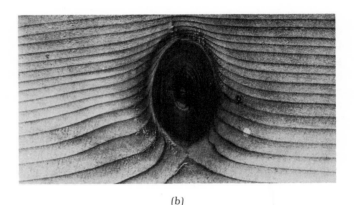

(b)

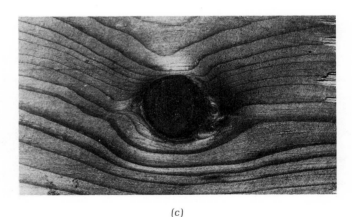

(c)

Fig. 5-2 Knots in lumber: (a) spike knot with partially decayed spur; (b) ingrown knot; (c) encased knot. (*U.S. Forest Products Laboratory.*)

characteristics of the various portions of wood cause warping and cracking in lumber. A great many checks appear in the ends of lumber, which dry faster than the interior. It is important that most shrinkage take place before lumber is used for construction.

Seasoning

The process of drying lumber to the point where it is ready for use is called *seasoning*. When trees have been cut into lumber, the green lumber is stored at the mill or in lumber yards to *air dry*. In order for lumber to dry properly it must be stacked in covered piles, with each successive layer separated by 1-in. strips so that air can flow between the layers. The time necessary to bring lumber to the proper moisture content varies with the area and the weather conditions at the place of storage. In the United States lumber is seldom stacked for more than 3 or 4 months.

Wood will absorb moisture after it has dried, causing it to swell. The best practice is to dry structural lumber until it reaches a moisture content equal to the average moisture content of the air in the area where it will be used. The recommended moisture content varies from 7 percent in dry southwestern states to 18 percent in damp coastal portions of the country. It is a good practice to store lumber on the job site for several months before it is incorporated into a building. This will allow lumber to reach an equilibrium so that the shrinking and swelling will be minimized.

Kiln drying

After drying for certain periods of time in the air, the lumber may be *kiln dried*. It is put into ovens, or kilns, and exposed to an elevated temperature in a controlled atmosphere for periods ranging from 4 to 10 days. Drying temperatures of 70 to 120°F are usually employed to reduce the cracking and checking of certain types of lumber. Interior-finish lumber and trim is usually kiln dried. When kiln-dried lumber is delivered on the job, it must be stored in locations where it will not take on moisture.

Cutting

The manner in which a piece of lumber is cut from the tree affects its appearance and strength. Lumber sawed in parallel slices is said to be *flat sawed, plain sawed,* or *slash cut*. A piece of lumber that has been cut across the annular rays, or perpendicular to the exterior of the tree, is said to be *edge grain, comb grain,* or *vertical grain*. If the log is first quartered, and lumber is cut from each quarter on a diagonal, it is said to be *quarter sawed*. The beauty of quarter-sawed oak and other hardwoods is brought out through this manner of sawing.

FLAT-SAWED LUMBER Flat-sawed wood produces what is called *flat-grain lumber* in softwoods and *plain-sawed lumber* in hardwoods. Each type of cutting has its advantages. Flat-grain lumber is produced with less waste and is consequently cheaper. Growth-ring patterns are distinct in plain-sawed lumber, and the grain and decorative patterns of many hardwoods are brought out when they are

Fig. 5-3 Defects in wood: (*a*) intergrown round knots in yellow pine; (*b*) pronounced compression failure in sitka spruce; (*c*) pith flecks in basswood; (*d*) shake in flat-grain board; (*e*) checks in a flat-grain board; (*f*) ring shake; (*g*) top, pitch streak; bottom, mineral streak; (*h*) top, pith pocket and streaks; center, decay stain; bottom, pocket rot. (*U.S. Forest Products Laboratory.*)

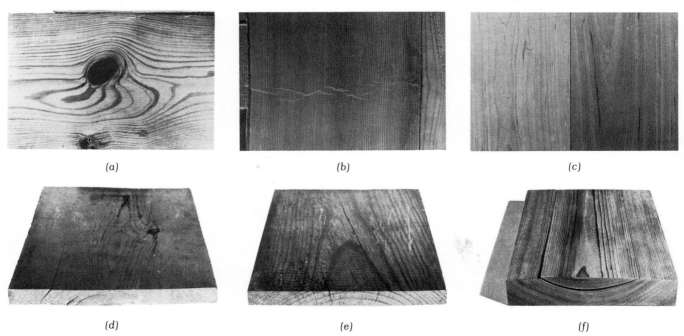

(*a*)   (*b*)   (*c*)

(*d*)   (*e*)   (*f*)

(g)

(h)

plain sawed. Flat-sawed or plain-sawed lumber has certain disadvantages. It tends to warp, check, split, and show separations of the growth rings. It shrinks and swells in width.

QUARTER-SAWED LUMBER Quarter-sawed lumber is more expensive because of the additional labor in the cutting, but it has several advantages. It swells and shrinks less than plain-sawed lumber and develops fewer cracks and

Fig. 5-4 A modern metal prefabricated dry-lumber kiln. *(U.S. Forest Products Laboratory.)*

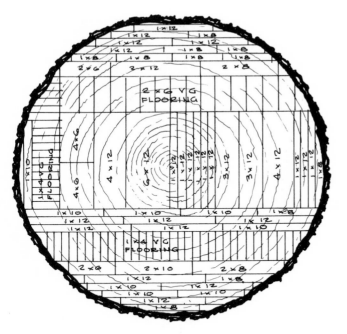

Fig. 5-5 Cutting plan of a log.

checks during seasoning and use. It is usually denser and allows less water to pass through it. The denser, more uniform texture of quarter-sawed lumber produces a surface that wears uniformly, a necessity for softwood flooring and decking and in areas subject to weathering.

Lumber is seldom cut to produce all flat-sawed or quarter-sawed boards. A combination of the two is usually

produced from one log. The experienced sawyer in the mill will study the log, and through a series of cuts at right angles to each other, produce many sizes of lumber. If the grain runs from 90 to 45° through the piece of lumber, it is considered vertical grain. The angle or *slope of the grain* is measured from the horizontal axis of the piece of lumber.

Lumber Sizes

Lumber is usually sawed in dimensions of even inches in thickness and width and in 2-ft increments of length, generally from 8 ft up to 20 or 24 ft. These are the nominal dimensions of the lumber. However, the actual sizes, due to sawing, planing, and surfacing, are 1/4 to 3/4 in. less than the nominal dimensions. Standard sizes of lumber have been established by the United States Department of Commerce for various types and species of lumber.

In 1966 a committee of the National Lumber Manufacturers recommended to the Department of Commerce that the sizes of finished softwood lumber be revised. The new sizes were incorporated into the new lumber standard PS 20-70. There have been many problems in specifying sizes of lumber in the past. Green lumber cut at mills to the standard sizes may arrive on the job site undersize, whereas boards cut after they have been seasoned, or from dry lumber, must be cut to exact dimensions. The new sizes are smaller than those previously used, but they are calculated at a specific moisture content of 15 percent (see Table 5-1). The size is then correlated with a specific moisture content near that which will be present when lumber is incorporated into a building.

TABLE 5-1 New softwood lumber sizes*

PRODUCT CLASSIFICATION, NOMINAL SIZE	OLD SIZES, UNSEASONED OR DRY	NEW SIZES	
		UNSEASONED †	DRY †
For Dimension Lumber:			
2 × 4	$1^5/_8 \times 3^5/_8$	$1^9/_{16} \times 3^9/_{16}$	$1^1/_2 \times 3^1/_2$
2 × 6	$1^5/_8 \times 5^1/_2$	$1^9/_{16} \times 5^5/_8$	$1^1/_2 \times 5^1/_2$
2 × 8	$1^5/_8 \times 7^1/_2$	$1^9/_{16} \times 7^1/_2$	$1^1/_2 \times 7^1/_4$
2 × 10	$1^5/_8 \times 9^1/_2$	$1^9/_{16} \times 9^1/_2$	$1^1/_2 \times 9^1/_4$
2 × 12	$1^5/_8 \times 11^1/_2$	$1^9/_{16} \times 11^1/_2$	$1^1/_2 \times 11^1/_4$
For Board Lumber:			
1 × 4	$^{25}/_{32} \times 3^5/_8$	$^{25}/_{32} \times 3^9/_{16}$	$^3/_4 \times 3^1/_2$
1 × 6	$^{25}/_{32} \times 5^1/_2$	$^{25}/_{32} \times 5^5/_8$	$^3/_4 \times 5^1/_2$
1 × 8	$^{25}/_{32} \times 7^1/_2$	$^{25}/_{32} \times 7^1/_2$	$^3/_4 \times 7^1/_4$
1 × 10	$^{25}/_{32} \times 9^1/_2$	$^{25}/_{32} \times 9^1/_2$	$^3/_4 \times 9^1/_4$
1 × 12	$^{25}/_{32} \times 11^1/_2$	$^{25}/_{32} \times 11^1/_2$	$^3/_4 \times 11^1/_4$

NOTE: The dry thicknesses of nominal 3 and 4 in. lumber are $2^1/_2$ and $3^1/_2$ in., respectively, and unseasoned thicknesses are $2^9/_{16}$ and $3^9/_{16}$ in. Widths for these thicknesses are the same as shown for dimension lumber.

*By permission of the Western Wood Products Association.

†Product Standard 20-70, published by the U.S. Department of Commerce, defines dry lumber as being 19% or less in moisture content and unseasoned lumber as being over 19% moisture content. The size of lumber changes approximately 1% for each 4% change in moisture content. Lumber stabilizes at approximately 15% moisture content under normal use conditions.

Rough lumber is unfinished, as it comes from the saw. Sizes of *finished lumber* are the dimensions of the lumber after it has been run through a planer, or *dressed*. Lumber may be surfaced on one or more sides and is designated as shown in Table 5-2. Boards may be further

TABLE 5-2 Designations for dressed lumber

DESIGNATION	DESCRIPTION
S1S	Surfaced one side
S2S	Surfaced on two sides
S1E	Surfaced on one edge
S2E	Surfaced on two edges
S1S1E	Surfaced on one side, one edge
S2S1E	Surfaced on two sides, one edge
S4S	Surfaced on four sides

TABLE 5-3 Western softwoods

SPECIES	DESCRIPTION
Douglas fir West Coast hemlock Larch	These are some of the strongest of the softwoods. They have a dense, close, prominent, straight grain of an orange-red color in contrast to a narrow white band of sapwood. These heavy, stiff woods provide the most widely used structural lumber in the United States and Canada.
White fir	There is an almost imperceptible line of demarcation between heartwood and sapwood in this abundant, nonresinous, finely textured, lightweight, easily worked wood. Fir takes paint well and is suitable to natural finishes. In addition to being used for all types of interior finish, it is also widely used as structural lumber in residential and light commercial construction.
Ponderosa pine	Summerwood is only slightly denser than springwood in this soft-textured wood. Color varies from white to a light straw, with little difference between heartwood and sapwood. This wood has little tendency to warp and twist, and its easy working characteristics and excellent finishing qualities make it suitable for paneling, exterior and interior trim, millwork, moldings, sash, and doors.
Idaho white pine Sugar pine	Uniformly soft, white, lightweight woods such as these offer unexcelled smooth surfaces for finishing. They are not structural woods, but because of their stability and freedom from defects, they are well suited for interior cabinetwork and trim.
Engleman spruce Sitka spruce	The Western spruces were used at one time as framing members for airplanes.

worked by running them through matching machines, stickers, or molders. These boards, usually used as siding or sheathing, are classed as *shiplap, tongue and groove,* or *patterned*. The boards may be square ended or they may be *end matched*. End-matched boards have tongues and grooves cut into the ends of the pieces to form tight joints.

CHARACTERISTICS OF SOFTWOODS AND HARDWOODS

Most framing or structural lumber used in the United States and Canada consists of softwoods, which are generally more abundant, and therefore less expensive. Softwoods are also usually available in larger sizes. Some lumber uses demand a material that is stiff, durable, and strong, with appearance being of secondary importance.

TABLE 5-3 Western softwoods (*Continued*)

SPECIES	DESCRIPTION
	Because of their light weight, resiliency, and stability they are now widely used for sash, doors, paneling, and interior finish. Although they are not as strong as douglas fir, their small, tight knot characteristics make them suitable for general construction.
Western red cedar	This wood, one of the largest and most generally used of several types of cedars, is found in the Pacific Northwest. It is moderately light in weight, with a high degree of dimensional stability. The predominant feature of cedar is its extreme resistance to decay and insects. Its reddish-brown color weathers to a driftwood grey with a silvery sheen. Western red cedar is suitable for paneling, shingles, siding, decking, fences, exterior trim, and other outside exposures.
Redwood	Wood cut from the giant redwoods, which grow only along the Pacific slope of the coastal mountains of California, has been used for years. Even though the range of the forest is relatively small, the size of many trees (20 ft in diameter and 300 ft tall) and the closeness of their growth in the forest, assure a continuing supply for many years to come. The heartwood is a reddish-brown with inconspicuous growth rings, while the sapwood is nearly pure white. The heartwood has outstanding resistance to decay and insects. Because of its deep red color and its resistance to the elements redwood is suitable for both interior and exterior paneling, siding, shingles, posts, fences, and garden structures. It may be finished in many ways or be left to weather to a driftwood grey.

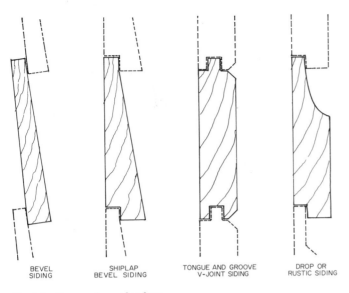

BEVEL
SIDING

SHIPLAP
BEVEL SIDING

TONGUE AND GROOVE
V-JOINT SIDING

DROP OR
RUSTIC SIDING

Fig. 5-6 Types of wood siding.

Other uses demand wood that is particularly resistant to weather and the attack of insects or decay. For interior-finish lumber ease of working and the ability to accept a good finish are important.

Softwoods

The most widely used softwoods on the North American continent, listed according to their origin or availability in the western and eastern parts of the United States, are described in Tables 5-3 and 5-4.

Hardwoods

Hardwoods are generally used for wood furniture, as decorative paneling, and as interior trim. Some hardwoods are extremely strong, but because of their scarcity and higher cost, they are seldom used structurally. Much hardwood is used in the form of veneer bonded onto a core of softwood.

Many different kinds of hardwood, both native and imported, are used in fine furniture and woodwork. Each

Fig. 5-7 The world's tallest trees: (a) coast redwoods growing in Redwood National Park, near Orick, California: Redwood Creek holds the tallest known tree, 367 ft, and the second, third, and sixth tallest trees; (b) a 7-ft sprout from redwood tree, cut 150 years ago; (c) measuring first-growth redwood lumber. (*Redwood Association.*)

(a)

(b)

TABLE 5-4 Eastern softwoods

SPECIES	DESCRIPTION
Southern pine	Southern pine includes longleaf, shortleaf, slash, and loblolly pine; however, there is little difference in the strength and appearance of the same grades of lumber taken from these trees. Southern pine has a reddish-brown hue with prominent growth rings. Its major characteristics are strength, hardness, stiffness, and resistance to shock. The strength, bending characteristics, and structural uses of Southern pine are similar to those of douglas fir.
Eastern white pine	This soft, easily worked wood was once abundant in the Northeastern portion of the United States but has become scarce and quite expensive. Wherever a softwood with minimum shrinkage is desired, as in doors, windows, and interior trim, it is extremely valuable.
Eastern hemlock	Strong, hard eastern hemlock is used in construction for studding, joists, and sheathing. This reddish-brown wood tends to splinter and is low in shock resistance.

TABLE 5-4 Eastern softwoods (*Continued*)

SPECIES	DESCRIPTION
Eastern spruce	Although it is heavier than the western variety, eastern spruce is strong, hard, and low in shrinkage. It has limited use as light framing lumber in certain areas.
Southern cypress	Cypress is a soft, easily worked wood from the swamp areas of the southeastern states. It is one of the most decay-resistant woods in the presence of water and is therefore in great demand for exterior siding, trim, posts, fences, and water tanks.
Yellow poplar	Poplar is a moderately strong, soft, lightweight wood that has a very high shrinkage. This yellowish-brown wood is used for paneling and as the core for plywood.
Eastern red cedar	This highly aromatic wood has dark-red heartwood with contrasting pure white sapwood. It has long been used as a mothproofing paneling in closets and is used as a decorative paneling because of its distinctive grain.

(c)

TABLE 5-5 North American hardwoods

SPECIES	DESCRIPTION
Alder	Red alder ranges from white to a pale pinkish-brown. This wood is light in weight, low in strength, and moderately soft and is used for some painted furniture, novelties, and cabinetwork.
Ash	Ash is a heavy, light-colored wood with a pronounced grain. It takes a good finish, either stained or clear, and is used for handles, sporting goods, paneling, and interior trim.
Basswood	This soft, easily worked wood has light-brown heartwood and sapwood that is nearly white. Its soft even texture makes it ideal for drawingboards, millwork, and cabinetwork.
Beech	Hard, stiff, strong beech, with reddish-brown sapwood, is used for furniture, flooring, and interior finish.
Birch	The birches include red birch and yellow birch. The hardness, strength, stability, and even texture of birch make it ideal for quality cabinets and doors. It can be given a natural finish, a stained finish, or a satin-smooth painted finish.
Cherry	American cherry has a light brownish-red heartwood with dark-brown growth rings. It is a hard, dense, strong wood. The figure caused by the grain ranges from plain to rich swirls.
Elm	Honey-yellow elm is a cool-toned wood that accepts natural and stained finishes equally well.
Hickory	Similiar to ash in appearance and use.
Gum	Figured red gum has a strong texture and ranges in color from pink to reddish brown. The patterns formed by the grain are varied, with wide ranges and sharp contrasts of color.
Maple	Maple is a hard, dense, durable wood that has great strength. These qualities, and the wide varieties of grain patterns

TABLE 5-5 North American hardwoods (*Continued*)

SPECIES	DESCRIPTION
	that can be produced by selection and cutting, make it extremely well suited for furniture, flooring, stair treads, doors, and paneling.
Oak	This hard, heavy, strong wood was at one time used for structural posts, beams, and heavy framing members. These functions have now been taken over by douglas fir and southern pine. However, both red and white oak are widely used for flooring, stair treads, railings, paneling, and furniture.
Poplar	Yellow poplar is a lightweight wood with a soft, uniform texture. It has a yellowish-brown color with a greenish tinge that produces a striking paneling when given a clear finish. It is also used as interior trim and cabinets.
Walnut	American black walnut is a strong, hard wood with dark-brown heartwood contrasting with a rather light sapwood. Walnut can be obtained with a plain grain or in cuts with many types of beautiful patterns. Other walnuts, which are not all true walnuts, are imported under the names of English walnut, French walnut, Italian walnut, and East Indian walnut, and others. Walnut offers an infinite range of grains and figures, providing a uniquely creative medium for architectural installations.
Mahogany	All true mahogany is grown in Florida or Central and South America. This hard, durable, reddish-brown wood can be cut to show a ribbon grain or a beautifully figured grain that takes a high polish. Several so-called mahoganies are imported from Africa, the Philippines, and Malaysia. Those from the Philippines consist of several species grown on neighboring islands called Lauan, Toon, or Philippine Mahogany. Khava, Sapole, Cameroon, and Makore are imported from Africa and are sometimes called mahogany.

species has its own grain and distinctive characteristics. Within each species there are also numerous variations provided by different types of cuts from the log. Irregularities in the tree growth and defects in the wood may produce uneven grain and further variations prized for their appearance.

Hardwoods from Avodire to Zebrawood are imported from forests throughout the world. Most imported hardwood is made into veneers for furniture construction or custom paneling. Many fine North American hardwoods are available for fine cabinetwork or interior finish (see Table 5-5).

LUMBER GRADES

The grading of lumber according to strength, appearance, or usability has been the subject of extensive studies and testing. The United States Department of Agriculture, the National Bureau of Standards, and lumber associations have spent many years attempting to simplify sizes, nomenclature, and grades of lumber and to obtain uniformity of practice. Since 1922 interested members of the lumber industry have from time to time met with members of the National Bureau of Standards to develop standards and methods of interpreting and applying these standards.

When lumber is cut from a log, the individual pieces vary in appearance and strength, depending on the imperfections and the defects in each piece. Grades of lumber are based on the number and placement of such defects as knots, checks, splits, and pitch pockets. The highest grades are practically free of these defects, while each successively lower grade allows more imperfections. This does not preclude the use of the lower grades for many purposes. A piece of softwood lumber with knots is not necessarily seriously defective.

Hardwood Grades

Hardwood grades are based on the amount of usable lumber in each piece of a standard length, from 4 ft to 16 ft. The hardwood is inspected on the poorest side of the piece, and the grade is based on the appearance of this side.

Hardwoods are classified as firsts, seconds, and selects, and Nos. 1, 2, 3A, and 3B common. In general each grade allows smaller portions of clear pieces. Firsts and seconds are nearly always combined into one grade (FAS). Hardwoods whose unique appearance is based on worm holes and other imperfections are called *sound wormy* and are classed as No. 1 common.

Softwood Grades

The "American Lumber Standards for Softwood Lumber," R16, divides softwoods into three basic classifications: yard, structural, and factory and shop. These classifications are shown in Table 5-6. Yard lumber is further classified as selects and finish or boards. The grades for each, as established by the Western Wood Products Association (WWPA) and the West Coast Lumber Inspection Bureau (WCLIB), are shown in Table 5-7.

TABLE 5-6 Softwood lumber grades

GRADE	USE
Yard	In general, used for framing in residences and other light construction.
Structural	Pieces 2 in. or more in thickness, graded according to the actual working stresses resisted by an entire piece of lumber. Working stresses vary with location and number of knots, checks, and splits, direction of grain, and presence of wane.
Factory and shop	Finish lumber used for sash, doors, and trim, graded according to the number of smaller pieces that can be obtained from each piece of lumber.

TABLE 5-7 Yard-lumber grades

GRADE	USE
Selects and finish	Graded from the best side. Used for interior and exterior trim, molding, and woodwork where appearance is of prime importance.
B & BTR	Highest grade of lumber, used where appearance is the primary factor. Many pieces are clear, but minor appearance defects are allowed which do not detract from their appearance.
C select	Used for all types of interior woodwork. Appearance and usability slightly less than B & BTR - 1 & 2 clear.
D select	Used where finishing requirements are less severe. Many pieces have finish appearance on one side with larger defects on back.
Boards	Lumber with defects that detract from appearance but which is suitable for general construction.
No. 1 common (WWPA) Select merchantable (WCLIB)	All sound, tight knots, with serviceability determined by size and placement of knots. Used in exposed interior and exterior locations where knots are not objectionable.
No. 2 common (WWPA) Construction (WCLIB)	All sound, tight knots and some defects, such as stains, streaks and patches of pitch, checks and splits. Used as paneling and shelving, subfloors, and roof and wall sheathing.
No. 3 common (WWPA) Standard (WCLIB)	Some unsound knots and other defects. Used for rough sheathing, shelving, fences, boxes, and crating.
No. 4 common (WWPA) Utility (WCLIB)	Loose knots and knotholes, up to 4 in. diameter in 14 in. widths, and other defects. Used for general construction purposes, such as sheathing, bracing, low-cost fencing, and crating.
No. 5 common (WWPA) Economy (WCLIB)	Large knots or holes, unsound wood, massed pitch, splits, and other defects. Used for low-grade sheathing, bracing, and temporary construction. Pieces of higher-grade wood may be obtained from this grade by crosscutting or ripping individual boards.

Structural Lumber Grades

Structural lumber is graded according to its intended use. Each piece is assigned a *stress grade*, designed to meet exacting requirements and strength values. These grades are shown in Table 5-8.

TABLE 5-8 Structural lumber grades

GRADE	USE
Light framing (LF)	Thicknesses 2″ to 4″, widths 3″ and 4″. Used for general light framing, such as studs, joists, and rafters, without regard to the position of the piece in the final structure.
Joists and planks (J&P)	Thicknesses 2″ to 4″, widths 2″ and over. May be used on edge as joists and rafters or flat as plank flooring. The same working stresses may be applied whether the wide faces are vertical or horizontal.
Beams and stringers (B&S)	Thicknesses 2″ to 4″, widths 2″ and over. Provisions of this grade are based on the expectation that the material will be loaded on the narrow edge.
Post and timbers (P&T)	5″ × 5″ and larger, approximately square. Graded primarily for use as posts or columns, but also suitable for use where resistance to bending is not critical.

Grade Marking

The lumber industry is responsible for grade marking its lumber. In some areas private agencies provide grade-marking services. Various lumber associations establish grade requirements and grade-marking procedures for species of lumber produced in their regions. In general the grade names and the broad divisions into grades conform to requirements set forth in "American Lumber Standards" by the National Bureau of Standards. Lumber-grading agencies or associations use grade stamps or grade marks which identify the grading agency, the individual mill, and the grade of each piece of lumber. This stamp, usually placed on the lumber at the mill, identifies the grade of each piece of lumber (see Table 5-9). If there is any question about the grade on delivery of the lumber, the grading agencies offer a reinspection service. A competent lumber inspector is sent out by the grading agency to retally the lumber and certify its grade. He will report exactly what he has found to all interested parties. The cost of this reinspection is usually borne by the party in error in any dispute over the grade marking of the lumber.

VISUALLY GRADED LUMBER Lumber is usually graded on the basis of visual inspection. The number, size, type, and placement of defects determine the possible strength of a given piece of lumber. The visual grading is based on rules established by various lumber associations. Each association publishes standard grading rules for use by its inspectors. The ground rules for strength, span, size, and the placement of defects in a piece of lumber are based on what experience has shown to be reasonable.

MACHINE-STRESS-RATED LUMBER Lumber which has been individually pretested by nondestructive mechanical means, supplemented by visual grading in order to establish unit working stresses, is classed as *machine stress-rated lumber* (MSR). Machines continuously measure strength and elasticity, and each piece is stamped with the proper strength and stiffness value as it leaves the machine. The stamp indicates that the piece has been stress rated, states the number of the mill where the lumber was processed, and states the allowable *f* and *E* values. Under this system the lumber is not graded on the basis of the weakest piece, but on its own merits. In addition to machine stress rating, each piece must be visually examined to eliminate certain defects that occur at the end of individual pieces of lumber.

Stress in Lumber

Stress in lumber is based on the amount of tension or compression exerted on the wood fibers at the extreme top and bottom of a beam when it is subjected to a bending load. This is called the strength of extreme fiber in bending, or *f value* of the beam, and is given in pounds per square inch. Thus in a beam rated at 1200*f* the extreme fibers at the top and bottom will resist a force of 1200 psi, in a beam rated at 1600*f* the extreme fibers at the top and bottom will resist a force of 1600 psi, and so on.

The amount that a beam bends under a load, or its *deflection*, varies with the species of lumber. The relationship between load and the amount of deflection is called the beam's stiffness or *modulus of elasticity E*. When a beam bends, stresses are produced in its central cross section which tend to separate the fibers of the wood. This is called the *horizontal shear*, designated as the *H* value.

Building codes and standards include tables of stress grades and the allowable working stresses under normal loads, for each species and grade of wood used in a structure. These tables allow the designer to calculate the size of beam, post, or structural member needed to support a given weight. Further information and the formulas for calculating the size of wood members and their connections are given in "National Design Specification for Stress Grade Lumber and Its Fastenings," published by the National Lumber Manufacturers' Association.

TREATED LUMBER

The principal causes of deterioration in wood are decay, insects, and fire. Different species of wood vary in their

TABLE 5-9 New lumber grades using the NBS Voluntary Product Standard 20-70

boards

APPEARANCE GRADES	SELECTS	B & BETTER (IWP—SUPREME) C SELECT (IWP—CHOICE) D SELECT (IWP—QUALITY)	**SPECIFICATION CHECK LIST** ☐ Grades listed in order of quality. ☐ Include all species suited to project. ☐ For economy, specify lowest grade that will satisfy job requirement. ☐ Specify surface texture desired. ☐ Specify moisture content suited to project. ☐ Specify Ⓦ grade stamp. For finish and exposed pieces, specify stamp on back or ends.
	FINISH	SUPERIOR PRIME E	
	PANELING	CLEAR (ANY SELECT OR FINISH GRADE) NO. 2 COMMON SELECTED FOR KNOTTY PANELING NO. 3 COMMON SELECTED FOR KNOTTY PANELING	
	SIDING (BEVEL, BUNGALOW)	SUPERIOR PRIME	

BOARDS SHEATHING & FORM LUMBER	NO. 1 COMMON (IWP—COLONIAL) NO. 2 COMMON (IWP—STERLING) NO. 3 COMMON (IWP—STANDARD) NO. 4 COMMON (IWP—UTILITY) NO. 5 COMMON (IWP—INDUSTRIAL)		
	ALTERNATE GRADES SELECT MERCHANTABLE CONSTRUCTION STANDARD UTILITY ECONOMY	**WESTERN RED CEDAR**	
		FINISH PANELING AND CEILING	**CLEAR HEART** A B
		BEVEL SIDING	CLEAR — V.G. HEART A — BEVEL SIDING B — BEVEL SIDING C — BEVEL SIDING

dimension/all species*

LIGHT FRAMING	CONSTRUCTION STANDARD UTILITY ECONOMY	**STUDS** STUD ECONOMY STUD
LIGHT FRAMING	SELECT STRUCTURAL NO. 1 NO. 2 NO. 3 ECONOMY	
APPEARANCE FRAMING	APPEARANCE	*Design values are assigned to all dimension grades except Economy. See pages 8, 9, 10, this book.
STRUCTURAL JOISTS & PLANKS	SELECT STRUCTURAL NO. 1 NO. 2 NO. 3 ECONOMY	
DECKING	SELECTED DECKING COMMERCIAL DECKING	

timbers

BEAMS & STRINGERS	SELECT STRUCTURAL NO. 1 NO. 2 (NO. 1 MINING) NO. 3 (NO. 2 MINING)	POSTS & TIMBERS	SELECT STRUCTURAL NO. 1 NO. 2 (NO. 1 MINING) NO. 3 (NO. 2 MINING)

By permission of the Western Wood Products Association.

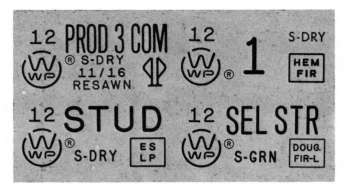

Fig. 5-8 Typical grade marks on lumber. (*Western Wood Products Association.*)

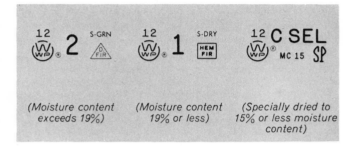

Fig. 5-9 New grade marks identifying seasoned, unseasoned, or specially dried structural lumber. (*Western Wood Products Association.*)

Fig. 5-10 When a lumber inspector's certificate issued by the association is required on a shipment of lumber and specific grade marks are not used, the stock is identified with the association mark and the number of the shipping mill. (*Western Wood Products Association.*)

Fig. 5-11 Grade stamp for machine-rated lumber. (*Western Wood Products Association.*)

durability and resistance to all these factors. However, lumber may be treated in various ways to protect it against deterioration. Preservatives may be painted or brushed on the surface, or the lumber may be dipped into large tanks. These methods are only partially successful, because only a thin coating can be applied in this manner. The preservative must be drawn or forced in under pressure into the wood for maximum effectiveness.

The lumber may be *pressure treated* by dipping it into tanks containing hot solutions of preservative. This converts the water in the wood into steam. The wood is then quickly transferred into vats containing cold preservative, and as the steam in the wood condenses, a partial vacuum is produced which draws the preservative deep into the wood. Lumber may also be placed in pressure tanks to force preservatives into the wood. In order to increase the penetration of preservative, the wood may be *incised*. This is done by passing lumber between rollers with thin knifelike teeth that separate the wood fibers, allowing the preservatives to penetrate more efficiently. When treated lumber is cut or drilled on the job site, the cut ends must be painted with preservative to maintain an unbroken protective surface.

Types of Preservatives

Preservatives used to combat the destructive agents of wood can be generally classified as oil- or petroleum-base products such as creosote, water-soluble salts such as zinc chloride and copper salts, and solvent-soluble products such as chlorinated phenols.

CREOSOTE Creosote forms an effective barrier against decay and insects. However, the objectionable odor limits its use to pilings, power poles, and waterfront structures. Creosote is insoluble in water, so it will not wash out of timbers used in structures subject to the action of water. Creosoted wood cannot be painted successfully.

WATER-SOLUBLE SALTS Wolman Salts (a product of the Koppers Company) and similar products, either painted on the surface or forced into the wood by pressure, give good protection against decay and insects. Lumber can be successfully painted after treatment with these salts.

ORGANIC MATERIALS Materials such as pentachlorophenol are used as a preservative on fenceposts, structural lumber, sash, and doors. When the solvent evaporates, a coating of nonsoluble material is left on the wood. The wood can then be successfully painted.

Decay

Decay in wood is caused by fungi, microscopic organisms that depend on wood fibers for food. As they eat through the wood fibers, the wood becomes soft, spongy, or pitted, depending on the type of fungus. The heat of curing kilns will kill most fungi by drying up the moisture they require. As long as the lumber is kept dry, through coatings or placement in a structure, fungi will not develop. Fungi also require air; hence wood that is completely immersed in water will not be affected by fungi. Fungi can also be removed by chemicals that poison the wood fibers, their source of food.

Termites

The insects most destructive to wood in buildings are termites, sometimes called white ants. The two main species are drywood termites and subterranean termites.

DRYWOOD TERMITES Drywood termites, which occur in a relatively narrow strip in the southwestern United States, are capable of surviving without moisture. Although their range is rather limited, protection against them is difficult, and they cause extensive damage. They can enter any exposed unprotected wood. At certain seasons drywood termites develop wings and can attack structures many feet above the ground. They may also be brought into structures in wood that has been infested before delivery to the building site.

SUBTERRANEAN TERMITES These termites are found throughout the United States, except in the extreme northern portions. They cause extensive damage in the warmer, damper climates of the southern states. Subterranean termites live in colonies in the ground and must have moisture and food to survive. They do not enter a building by means of infested wood, but from ground nests after the building has been constructed. Subterranean termites infest any wood in contact with the ground, and even wood that is several feet above the ground. They are capable of penetrating through minute cracks in concrete or masonry.

The best protection against termites is to prevent their entry into a structure. All wood must be above the ground and, if possible, shielded by metal. Wood scraps left under a building provide food for colonies of termites that will eventually attack the structure. Proper ventilation under buildings tends to discourage termites. As discussed in Chapter 2, soil poisoning is also helpful. Many preservatives used to prevent decay are also effective against termites.

Fire Protection

When wood is subjected to a temperature of 300°F, inflammable gases are produced and the wood begins to char. While small pieces of wood burn through quickly, a large timber will develop a layer of char which tends to insulate its interior. Large timbers may stand up better than steel under fire conditions. Steel will lose strength when its softening point is reached, whereas heavy timbers, because of this insulating layer of char, may resist the action of severe fires. Lumber may be coated with layers of fire-retarding paints. Coatings give only a limited protection to lumber by forming blisters which tend to insulate wood. Mineral salts forced into lumber will prevent the spread of flame by causing the wood to stop burning when the source of ignition is removed. Nationally recognized codes permit fire-protected wood to be used as framing members for interior walls, partitions, and roof assemblies in fire-resistive construction. Treated wood provides the opportunity to enjoy the many benefits of wood in noncombustible types of construction.

Fig. 5-12 Loading lumber in a pressure vessel for applying preservatives. (*American Wood Preservers' Institute.*)

Fig. 5-13 Termite-damaged wood.

Fig. 5-14 Gluing a laminated beam. (*Weyerhaeuser Company.*)

GLUED-LAMINATED TIMBER

Construction with solid timber is limited by the size and shape of the timbers available. Modern methods and the development of new materials have made it possible to fabricate wood members of almost any size and shape. Glued-laminated construction has made possible fabrication of curved wood trusses, long-span wood beams, two- and three-hinged wood arches, and other interesting structures. Many of these are produced under the trade name Glu-Lam.

Fabrication

Small pieces of wood may be bonded together to form a laminated structural member that is strong and durable. High-strength material is used at stress points, with less expensive lumber used where strength is not important. Lumber may be selected for appearance where it can be seen but need not be used where appearance is not a factor. Laminated beams are usually made of dry lumber, so the tendency of heavy members to warp, crack, and check is minimized. Glues used in laminating beams for interiors are usually of the casein type with a mold inhibitor. Exterior-grade members require a waterproof glue of the resorcinol or phenol-plastic type.

Since beams for interior use are fabricated of kiln-dried lumber and glued with nonwaterproof glue, they are usually delivered to the job site prefinished and enclosed in plastic membranes. These membranes must be kept in place until the beam is covered and protected against moisture. They must be unloaded and moved into place by means of nonmarring slings or otherwise protected from damage. They should be stored off of the ground and covered to protect all portions from the elements.

Laminated members must be constructed in shops that have facilities to control the temperature. The pressure that must be exerted to form complex shapes requires special forms that can be firmly secured. Small pieces of wood are bent around a form, and glue is applied to the face of the piece. Successive pieces are added until the desired shape and thickness is reached. *Scarfed joints* are usually used to join the ends of the individual pieces. These long, sloping joints are well scattered throughout the member.

Grades

Glued-laminated members are graded according to use and appearance. Appearance grades are based on such factors as grain, fillers, and surface imperfections, characteristics which do not affect the strength of the member. Table 5-10 describes the three most commonly used appearance grades.

TABLE 5-10 Glued-laminated appearance grades

GRADE	USE
Industrial appearance	This grade is suitable for garages, industrial plants, and other locations where appearance is not the primary concern.
Architectural appearance	Used where appearance is an important consideration. This grade allows some imperfections, such as small voids, tight knots, and other defects that must be filled or corrected on the job, and is suitable for a painted finish.
Premium appearance	The highest grade obtainable. Used for natural finishes and in locations where appearance is of primary importance.

STRUCTURAL PLYWOOD

Plywood, which is also a glued-laminated wood product, is an engineered panel constructed of thin sheets of wood 1.10 to $\frac{1}{4}$ in. thick. Thin sheets of wood, or *veneers*, are peeled from logs mounted in giant lathes. The veneers are bonded together with glue under high pressure, with the grain of alternate layers running in opposite directions.

The resulting composite material is therefore stronger than solid wood. Plywood is strong across the panel as well as along its length. (The lateral strength is not quite equal to the longitudinal strength because there is one less ply running across the panel.)

Plywood resists splitting, checking, and splintering and is more dimensionally stable than solid wood. Solid wood shrinks from 5 to 8 percent across the width of boards; plywood panels shrink less than 0.5 percent across the width of a 4-ft panel. Thus a plywood panel has less warp and twist than most solid-wood panels of comparable size. It is easy to work with ordinary tools and lends itself to speedy fabrication.

Plywood is generally produced in 4′ × 8′ sheets and standard thicknesses of ¼″, ⁵⁄₁₆″, ½″, ⅝″, ¾″, 1″, and 1⅛″. Approximately 75 percent of all plywood manufactured is in 4′ × 8′ sheets, but sheets up to 50 ft long may be ordered.

Plywood may be 3-ply, 5-ply, or 7-ply. The wood sheets, or *plies*, are bonded together in odd-numbered layers, so that the outside layers on both sides will have the grain running with the length of the sheet. This minimizes the warpage that could occur if the outer layers were at right angles.

Characteristics of Softwood Plywood

Most softwood plywood is constructed of douglas fir, although southern pine, western larch, western hemlock, white fir, cedar, and other species are also used. The species used for plywood are grouped according to their strength and stiffness properties as shown in Table 5-11.

Plywood Types

Plywood is classified as either *exterior* or *interior*, depending on the type of glue with which it is fabricated. Exterior plywood will retain its original form and strength when repeatedly wet and dried. It is made with hot-pressed phenolic-resin adhesives that are insoluble and waterproof. Exterior plywood is designed for those applications where there is permanent exposure to the weather or unusual moisture conditions. Interior plywood is bonded with soybean or extended resin glues to which a mold

Fig. 5-15 Completed Glu-Lam beam, ready to receive protective covering for shipment. (*Weyerhaeuser Company.*)

TABLE 5-11 Classification of species*

GROUP 1		GROUP 2	GROUP 3	GROUP 4	GROUP 5
Birch	Cedar, port orford	Maple, black	Alder, red	Aspen	Fir, balsam
Yellow	Douglas fir 2‡	Meranti	Cedar	Bigtooth	Poplar, balsam
Sweet	Fir	Mengkulang	Alaska	Quaking	
Douglas fir 1†	California red	Pine	Pine	Birch, paper	
Larch, western	Grand	Pond	Jack	Cedar	
Maple, sugar	Noble	Red	Lodgepole	Incense	
Pine, caribbean	Pacific silver	Western white	Ponderosa	Western red	
Pine, southern	White	Spruce, sitka	Spruce	Fir, subalpine	
Loblolly	Hemlock, western	Sweet gum	Redwood	Hemlock, eastern	
Longleaf	Lauan	Tamarack	Spruce	Pine	
Shortleaf	Red		Black	Sugar	
Slash	Tangile		Red	Eastern white	
Tanoak	White		White	Poplar, western§	
	Almon			Spruce, engelmann	
	Bagtikan				

*Courtesy of American Plywood Association.
†Douglas fir 1 consists of lumber from trees grown in the states of Washington, Oregon, California, Idaho, Montana, Wyoming, and the Canadian Provinces of Alberta and British Columbia.
‡Douglas fir 2 consists of lumber from trees grown in Nevada, Utah, Colorado, Arizona, and New Mexico.
§Black cottonwood.

inhibitor is added. Even though interior grades of plywood are not constructed with waterproof glue, they will maintain strength and form when subjected to occasional wetting and drying.

Most softwood plywood is produced in accordance with nationally recognized standards established by the Product Standards Section of the National Bureau of Standards, in cooperation with manufacturers, distributors, and users. The American Plywood Association has taken a leading role in the development of the current standard (PS 1-66), published in 1966. This organization, formerly the Douglas Fir Plywood Association, is a nonprofit, industrywide organization devoted to research and quality control of plywood. Through licensing, it maintains a program of quality control based on grade trademarks. Panels bearing these marks have been inspected in accordance with U.S. Product Standards PS 1-66 and the requirements of the American Plywood Association. The registered DFPA grade trademark appears on the back or edge of each sheet of plywood produced, indicating whether the panel is exterior or interior grade.

Veneer Grades

Each layer of plywood veneer is graded for allowable defects. Grades are based on the percentage of heartwood and the presence of stains, knots, splits, checks, open sections, and other defects. Repairs are permitted in some grades of veneer. Round, boat-shaped, or oval patches are used to fill holes in the veneer. Narrow shims are used to fill voids left by pitch pockets and splits.

The six grades of veneer, designated by letters, are shown in Table 5-12.

TABLE 5-12 Veneer grades

GRADE	DESCRIPTION
N	A special-order cabinet-grade veneer of 100 percent heartwood, free of knots and open defects and selected to receive a natural finish.
A	The highest standard veneer grade, used for panel faces. Neatly made repairs are permitted, but no open defects are allowed. Suitable for a smooth painted finish.
B	Presents a solid surface with tight knots, limited sander skips, circular plugs, and splits not wider than $1/32$ in., as well as repairs admitted in A-grade veneer.
C	Plugged, improved veneer with splits limited to $1/8$ in. and holes limited to $1/4'' \times 1/2''$.

Appearance Grades

Sanded plywood panels are graded primarily by the appearance of their front and back faces. The grade of the panel is thus indicated by two letters; an A-C panel is one having an A-grade face and a C-grade back. In exterior plywood the internal plies must be grade C or better; interior plywood may consist of D-grade inner plies. Appearance grades for interior and exterior panels and the grade trademarks that identify them are given in Table 5-13.

Construction Grades

Unsanded plywood panels used for sheathing, subfloors, underlayment under resilient floor coverings or carpeting, and structural applications are graded according to strength

TABLE 5-13 Grade-use guide for appearance grades of plywood[1]

Use these symbols when you specify plywood	Description and Most Common Uses	Typical Grade-trademarks (2)	Face	Back	Inner Plys	1/4	5/16	3/8	1/2	5/8	3/4
Interior Type											
N-N, N-A, N-B INT-DFPA	Cabinet quality. One or both sides select all heartwood or all sapwood veneer. For natural finish furniture, cabinet doors, built-ins, etc. Special order items.	N-N · G-1 · INT-DFPA · PS 1-66 ; N-A · G-2 · INT-DFPA · PS 1-66	N	N,A, or B	C						3/4
N-D-INT-DFPA	For natural finish paneling. Special order item.	N-D · G-3 · INT-DFPA · PS 1-66	N	D	D	1/4					
A-A INT-DFPA	For interior applications where both sides will be on view. Built-ins, cabinets, furniture and partitions. Face is smooth and suitable for painting.	A-A · G-3 · INT-DFPA · PS 1-66	A	A	D	1/4		3/8	1/2	5/8	3/4
A-B INT-DFPA	For uses similar to Interior A-A but where the appearance of one side is less important and two smooth solid surfaces are necessary.	A-B · G-4 · INT-DFPA · PS 1-66	A	B	D	1/4		3/8	1/2	5/8	3/4
A-D INT-DFPA	For interior uses where the appearance of only one side is important. Paneling, built-ins, shelving, partitions and flow racks.	A-D GROUP 1 INTERIOR	A	D	D	1/4		3/8	1/2	5/8	3/4
B-B INT-DFPA	Interior utility panel used where two smooth sides are desired. Permits circular plugs. Paintable.	B-B · G-3 · INT-DFPA · PS 1-66	B	B	D	1/4		3/8	1/2	5/8	3/4
B-D INT-DFPA	Interior utility panel for use where one smooth side is required. Good for backing, sides of built-ins. Industry: shelving, slip sheets, separator boards and bins.	B-D GROUP 3 INTERIOR	B	D	D	1/4		3/8	1/2	5/8	3/4
DECORATIVE PANELS	Rough-sawn, brushed, grooved or striated faces. Good for paneling, interior accent walls, built-ins, counter facing, displays and exhibits.	DECORATIVE · B-D · G-1 · INT-DFPA	C or btr.	D	D		5/16	3/8	1/2	5/8	
PLYRON INT-DFPA	Hardboard face on both sides. For counter tops, shelving, cabinet doors, flooring. Hardboard faces may be tempered, untempered, smooth or screened.	PLYRON · INT-DFPA			C & D				1/2	5/8	3/4
Exterior Type											
A-A EXT-DFPA (4)	Use in applications where the appearance of both sides is important. Fences, built-ins, signs, boats, cabinets, commercial refrigerators, shipping containers, tote boxes, tanks, and ducts.	A-A · G-4 · EXT-DFPA · PS 1-66	A	A	C	1/4		3/8	1/2	5/8	3/4
A-B EXT-DFPA (4)	For use similar to A-A EXT panels but where the appearance of one side is less important.	A-B · G-1 · EXT-DFPA · PS 1-66	A	B	C	1/4		3/8	1/2	5/8	3/4
A-C EXT-DFPA (4)	Exterior use where the appearance of only one side is important. Sidings, soffits, fences, structural uses, boxcar and truck lining and farm buildings. Tanks, trays, commercial refrigerators.	A-C GROUP 2 EXTERIOR	A	C	C	1/4		3/8	1/2	5/8	3/4
B-B EXT-DFPA (4)	An outdoor utility panel with solid paintable faces.	B-B · G-1 · EXT-DFPA · PS 1-66	B	B	C	1/4		3/8	1/2	5/8	3/4
B-C EXT-DFPA (4)	An outdoor utility panel for farm service and work buildings, boxcar and truck lining, containers, tanks, agricultural equipment.	B-C GROUP 3 EXTERIOR	B	C	C	1/4		3/8	1/2	5/8	3/4
HDO EXT-DFPA (4)	Exterior type High Density Overlay plywood with hard, semi-opaque resin-fiber overlay. Abrasion resistant. Painting not ordinarily required. For concrete forms, cabinets, counter tops, signs and tanks.	HDO · A-A · G-1 · EXT-DFPA · PS 1-66	A or B	A or B	C plgd		5/16	3/8	1/2	5/8	3/4
MDO EXT-DFPA (4)	Exterior type Medium Density Overlay with smooth, opaque, resin-fiber overlay heat-fused to one or both panel faces. Ideal base for paint. Highly recommended for siding and other outdoor applications. Also good for built-ins, signs and displays.	MDO · B-B · G-2 · EXT-DFPA · PS 1-66	B	B or C	C (5)		5/16	3/8	1/2	5/8	3/4
303 SIDING EXT-DFPA (7)	Grade designation covers proprietary plywood products for exterior siding, fencing, etc., with special surface treatment such as V-groove, channel groove, striated, brushed, rough-sawn.	303 SIDING 16 o c GROUP 4 EXTERIOR	(6)	C	C			3/8	1/2	5/8	
T 1-11 EXT-DFPA	Exterior type, sanded or unsanded, shiplapped edges with parallel grooves 1/4" deep, 3/8" wide. Grooves 2" or 4" o.c. Available in 8' and 10' lengths and MD Overlay. For siding and accent paneling.	T 1-11 GROUP 1 EXTERIOR	C or btr.	C	C					5/8	
PLYRON EXT-DFPA	Exterior panel surfaced both sides with hardboard for use in exterior applications. Faces are tempered, smooth or screened.	PLYRON · EXT-DFPA			C				1/2	5/8	3/4
MARINE EXT-DFPA	Exterior type plywood made only with Douglas fir or Western larch. Special solid jointed core construction. Subject to special limitations on core gaps and number of face repairs. Ideal for boat hulls. Also available with overlaid faces.	MARINE · A-A · EXT-DFPA · PS 1-66	A or B	A or B	B	1/4		3/8	1/2	5/8	3/4

(1) Sanded both sides except where decorative or other surfaces specified.

(2) Available in Group 1, 2, 3, 4, or 5 unless otherwise noted.

(3) Standard 4x8 panel sizes, other sizes available.

(4) Also available in STRUCTURAL I (face, back and inner plys limited to Group 1 species).

(5) Or C-Plugged.

(6) C or better for 5 plys; C-Plugged or better for 3 ply panels.

(7) Stud spacing is shown on grade stamp.

By permission of the American Plywood Association.

and rigidity as shown in Table 5-14. These grades have been established to meet the needs of construction and industrial buyers.

TABLE 5-14 Plywood construction grades

GRADE	DESCRIPTION
Standard	Designed to meet all requirements for simple structural and industrial applications, including subflooring, roof sheathing, wall sheathing, and other interior uses.
Structural, Class I and Class II	Designed in two strengths to withstand stresses other than simple bending. Used for engineered diaphragms, box beams, stressed-skin panels, and applications where such factors as tension, compression, shear, and nail-holding properties are important. Grade and glue bonds are closely controlled.
C-C exterior	Manufactured to meet all of the requirements of exterior plywood.
B-B concrete-form panels Class I and Class II	Made in two bending strengths especially for concrete forms. The American Plywood Association's registered grade trademark for concrete-form panels is Plyform. Plyform is oiled at the mill and the edges are sealed.

Exterior, structural, and standard panels are identified with an index number that designates its performance rating. This index consists of two numbers; the first refers to the maximum recommended roof span in inches and the second the recommended span for structural flooring or subflooring. A panel identified as 48/24, for example, can be used as roof sheathing over rafters or beams spaced 48 in. on center and as flooring over studs spaced 24 in. on center.

Specialty Plywoods

There are also a number of plywood products on the market to serve special needs. In general, these products follow the grading rules of PS 1-66 as to the construction of the interior plies. Special surface patterns or coatings have been developed to create a textured surface, superior paint base, or weather-resistant qualities. The outer veneer of plywood intended for use as paneling may be brushed, etched, or sandblasted to expose harder portions of grain and create highlights. Plywood panels may be run through rollers or glued between patterned forms to create a textured or embossed surface. Striated or combed surfaces are produced by running the panels over shaped cutting blades. Parallel grooves $3/8$ in. deep, spaced 2 in. or 4 in. on center, are cut in the face of douglas fir plywood to simulate vertical planks. Plywood imitations of rough-sawed beveled siding have been developed as exterior siding or as accent panels for interior.

OVERLAID PLYWOOD Plywood may be coated with resin-impregnated paper or fibers. The coating is cured under heat and pressure and is bonded to the plywood panel to provide a dense surface that is impervious to water. Plywood panels so coated are called *overlaid* or *plastic-surface plywood*. Overlaid plywood may be medium density or high density. High-density overlaid plywood has a coating that is 40 percent resin; medium-density overlay is 20 percent resin. Medium-density overlaid

Fig. 5-16 Peeling a log for plywood. (*American Plywood Association.*)

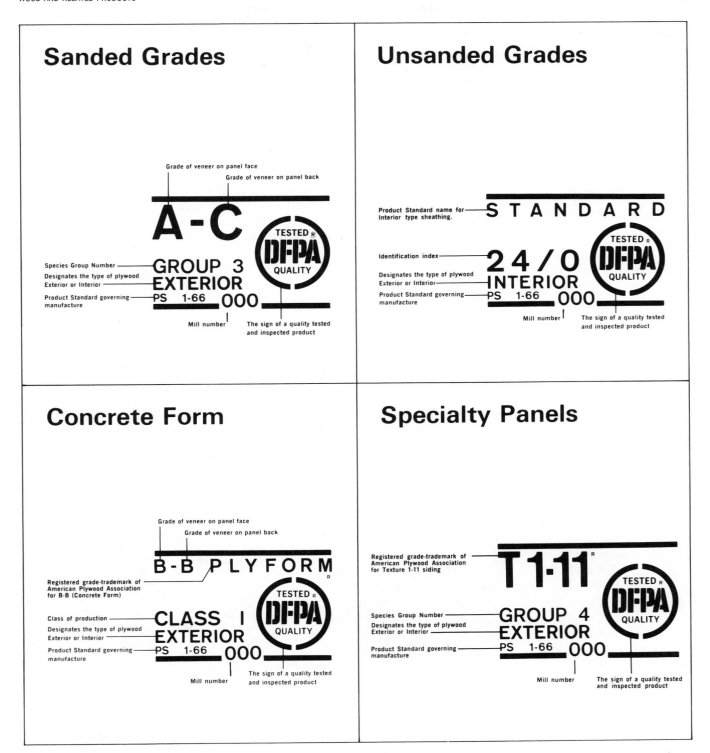

Fig. 5-17 Typical grade trademarks. (*American Plywood Association.*)

Grade-Use Guide for Concrete Forms*

Use these symbols when you specify plywood	Description	Typical Grade-trademarks	VENEER GRADE	
			Faces	Inner Plys
B-B Plyform Class I & Class II**	Specifically manufactured for concrete forms. Yields many reuses. Smooth, solid surfaces. Edge-sealed. Mill-oiled unless otherwise specified.	B-B PLYFORM CLASS I (DFPA) EXTERIOR	B	C
HDO Plyform Class I & Class II**	Hard, semi-opaque resin-fiber overlay, heat-fused to panel faces. Smooth surface resists abrasion. Yields up to 200 reuses. Edge-sealed. Light oiling recommended after each pour.		B	C Plugged
Structural I Plyform	Especially designed for engineered applications. Contains all Group I species. Stronger and stiffer than Plyform Class I and II. Especially recommended for high pressures where face grain is parallel to supports. Also available with HD Overlay.	STRUCTURAL I B-B PLYFORM CLASS I (DFPA) EXTERIOR	B	C or "C" Plugged
Special Overlays, proprietary panels and MDO plywood specifically designed for concrete forming.**	Panels produce a smooth uniform concrete surface. Generally mill treated with form release agent. Check with manufacturer for design specifications, proper use, and surface treatment recommendations for greatest number of reuses.			

*Commonly available in 5/8" and 3/4" panel thicknesses (4' x 8' size).

**Check dealer for availability in your area.

Fig. 5-18 Plywood grade-use guide for concrete forms. (*American Plywood Association.*)

Fig. 5-19 Textured plywood paneling. (*American Plywood Association.*)

plywood is an exterior plywood with the resin-impregnated fiber added to one or both faces of the panel. The hard, impervious surface makes an excellent, smooth base for painted finishes. High-density overlaid plywood is an exterior plywood, coated on two sides, that is highly resistant to abrasion. High-density overlaid plywood shows a slight grain pattern.

PARTICLE-BOARD AND LUMBER CORES Plywood panels are also made with solid rather than veneer cores. Plywood that has a core of solid wood and two veneer faces is called *lumber core* or *solid core*. Lumber-core panels are used where warpage is a factor, as in cabinet doors. Pressed wood-fiber or wood-flake cores, termed *particle-board cores*, are widely used in softwood and hardwood panels. These panels are exceptionally warp free and have a dimensional stability that make them valuable for sliding and hinged cabinet doors.

Plywood Structural Members

The use of plywood extends far beyond the traditional floor, wall, and roof sheathing. *Shear panels* of plywood are effective in resisting lateral forces developed by wind and earthquakes. When plywood sheathing is applied over wood studs, diagonal braces are unnecessary. Even a small

Fig. 5-20 Plywood cores.

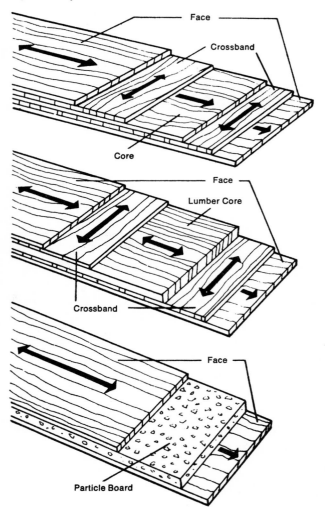

plywood shear wall adds considerable strength to a building. Plywood 1⅛ in. thick with tongue-and-groove edges has been developed for use as a structural flooring material that will span up to 4′-0″ in a residential floor. This system is called T&G 2·4·1 by the American Plywood Association.

PLYWOOD BOX BEAMS   Box beams are an assembly of plywood and solid lumber that develops the greatest potential of each of the materials. They consist of solid-wood members on the top and bottom to resist the bending moment of the load put on the beam, held apart by two or more webs of plywood. Stiffeners are placed at intervals along the beam to prevent the plywood from buckling. Lightweight douglas fir box beams can be designed to span up to 120 ft.

Box beams may be nailed, screwed, or bolted together; however, gluing is considered the most satisfactory method. Box beams can be made up on the job site or fabricated at a plant. In the plant such important factors as moisture content, temperature, and the application of glue can be closely controlled.

STRESSED-SKIN PANELS   Stressed-skin panels are similar to box beams, except that the upper and lower compression and tension members are plywood, held apart by solid-wood webs. They are usually factory made and custom manufactured for each job.

The bottom sheet of plywood of a stressed-skin panel must be strong enough to resist the tension developed

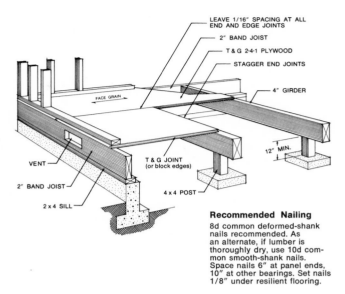

Recommended Nailing

8d common deformed-shank nails recommended. As an alternate, if lumber is thoroughly dry, use 10d common smooth-shank nails. Space nails 6″ at panel ends, 10″ at other bearings. Set nails 1/8″ under resilient flooring.

Fig. 5-22   2•4•1 plywood with joists 48 in. on center.

when loads are applied. The upper sheet of plywood must withstand the compression exerted when the panel is loaded and must also support the loads between the interior web members. The glued joints must therefore be sound to resist the shearing action which takes place when the panel deflects.

Fig. 5-21 Installing tongue-and-groove (T&G) 2•4•1 douglas fir plywood structural floor. (*American Plywood Association.*)

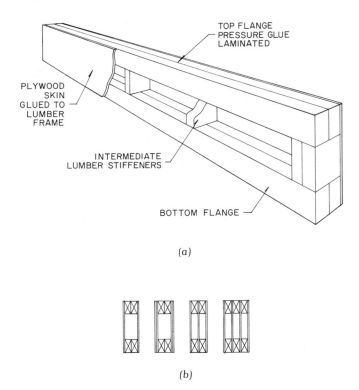

(a)

(b)

Fig. 5-23 Plywood box beams; (a) typical beams; (b) typical cross sections.

Flat stressed-skin panels are best suited for spans of 12 to 24 ft, although longer spans are feasible under special conditions. They are particularly effective as components in a folded-plate roof. Curved panels can be used to span large areas as part of a multiple-barrel-vault roof.

HARDWOOD PLYWOOD

The term *hardwood plywood* denotes a wide range of products, from plywood in which all plies are hardwood veneer to plywood with hardwood outer layers and a core of softwood veneer, lumber, or particleboard.

Many expensive and rare hardwoods have color, figure, or grain characteristics that make them highly prized for paneling and cabinetwork. Modern methods of peeling or slicing thin veneers from rare and exotic woods have made it possible to use these woods in moderately priced construction. Imported hardwood plywood accounts for over 60 percent of the American market.

Types of Veneer Cuts

The manner in which veneers are cut from the log is important in producing the varied effects seen in hardwood plywood. Two pieces of veneer cut from the same log may look entirely different. Some woods are best cut by centering the log on a large lathe and revolving it against a

razor-sharp knife. Such *rotary-cut veneer* can be produced in extremely long and wide sheets. This type of cutting, which generally follows the annular rings, results in a veneer with a bold, variegated grain.

The log may be *plain sliced,* or *flat sliced.* A half-log, or *flitch,* is mounted against a guide, and parallel slices are made through it, producing plain-sliced veneers. If a log is quartered and then sliced perpendicular to its outside perimeter, the veneer is said to be *quarter-sliced.* This process produces veneer showing a fairly even pattern of thin stripes. If a log is mounted off center in a lathe and revolved against a knife, sections of veneer will show modified annular growth rings. This is called *half-round*

Fig. 5-24 Stressed-skin panels: (a) flat panel connections; (b) plywood vault construction.

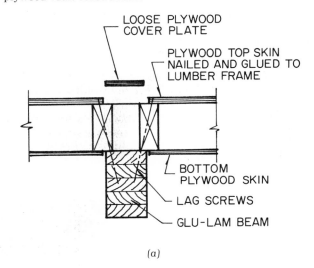

(a)

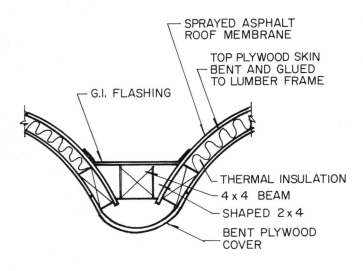

(b)

slicing. If the half-log is reversed in the lathe, so that the bark portion is in the center, rotary slicing will produce veneer with an enhanced striped figure and some sapwood. This is called *back-cut veneer*.

Various species of oak are *rift cut* to expose the medullary rays and produce a combed effect of pin stripes. Rift-cut oak is cut from quarter sections of log mounted off center in a lathe and revolved against a knife. Cuts from the intersection of two large limbs, or from *burls*, or protuberances from the trunk, or from the roots of a tree, will produce beautiful and varied veneers.

Plywood Types and Sizes

Hardwood plywoods are divided into three grades as shown in Table 5-15, based on the type of glue used and the resistance to moisture. Veneer-core panels are preferable where bending or molding are required, or for exterior applications. Lumber-core construction, although it is expensive, is preferable where freedom from warping is essential. Individual strips of lumber are so placed in the core that the tendency of the panel to warp is minimized.

Lumber-core panels are also preferred for some installations because the lumber edges can be shaped and finished to match the veneer faces without filling. Where butt hinges are to be used, as in cabinet doors, the lumber core affords better holding power than a veneer core.

Standard panels range from 2 to 4 ft in width and 3 to 12 ft in length. Matched panels, with scarfed joints, can be obtained in almost any length or width on special order. Thicknesses of veneer-core hardwood panels are shown in Table 5-16; however, the number of plies for a given thickness may vary with the wood, the cut, and the mill. Standards and appearance grades, adopted by the Hardwood Plywood Institute and included in the "U.S. Commercial Standard for Hardwood," CS 35-61, are shown in Table 5-17.

Veneer Matching

The matching of individual panels of hardwood can alter the appearance of a finished installation as much as the

TABLE 5-15 Hardwood plywood types

TYPE	USE
I	Constructed with waterproof glue to withstand full weather exposure and constant wetting and drying cycles
II	Weather resistant and will withstand occasional thorough wetting and drying
III	Suitable for applications not to be subjected to water, moisture, or high humidity

TABLE 5-16 Hardwood plywood thicknesses

THICKNESS, IN.	CONSTRUCTION
$1/8$	3 ply
$3/16$	3 ply
$1/4$	3 ply
$5/16$	3 ply
$3/8$	5 ply
$1/2$	5 ply
$5/8$	5 ply and 7 ply
$3/4$	5 ply, 7 ply, and 9 ply

Fig. 5-25 Barrel-vault roof on St. Paul's Lutheran Church, Monrovia, California, architects Smith and Williams.

different methods of cutting veneers from a log. For special installations the veneer cut or sliced from a single log or flitch may be specified by the designer. As the thin pieces of veneer are cut from the log, they are kept in sequence and are then joined consecutively by means of a *tapeless splicer*, which glues the edges together in whatever pattern is desired.

Several standard types of veneer matching are used for stock panels. The panels may be *random matched, slip matched*, or *center matched*. Not all of these patterns will be available from all manufacturers. Numbered sets of panels marked to indicate flitch, panel number, and number of panels in a flitch are available on special order. The type of matching and preparation of the paneling must be worked out between the designer and the manufacturer.

Prefinished Panels

Hardwood plywood is available factory finished for use as wall paneling, often with V-jointed grooves to simulate wood planking. This pre-stained and lacquered paneling enables the buyer to visualize how the installed product will look. Prefinished plywood paneling is simple to install. However, it is not always possible to obtain solid hardwood stock or trim to match it.

PRESSED BOARDS

Pressed boards may be composed of any vegetable, mineral, or synthetic fiber mixed with a binder and pressed into a flat sheet. They are widely used in the construction industry as insulation, sheathing, and finish panels. Pressed boards may be soft-textured panels of loosely held fibers which have little strength but excellent insulating and acoustical properties. Other types of boards are pressed into dense sheets that are impervious to water or are of fireproof construction.

Fiberboard

CANE-FIBER BOARD Cane-fiber board is made from the fiber *bagasse*, obtained from the stalks of sugar cane. Cane-fiber board such as Celotex (produced by the Celotex Corporation), given a factory finish, is widely used as bulletin boards or tack boards. It is also used as rigid insulation for walls and roofs, and for its sound-deadening qualities inside doors. Cane fiber, which is a springy, sawtoothed material, makes an excellent insulating product; however, this type of board will not withstand moisture. In order to increase its water resistance, the board is asphalt impregnated. This asphalt-impregnated board is used for roof insulation or in locations where moisture is a factor.

Fig. 5-26 Flat slicing on a veneer slicer. (*Hardwood Plywood Manufacturers' Association.*)

Fig. 5-27 Half-round slicing on a veneer lathe. (*Hardwood Plywood Manufacturers' Association.*)

TABLE 5-17 Grade standards for hardwood plywood faces and backs

GRADE	DESCRIPTION
Custom	Selected veneers or matched-grain panels for special effects, as agreed upon by the customer.
1. Good	The highest standard quality, suitable for natural finish, with matched joints to avoid sharp variations in color and grain characteristics. Panels may have some small, inconspicuous, well-made patches, but no defects or knots other than pin knots.
2. Sound	Suitable for painted surfaces. Tight knot patches are allowed but no open defects, discoloration, rough-cut veneer, or sander skips.
3. Utility	Panels may have open defects, such as ³⁄₄-in. knotholes, splits, and open joints of a certain size, and small areas of rough grain, but no decay.
4. Backing	No selection of grain or color. Panels may have knotholes up to 2 in., splits up to 1 in. wide, and other defects that do not impair over-all strength or serviceability.

MINERAL-FIBER BOARD This insulating board, similar in appearance and use to cane-fiber board, is manufactured of asbestos fibers or rock wool. These mineral fibers, combined with a suitable binder, form boards that are rated as incombustible. Mineral-fiber board is not recommended where moisture is likely to be present.

Fig. 5-28 Samples of hardwood plywood: (*a*) American walnut, quartered-sliced; (*b*) American walnut, sliced-figured; (*c*) American walnut, figured; (*d*) American walnut, stumpwood; (*e*) claro (California) walnut. (*Hardwood Plywood Manufacturers' Association.*)

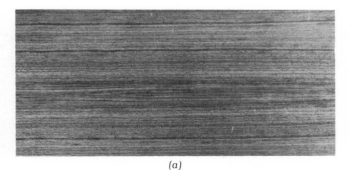

(*a*)

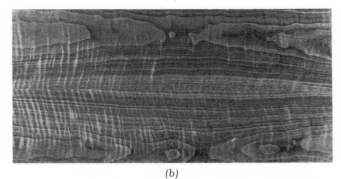

(*b*)

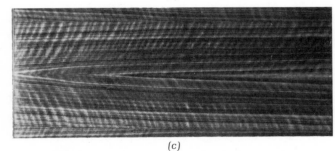

(*c*)

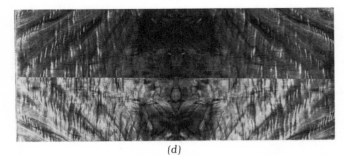

(*d*)

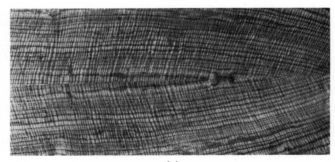

(*e*)

RANDOM MATCH

VENEERS CAREFULLY MIS-
MATCHED; COLOR SELECTED
FOR MOST EFFECTIVE
APPEARANCE

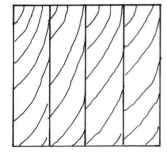

SLIP MATCH

VENEER JOINED SIDE BY
SIDE WITHOUT TURNING
FLITCH

BOOK MATCH

EVERY OTHER SHEET IS
TURNED OVER

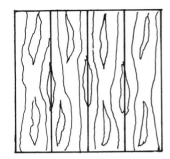

CENTER MATCH

EQUAL NUMBER OF PANELS;
VENEER JOINT ON CENTER
LINE OF PANEL

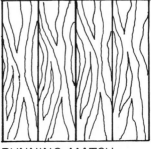

RUNNING MATCH

VENEERS ARE LAID UP IN
NUMBERED SEQUENCE

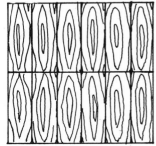

VERTICAL BUTT MATCH

USED WHERE CEILING
HEIGHT EXCEEDS FLITCH
LENGTH

Fig. 5-29 Basic veneer and panel matching.

GLASS-FIBER BOARD   Glass fibers mixed with a binder, placed between layers of kraft paper, and pressed into boards form a rigid insulating board. However, this board cannot be used in locations where it is subject to loads, such as roofs that will be walked on. Foam-glass board (produced by Pittsburgh-Corning), an insulation board of glass that has been foamed or aerated, also forms an efficient insulation. This board is covered with laminated sheets of kraft paper. It is strong and is not damaged by moisture.

PARTICLEBOARD   Panels made of wood fibers bonded with urea-type resins and pressed under high temperatures are classed as *particleboard*. The small particles or chips are positioned in a criss-cross arrangement to form a board that has equal strength in any direction. Its smoothness, outstanding uniformity in thickness, and dimensional stability make it an ideal backing material for plastic laminates and veneer. It may be used for cabinetwork and given a natural or a painted finish. Some types of particleboard have larger wood flakes on the surface, with the inner portion made up of smaller wood chips. Others have a fine-grained outer surface and an inner core of course flakes.

HARDBOARD   Hardboard panels are made of wood chips that have been exploded, leaving cellulose fibers and lignin. These are fused under heat and pressure into hard, durable boards which are available in a variety of finishes and thicknesses. Products such as Masonite (produced by Masonite Corporation) are manufactured in thicknesses of $\frac{1}{10}''$ to $\frac{5}{16}''$, with one smooth side and a screen pattern on the back or smooth on both sides.

Standard types of hardboard are suitable for interior uses, but for locations exposed to weather or moisture, *tempered hardboard* is recommended. Tempered hardboard has been given a coating of oils and resin and then baked. This produces a dark-brown board that is stronger, denser, and considerably more durable than standard hardboard. It is, however, stiffer and more brittle.

Hardboard can be obtained with special acid-resistant finishes or finishes for exterior siding in a number of patterns. A wide variety of hardboard panels have been developed for use as paneling and furniture. Several manufacturers offer a choice of prefinished wood-grained panels reproducing tones and patterns of fine woods. Other panels are embossed in striated or burlap textures. Perforated hardboard, called Pegboard by one manufacturer, may be used in garages, storage areas, and workshops to hang tools and other equipment on specially made hooks which fit into the perforations.

Asbestos-cement Board

Asbestos fibers are combined with portland cement to form asbestos-cement sheets or boards. Wood or cane fiber is sometimes added to the sheet to promote resiliency and ease of working. Asbestos-cement boards are strong, fire-resistant, stone-grey boards which are impervious to decay and insects. They can be obtained in thicknesses of $\frac{1}{8}''$ to $\frac{1}{2}''$. Depending on the type, they may be 2' to 4' wide and 4' to 12' long. There are four types of cement asbestos board, as shown in Table 5-18.

Asbestos-cement board is produced in many finishes and colors. Mineral pigments may be added to the mixture of portland cement and asbestos fibers to produce integrally colored sheets. Baked-enamel finishes may be applied to the surface to produce colorful panels for inte-

TABLE 5-18 Types of asbestos-cement board

TYPE	DESCRIPTION
I	Utility flat sheets suitable for general construction purposes. Panels are easy to cut and bend and need not be drilled for nailing in thicknesses of $1/4''$ or less.
II	Rigid, high-strength sheets suitable for interior and exterior applications where high density and a glossy finish are needed. Panels must be drilled for fastening.
III	Flexible, high-strength sheets suitable for interior and exterior applications where a smooth surface is desirable. Panels can be bent to fit curved walls or ceilings and need not be drilled for nailing.
Corrugated	Standard and lightweight types from $3/16''$ to $3/8''$ thick, originally designed for factory roofs and side walls and now used as decorative wall panels in many types of buildings.

rior or exterior use. Textured or patterned surfaces may be produced by pressure rolling as the material is formed. Special sizes and textures are produced for use as siding and roofing material.

COMPOSITE BOARDS

The use of laminated panels has greatly increased as architects have taken advantage of their durability, ease of maintenance, and economy. Such panels range from the plastic-laminated counters and drainboards used in kitchens to sandwich panels that form a finished interior and exterior, with all necessary insulation between.

Plastic Laminates

Plastic laminates are widely used in residential construction. Most of these materials, manufactured under such various trade names as Formica, Micarta, Panelyte, and Wilson Art, are *high-pressure laminates*, cured at pressures not less than 1000 psi. These high-pressure laminates comply with standards set by the National Electrical Manufacturers Association (NEMA).

The plastic laminates most widely used in architectural construction consist of several layers of kraft paper impregnated with phenolic or melamine resins, a layer of translucent colored or printed paper, and a final finish layer of paper treated with a melamine resin. The layers of melamine-impregnated kraft paper are laid up, the pattern or color sheet is placed on top, and the entire sandwich is placed in a press and subjected to a heat of over 300°F for approximately an hour. The finish of the sheet can be made glossy by including a polished stainless-steel plate in the press. The final product is a thin, flexible sheet from $1/32''$ to $1/16''$ thick which is then applied to plywood or other materials with adhesives. Many types of plastic laminate can be formed into sharp curves or molded into special shapes. Plastic laminates provide tough surfaces that will withstand boiling water and temperatures up to 275°F, although they can be damaged by misuse.

Many manufacturers will produce custom-designed plastic-laminate sheets or panels to order. Such panels may include patterns, trademarks, or decorative murals. Special compositions have been developed that increase the resistance to fire and the spread of flame.

Plastic laminates are surface materials only. They must be bonded to a base material, such as plywood, particle board, or hardboard. The resistance of the surfacing material to impact and other damage, as well as the smoothness

Fig. 5-30 Portion of a building covered with corrugated asbestos-cement board. (*Philip Carey Company.*)

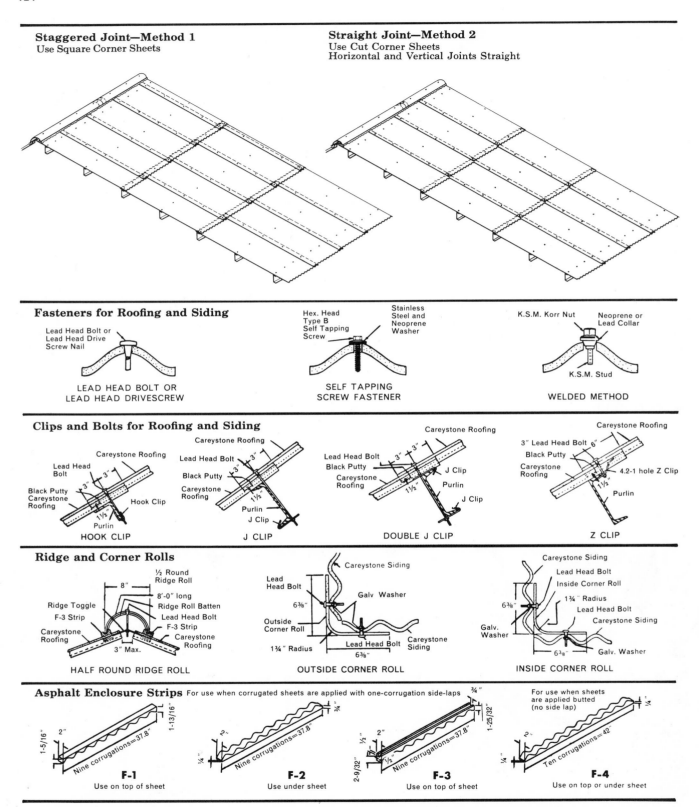

Fig. 5-31 Methods of attaching corrugated asbestos-cement board. (*Philip Carey Company.*)

of surface, depends to a great extent on the base to which it is bonded, the adhesives used, and the fabrication methods. Some types of laminates can be bent cold into a fairly small arc. Others require the application of heat. Phenolic and melamine plastics are thermosetting. A *thermosetting plastic* is one that undergoes a chemical change and hardens permanently when it is heated. Most manufacturers produce a special grade of plastic laminate called *postforming grade*, which can be bent to a ¾-in. arc through the use of heat (315 to 325°F).

The plastic-laminate tops used in typical residential construction are usually fabricated in shops that specialize in this type of work. They are delivered to the job site bonded to ¾″ plywood, ready for installation. The characteristics of each manufacturer's plastic laminates are different; hence the manufacturer's instructions regarding a particular application, the method of forming, and the recommended adhesives should be followed carefully.

Sandwich Panels

Panels consisting of an impregnated insulating board core faced with hard, smooth-surfaced asbestos-cement sheets can be used to form curtain walls in small buildings. They have a high insulating value and provide finished surfaces for both interiors and exteriors. Several types of prefabricated roof-deck panels are made of layers of different kinds of material laminated together as a structural unit. The top layer may be pressed vegetable or wood fibers impregnated with asphalt, which forms a base for the exterior roofing. A center layer consisting of low-density board forms an efficient insulator, and the bottom layer may be standard fiberboard with an interior finish. Thus the entire sandwich serves as everything from the roofing base to the finished ceiling.

WOOD FASTENERS

A wide variety of fastenings have been developed for joining wood. The oldest known form of fastening was the peg, or trunnel. Wooden dowels are still used in custom work. However, they are time consuming and expensive.

Nails

Hand-wrought nails were used by the ancient Egyptians, but the most significant advance in nail making came about in the late nineteenth century when a *wire-nail* machine was developed in France. Since that time hundreds of different types and sizes of nails have been developed.

The length of nails is designated in *pennies*, abbreviated as "d." This designation is an old English term which may originally have designated the number of nails that could be bought for a penny. The diameter of the shank and the size of the head vary with the length of the nail and the type of nail. The three basic types, from the smallest diameter to the largest, *box nails, common nails,* and *spikes.*

(a)

(b)

(c)

Fig. 5-32 Manufacturing plastic-laminate sheets: (a) laying up melamine impregnated layers; (b) sandwich ready for laminating; (c) laminating plastic coating in the hot press. (*Ralph Wilson Plastics Company.*)

Nails may have normal flat heads for use in general construction or large flat heads where extra gripping power is necessary, as with roofing and plasterboard. Nails for finish, which are to be *countersunk*, or driven below the surface, have small spherical or conical heads.

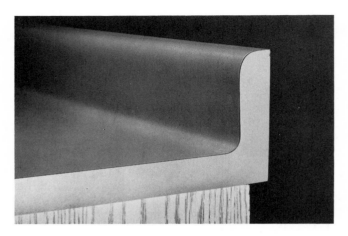

Fig. 5-33 Installation of a high-pressure-laminate countertop with integrally molded corners. (*Ralph Wilson Plastics Company.*)

Double-headed nails have been developed for temporary work. Round heads, oval heads, square heads, offset heads, and many others are available for special applications.

Most nails are made of cold-drawn wire with a bright, smooth finish and are covered with a thin film of lubricating oil. Tacks, plasterboard nails, and roofing nails are *blued* by a process of heating and sterilizing so that they can be held in the mouth. Certain applications re-

quire nails that will resist rust and will not stain the surrounding material. Such nails are made of copper, zinc, brass, aluminum, and stainless steel. Coatings of cement, zinc, copper, cadmium, tin, and brass may be applied to steel-shanked nails.

Several special types of nails have been developed with increased holding power, to overcome their tendency to work their way out of the wood. This is called *nail pop*. Surfaces may be roughened by chemical etching, coatings of cement, barbs, and circular or spiral grooves cut or formed into the shank.

Staples

The development of hand- and machine-powered stapling devices has led to wide use of staples of many types and sizes. In some applications an unskilled workman can drive 200 such fastenings per minute. Plaster lath, insulating materials, hardboard, plywood, ceiling tiles, and many other products are installed with stapling guns.

Powder-set Fasteners

Hardened-steel nails have been developed for attaching wood and other materials to concrete masonry and steel. These hardened-steel pins are designed to fit into a specially constructed gun that fires them into the material. These fastenings are termed *powder set*. This type of

Fig. 5-34 Building covered with structural insulating panels, $1/8''$ asbestos-cement board bonded to both sides of asphalt-treated insulation board. (*Philip Carey Company.*)

Fig. 5-35 Methods of attaching insulated structural panels. (*Philip Carey Company.*)

Wall Framing Application Details

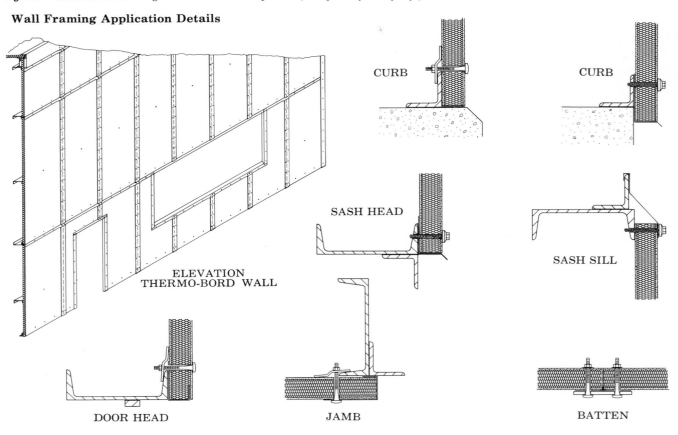

ELEVATION
THERMO-BORD WALL

CURB

CURB

SASH HEAD

SASH SILL

DOOR HEAD

JAMB

BATTEN

Application in Curtain Walls—Aluminum Exterior Batten & Mullion

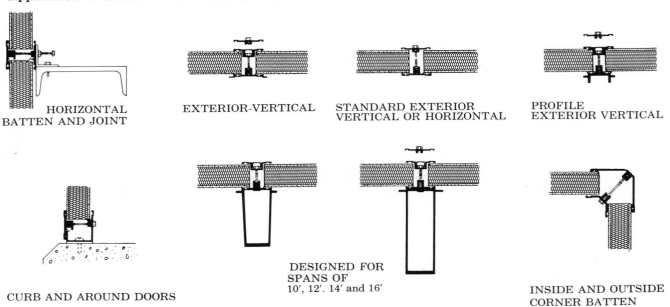

HORIZONTAL
BATTEN AND JOINT

EXTERIOR-VERTICAL

STANDARD EXTERIOR
VERTICAL OR HORIZONTAL

PROFILE
EXTERIOR VERTICAL

CURB AND AROUND DOORS

DESIGNED FOR
SPANS OF
10′, 12′. 14′ and 16′

EXTERIOR VERTICAL MULLIONS

INSIDE AND OUTSIDE
CORNER BATTEN

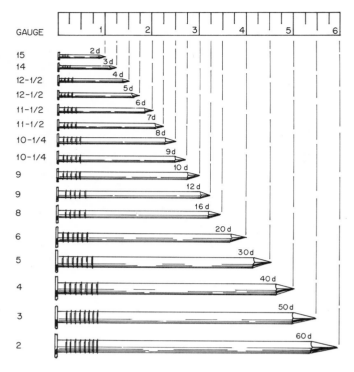

Fig. 5-36 Size of common nails. The gauge is adapted from the American Wire Gauge.

Fig. 5-37 Nail types.

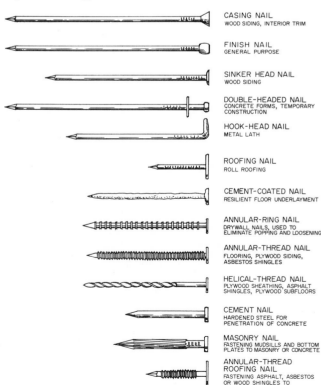

CASING NAIL
WOOD SIDING, INTERIOR TRIM

FINISH NAIL
GENERAL PURPOSE

SINKER HEAD NAIL
WOOD SIDING

DOUBLE-HEADED NAIL
CONCRETE FORMS, TEMPORARY
CONSTRUCTION

HOOK-HEAD NAIL
METAL LATH

ROOFING NAIL
ROLL ROOFING

CEMENT-COATED NAIL
RESILIENT FLOOR UNDERLAYMENT

ANNULAR-RING NAIL
DRYWALL NAILS, USED TO
ELIMINATE POPPING AND LOOSENING

ANNULAR-THREAD NAIL
FLOORING, PLYWOOD SIDING,
ASBESTOS SHINGLES

HELICAL-THREAD NAIL
PLYWOOD SHEATHING, ASPHALT
SHINGLES, PLYWOOD SUBFLOORS

CEMENT NAIL
HARDENED STEEL FOR
PENETRATION OF CONCRETE

MASONRY NAIL
FASTENING MUDSILLS AND BOTTOM
PLATES TO MASONRY OR CONCRETE

ANNULAR-THREAD
ROOFING NAIL
FASTENING ASPHALT, ASBESTOS
OR WOOD SHINGLES TO
PLYWOOD SHEATHING

fastener is widely used in setting wood sills or plates on concrete slabs and for similar installations. Powder-set fasteners can be driven into steel for future attachment of wood framing members. They must be used with care, however. It is possible to shoot a fastener completely through a backing material.

Screws and Bolts

Wood may be attached to concrete or masonry with bolt *anchors* and *expanding shields*. A hole is drilled into the concrete, and a hollow or split shield is placed in the hole. The inside of the shield is threaded so it will expand and grip the side of the hole to form a solid anchor for the installation of other materials. *Toggle bolts* have been developed primarily for attaching various materials to plastered walls. These bolts are equipped with winged devices that fall or spring into place to bear on the back of the plasterboard. In this way material can be attached to a plaster wall where there is no backing or stud.

Wood screws are made with various types of heads and threads. The most common types used in woodwork are the flat-head, round-head, and oval-head screws. They may be made of steel or brass or with special platings, depending on their use. The length of wood screws is measured in inches and fractions of an inch. The diameter of the shank is designated by wire gauge. The larger the gauge number, the larger the diameter. A No. 0 wood screw is 0.06 in. in diameter and a No. 24 wood screw is 0.372 in. in diameter. *Lag screws* or *lag bolts* are large wood screws with square heads, used for connecting heavy wood framing members.

Bolts are used to fasten wood sills to a concrete foundation and to make other connections in heavy timber framing. Square-headed bolts and square nuts are the most commonly used. Special bolts are manufactured with L-shaped ends for use as foundation bolts. The bent end forms a better bond with the concrete in the foundation than a small square head. Bolts are manufactured from 1/4" to 1 1/4" in diameter and from 3/4" to 30" long.

Rings and Clamping Plates

To increase the strength of joints in heavy timber construction, particularly in the construction of wood trusses, the *split ring* has been widely used. This is a steel ring, either 2" or 4" in diameter, that is fitted into precut circular grooves made by a special power-driven tool. The ring is inserted in matching grooves between two pieces of timber, and the two pieces are held together by a bolt through the center of the ring. *Clamping plates* and *spike grids* are steel-toothed plates that are placed between two timbers of a bolted joint in heavy-timber construction.

Framing Anchors and Joist Hangers

Metal fittings have been developed for use in wood framing. These metal fittings, sometimes called *clips*, help to eliminate the problems of toenailing abutting

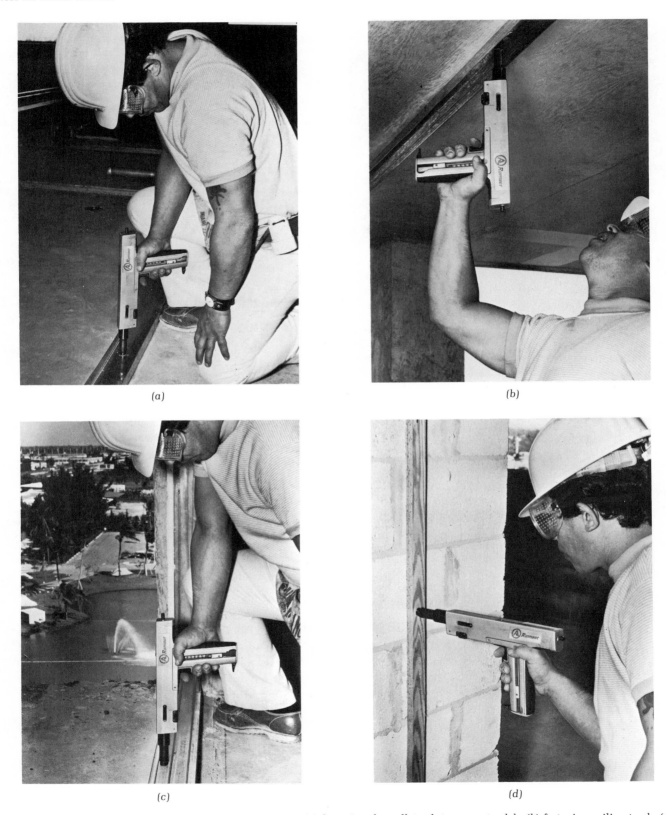

Fig. 5-38 Use of nail gun for anchoring interior partitions: (a) fastening drywall track to concrete slab; (b) fastening ceiling track; (c) fastening sliding-door track; (d) fastening furring strips to concrete-block wall. (*Ramset Fastening Systems.*)

Fig. 5-39 Assembling a wood truss with split rings. (*Timber Engineering Company.*)

wood framing members, and provide a stronger joint. One type of fitting consists of a specially shaped and bent 18-gauge steel plate used where joists butt into a header or beam. The plate has prepunched holes for nails. Specially shaped light-gauge steel plates have been developed for connecting wood beams to the top of wood posts.

QUESTIONS

1. Explain the difference between hardwoods and softwoods.

2. Explain the following terms: cross grain, intergrown knot, encased knot, spike knot, pitch pocket, dote, stain, wane, shake, cup.

3. What causes decay of wood fibers?

4. What is the reason for seasoning wood?

5. Why is some lumber kiln dried?

6. What are the actual finished sizes of a 2 × 4, a 3 × 3, a 4 × 4, a 4 × 6, and a 4 × 12?

7. Who establishes lumber grades, and why are they used?

8. Explain the differences in hardwood and softwood grades.

9. Who is responsible for the grade marking of lumber?

10. What is treated lumber, and where would it be used?

11. Describe the process of fabrication used in constructing glued-laminated beams.

12. What grade of douglas fir plywood would you specify for each of the following uses? Cabinet doors, cabinet sides, fences, concrete forms, structural sheathing, underlayment under resilient flooring.

13. What are the differences between exterior and interior plywood?

14. What is medium-density overlaid plywood, and where is it used?

15. Describe three types of cores used in the manufacture of plywood.

16. Describe five veneer appearance grades of softwood plywood.

17. How are hardwood veneers removed from a log?

18. What are the properties of a high-pressure laminate?

19. What are the advantages of pressed board over solid lumber or plywood?

20. Compare the qualities and uses of cane-fiber board, mineral-fiber board, wood-fiber board, and cement-asbestos board.

21. Describe the construction and use of sandwich panels.

22. Describe three uses of asbestos-cement board.

23. What types of finishes are usually available on asbestos board?

24. Describe a stressed-skin panel.

25. What are some of the advantages of a box beam?

26. What type of nail would you use to apply plywood underlayment for vinyl tile? Why?

27. Describe powder-set fasteners.

28. Of two screws the same length, which is the largest, a No. 6 or a No. 10 wood screw?

29. Describe an anchor bolt to be set in a foundation wall.

30. Where would a double-headed nail be used?

REFERENCES FOR FURTHER STUDY

American Wood Preservers Institute: 1651 Old Meadow Road, McClean, Va., 22101. *Wood Preserving*, a monthly publication.

Dana-Deck and Laminates, Inc.: Rogue River, Ore., 97537. "Dana's Lumber Dictionary and Handbook," 1967.

National Bureau of Standards: Washington, D.C. "Lumber: American Lumber Standards for Softwood Lumber," R16.

National Lumber Manufacturers' Association: 1619 Massachusetts Avenue, N.W., Washington, D.C., 20036, "Lumber and Wood Products Literature: A Listing of Technical and Non-technical Literature on Wood Technology and Products," 1970.

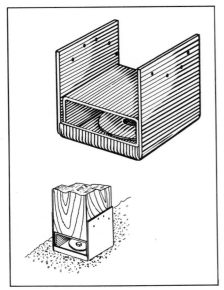

(a) TECO Post Anchor

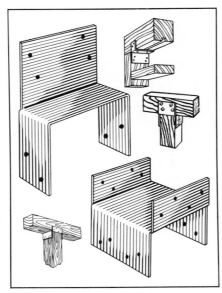

(b) TECO Post Caps (2 types)

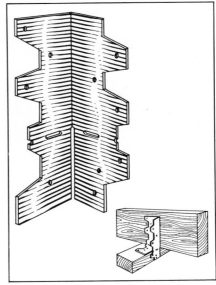

(c) TECO All Purpose Framing Anchor

(d) TECO Trip-L-Grip Framing Anchor

(e) TECO Ty-Down Rafter Anchors

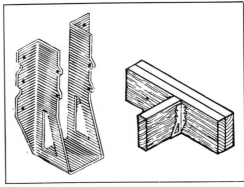

(f) TECO U-Grip Joist Hangers

Fig. 5-40   Typical framing anchors. (*Timber Engineering Company.*)

Fig. 5-41 Framing anchors in place.

Timber Engineering Company: 1619 Massachusetts Avenue, N.W., Washington, D.C., 20036. "Timber Design and Construction Handbook," 1956.

U.S. Forest Service: Forest Products Laboratory, Washington, D.C. "Wood Handbook."

Western Pine Association: 510 Yeon Building, Portland, Ore., 97204. "Lumber Technical Manual," 1966. "From the Woods," 1965.

Western Wood Products Association: Yeon Building, Portland, Ore., 97204. "West Coast Hemlock," 1956. "Grading and Dressing Rules 15." "National Design Specifications for Stress Grade Lumber and Its Fastenings." "Heavy Timber Construction Details." "Western Red Cedar Lumber." "Douglas Fir Use Book."

IRON

Metals are traditionally classified as ferrous and non-ferrous. The term *ferrous*, derived from the Latin word *ferrum*, meaning iron, refers to those metals which contain a large percentage of iron (Fe). Two or more metals combined in molten form into a substance which has metallic qualities is an *alloy*. Alloys may be classed as ferrous or nonferrous, depending on the percentage of iron they contain. The ferrous metals important in construction include cast iron, wrought iron, and steel, which is an iron alloy.

Metallic iron, which was probably used before 4000 B.C., has had more influence on civilization than any other material. Relatively pure metallic iron, containing some nickel, was broken off fallen meteorites and was first used in its natural form. Iron knife blades found in ancient tombs dating back to 3000 B.C. indicate that the Assyrians, Babylonians, and Greeks had learned to separate iron from ore and forge it into useful tools.

The first forged iron was probably produced in open limestone fire pits. Ore, mixed with charcoal, was added to the fire, and the limestone acted as a *flux* to promote fusion of metals or minerals. As the ore, mixed with impurities, melted, it flowed to the bottom of the pit, where it formed a spongy mass. This spongy mass was then removed from the fire and hammered into shape. The use of iron, for the most part, was confined to the manufacture of weapons, armor, and small tools.

The flow of civilization, the migration of peoples, and the development of new cultures were greatly affected by iron. Invading armies equipped with iron weapons and armor defeated and destroyed established civilizations which had only copper, brass, or bronze weapons. The Greeks and Romans made wide use of iron and steel from 1000 B.C. to 300 A.D. During the Dark Ages, from 300 A.D. to 1300 A.D., much of the knowledge of how to produce quality iron and steel was lost to the Western world. While steel was still produced in the Far East and by civilizations to the north of the Arabian desert, the Western world reverted to the open fire pit and iron of an earlier era.

Use of the blast furnace to melt iron and reduce the ore

to cast iron dates from about 1440. The first known cast-iron cannon was made in 1509. From that time on a series of technical developments increased the production and quality of iron. Steel was made from wrought iron, and in limited quantities from pig iron. The age of steel was ushered in with the development of the bessemer converter in 1856.

Properties of Iron

Iron is one of the most abundant metals in the earth's crust. About 5 percent of the earth's crust is iron. Pure metallic iron contains not over 0.025 percent carbon. This tough, silvery-white metal is as *ductile*, or capable of being drawn out, and as *malleable*, or capable of being hammered or rolled to shape, as copper. It is easy to work, can be readily magnetized, oxidizes (rusts) rapidly in air, and is destroyed by most acids. The purest commercial iron is in powdered form and is 99.965 percent pure. Most commercial metallic iron contains carbon, manganese, silicon, phosphorus, and sulfur. Minute percentages of these and other substances are combined with iron to produce commercially usable iron alloys and many types of steels. The differences in appearance, strength, brittleness, and workability of various irons depend to a great extent on the percentage of carbon alloyed with the pure iron.

Irons that contain less than 0.1 percent carbon are usually referred to as wrought iron. Those that contain 2 to 4 percent carbon are referred to as pig iron or cast iron. *Steel* refers to iron alloys that contain not more than 2 percent carbon and some manganese and are capable of being shaped at some temperature range as initially cast.

The physical properties of irons are governed by several factors: (1) characteristics and composition of the iron ore used in *smelting*, the process of melting or fusing the ore; (2) the percentage of carbon in the finished iron; (3) the inclusion of other elements, either in the iron ore or added during the melting process; (4) the manner in which the metal is allowed to cool from a liquid to a solid state; (5) and the conditions of cooling after the iron has reached a solid state. The properties of iron may be further altered by working, rolling, forging, and reheating.

Materials for Iron Production

The production of iron requires iron ore, fuel, and a flux to remove the impurities. The fuel used in the blast furnace

Fig. 6-1   Mining and shipping iron ore from an open-pit mine, Sherman, Minnesota. (*United States Steel Corporation.*)

is coke; the flux used is crushed limestone. Approximately 350 tons of iron ore, and 200 tons of coke, and 100 tons of limestone are used to produce 200 tons of pig iron.

IRON ORE   Most of the important iron ore used in the United States is in the form of iron oxides. These ores usually contain impurities such as phosphorus, silica, sulfur, manganese, and silicon, most of which must be removed during the production of iron. Although most of the earth's crust contains iron, only those ores that contain a high percentage of iron ore can be used economically. Before the ore is smelted in a blast furnace, it is ground, screened, and washed, and the fine particles are sintered, or formed into larger particles without melting.

COKE   The fuel used to melt iron is coke, a light, porous material made from coal. Coal is placed in large fire-brick-lined ovens, where it is heated to drive off the volatile portions as gas. The residue is coke, which is removed from the oven and quenched with water.

By-products of the coking process are extremely valuable. Coking of one ton of coal produces 600 cu ft of gas

that can be used in the firing of the blast furnace or sold as a by-product. Ammonium sulfite, tar, and light oils are also produced.

LIMESTONE   To remove impurities in iron ore crushed limestone is used as a flux when the ore is melted. Limestone combines with impurities in the iron ore and forms slag, which floats on top of the molten iron and is removed separately.

Blast-furnace Operation

The modern blast furnace consists of a 20- to 30-ft round steel stack, 100 to 200 ft high, lined with special refractory fire brick. The top of the furnace is sealed with double bells and hoppers to allow the addition of iron ore, coke, and limestone while the furnace is in operation. Once a blast furnace is put into operation, it is run continuously, 24 hr a day, 7 days a week. If the furnace is shut down for any reason and allowed to cool, the entire refractory fire brick lining must be replaced. In order to reduce ore, a blast of hot air at a temperature of 1100°F or more is introduced near the bottom of the furnace. Preheated air is

Fig. 6-2   Blast-furnace operation. (*American Iron and Steel Institute.*)

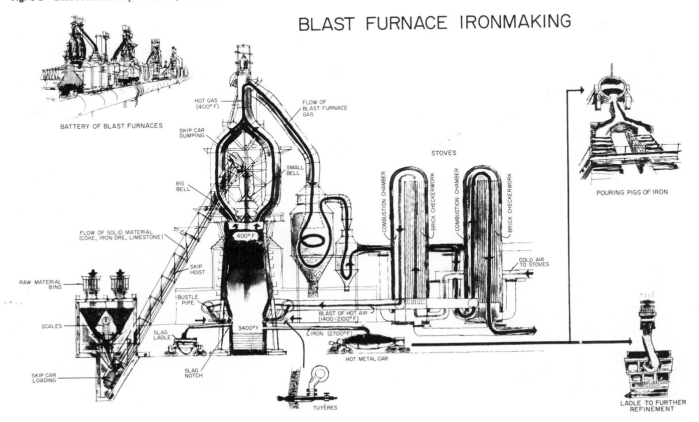

BLAST FURNACE IRONMAKING

blown through a series of *tuyères*, or water-cooled holes, near the bottom of the furnace. Iron ore, coke, and limestone are conveyed to the top of the furnace and deposited in alternate layers. The heat around the tuyeres is so intense that the coke burns, forming carbon monoxide gas. As this gas passes upward through the ore, coke, and limestone, it reduces the iron ore to metallic iron. The iron picks up carbon from the carbon monoxide gas and flows to the bottom in a puddle. The limestone flux unites with sulfur, alumina, silica, and other impurities in the ore, to form slag, which floats on top of the iron.

Hot, combustible gases are drawn off the top of the furnace, where they are cleaned, washed, and filtered and then used to generate steam or to heat the air blast. Combustible gas may be used to run blowers for hot air or as fuel for plant machinery.

At the bottom of the furnace are two tap holes one above the other. The molten slag floating on top of the iron is drawn off into ladles through the top hole. The bottom hole is tapped, and iron is allowed to flow into sand or metal molds to form pigs, or into large ladles where it will be transported, in liquid form, to be used in the manufacture of various iron alloys. During operation the blast furnace will usually be tapped for slag and iron five or six times a day.

PIG IRON   The characteristics of pig iron produced by the blast furnace will depend on the type of ore, limestone, and percentage of coke used in relation to the ore. The regulation of heat during the smelting process also affects the quality of pig iron. Pig iron, as it comes from the blast furnace, has no structural use; it must be remelted to eliminate unwanted elements.

BLAST-FURNACE BY-PRODUCTS   Blast-furnace slag consists of earthy materials from the iron ore and lime from limestone. Because of its high lime content, much slag is used in the manufacture of cement. Crushed or expanded slag is used as an aggregate in concrete, especially in lightweight or insulating concrete, and as fill or subbase under roads and asphaltic concrete pavement. Insulating material such as rock or mineral wool is also manufactured from blast-furnace slag.

Fig. 6-3   United States Steel Corporation blast furnace at Duquesne, Pennsylvania. (*United States Steel Corporation.*)

CAST IRON

Irons containing over 1.7 percent carbon, poured into molds, are cast irons. Cast iron is brittle, high in compressive strength, low in tensile strength, hard, and relatively crystalline in nature. It can be easily molded into intricate shapes. At one time cast iron was used structurally. Its uses are now confined to pipe, fittings, bases for plumbing fixtures, and ornamental grilles. It is used to a limited extent for machinery, bearing plates, and minor structural parts.

Manufacture of Cast Iron

The amount of carbon and the percentages of phosphorus, silicon, sulfur, and manganese in the pig iron determine the physical characteristics of cast iron. To control these elements the pig iron is remelted with iron or steel scrap in a cupola furnace, an air furnace, or an electric furnace.

The *cupola furnace* is essentially a small blast furnace charged with alternate layers of pig iron, scrap iron, and coke. Air is introduced through tuyères near the bottom of the furnace. As the red-hot coke is oxidized, the iron melts and trickles to the bottom, and when enough iron has accumulated, the furnace is tapped. This is accomplished by piercing through a clay plug, or *bod*, at the bottom of the furnace with a pointed iron bar. The iron is then allowed to flow into ladles or sand molds that have been formed by wood forms. When enough iron has flowed, the hole is stopped with a new bod. Unlike a blast furnace, a cupola furnace is never run continuously. It is fired anew for each series of castings and is dumped at the end of the run.

An air furnace is a horizontal furnace fired with coal, fuel oil, or gas. The heat of the flame is reflected from the roof of the furnace down onto a bath or puddle of material. As the iron begins to melt, slag forms and covers the metal, preventing direct contact between the flame and the molten iron. Less sulfur and carbon are absorbed by the iron, resulting in a strong high-grade iron. The time required for melting iron is greater in an air furnace than in a cupola furnace. However, the heat of the melt can be accurately controlled in an air furnace, resulting in a cast iron of high quality, although at a higher cost.

Many modern foundries use an *electric furnace* for melting cast iron. In an electric furnace the temperature and composition of the iron can be closely controlled. Pig iron and scrap iron are charged into the furnace and melted by an electric arc. In some instances the metal is melted in a cupola and charged into an electric furnace in liquid form.

Properties and Use

GREY CAST IRON   The output of a cupola furnace is *grey cast iron*, so called because of the grey, crystalline, coarse flakes of graphite in the casting. Grey graphite flakes are either embedded in a matrix of iron or combined chemically with the iron. The hardness and strength of the cast iron depends on the way the graphite is combined with the iron and on the amounts of carbon, silicon, sulfur, and manganese. Grey cast iron is widely used for ordinary castings. It is inexpensive to produce and easy to machine.

WHITE CAST IRON   Cast iron from an air or electric furnace, in which most of the carbon is combined chemically with the iron, is *white cast iron*. It presents a shiny, white fracture when broken. White cast iron is used where resistance to abrasion is important. It is harder than grey cast iron, but it is more brittle. The chief industrial use of white cast iron is in the manufacture of *malleable cast iron*.

MALLEABLE CAST IRON   Both white and grey cast iron can be made stronger and more ductile by *annealing*. After the castings are made, they are cleaned, inspected, and packed in an oxidizing agent. They are then heated for several days to a temperature below the melting point of iron. This changes the hard, brittle cast iron into a strong, tough, easily machined product. The flakes of graphite are changed into well-distributed fine grains. Malleable cast iron cannot be forged or rolled but must be cast into its final form. It is used where it must withstand some twisting and bending. Inserts for concrete, some hardware items, and bearing plates that must withstand a fair amount of vibration and shock are made of malleable cast iron.

WROUGHT IRON

Wrought iron is a soft, easily worked material that has a high resistance to corrosion and repeated stress. It consists of high-purity iron mechanically mixed with an inert glasslike slag of iron silicate. The threadlike fibers of slag are evenly distributed throughout the iron, arranged in the direction of the rolling. Wrought iron usually contains less than 0.12 percent carbon. The ASTM defines it as follows: "A ferrous material aggregated from a solidifying mass of pasty particles of highly refined metallic iron, with which without subsequent fusion, is incorporated a minutely and uniformly distributed quantity of slag."

Manufacture of Wrought Iron

Wrought iron may be manufactured by a process called *puddling*. In this process iron is melted in a shallow puddling furnace. The bottom of the furnace is lined with a layer of iron oxide, and as the charge melts, the carbon, silicon, manganese, phosphorus, sulfur, and other impurities in the pig iron are oxidized and eliminated. The iron becomes pasty during this process, and as it cools a workman called a puddler gathers a lump of the pasty iron on the end of a long bar. This lump of iron, called a *muck ball*, weighs approximately 100 lb. The muck ball is put under a squeezer or hammer, and much of the slag is squeezed out. The balls are then rolled into bars, which are cut off, piled on top of one another, and, while still

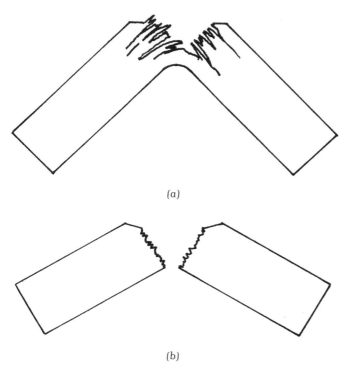

Fig. 6-4 Bending tests: (a) wrought iron; (b) steel.

mixed with molten slag to form wrought iron. The molten iron, at a temperature of 2800°F, is poured into a ladle of molten slag at 2300°F. As the molten iron hits the relatively cooler slag, it solidifies and sinks to the bottom of the ladle in small particles. Since the iron is at welding temperature, and owing to the fluxing nature of the slag, the fragments of the slag and iron cohere to form a spongey ball at the bottom of the ladle. This *puddle ball*, which may weigh 6000 lb or more, consists of a loose mass of pasty iron and slag. It is hammered or squeezed to remove excess slag and to weld it into a solid mass. The iron is immediately transferred to the rolling mill, where it is rolled into rectangular bars, or *billets*, of the desired size. These billets are then reheated and rolled into plate, bars, pipe, or other desired shapes.

Properties and Use

Wrought iron is nearly pure iron and slag. Since the slag fibers parallel to the long dimension of the bar, the strength of wrought iron is noticeably greater in a direction parallel to the direction of rolling. Wrought iron is very similar to mild steel but is distinguished by its fibrous character when it is broken. Steel will snap after a small bend, whereas wrought iron will tear gradually with a distinctive fibrous fracture. Wrought iron shows good resistance to fatigue. The strength of wrought-iron bars is increased by cold working or hammering. The purity of the iron and the glasslike nature of the slag ensure good resistance to rust and corrosion. The relatively rough surface of wrought iron provides a good base for paints and finishes.

Before the advent of modern steel-manufacturing methods wrought iron was used extensively for structural purposes. Because of its relatively lower tensile strength (25,000 to 35,000 psi for wrought iron, compared with 60,000 to 400,000 psi for steel), its use is now confined to rods, wire, and ornamental grilles, grates, handrails, and

at welding heat, rolled into bars and special shapes. The slag is never entirely removed in the hammering and rolling process but is formed into thin, evenly spaced, threadlike particles running parallel to the rolled sheet or bar.

The puddling process has been largely supplanted by a process in which nearly pure, molten iron is mechanically

Fig 6-5 Wrought-iron balcony rail at Casa Mila, Barcelona, Spain, architect Antonio Gaudi.

ballustrades. Wrought iron is used extensively for hot-water pipes because of its resistance to rusting.

STEEL

Steel is a malleable alloy of iron and carbon (by definition, not over 2 percent) with substantial quantities of manganese. *Mild steel* is similar in structure to wrought iron, except that it is melted and poured into billets that can be cooled, reheated, and rolled into shape. As the steel is rolled and worked, it attains a finer grain structure without slag. Because of its greater strength in both tension and compression, steel has replaced wrought iron for most construction purposes. Steels can be produced with a remarkable range of properties through the addition of only 2 or 3 percent of other elements. The amount of carbon in steel largely governs its strength. As the carbon content of steel is increased up to 0.8 percent, the strength of steel is increased and its ductility is decreased in proportion. Other elements present in steel further modify its properties. *Plain carbon steels* contain small amounts of sulfur, phosphorus, silicon, and manganese. Carbon steels are classified as *low carbon*, with up to 0.25 percent carbon; *medium carbon*, with 0.25 to 0.50 percent carbon; or *high carbon*, with over 0.50 percent carbon. Plain car-bon steels can be given a wide range of physical properties by working, rolling, and heat treating. Steel can be given additional properties by adding or alloying other elements such as aluminum, chromium, copper, molybdenum, nickel, titanium, tungsten, vanadium, and cobalt. These steels are classed as *alloy steels*.

Early Types of Steel

The discovery of steel was in all probability an accident. Ores containing a high percentage of molybdenum were used to produce the famous *Toledo steel* sword blades and armour of Spain in the twelfth century. The equally famous *Woots steel* of India contained traces of aluminum, either in the ore or added to the iron during the forging process. *Damascus steel* contained certain alloying agents that accounted for its superior qualities. Small quantities of steel were made in Europe by packing wrought-iron bars with charcoal and heating them for several days to produce what was known as *blister steel*. This method produced a high quality of steel, but in limited quantities. A method of producing steel by placing scrap iron and other elements in a crucible made of carbon or clay and maintaining the metal in a molten form for several hours was developed in England during the eighteenth century.

Fig. 6-6 A bessemer converter in operation (no bessemer converters are presently used in the United States). (*United States Steel Corporation.*)

The Bessemer Process

In 1855 Henry Bessemer of England patented a process that was to be the start of the steel industry as we know it today. He discovered that if air were blown through a molten bath of pig iron (2300°F), the oxygen would cause the silicon and carbon to burn off. The temperature of the mix could be raised by 300 to 500°F to eliminate other impurities from the iron. This new process meant that quality steel could now be produced from pig iron direct from the blast furnace.

For many years, the bessemer process was widely used throughout the world to produce high-quality steel. As late as 1961 over 800,000 tons of bessemer steel was produced in the United States. The process has now been entirely superseded in the United States by more efficient methods of steelmaking.

Manufacture of Steel

The making of steel involves the oxidation (burning) and removal of unwanted elements from the product of the blast furnace, and the subsequent addition of certain elements to produce a desired composition. Regardless of the type of furnace used to produce steel, the metal is worked until the sulfur and phosphorus contents reach acceptably low concentrations. These elements cause undesirable characteristics in both hot and cold steel. Carbon and other elements are usually added after the steel has been poured from the furnace into a ladle.

Most steels are made by adding scrap steel to the pig-iron melt. The average charge in the United States involves the addition of about 50 percent scrap. In that the scrap may consist of several types of steel alloys with various percentages of carbon, the output of the furnace may contain limited amounts of unwanted elements. These residual elements, such as copper and tin, that have not been separated from the scrap, must be carefully considered by the steel maker. The temperature of the furnace or the melt and the length of time the charge is held in molten form is closely controlled.

Four principle methods of making steel are in use today: the open-hearth process, the oxygen process, the electric-furnace process, and the vacuum process.

OPEN-HEARTH PROCESS   The open-hearth furnace is a shallow hearth, roofed over with refractory fire brick. Limestone and scrap steel are charged into the furnace, and when the bath is molten, hot metal from the blast furnace is put in.

Fig. 6-7   Open-hearth steelmaking. (*American Iron and Steel Institute.*)

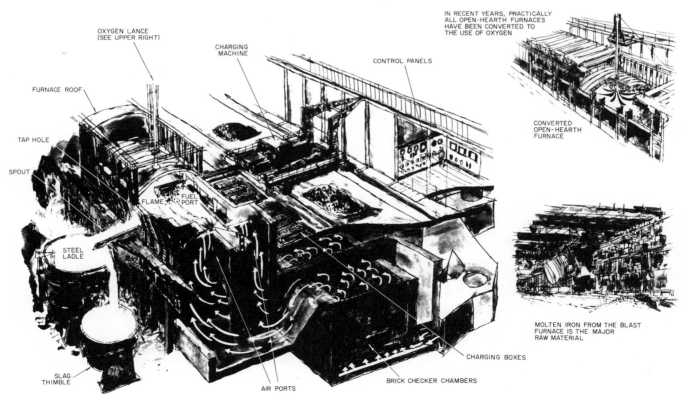

OPEN-HEARTH STEELMAKING

The oxidization and removal of impurities is accomplished by the action of a flame which sweeps over the bath. The heat of the flame is intensified by reflection from the brick at the top of the furnace. Preheated gas and air are blown into the furnace to maintain the temperature of the metal between 2912 and 3090°F. As the flame passes over the charge, the heat is absorbed by the metal through a layer of slag. The slag prevents direct contact of the gas flame with molten metal. American open-hearth furnaces hold 50 to 250 tons of steel. The entire refining process takes from 6 to 10 hr.

Near the end of the refining process the molten metal is tested frequently with optical *pyrometers*, recording devices that chart the temperature continuously. Samples of the molten metal are taken, cast, broken, and analyzed. The character of the break and the grain size and placement indicate the composition of the melt. The temperature of the furnace may be altered to adjust the composition of the metal at this time. Lime or iron ore may be added to change the composition of the slag. Other elements may be added to increase or decrease the fluidity of the molten metal. At this point the elements necessary for the production of alloy steels are added. Before the melt is poured, its composition is tested by an adjacent laboratory to see that it meets the standards established for that particular type of steel or alloy.

At the completion of the melt a hole at the bottom of the furnace is opened, and the molten metal is allowed to flow into a ladle, whose capacity is as near that of the furnace as possible. The slag flows over the molten metal into a separate ladle.

OXYGEN PROCESS The *oxygen-lance process*, sometimes called the *L-D process* after the two Austrian cities of Linz-Donawitz in which it was developed, is being increasingly adopted. Molten metal from the blast furnace and steel scrap are charged into an open-mouthed vessel. Scrap usually makes up 30 percent of the charge. An oxygen lance is lowered into the vessel to a point above the metal, lime is charged on top of the metal, and pure oxygen is then blown through the lance into the metal.

The substitution of oxygen for air eliminates some of the control problems inherent in the bessemer process. The oxygen process will handle certain grades of ore that are unsatisfactory for the bessemer process. The size of a single melt in the oxygen process is considerably smaller than that of the open-hearth furnace, usually not over 100 tons. The process is much quicker and can, in some in-

Fig. 6-8 Basic oxygen steelmaking (BOP). (*American Iron and Steel Institute.*)

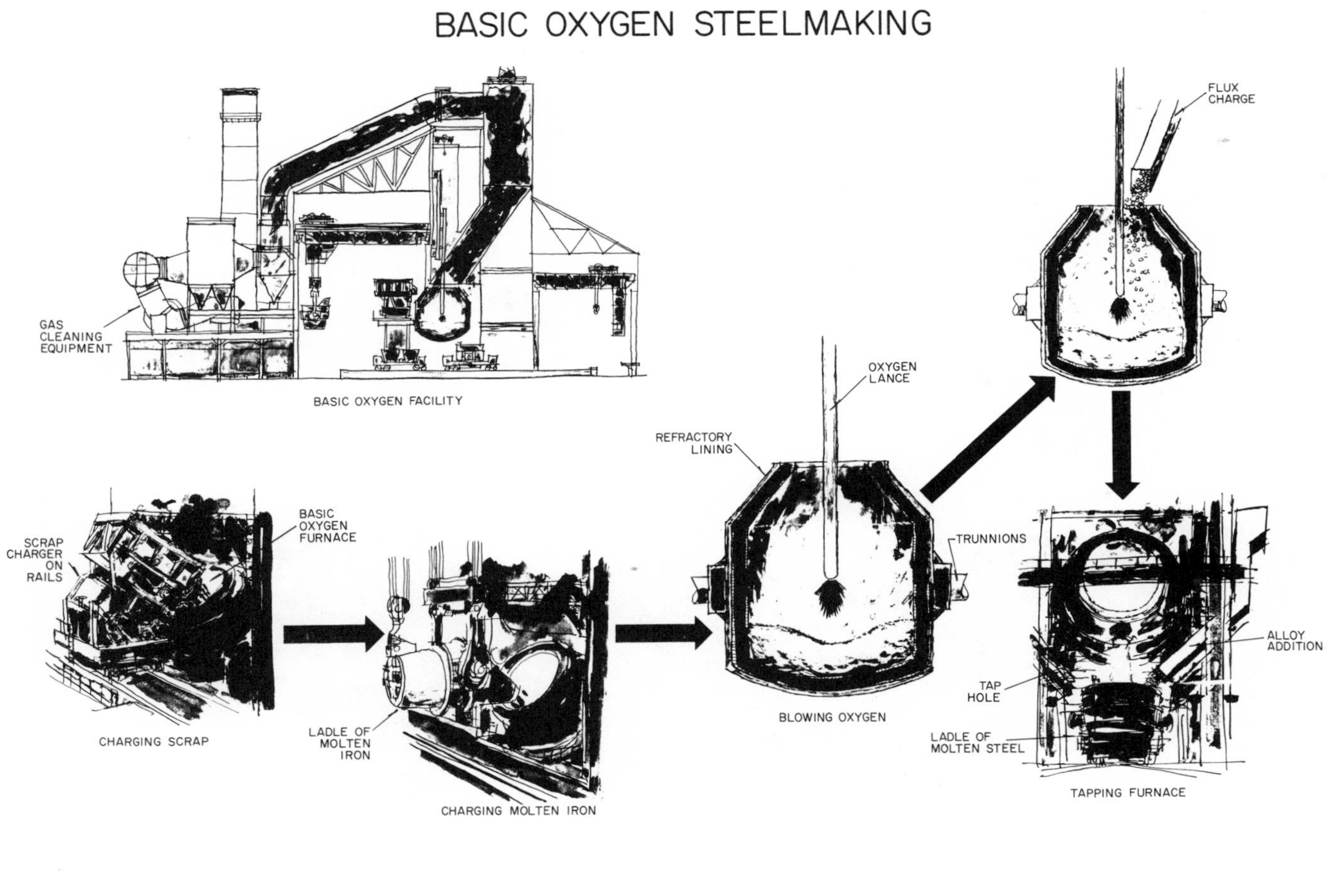

BASIC OXYGEN STEELMAKING

stances, produce more tonnage per hour than an open-hearth furnace.

An oxygen furnace can produce a *heat*, or batch, of steel from a charge of pig iron and scrap in 40 min, as opposed to the 6 to 10 hr required by the open-hearth process. Thus a producer may average 419 tons of steel an hour in a large oxygen furnace, in contrast to the 120 tons from a well-run open-hearth furnace.

ELECTRIC-FURNACE PROCESS   The electric steelmaking process is usually confined to the production of small quantities of alloy steel. The charge is generally restricted to 100 percent scrap steel. The operation of an electric furnace is similar to that of the open-hearth furnace, except that the source of heat is the electric arc, or the resistance of steel to the flow of electricity.

The electric furnace is capable of heating and melting scrap steel very rapidly under accurate control. The conditions inside the furnace can be maintained so that harmful gases are not formed. Thus expensive alloys which would be oxidized and lost in other types of furnaces can be incorporated in the mix. Electric furnaces range in capacity from one to several tons, which gives them a wide range of use in the production of alloy steels.

THE VACUUM PROCESS   Special steels are often melted or processed in a vacuum or a controlled atmosphere. Steels with improved physical and mechanical properties can be produced in a vacuum that are unobtainable in any other way. When steels are melted in a vacuum, gases such as oxygen, nitrogen, and hydrogen can be removed from the molten metal to produce higher-purity steel.

Vacuum melting may be accomplished in an *electric induction furnace*. The electric induction furnace is surrounded by an electric coil. When alternating current is introduced to this coil, a secondary current is induced in the steel to provide the melting heat. Scrap or molten steel is charged in the furnace and the air is evacuated so the entire furnace is in a vacuum. When the steel has been melted and the unwanted gases removed, it is poured into a holding ladle from which it is cast into ingots. The melting furnace, the holding ladle, and the ingot mold are each in a separate vacuum chamber. Each operation is carried out with remote controls.

Fig. 6-9 Electric-furnace steelmaking. (*American Iron and Steel Institute.*)

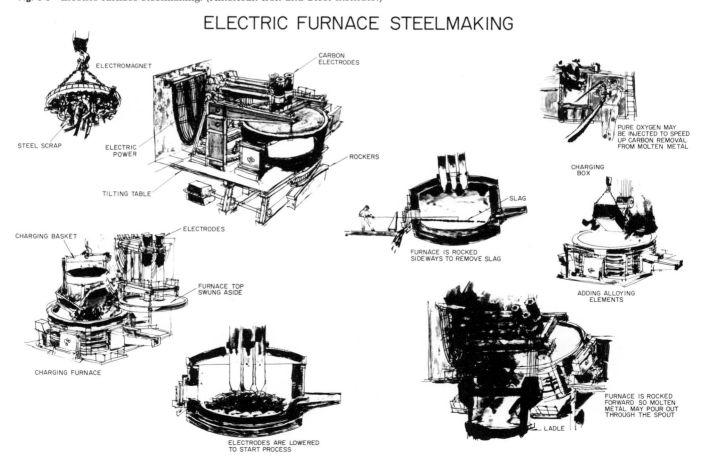

ELECTRIC FURNACE STEELMAKING

A *vacuum arc process* is used to remelt and refine steel ingots which have been produced by other methods. The ingot is introduced into a vacuum chamber. The steel ingot acts like a welding electrode. As the end of the ingot melts, the molten steel falls into a cooled mold below, where it solidifies into an extremely dense ingot with practically no center porosity.

Vacuum degasing is a process of refining melted steel that has been produced by other methods. Ingot molds are placed in vacuum chambers. Melted steel is poured into a small ladle on top of the vacuum chamber. As the steel flows from this ladle into the vacuum chamber, it is broken into small droplets. As the droplets are falling to the bottom of the mold, the unwanted gases are removed. Special vacuum degasing ladles have been developed to process steel.

CONTINUOUS-CASTING PROCESS   In the continuous-casting process, instead of casting steel into ingots for later rolling and shaping, molten steel is poured into an electric reheating furnace and then into a chilled bottomless brass mold. The steel is solidified in the brass mold and extruded in the form of a red-hot rod. It is said that this process simplifies the operations necessary in the forming of steel shapes. However, it is presently used only by the smaller steel companies.

ACID AND BASIC STEEL   Steel is produced by either an acid or a basic process. Pig iron and scrap of low phosphorus content must be used in the acid process, as phosphorus and sulfur are not eliminated by this process. In the basic process the refractory material used to line the furnace is limestone, dolomite, or magnesite, which are chemically basic in character. Burned lime is used as a flux to absorb and hold the phosphorus oxides that develop during the refining process.

The steel produced by these processes is referred to as *acid electric, basic electric, acid open-hearth, basic open-hearth*, and so on. The most commonly used processes in the United States are basic open-hearth, basic oxygen, and basic electric.

SHAPING STEEL

Regardless of the type of furnace used to process steel, the output of the furnace is usually tapped, and the molten metal is poured into cast-iron *ingot* molds. The size of ingots ranges from 100 lb in small mills to 25 tons in large mills. The ingots may be square or rectangular, depending on the shape needed for subsequent processing.

An ingot cannot be sent directly to the rolling mills just as it comes from the mold. If the mold is removed as soon as the outside has solidified, the interior is still in a molten state. If the ingot is allowed to stand until the center has solidified, the exterior is too cold to be worked. The ingot must therefore be allowed to solidify and then be reheated

Fig. 6-10   Removing ingots from soaking pit. (*United States Steel Corporation.*)

to a uniform temperature throughout. This is done in a furnace called a *soaking pit*. The ingot is held in the soaking pit until it reaches a uniform temperature of about 2300°F. The exact temperature depends on the size of the ingot, the composition of the steel, and the method of rolling.

Blooming Mill

When the ingot has reached the desired temperature throughout, it is conveyed to a *primary mill*, a *cog mill*, or a *blooming mill*. To be rolled to its final shape the steel must be passed through many sets of rollers. These rollers are made of cast iron or steel which has been chilled to produce a hard exterior.

The blooming mill consists of several sets of rollers, one on top of another, arranged so the steel billet passes back and forth through them without changing its direction of rotation. Most mills are equipped with roller tables that can be raised, lowered, and reversed to direct the steel to upper or lower rollers. Through a series of guides and levers, the steel is guided and turned so that it can be reduced in both width and thickness.

The product of the blooming mill may be a bloom, a slab, or a billet. Although the distinctions are not clear cut, a *bloom* is usually a section ranging from 6″ × 6″ to 12″ × 12″; a *slab* is generally 2 to 6 in. thick and over 24 in. wide; a *billet* ranges from 2″ × 2″ to 5″ × 5″.

Besides forming the ingot to a uniform size for further rolling, the blooming mill serves another important function. The initial rolling operation breaks down the coarse, cast structure of the ingot so that internal contraction cavities and other voids in the ingot are sealed. Surface defects, such as scabs, seams, and folds that are formed during the casting process may be removed at this stage or at a later point in the rolling process. In some mills the bloom is rolled into a final product; in others it is sheared at each end to remove irregularities, cut in two, returned to a reheating furnace, and brought again to the proper temperature for further rolling.

Structural Mill

Large structural members may be rolled directly from the bloom without reheating. Smaller members are produced from billets. The red-hot steel is passed through a succession of rollers which gradually form it into the desired shape. Structural shapes are formed by passing the steel back and forth through one set of rollers, with the space between them decreased for each pass until the member has reached the desired thickness and shape. In some mills, the steel passes through a series of continuous rollers, each of which makes a given reduction in size or change in shape. As the steel passes through each stand, it lengthens, becomes smaller in section, and speeds up. At the end of this process the structural shapes are cut to length and allowed to cool. After cooling, they are straightened by a final set of rollers. Typical shapes are shown in Table 6-1.

Plate Mill

Steel plate is rolled from slabs. The slabs are passed through successive stands of rollers that reduce the thickness with each pass. The hot steel plates may be ⅛″ to 3″; thinner sections of plate may be produced continuously and formed into rolls for further rolling into thin sheets. The product is called *hot-rolled plate, strip,* or *sheet.* This material may be subsequently cold rolled.

Cold rolling

To form a smooth-surfaced sheet or strip to close dimensional tolerances, the hot-rolled strip or sheet is cooled, pickled, cleaned, and passed through a series of rollers that reduce its thickness by 40 to 85 percent. As the steel is cold rolled, it gains strength. However, it also loses ductility, which makes it unsatisfactory for some forming operations. Cold-rolled steel may be annealed to soften it. This process involves heating the steel above a certain critical temperature and then allowing it to cool at a controlled rate. After annealing the steel is given a final cold rolling through one or more stands of rollers that reduce its thickness by 1 or 2 percent. This finishing operation re-

Fig. 6-11 Blooming mill in operation. (*United States Steel Corporation.*)

TABLE 6-1 Structural steel shapes

SHAPE	DESCRIPTIVE NAME	OLD AISC IDENTIFYING SYMBOL	NEW IDENTIFYING SYMBOL	*TYPICAL DESIGNATIONS
I	WIDE FLANGE SHAPES	W̄F	W	W 36 x 300 W 4 x 13
I	MISCELLANEOUS SHAPES	JR & M	M	M 14 x 17.2 M 4 x 13
I	AMERICAN STANDARD BEAMS	I	S	S 24 x 120 S 3 x 5.7
[	AMERICAN STANDARD CHANNELS	[	C	C 15 x 50 C 3 x 4.1
[	MISCELLANEOUS CHANNELS	[	MC	MC 18 x 58 MC 3 x 7.1
L	ANGLES-EQUAL LEGS	∠	L	L 8 x 8 x 1 1/8 L 3 x 3 x 3/16
L	ANGLES-UNEQUAL LEGS	∠	L	L 9 x 4 x 1 L 3 1/2 x 3 x 1/4
⌐	BULB ANGLES	bulb ∠	BL	BL 10 x 3 1/2 x 32.3 BL 3 x 2 x 3.8
T	STRUCTURE TEES-CUT FROM WIDE FLANGE SHAPES	ST — W̄F	WT	WT 18 x 150 WT 9 x 32
T	STRUCTURAL TEES-CUT FROM MISCELLANEOUS SHAPES	ST — JR ST — M	MT	MT 7 x 8.6 MT 4 x 9.25
T	STRUCTURAL TEES-CUT FROM AMERICAN STANDARD BEAMS	ST —	ST	ST 12 x 60 ST 1.5 x 2.85
T	TEES	T	T	T 5 x 13.6 T 3 x 6
T	WALL TEES		AT	AT 8 x 29.2
I	ELEVATOR TEES		ET	ET 5 x 33 .2 ET 2.5 x 8.9
⌐	ZEES	Z	Z	Z 6 x 21.1 Z 3 x 6.7

*For a complete description of sizes and shapes of standard structural steel shapes see: STANDARD NOMENCLATURE FOR STRUCTURAL STEEL SHAPES, published by Committee of Structural Steel Producers, AMERICAN IRON AND STEEL INSTITUTE.

duces the material to specific dimensions, gives it a bright surface finish, and permits a final control on mechanical properties.

Cold-rolled steel sheet and strip are designated by gauge number according to thickness, as established by the "Manufacturer's Standard Gauge," or the "U.S. Standards Revised." The larger the gauge number, the thinner the sheet. Table 6-2 shows the variations in standard gauge measurements between different metals. For example, a 16-gauge steel sheet (0.0598) is a different thickness than

a 16-gauge stainless steel sheet (0.0625) or a 16-gauge aluminum- or copper-alloy sheet (0.05082). By referring to the column showing decimals and fractions of an inch, the comparable thickness in inch decimals of the metal to be specified may be checked. Because of variations in metal thickness when measured by the gauge for different alloys, it is often advisable to designate thickness by decimals of an inch instead of a gauge number. If the gauge number is used, the name of the gauge referred to should be specified.

TABLE 6-2 Standard gauge tables for sheets, tubing, wire, and screws

Gage No.	United States Standard Revised Manufacturers' Gage — For Sheets— Hot and Cold Rolled Steel	United States Standard (U.S.S.) Gage — For Sheets— Stainless Steel Monel Metal	Birmingham Wire (B.W.G.) or Stubs' Iron Wire Gage — For Strip— Hot and Cold Rolled Steel Rivets— Spring Steel— Flat Steel Wire— Tubing— Steel, Aluminum, †Copper, Bronze, ††Brass, Monel and Stainless Steel	Brown and Sharpe (B. & S.) or American Wire (A. W.) Gage — For Sheets, Strip and Wire— Aluminum, Copper, Brass, Bronze and Nickel Silver Tubing— †Copper ††Brass	American Steel Wire or Washburn and Moen (W. & M.) Gage — For Wire — Iron and Steel	Machine and Wood Screw Gage — For Machine Screws Wood Screws— Ferrous and Non-Ferrous	Fractions and Decimal Equivalents of an Inch, For Each 64th of an Inch	
							1/64	.015625
							1/32	.03125
							3/64	.046875
							1/16	.0625
							5/64	.078125
							3/32	.09375
							7/64	.109375
							1/8	.125
							9/64	.140625
6-0's	.46875	.46875		.5800	.4615		5/32	.15625
5-0's	.4375	.4375	.500	.5165	.4305		11/64	.171875
4-0's	.40625	.40625	.454	.4600	.3938		3/16	.1875
3-0's	.3750	.3750	.425	.4096	.3625		13/64	.203125
2-0's	.34375	.34375	.380	.3648	.3310		7/32	.21875
1-0	.3125	.3125	.340	.3249	.3065	.060	15/64	.234375
1	.28125	.28125	.300	.2893	.2830	.073	1/4	.250
2	.26562	.26562	.284	.2576	.2625	.086	17/64	.265625
3	.2391	.2500	.259	.2294	.2437	.099	9/32	.28125
4	.2242	.2343	.238	.2043	.2253	.112	19/64	.296875
5	.2092	.2187	.220	.1819	.2070	.125	5/16	.3125
6	.1943	.2031	.203	.1620	.1920	.138	21/64	.328125
7	.1793	.1875	.180	.1443	.1770	.151	11/32	.34375
8	.1644	.1718	.165	.1285	.1620	.164	23/64	.359375
9	.1495	.1562	.148	.1144	.1483	.177		
10	.1345	.1406	.134	.1019	.1350	.190	3/8	.375
11	.1196	.1250	.120	.09074	.1205	.203	25/64	.390625
12	.1046	.1093	.109	.08081	.1055	.216	13/32	.40625
13	.0897	.0937	.095	.07196	.0915		27/64	.421875
14	.0747	.0781	.083	.06408	.0800	.242	7/16	.4375
15	.0673	.0703	.072	.05707	.0720		29/64	.453125
16	.0598	.0625	.065	.05082	.0625	.268	15/32	.46875
17	.0538	.0562	.058	.04526	.0540		31/64	.484375
18	.0478	.0500	.049	.04030	.0475	.294	1/2	.500
19	.0418	.0437	.042	.03589	.0410		33/64	.515625
20	.0359	.0375	.035	.03196	.0348	.320	17/32	.53125
21	.0329	.0343	.032	.02846	.0317		35/64	.546875
22	.0299	.0312	.028	.02535	.0286		9/16	.5625
23	.0269	.0281	.025	.02257	.0258		37/64	.578125
24	.0239	.0250	.022	.02010	.0230	.372	19/32	.59375
25	.0209	.0218	.020	.01790	.0204		39/64	.609375
26	.0179	.0187	.018	.01594	.0181		5/8	.625
27	.0164	.0171	.016	.01420	.0173		41/64	.640625
28	.0149	.0156	.014	.01264	.0162		21/32	.65625
29	.0135	.0140	.013	.01126	.0150		43/64	.671875
30	.0120	.0125	.012	.01003	.0140	.450	11/16	.6875
31	.01094	.01094	.010	.00893	.0132		45/64	.703125
32	.01016	.01016	.009	.00795	.0128		23/32	.71875
33	.00938	.00938	.008	.00708	.0118		47/64	.734375
34	.00859	.00859	.007	.006304	.0104	.502	3/4	.750
35	.00781	.00781	.005	.005614	.0095			
36	.00703	.00703	.004	.005000	.0090			
37	.00664	.00664		.004453	.0085			
38	.00625	.00625		.003965	.0080			

†Copper tubing in small sizes measured by both B. & S. and Stubs' gauge.
††Brass tubing under 3/8" O.D. measured by B. & S. Gauge.
By permission of the National Association of Architectural Metal Manufacturers.

STEEL PIPE, TUBING, AND WIRE

Pipe

Finished pipe is not usually produced in the steel mill; however, it is produced from billets, or strip, usually called *skelp*, made by the mill. Pipe, which has become an important structural material, is classed according to the process by which it is manufactured. The two principal forms of pipe are seamless and welded pipe.

SEAMLESS PIPE   Seamless pipe may be produced by one of three processes. In the most common method a heated billet is forced over the pointed nose of a piercing mandrel. The mandrel punches a hole in the center of the billet while rolls on the outside control the diameter. A typical piercing operation consists of two piercing operations and two or more passes in a *plug mill*, which gives the seamless pipe a uniform size and finish.

In the second method a partially pierced billet, called a *bottle*, is forced through a series of progressively smaller dies to bring the pipe down to the required diameter. The pipe is then sized and straightened in a plug mill.

The third method involves the forming of a flat steel plate, in the form of a round disk, into finished pipe. The disk is heated to forging temperature and is formed over a round-nosed mandrel into a cup shape. The cup-shaped steel is then forced through rollers to reduce its size and provide a uniform wall thickness.

Seamless pipe can be produced in diameters up to 26 in. The length, governed by the length of the mandrel, is usually not more than 40 ft. While seamless pipe can be pro-

duced with exceptionally smooth round surfaces, the thickness of the walls tends to vary. Small-diameter pipe may be produced by stress reduction. The pipe is run through a series of rollers that induce tension, stretching the pipe and reducing its diameter.

WELDED PIPE   Welded pipe is also manufactured by several methods. Large-diameter pipe is formed by large presses that first form plate or strip into a U shape and then into a circle. Smaller pipe may be formed in a continuous operation by passing a continuous hot strip through an appropriately formed series of rollers that mold the strip into a circular section and press the edges together to form a butt-welded seam the length of the pipe. The pipe is then straightened by a series of rolls. The edges of the formed strip may be heated to welding temperature by means of an oxygen blast just before welding or by passing an electric current between the edges.

Welded pipe can be produced to very close tolerances, both in outside and in inside diameters. The welded seams are closely inspected, and if the manufacturing process is carefully controlled, the welded seam is not necessarily a point of weakness.

Most pipe used for structural and mechanical purposes is produced in relatively few sizes in both seamless and welded form. This pipe, designated *mechanical-service pipe*, is available in standard, extra-strong, double-extra-strong weights. Sizes (up to 12 in.) are nominal equivalents of the inside diameter of standard-weight pipe. The outside diameter is the same for each size so that the increase in wall thickness necessary to produce the extra-strong

Fig. 6-12   Flow chart of electric-resistance-welded pipe. (*Republic Steel.*)

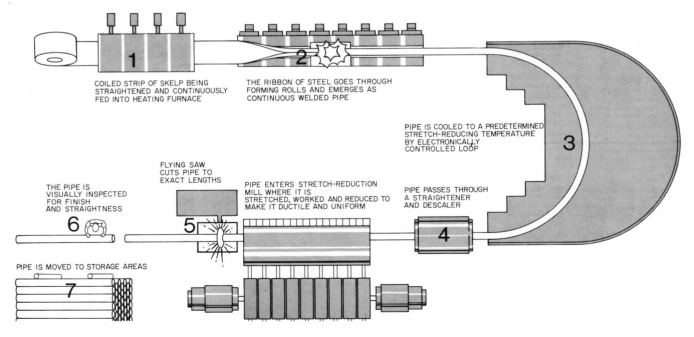

1 COILED STRIP OF SKELP BEING STRAIGHTENED AND CONTINUOUSLY FED INTO HEATING FURNACE

2 THE RIBBON OF STEEL GOES THROUGH FORMING ROLLS AND EMERGES AS CONTINUOUS WELDED PIPE

3 PIPE IS COOLED TO A PREDETERMINED STRETCH-REDUCING TEMPERATURE BY ELECTRONICALLY CONTROLLED LOOP

4 PIPE PASSES THROUGH A STRAIGHTENER AND DESCALER

PIPE ENTERS STRETCH-REDUCTION MILL WHERE IT IS STRETCHED, WORKED AND REDUCED TO MAKE IT DUCTILE AND UNIFORM

5 FLYING SAW CUTS PIPE TO EXACT LENGTHS

6 THE PIPE IS VISUALLY INSPECTED FOR FINISH AND STRAIGHTNESS

7 PIPE IS MOVED TO STORAGE AREAS

TABLE 6-3 Mechanical service pipe sizes

NOMINAL SIZE, IN.	WT. CLASS*	OUTSIDE DIAMETER, IN.	INSIDE DIAMETER, IN.	WALL THICKNESS, IN.	WT/FT, LB.
1/8	STD	0.405	0.269	0.068	0.24
	XS		0.215	0.094	0.31
1/4	STD	0.540	0.364	0.088	0.42
	XS		0.302	0.119	0.54
3/8	STD	0.675	0.493	0.091	0.57
	XS		0.423	0.126	0.74
1/2	STD	0.840	0.622	0.109	0.85
	XS		0.546	0.147	1.09
	XXS		0.434	0.308	2.44
1	STD	1.315	1.049	0.133	1.68
	XS		0.957	0.179	2.17
	XXS		0.599	0.358	3.66
1 1/4	STD	1.660	1.380	0.140	2.27
	XS		1.278	0.191	3.00
	XXS		0.896	0.382	5.21
1 1/2	STD	1.900	1.610	0.145	2.72
	XS		1.500	0.100	3.63
	XXS		1.100	0.400	6.41
2	STD	2.875	2.469	0.203	5.79
	XS		2.323	0.276	7.66
	XXS		1.771	0.552	13.70
2 1/2	STD	3.500	3.068	0.216	7.58
	XS		2.900	0.300	10.25
	XXS		2.300	0.600	18.58
3	STD	3.500	3.068	0.216	7.58
	XS		2.900	0.300	10.25
	XXS		2.300	0.600	18.58
3 1/2	STD	4.000	3.548	0.226	9.11
	XS		3.364	0.318	12.51
4	STD	4.500	4.026	0.237	10.79
	XS		3.826	0.337	14.98
	XXS		3.152	0.674	27.54
5	STD	5.563	5.047	0.258	14.62
	XS		4.813	0.375	20.78
	XXS		4.063	0.750	38.55
6	STD	6.625	6.065	0.280	18.97
	XS		5.761	0.432	28.57
	XXS		4.897	0.864	53.16
8	STD	8.625	7.981	0.322	28.55
	XS		9.750	0.500	43.39
	XXS		6.875	0.875	72.42
10	STD	10.750	10.020	0.365	40.48
	XS		9.750	0.500	54.74
	XXS			1.000	104.13
12	STD	12.750	12.000	0.375	49.56
	XS		11.750	0.500	65.42
	XXS			1.000	125.49

*STD is standard weight.
XS is extra strong.
XXS is double extra strong.

and double-extra-strong weights results in a decrease in inside diameter.

Mechanical Tubing

Tubing is produced in the mill by the same method as pipe. However, it is produced to exact dimensions in inches, and not to standard sizes. Round, square, or rectangular tubing is produced by hot rolling steel strip or sheet and using flash or resistance welding for the seams. Portions of the welding bead that extend beyond the exterior surface are removed with a cutting tool to provide a smooth, unbroken surface. The tubing may be further sized or finished to obtain sharp, square corners by cold rolling or die forming. Seamless tubing is produced by piercing, extrusion, and cupping. The size and weight of tubing is designated by outside diameter, inside diameter, and wall thickness.

Wire

Each year 5,500,000 tons of wire are produced in the United States. This is approximately one-twentieth of the entire output of steel products. A virtually limitless variety of wire can be produced by controlling the composition of the steel and the manufacturing processes. Wire is usually thought of as round; however, it may also be square, rectangular, polygonal, and many other shapes. A variety of strengths, hardnesses, and surface finishes can be produced by controlled processing during manufacture. In addition to the long rolls of finished wire used for construction purposes, wire is the starting material for nails, bolts, screws, rivets, welding electrodes, and similar products.

Wire is drawn from wire rods that have been hot rolled in the mill. This process consists of drawing the unheated rod through a number of dies that progressively reduce its diameter as they increase its length. Each successive pass through a die must therefore be made at a higher speed. This process, like cold rolling of steel, generally increases the hardness, brittleness, stiffness, and tensile strength of the wire. The extent of the physical change in the metal depends on the amount of reduction with each pass and the number of passes used to achieve the final size.

It is not always possible to produce wire from wire rod without annealing. After 3 to 10 passes through the dies, the wire is heated in a closed furnace and allowed to cool at a given rate. This relieves the stresses built up in the steel during successive passes through the dies. The temper of the wire—its hardness, stiffness, and strength— is affected by the amount of carbon and alloying agents, the number of passes through the dies without annealing, and the final heat treatment. The tempers of low-carbon steel wire are usually designated as hard, medium hard, bright soft, soft, and extra soft.

A variety of finishes may be produced by varying the drawing process. A *bright finish* may be obtained by passing the wire through the last die in a dry condition. A *liquor finish* is imparted to the wire by passing it through the last die in a wet condition. Annealing or heat treatment after the last draw leaves the metal *black annealed*. To further protect the surface the wire may be coated, painted, or plated as part of the last operation.

Wire sizes are usually designated by gauge numbers. Three standard gauges are used in the United States: the American Steel Wire Gauge (ASW) for ferrous wire, the American Wire Gauge (AWG) or Brown & Sharp Gauge (B&S) for nonferrous wire, and the Music or Piano Wire Gauge for music or piano wire.

STEEL CASTINGS

Most of the steel castings used in construction are produced from medium-high-carbon steel. Sound steel castings have properties similar to those of wrought steel products. For normal commercial application very thin steel sections cannot be cast, since the melting point of steel is extremely high. Most steel castings must be an-

nealed or heat treated to impart the required physical properties. Only about 1 percent of the world's steel production is represented by castings.

Steel castings of medium-carbon and low-alloy steels are produced by pouring molten steel of the desired composition in a mold and allowing it to solidify. Steel castings and wrought or rolled steel respond similarly to heat treatment and have the same weldability and mechanical properties.

Castings produced to resist high stresses, high temperatures, or high pressures must be tested carefully for hidden flaws. To locate surface flaws or cracks a dye that will penetrate minute cracks is applied to the part. The part is then wiped clean, and a fine powder is spread over the surface, which absorbs the dye as it is released from the crack and reveals the flaw. X rays and gamma rays can be used to detect flaws or blow holes in the interior of the casting. With magnetic testing the part is magnetized and the magnetic flux surrounding it is tested. Very-high-frequency sound waves may also be transmitted through the metal to expose defects.

Fig. 6-13 Production of welded steel pipe. (*United States Steel Corporation.*)

CLASSIFICATION OF STEELS

The classification and identification of steels is complicated by the many factors that govern their physical properties. Complete identification of a steel requires four specifications: method of manufacture, heat treatment, chemical composition, and reference to a recognized standard.

The method of manufacture includes the basic reducing process, such as basic open-hearth, basic oxygen, etc. It also includes the forming, rolling, or casting process used to shape the product, such as hot rolling, cold rolling, drawing, extrusion, or casting. Certain steels can be hardened by tempering or softened by annealing. The heating of hardenable steel and fast or slow cooling with air, water, oil, or molten lead will alter its characteristics. There are four broad and sometimes overlapping classifications of steel: carbon steel, alloy steels, high-strength low-alloy steels, and stainless steels. The most commonly encountered standards in the steel industry have been established by the following associations:

The American Iron and Steel Institute (AISI)
The American Institute of Steel Construction (AISC)

American Society for Testing and Materials (ASTM)
Society of Automotive Engineers (SAE)
Concrete Reinforcing Steel Institute (CRSI)
Steel Joist Institute (SJI)

Carbon Steels

Steels containing over 95 percent iron, not over 2 percent carbon, 0.60 percent copper, 1.65 percent manganese, and 0.60 percent silicon are classed as *carbon steels*, also termed *plain carbon steel, ordinary steel,* and *straight carbon steel.* Oxygen, nitrogen, and sulfur are present as residual impurities. Various other elements such as phosphorus, aluminum, and chromium may be used in small amounts to impart different properties. Aluminum imparts a fine grain structure; manganese is added to eliminate oxygen, sulfur to increase resistance to abrasion, and silicon and phosphorus to increase strength. The properties of carbon steel are determined to a great extent by heat treatment and method of manufacture.

Carbon steels are usually classified according to their carbon content. Up to a point, the more carbon, the stronger, harder, and stiffer the steel. As the carbon con-

Fig. 6-14 Galvanized wire coiled onto tubular carriers in large bundles for shipment. (*United States Steel Corporation.*)

tent increases, the steel also becomes less ductile and more brittle. Table 6-4 indicates the general classifications based on the amount of carbon present.

TABLE 6-4 Carbon-steel characteristics

TYPE	DESCRIPTION
Very mild	0.05 to 0.15 percent carbon. An easily worked steel that is tough and soft, used for sheets, wire, rivets, pipe, and fastenings
Mild structural	0.15 to 0.25 percent carbon. A strong, ductile, machinable steel used for buildings, bridges, boats, boilers
Medium	0.25 to 0.35 percent carbon. Stronger and harder than mild structural grade, used for machinery, in shipbuilding, and for general structural purposes
Medium-hard	0.35 to 0.65 percent carbon. Used in locations subject to wear and abrasion
Spring	0.85 to 1.05 percent carbon. Used in the manufacture of springs
Tool	1.05 to 1.20 percent carbon. The hardest and strongest of the carbon steels

Alloy Steels

Much of the steel used for construction is low- to medium-carbon steel that is tough, strong, and easy to work. Elements such as manganese, nickel, chromium, vanadium, and copper may be alloyed with carbon steel to provide properties that are unobtainable in carbon steel. An *alloy steel* is one in which alloying elements have been added to the mix in excess of those allowed in carbon steel.

Alloy steels are usually designated by the element or elements from which the alloy derives its particular characteristics. Copper alloys have improved resistance to corrosion and are used for such products as wire lath, and sheet steel subject to moisture. Nickel added to the steel increases its strength. Chromium increases strength and acts as a hardener. There are also alloy steels based on two or more elements, such as chrome-molybdenum steel, chrome-vanadium steel, and manganese-silicon steel.

High-strength Low-alloy Steels

A recent development in steel construction has been in the use of a group of patented alloy steels classed as high-strength low-alloy steels, sometimes called *weathering steels*. These steels marketed under such trade names as Cor-Ten, Mayari-R, and Dynalloy, develop strengths up to 40 percent higher than structural carbon steel and have a high resistance to corrosion. Because of their strength, they can be used in thinner sections to reduce weight, or in the same thicknesses as carbon steel to support heavier loads. These steels can be easily fabricated by shear-

Fig. 6-15 Exposed high-strength low-alloy of the U.S.S. Cor-Ten steel frame of United States Steel's headquarters building, Pittsburgh, Pennsylvania. (*United States Steel Corporation.*)

ing, cutting, forming, punching, riveting, and welding.

These steels are generally produced to meet specific physical requirements, such as strength and resistance to corrosion. The chemical composition varies slightly with the individual producer. The composition of Cor-Ten,

Fig. 6-16 Stainless-steel installed in 1930 on the tower of the Chrysler Building, New York City. (*American Iron and Steel Institute, Committee of Stainless Steel Producers.*)

produced by the United States Steel Corporation, is as follows:

Carbon	0.12% maximum
Manganese	0.20 – 0.50%
Phosphorus	0.07 – 0.15%
Sulfur	0.05% maximum
Copper	0.25 – 0.75%
Chromium	0.30 – 1.25%
Nickel	0.65% maximum

The corrosion resistance of these alloys is provided by a tightly adhered, protective oxide film that seals the surface of the member against further corrosion. During the formation of the oxide film, the steel will lose about 0.002 in. in thickness. This protective oxide film gradually assumes a pleasing texture and darkens to a color ranging from brown to warm purple, depending on the condition of exposure. The atmospheric corrosion resistance eliminates the need for protection of surfaces exposed directly to the weather. The texture and color of the oxide film depends on the eroding action of wind and rain and the drying action of sunlight. Sheltered locations will develop a rougher texture than those exposed directly to the wind and weather. Unpainted corrosion-resistant steels must be used with care in conjunction with materials that stain readily. Exposure of these steels is not generally recommended for structures exposed to recurrent wetting by salt water.

Stainless Steels

The corrosion resistance of iron is improved as increasing quantities of chromium are added. At 11.5 percent there is sufficient chromium to form an inert film of chromic oxide over the entire metal surface, and the steel is considered *stainless*. The film of oxide varies in composition from alloy to alloy and with different treatments, such as hot rolling, cold working, and heating. If the film is broken, it will reform when reexposed to a suitable oxidizing agent. If the film is prevented from reforming by constant abrasion, the steel will rust. Stainless steels have low heat conductivity but high expansion with changes in temperature.

Elements other than chromium are added to stainless steels to produce special characteristics, such as improved corrosion resistance, increased strength, toughness, ease of fabrication, hardenability, and weldability. Nickel added to chromium stainless steels in excess of about 6 percent produces a series of strong, ductile alloys of improved corrosion-resistant steels known as chromium-nickel stainless steels. Other elements, such as sulfur, columbium, and molybdenum, are sometimes added to give special properties. Manganese and nickel increase the ductility and acid resistance of stainless steel.

TYPES   There are nearly 40 standard types of stainless steel, and many others under various trade names. Through the modification of the kinds and quantities of alloying elements, the producer can adapt the steel to specific applications. However, stainless steels can be classed in four basic series:

200 series	Chromium-nickel-manganese; nonhardenable, nonmagnetic
300 series	Chromium-nickel; nonhardenable, nonmagnetic
400 series	Chromium; hardenable, magnetic
500 series	Chromium; low-chromium, heat resistant

Within these basic groups the standard types are designated by a numerical system developed by the AISC which describes the specific alloy content of each type. The most commonly used alloys for architectural purposes are shown in Table 6-5.

TABLE 6-5   Stainless-steel alloys

TYPE	DESCRIPTION
302	Basic chromium-nickel stainless steel, used for a wide range of applications in all kinds of architectural work. It is easy to form and fabricate and has excellent resistance to corrosion from exposure to weather.
301	A variation of 302 which can be cold rolled to high tensile strengths for special applications. Used primarily in strip form for flashing.
304	A low-carbon form of 302 with medium corrosion resistance. It is sometimes specified where extensive welding of heavy sections will be done.
305	Used for bolts, nuts, screws, and other fasteners.
316	Offers more corrosion resistance owing to the addition of molybdenum. This type is desirable where corrosion conditions are severe, as in salt water and heavy industrial atmospheres.
201	An alloy with higher strength and better drawing and spinning characteristics than 301.
202	A variation of 201 with slightly less strength. Usually used in an annealed condition.
410	Used for nuts, bolts, screws, and other fastenings.
430	A chromium stainless steel with lower corrosion resistance than the 300 or 200 series, usually the least expensive of the stainless steels. Used primarily for interior work, with limited use in the automobile industry because of its resemblance to chromium.

FINISHES   The finishes of stainless steel products vary from a nonreflective matte finish to a highly polished reflective surface. Finishes available from the mill will vary on different fabricated shapes. The basic finish on round bar and

Fig. 6-17   Latticed steel load-bearing walls sheathed in stainless steel, Gateway No. 5, Pittsburgh, Pennsylvania, architects Curtis and Davis. (*American Iron and Steel Institute, Committee of Stainless Steel Producers.*)

wire is a smooth, moderately reflective surface that is suitable for many products. These shapes can be obtained with a ground or polished surface for brighter appearance. Square, rectangular, hexagonal, and irregular shapes are usually furnished in a cold-drawn or an unfinished pickled finish. Any of these shapes can be given a wide variety of finishes by the fabricator.

Standard finishes established for flat-rolled stainless steel are shown in Table 6-6.

Structural Steel

Structural steel consists of hot-rolled steel sections, shapes, and plates not less than $1/8$ in. thick, including all bracing, bolts, rivets, or devices necessary to hold a structural frame in place. The cutting of steel plates, the drilling or punching of holes for bolts or rivets, and the joining of

Fig. 6-18 Mirror-finish stainless-steel trim on escalator in the Toronto store of Robert Simpson Company, Ltd., architect Maxwell Hiller. (*American Iron and Steel Institute, Committee of Stainless Steel Producers.*)

TABLE 6-6 Stainless-steel finishes

TYPE	DESCRIPTION
1	Unfinished surface, annealed and pickled, used where appearance is not important
2D	Nonreflective surface, used where reflectivity is not important
2B	Bright, moderately reflective with a satin sheen, the most widely used finish
Matte	Produced in the mill by the use of special rolls
Scratch	A simulated polish finish produced in the mill
3	Polished with an abrasive to a bright, grained finish, suitable for exterior and interior trim
4	Polished with a finer abrasive
6	Polished with a fine grit abrasive and finished with a tampico brush to a velvety luster, used where appearance warrants the additional cost
7	A highly reflective surface produced by grinding, polishing, and buffing, used for special effects
8	A mirrorlike finish with the reflectivity of a plate-glass mirror
Specials	Most mills have developed special finishes to expand the design possibilities of stainless steel

structural steel assemblies, ready for shipment, is performed in a fabricating shop. The steel assemblies are erected on the job site by ironworkers.

Not all steel used in a building is classed as structural steel. Miscellaneous steel members that are architecturally necessary but are not required for the completion of the steel structural frame are classed as *miscellaneous metals*. These include such items as metal stairs, ladders, floor gratings, construction castings, curb angles, corner guards, and ornamental metalwork. Bolts, clips, joist anchors, and similar items that would be installed by the carpenter on the job are classed as *carpenter's iron*. Lintels, spanning openings in masonry walls, anchors, bolts, inserts, and ties embedded in masonry or concrete are usually not considered to be structural steel except when they are an integral part of a structural steel member. Metal flooring and lightweight steel joists or studs are seldom classed as structural steel.

STEEL CONSTRUCTION

There are three basic types of steel construction. These may be designated as wall-bearing, skeleton-framing, and long-span construction. One or more of these types may be used in a single structure.

Wall-bearing Construction

One of the oldest and most common types of construction consists of exterior or interior masonry walls supporting the ends of the structural elements which carry the floors and walls. The walls must be thick enough to carry the loads and resist the horizontal forces that may be applied to them by wind and earthquake. Modern developments in reinforced masonry construction have made this method economical for high-rise buildings in some areas. However, it is usually restricted to relatively low structures, such as residences and light industrial-type buildings, as unreinforced load-bearing masonry walls tend to become massive and uneconomical in taller buildings.

Steel beams used to span basement areas or wide openings in residences are an example of wall-bearing construction. Steel lintels supporting masonry over openings such as doors, windows, and fireplaces are another example. The relatively shallow dimension of a steel beam in comparison to the sizes of timbers necessary to carry heavy loads over long spans makes it possible to gain additional headroom where needed. The beam may be supported by steel-pipe columns at intermediate points for longer spans.

When steel beams are to rest on masonry, *bearing plates* are usually welded to the bottom, at each end of the beam. These bearing plates distribute the load safely to the masonry wall or pier. The ends of such members resting on masonry or reinforced concrete are usually provided with joist anchors thoroughly embedded in the masonry or concrete. It may be necessary to increase the wall thickness at beam bearing points to form a square engaged pillar or pilaster. It is sometimes feasible to introduce steel columns in the masonry wall to support the beams and keep the wall and pilaster thicknesses to the permissible minimum.

Skeleton Framing

A tall building with a steel frame is often referred to as *skeleton construction*. The first building with true skeleton construction was erected between 1884 and 1885. The Home Insurance Building in Chicago, designed by William Le Baron Jenny, embodied most of the features of the fully developed skyscraper.

All loadings, both live loads and dead loads, including walls, are supported by this steel skeleton. The exterior walls are thus non-bearing walls or curtain walls. Exterior and interior columns are spaced to provide support for the beams running between them. There is no limit to the area of floor or roof that can be supported by adding another row of columns and beams or a *bay*. The horizontal members or beams connecting the exterior columns, called *spandrel beams*, are equipped with *shelf brackets* to support the masonry spandrel over window and door openings.

Long-span Steel Construction

Large industrial buildings, auditoriums, sports arenas, exhibit halls, aircraft hangers, and similar structures may require greater distances between supports than can be spanned by the post-and-beam frame. When it is not possible to use a rolled-steel beam (36-in. maximum) to span the distance between supports, a girder, truss, arch, rigid frame, cable-hung frame, or several other types of framing systems may be used.

Where depths are limited, a *built-up girder* may be used. This consists of plates and shapes built up to the necessary strength. The top and bottom flanges of the built-up member resist the bending moment, and the web acts as a spacer to keep the two flanges apart. Holes may be cut in the web for electrical conduit and heating ducts. The flange plates may be tapered or arched rather than parallel to suit design requirements. The individual parts may be assembled by welding or riveting.

Fig. 6-19 High-rise building with load-bearing brick masonry walls. (*Masonry Research.*)

Where the depth of the structural member is not the limiting factor, it is usually more economical to use a *truss* to span large areas. The truss consists of a top chord and bottom chord, held apart by structural members called *struts*. The truss may be riveted or welded. The top and bottom chord may be parallel, as for floor construction, or the top chord may be tapered or formed as the arc of a circle. Figure 6-21 shows some of the most commonly used trusses.

When extremely long clear spans are needed, transverse framing, or *bents*, may take the form of solid or open-web *arches* which will support not only the roof structure, but the walls as well. The arches may be hingeless or

Fig. 6-20 Typical built-up girders.

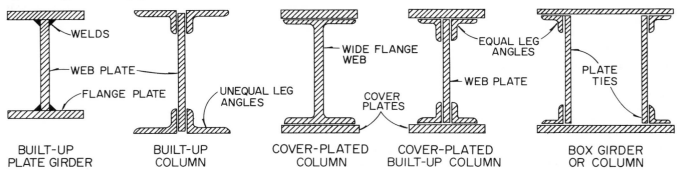

| BUILT-UP PLATE GIRDER | BUILT-UP COLUMN | COVER-PLATED COLUMN | COVER-PLATED BUILT-UP COLUMN | BOX GIRDER OR COLUMN |

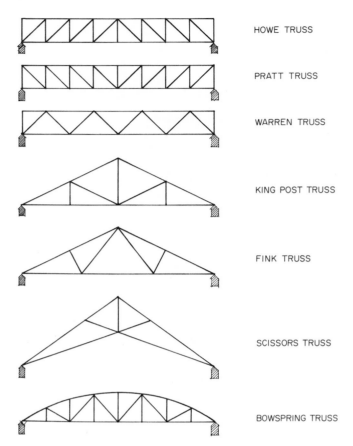

HOWE TRUSS

PRATT TRUSS

WARREN TRUSS

KING POST TRUSS

FINK TRUSS

SCISSORS TRUSS

BOWSPRING TRUSS

Fig. 6-21 Typical steel trusses.

welding. However, tapered columns with smooth transitions at the haunches to variable-depth beams may be exposed for design reasons. A smooth welded joint and the absence of rivet heads affords cleaner lines.

Cable-supported Construction

In recent years there has been substantial upsurge in the design and construction of structures with cable roofs. The first permanent large structure in the United States to use a cable roof was constructed in Raleigh, North Carolina, in 1953. A cable is the most economical steel span over wide areas. The roof deck may be constructed directly on the cables, or loads such as ceiling and roof framing, may be supported under the cables.

STEEL FASTENERS

There are several different methods of connecting steel members, such as rivets, unfinished bolts, high-strength structural bolts, and welds. The selection of a particular fastening system is based on many criteria, such as code requirements, fabricator's preference, and economic consideration. The common shop methods of fabrication are

Fig. 6-22 Typical steel arches.

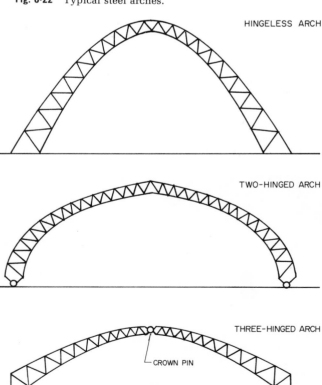

HINGELESS ARCH

TWO-HINGED ARCH

THREE-HINGED ARCH

CROWN PIN

BASE PIN

CONCRETE PIER

hinged. A *hingeless arch*, shown in Figure 6-22, may be used if soil conditions are suitable and loads are light. The more common practice is to use either the two-hinged or the three-hinged arch. A *two-hinged arch* consists of a trussed arch resting on large pins at the foundation. A *three-hinged arch* rests on two large pins used to connect the arch to the foundation and a third pin connecting the two halves at the center. There are two main advantages for the use of pin connections. The pin connections can be fabricated in the shop, they are simple to erect and align, and the design is greatly simplified.

Another type of long-span frame is the *rigid-frame bent*. The stiffness of the rigid bent is developed by careful detailing of the beam-to-column connection. This connection is made rigid by means of a *knee brace, gusset,* or *haunch,* as shown in Figure 6-23.

When fully assembled in the field, rigid bents are fully continuous and rigid. No pin connection is used in the center of the arch. The connection to the ground may have a pin connection or be bolted through a base plate to the foundation. Beams called *purlins* run perpendicularly to the bents to hold them in alignment and support the roof structure. The frames may be fabricated by riveting or welding and riveting, although high-strength bolts are replacing rivets in many shops. All methods may be used in the field. It is not uncommon to find one method of fastening used in the shop and another used in the field. Welded subassemblies delivered to the job site may be erected with bolts or rivets.

Rivets

Rivets are made of either an annealed, soft, carbon steel, for use with standard ASTM A36 structural steel, or as carbon-manganese steel rivets, suitable with proper driving techniques for use with high-strength carbon and high-strength low-alloy structural steel. The composition and characteristics of rivets are covered by ASTM A502. Rivets usually consist of a rounded buttonhead, and a cylindrical shank long enough to form a head at the other end after the rivet has been driven. This second head may be a *buttonhead*, a *flattened head*, a *countersunk head*, or a *countersunk* and *chipped head*.

The buttonhead is the most common type. Flattened and countersunk heads may be necessary in some locations. Countersunk and chipped heads are used where one side of the member may be a bearing surface.

Rivets are heated to a cherry red and placed in holes $1/16$ in. larger than the shank diameter. The rivet head is formed with a pressure-type or impact-type riveter. The *pressure-type riveter* consists of a heavy, C-shaped frame suspended from a crane. The rivet head is formed in one

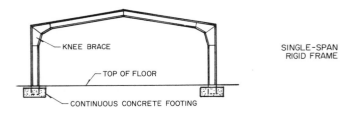

SINGLE-SPAN RIGID FRAME

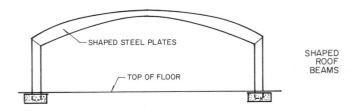

SHAPED ROOF BEAMS

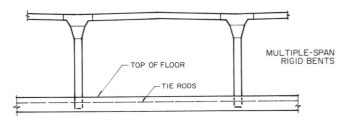

MULTIPLE-SPAN RIGID BENTS

Fig. 6-23 Rigid bents.

Fig. 6-24 First major building with a cable-hung roof, the State Fair arena at Raleigh, North Carolina, completed in 1953, architect William Henley Deitrick. (*Bethlehem Steel Corporation.*)

stroke, with a force of as much as 80 tons. The use of pressure-type riveters is usually confined to the fabrication shop. Impact riveters, called *riveting guns*, are powered by compressed air. The head is formed by repeated blows of a plunger that moves back and forth in the barrel of the riveting gun. A skillful operator can form a rivet head that is as satisfactory as that formed by a pressure riveter. As the rivet cools it contracts, exerting a clamping force on the material included.

Unfinished Bolts

Unfinished bolts may be called *machine, ordinary, common,* or *rough bolts* in the construction trade. They are designated as ASTM A307 and are made of low-carbon steel with rough, unfinished shanks. They are inserted in holes $1/16$ in. larger than the shank. Unfinished bolts are relatively inexpensive and can be tightened with a hand wrench. They may be used to hold structural steel members in place temporarily while field rivets are being driven.

When unfinished bolts are used for permanent connections, building codes limit the location and the stress that may be applied. Allowable working stresses are usually about two-thirds less than those of similar-sized rivets. The disadvantage of a larger number of bolts and possibly larger connections may be offset by less labor in making the joint.

High-strength Structural Bolts

One of the newest type of fasteners in steel construction is the *high-strength structural bolt.* These fasteners offer advantages in speed of construction, strength, simplicity, and safety. Their allowable carrying capacity is equal to that of rivets of the same size, and they are usually given

the same rating by building codes. Because of the high tensile strength of these bolts, they can be tightened so that friction between the parts is adequate to prevent a sliding motion in the joint. Cooled rivets tend to loosen and vibrate, and eventually to need replacement. The high initial tension of high-strength structural bolts is increased to the point that they afford sufficient resistance to vibration.

Two types of high-strength structural steel bolts are currently being produced: ASTM A325 and ASTM A490. ASTM standards (1970) provide for three types of A325 high-strength structural bolts: (1) bolts of medium-carbon steel, supplied in diameters of $1/2''$ to $1\frac{1}{2}''$; (2) bolts of low-carbon martensite steel, supplied in diameters of $1/2''$ to $1''$; and (3) bolts with atmospheric corrosion resistance and weathering characteristics comparable to those of A588 and A242 steels, supplied in diameters of $1/2''$ to $1\frac{1}{2}''$. All three types have the same allowable working stresses. The allowable applied working stress in tension for A325 bolts is 40,000 psi. For A490 bolts the allowable applied working stress in tension under static loading is 54,000 psi.

High-strength structural bolts and nuts manufactured to ASTM specifications for A325 and A490 are identified as shown in Figure 6-27.

High-strength bolts are inserted in holes $1/16$ in. larger than the shank. The head of the bolt is initially kept from turning by means of a hand wrench. The bolt is tightened with a pneumatic impact wrench, which can be adjusted to tighten each bolt to a predetermined tension, which is then checked with a torque wrench. Washers are not required under A325 nuts; however, the extremely hard material of the A490 bolt tends to roughen or *gall* the surface of standard A36 structural steel. The washers used are hardened to resist this galling.

Fig. 6-25 Interior of Raleigh State Fair arena. (*Bethlehem Steel Corporation.*)

Welding

Today welding is the principal method of joining steel building frames in the shop and ranks with high-strength structural bolts as one of the two principal methods for erecting structural steel. It has the inherent advantage of fusing the metals to be joined, thereby eliminating the need for reinforcing angles and cover plates. It is particularly advantageous for rigid frames and architecturally exposed structural steel members.

SHIELDED-METAL ARC WELDING This is the most commonly used process for structural steel work. An electric arc is formed between a coated metal electrode and the parts to be joined, generating enough heat to melt the base metal at the point of welding. The molten metal forms a puddle at the point of the arc, and additional metal from the metal electrode is fed into the puddle as tiny globules. The coating on the electrode melts and forms a gas that protects the molten metal from contact with the air. As the electrode is moved along the joint by the welder, the molten metal solidifies to form the weld. The coating forms slag or flux, which floats on top of the molten metal as a protection from the air. Molten metal exposed to the air tends to absorb oxides and nitrates which produce brittle welds. When the weld has cooled, the slag is easily removed with a chipping hammer.

SUBMERGED ARC WELDING In this type of welding a machine moves along a joint with a roll of uncoated wire and feeds it automatically into the joint. Heating is obtained by an electric arc between the wire, or electrode, and the metal to be welded. The welding is shielded by a blanket of granular, fusible material. The filler metal is obtained from the electrode and sometimes from a supplementary welding rod. It is difficult to use this process on anything but flat plates in a horizontal position. It is generally confined to the fabricating shop.

WELD TYPES There are several types of welds. The *fillet weld* is formed between two surfaces that are approximately at right angles to each other. The size of a fillet weld is measured along sides of the triangle formed. The strength of the weld is calculated by measuring from the intersection of the two plates perpendicular to the surface of the weld. A *lap weld* consists of two fillet welds applied to both ends of lapped plates. A *butt weld* is made by depositing metal in the joint formed when two plates or members are butted. If the edges butted are cut or shaped to form a groove, which may be V-, U-, or J-shaped, it is called a *groove weld*. These shapes may be formed on one side only or on two sides. If the plates are beveled on only one side, the joint is called a *single V*, and on two sides, a *double V*. *Plug welds* or *slot welds* are made in a circular or elongated hole in one member of a lapped joint. The

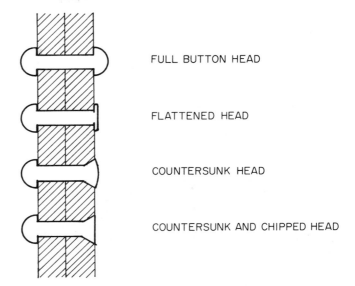

Fig. 6-26 Rivet types.

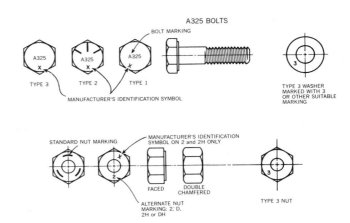

Fig. 6-27 Markings on high-strength steel bolts, from "Specification for Structural Joints Using ASTM A325 or A490 Bolts," 7th ed., March 31, 1970, endorsed by the American Institute of Steel Construction. (*By permission of the Industrial Fasteners Institute.*)

hole or slot is filled with weld metal, thereby joining the two members together.

The American Welding Society has set up standard welding symbols for use on drawings. These symbols indicate the type and size of the groove to be cut, the type and size of the weld, the finish expected, and the process to be used. Figure 6-31 shows an example of welding symbols. A complete explanation of welding symbols is given in the "Welding Handbook," published by the American Welding Society.

Fig. 6-28 Installing high-strength structural bolts. (*Republic Steel Corporation, Nut and Bolt Division.*)

STEEL FLOOR AND ROOF FRAMING

The selection of a suitable floor or roof system for a steel or masonry framed building is based on several considerations: span, load to be applied, depth, weight, fire resistance, sound transmission, air-conditioning system, heating ducts, appearance, construction time, and cost. As the floor and roof systems are intimately related to the structural system, it is well to consider them together. Building codes set minimum live loads that each system must carry, and most floor or roof systems can be designed to carry any reasonable load.

Concrete-arch Floors

One of the earliest types of floor used with steel-framed structures consists of intermediate steel beams approximately 8 ft apart, attached to the structural steel frame. Concrete is poured around the steel beam, and an integral floor slab about 4 in. thick is formed. The steel beam acts as reinforcement for the beams. This type of floor construction is called *concrete arch* because it resembles an older type of construction which used flat-brick arches to support the floor structure. To a great extent it has been superseded by lighter-weight flooring systems, except for

floors that must support exceptionally heavy loads. There are several variations of this type of floor or roof structure, such as the *metal-pan system*, which uses removable metal pans to form the beams in a poured concrete floor. This may be further modified by casting the floor in a ribbed, grid, or waffle pattern. In these floor or roof systems the steel beams are replaced by steel-bar reinforcement.

Open Web Steel Joists

One of the lightest roof and floor support systems in use today is the open web steel joist. Open web steel joists generally consist of parallel top and bottom chords of steel angles held apart by diagonally placed round steel bars. If the joists are to support a roof, the top chord may be sloped 1/8 in. to 1 ft from the center to one side. Steel decking can be welded directly to the top chord or the joist, or 2″ wood *nailers* can be installed on top of each to receive wood rafters.

Open web steel joists are manufactured in a wide range of spans to provide an economical floor or roof support system. Floor joists are produced to span up to 144 ft with a depth of 72 in. Specifications and load-bearing capacity for standard sizes of steel joists have been established by the Steel Joist Institute and the American Institute of Steel Construction. These specifications are for standard depths of 8″ to 24″ in 2-in. increments, or 18″ to 48″ in 4-in. increments, in lengths to accommodate all spans from 25 to 96 ft. For longer spans *open web deep longspan steel joists* are manufactured on special order by some companies.

Table 6-7 indicates standard designations and characteristics of steel joists. Full information on the load-bearing capacities of all standard sizes is given in "Standard Specifications and Load Tables Catalog," published by the Steel Joist Institute.

Open web steel joists are hung from the top chord of the truss. The ends of the joists are extended at least 4 in. for installation over or in masonry or concrete, and at least 2½ in. over steel supports. Special anchors are attached to the ends of the joist for anchorage in masonry or concrete and bearing plates for attachment to steel. The ends of the joist are welded or bolted to the steel framing member. If a ceiling is to be hung from the bottom chord of the truss, a ceiling extension is furnished to extend the bottom chord to the wall. Bracing or bridging must be installed between the joists to keep them from twisting when a load is applied. Since joists must be selected and spaced so that they carry no more than the recommended load, the type of decking which will span between the joists must be considered.

Steel Decks

The roof and floor decks of structural-steel-framed buildings or masonry buildings with open web steel joists, interlocking panels of light-gauge galvanized or painted

TABLE 6-7 Product designation for open web steel joists

SERIES	BASIC USE
J	Depths of 8″ to 24″ in 2-in. increments, spans up to 48′. 36,000 psi, minimum-yield-point steel in all component parts.
H	Depths of 8″ and 24″ in 2-in. increments, spans up to 48′. 50,000 psi, minimum-yield-point steel in chord sections.
LJ (longspan)	Depths of 18″ and 20″ up to 48″ in 4-in. increments, spans from 25′ to 96′. 36,000 psi minimum-yield-point steel in all components.
LH (longspan)	Depths of 18″ and 20″ up to 48″ in 4-in. increments, spans from 25′ to 96′. 50,000 psi minimum-yield-steel in chord sections, 35,000 to 50,000 psi minimum-yield-point steel in web sections.
DLJ (deep longspan)*	Depths of 52″ to 72″ in 4-in. increments, spans up to 144′. 36,000 psi minimum-yield-point steel.
DLH (deep longspan)*	Depths of 52″ to 72″ in 4-in. increments, spans up to 144′. 50,000 psi minimum-yield-point steel.

*Product of the Armco Steel Corporation, not shown in the SJI load tables. For deep longspan joist designations of other companies see the manufacturer's literature.

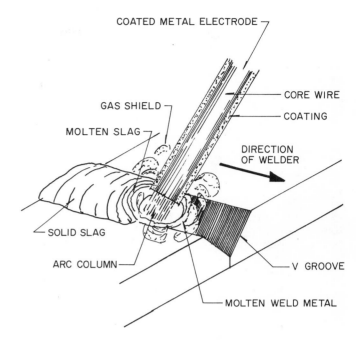

Fig. 6-30 Diagram of shielded-metal arc welding.

steel, either corrugated single sheets or built-up cellular units, are often used as the base for poured lightweight-concrete floors or roofing materials. The steel deck spans between the steel beams, joists, trusses, or structural frame. It may span as much as 25 ft, depending on the load, and is usually welded to the steel framing members. The deck may extend over the structural frame to form overhangs. The choice of a particular floor or roof decking system will be based on the required fire rating, span, load to be carried, ceiling to be installed under or hung from the deck, acoustical properties desired, electrical and telephone circuits to be embedded under the finished floor, and cost.

The simplest type of steel decking is the corrugated or ribbed type. This type of metal decking makes an efficient system because it serves as a reinforcing for a concrete

Fig. 6-29 Shielded-metal arc welding on structural steel frame. (*H. H. Robertson Company.*)

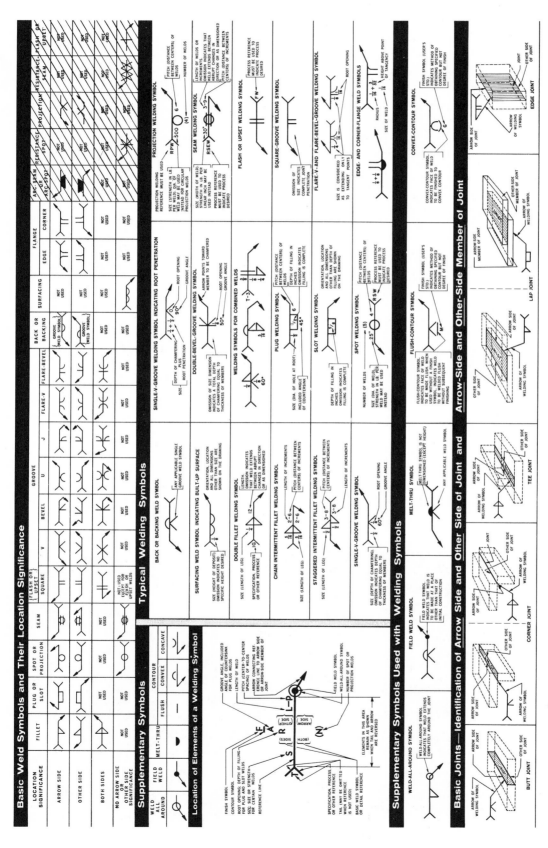

Fig. 6-31 Types of welds and welding symbols. (By permission of the American Welding Society.)

floor slab poured on top. Reinforcing steel is placed at right angles to the corrugations or ribs and welded to the steel deck, so that the entire assembly acts as a unit. Utilities may be embedded in the concrete floor slab. Rigid insulation board may be applied directly over the ribbed type decking. Certain types of ribbed steel decking have perforated fins, into which insulation may be placed to increase the sound-absorbing qualities of the assembly. The required fire resistance for the underside of the floor or roof deck is provided by ceilings of lath and plaster or other fire-resistant materials hung below.

Many types of cellular steel decking have been developed. Cellular steel decking has a decided advantage over corrugated decking in that the hollow cells can be used for utilities, which simplified the installation or modification of electrical or telephone outlets. Certain types have perforated bottom panels suitable for insulation. Types, spans, and loading capacities for steel deckings are given in publications of the Steel Deck Institute.

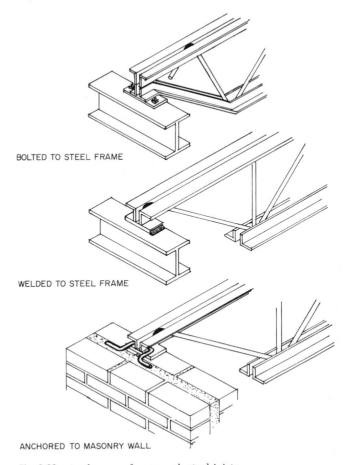

BOLTED TO STEEL FRAME

WELDED TO STEEL FRAME

ANCHORED TO MASONRY WALL

Fig. 6-33 Anchorage of open web steel joists.

Fig. 6-32 Open web steel floor joists.

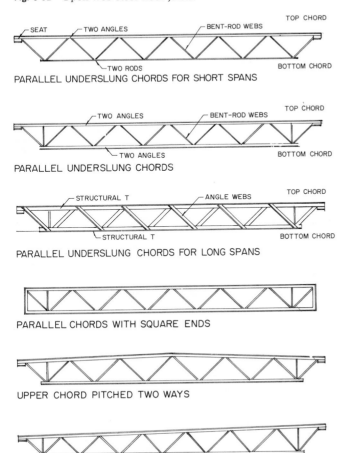

SEAT — TWO ANGLES — BENT-ROD WEBS — TOP CHORD
— TWO RODS — BOTTOM CHORD
PARALLEL UNDERSLUNG CHORDS FOR SHORT SPANS

— TWO ANGLES — BENT-ROD WEBS — TOP CHORD
— TWO ANGLES — BOTTOM CHORD
PARALLEL UNDERSLUNG CHORDS

— STRUCTURAL T — ANGLE WEBS — TOP CHORD
— STRUCTURAL T — BOTTOM CHORD
PARALLEL UNDERSLUNG CHORDS FOR LONG SPANS

PARALLEL CHORDS WITH SQUARE ENDS

UPPER CHORD PITCHED TWO WAYS

UPPER CHORD PITCHED ONE WAY

QUESTIONS

1. Define a metal.

2. Explain the difference between a ferrous and a nonferrous metal.

3. What is an alloy?

4. Define the terms *ductile*, *malleable*, and *oxidation*.

5. What is the maximum percentage of carbon in wrought iron?

6. What three substances are fed into a blast furnace to produce pig iron?

7. Make a simple drawing showing the operation of a blast furnace.

8. What are some of the by-products of a blast furnace?

9. Describe the properties and uses of three types of cast iron.

10. What is the major difference between cast iron and wrought iron?

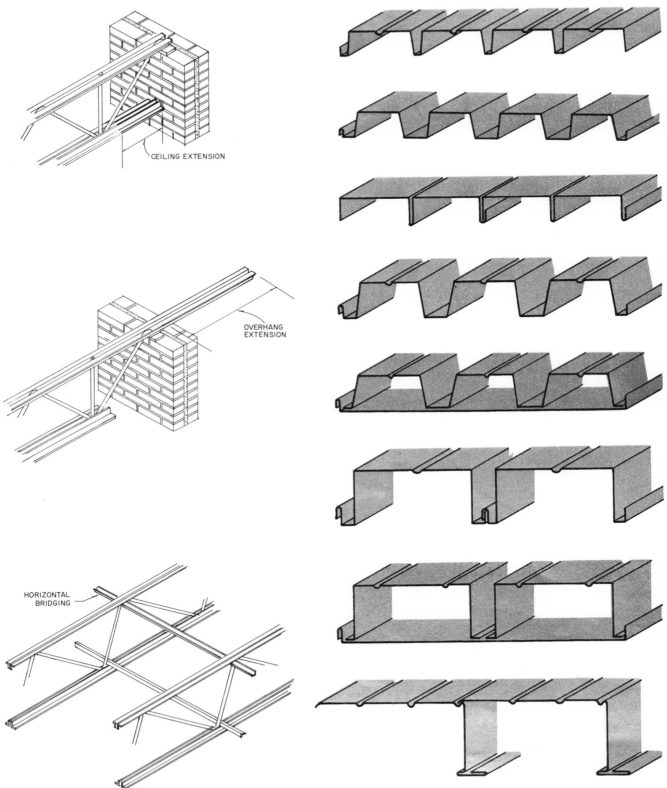

Fig. 6-34 Extension and bridging of open web steel joists.

Fig. 6-35 Types of cellular steel decking. (*By permission of the Sheet Metal and Air Conditioning Contractors' National Association.*)

11. What is steel?

12. Describe the four principal methods of making steel in use today.

13. What is the difference between acid steel and basic steel?

14. What is a soaking pit, and why is it needed in the production of structural steel shapes?

15. What are the characteristics and uses of cold-rolled steel?

16. Describe the process of making seamless steel pipe.

17. What is the feature that distinguishes tubing from pipe?

18. Give a brief description of the process of making wire.

19. What is meant by the temper of steel?

20. What are the basic properties of low-, medium-, and high-carbon steels?

21. What are the advantages of high-strength low-alloy steels?

22. What constitutes a stainless steel?

23. What stainless-steel alloy would you specify for use as flashing?

24. What is the ASTM designation for most structural steel in use today?

25. What is the most commonly used standard finish on stainless steel in architectural construction?

26. List 10 steel items that are not classed as structural steel.

27. Describe an open web steel joist.

28. Describe four types of longspan steel framing.

29. What is a rigid bent?

30. List the advantages and disadvantages of riveting in steel construction.

31. Sketch five types of welded joints.

32. Describe four types of floor systems used in conjunction with steel framing systems.

REFERENCES FOR FURTHER STUDY

American Institute of Steel Construction: 101 Park Avenue, New York, N.Y., 10017. "Specification for Design, Fabrication and Erection of Structural Steel for Buildings," 1963. "Manual of Steel Construction," 1963. "Specification for the Design, Fabrication and Erection of Structural Steel for Buildings," 1968. "Code of Standard Practice for Steel Buildings and Bridges," 1970.

American Iron and Steel Institute: 150 East 42d Street, New York, N.Y., 10017. *Building Report*, a periodical. "Steel Architectural Products," 1967. *Contemporary Steel Design*, a periodical. *Stainless Steel in Architecture*, a periodical. "Picture Story of Steel," 1958. *Steel Pipe News*, a periodical. "Standard Nomenclature for Structural Steel Shapes," 1970.

American Society for Testing and Materials: 1916 Race Street, Philadelphia, Pa., 19103. "ASTM Standards in Building Codes," published annually.

Armco Steel Corporation: Middletown, Ohio. "Building Picture," a series of pamphlets, 1968.

Hanson, Albert, "The Engineer's Guide to Steel," Addison-Wesley, Reading, Mass., 1965.

Hornbostel, Caleb, "Materials for Architecture," Reinhold, New York, 1963.

International Nickel Company, Inc.: 67 East 11th Street, New York, N.Y. "Architect's Guide to Nickel Stainless Steel Flashings," 1961.

Merrit, Frederick S., "Building Construction Handbook," McGraw-Hill, New York, 1958.

Steel Joist Institute: 2001 Jefferson Davis Highway, Arlington, Va., 22202. "Standard Specifications and Load Tables," 1970.

United States Steel: 525 William Penn Place, Pittsburgh, Pa., 15230. "The Making, Shaping, and Treating of Steel," 1964. "USS Cor-Ten Steel," 1966. "Ultimet Wall Framing Components: Architectural Details," 1966.

Other associations offering published material covering ferrous metals:

American Welding Society: 345 East 47th Street, New York, N.Y., 10017.

Cast Iron Pipe Research Association: Suite 3440, Prudential Plaza, Chicago, Ill., 60601.

Cast Iron Soil Pipe Institute: 1824-26 Jefferson Place, N.W., Washington, D.C., 20036.

Institute of Boiler and Radiator Manufacturers: 393 Seventh Avenue, New York, N.Y., 10001.

Steel Door Institute: 2130 Keith Building, Cleveland, Ohio, 41115.

Steel Joist Institute: 1346 Connecticut Avenue, N.W., Washington, D.C., 20036.

Steel Kitchen Cabinet Manufacturers' Association: 1120 Chester Avenue, Cleveland, Ohio, 44114.

Steel Window Institute: 18445 Harvest Lane, Brookfield, Wisc., 53005.

Wire Reinforcement Institute: 5034 Wisconsin Avenue, N.E., Washington, D.C., 20016.

NONFERROUS METALS AND ALLOYS

7

ALUMINUM AND ALUMINUM ALLOYS

Almost all nonferrous metals used in construction, with the possible exceptions of copper, lead, and zinc, are alloys. Nonferrous alloys are generally classified in terms of their predominant metal; thus most aluminums are aluminum-based alloys, tins are tin-based alloys, and so on. These metals may contain nonmetallic elements as well as some iron and still be classed as nonferrous metals.

The commercial history of aluminum covers less than 90 years. In that time aluminum has progressed from a curiosity to the leading nonferrous metal. Aluminum and its alloys are now essential in the manufacture of thousands of kinds of equipment and component parts used in the construction industry. There are two basic reasons that aluminum has become one of the most useful materials in the construction industry. One is its adaptability to many forming methods and the wide range of physical properties that may be imparted by the addition of alloying agents; another is its availability. Aluminum oxide, or *alumina*, is the most abundant element in the earth's crust. Whereas the known reserves of some metals have been steadily diminishing, bauxite, the major source of aluminum, has scarcely been tapped. The development of new sources of hydroelectric and atomic power necessary for the production of aluminum is constantly increasing.

The word *aluminum* (*aluminium* in Canada, Europe, and England) comes from the Latin *alumen*. Naturally occurring salts of aluminum were used by the Romans as long ago as 500 B.C. However, it was not until 1825 that Oersted produced the first metallic aluminum as a powder. In 1845 a process was developed to change this powder to small metallic particles. At this time aluminum was considered a precious metal and sold for $34 an ounce. Napoleon III reserved table settings made of this precious metal for honored guests; his other guests had to be content with solid gold or silver utensils. In 1855 several bars of aluminum, made by Deville of France, were displayed at the Paris Exhibition. The first known architectural use of aluminum in the United States was in 1884, when the Washington Monument was capped with aluminum, which is still in place.

In 1886 two scientists independently discovered the process that was to make possible the production of aluminum in large quantities. Charles M. Hall, an American, and Paul L. T. Heroult, a French chemist, developed an electrolytic process for reducing aluminum from aluminum oxide. They dissolved it in a solution of molten cryolite (sodium aluminum flouride, Na_3AlF_6), and when current from a battery or dynamo was passed through this solution, the aluminum was separated from other elements by the action of positive and negative electrodes. The oxygen passed off in the form of carbon monoxide, and molten aluminum flowed to the bottom of the tank. By 1892 the price of aluminum had dropped to 57 cents a pound. By 1950 the cost of aluminum ingots had dropped to approximately 16 cents a pound. In 1961 the United States produced or imported 4900 million lb of aluminum.

Properties of Aluminum

Aluminum is highly resistant to weather and to corrosive industrial and seacoast atmospheres. Although exposure causes surface oxidation and dulling, the metal is not weakened structurally. The oxide forms an added protective coating, so that the weathering rate soon tends to level off. The average penetration of weathering on architectural alloys is not much deeper after half a century than after 2 years. Exposure in a typical industrial atmosphere produces pitting to an average depth of only 0.003 in. after 52 years.

Pure aluminum (99.996 percent pure) is the most corrosion-resistant form of aluminum or its alloys, but it is extremely soft and weak. Alloys of aluminum with chromium, manganese, and silicon are still highly resistant to corrosion; alloys containing appreciable amounts of copper are more susceptible to corrosion. The addition of zinc improves the machining qualities of aluminum. Nickel increases its hardness. Manganese-aluminum alloys have been found to be nearly as resistant as commercially pure aluminum, and even more resistant to salt water and some alkaline solutions.

Some 50 standard aluminum alloys are currently available, and many others can be produced for specific purposes. The selection of a particular alloy depends largely on whether it will be formed by casting, rolling, or extrusion as well as on the mechanical properties and finishing characteristics desired.

Production of Aluminum

The basic raw material from which aluminum is produced is bauxite, an ore containing a high percentage of aluminum oxide. One of the world's largest bauxite deposits is on the Caribbean island of Jamaica, where there are extensive mining operations.

Alumina (aluminum oxide, Al_2O_3) is separated from bauxite by the *Bayer process*. Finely ground bauxite is mixed in a digester with soda ash, crushed lime, sodium hydroxide, and hot water. Live steam and agitators stir the mixture to bring all the materials into close contact to form sodium aluminate. Impurities settle to the bottom and are removed. The sodium aluminate is then pumped through filters to precipitators, where it is mixed with aluminum hydrate. As the mixture cools, aluminum hydrate settles to the bottom, and sodium hydroxide rises to the top. The sodium hydroxide is pumped back to the

Fig. 7-1 Mining bauxite. Power shovels scoop up bauxite and load it into huge trucks in mining operations of the Kaiser Bauxite Company in Jamaica, West Indies. (*Kaiser Aluminum and Chemical Corporation.*)

Fig. 7-2 Unloading bauxite from Jamaica at the Mississippi River dock of the Kaiser plant in Baton Rouge, Louisana. (*Kaiser Aluminum and Chemical Corporation.*)

precipitators for reuse, and the aluminum hydrate is *calcined* (heated) in rotary kilns at temperatures of 2000°F, where it becomes alumina. By this process 4 lb of bauxite ore become 2 lb of alumina, which convert to 1 lb of metallic aluminum.

The alumina is converted to aluminum in an electric furnace by the *Hall-Heroult process.* The furnace consists of a large steel tank which is lined with carbon and filled with a solution of melted cryolite and alumina. Large anodes of carbon are suspended in the electrolytic bath from overhead bars. When a current of 8000 to 20,000 amp is passed through the solution, the metallic aluminum separates out and settles to the bottom of the tank, where it is drawn off through a taphole. The molten aluminum may be cast into molds as *pigs* or conveyed to an alloying furnace for the production of standard or special alloys.

CASTING ALLOYS   There are several processes of casting aluminum alloys. The molten aluminum alloy may be poured into sand molds or into metal molds. Aluminum alloys are also poured into plaster molds to produce plaster-process and *investment* castings. In the die-casting process the molten alloy is forced into steel molds under pressure.

Aluminum alloys used for casting are designated by a two- or three-digit number indicating their composition.

These number designations are sometimes followed by a letter indicating the temper.

WROUGHT ALLOYS   Aluminum alloys used in the production of sheet products and extruded shapes are heat-treatable or non-heat-treatable alloys. *Heat-treatable alloys* attain maximum strength through controlled heat treatment, either before or after forming operations. These are the highest-strength alloys. They are hard, retain their appearance, and generally have good resistance to corrosion and abrasion. These alloys are particularly suited for structural applications and other uses requiring a combination of formability and strength, and are produced commercially in the form of extrusions and forgings. *Non-heat-treatable alloys* attain maximum strength, beyond the annealed condition, through work hardening as a result of cold rolling. They have high corrosion resistance, good formability, pleasing appearance, and good weldability, and are widely used for manufactured products and general sheet applications.

Alloy Designations

The designations for casting alloys are arbitrarily assigned numbers. However, the Aluminum Association has devised a four-number system which is used by most producers to identify wrought aluminum and aluminum alloys. The first digit identifies the alloy type or major alloying element, as shown in Table 7-1. The second digit

TABLE 7-1   Wrought-alloy designations

DESIGNATION	DESCRIPTION
EC	A special electrical-conductor series
1xxx	Commercially pure aluminum, 99.00 percent pure and greater
2xxx	Copper-based alloys
3xxx	Manganese-based alloys
4xxx	Silicon alloys
5xxx	Magnesium alloys
6xxx	Magnesium-silicon alloys
7xxx	Zinc
8xxx	Other elements
9xxx	Unused series

in the alloy designation indicates the amount of control of impurities, and the last two digits identify the proportion of aluminum, or the specific alloy. For alloys in use before adoption of the four-digit system the digits are the same as the numbers in the old designation. For example, 1060 indicates aluminum that is 99.60 percent pure, or 0.60 percent more than required for the 1xxx series, with only minimal control of impurities, and 1175 designates an aluminum that is 99.75 percent pure with some control of impurities. The designation 2014 indicates an aluminum-copper alloy which is used widely for rolled structural shapes; 2017 is an aluminum-copper alloy used for rivets; 2911 is a modified aluminum-copper alloy used for screws. Architectural aluminum alloys are listed in Table 7-2.

Temper and Heat Treatment

Temper in nonferrous alloys indicates the hardness and strength produced by mechanical or thermal treatment, or both, as characterized by mechanical properties or reduction in area during cold working. Heat-treatable alloys contain elements that cause increase in strength when the alloy is heated to a certain point and then quenched in a cooling medium. This process is called *solution heat treating*. Some alloys can be further strengthened by *precipitation hardening*, or aging. If they are allowed to stand for several days at room temperature, or slightly above room temperature, they will increase in strength and hardness.

For many fabrication processes alloys must be softened or annealed to remove the effects of work hardening. The piece is heated in a closed furnace until it has reached the specified temperature throughout, and then it is cooled slowly in still air.

Because of the various combinations of heat treatment, aging, and annealing possible for aluminum alloys, a system of letter and number designations is used to indicate the type of heat treatment and the temper of the various products of the mill. These designations, shown in Table 7-3, follow the alloy designations; for example, alloys might be designated as 1100-H16, 3003-0, 6061-T13.

Aluminum Finishes

Pure aluminum spontaneously forms a transparent oxide film which inhibits further oxidation. As a result, it is highly resistant to corrosion. However, it is very soft. Aluminum alloys can be formulated that will achieve

Fig. 7-3 Production of aluminum. Overhead crane moves a crucible of molten aluminum which has just been tapped from the electrolytic cells, or pots, in this potline at the Kaiser works in Ravenswood, West Virginia. (*Kaiser Aluminum and Chemical Corporation.*)

TABLE 7-2 Architectural aluminum alloys

ALLOY	TYPE
	Sheets and plates
1100 Sheet, plate	Used for sheet-metal applications where high strength is not required. It has excellent weldability, resistance to corrosion, and a high degree of forming or drawing. When anodized it is moderately bright. It can be porcelain enameled.
3003 Sheet, plate	A general-purpose alloy, commonly used for sheet-metal applications. It has higher strength than alloy 1100, is readily welded, and has good corrosion resistance. Assumes a slight yellow cast when anodized.
3004 Alclad sheet	A moderately high-strength alloy. Used for corrugated, ribbed, or V-beam sections and various embossed patterns.
5005 Sheet, plate	Comparable to alloy 3003 in strength and workability, is readily welded, and has good corrosion resistance. When anodized it is a close color match for anodized alloy 6063 extrusion.
5050 Sheet, plate	A stronger alloy than 3003 or 5005. It is readily welded and has good corrosion resistance and a comparatively clear white appearance after anodizing.
5052 Sheet, plate	Has higher strength than alloy 5050 and has good weldability and corrosion resistance. A thin anodic coating is a fair color match with anodized alloy 6061 sheet and 6063 extrusion.
6061 Sheet, plate	Is a high-strength heat-treatable alloy with good workability in the annealed condition after solution heat treatment. It is readily welded and has good corrosion resistance. Because of its strength it is frequently used for formed structural shapes. When anodized it is a good color match for alloy 6061 extrusion, but not with other alloys.
	Extrusions
6061 Extrusion	Used principally for extruded structural shapes, pipe and tubing, or other applications requiring high strength. When anodized it is a good color match with alloy sheet 6061 but not a close color match with other alloys.
6063 Extrusion	The most commonly used extrusion for building and ornamental metal products. When heat-treated it develops moderately high strength. It is readily welded and has good corrosion resistance. When anodized it is a good color match with alloy sheet 5005.
	Castings
43 Casting	Used for hardware and ornamental metalwork where low-strength castings are satisfactory. Will turn gray shades when anodized.
214 Casting	Best appearance match with 6063 extrusions and 5005 sheet when anodized. Higher strength than alloy 43 casting.
356 Casting	High-strength casting alloy. Turns gray when anodized.

TABLE 7-2 Architectural aluminum alloys (*Continued*)

ALLOY	TYPE
	Fasteners
1100	For low-strength rivets and washers. Plain or anodized.
2024	For bolts, nuts, and screws. Plain or anodized.
6061	For high-strength rivets and bolts. Plain or anodized.

By permission of the National Association of Architectural Metal Manufacturers.

strengths of 20,000 to 68,000 psi, but the alloying elements tend to decrease the resistance of the metal to corrosion. A number of finishes and coatings may be applied to aluminum that greatly extend its usefulness. Mechanical and chemical finishes may be used to produce a variety of surface textures, and electrolytic finishes, organic coatings, and porcelain enamel may be used for protection.

MECHANICAL AND CHEMICAL FINISHES Aluminum may be produced with various surface textures, from smooth to rough, in addition to the natural mill finishes. These mechanical and chemical finishes may be used as final finishes, but they should be protected during handling and construction with lacquer or some other coating. Aluminum products are usually available with the surface textures shown in Table 7-4. Additional finishes are available from individual manufacturers.

ELECTROLYTIC FINISHES One of the protective treatments used to improve the corrosion and abrasion resistance of aluminum is *anodizing*. Aluminum pieces are placed into an electrolytic bath of sulfuric or chromic acid, at a temperature of around 70°F. The aluminum part is made the positive pole, or *anode*, of an electric couple, and current of 10 to 20 amp/sq ft of surface area to be anodized is forced through the solution. This treatment does not apply a coating, but converts an extremely thin layer of aluminum on the surface to an oxide that is almost diamond hard. This film of hard aluminum oxide does not necessarily change the appearance of the surface. The thickness of the coating, and therefore its corrosion resistance, depends not only on time in the bath, but on the composition, concentration, and temperature of the electrolyte, intensity of current, agitation of the bath, and sealing of the film after anodizing. Times for clear oxide coatings range from 20 to 60 min for coatings of 0.00025″ to 0.0008″. After the coating has reached the desired thickness it is sealed by immersing the part in boiling water. Standard anodized coatings are given in Table 7-5.

The anodized coatings on aluminum may be colored by forcing dyes into the relatively spongy oxide coating before it is sealed. A wide range of colors may be produced by this method for use in interiors and protected locations.

TABLE 7-3 Temper designation of aluminum alloys

DESIGNATION	DESCRIPTION
F	As fabricated. Some temper is acquired during rolling, but properties may vary considerably, depending on the size and shape of the piece.
O	Fully annealed, recrystallized. This is the softest temper of alloy products.
H1	Strain hardened. Strength has been increased by working without subsequent heat treatment. A second digit indicates the degree of hardness; for example, H14 is a cold-rolled material midway between O and H19, H18 is full-hard commercial temper, and H19 is extra-hard temper.
H2	Strain hardened and then partially annealed. A second digit (2 to 8) indicates degree of strain hardening remaining after annealing.
H3	Strain hardened and then stabilized. A second digit indicates the degree of strain hardening remaining after stabilization.
W	Solution heat-treated. Temper is unstable owing to natural aging after heat treatment.
T	Thermal treatment to produce stable temper without supplementary strain hardening.
T2	Applies to castings only, improved ductility and dimensional stability through annealing.
T3	Solution heat treated and cold worked to improve strength.
T4	Solution heat treated and naturally aged to stable condition.
T5	Artificially aged only.
T6	Solution heat treated and artificially aged.
T7	Solution heat treated and then stabilized.
T8	Solution heat treated, cold worked, and then stabilized.
T9	Solution heat treated, artificially aged, and then cold worked to improve strength.
T10	Artificially aged and then cold worked.

Fig. 7-4 Painting aluminum sheet. Paint line at the Reynolds sheet and plate plant in McCook, Illinois. (*Reynolds Metals Company.*)

Because of the nature of the finishing process, minor variations in shading can be expected from one colored element to another. The differences are particularly noticeable between sheet and extrusions. The colors have the same susceptibility to fading as do other dyed objects.

Most aluminum producers have developed anodic treatments that produce a colored hard oxide finish without the use of dyes. In this process, called *hard coating*, the color comes from the nature of the alloy and the electrolyte. The result is a colored surface that is weather and abrasion resistant. The Reynolds Aluminum Company's Reyno Color 5000 series, Alcoa's Duranodic finishes, and Kaiser's Kalcolor are examples of this process.

Exterior doors, windows, and other members that will be subject to construction marring or plaster and mortar droppings should be protected by coatings of clear methacrylate lacquer. This clear lacquer offers a reasonably effective barrier against chemical and physical damage during installation. It wears off in time, leaving the metal surfaces undamaged.

PORCELAIN-ENAMEL COATINGS Aluminum may be given a colorful, hard, resistant surface by fusing glass and finely ground pigments to the surface at high temperature (in excess of 800°F). The resulting opaque porcelain coating is highly resistant to alkali and acid and relatively unaffected by weather. Since porcelain enamel can be applied in thinner coats and has better adhesion to aluminum than to other metals, it has been said that it can withstand much greater impact deformation without chipping. Most colors can be obtained in porcelain enamel, with finishes in any degree of gloss. Color match is accurate, and there is relatively little fading.

Wrought Aluminum

Aluminum is one of the most workable of all common commercial metals. With careful control of temperatures

Fig. 7-5 Aluminum ingots. Crane lowers a huge aluminum ingot to await its turn on the plant's hot rolling line. Ingots weighing 10,000 lb or more are rolled in successive operations to plate, sheet, or foil as thin as two ten-thousandths of an inch. (*Kaiser Aluminum and Chemical Corporation.*)

TABLE 7-4 Standard aluminum finishes

FINISH	DESCRIPTION
Bright buffed	A smooth, highly lustrous surface produced by muslin buffing wheels and sometimes by hand buffing. Suitable for a high-gloss finish on narrow elements, but usually too costly and difficult to apply on large areas.
Scratch brushed	A coarse, lined texture imparted by rotary stainless-steel brushes.
Satin	A soft texture of fine parallel lines produced by polishing with abrasive cloth belts or canvas wheels with 180- to 220-grit abrasives.
Sandblasted	A rough texture produced by blasting with compressed air and washed silica sand in varying grades of fineness. This texture must be protected by further finishing.
Frosted or caustic etched	A low-cost chemically produced matte surface with the appearance of finely etched glass. Used for windows, mullions, and large sheet areas such as wall panels.
Chemical polish	A mirror-bright finish for high-purity alloys. Can be used to brighten textured surfaces not amenable to buffing.
Conversion coating	A low-cost chemically produced coating applied as surface preparation for paint films. Produced in durable colors of pale green, grey-green, and tan also suitable as final finishes on roofing.

and mechanical factors that would affect the properties of the finished product, it can be extruded or rolled to exact dimensions with the proper temper in an extensive variety of shapes.

PLATE   The first step in producing plate is the melting, alloying, and pouring of *billets*, which may weigh from 2000 to 9000 lb. The billets are *scalped* (cleaned), and preheated in electric soaking pits to bring them to a uniform temperature for rolling. The first rolling is done in a slab mill, which reduces them to nearly 30 percent of their original thickness. The resulting slab is usually taken to its final reduction in a hot reversing mill. It is then given a solution heat treatment and stretched at least 2 percent of its length in a plate stretcher. This improves the flatness and gives the plate a permanent set which minimizes any tendency of the plate to warp or twist during fabrication. As a final operation, the plate is either sheared or cut to the required dimensions.

SHEET   When plate comes from the reversing mill, it may be fed into a continuous hot mill, where it passes directly from one stand to the next and is rolled progressively

thinner. It is then coldrolled through a succession of rollers to its final thickness. As the sheet is rolled, it loses its ductility and becomes brittle. Sometimes it must be annealed between the rolls before it can be reduced to the required thickness.

The sheet may be given any one of many finishes during coldrolling, from a dull, matte finish to a bright, buffed polish. It may also be *embossed*. This process produces a sheet with a raised pattern on one side and the same pattern impressed on the reverse. Embossed sheet is stiffer than regular flat sheet and provides an attractive mar-resistant surface that diffuses incident light. The pattern on either side of the sheet may be used, for variations in appearance. Sheets may also be embossed with the pattern on one side and the other side smooth.

ROLLED STRUCTURAL SHAPES   The same structural shapes that are produced in steel are available in aluminum alloys. H beams, I beams, angles, and other structural shapes are produced of alloys that rival steel on the basis of comparative weight. These structural shapes may be produced by rolling or extrusion.

Rolled structural shapes start, as does sheet and plate,

with a billet. The billet is passed through a series of rolls, each of which forms a cross-sectional shape more nearly approaching the final form. The rollers are shaped and spaced so that each pair produces only a small deformation. The last pair produces the final shape. No straightening is required, since roll-formed products are normally very straight and free from distortion.

Extrusions

To produce extruded shapes a hydraulically operated ram forces a hot (but not molten) aluminum billet through openings in a precision-made die. The result is a fine-grained extrusion conforming exactly to the configurations and dimensions of the die. The versatility of this process makes it possible to form an infinite variety of uniform precision products. One extrusion may replace complex assemblies of roll- and brake-formed shapes. It is possible to produce extrusions having a cross-sectional area of more than 60 sq in. and lengths up to 30 ft.

Voids or hollow members are formed by pressing a hollow cast ingot over a mandrel. As it is forced through the die and over the mandrel the specified void is formed. Irregularly shaped voids and thin-walled sections may be extruded as open sections, which are then pulled at welding heat through a second die that closes them and so forms the void.

Aluminum extrusions are widely used as window and door components, framing members in curtain-wall construction, and structural framing members. A wide variety of ornamental and functional shapes are extruded. Aluminum thresholds and weatherstripping shapes are produced for both residential and commercial applications. Extruded copings, gravel stops, and fascias are produced for use as roofing accessories.

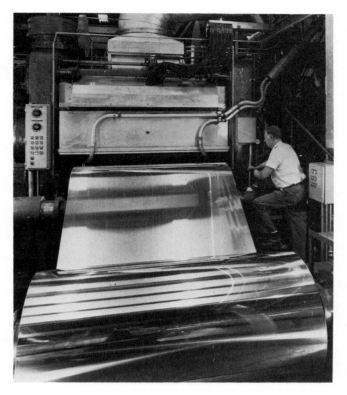

Fig. 7-6 Aluminum foil for the nation's kitchens rolls off an 84-inch mill at a Reynolds plant. (*Reynolds Metals Company.*)

ALUMINUM PRODUCTS

Today there are over 7000 manufacturers of aluminum building products, and the number is growing. Over 25 percent of all the aluminum produced (over 1.3 billion lb in 1970) is used in the construction industry. In general, sheet is the most economical form of aluminum for construction use. It is adaptable to a broad range of applications and may be fabricated into many shapes by brake forming, roll forming, or die forming. However, extrusions are more widely used because of the variety of shapes that are not possible in roll or brake forming. Aluminum castings offer a wide latitude in both configuration and texture, since intricate detail can be accurately reproduced. However, patterns are expensive, and thickness requirements are greater for casting than for either sheet or extrusions.

Tube and Pipe

The Aluminum Association defines aluminum tube quite broadly as "a hollow wrought product that is long in relation to its cross section, which is round, a regular hexagon, a regular octagon, elliptical, or square or rectangular with sharp or rounded corners, and that is uniform wall thickness except as affected by corner radii." Thus *aluminum tube* also includes pipe. Table 7-6 indicates the various types of aluminum tube and pipe.

TABLE 7-5 Standard anodized coatings

SYMBOL	MIN. THICK-NESS, IN.	MIN. WEIGHT PER SQ IN., MG	USE
202	0.00025	12	Minimum abrasion resistance, suitable for interior moldings, balusters, interior fascias
204	0.004	17	Medium abrasion resistance, suitable for interior and exterior door and window frames, baseboards, and hardware
215	0.0008	35	Maximum resistance to abrasion, suitable for handrails, store fronts, and exterior trim

Wire

Aluminum wire is produced by hot rolling a rod to a size slightly larger than the desired diameter and drawing it to the final dimension through a series of progressively smaller dies. Much of the aluminum wire that is produced is fabricated into insect screens, which are usually made from 22-gauge (0.029″) wire. Over 90 percent of the electrical transmission lines in the United States use aluminum cable or steel-reinforced aluminum cable.

The EC alloy used for electrical conductors is 99.45 percent aluminum with close control of impurities and trace additions of copper and boron. This alloy provides high conductivity at low cost. The conductivity of aluminum is 61 percent that of copper on the basis of size. However, on the basis of weight, aluminum can carry twice the amount of electricity. Steel-reinforced aluminum conductors consist of one or more strands of aluminum wire around a high-strength galvanized-steel wire core. This type of conductor permits longer spans and fewer poles on high-voltage transmission lines.

Sheet Products

CORRUGATED SHEET   In the last 25 years aluminum corrugated roofing and siding, developed for use on industrial buildings, has found increasing acceptance in nonindustrial construction because of its excellent weathering qualities. Corrugated panels are available with a plain mill finish, in embossed patterns, as perforated sheet, and in color. They usually consist of an inner core of aluminum alloy with an alloy coating that is resistant to industrial gases, fumes, and salt spray.

Aluminum corrugated industrial sheet is produced in thicknesses of 0.024″, 0.032″, 0.040″, and 0.050″ and in lengths from 3 to 30 ft in 6-in. increments. The two lighter gauges are formed with regular corrugations ⁷/₈ in. deep and 2.67 in. apart. The heavier gauges are usually produced with 1³/₄-in. deep V-shaped corrugations 4³/₄ in. apart. Several types of ribbed roofings and sidings are produced by different manufacturers. Curved corrugated sheets, produced for specialized applications such as storage tanks or curved roofs, are available with a radius from 1½ to 20 ft or more.

Perforated corrugated sheet is used with sound-absorbing materials to provide an exceptionally low-cost, noise-reducing wall. The holes admit and trap sound. These sheets are usually used as an inner panel in industrial sandwich walls. These are insulated walls fabricated, either in the shop or in the field, by sandwiching a layer of insulating material, such as glass fiber, between two sheets of aluminum. The exterior facing may be round or V-shaped siding and the interior facing 0.032″ corrugated or perforated sheet.

ALUMINUM SIDING   More than 3 million residences have been clad in aluminum siding. Most aluminum siding has a factory-applied coating of sprayed-on enamel, baked-on enamel, or porcelain enamel. The baked-enamel coatings

Table 7-6 Types of aluminum tube and pipe*

TYPE	DESCRIPTION
Alclad tube	Composite tube consisting of an aluminum-alloy core and, on either the inside or the outside surface, an anticorrosive aluminum or aluminum-alloy coating metallurgically bonded to the core
Brazed tube	Tube produced by forming and seam brazing sheet
Drawn tube	Tube brought to final dimensions by drawing through a die
Extruded tube	Tube formed by hot extruding
Lock seam tube	Tube produced by forming and mechanically lock seaming sheet
Open seam (butt seam) tube	Normally produced from sheet of nominally uniform wall thickness; approximately tubular, but with longitudinal unjointed seam or gap no wider than 25 percent of the outside diameter or greatest over-all dimension
Seamless tube	Tube which has no line junctures resulting from the method of manufacture
Stepped drawn tube	A drawn tube whose cross section changes abruptly at intervals along its length (as, for example, in aluminum golf-club shafts)
Structural tube	Extruded tube which may contain an extrusion seam, suitable for applications not involving internal pressure
Welded tube	Produced by forming and seamwelding sheet longitudinally
Butt welded	Formed by positioning one edge of the sheet against the other for welding
Helical welded	Formed by winding the sheet into a closed helix and joining the edges of the seam by welding
Lap welded	Formed by lapping the edges of the sheet for welding
Pipe	Tube in standardized combinations of outside diameter and wall thickness, commonly designated by national pipe sizes and ANSI schedule numbers
Seamless	Pipe produced from a hollow extrusion billet
Structural	Extruded pipe, which may contain an extrusion seam, suitable for applications not involving internal pressure

*From "Nomenclature for Aluminum Mill Products," published by the Aluminum Association, 4th ed., April 1968.

are usually guaranteed up to 15 years. Porcelain-enamel coatings are available in a range of finishes, from high gloss to matte. Porcelain enamel, which consists of a ceramic base permanently fused to the metal, has been used successfully for exterior surfaces for more than 50 years.

Aluminum siding for residential use is produced in many designs and textures. The textures are rolled into the sheet before fabrication to simulate wood grains, and the siding is usually produced in interlocking strips, to represent horizontal or vertical wood siding. The individual strips range from 8″ to 16″ in width. Several manufacturers produce horizontal siding with fiberboard laminated to the back for increased insulation and maximum ease of installation. The siding is usually nailed over waterproof paper to solid wood sheathing or stripping. When the siding is cut, extreme care must be taken to seal the raw aluminum edges. Otherwise water in direct contact with the metal will cause discoloration.

ALUMINUM CURTAIN WALLS   A metal curtain wall is attached to the structural frame of a building. It may consist of metal panels or combinations of metal panels and glass. In addition to protection from the elements, a curtain wall must provide a barrier to the passage of heat. It must also be esthetically appropriate for the building and sufficiently permanent to last for the expected life of the building. Most curtain walls are custom designed for specific projects, especially on the larger buildings.

Curtain-wall systems are usually based on mass-produced components. Some systems consist of sandwich panels of sheet aluminum, with insulation enclosed between a color-anodized or enameled exterior sheet and a vinyl-covered interior sheet. Other curtain walls may

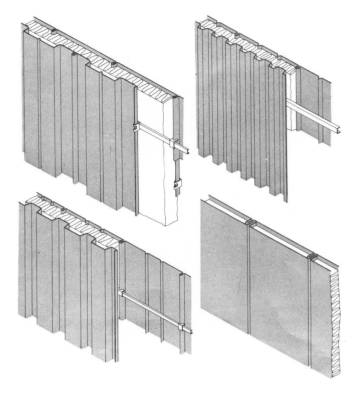

Fig. 7-7   Types of corrugated aluminum sandwich panels. (*By permission of the Sheet Metal and Air Conditioning Contractors' National Association.*)

Fig. 7-8   Aluminum sun-control screen on United States Aluminum's general offices, Monterey Park, California. (*United States Aluminum; photo by Leigh Wiener.*)

Fig. 7-9 Lead pipe in Pompeii installed before 79 A.D. (*By permission of The California Plumbing Contractor.*)

consist of glass held both vertically and horizontally in extruded aluminum shapes. Curtain walls are discussed further in Chapter 12.

ALUMINUM COLUMN COVERS One of the newest innovations in steel framing is the use of external structural steel members covered with aluminum cladding for protection (not to be confused with clad metal). One outstanding example of this type of construction is the John Hancock Center in Chicago, completed in 1968. This 100-story building extends 1125 ft above a depressed concourse level and is topped with twin television towers that extend up another 344 ft. It is supported by vertical steel columns and long double diagonals across every 18 stories. Both the vertical columns and the diagonals are protected by aluminum cladding.

The cladding panels from the second to the twenty-first floor are constructed of ³⁄₁₆″ aluminum sheet, and those

from the twenty-second to the hundredth floor are constructed of ⅛″ aluminum sheet. A black anodized finish was used for the column and diagonal cladding, and a bronze anodized finish was for the window frames and panels. Between the aluminum cladding and the structural steel frame is 2 to 4 in. of urethane foam to accommodate expansion and contraction of the frame under a possible 85°F temperature difference between the interior of the building and the exterior surface.

Ornamental Products

Many types of rods, bars, and other shapes are manufactured as stock items for assembly as ornamental railings, balustrades, screens, and grilles. Expanded metal sheet is used for decorative screens or sun shades. New types and designs are being produced by extrusion as hand rails, thresholds, brackets, and connections. Many of these are patented products or produced on special order.

Windows account for the greatest amount of heat entering buildings, and therefore the method of shading them offers the greatest opportunity for improved performance. An infinite variety of patterns are available in aluminum grillework that acts as a sun shade as well as ornamentation. Any degree of shading and visibility can be achieved by varying the thickness and angle of the screen elements. Screens may be produced from expanded or formed sheets or fabricated by welding or special connections. Aluminum shades and grilles may be color anodized for a permanent finish or factory finished in baked enamel.

Joining Aluminum

Aluminum parts may be joined or attached with screws or special fasteners. When fasteners of a metal other than aluminum are used, care must be taken that the metal is compatible with the aluminum; otherwise galvanic action may destroy the joint. (The problem of galvanic action is discussed at the end of this chapter.) Most aluminum alloys may be welded. Practically all aluminum is welded by the *inert-gas shielded arc method*. In this process an electric arc is used to heat and fuse the metal, and the melted metal is shielded from contact with the air by an inert gas (usually helium). Aluminum alloy 4030 is usually used as the electrode. If the parts to be welded are anodized, the weld points must be in inconspicuous locations, as there is usually some discoloration in the heat-affected areas around the weld.

LEAD

The use of lead in construction can be traced back more than 2000 years, but its applications for waterproofing, sound and vibration insulation, corrosion resistance, and decorative treatment have continued to increase. The Romans made extensive use of lead for water pipes. In fact the chemical symbol for lead, Pb, comes from the Roman word for water pipe, *plumbum*. Examples of these lead pipes have been uncovered in Italy, Spain, and England in a remarkable state of preservation. In many buildings constructed in the fifteenth and sixteenth centuries the original lead roofs are still intact.

Production of Lead

Zinc, silver, and several other metals are commonly associated with lead ore. These metals are separated from the lead by flotation techniques and are extracted separately. The lead concentrate (lead sulfide) is then roasted to form lumps of lead oxide, which are fed into a blast furnace with coke, iron oxide, and lime. As the lead collects at the bottom of the furnace, it is tapped off at intervals for further refining and alloying. The principal metal used in commercial lead alloys is antimony (6 to 7 percent), which provides hardness and strength. This alloy is called *hard lead*. Lead may also be alloyed with tin to form soft solder. Copper, nickel, silver, iron, manganese, and other elements may be added to impart useful qualities to the finished product.

The physical properties of lead that make it valuable for construction are its resistance to corrosion, its malleability, and its high density (707 lb/cu ft). Lead can easily be rolled into thin sheets for roofing and flashing, and its extreme pliability enables it to be fit over uneven surfaces.

Types and Uses

Although lead cannot be used where low weight is critical, for weights and counterbalances its high relative cost is offset by the saving in space and materials. Because of the low melting point of lead and the ease with which it can be cast, it can be formed into intricate shapes. Its high density makes it the favored material for shields against X rays and radiation from atomic reactors, and its softness and flexibility make it an ideal material for soundproofing blankets.

The thickness of sheet lead is specified in pounds per square foot rather than by gauge or fractions of an inch. Sheet lead $1/64$ in. thick weighs approximately 1 lb/sq ft. Thus 1 lb designates $1/64''$ sheet; 4 lb designates $(4 \times 1/64)$ $1/16''$ sheet; 8 lb designates $(8 \times 1/64)$ $1/8''$ sheet. Lead used for residential flashing and roofing is usually $2^{1}/_{2}$-lb sheet.

LEAD ROOFING Lead has a high coefficient of thermal expansion and is therefore difficult to hold in place. This limits the size of sheets that may be successfully used as roofing. The maximum sheet size is usually considered to be $4' \times 8'$. Lead sheets are joined by standing, batten, or lock seams (see Chapter 9).

LEAD MEMBRANES Sheet lead is often used as a waterproof lining for indoor and outdoor pools, and as a waterproof pan under tile showers. Sheets of 6- or 8-lb lead are placed over a concrete slab, and the joints are burned or welded, to form a continuous membrane. Terrazzo, tile, or marble is then placed over the lead sheet as a finish. Lead is, however, reactive with uncured concrete or mortar and must be protected by a heavy coating of asphalt or similar protective compound.

LEAD-COATED STEEL Lead-coated copper-bearing steel, called *terneplate*, combines the corrosion resistance of lead and the strength of steel. The steel is chemically cleaned, coated with a flux, and passed through a bath of molten tin-lead alloy, which is 90 to 95 percent lead and $2^{1}/_{2}$ percent or less tin, with small amounts of antimony, silver, and zinc. The sheet is immediately passed through rollers

Fig. 7-10 Sound barrier of 1-lb ($1/64''$) sheet lead over movable partition. (*Lead Industries Association, Inc.*)

which remove excess oil and give a smooth surface. Terne-plate is used for roofing, gutters, leaders, flashing, and metal doors, where a strong corrosion-resistant material is needed. Monticello, Thomas Jefferson's home in Virginia, still has its original terneplate roof.

LEAD ACOUSTICAL BARRIERS   The primary requirements for a good sound-barrier material are high density, natural limpness, good damping capacity, and nonpermeability. Weight is important in that the sound vibrations are reduced in intensity in overcoming the inertia of a barrier. The limpness of lead sheet reduces the vibration tendency that is common in other acoustical materials (see Chapter 8). Lead barriers are particularly effective over partitions used in conjunction with hung ceilings. Lead sheet can be used in many thin partitions to deaden sound without increasing bulk. It is easily attached to other materials with an elastomer adhesive to add weight without increasing stiffness.

ANTIVIBRATION PADS   For 50 years lead and asbestos pads have been used in building foundations to reduce transmission of vibration from the ground into the structure, especially where railroad tracks, subways, or heavy street traffic might be a source of troublesome vibration. More recently smaller pads of the same construction have been successfully used to isolate rooftop cooling towers from the steel-work of buildings. Lead is used for the same purpose, either alone or in combination with asbestos or other materials, under machinery and air-conditioning equipment that could become irritating sources of vibration. The top and bottom layers of sheet lead are burned together while the pad is recompressed at 200 psi to form a watertight envelope around the inside layer of asbestos. Before the pads are set in place, they are given a coat of asphalt paint.

LEAD PIPE AND DRAINAGE SYSTEMS   In chemical-processing plants the piping, storage tanks, and other equipment for handling corrosive chemicals may be designed with reference to specific chemicals. Since lead is generally resistant to a greater variety of corrosive chemicals than any other common metal, it is one of the most useful materials for laboratory piping, fittings, sinks, and related equipment. Lead pipe, fittings, and sheet lead for laboratory work are

Fig. 7-11   Building completely sheathed in lead, Marina City, Chicago, Illinois, architect Bernard Goldberg. (*Lead Industries Association, Inc.; photo by Harvey Shaman.*)

standard items throughout the country. The fact that lead pipe needs no expensive fittings for joints or changes of direction reduces the over-all cost (for more information on lead pipe see Chapter 14). Lead pipes cannot be used in supply lines for drinking water because of the danger of lead poisoning.

LEAD COMPOUNDS   Lead is classified according to use either as an ingredient of a chemical compound or as a metal, either alone or alloyed with some other metal. The chemical forms of lead most commonly encountered in the construction industry are those used in the manufacture of paints and primers. Lead carbonate, or *white lead*, is a white powder used mainly as a stabilizer in exterior paints to provide toughness, elasticity, and durability. Lead monoxide, or *litharge*, is a yellow powder used for yellow pigments and as a filler in linoleum and cork coverings. Lead oxide, or *red lead*, is still one of the most effective rust-inhibiting primers or paint ingredients for structural steel. These materials are discussed further in Chapter 13.

ZINC AND ZINC COATINGS

Zinc is a bluish-white metal characterized by low strength and brittleness. It is readily attacked by alkalis and acids, but is resistant to corrosion by water. It can be rolled, extruded, formed, cast, and machined by ordinary methods. Upon exposure to air a coating of zinc carbonate forms on the outside of a zinc sheet which protects the metal from further oxidation. Thin slabs or sheets of zinc are called *spelter*. The widest use of zinc in the construction industry is as a coating on steel. The process of coating steel with zinc is called *galvanizing*. The sheet produced is sometimes referred to as galvanized iron (G.I.).

Production of Zinc

The main ore from which zinc is extracted is *sphalerite*, or *zincblende*. The ore is ground, and the ore particles are separated from the waste rock. Lead, copper, and iron sulfides which are usually associated with zinc, are then separated by flotation, a process in which the finely pulverized ores segregate according to their relative capacity for floating on a given liquid. Lead and copper sulfides are floated off on top of large flotation tanks. Other chemicals are added to the bath, and the zinc sulfide is floated off. The zinc concentrates are then thickened, dried, and removed, ready for reduction to metal.

There are two basic methods of converting the zinc into metal. The zinc concentrates may be mixed with coking coal and pressed into briquettes, which are fed into the top of a vertical furnace and heated above the *volatilizing point*, the point at which the element zinc turns to a vapor. The zinc vapor is drawn off and condensed at a temperature above the *point of fusion*, the point at which the liquid turns to a solid, and is cast into slabs for further shaping and forming.

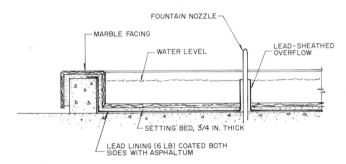

Fig. 7-12 Lead-lined pool.

Fig. 7-13 Sheet-lead blankets hung above a suspended ceiling. (*Lead Industries Association, Inc.*)

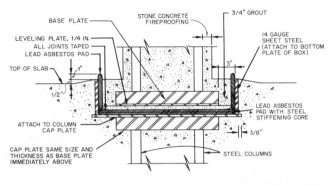

Fig. 7-14 An antivibration pad at John F. Kennedy Center for the Performing Arts, Washington, D.C., architect Edward Durell Stone. (*By permission of Lead Industries Association, Inc.*)

Zinc may also be produced by an electrolytic process. In this process the zinc concentrates are roasted and *leached* (soluble parts are removed) with a weak solution of sulfuric acid. Other metals are filtered out, and the solution is then pumped into electrolytic tanks. Cathodes of pure aluminum and anodes, either of lead or lead-silver alloys, are lowered into a tank containing electrolyte, and electric current is forced through the solution. Pure zinc is deposited on the cathodes. It is then stripped off the cathodes and melted into slabs for further processing.

Types and Uses

Zinc is used for roofing and flashing and for die-cast hardware and fixtures where high resistance to corrosion is required. Its chief use is as a protective coating for steel.

SHEET AND STRIP PRODUCTS Rolled zinc sheet or strip may be obtained either soft or medium hard. Zinc sheet and strip are identified according to thickness and weight by a special gauge system, the American Zinc Gauge. Sheet and strip zinc ranges from gauge 3, which is 0.006 in. thick and weighs 0.22 lb/sq ft, to gauge 28, which is 1 in. thick and weighs 37.5 lb/sq ft. Gauges 9 to 12 are the ones most commonly used for roofing, siding, and flashing. Many manufacturers have discarded this gauge system and designate thicknesses in thousandths of an inch.

DIE CASTINGS Because of its low casting temperature, zinc is widely used for die-cast hardware, electrical fixtures, and bathroom accessories. Zinc die castings have high dimensional accuracy and adequate strength for these products. The zinc may contain various alloying agents such as aluminum, magnesium, or copper. The castings can be finished by buffing or polishing or by plating with nickel, chromium, brass, or silver. Zinc castings find many uses where a material is needed that can withstand extreme corrosion or must be nonstaining.

HOT-DIP GALVANIZING Steel sheets may be protected against rust and corrosion by a galvanized zinc coating. Galvanizing serves as a double protection by forming a mechanical barrier against moisture as well as preventing oxidation, or rusting, of the steel base. If the barrier is broken, moisture will induce an electric current that consumes the zinc, thus sparing the steel.

The most common method of placing a zinc coating on steel is to immerse cleaned steel in a bath of molten zinc. The zinc adheres to the base metal in a smooth, even covering which usually has a crystalline, or *spangled*, appearance. After the sheets have been galvanized, they may be used flat; when they are to be used for roofing and siding they are usually corrugated to give additional stiffness. Galvanized steel may be formed, rolled, shaped, or assembled with little damage to the coating. However,

Fig. 7-15 Installing an antivibration pad. (*Lead Industries Association, Inc.*)

welded areas, trimmed edges, or damaged spots must be repaired and protected.

Practically all galvanized sheets are now produced by automatic equipment which passes the sheets, in continuous or cut lengths, between rollers through a tank of molten zinc. The rollers are adjusted to control the thickness or weight of the zinc coating. The coating on such sheets is usually 1 to 1.25 oz/sq ft, but may be as thin as 0.75 oz/sq ft. Heavier coatings, which provide greater resistance to rust and therefore greater durability, are also available. Standard galvanized coatings can usually be specified, in quarter-ounce increments, up to 2.75 oz/sq ft.

METALLIZING   Assembled structures as well as components may be sprayed with molten zinc by a compressed-air gun. This process, called *metallizing* or *flame spraying*, may be used on new metal or on installations that are partially corroded. The chief advantage of metallizing is that welds, ends, bolts, and fastenings receive the same protective coating as the steel sheet. Whereas certain sizes or shapes might be distorted by the hot-dipping process, metallizing will produce a smooth uniform surface which, according to reports of the American Zinc Institute, should have a life of 10 years.

Fig. 7-16 Zinc die castings for use with folding partitions. (*American Die Casting Institute.*)

Fig. 7-17 Hot-dip galvanizing of structural members at Corbec Corporation, Montreal, Canada. (*Ametalco, Inc.*)

SHERARDIZING   Small parts and architectural components may be protected by a dry zinc coating. The parts are tumbled at a high temperature in a container full of zinc dust. This process, called *sherardizing*, applies a uniform coating which is highly abrasion resistant. Since the coating is less than one-thousandth of an inch thick, the parts do not have to be remachined. Electrical conduits, nuts, bolts, screws, lock cases, and similar small items are often sherardized to furnish a base for varnish or paint (see Chapter 13 for painting of galvanized steels).

ELECTROPLATING   Steel can also be coated by electroplating. The cleaned steel object is placed in a solution of zinc sulfate and cyanide, and an electrical current is then passed through this electrolytic solution, depositing a thin coating of zinc on the object. This coating is usually 0.0001″ to 0.0005″. When the grey matte finish of electroplated pieces is not suitable, special brightening agents can be added to the solution. The bright finish can be protected by clear dips.

COPPER AND COPPER ALLOYS

Copper occurs in its pure metallic form in some parts of the world. Copper weapons, utensils, and ornaments have been found with the remains of Neolithic man dating from 8000 B.C. By 2000 B.C. copper implements were in common use around the Mediterranean and in China. The Greeks and Romans obtained this reddish metal from the island of Cyprus, which received its name from the Greek word for copper, *cyprium*. The chemical symbol for copper, Cu, is from the Roman word *cuprum*.

The properties of copper that are of greatest importance in the construction industry are its resistance to corrosion, tensile strength, workability, and electrical conductivity. Copper can be rolled, drawn, extruded, spun, formed, hammered, welded, brazed, and soldered. Soft copper can be hardened by cold working and resoftened by annealing. The excellent resistance of copper to corrosion makes it suitable for such applications as roofing, gutters, screens, and flashing. Its conductivity of electricity and heat is greater than that of any metal except silver.

Copper does not corrode readily, but it oxidizes on exposure to form a green *patina* of copper carbonate. This patina protects the underlying metal against further oxidation. The patina passes through various shades of brown and green before it ultimately weathers to a grey-green color. This process takes 5 to 10 years depending on the atmosphere. In seacoast areas the patina weathers rapidly;

Fig. 7-18   Hot-dip galvanizing water-heater tanks. (*Cominco Ltd.*)

in the dry climates of the southwestern United States the patina may never even turn green.

Production of Copper

Most copper produced in the United States is obtained from low-grade sulfite ores. These ores are crushed and pulverized, and the copper is concentrated by flotation. The concentrated ore is then put through several smelting processes to remove impurities. The metal taken from the last smelting process, call *blister copper*, is too impure for most uses. It may be transferred to a reverberatory furnace for further refining or cast into anodes for electrolytic refining.

Pure sheets of refined copper are placed alternately between anodes of blister copper, in a solution of water, sulfuric acid, and copper. When an electric current is passed through the solution, the copper anodes are dissolved, and pure copper is deposited on the cathode sheets. The impurities fall to the bottom of the tank, where they can be removed and processed to recover platinum, gold, silver, and other valuable metals. The resulting electrolytic copper may be further refined to remove any remaining sulfur and oxygen that would be harmful when the metal was cast. Much copper is also salvaged by this process from brass, bronze, and copper scrap. This product is classified as secondary copper.

Types and Uses

ELECTRICAL WIRE Electrolytic copper, which is 99.90 percent pure copper, is used for most electrical conductors and wire. Copper wire is manufactured either by hot rolling or by extrusion. In the extrusion process the hot billet is reduced to ¼-in. rods, which are then reduced to final size by cold drawing. Electrical conductors are usually

Fig. 7-19 Flame spraying a filigreed iron chair with zinc by the Schorie process (*Zinc Institute, Inc.; photo by David B. Hecht.*)

protected by some kind of coating. If the coating is to be rubber compound, the wire must be tinned first. Rubber or plastic electrical insulation is then applied over the tinned copper wire.

The sizes of copper wire, designated by the "American Wire Gauge" (AWG), are based on the circular mils of cross-sectional area. This measure is used, rather than the diameter, because the amount of electricity (amperage) that the wire will carry is calculated on the basis of circular mils, the area of a circle with a diameter of one-thousandths of an inch. Table 7-7 is a partial list of the standard gauges of bare copper wire as established by the National Bureau of Standards.

Fig. 7-20 Metallized 110,000-gal water wash tank at the Erie Water Works, Erie, Pennsylvania. Inspection after 23 years reveals continued positive protection by metallized zinc coating. (*Zinc Institute, Inc.*)

TABLE 7-7　Sizes of copper wire

GAUGE	AREA, CIRC. MILS	DIAMETER, IN.	AREA, SQ IN.
18	1,620	0.0403	0.0013
16	2,580	0.0508	0.0025
14	4,110	0.0641	0.0032
12	6,530	0.0808	0.0051
10	10,380	0.10119	0.0081
8	16,510	0.1285	0.0130
6	26,240	0.184	0.027
4	41,740	0.232	0.042
2	66,360	0.292	0.067
1	83,690	0.332	0.087
0	105,600	0.372	0.109
00	133,100	0.418	0.137
000	167,800	0.470	0.173
0000	211,600	0.528	0.219

COPPER SCREEN　Copper wire is also used for woven mesh and screen, available in several mesh sizes and weaves. The mesh size is defined by openings per linear inch. For example, 2-gauge screen has two openings per linear inch, and 100-gauge screen has 100 openings per linear inch. The standard copper screen used for most construction purposes is square 18 × 18 mesh. Copper screen is available in 100-ft rolls in widths of 24″ to 72″.

TUBE AND PIPE　Seamless copper tube and pipe may be produced by either hot-working or cold-working operations in round, square, and rectangular sections. The composition of the tube is designated according to the elements alloyed with the copper, as given in Table 7-8.

TABLE 7-8　Copper tube and pipe alloys

DESIGNATION	COMPOSITION
DPL	Phosphorized copper
DHP	Phosphorized copper with high residual phosphorous
DPA	Phosphorized arsenical copper
OF	Oxygen-free copper without residual metallic deoxidants

The copper tube or pipe is finished by cold-working, annealing, or heat treatment according to the requirements of use. Annealed tube, specified as *soft annealed* or *light annealed*, is used where the tube must be soft enough to be bent around corners, as in air-conditioning and refrigeration equipment. Drawn tube is designated as *light drawn, drawn,* or *hard drawn.* Light-drawn tube has some

Fig. 7-21　Copper roof on the Stock Exchange, Copenhagen, Denmark.

stiffness but is capable of being bent. Drawn tube is a general-purpose temper. Hard-drawn tube is used only where strength is the major requirement.

Seamless copper water tube is used in general plumbing. The type of tube is governed by service conditions and local codes. Annealed tube is satisfactory where flared, compression, or soldered fittings are to be used. Drawn tubes are suitable for use with soldered fittings.

Seamless copper water tube is produced in three wall thicknesses, designated K, L, and M; K is the thickest and M is the thinnest. The nominal size of the tubing refers to the outside diameter. Tubing is available in either coils or straight lengths. For further discussion on copper tube and pipe, see Chapter 14.

SHEET AND STRIP Copper is designated either sheet or strip on the basis of its width. Widths 24 in. or less are termed *strip copper*. Widths over 24 in. are termed *sheet copper*. The thickness, or gauge, of copper sheet and strip is designated in ounces per square foot; thus 16-oz copper sheet is sheet of a thickness that weighs 16 oz/sq ft. The weights most generally used in the building industry are given in Table 7-9.

TABLE 7-9 Weights of copper sheet

WEIGHT PER SQ FT		THICKNESS, IN.		NEAREST GAUGE NO. (B&S)	NEAREST FRACTIONAL IN.
OZ	LB	NOMINAL	MIN.		
32	2	0.0431	0.0405	17	
24	1½	0.0323	0.0295	20	¹⁄₃₂
20	1¼	0.0270	0.0245	21	
16	1	0.0216	0.0190	23	
10	⅝	0.0235	0.0115	27	¹⁄₆₄
8	½	0.0108	0.0090	29	

The most commonly used types of sheet copper are 110 soft copper and 110 cold-rolled copper. *110 soft copper* is used only where extreme malleability is required, as for intricate ornamental copper work. *110 cold-rolled copper* is used for roofing, flashings, gravel stops, gutters, and similar applications. It is less malleable than soft copper, but far stronger.

The weight of copper to be used for a particular application depends on the structural, physical, and chemical properties required, such as the shape of the section, the types of joints, seams, and fastenings, anticipated thermal movement, and expected degree of corrosion. Copper is subject to galvanic corrosion where it is in contact with aluminum or ferrous metals. Sheet lead is recommended as a barrier between copper and ferrous metals.

Beryllium-Copper

Alloys of beryllium and copper provide a strong, nonmagnetic, nonsparking material that will withstand temperatures up to 4000°F. These alloys are used as springs,

Fig. 7-22 Gates of Paradise, cast-bronze doors by the sculptor Ghiberti for the Baptistry of Florence Cathedral.

bellows, and controls. They can be worked easily in an annealed condition and can be accurately hardened by simple heat treatment.

Brass and Bronze

Many types of brass and bronze are available for a variety of end uses. *Brass* is an alloy of copper and zinc with small quantities of other elements sometimes added to provide special qualities. The proportions of copper to zinc range from 95% copper : 5% zinc to alloys containing only 55% copper : 45% zinc.

Bronze is a rich brown metal suitable for casting, where its dense grain, corrosion resistance, and ability to take delicate mold impressions make it particularly suitable for cast statuary. Bronze was originally an alloy of copper and tin; however, the term now includes copper alloys with other metals, designated according to the alloying element as silicon bronze, phosphor bronze, or manganese bronze. These alloys may or may not include tin as an ingredient.

Brasses and bronzes are classified, generally, on the basis of their color and alloying element. Table 7-10 shows the characteristics and uses of the alloys most commonly used in architectural construction.

Fig. 7-23 Cast-bronze fireplace by Roger Darricarrere, originally made for the Elliot Handler residence in Los Angeles. (*Photo by George Szanik.*)

Fastenings

Copper and brass may be fastened to a substrate by cleating, nailing, or screwing. Cleats are most frequently used because they permit movement and thereby ensure against buckling. Screws are used where the material must be held rigidly in place, as at a ridge roll subject to severe wind vibration or where it is secured to a masonry surface hard enough to require the use of expansion shields. Nailing is more practical for applications such as base flashings, gravel stops, and eave strips. For nailing to wood or concrete, nails should be at least 12-gauge copper or brass.

NICKEL, CHROMIUM, CADMIUM, AND TITANIUM

Nickel Alloys

Most nickel is used as an alloying agent with other metals to impart hardness, toughness, strength, corrosion resistance, increased magnetism, electrical resistance, and many other qualities. Nickel or nickel alloys are widely used as a plating for decorative purposes or as a corrosion-resistant coating. Pure-nickel coatings are off-white in color and can be given a satin finish or a bright polish. Nickel plating is often used as an undercoating for platings

TABLE 7-10 Characteristics of brass and bronze

DESIGNATION	CHARACTERISTICS
Commercial bronze	90% copper : 10% zinc, bronze-red color. Ductile and easy to form; used for forgings, screws, and stamped hardware.
Brass	85% copper : 15% zinc, golden or reddish color. Has greater strength and ductility than copper, with excellent resistance to corrosion; used generally for plumbing pipe and tubing.
Cartridge brass	70% copper : 30% zinc, yellow brass color. One of the best combinations of strength and workability; used for processes requiring deep drawing, stamping, or rolling.
Silicon bronze	96% copper : 3% silicon : 1% manganese, light copper color. Has the corrosion resistance of copper and the strength of mild steel; used for tanks, weatherstripping, and pressure vessels.
Copper nickel	70% copper : 30% nickel, silver-white color. A ductile metal used where resistance to corrosion is important, as in condenser tubes, automotive parts, and refrigerator pump bodies.
Muntz metal	60% copper : 40% zinc, similar in color to architectural bronze. Has high strength but low ductility; usually used in sheet form for architectural work.
Nickel silver extr. 10.	45% copper : 42% zinc : 1% lead : 2% manganese : 10% nickel, yellow-white in color. This is only one of the nickel silvers used in construction, fabricated into intricate shapes for plumbing fixtures, stair railings, and other decorative items.

of decorative metals such as chromium, platinum, or gold.

The two major nickel alloys used in the construction industry are the trade-marked products Monel and Inconel. These alloys are widely used in kitchen equipment.

MONEL   This nickel-copper alloy was first produced by the International Nickel Company in 1905. Monel is nominally composed of 67 percent nickel and 30 percent copper, plus some iron, manganese, silicon, and carbon. It is highly resistant to corrosion, does not tarnish easily, and will take a high polish. Monel is readily workable. It is available in rod, wire, sheet, or strip form and can be successfully joined by welding or soldering.

The lighter gauges of Monel are used as roofing and flashing, where its low coefficient of expansion and its good fatigue resistance makes it extremely efficient. Monel alloy is available in gauges 22 to 26 for use as gutters, copings, cornices, and flashings. Gauges 16 to 20 are usually used for kitchen, laboratory, and hospital work.

INCONEL This nickel-chromium alloy has a nominal composition of 78 percent nickel, 0.2 percent copper, 14 percent chromium, and 6.5 percent iron, with some manganese, silicon, and carbon. It is almost completely resistant to corrosion by food products and dilute organic acids. It resists oxidizing acid salts. Inconel is available as sheet stock in most standard sheet-metal gauges.

Chromium

Chromium is a very hard, nonmagnetic metal that is used primarily as an alloying ingredient in both ferrous and nonferrous metals or as a bright protective coating for other metals. When chromium is deposited on base metal, the resulting coating usually contains microscopic holes which permit moisture and corrosive liquids to penetrate to the underlying metal. The protective value of chromium plating is usually dependent on the undercoatings of copper and nickel.

Chromium plating, in thicknesses of 0.0001″ to 0.0002″, are widely used where a bright, decorative, tarnish-free surface is desired. The major chromium-plated items encountered in construction are plumbing fixtures, lighting fixtures, hardware, and decorative trim.

Cadmium

Cadmium is a blue-white metal similar in several ways to zinc. On exposure it develops a film which protects the parent metal from further corrosion. Cadmium is used chiefly as a protective coating for small steel fastenings. Since it is not subject to serious galvanic action with

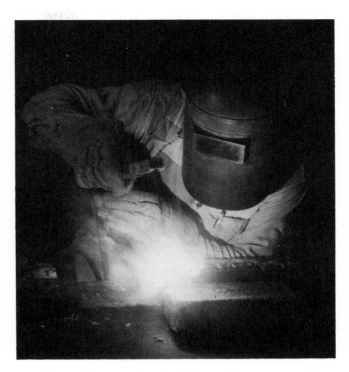

Fig. 7-24 Welder puts down nickel overlay on copper (*International Nickel Company, Inc.*)

Fig. 7-25 Strip zinc Titanaloy (zinc-copper-titanium alloy) roofing, a product of Matthiessen and Hegeler Zinc Company.

aluminum, cadmium-plated steel screws, bolts, and small parts are extremely effective for aluminum assemblies such as sliding glass doors and windows.

Titanium

The element titanium was discovered in 1790, but it was not used in metallic form until 1948, when it was produced commercially as a strong ductile metal. A titanium-aluminum alloy used as a structural metal, with an ultimate strength of 200,000 psi, has been developed for use in aircraft landing gear.

In the architectural field a zinc-copper-titanium alloy has been used successfully for roofing, fascias, gravel stops, flashing, and other members requiring a lightweight, strong, easily formed, corrosion-resistant material. The metal comes from the mill with a bright finish which weathers to a pleasing dark-grey patina. This alloy is also recommended by its manufacturers for use in air-conditioning ducts exposed to condensation. It is said to be as strong as copper, 25 percent lighter, and approximately 40 percent less expensive.

COMBINED METALS

Clad Metals

Clad metals can effectively combine the best qualities of two or more different metals, frequently at a lower cost than that for solid metal. A clad metal is one with a metallurgical bond between layers of dissimilar metals.

ALUMINUM CLADDING A corrosion-resistant layer of nearly pure aluminum may be rolled onto both sides of an aluminum base whose corrosion resistance has been reduced by other elements added to increase the strength of the sheet. Such sheets are produced under various trade names, such as Alclad and Anoclad.

The Armco Steel Corporation produces carbon-steel sheet with a coating of aluminum on two sides which they call Armco Aluminumized Steel. The steel sheet is immersed in a bath of commercially pure aluminum. The cladding process creates a strong metallurgical bond between the steel base and the aluminum coating, which is approximately 0.002″ thick. This sheet is used as siding, roof decks, building panels, and other applications that require resistance to atmospheric corrosion and the strength of steel.

COPPER CLADDING Another bimetal sheet that is produced consists of an inner carbon-steel or stainless-steel core covered with a heavy layer of copper. Texas Instruments produces a copper-clad stainless steel called TiGuard Type S for applications where a strong, lightweight, easily formed, corrosion-resistant material is desired.

LEAD CLADDING Lead-coated copper is similar in workability, ease of joining, and strength to 110 cold-rolled copper. It is used where the copper might stain metals or wood surfaces and in industrial applications where the patina of copper might be objectionable.

Galvanic Action

When two dissimilar metals are in contact in the presence of an *electrolyte*, an electric current is generated (as in a battery) which causes one of the metals to corrode away. This process, called *galvanic action*, is particularly significant in the choice of nails or fastenings for metal roofing or flashings. The electrolyte may be rainwater running from one area to another, salt spray, or chemical vapors such as those in industrial atmospheres. In dry desert climates and in inland rural regions, the problem is not so great as in urban areas.

The severity of the galvanic attack, or corrosion, varies with the combination of metals and their electrolytic properties. In order to determine the possible corrosive effects of the two metals in contact, it is necessary to know their place in the galvanic or *electropotential series*, the sequence in which each metal will be corroded by any metals above it in the series. Generally, the further apart two metals are in the electropotential series, the greater the corrosion. Table 7-11 shows the position of some of the metals and alloys more commonly used in construction.

TABLE 7-11 Galvanic or Electropotential Series of Metals

Magnesium	Bronze
Aluminum	Stainless steel 301, 302
Manganese	Cadmium
Zinc	Nickel
Mild Steel	Inconel
Tin	Monel
Lead	Silver
Brass	Platinum
Copper	Gold

QUESTIONS

1. What does nonferrous mean?

2. What is the process that made commercial production of aluminum possible? When was it invented?

3. What is the basic ore from which aluminum is produced?

4. Where is the world's major deposit of aluminum ore?

5. Why is aluminum resistant to weather?

6. How can the strength of aluminum be increased?

7. Name three types of aluminum casting processes.

8. Describe the characteristics of wrought-aluminum alloys designated as 1100-H19 frosted and 3003-T9 satin.

9. Describe the process of anodizing and explain why it is used.

10. What are two methods other than paint and enamel by which color can be imparted to aluminum?

11. What is porcelain enamel?

12. Name three types of aluminum products used in industrial building.

13. Describe three methods of shaping aluminum.

14. What gauge of aluminum wire is usually used in screens for residences?

15. What are three physical properties that make lead valuable for construction?

16. What is the thickness in inches of a 6-lb lead sheet?

17. What are the limitations of lead as a roofing material?

18. Explain the advantages of three types of aluminum siding used for residential construction.

19. What is terneplate, and what is its use?

20. What is the major use of zinc in building construction?

21. Give three uses of zinc die castings in construction.

22. Describe the process of sherardizing.

23. What are five uses of copper in building construction?

24. Describe electrolytic refining of copper.

25. What dimension does the nominal size of copper indicate?

26. What is the thickness in inches of a 10-oz sheet of copper?

27. Bronze was originally an alloy of what two metals?

28. What is the composition of nickel silver extra?

29. What are some of the principal uses of Monel in construction?

30. What are the advantages of cadmium-plated steel fastenings?

31. Define a clad metal.

32. Explain the principle of galvanic action.

REFERENCES FOR FURTHER STUDY

Aluminum Company of America: 1205 Alcoa Building, Pittsburgh, Pa., 15219. "Aluminum in Architecture," 1961. "Industrial Building Products," 1960. "Alcoa Structural Handbook," 1956. "Alcoa Aluminum Handbook," 1957.

American Iron and Steel Institute, Committee of Galvanized Sheet Products: 150 East 42d Street, New York, N.Y., 10017. "Painting Tips for Best Results on Galvanized Steel." 1966.

American Zinc Institute, Inc.: 292 Madison Avenue, New York, N.Y., 10017. *Zinc Spotlight*, a periodical. "Facts about Galvanized Sheets," 1955.

Architectural Aluminum Manufacturers' Association: 35 East Wacker Drive, Chicago, Ill., 60601. "Certified Products Directory," 1968.

Copper Development Association, Inc.: 405 Lexington Avenue, New York, N.Y., 10017. "Copper, Brass, and Bronze in Architecture," 1965. "Contemporary Copper," 1966.

Harvey Aluminum Sales, Inc.: 19200 South Western Avenue, Torrance, Calif., 90505. "Mill Products and Alloys," 1966.

Hornbostal, Caleb: "Materials for Architecture," Reinhold, New York.

Kaiser Aluminum and Chemical Sales, Inc.: Kaiser Center, 300 Lakeside Drive, Oakland, Calif., 94604. "Kaiser Aluminum in Architecture," 1958.

Lead Industries Association, Inc.: 292 Madison Avenue, New York, N.Y., 10017. *Lead*, a periodical.

Matthiessen and Heggeler: La Salle Street, Chicago, Ill., 61301. "Titanaloy-Hydro-Metal," 1969.

Merrit, Frederick S.: "Building Construction Handbook," McGraw-Hill, New York, 1958.

National Association of Architectural Metal Manufacturers: 228 North La Salle Street, Chicago, Ill., 60601. "Metal Product Outline," 1968.

Reynolds Metals Company, 530 East Main Street, Richmond, Va., 32218. "Reynolds Aluminum Architectural Finishes," 1966. "Reynolds Aluminum in Architecture," 1965. "Reynolds Aluminum Data Book," 1958.

Smith, R. C.: "Materials of Construction," McGraw-Hill, New York, 1966.

Texas Instruments, Inc.: Attleboro, Mass., 02703. "Clad Metals," 1968.

United States Aluminum Corporation: 4950 Triggs Street, Los Angeles, Calif., 90022. "Architectural Building Products," 1968.

LATH
PLASTER
AND
ACOUSTICAL
MATERIALS

8

PLASTER

Approximately 400 million square yards of plaster is applied in the United States each year. This is the equivalent of plastering both sides of a wall 8 ft high and 33,750 miles long. Although plaster is basically a finishing material, constant research in the construction industry has led to improved materials and methods which have made lath and plaster increasingly important.

Plastic materials have been used since recorded history to provide a smooth finish over a rough surface and as a base for painted and carved decoration. In ancient Greece during the Minoan Period (3500 to 1700 B.C.), intricately painted surfaces were used to cover structural elements of palaces. Chambers in the Egyptian pyramids were plastered to form a base for paintings depicting the life of the Pharaoh. Greek colonists, who spread their classic civilization to what is now Italy and Turkey, used plaster made of marble granules to reproduce the marble of their homeland in Greece. Much later, from 700 to 1492 A.D., the Moors in Spain created masterpieces in precast plaster ceilings and wall decorations for the Alhambra in Granada.

During the Renaissance the art of fresco painting reached a high point. In this process tempera colors are applied to a wet plaster surface, so that they saturate the plaster and the color and the plaster dry together. Frescos such as Michelangelo's famous paintings on the ceiling of the Sistine Chapel, in the Vatican, still retain their original brilliant color after 400 years. A highly decorative type of plaster work called *sgraffito* also developed in Italy during the Renaissance. In sgraffito work several thin layers of plaster, each of a different color, are applied. Before the plaster has hardened, one or more layers are scratched through or removed, revealing different undercoats, to produce a colored three-dimensional design.

In the Baroque and Rococo periods of architecture, plastered surfaces became the basis of an entirely different system of design. Structural elements became merely a base for smooth, glazed plaster surfaces. Le Corbusier's chapel at RonChamp, France, illustrates the plastic quality of exterior stucco. The curving walls turn smoothly around corners and the simple curved surfaces of the plaster walls and bell tower are enlivened by variations in texture.

Because of the decline in use of carved and cast orna-ment, the skills and techniques of ornamental plastering have largely disappeared over the years. However, new techniques have taken their place. Plaster is still used as a surfacing material to cover structural elements. It is also used in itself as a structural element. Movable, temporary, and permanent plaster partitions in office buildings are commonplace. Lath and plaster provide excellent fire-proofing for structural steel with a minimum of cost and labor. Coatings of lightweight plaster can be sprayed for fire protection, acoustical treatment, and thermal insula-tion as well as serving as a finish material.

Cementitious Materials

The *cementitious* materials in a plaster mix, those mate-rials that undergo a physical or chemical change during the mixing or curing process, are usually gypsum, lime, or portland cement. Certain clays and other materials may be added to improve acoustical properties, fire resistance, moisture resistance, strength, or to act as binders. The quality of the plaster mix is governed by the properties of the cementitious materials.

GYPSUM   Gypsum (hydrous calcium sulfate) is the mineral residue that remains after the evaporation of sea water. The sedimentary rock formed may be gray, pink, or white. The word *gypsum* came from the Greek word *gypsos*, meaning chalk. Gypsum, which is found in abundance throughout the world, is from open pits or underground mines. Most gypsum used in the construction industry has been *calcined*. The rock is crushed and heated (cal-cined) in kettles or rotary kilns to temperatures of 325 to 350°F until about three-fourths of its combined water is driven off. When calcined gypsum is later recombined with approximately the same amount of water it has lost during calcination, it reverts to its original rocklike crystal-line form.

Pure calcined gypsum is termed *plaster of paris*, named after a plaster originally produced from the vast beds of very pure white gypsum which lie beneath the city of Paris. Plaster of paris sets in only a few minutes. Late in the nineteenth century retarders were found which delayed the setting action, thus opening the way to broadly ex-panded commercial applications.

If the gypsum is further heated to temperatures of 1000 to 1400°F in the presence of alum and other materials, virtually all the combined water is driven off. The resulting material is called *Keene's cement*. Keene's cement is used as a finishing material to produce dense, hard surfaces.

After gypsum has been calcined, it is ground uniformly to a fine powder in a tube mill, and various materials are added to control physical or chemical properties and govern the setting time, the time from the addition of water to the start of recrystallization. When gypsum is used as plaster, a retarder is added so that there will be time for mixing, handling, application, and finishing before the material begins to change from a plastic to a rigid state. Once gypsum plaster has begun to harden or set, it cannot be retempered, or remixed with water.

Fig. 8-1   Plaster walls of King Minos' palace, circa 1700 B.C., Knossos, Crete.

LIME Lime is obtained from limestone, marble, coral, or shells which have been heated, or burned, to 2000°F in a furnace or kiln to drive off carbonic acid gas. Most lime used for construction in the United States is produced from Dolomite limestone, found mostly in the states of Ohio, Missouri, Pennsylvania, Texas, and Virginia. Only the purest limestones (97 to 99 percent) are used to produce plastering lime. Lime to be used for plastering is classed as *finishing lime*. Limes produced with special properties for use in masonry construction are called *mason's limes*.

The product of the lime kiln is *quicklime*. The outstanding characteristic of quicklime is its capacity for *slaking*, or *hydration*, a chemical reaction that takes place when quicklime is allowed to soak up two or three times its weight in water. As the calcium oxide combines with water to form calcium hydroxide, the chemical reaction causes the temperature of the mixture to rise rapidly. After the mixture cools, it stiffens to the consistency of putty and can be carried on a shovel. The lime putty must be allowed to stand on the job site for 2 to 3 weeks before is can be used as an ingredient in plaster. Quicklime has a limited shelf life, because it combines with air and is then said to be *air slaked*.

When quicklime is slaked, it is transformed into a hydroxide of lime. If only a limited quantity of water is added to quicklime, there is still a chemical reaction. In this case, however, when the product ceases to produce heat, the result is a fine, dry powder called *hydrated lime*. For all practical purposes hydrated lime has replaced quicklime in plastering. Hydrated lime is produced as either Type N (normal) or Type S (special). The normal type must be soaked for 12 to 16 hr before it can be used. The special type can be used immediately after being mixed with water. Either type of hydrated lime can be mixed dry with other dry plastering materials and packaged for use. Only water is added at the job site.

PORTLAND CEMENT Portland cement, which is essentially a combination of limestone and claylike substances, is used chiefly as an ingredient in concrete (for a detailed description of the manufacture of portland cement see Chapter 3). In the plastering trade portland cement is limited to exterior or interior applications subject to wetting or severe dampness. Portland cement plaster is extremely durable, is unaffected by water, and is capable of withstanding repeated freezing and thawing cycles. Portland cement plaster is difficult to trowel. For this reason a plasticizing agent, such as hydrated lime, ground asbestos, or certain clays, are added in small quantities to improve workability.

Fig. 8-2 Wall paneling of the Queen's Balcony in the Alhambra, Granada, Spain.

Aggregates

Aggregates in plaster consist of inert materials which do not combine chemically with cementitious materials. Their most important function is to provide dimensional stability. Volume changes in plaster, for the most part, stem from the cementitious materials. For example, portland cement shrinks as it loses water, and after it sets it swells and shrinks with temperature and moisture changes. The aggregate materials are generally stable and provide a cushioning effect. The correct selection and proportioning of aggregates helps to reduce cracking in plaster.

The second function of aggregates in plaster is as bulk to replace the more expensive cementitious ingredients. In addition, aggregates can effect the texture and color of finish plaster.

SAND   Most plaster sands come from natural sources, although crushed stone of proper size and grading can also be used. Gradation of the sand will affect the *void content*, the air space between the individual pieces of sand. Sand for plaster should be graded with particles ranging from a maximum size of $\frac{1}{8}$ in. to fine. In well-graded sand the smaller particles will fill in most of the spaces between the larger ones, so that there will be a minimum of voids. Where the sand contains organic or chemical impurities, there may be chemical reactions with the cementitious materials. Only sand meeting recognized standards of purity should be used as aggregate in plaster.

VERMICULITE   Lightweight aggregates such as vermiculite are sometimes used in plaster. Vermiculite, a micalike material of magnesium–aluminum–iron silicate, is characterized by its foliated structure (separated into thin layers or leaves). Between each layer of the material is a thin layer of water. When vermiculite ore is crushed and heated to 2000°F, the water turns to steam and expands the layers to as much as sixteen times their original size. Expanded vermiculite is a soft, pliable material of low density, low thermal conductivity, and good resistance to high temperatures. Combined with gypsum plaster and a special binder, it produces an excellent acoustical material for interior plastering.

PERLITE   Raw perlite is a glassy, porous volcanic rock which is 10 to 20 percent water. When the perlite ore is heated to 1500°F, the water in the pores turns to steam, and the material is expanded to form frothy particles of irregular shape, containing millions of closed air cells. Perlite expands from four to twenty times its original volume. Thus

Fig. 8-3   Interior of Weldon Church, Innsbruck, Austria.

the weight of plaster with perlite as an aggregate is less than half the weight of sanded plaster. Expanded perlite produces a lightweight, fireproof plaster having good thermal and acoustical properties.

WOOD FIBER   Although the most commonly used plaster aggregates are sand, vermiculite, and perlite, other materials are employed to provide particular qualities. Wood fiber added to gypsum plaster during the manufacturing process is considered an aggregate. Plaster with wood-fiber aggregate is approximately half the weight of sanded plaster. Wood fiber imparts high compressive and tensile strength to gypsum plaster.

GYPSUM PLASTERS

Base-coat Plasters

Base-coat plasters are specifically formulated to control setting time and develop other important characteristics. The formulation depends on the intended method of application and the climatic conditions of the area in which they will be used. Gypsum base-coat plasters are suitable for all interior uses except where they will be exposed to water or severe moisture conditions. Base-coat plasters

are used to form the *scratch coat* (first coat) and the *brown coat* (second coat) on walls and ceilings.

NEAT PLASTER   Gypsum neat plaster requires the addition of aggregate and water at the job site. It is used as a base coat to receive the finish coat of plaster. Gypsum neat plaster is low in cost and may be mixed with any type of aggregate needed to fulfill the requirements of the job.

WOOD-FIBERED PLASTER   This type of plaster is a factory-prepared gypsum base-coat plaster containing finely shredded select wood fiber. Only water must be added on the job. Wood-fibered plaster has approximately three times the strength of sanded plaster. It has greater resistance to lateral impact and greater surface hardness, which causes it to have greater resistance to cracking. Wood-fibered plasters have significantly greater fire resistance than sanded plasters.

READY-MIXED PLASTER   Ready-mixed plasters consist of gypsum and an aggregate mixed at the mill. It is necessary to add only water on the job. The aggregate is usually perlite or vermiculite. Plaster with perlite aggregate has greater fire resistance than sanded plaster. It is ideal where building codes require maximum fire ratings, not attain-

Fig. 8-4   Sgraffito by Picasso on a modern building, Barcelona, Spain.

able with sand. The precise proportioning and mixing that can be achieved in the factory assures a uniform mix conforming to exact specifications for density, strength, and gradation. Ready-mixed plaster, either sanded, fibered, or with lightweight aggregate, should not be applied directly to concrete.

BOND PLASTER   A plaster having special bonding properties is produced for application to concrete surfaces that have been sufficiently roughened to provide a mechanical key. It is formulated so that its coefficient of expansion approximates that of concrete. Ordinary plasters have a higher thermal expansion than concrete and therefore do not perform satisfactorily over concrete surfaces.

Finish-coat Plasters

There are several types of gypsum finish plasters. Some consist only of gypsum; others are mixed with lime or lime and sand. Since the finish coat must be compatible with the base coat, the finish-coat materials must be carefully evaluated in relation to the characteristics of the base coat. The finish coat serves as a leveling coat, as a base for decoration, and to provide the required resistance to abrasion. The finish coat, or *putty coat*, is applied to a thickness of $1/16$ to $1/8$ in. over a plaster base coat.

READY-MIXED FINISH PLASTERS   These are mill-mixed gypsum plasters that require the addition of water only. Prepared gypsum finish plasters are available in white or gray or in specially prepared colors. They are produced for either a smooth-troweled finish or a sand-float finish. Most prepared gypsum finish plasters have no alkali reaction with paint and can be painted as soon as they have set.

GAUGING PLASTERS   Gauging plasters are used with finish lime to produce a smooth, white finish called *whitecoat*.

Fig. 8-5   Textured plaster walls of the Chapel Nôtre Dame du Haut at RonChamp, France, architect Le Corbusier.

CRUDE ORE

GRADED AND CLEANED ORE

PROCESSED OR EXPANDED VERMICULITE

Fig. 8-6 Three forms of vermiculite. (*W. R. Grace and Company.*)

They consist of specially ground, calcined gypsum which mixes readily with water and lime putty. The function of lime in finish plaster is to provide the spread and plasticity to permit fast, easy application with full flexibility. The gypsum *gauging* adds strength and hardness to the finish surface by reinforcing the plastic, nonsetting lime against shrinkage and cracking. It must be blended into the lime

in proper proportions for the required initial set, strength, and stability.

MOLDING PLASTER   Molding plaster is a very white, finely ground gypsum used primarily for ornamental plastering. It is adaptable for casting in rubber, gelatin, and other types of molds. When it is used for casting, only water is added. For *run-in-place* ornamental work, such as cornices and moldings, it is used with lime putty.

LIME–KEENE'S CEMENT PLASTER   Keene's cement is manufactured from select white gypsum rock burned at high temperatures to produce an extremely dense plaster surface. It is mixed with lime putty for finish coats. Lime–Keene's cement produces a high-quality smooth-troweled or sand-float finish that is highly resistant to cracking. It may be obtained in either slow-setting or fast-setting types. Lime–Keene's cement finishes are for interior use over gypsum-base plasters. Since lime–Keene's cement is somewhat less permeable than ordinary gauged lime-putty finishes, it is used in areas of high humidity, such as bathrooms and kitchens. However, it cannot be used where exposure to water is extreme or continuous. It must be painted and maintained properly to perform satisfactorily.

Fire-resistant Coatings

Calcined gypsum has a great affinity for water and completely recombines with two or three times its weight in water while setting. This combined water in gypsum plasters makes them an effective fire barrier. When plaster is exposed to fire, the water in the gypsum is slowly released as steam, which effectively retards heat transfer. This phenomenon is called *calcination*.

The manner in which gypsum insulates against the

Fig. 8-7 Microphoto of vermiculite granules after expansion. (*W. R. Grace and Company.*)

transfer of high temperatures is best likened to what happens when the intense heat from a blow torch is directed against a solid block of ice. Even though the ice melts, one can safely hold his hand on the opposite side. The low temperature on that side will be maintained until the intense heat has completely melted the ice.

The chemically combined water in plaster continues to function as a heat barrier until the slow process of calcination is complete. As the surface is heated to 212°F (the boiling point of water), the resulting steam acts as a built-in sprinkler system, which repels the fire and dissipates the heat. After 30 min of intense heat, the water in the gypsum will be released to a depth of 1/2 in. Theoretically, at a depth of 5/8 in. the temperature will not exceed 212°F. Thus a 2-in. thickness of gypsum protects a steel column or beam for 4 hr. Most gypsum plasters used as fire-resistant coatings or membranes contain vermiculite or perlite aggregates.

PORTLAND CEMENT PLASTERS

Portland cement plaster is a combination of portland cement or masonry cement, sand, water, and a plasticizing agent such as lime. It can be applied to exterior or interior surfaces to provide a hard, durable surface that possesses the properties of concrete. Portland cement plaster used on exterior surfaces is generally called *stucco*. In some areas stucco refers only to the finish coat, and in others it refers to the entire thickness. Portland cement

Fig. 8-9 Applying the brown coat of plaster. (*Ceramic Tile Institute.*)

Fig. 8-10 Using a darby to bring the brown coat to a true plane. (*Ceramic Tile Institute.*)

Fig. 8-8 Scratching the base coat. (*Ceramic Tile Institute.*)

plasters can be applied in numerous textures over a wide variety of bases. When it is used as a finish coat, color pigments may be added and blended at the factory.

Characteristics and Uses

Portland cement plaster is used primarily for surfaces that are likely to be exposed to wetting or severe dampness. It is very durable, unaffected by water, and capable of withstanding repeated freezing and thawing cycles. Portland cement, mixed only with sand and water, is difficult to manipulate with a trowel in plastering. Lime, ground asbestos, diatomaceous earth, or other plasticizing agents are added in small quantities to improve the workability of the mix. Lightweight aggregates may be used for interior plastering, but for exterior plastering sand must be used as an aggregate.

Portland cement plaster may be applied by hand or machine to metal lath, masonry, or properly prepared concrete surfaces. It cannot be used over gypsum base coats or gypsum lath, as the bond may be destroyed by chemical reaction between the two materials. Portland cement plaster may be used for scratch and brown coats under a lime–Keene's cement finish and for scratch and brown coats under ceramic-tile walls or wainscots. It can also be applied as a finish coat in an unlimited variety of patterns and colors. Deep textures such as Spanish brocade, scoring, dashing, and combing add visual interest. Machine-applied dash finishes will produce surface textures of a very even color. Fresh coats may also be sprayed with "diamond dust" (ground glass) or "glitter" (bits of mica or colored metal) before they have set.

One limitation of portland cement plaster is its tendency to shrink as it dries. Unless this shrinkage is taken into consideration and controlled by careful detailing and expansion joints, unsightly cracks and faulty plaster surfaces will result.

Fig. 8-11 Applying a finish coat of plaster.

Types of Portland Cement Used in Plastering

Five basic types of portland cement are manufactured. Types I and II, also available as air-entraining cements (Types I-A and II-A), are generally used for plastering.

TYPE I PORTLAND CEMENT Type I portland cement plaster, available in grey or white, is used for both base coats and finish coats. If integral coloring or decorative aggregates are to be used, white portland cement is usually specified. Type I-A, air-entraining cement, is finding increased use in plastering. The millions of tiny bubbles formed in the plaster coat provide improved workability, durability, and resistance to bleeding, the concentration of fines at the surface. Type I-S cements are made by intergrinding *granulated slag* with Type I portland cement.

TYPE II PORTLAND CEMENT This type of portland cement was developed to offer greater resistance to the action of sul-

fates. It is particularly valuable where a plastered surface must be applied over certain types of concrete block or brick that contain soluble sulfite materials. Type II develops a higher heat during hydration than Type I. This property is useful when application or curing may occur during subfreezing weather.

READY-MIXED PORTLAND CEMENT PLASTERS Several portland cement plaster mixes are available that require only the addition of water at the job site. These are finish-coat materials for either machine or hand application over portland cement base coats. They are sometimes called *finishing stuccos* and come in a variety of colors. The ready-mixed products usually provide a more uniform color and texture than aggregate and color mixed on the job. Most of the ready-mixed products are designed for a rough-troweled or textured finish rather than a smooth-troweled finish.

Fig. 8-12 Fireproofing structural steel. (*H. H. Robertson Company.*)

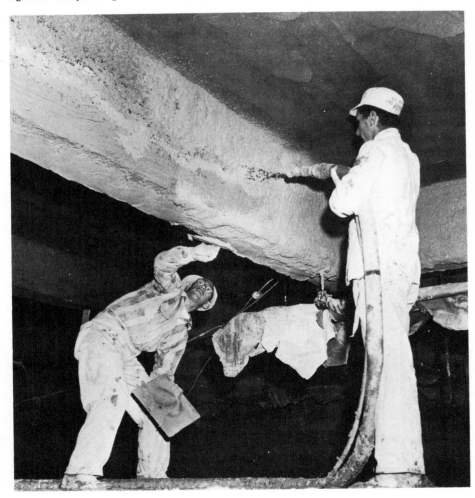

Acoustical Plasters

Plaster is distinctive, in that it can be easily adapted to the many requirements of acoustical design. It can be made porous for sound absorption, or it can be troweled to a dense surface to resist the transmission of sound through a structural assembly. Hard plaster is one of the most efficient surfaces for reflecting sound; it is capable of reflecting 97 percent of the sound waves that strike it at a right angle.

Most so-called acoustical plasters are of the sound-absorption type. The most common cementitious or binding materials are gypsum, lime, and certain types of clay. Vermiculite, perlite, and pumice are commonly used as aggregates. Most acoustical plasters contain air-entraining agents which act as foaming agents, producing minute air bubbles in the wet plaster which form interconnecting pores to absorb sound. Sound-absorbing plasters can be produced and applied to form many interesting textures and to unify the appearance of large and irregular surfaces. They are especially useful for rounded structures and domed ceilings, where rigid tiles and boards cannot be used.

Acoustical plasters are generally softer and more easily damaged than conventional finish coats. For this reason their use is usually confined to ceilings and the upper portions of walls, where damage by abrasion is not a factor. Although they also have considerably less strength than other plasters, the material need only to support itself and remain in place. To maintain their light-reflecting qualities ceilings must periodically be cleaned and painted. Some acoustical-plaster ceilings can be scrubbed with water and mild soap without affecting their acoustical properties. Others can be cleaned only with dry wallpaper cleaners or vacuumed with a brush attachment. Some can be painted with a brush or roller; others must be sprayed. It is necessary to follow the manufacturer's instructions carefully for each type of surface.

GYPSUM BASE Gypsum-base acoustical plasters consist of special gypsum binders combined with vermiculite, per-

Fig. 8-13 Acoustical-plaster ceiling.

lite, or pumice aggregates. The acoustical properties are developed in the setting of the gypsum, which leaves voids between the particles. Air-entraining agents are sometimes used to create an open cellular structure. The material is applied by machine or by hand over a standard gypsum base coat. The finish coat consists of a first coat $\frac{1}{4}$ to $\frac{3}{8}$ in. thick, which is allowed to dry overnight, and a second coat applied to bring the total thickness to a minimum of $\frac{1}{2}$ in.

LIME–KEENE'S CEMENT BASE Acoustical plasters with a lime–Keene's cement base are similar in some ways to gypsum-base plasters. The lime–Keene's cement base is combined with lightweight aggregates and is applied by machine or by hand. This material, when applied over portland cement base coats, provides a highly durable surface in areas of moderate humidity, such as bathrooms and kitchens. For acoustical properties the surface must be opened by stippling or mechanical perforation.

LIME BASE Lime plasters differ from other types, in that the surface of the materials becomes hard while the material under the surface remains soft. Lime acoustical plasters are mixed with perlite, vermiculite, mineral fiber, or other aggregates. A chemical foaming agent may be added to increase the porosity, but the hard surface must be pierced for maximum acoustical performance. The hard, durable surface may be painted repeatedly with little loss of sound absorption.

CLAY-ADHESIVE BASE Nonsetting clay base materials with adhesive qualities are combined with lightweight aggregates or mineral fibers such as asbestos to form a porous plaster surface. Fissures form during drying to add to its acoustical properties. This material can be applied over gypsum, concrete, metal, or paint. The surface may be vacuumed clean with soft brushes and may be refinished by applying a thin coat of the same material.

LATH

The primary function of lath is to form a bridge between structural elements and provide a rigid base for the application of plaster. The lathing material may have open spaces, perforations, or keys to provide a mechanical lock or grip to hold the plastering materials in place, or it may be of such a nature that plaster will bond with it to form an integral unit.

Interior chambers of the Pyramids, built about 3700 B.C., were surfaced with three coats of gypsum plaster on laths made of intertwined reeds. The openings of English half-timber houses of the Middle Ages were filled with *daub* applied over *wattle*, a woven framework of saplings and reeds. Wood lath, sawed into strips and nailed $\frac{3}{8}$ in. apart over wood studs, was the standard base for plaster until after World War I. Wood lath has been replaced by gypsumboard and metal lath in modern construction.

Fig. 8-14 Applying acoustical plaster by machine.

Gypsum Lath

Gypsum lath, sometimes called *rock lath* or *plasterboard*, consists of a core of gypsum plaster between two layers of specially formulated, fibrous, absorbent paper. The calcined gypsum is mixed with water, fiber, and additives and is fed into a board machine in continuous streams between two sheets of paper. As the board travels down a moving belt the gypsum starts to set, and in 3 to 4 min it is hard enough to be cut to length.

Gypsum lath is generally $\frac{3}{8}''$ or $\frac{1}{2}''$ thick, 16″ wide (16.2″ on the West Coast), and 48″ long. Other sizes and thicknesses are available for special uses. Special $\frac{1}{2}''$ gypsum lath up to 12 ft long is produced for use in plaster veneer systems. There is also a $\frac{1}{2}''$ lath for fireproofing applications and for installation when studs or ceiling joists are spaced 24 in. on center. Long-length lath is available in $\frac{3}{8}''$ or $\frac{1}{2}''$ thicknesses, 16″ or 14″ wide, and cut to any length up to 12 ft.

Gypsum lath may be nailed, stapled, screwed, or clipped to wood, metal framing, or furring members. It is economical because plaster need be applied to a thickness of only $\frac{1}{2}$ in. over $\frac{3}{8}''$ lath for the fire protection provided by $\frac{7}{8}$ in. of plaster. Lath is usually applied with the long dimension perpendicular to the framing and with the end joints staggered between courses. All lath ends must bear on framing members. Any spaces of more than ³/₈ in. between the laths should be reinforced with 3-in.-wide metal furring strips secured to both pieces. Metal lath may be nailed directly to the wood studs or it may be fastened by special spring clips to decrease the transmission of sound.

PERFORATED GYPSUM LATH Perforated gypsum lath, sometimes called *buttonboard*, has holes punched through it at regular intervals. The lath may be perforated by a wet-punch press or a mechanical perforator located just before the cutoff knife on the board machine or by a gang drillpress after the board has been bundled. Perforated gypsum lath is identical to plain or standard gypsum lath except for the perforations. These perforations at regular intervals allow the plaster to "rivet" itself to the lath with a mechanical key for greater fire protection. Most perforated gypsum lath contains ³/₄-in. holes at 4 in. on center.

INSULATING GYPSUM LATH Insulating gypsum lath is plain gypsum lath with a sheet of aluminum foil cemented to one side. This lath, installed with the foil facing the studs or ceiling joists, provides all the advantages of gypsum lath plus thermal insulation. Aluminum foil is well established as a reflective insulation and is one of the best vapor barriers known. Aluminum-foil insulation gypsum lath effectively reduces vapor condensation within outside walls and ceilings, which helps to prevent rotting of framing members and damage to both exterior and interior painted surfaces.

Metal Lath

Metal lath, formed from copper-bearing steel, is one of the most versatile lathing materials. It may either be galvanized or have a rust-inhibitive coat of paint. It may be used with any type of plaster and is particularly adaptable for curved forms and surfaces.

Metal lath is second only to gypsum lath in volume of use. Whereas gypsum lath develops a plaster bond by suction, metal lath provides only a mechanical bond.

Fig. 8-15 Applying gypsum lath. (*Gypsum Association.*)

However, as the plaster is forced through the metal lath, it forms into keys. Thus the steel becomes embedded within the plaster to produce a reinforced plaster slab. If the lath is plastered on both sides, the metal lath acts as a tension member, like the reinforcing bars in reinforced concrete. Extremely thin shell structures have been produced with metal lath as the core reinforcing element.

Several types of metal lath are available. Some are produced from thin sheet metal and others are woven wire.

DIAMOND-MESH LATH   In 1884 J. F. Golding developed a process of punching parallel staggered slits in sheet metal so that they could be expanded to form diamond-shaped openings by pulling on each end of the sheet. Diamond-mesh lath is produced in standard sheets 24″ or 27″ wide and 96″ long, although longer lengths are available for use in solid partitions. Diamond-mesh lath is suitable for most types of plastering. When it is installed over wood studs, waterproof building paper or building felt is placed between the lath and the studs to protect the wood from water and other ingredients in the plaster. The lath is attached with *furring nails*, special nails with a fiber wad that holds the lath out from the paper. This provides a space for plaster keys to develop between the paper and the metal lath.

There is also a *self-furring diamond-mesh lath*. This lath is indented at regular intervals to form dimples in the surface. On the reverse side the dimples project to hold the mesh ¼ in. away from the building paper or other surface, thus performing the function of furring nails. This type of lath is particularly useful where old plaster walls must be furred out for replastering. It can be attached to concrete or masonry and wrapped around structural steel.

STUCCO MESH   Expanded-metal stucco mesh was developed for use under stucco or portland cement plaster. It is applied with furring nails designed to hold the metal lath ⅜ in. away from the sheathing and waterproof building paper. This lath is similar to diamond mesh, except that it has larger openings (approximately 1½ × 3 in).

Stucco mesh fabricated from 18-gauge galvanized wire is produced in 1½-in. hexagonal mesh, sometimes called chicken wire. The mesh is applied over waterproof building paper with furring nails, assuring ample embedment of the mesh in the finish plaster. Stucco mesh may be obtained in a hexagonal pattern that is crimped every 3 in. to eliminate the need for furring nails. The built-in crimp maintains the proper spacing of reinforcing wire from the building paper. The open mesh permits rapid troweling of a full, even coat.

RIB LATH   Flat-rib laths are expanded like diamond-mesh laths; however, additional longitudinal ribs of stiffening are left in each sheet. The ribs increase the rigidity of the sheet, permitting wider spacing of supports with a savings

Fig. 8-16 Metal lath used as a base for fireproofing structural steel beams and decking. (*H. H. Robertson Company.*)

Fig. 8-17 Applying plaster base coat to metal lath. (*Ceramic Tile Institute.*)

in installation time and materials costs. This type of lath is well suited for two-coat work, or *back plastering*.

A self-furring rib lath with ⅜-in. raised ribs is made for use on long-span ceilings and a centering material for floor reinforcing over steel joists. There is also a ¾-in. ribbed lath, frequently used as a self-furring lath on walls. It is installed with ribs fastened directly to the surface, so that furring channels are not required, and is used in locations where long spans between supports are desirable.

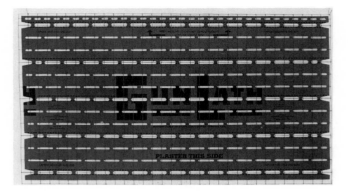

Fig. 8-18 Paper-backed wire lath. (*K-Lath Corporation.*)

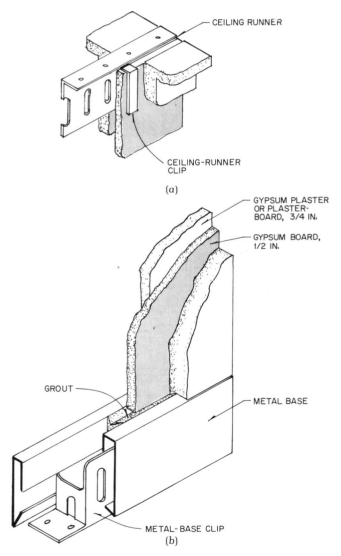

Fig. 8-19 Details of gypsumboard solid partitions: (*a*) with ceiling attachment; (*b*) with metal base.

SHEET LATH   Metal sheet lath consists of perforated copper-alloy steel sheet. It is not expanded. Because of its stiffness, it is sometimes used as tensile reinforcement in concrete floor slabs.

WIRE LATH   Wire-mesh lath is manufactured by weaving or welding wire of various gauges in either square, hexagonal, or diamond patterns. The wire is 19 gauge or larger, and is galvanized or given a coat of rust-inhibitive paint. This type is used as a base for interior or exterior plaster.

One such product consists of galvanized wire electrically welded at each intersection through specially perforated heavy kraft paper inserted between the front and back wires. The paper is thus an integral part of the lath and cannot tear loose. Deep embedment of the vertical wires in plaster is obtained through perforations in the paper formed around the horizontal wires.

Lathing Accessories

A wide variety of metal accessories are produced for use with gypsum and metal lathing. Lathing accessories are usually installed before plastering to form true corners, to act as screeds for the plasterer, to reinforce possible weak points, to provide control joints, and to provide structural support.

SCREEDS   Base or parting screeds are used to separate plaster from other flush surfaces, such as terrazzo or concrete. Ventilating expansion screed is used on the underside of closed soffits and in protected vertical surfaces for ventilation of enclosed attic spaces. Drip screeds act as terminators of exterior portland cement plaster at concrete foundation walls. They are also used on external horizontal corners of plaster soffits to prevent drip stains on the underside of the soffit. Metal base acts as a flush base at the bottom of a plaster wall. It also serves as a plaster screed.

BEADS   Corner beads fit over gypsum lath exterior corners to provide a true, reinforced corner. They are available in either small-nose or bullnose types, with either a solid flange or a woven-mesh flange.

Casing beads are used both as finish casings around openings in plaster walls and as screeds to obtain true surfaces around doors and windows. They are also used as a stop between a plaster surface and another material, such as masonry or wood paneling. Casing beads are available as square sections, modified-square sections, and quarter-rounds.

REINFORCEMENT   Corner reinforcement fabricated from expanded metal with large openings is used for exterior corners under stucco. It is placed over stucco mesh and waterproof building paper to reinforce the corner and provide a true line. Cornerite is made of expanded metal lath shaped to act as reinforcement for interior corners. Cornerite may also be obtained as shaped, galvanized wire.

Strip reinforcement is used in the reinforcement of continuous joints of gypsum lath or to reinforce joints of dissimilar materials in the same plane. Strip reinforcement is placed at corners of windows and doors to prevent cracks.

CONTROL JOINTS   These are formed metal strips used to relieve stresses and strains in large plaster areas of walls and ceilings. The control joint minimizes plaster cracking and assures proper plaster thickness. The use of control joints is extremely important when portland cement plaster is being installed.

CONCEALED PICTURE MOLDING   Metal picture molding may be attached directly to the lath around the entire perimeter of the room as a support for pictures or draperies.

LATH-AND-PLASTER CONSTRUCTION

The lather installs not only gypsum and metal lath and accessories, but also certain types of supporting structures. His work includes the installation of interior partitions of metal studs and suspended ceilings with a framework of steel channels.

Interior Partitions

There are two types of plaster partitions whose base is installed by the lather: solid partitions, with either a plasterboard or a metal-lath core, and hollow partitions, which consist of outer plaster membranes over structural metal studs.

SOLID PLASTERBOARD PARTITIONS   Solid gypsum-wallboard partitions are non-load-bearing units that may be constructed in place by laminating two layers of ½″ gypsum wallboard to a 1 in.-thick gypsum core. Solid gypsum-wallboard partitions are seldom less than 2 in. thick. The height to which they can be carried, usually a maximum of 12 ft, depends on the thickness and the structural rigidity required.

Solid plasterboard partitions are economical to install. Their overall thinness increases available floor space. They are durable, with relatively high crack resistance, and can be installed rapidly and easily. Their two major limitations are their poor soundproofing qualities and the difficulty of installing electrical and plumbing services in thin walls.

The partitions are held in place at the floor and ceiling by metal or wood runners. Gypsumboard is nailed to the wood runners or attached to the metal runners with sheet-metal screws. Gypsumboard facings may be taped at the joints and serve as a base for any decorative treatment, such as paint, wallpaper, fabric, and vinyl films. Panels which are factory covered with vinyl or wood-grained surfaces may be used as the finished wall surfaces.

Solid gypsum partitions may also be constructed with a core or base of ½″ gypsumboard plastered on both sides

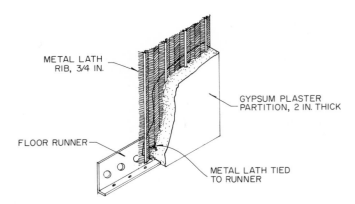

Fig. 8-20   Studless metal-lath-and-plaster partition.

Fig. 8-21   Applying gypsum wallboard to steel studs. (*Gypsum Association.*)

with ½ in. of gypsum plaster. Temporary bracing must be used while the partition is being plastered. The bracing is moved from one side to the other as successive coats of plaster are being applied. Either flush metal plaster base is applied to the bottom of the partition before plastering is begun, or wood, metal, rubber, or vinyl base is applied later.

Fig. 8-22 Applying gypsumboard to wood studs. (*Gypsum Association*.)

Fig. 8-23 Metal lath attached with resilient clips.

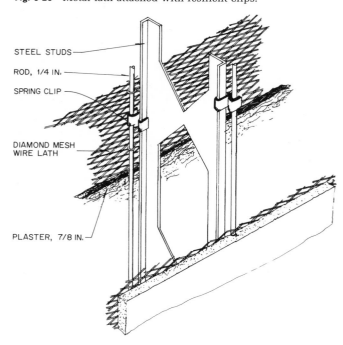

STEEL STUDS

ROD, 1/4 IN.

SPRING CLIP

DIAMOND MESH
WIRE LATH

PLASTER, 7/8 IN.

STUDLESS PARTITIONS Studless metal-lath-and-plaster partitions are constructed over ³/₈″-rib lath hung vertically as a plaster base. This type of partition eliminates the need for studs, reduces dead load, and cuts materials costs. However, it requires the use of special door frames and shallow electric switches, outlets, and wiring devices.

STEEL-STUD PARTITIONS These lightweight, non-load-bearing, noncombustible partitions consist of lightweight galvanized steel studs (1⅝ to 6 in. thick), either punched sheet steel or welded-truss construction, faced on each side with gypsum wallboard. The wallboard is nailed to the studs or attached with self-tapping screws. A single layer of ³/₈″, ½″, or ⅝″ gypsum wallboard may be applied by attaching a base layer to the studs and laminating or nailing a face layer of wood-grained gypsumboard or vinyl-covered gypsum wallboard.

Hollow metal-stud partitions may be constructed by wiring diamond-mesh lath, flat-rib lath, ³/₈″-rib lath, or gypsum lath to studs. For additional soundproofing, the lath may be attached to metal studs with resilient spring clips. This allows for independent movement of the plaster surfaces. Another advantage of this type of system is reduced plaster cracking, since movement of the walls is not transmitted to the plaster surfaces.

CHANNEL-STUD HOLLOW PARTITIONS For maximum soundproofing, partitions may be constructed of a double row of parallel ³/₄-in. channel studs covered with metal lath and plaster or with plasterboard. Each row of channel studs is attached independently to the floor and ceiling with no other connection between them. This type of partition offers the greatest resistance to the passage of sound.

Ceilings

Lath-and-plaster ceilings are of three basic types, depending on the method of supporting the lath. In *contact*

Fig. 8-24 Channel-stud hollow partition.

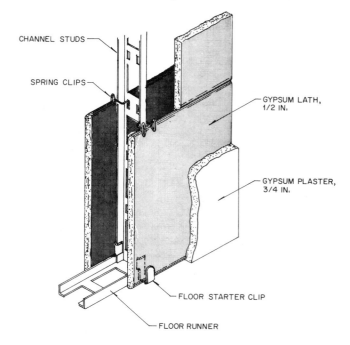

CHANNEL STUDS

SPRING CLIPS

GYPSUM LATH,
1/2 IN.

GYPSUM PLASTER,
3/4 IN.

FLOOR STARTER CLIP

FLOOR RUNNER

ceilings the lath is attached directly to the overhead structure. In *furred ceilings* it is separated from the structure by furring channels, rods, or other special devices. *Suspended ceilings* are hung from the main structural elements by wires, rods, or hangers.

CONTACT CEILINGS   Metal lath or paper-backed wire-fabric lath may be attached directly to the underside of concrete joists with hairpin, hook, or loop hangers. These devices are cast in the concrete when the structural member is poured. Metal lath may be attached to the underside of steel joists by tie wires over the bottom flange. Metal or gypsum lath may be nailed or stapled to the bottom of wood ceiling joists. Expanded-metal lath or paper-backed welded-wire lath will span 16 in. when attached to wood or concrete or 13½ in. when attached to metal. For longer spans flat-rib or ³/₈″-rib expanded-metal lath must be used. Contact ceilings are suitable only when the joists or structural supports are within the permissible span for metal lath.

FURRED CEILINGS   In furred ceilings ³/₈-in. round steel *pencil rods* or steel channels (³/₄ to 2 in. deep, depending on the span) are securely tied, clipped, or welded to the underside of steel joists. In concrete-joist construction the runner channels are tied with wires that have been cast into concrete. When concrete joists are too far apart for the channel to span, cross channels are hung between concrete joists to support runner channels. When runner channels are to be attached to wood joists, 16-penny nails are driven in a horizontal position completely through the joist at least 2 in. above the bottom of the joist. The runner channels are attached snugly against the bottom of the joists with wire.

Metal lath is then attached to the runner channels, either with wire or with specially designed clips. Furred ceilings are useful where the structural members are too far apart for metal or gypsum lath to span.

SUSPENDED CEILINGS   Suspended ceilings are adaptable to most types of structural systems. They allow maximum freedom of positioning of the structural elements. The space above contact or furred systems for ducts, conduits, and mechanical equipment is governed by the depth of joists or trusses. Suspended ceilings permit virtually any type of mechanical equipment to be installed above them; the length of hangers may be adjusted as necessary. There is also no restriction on the direction in which ducts and services may be run.

In the normal suspended ceiling carrying channels, or main runner channels, are hung from structural members with hanger wires, and ³/₄-in. cross-furring channels are tied to the runner channels. Metal lath, wire-fabric lath, or gypsum lath is then attached to the furring channels by wire or special clips.

The size and spacing of hanger wires depend on the structural system and the area of ceiling that is to be sup-

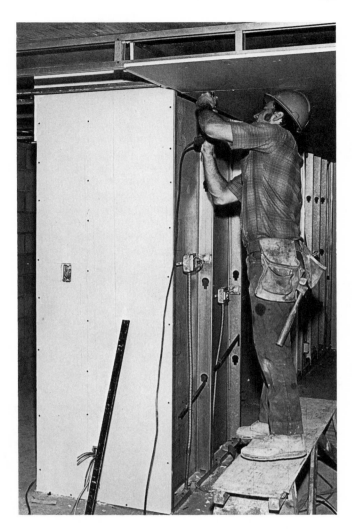

Fig. 8-25   Applying gypsumboard to a furred ceiling. (*Gypsum Association.*)

ported by each hanger. Building codes specify the required size and spacing for hangers, runners, and furring channels. Wire hangers are wrapped around, inserted through, or clipped to steel supports. For concrete joists or concrete-slab construction the wires are secured to reinforcing bars or reinforcing wire mesh before the concrete is poured. They are allowed to extend through the underside of the concrete far enough to allow a positive tie to the runner channels. In wood construction the hanger wires may be inserted in holes drilled 3 in. above the bottom of the joists, or they may be attached to the side of the joists with two 1½-in. 9-gauge wire staples.

The main runners or cross-furring channels are not allowed to touch abutting masonry or concrete walls. A main runner must be placed within 6 in. of parallel walls. The main runner must be supported at both ends.

Metal lath, wire-fabric lath, or gypsum lath is tied or clipped across the cross-furring channels.

Column and Beam Fireproofing

A steel column or beam can be fireproofed efficiently by surrounding it with gypsumboard or a membrane of lath and gypsum plaster. The gypsum increases the time that a steel structural member can sustain its full load. A steel column or beam can be protected for periods of 1 to 4 hr. There are four common methods of fireproofing: (1) lath and plaster applied directly to the member, (2) furred lath and plaster, (3) plaster applied over gypsum, and (4) clay or concrete block which have been built up around the member. The type and thickness of the fireproofing materials depend on the location of the member and building codes governing the construction.

Drywall Systems

Drywalls are constructed of a wide variety of materials, but the primary one is gypsum. *Gypsum drywall* consists of paper- or vinyl-covered gypsum wallboard $\frac{1}{4}''$ to $1''$ thick, either $24''$ or $48''$ wide, and from 7 to 16 ft long. The edges may be squared, tapered, or beveled. Many boards have factory finishes that require no taping and decorating. These range from heavy vinyls to inexpensive papers, and come in several shapes, including planks as well as panels. The vinyls give rugged protection to areas subject to heavy wear. Papers in simulated wood grains are used to produce a low-cost finish.

Drywall systems with concealed joints use boards with tapered edges. In wood construction the boards are nailed to ceiling joists and studs with special nails called *cooler nails*. The wallboard must be nailed with great care. Not only must the nail be driven solidly into the stud without denting the wallboard, but it must be slightly countersunk without breaking the paper skin, so that it can be concealed by a nail-spotting compound.

TAPING AND FINISHING   Contemporary drywall construction began with the advent of concealed joints, made possible by the development of joint-treatment tapes, taping compounds, and topping-finishing compounds. *Joint-treatment tapes* are generally made of high-quality papers. They are strong, uniform in thickness and width, and processed to

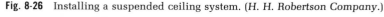

Fig. 8-26 Installing a suspended ceiling system. (*H. H. Robertson Company.*)

achieve proper porosity yet have low absorption and expansion when moistened by embedding compounds. *Taping compounds* are generally water-soluble adhesive materials having controlled shrinkage properties. The taping compound is applied along shallow channels formed by the tapered edges, where boards are butted, and along both sides of inside corners. The joint-treatment tapes are pressed smoothly into the taping compound.

Topping-finishing compounds are then applied over the tape and nailheads to bring the surface to a true plane. After the first application is dry, it is sanded where necessary, and a second, or fill coat, of topping compound is applied. The edges are feathered, and the surface is sanded to conceal all imperfections.

LAMINATED DRYWALL   Laminated wallboard, alone or in combination with other materials, provides any degree of fire and sound protection desired. On wood studs the most common lamination system is two layers of $^3/_8''$ gypsum board. The base layer is nailed, and the second layer is applied adhesively. Taping compound or other adhesives are applied to the entire back surface of the face layer. This layer is applied to the layer that has been nailed or stapled to the studs. Joints in the face layer must be staggered so as not to coincide with those of the base layer.

The base layer may be backing board, manufactured especially for this purpose, and may be power stapled instead of nailed. The face layer may be shop or factory finished with a wood-grained paper or vinyl. Wallboards designated as Type X are specially engineered for fire protection. Drywall on wood studs can be laminated with sound-deadening boards for soundproofing. Insulation blankets placed between studs will further deaden sound.

VENEER PLASTERING   Veneer plastering consists of a monolithic plaster surface applied in one or more coats to a thickness of $^1/_{16}$ in. over large gypsum sheets (4 ft wide and up to 12 ft long) attached to wood or metal supports. The gypsum lath is usually coated with a catalyst that permits the plaster to form a good bond. All joints are reinforced either by stapling or by embedding in veneer plaster. Veneer plaster is a high-strength gypsum-base plaster specially formulated for hand or machine application. It may contain polyvinyl or other materials to allow the finish to set in 20 to 90 min and cure in 24 hr. Veneer-plastered surfaces may be troweled smooth or given a textured finish. They can usually be painted within 24 hr after plastering.

Veneer-plastering systems produce a hard, durable surface. The speed of application, setting, and curing make them extremely valuable for remodeling and for speeding up construction.

ACOUSTICS

Acoustics concerns the propagation, transmission, and effects of sound. The word *acoustics* is taken from the

Fig. 8-27 Applying gypsumboard to suspended ceiling runners. (*Gypsum Association.*)

Greek *akoustikos,* relating to hearing. Today's living is noisy. Television, stereo, electric guitars, garbage-disposal units, dishwashers, vacuum cleaners, washers and driers, and heating and cooling equipment make life easier and pleasanter, but at the same time they create noise. Outside noise is ever increasing as high-speed freeways or expressways cover the country and jet planes become larger and noisier.

Modern construction materials and methods can contribute to the problem. Smooth-troweled plaster can reflect up to 98 percent of the sound that strikes it. Lightweight plastic or thin plaster partitions can create problems in confining sound to one room. As apartment living continues to increase, the control of sound transmission between living units is a growing problem. In selecting materials for sound control, the designer must consider two aspects of sound: sound absorption and sound transmission. Materials that act as efficient sound-absorption mediums may transmit it readily from one room to another. Materials that resist the passage of sound through walls and ceilings may create problems with reverberations or echoes in enclosed spaces.

Nature of Sound

Sound is produced by vibrations transmitted in air or any elastic medium. A vibrating body will impart a portion of its energy to the surrounding air in the form of *sound waves*. These sound waves travel through air at approximately 1130 ft/sec, or 1 mile every 5 sec. When these vibrations strike the eardrum, they are multiplied through a series of bones in the inner ear and transmitted to nerve endings that convey impulses to the brain. It is the *frequency* of vibration, or the *cycles per second* (Hz), that determines the *pitch* of the sound. The apparent loudness perceived by the ear depends on both the intensity and the frequency of the vibrations.

SOUND FREQUENCY   The range of sound frequencies that can be heard by the average human ear is limited to a low of 16 Hz and a high of 20,000. Thunder is in a very low frequency range. A police siren generates primarily high-frequency sound. Most common sounds cover a wide range of frequencies, as shown in Table 8-1.

TABLE 8-1   Frequencies of some common sounds

SOUND	APPROX. FREQUENCY, Hz
Piano	30–4000
Violin	196–2100
Female voice	196–1050
Male voice	82–500

Materials are usually rated by their ability to absorb or resist the passage of sound at a particular frequency. Certain materials have good sound-absorption qualities in the higher frequencies, but are poor in the lower frequencies. However, high-pitch sounds are generally more annoying than those in the lower frequencies. Our sensitivity to

Fig. 8-28 Beam fireproofing. (*H. H. Robertson Company.*)

sound is most acute in the middle frequencies, around 1000 Hz. The sound-absorption qualities of a material are usually tested at 125, 250, 1,000, and 4,000 Hz.

SOUND INTENSITY The ear responds to an enormous range of sound intensity. A loud noise may develop 3 trillion times the intensity of one that is barely audible. However, the ear does not perceive changes in loudness in direct relation to changes in the actual intensity of the sound. For this reason sound intensity is measured in terms of *apparent loudness*. The unit measure is the *decibel* (dB), the smallest change in sound intensity that can be discerned by the average human ear. The decibel scale starts at the *threshold of hearing*, 0 dB, and terminates at the *threshold of pain*, 130 dB.

Generally, in a quiet room a 3-dB change is barely perceptible. A 5-dB change is clearly noticeable, and a 10-dB change is perceived as twice as loud. This is because there is nearly always a minimal amount of sound or background noise in a room which masks specific sounds. It may be the sound of distant traffic, noise from a ventilating duct, the electric motor in a refrigerator, or the fan in a forced-air heating unit. The simplest way to understand decibel levels of such background noise is in terms of specific easily recognizable sounds. Table 8-2 lists the approximate sound levels of some noises encountered in everyday life.

Sound Reduction

Sound-absorbing, or acoustical materials have the property of absorbing the sound waves striking their surfaces and reflecting less than 50 percent back into the room. They serve as a cushion to counteract the undesirable effects of sound reflection. The amount of sound a material absorbs depends on the size, depth, and number of pores in the material and the frequency of the sound. Air particles set in motion by sound move in and out of pores,

causing friction. The sound energy is dissipated as heat, transmitted through the barrier, or reflected back into the room. In practice, it is seldom feasible to obtain reductions of much more than 10 dB by the use of sound-absorbing materials. A reduction of 5 to 7 dB is usually obtained when the ceiling of a residence or office is covered with acoustical tile.

NOISE-REDUCTION COEFFICIENT Theoretically, a perfectly reflective surface would reflect all sound back into a room. The more sound energy a material absorbs, the less it reflects as noise. The percentage of sound energy absorbed by a material is expressed as its *noise-reduction coefficient* (NRC). An NRC of 0 represents a material that will absorb no sound, and an NRC of 1 represents a material that will absorb all sound reaching it.

In order to find a single figure for the noise-reducing qualities of a material it is customary to average the reflective qualities of that material when subjected to sound at 250 to 2000 Hz. This average value is then expressed

Fig. 8-30 Dissipation of sound by sound-absorbing materials. (a) In fibrous or porous acoustical materials friction of moving air within interconnecting air spaces transforms sound into heat. (b) In perforated acoustical materials sound is transformed into heat by friction on the sides of perforations.

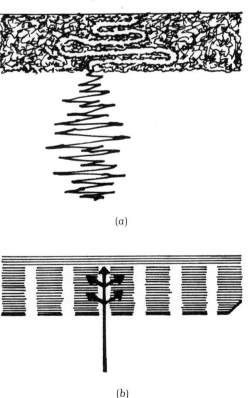

(a)

(b)

Fig. 8-29 Reinforcing drywall joints with tape to prevent cracks at filled gypsumboard joints. (*Gypsum Association.*)

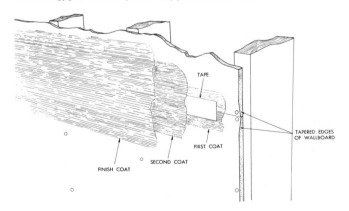

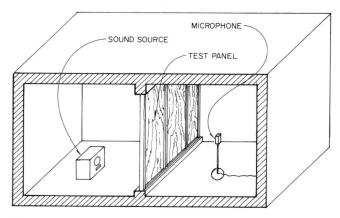

Fig. 8-31 Facility for testing sound transmission loss.

Fig. 8-32 Facility for testing impact noise.

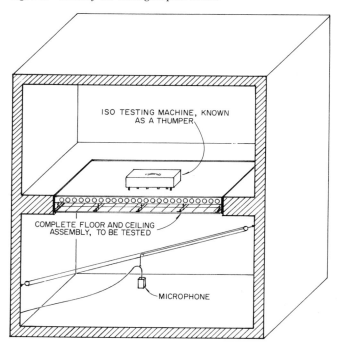

TABLE 8-2 Sound levels of common environmental noises

DECIBELS	SOURCE	SENSATION
110–130	Jet plane	Painful
100	Thunder Artillery fire Passing train Boiler factory	Deafening
90	Noisy industrial plant Rock-and-roll music	Extremely loud
80	Truck traffic Cabin of airplane Usual hi-fi level	Very loud
70	Noisy office (20 typewriters) Average street noise	Loud
60–70	Average radio or TV level Average factory Average office	Moderately loud
50–60	Noisy home Average conversation Quiet radio	Moderate
40–50	Private office Quiet home	Quiet
30–40	Bedroom Empty theater	Faint
20–30	Average auditorium Quiet conversation	Very faint
10–20	Rustle of leaves Whisper Soundproof room	Whisper
0	Threshhold of audibility	Silence

as the NRC to the nearest 0.05. A material with an NRC of 0.50 would absorb 50 percent of the sound and reflect 50 percent back into the room. A material with an NRC of 0.70 would absorb 70 percent of the sound and therefore be a better sound-absorption medium.

SOUND-TRANSMISSION CLASS   The effectiveness of a sound barrier, such as a door, a partition, or a floor, in reducing the transmission of airborne noise is measured in terms of the loss in transmitted sound. This is the ratio of the sound impinging on one side of the barrier to the sound emerging on the opposite side, expressed in decibels.

Sound transmission loss is measured in accordance with tests outlined in ASTM E90 on a specimen panel of at least 80 sq ft. The panel is located in a wall between two isolated testing rooms, and the losses are measured at 16 different frequency bands within a range of 125 to 4000 Hz. The material is then assigned to a *sound-transmission class* (STC), a single-figure rating derived by comparing the sound transmission losses against predetermined standards. In the range of sound tested, the STC is in effect a rating reduction of the sound of speech. Various STC ratings are described in Table 8-3.

IMPACT-NOISE RATING   Impact noise is the sound generated by an object striking, skidding, vibrating, or sliding against a floor. Footsteps, moving of furniture, or dropped objects will start a floor vibrating and cause it to radiate sound. The level of impact noise in the room below indicates the ability of the floor construction to deaden impact noise.

TABLE 8-3 STC ratings

STC RATING, dB	SOUNDPROOFING PROPERTIES	SPEECH COMPARISON
25–30	Poor	Normal speech understood easily and distinctly through the wall
30–35	Fair	Loud speech understood, normal speech audible but understood with difficulty
35–40	Good	Loud speech audible but not understood, normal speech inaudible
40–50	Very good	Loud speech, and average radio or TV only faintly audible
50 or over	Excellent	Very loud noises and hi-fi faint or inaudible

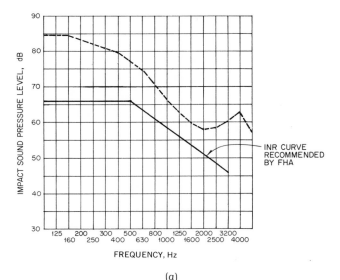

(a)

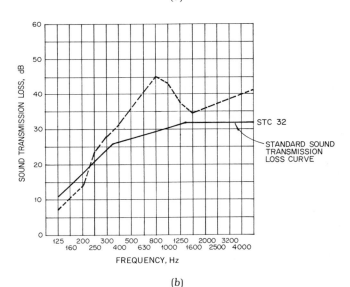

(b)

Fig. 8-33 Standard impact-noise rating and standard sound-transmission class. (a) INR is found by comparing impact-sound-pressure level (dotted) with standard curve (solid); (b) STC is found by comparing standard curve with test results of assembly.

The *impact-noise rating* (INR) of a floor-ceiling construction is determined by a standard means of generating and measuring known impacts. The floor is subjected to a series of impacts at different frequencies by a tapping machine. This establishes an impact-noise curve for that particular floor construction, which is then compared with a standard curve that represents a minimum rating for floor construction. If the rating is above that of the standard curve, the INR is a plus value; if it is below that of the standard curve, it is a minus value.

An INR of 0 is considered to be the minimum for a floor construction for quiet environments. For corridor floors above living units in quiet areas an INR of +5 is considered the minimum. A floor construction that exceeds the minimum values for suburban and urban living provides the best solution for impact-noise problems. An INR greater than +10, for instance, would be desirable for a luxury apartment.

BACKGROUND NOISE   Background-noise levels should be taken into consideration in judging the adequacy of a construction for airborne and impact noise. The ambient or background noise associated with a given environment is the total noise produced by distant traffic, air-conditioning and heating units, and other sounds that are constantly present in a room. This background noise tends to cover up or mask specific sounds. The level of background noise must be taken into consideration in calculating the sound reduction needed for a partition or floor, because it determines whether or not transmitted sound will be heard.

FLANKING PATHS   The transmission loss of a particular construction is evaluated on the basis of a sealed structure with no openings. Noise transmitted through open windows, doors, ducts, or grilles or through the air space above suspended ceilings can make an efficient wall or partition valueless, since the sound may be transmitted around

or through it. This bypassing is called *flanking*. The paths can be medicine cabinets or electrical-outlet boxes installed back to back, air-conditioning or heating ducts common to two rooms, and even the crack below or around a loosely fitted door.

ACOUSTICAL MATERIALS

Acoustical materials comprise a wide range of substances and are produced under many trade names. Although their

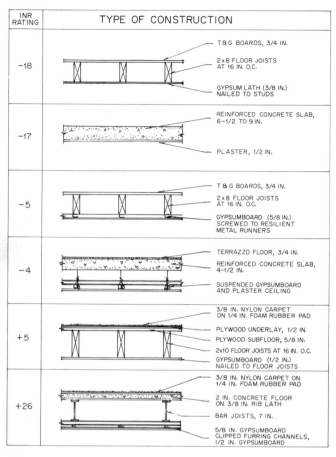

INR RATING	TYPE OF CONSTRUCTION
−18	T & G BOARDS, 3/4 IN. / 2 x 8 FLOOR JOISTS AT 16 IN. O.C. / GYPSUM LATH (3/8 IN.) NAILED TO STUDS
−17	REINFORCED CONCRETE SLAB, 6-1/2 TO 9 IN. / PLASTER, 1/2 IN.
−5	T & G BOARDS, 3/4 IN. / 2 x 8 FLOOR JOISTS AT 16 IN. O.C. / GYPSUMBOARD (5/8 IN.) SCREWED TO RESILIENT METAL RUNNERS
−4	TERRAZZO FLOOR, 3/4 IN. / REINFORCED CONCRETE SLAB, 4-1/2 IN. / SUSPENDED GYPSUMBOARD AND PLASTER CEILING
+5	3/8 IN. NYLON CARPET ON 1/4 IN. FOAM RUBBER PAD / PLYWOOD UNDERLAY, 1/2 IN. / PLYWOOD SUBFLOOR, 5/8 IN. / 2x10 FLOOR JOISTS AT 16 IN. O.C. / GYPSUMBOARD (1/2 IN.) NAILED TO FLOOR JOISTS
+26	3/8 IN. NYLON CARPET ON 1/4 IN. FOAM RUBBER PAD / 2 IN. CONCRETE FLOOR ON 3/8 IN. RIB LATH / BAR JOISTS, 7 IN. / 5/8 IN. GYPSUMBOARD CLIPPED FURRING CHANNELS, 1/2 IN. GYPSUMBOARD

Fig. 8-34 Impact-noise rating of a typical floor construction.

sound-absorption characteristics may be similar, the designer must select the material that will perform under the particular conditions of each project.

Acoustical materials may be either prefabricated or job assembled. Prefabricated tiles and boards range in size from $12'' \times 12''$ to $4' \times 4'$. Most are manufactured from cane fiber, asbestos fiber, mineral fiber, or glass fiber matted and bonded into boards of various thicknesses. Tiles are usually limited to ceilings, where they may be attached directly to the underside of structural floor systems or suspended by wires or hangers supporting T-grid systems. Job-assembled materials include acoustical plasters and various combinations of sound-absorbing units.

For an acoustical ceiling to be completely successful, many factors in addition to its sound-absorbing qualities must be considered. These include, but are not limited to, the following properties:

Insulating qualities
Thickness
Light reflection
Flame resistance
Moisture resistance
Maintenance
Ease of installation
Cost

Acoustical Tiles and Boards

CELLULOSE-FIBER TILES   Cellulose tiles are usually made from bagasse (sugar-cane fiber). Cane-fiber tiles are the oldest, and generally the cheapest, type of acoustical tile. The fibers are pressed into boards, with tiny voids between the fibers throughout the tile. Cane-fiber tile is usually perforated to allow the sound to reach the voids between the fibers. This gives the tile its sound-absorbing qualities.

Fig. 8-35 Reduction in intensity of sound passing through a wall.

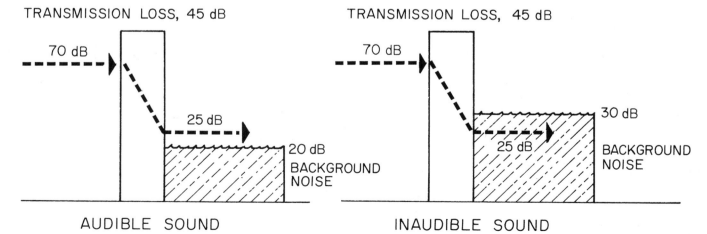

TRANSMISSION LOSS, 45 dB

70 dB

25 dB

20 dB BACKGROUND NOISE

AUDIBLE SOUND

TRANSMISSION LOSS, 45 dB

70 dB

30 dB BACKGROUND NOISE

25 dB

INAUDIBLE SOUND

Variations in texture and appearance are obtained by variations in the pattern of holes and surface.

Cane-fiber tiles are subject to dimensional changes and loss of strength when subjected to moisture. They are also not fireproof, although their rate of burning is low. Federal specifications establish specific criteria by which the fire resistance of material is rated, from A for incombustible materials through D for varying degrees of flame resistance. Cane-fiber tile with a standard paint finish is usually classed as D, although some tiles with a factory-applied finish are classed as C. They are usually furnished factory finished with beveled edges in sizes ranging from 12″ × 12″ to 24″ × 24″.

MINERAL-FIBER TILE   Mineral wool is the major component of mineral-fiber tile. Most of the mineral wool produced in the United States is made from blast-furnace slag. The slag is remelted in a small cupola, and after it reaches a desired temperature it is blown into wool by a jet of high-pressure steam or compressed air, or spun into filaments by the action of a high-speed rotating disk. A binder is added to provide strength and toughness, and the combined materials are *felted* into the finished product.

Mineral-fiber tile may be fissured or perforated to develop its sound-absorbing qualities. Fissured material dissipates the sound energy by friction in the small voids between individual fibers of the material. Perforations may be added to obtain maximum sound attenuation. Fissured tile is generally used where appearance is of primary importance. The perforated tile is more often used in industrial or institutional buildings, where maximum permeability and paintability is desired.

Mineral-fiber tiles have a fire rating of class A and are used where building codes require a material that is incombustible, as in places of public assembly and exit areas. They are manufactured in a variety of sizes, textures, thicknesses, and efficiencies. Extreme care must be exercised in painting fissured or textured tiles. A non-bridging paint must be used so not to close the pores and thus destroy the acoustical characteristics of the material.

Fig. 8-36   Flanking paths for sound.

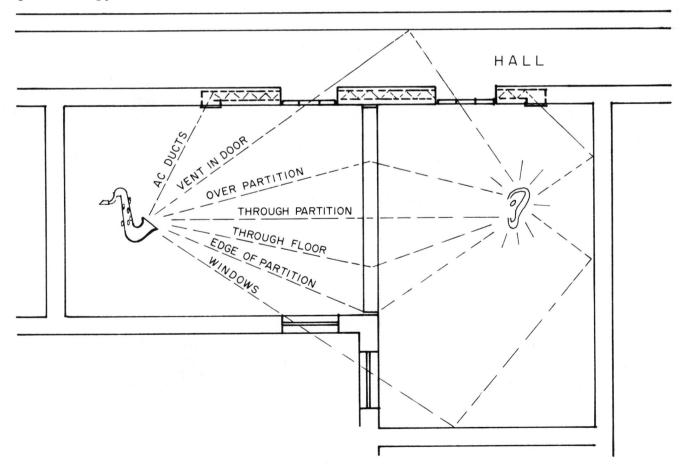

PERFORATED METAL TILE   This type of tile consists of a perforated metal pan filled with a pad of some acoustical material such as mineral wool. The thin perforated metal pan does not decrease the sound-absorbing qualities of the acoustical material above. Rather, it acts as a diaphragm in transmitting the sound to the insulating material, where it is absorbed. The pan may be made of aluminum or light-gauge steel and is usually finished with a white baked-on enamel.

Although the initial cost is relatively high, this type of tile is economical from the standpoint of durability and upkeep. The surface can be cleaned with a damp cloth, so that it does not require repainting or replacement, and the hard enamel finish provides high reflective values.

PERFORATED CEMENT-ASBESTOS TILE   Acoustical units are manufactured of perforated cement-asbestos. The perforated panel supports a sound-absorbant pad or blanket and provides a decorative, long-wearing surface. The cement-asbestos facings will not corrode or deteriorate under extreme moisture conditions, and they are incombustible. This tile is particularly useful in restaurant kitchens and swimming pools because of its resistance to moisture and its low maintenance requirements.

Installation of Acoustical Materials

In order to achieve the best performance and appearance acoustical materials must be installed by the correct techniques under the best of conditions. The materials should be installed when the environment inside the room closely approaches the temperature and humidity that will exist when the room is in service.

CEMENTING   Approximately 50 percent of all acoustical tile is mounted by cementing to solid surfaces of concrete, plaster, or gypsumboard. This is the most common and least expensive method of applying acoustical tile to existing ceilings. Cementing requires a smooth, solid base. Old surfaces must be cleaned thoroughly, and new plaster must be sized to assure proper bond with the cement. The adhesive cement must be one recommended or manufactured by the producer of the tile, to assure proper bonding of the tile to the base material.

Cement is applied to the back of the acoustical tile in walnut-sized dabs, at each corner for 12″ × 12″ tiles and at intervals no greater than 12 in. for larger tiles. When the tile is pressed into place, each spot of cement provides an area of contact approximately 2½ in. in diameter and 1/16 in. thick. The tile is slid diagonally into place and pressed into position flush with the surrounding tiles.

NAILING   When ceilings are not level or true enough for adhesive application of tile, 1″ × 3″ wood furring strips are attached to the structural ceiling every 12 in. on center and *shimmed*, or wedged out, as necessary to furnish an even, level surface. Where floor or ceiling joists are left exposed,

Fig. 8-37 Acoustical-tile ceiling. (*Ceiling and Interior Systems Contractors' Association.*)

the furring strips are placed 12 in. on center perpendicular to the joists.

Perforated acoustical tiles usually have shallow holes at each corner for nailing. Screws may be used in place of nails to provide a more secure fastening for tiles located in areas subject to shock or impact. Tiles with tongue-and-groove joints usually have a wide flange through which the tiles may be nailed or stapled. Stapling is an economical method of installing wide-flanged tiles.

Fig. 8-38 Installing a cemented acoustical-tile ceiling. (a) Tile is cemented to an old ceiling in remodeling, to an unfinished surface, or to backing board which is part of furring-bar suspension system; (b) adhesive is placed on back of tile in daubs; (c) tiles are pressed into place. (*Ceiling and Interior Systems Contractors' Association.*)

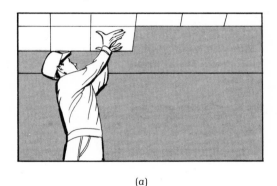

(a)

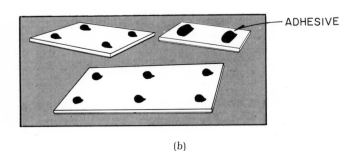

(b)

(c)

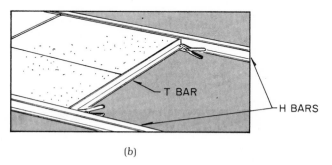

(a)

(b)

Fig. 8-39 Concealed H and T system: (a) concealed H and T bars attached to runner channel; (b) installing cross T's to H bars. (*Ceiling and Interior Systems Contractors' Association.*)

Mechanical Suspension Systems

Mechanical suspension systems for acoustical tile and board are similar to those for suspended plaster ceilings. Mechanically supported ceilings are suited to receive flush lighting fixtures and heating or air-conditioning grilles, which fit into the grid of the supporting structure. Luminous ceilings can be developed by substituting translucent plastic panels for acoustical panels over a portion of the room. Some perforated or slotted exposed runners are used in connection with air-conditioning systems to introduce air into the room. With the proper choice of system and materials, time-rated fire-resistant suspended ceilings can be obtained with some of the newer acoustical tiles.

Suspended ceilings may be installed in concealed systems, semi-exposed systems, or exposed systems. Almost every type of acoustical material can be suspended. The type of suspension system to be used depends on the material.

CONCEALED SYSTEMS   Several systems have been developed in which none of the suspension metal is visible, with the possible exception of wall angles. When concealed systems are installed none of the supporting members need be painted or finished. Metal-pan acoustical tiles are usually supported by patented systems designed to fit the metal-pan tiles of a particular manufacturer. The pans are held in place with specially designed spring T's. Sound-absorbing pads are placed in the pans as they are installed. The major disadvantage of a concealed suspension system is the difficulty of providing access to the space above

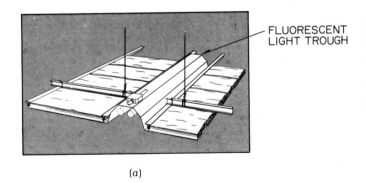

(a)

Fig. 8-40 Concealed Z-bar system: (a) Z bars can be attached directly to steel bar joists, wood joists, or runner channels; (b) Z bar clipped to runner channel; (c) channel and springs at wall. (*Ceiling and Interior Systems Contractors' Association.*)

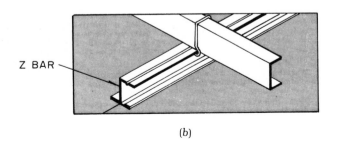

(a)

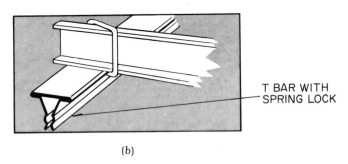

(b)

Fig. 8-41 Metal-pan suspension system; (a) fluorescent-light trough incorporated in a metal-pan system; (b) T bar with spring lock which grips metal pans. (*Ceiling and Interior Systems Contractors' Association.*)

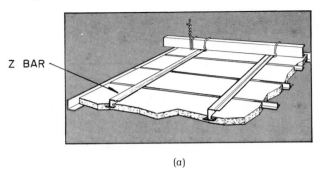

(b)

Fig. 8-42 (a) Exposed Z-bar system; (b) Z bar attached to runner channels with clips. (*Ceiling and Interior Systems Contractors' Association.*)

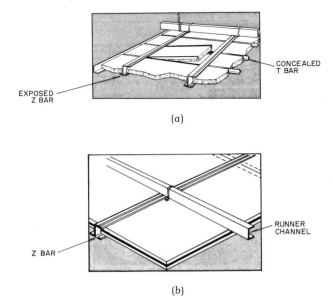

(a)

(b)

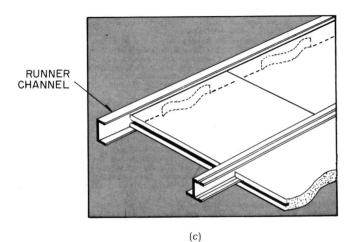

(c)

the ceiling. In this system the pans can be removed with a special tool to permit access to piping, duct work, and electrical conduit. The supporting members fit into a *kerf* on the edges of the tile. In one such system 1½-in. furring channels are hung at 4 ft on center, just as in suspended plaster construction, and H runners are fastened to the runners at 2, 3, or 4 ft on center by wire clips. T sections span the distance between the H runners, and flat metal or fiber splines installed parallel to the H runners support the tile joint.

There are several variations of this system. In one a modified Z section is used in place of the H and T sections. In others special tongue-and-groove tile is used to eliminate the need for the flat spline.

SEMIEXPOSED SYSTEMS   In semiexposed systems the main runners are exposed, showing parallel tracks in one direction. These systems are designed to hold larger acoustical units,

Fig. 8-43 Exposed grid system. (*a*) Tiles rest on flange of T bars and may be held in place with clips; (*b*) T bars are held in place with hanger wires; (*c*) cross runners are cut to length and fitted into prepunched slots; (*d*) special clips hold runners in place; (*e*) pop rivets are used at every other cross runner to stabilize the ceiling. (*Ceiling and Interior Systems Contractors' Association.*)

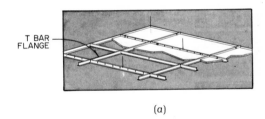

(*a*)

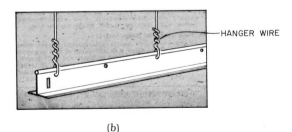

(*b*)

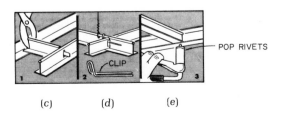

(*c*)   (*d*)   (*e*)

Fig. 8-44 Metal-pan acoustical-tile ceiling. (*Ceiling and Interior Systems Contractors' Association.*)

classed as board rather than tile. With proper selection of acoustical material and suspension system, the exposed supports can be spaced as far apart as 4 ft on center. Cross T's or flat splines are inserted in kerfs at right angles to the exposed supporting members.

EXPOSED SYSTEMS   Large acoustical boards are usually supported by exposed suspension systems, with the bottom flange of the suspension member carrying the weight. Perforated cement-asbestos board can be laid onto the bottom flange. An acoustical pad is then placed on top of the cement-asbestos board to act as a sound absorbing material. Individual acoustical panels may be removed at any time for access to mechanical equipment or ducts located above the ceiling. Since the entire grid pattern is in view, the size of the grid should be chosen to fit the scale of the room.

QUESTIONS

1. What are the three cementitious materials most commonly used in plaster?

2. Name five aggregates commonly used in plastering.

3. Describe the source and characteristics of gypsum.

4. Why is it necessary to add a retarder to gypsum for plastering?

5. What are the differences between quicklime and hydrated lime?

6. List some of the advantages of portland cement plaster.

7. What are the functions of aggregates in plaster?

8. Describe the process of preparing vermiculite for use as a plaster aggregate.

9. What are the limitations of gypsum base-coat plasters?

10. What type of gypsum plaster must be used over concrete surfaces?

11. What are some of the advantages of gypsum wood-fibered plaster?

12. What is Keene's cement, and where is it used?

13. List the advantages and disadvantages of portland cement plaster.

14. What are some of the limitations of acoustical plasters?

15. Name three types of aggregate commonly used in acoustical plaster.

16. How is metal lath installed over wood studs?

17. Name six items classed as lathing accessories and describe their uses.

18. Describe the construction and give the advantages and disadvantages of solid gypsum partitions.

19. How can a hollow metal-stud partition be made more soundproof?

20. Describe three ways of fireproofing columns with gypsum plaster.

21. What is veneer plastering, and what are its advantages?

22. What are the advantages and limitations of drywall construction?

23. Explain the differences between sound absorption and sound transmission.

24. What two factors determine the loudness of a sound?

25. How does the background noise affect acoustical design?

26. Define the following abbreviations: NRC, STC, INR.

27. What are flanking paths, and how do they affect acoustics?

28. Describe the four basic materials used in the manufacture of acoustical products.

29. Describe three types of mountings used in the construction of acoustical-tile ceilings.

30. Describe the three types of mechanical suspension systems used for acoustical ceiling tiles or boards.

REFERENCES FOR FURTHER STUDY

Acoustical Society of America: 335 East 45th Street, New York, N.Y., 10017. "Theory & Use of Acoustical Materials," 1950.

American Concrete Institute: P.O. Box 4754, Bedford Station, Detroit, Mich., 48217. "Recommended Practice for Portland Cement Plastering," Committee 624. "Guide to Portland Cement Plastering," Committee 524.

American National Standards Institute: 1430 Broadway, New York, N.Y., 10018. "American Standard Specifications for Gypsum Plastering," ANSI A42.1, 1955. "American Standard Specifications for Interior Lathing and Furring," ANSI A42.4, 1955. "American Standard Specifications for Portland Cement Stucco and Portland Cement Plastering," ANSI A42.2 and A42.3, 1946. "American Standard Specifications for Lime-cement Stucco," ANSI 42.5.

California Drywall Contractors' Association: 1830 West Eighth Street, Suite 305, Los Angeles, Calif., 90057. *California Drywall Industry*, a periodical.

California Lathing and Plastering Contractors' Association: 3558 West 8th Street, Los Angeles, Calif., 90005. "Reference Specifications for Lathing, Furring and Plastering in California," 1964.

Contracting Plasterers' and Lathers' International Association: 1343 H Street, N.W., Washington, D.C. "Recommended Specifications for Lathing, Furring, and Plastering," rev. October 1964.

Diehl, John R.: "Manual of Lathing and Plastering," National Bureau for Lathing and Plastering, 1960.

Gypsum Association: 201 North Wells Street, Chicago, Ill., 60606. "Specifications, Publications on Gypsum Products, Special Recommendations and Their Proper Use."

Knudsen, Vern O., and Cyril M. Harris: "Acoustical Design in Architecture," Columbia University Press, New York, 1962.

Perlite Institute: 45 West 45th Street, New York, N.Y., 10036. "Perlite Design Manual"; "Specifications; Technical Bulletins; Test Data."

Plastering Information Bureau: 3127 Los Feliz Boulevard, Los Angeles, Calif., 90027. "Reference Specifications for Machine-applied Plaster," June 6, 1961.

Texas Bureau for Lathing and Plastering and National Bureau for Lathing and Plastering: Austin, Tex. "Lathing and Plastering Selection Data Assemblies," 1960.

Texas Lathing and Plastering Contractors' Association: Perry Brooks Building, Austin, Tex. "Furring, Lathing and Plastering Specifications."

United States Gypsum: Chicago, Ill. "Sound Control in Design," 1959.

Vermiculite Institute: 208 South La Salle Street, Room 1906, Chicago, Ill., 60604. "Specifications; Technical Bulletins; Test Data."

ROOFING
SHEET METAL
DAMPPROOFING
AND
THERMAL INSULATION

9

ROOFING MATERIALS

The covering of a building consists of three major components: the skeletal framing or supporting members, a stiff membrane to support the outer skin, and a waterproof outer layer of roofing material. The framing may be rafters or trusses. The supporting decking may be a concrete slab, metal roof decking, poured or precast gypsum units, wood sheathing, or fiberboard; and the roofing may be any number of materials.

The earliest roofing materials were probably mud and sod, supported by wood beams and woven reeds. The Egyptians used heavy sandstone slabs over closely spaced columns to cover their temples. The early Greeks manufactured burned clay tile to cover their temples and dwellings. Clay tile brought to Mexico and California by the Spaniards is almost identical to that of the ancient Greeks. The ancient Chinese and Japanese fashioned beautiful tile, glazed in a wide range of colors.

Stone, in the form of slate, was used as roofing by the Romans, and throughout the Middle Ages it was used as a covering of the great Gothic cathedrals of Europe. Stone

roofs installed centuries ago are still in existence throughout Europe.

Copper sheet was first manufactured in 1500 A.D. The sheets were pounded out by hand and were used in limited quantities as roofing. In 1750 the techniques for rolling copper into sheets were developed. Copper is still used for lasting trouble-free roofing surfaces.

Asphalt came into use as a roofing material in 1892, when a chemist named William Griscom developed a single-ply asphalt-impregnated paper in roll form, ready for application as a roof covering.

The selection of roofing systems and materials depends on numerous factors, such as design of the structure, fire-rating requirements, climate, snow loads, cost, and expected life. One consideration is the weight of the roof covering, which affects the design and cost of the supporting members. Table 9-1 lists the approximate weight of some of the most commonly used roof coverings. The unit of measure in the roofing industry is the *square*, the amount of roofing material that will cover one hundred square feet. Thus the weights in Table 9-1 are given in pounds per square.

Another important consideration is the pitch or slope of the roof. Proper drainage of water from roof surfaces is essential if good service is expected from the roofing. The pitch or slope of a roof imposes limitations to the type of roofing material and installation method that can be used. The words *pitch* and *slope* are frequently confused. In former days, and in some locations at present, the word *pitch* is used to mean the total rise of a roof, divided by the total horizontal span. If a roof spans a building that is 20 ft wide and the high point of the roof is 5 ft above the eaves, the pitch is ⁵⁄₂₀, or ¼. Most architectural drawings simply indicate the *slope* of the roof rather than the pitch, as explained above. This slope would be designated as the number of inches the roof rises in each 12 in. of run. The slope would thus be written as 6:12.

TABLE 9-1 Weight of roofing materials

MATERIAL	LB WEIGHT/ SQUARE (100 SQ FT)
Tin	100
Roll roofing	100
Asphalt shingles	130–320
Copper	150
Corrugated iron	200
Wood shingles	300
Asbestos-cement shingles	500
Portland cement shingles	500–900
Built-up roof	600
Sheet lead	600–800
Slate, ³⁄₁₆″	700
¼″	1000
³⁄₄″	1500
Flat clay tile	1200
Clay shingles	1100–1400
Spanish clay tile	1900
laid in mortar	2900

Roof Decks

Good roofing requires a good roof deck or underlayment. In order to assure a lasting, waterproof roof that will stand up under abuse after it is installed, a roof deck must have a strong, smooth surface for the application of roofing material. Many roofing problems can be traced to roof decks that are not rigid. Movement resulting from the instability of roof sheathing may tear or buckle roofing membranes.

Roof decks must provide different types of service under different types of roofing material. Sheathing under wood shingles may be spaced to allow air and moisture to reach the underside of the shingles so that they do not curl as a result of uneven wetting of the top and bottom surfaces. Vapor seals are required under some types of roofing, expecially where low temperatures are encountered, or where rolled roofing is to be placed over a con-

Fig. 9-1 Twelfth-century stone roof, Conques, France.

Fig. 9-2 Tile roofs, Florence, Italy.

crete slab that contains moisture which will continue to evaporate for a long time after construction has ceased. Poorly seasoned wood sheathing may warp, causing asphalt shingles or rolled roofing to buckle. Lack of ventilation in attic spaces or the moisture of drying plaster as the building is under construction can cause solid sheathing to warp.

The surface of the roof deck, whether it is wood, concrete, or steel, must be clean, smooth, and dry. Many roofing failures are the result of applying roofing to moisture-laden roof decks. Pressures developed by the imprisoned moisture cause blisters and ruptures in the roofing material. Irregularities in the roof deck can puncture roof coverings. Cracks, openings, or other voids in roof decks do not provide proper support.

The method of applying roofing depends on the type of roof deck. Some roof decks are nailable and others are not. Nailable decks include materials such as wood or fiberboard, poured or precast units of gypsum, or nailable lightweight concrete. Nonnailable decks of concrete or steel require different techniques of roofing.

BITUMINOUS ROOFING MATERIALS

Hot bitumens are used with several types of roofing systems. Both asphalt or coal-tar pitch are bitumens. Although these two materials are similar in appearance, they have different characteristics. Asphalt is usually a product of the distillation of petroleum, whereas coal-tar pitch is a by-product of the coking process in steel manufacture.

ROOFING ASPHALTS   Some asphalts are naturally occurring or are found in combination with porous rock. Most roofing asphalts are manufactured from petroleum crudes from which the lighter fractions have been removed. Roofing asphalts are available in a number of different grades for different roof slopes, climatic conditions, or installation methods.

Roofing asphalts are graded on the basis of their *melting points,* which range from a low of 130°F to a high of 200°F. The melting point is not the point at which the asphalt begins to flow, but is determined by test procedures established by the ASTM. Asphalts begin to flow at a somewhat lower temperature than their melting points, depending on the slope and the weight of the asphalt and surfacing material.

Generally, the lower the melting point of an asphalt, the better its self-healing properties and the less tendency it has to crack. Dead flat roofs, where water may stand, or nearly flat roofs, require an asphalt that has the greatest waterproofing qualities and the self-healing properties of low-melting asphalts. A special asphalt known as *dead-flat asphalt* is used in such cases. As the slope of the roof increases, the need for waterproofing is lessened, and an asphalt that will not flow at normal expected temperatures must be used. For steeper roofing surfaces asphalt with a melting point of 190 to 200°F is used. This material is classed as *steep asphalt.* In hot, dry climates only the high-temperature asphalts can be used.

COAL-TAR PITCH   The melting point of coal-tar pitch generally ranges from 140 to 155°F. The low melting point of coal-tar pitch limits its usefulness; however, it has been used successfully for years in the Eastern and Middle Western parts of the United States on dead-level or nearly level roofs. In the Southwest, where roof surfaces often reach temperatures of 140 to 160°F in the hot desert sun, its low melting point makes coal-tar pitch unsuitable as a roof surfacing material.

When used within its limitations on flat and low-pitched roofs in suitable climates, coal-tar pitch provides one of the most durable roofing membranes. It is reputed to have *cold flow,* or self-healing qualities in closing up cracks that may have formed. One manufacturer states that this is because the molecular structure of pitch is such that individual molecules have a physical attraction for each other, so that self-sealing is not dependent on heat. Coal-tar-pitch roofs are entirely unaffected by water and, when covered by mineral aggregate, may actually be preserved by standing water, which protects the volatile oils.

Roofing Felts

Roofing felts are used as underlayment for shingles, for sheathing paper, and as laminations in the construction of built-up roofs. They are made from a combination of shredded wood fibers, mineral fibers such as asbestos, or glass fibers saturated with asphalt or coal-tar pitch. The fibers are formed into a flexible sheet by a method similar to that used in the manufacture of paper. Sheets are usually 36″ wide and available in weights of 7, 15, and 30 lb. These weights refer to weight per square (100 sq ft).

RAG FELTS   Asphalt-saturated felts composed of a combination of felted papers, shredded wood fibers, or rag fibers are all considered rag felts. They are among the least expensive of roofing felts and are widely used not only as roofing, but as water or vapor barriers. Seven-lb felt is used as a dry sheet to protect wood sheathing from dripping asphalt. Fifteen-lb felt is used under wood siding and exterior plaster to protect sheathing or wood studs. It is generally used in roofing for layers or plies in gravel-surfaced assemblies and is available either perforated or unperforated. Perforated felts allow entrapped moisture to escape during application. Thirty-lb felts require fewer layers in a built-up roof. They are usually used as underlayment for heavier cap sheets or tile on steeper roofs.

ASBESTOS FELTS   Felts manufactured from asbestos fibers are available in weights of 15, 45, and 55 lb/square in widths of 32″ and 36″. Fifteen-lb asbestos felts are usually perforated. When a built-up roof is being installed, the hot asphalt wells up through the perforations, completely sealing the felt from below. The subsequent layer of asphalt then seals it from above. This tends to reduce air bubbles that could develop into blisters.

The inorganic nature of asbestos felts tends to make them less subject to extremes of weather and moisture. They are particularly effective under the difficult climatic conditions encountered in the Southwest and where the interior humidity of a building is high.

GLASS-FIBER FELTS   Sheets of glass fiber, when lightly saturated with asphalt, retain a high degree of porosity, assuring a maximum escape of entrapped moisture or vapor during application and maximum bond between felts. Asphalt can flow through the pores so that the finished built-up roof becomes a monolithic slab reinforced with properly placed layers of glass fibers. The glass fibers, which are inorganic and do not curl, help to create a solid mass of reinforced waterproof roofing material.

TARRED FELTS   Both rag felts and asbestos felts are available saturated with coal-tar pitch, for use with bitumens of the same composition. Since coal-tar and asphalt are not compatible, in any construction the components must be limited to one bitumen or the other.

Built-up Roofs

A built-up roof, as the name indicates, is built up in alternate layers of felt and bitumen to form a seamless, waterproof, flexible membrane which conforms to the surface of the roof deck and protects all angles formed by the roof deck and projecting surfaces. Without the reinforcement of the felts, the bitumens would crack and *alligator* and thus lose their volatile oils under solar radiation.

Application of Bitumens

The temperature of asphalt and coal-tar pitch during application is very critical. At higher temperatures asphalt is seriously damaged and its life considerably shortened. Heating asphalt over 500°F may decrease the weather life by as much as 50 percent. Coal-tar pitch should not be heated above 400°F. Asphalt is applied to the roof at a temperature of 350 to 450°F, and coal-tar pitch is applied at 275 to 375°F.

Bitumens are spread between felts at rates of 25 to 35 lb/square, depending on the type of felt. An asphalt primer must be used over concrete before the hot asphalt is applied. It usually is unnecessary to apply a primer under coal-tar pitch. With wood and other types of nailable decks, the first two plies are nailed to the deck to seal the joints between the units and prevent dripping of the bitumens through the deck.

Built-up roofs are classed by the number of plies of felt that are used in their construction. The roof may be a three-ply, four-ply, or five-ply roof, depending on whether the roofing material can be nailed to the deck, whether insulation is to be applied underneath it, the type of surfacing desired, the slope of the deck, the climatic conditions, and the life expectancy of the roofing.

The felt-and-bitumen membrane of a built-up roof must form a flexible covering that has sufficient strength to withstand the normal expansion of structures. Most built-up roofs have a surfacing over the last felt ply. This protective surfacing may be applied in several ways.

GLAZE-COAT SURFACING   A coat of asphalt or coal-tar pitch may be flooded over the top layer of felt. This *glaze coat* protects the top layer of felt from the rays of the sun. The glaze coat is black, but it may be coated with white or aluminum surfacing to provide reflective coatings.

GRAVEL SURFACING   A flood coat of bitumens (60 lb of asphalt or 70 lb of coal-tar pitch per square) is applied over the top ply, and a layer of aggregate, such as rock, gravel, slag, or ceramic granules, is applied while the flood coat is still hot. If gravel or slag is used as an aggregate, the gravel would amount to 400 lb/square and the slag to about

Fig. 9-3 Types of built-up roofing: (*a*) three-ply roof over nailable deck, gravel surfaced; (*b*) three-ply roof over nonnailable deck, gravel surfaced; (*c*) four-ply roof over insulation, gravel or slag surfaced.

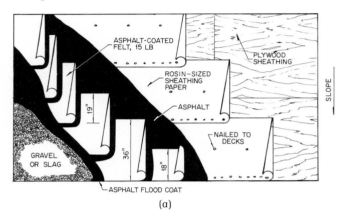

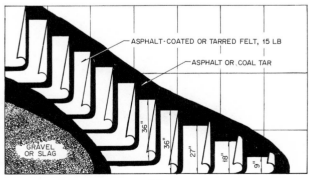

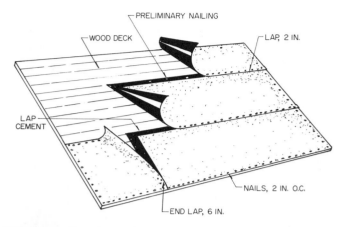

Fig. 9-4 Roll roofing with exposed nailing.

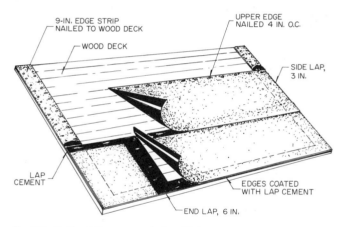

Fig. 9-5 Roll roofing concealed nailing.

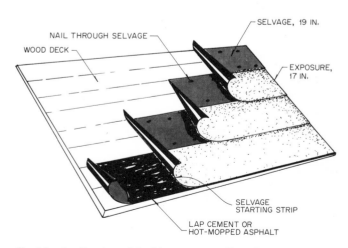

Fig. 9-6 Application of double-coverage roll roofing.

300 lb/square. Other aggregates would be applied at a rate consistent with their weight and opacity. The gravel protects the bitumen from the sun and provides a fire-resistant coating.

CAP SHEETS   This surface is similar to gravel-surfaced roofings, except that a mineral-surfaced *cap sheet* is used in place of the flood coat and job-applied gravel. Cap-sheet roofing consists of heavy roofing felts (90 to 105 lb) of rag, asbestos, or glass fibers, coated on both sides with asphalt or coal-tar pitch and surfaced on the exposed side with mineral granules, mica, asbestos, or similar materials. The cap sheets are applied with a 2-in. lap, or a 19-in. lap if two-ply construction is desired. The mineral surfacing is omitted on the portion that is lapped. The cap sheets are layed in hot asphalt along with the base sheet. Cap sheets are used on slopes between 1:12 and 6:12 where the weather is moderate.

COLD-PROCESS ROOFING   Cold-applied emulsions, cut-back asphalts, or patented products may be applied over the top felt of a hot-mopped roof or as an adhesive between felts. If emulsified asphalt is to be used as an adhesive between plies, special felts (such as glass) must be used that are sufficiently porous to allow the water in the emulsion to evaporate. Decorative and reflective coatings with asphalt-emulsion bases have been developed to protect and decorate roofing.

Roll Roofing

Roll roofing is made of heavy felt saturated with asphalt or coal-tar pitch, with an additional viscous bituminous coating. Finely ground talc or mica may be applied to both sides of the saturated felt to produce a smooth roofing.

Fig. 9-7 Conducting a flame-spread test. (*By permission of Underwriters' Laboratories, Inc.*)

Mineral granules in a variety of colors are rolled into the upper surface while the final coating is still soft. These mineral granules protect the underlying bitumen from the impact of sun rays. The mineral aggregates are nonflammable and increase the fire resistance and appearance of the product. Mineral-surfaced roll roofing comes in weights of 90 to 120 lb/square. Roll roofing may be obtained with one surface completely covered with granules or with a 2-in. plain-surface *selvage* along one side to allow for laps. Roll roofing split down the center to show a patterned edge when installed is classed as pattern-edge roll.

SELVAGE-EDGE ROLL ROOFING Roll roofing may be installed by either exposed or concealed nailing. The cheapest and least lasting type of installation is a 2-in. lap at the side and ends, cemented with special cement and nailed with large-headed nails. In concealed-nailing installations the roll roofing is nailed along the top of the strip and cemented with lap cement on the bottom edge. Vertical joints in the roofing are cemented into place after the upper edge is nailed. This method is used when maximum life in service is required.

DOUBLE-COVERAGE ROLL ROOFING Double-coverage roll roofing is produced with slightly more than half its surface covered with granules. This roofing is known as double coverage or 19 in. selvage edge. It is applied by nailing and cementing with special adhesives or hot asphalt. Each sheet is lapped 19 in., nailed in the lapped selvage portion, and then cemented to the sheet below. End laps are cemented into place.

SHINGLES, TILES, AND SLATE

Asphalt Shingles

Asphalt shingles, sometimes called composition shingles, are available in many patterns both in strip form and as individual shingles. Asphalt shingles are made of heavy rag, wood, or mineral-fiber felt saturated with asphalt and coated on one side with mineral granules which form a colorful weather-resistant surface. One of the most common shapes is a 12″ × 36″ strip with the exposed surface cut or scored to resemble three 9″ × 12″ shingles. These are called *strip shingles*. Asphalt shingles can be obtained in weights of 150 to 325 lb/square. The exposure varies with the dimension of the shingles. A lap of 2 to 3 in. is usually provided over the upper edge of the shingle in the course directly below. This is called the *head lap*.

STRIP SHINGLES The thickness of asphalt shingles may be uniform throughout, or the head lap may be beveled to give smoother, flatter shingle courses. The butts may also be thickened to accentuate the shadow lines when the shingles are installed. Strip shingles, slotted at the butts to give the illusion of individual units, are produced with

Fig. 9-8 Roofing after fire exposure. (*By permission of Underwriters' Laboratories, Inc.*)

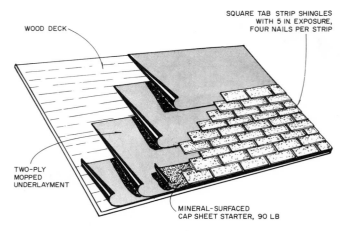

Fig. 9-9 Application of shingles over double underlay. Mopped double underlayment is recommended under square tab strip shingles for slopes less than 4:12.

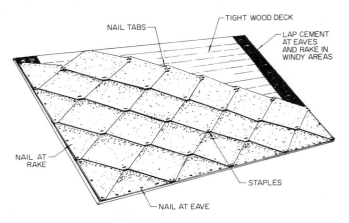

Fig. 9-10 Application of staple-type shingles.

228

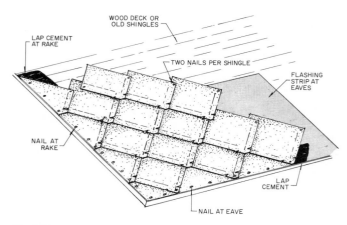

Fig. 9-11 Application of lock-type shingles.

Fig. 9-12 Asbestos-cement shingles.

of the sun and are intended to hold them firm through high winds, rain, and snow.

Special strip shingles, classed as *wind resistant*, are produced for use in areas subject to high winds. Some asphalt shingles are produced with a class A fire rating. This means that the shingle roof will withstand the heat generated by the burning of dried wood, which is 2000°F, ignited directly on the shingles and fanned by a 12-mph wind. The shingles must protect the wood deck from igniting to pass this test.

Strip shingles are usually laid over a single thickness of asphalt-saturated felt if the slope of the roof is 4:12 or greater. Square-tab strip shingles may be applied to decks having a slope of less than 4:12, but not less than 2:12, when special application methods are used.

SINGLE SHINGLES   Single shingles are produced to show either a square or a diamond-shaped edge and may be either a staple-down or lock-down type. In the staple-down type the lower tab is stapled to the shingle below it. This prevents the tab from being raised by wind or driving rain. Special stapling machines are used so that the staples will secure the shingles to the adjacent tabs of shingles in the course below, and not through the complete shingle assembly.

Lock-type shingles are nailed with two or four nails at the top or sides. The lower corners or sides are locked by inserting the locking tabs under the course directly below. Lock-type shingles are particularly resistant to wind damage and are economical in terms of coverage.

Asbestos-cement Shingles

Because of their resistance to rot, decay, and fire, shingles composed of portland cement and asbestos fibers have found widespread use as a roofing material. They usually consist of 25 to 35 percent asbestos fiber and 65 to 75 percent portland cement. Small quantities of ceramic granules and other inert materials are added to impart weathered and variegated colors. Surface patterns may be striated, veined to give the appearance of slate, or grained to look like wood.

Asbestos-cement shingles are produced in a variety of shapes, sizes, and textures and are usually available in thicknesses of $5/32''$, $1/4''$, and $3/8''$. Shingles can be obtained as individual units or as multiple units that cover the area of two to five single shingles. Multiple units come in straight-butt or staggered-butt patterns.

Asbestos-cement shingles are applied over one layer of 30-lb felt to roofs with a minimum slope of 5:12. For pitches of less than 5:12 two mopped layers of 30-lb felt are used. As the shingles are stiff and extremely brittle, they nail to the roof sheathing through prepunched holes and must be installed with care. Impact loads, such as workmen with hard shoes, will damage roof surfaces. One manufacturer has developed a product similar in composition which can be nailed and sawed with ordinary hand tools.

either straight-tab or random-tab design with heavy butts to simulate the appearance of wood shakes. Most strip shingles have spots of special thermoplastic adhesive spaced at intervals along the concealed portion of the strip. These spots of adhesive are activated by the warmth

Metal Shingles

Metal shingles provide an all-metal roofing system that will not warp, rot, split, or burn. They are obtainable in either 30-gauge steel or 0.020 gauge aluminum.

Aluminum shingles are produced in roughhewn textures and a deep shadow line, resembling wood shakes, or in smoother surfaces with a wide variety of baked-enamel coatings. The baked-enamel finishes assure uniformity in color and coating thickness. Accessories and trim molds in matching or complimentary colors are usually available. One manufacturer produces porcelain-enameled shingles purported to be unaffected by sun, rain, hail, snow, dust, smog, or industrial atmospheres.

Metal shingles are usually applied over 30-lb felt. A special type of metal shingle is manufactured to fit into steel framing members, for use on metal buildings such as ranch-style service stations. Purlins span between ribs of galvanized roof decks, and the shingles are locked into place with special support clips. The same shingles can be used as side-wall shingles attached to metal framing.

Most metal shingles have interlocking flanges to provide a positive lock between them. Tabs are provided to allow nailing to underlying sheathing. Complete sets of roof and sidewall accessories are available to meet all conditions for new and old construction.

Roofing Tiles

Roofing tile was originally a thin solid unit made by shaping moist clay in molds and drying it in the sun or burning it in a kiln. Gradually the term has come to include a variety of tile-shaped units made of clay, portland cement, and other materials. The designs of tile have come down to us relatively unchanged from the Greeks and Romans. Roofing tiles are durable, attractive, and resistant to fire; however, because of their weight (900 to 1300 lb/square), they usually necessitate additional structural framing members and heavier roof decks.

CLAY TILE The clays used in the manufacture of roofing tile are similar to those used for brick. Unglazed tile comes in a variety or shades, from a yellow-orange to a deep red, and in blends of grays and greens. Highly glazed tiles are used for landmark purposes on numerous ecclesiastical and commercial buildings.

Clay roofing tiles are produced as either flat tile or roll tile. Flat tile may be English tile (interlocking shingle tile) or French (ludowici) tile. Roll tiles are produced as in Greek or Roman style pan-and-cover tile, Spanish tile, or Mission tile.

Roll tile is usually installed over two layers of hot-mopped 15-lb felt. Double-coverage felts, laid shingle

Fig. 9-13 Metal roofing shingles. (*Hunter Aluminum Shakes.*)

TYPES OF CLAY ROOFING TILES

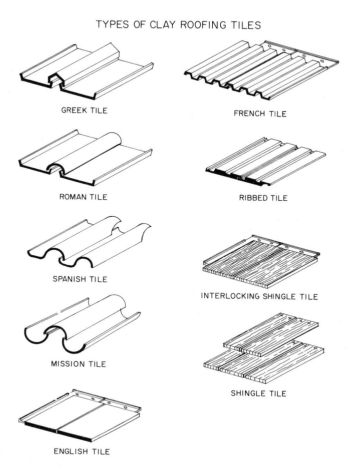

Fig. 9-14 Types of clay roofing tiles.

fashion, lapped 19 in., and mopped with hot asphalt, may be required as an underlayment. The individual tiles are nailed to the sheathing through prepunched holes. Special shapes are available for starter courses, rakes, hips, and ridges. Some manufacturers produce tiles in special tile-and-a-half units for exposed locations such as gables and hips.

Mission tiles, which are slightly tapered half-round units, are set in horizontal courses with the convex side and concave sides alternated to form *pans* and *covers*. The bottom edges of the covers may be laid with a random exposure of 6 to 14 in. to weather. Mission tile may be fastened to the prepared roof deck with copper nails, copper wire, or specially designed brass strips. The covers may be set in portland cement mortar. This gives the roof a rustic appearance, but it adds approximately 10 lb/square to the weight of the finished roof.

Flat tile may be obtained as either flat shingle tiles or interlocking tiles. Shingle tiles are butted at the sides and lapped shingle fashion. They are produced in various widths from 5″ to 8″, with a textured surface to resemble wood shingles, with smooth colored surfaces, or with

highly glazed surfaces. Interlocking shingle tiles have side and top locks which permit the use of fewer pieces per square. The back of this type of tile is ribbed, which reduces the weight without sacrifice of strength. Interlocking flat tile may be used in combination with lines of Greek cover-and-pan tile as accents.

CONCRETE TILE   The acceptance of concrete tile as a roofing material has been slow in the United States. However, European manufacturers have invested heavily in research and development to produce a uniformly high-quality product at a reasonable cost. Concrete tile is now used on more than 80 percent of all new residences in Great Britain. Modern high-speed machinery and techniques have revolutionized the industry in the United States, and American-made concrete tiles are now finding a wide market, particularly in the West.

Concrete roof tile, made of portland cement, sand, and water, is incombustible. It is also a poor conductor of heat. These characteristics make it an ideal roofing material in forested or brushy areas subject to periodic threats of fire. In addition, concrete actually gains strength with age and will withstand repeated freezing and thawing cycles.

Color pigments may be mixed with the basic ingredients during manufacture. To provide a glazed surface cementitious mineral-oxide pigments may be sprayed on the tile immediately after it is extruded. This glaze becomes an integral part of the tile. The surface of tiles may be scored to give the appearance of rustic wood shakes.

Most concrete tiles are formed with side laps consisting of a series of interlocking ribs and grooves, designed to restrict lateral movement and provide weather checks between the tiles. The underside of the tile usually contains weather checks to halt wind-blown water. Head locks, in the form of lugs, overlap wood battens nailed to solid sheathing or strips of spaced sheathing. Nail holes are prepunched. The most common size of concrete tile is $12\frac{3}{8}″ \times 17″$ for maximum coverage with minimum lapping.

Concrete tiles are designed for minimum roof slopes of $2\frac{1}{2}$:12. For slopes up to $3\frac{1}{2}$:12 roof decks are solidly sheathed and covered with roofing felt. For slopes greater than $3\frac{1}{2}$:12 the roof sheathing may be spaced. Roofing felt is placed between each row to carry any drainage to the surface of the next lower course of tile. The lugs at the top of the tiles lock over the sheathing or stripping. Except where roofs are exposed to extreme winds or earthquake conditions, generally only every fourth tile in every fourth row is nailed to the sheathing; the weight of the tile holds it in place.

Slate Roofing

Roofing slate is hand split from natural rock. It varies in color from black through blue-grey, grey, purple, red, and green. The individual slates may have one or more darker streaks running across them. These are usually covered in the laying. Most roofing slate is available in sizes from 10″ × 6″ to 26″ × 14″. The standard thickness is ³⁄₁₆″, but thicknesses of ¼″, ³⁄₈″, ½″, and up to 2″ can be obtained for special purposes. Slate may be furnished in a uniform size or in random widths. The surface may be left with the rough hand-split texture or ground to a smoother texture.

The weight of a slate roof ranges from 700 to 800 lb/square and may be more if rough-textured, thick slates are used. The size of framing members supporting a slate roof must be checked against the weight of the slate and method of laying. The type of underlayment used for a slate roof varies, depending on local codes, from one layer of 15-lb asphalt-saturated felt to 65-lb rolled asphalt roofing for slate over ¾″ thick.

Slate is usually laid like shingle, with each course lapping the second course below at least 3 in. The slates may be laid in even rows or at random. Each slate is pre-drilled with two nail holes and is held in place with two large-headed slaters' nails, which may be hard copper wire, cut copper, cut brass, or cut yellow metal. On hips and ridges and in other locations where nailing is not possible, the slates are held in place with waterproof elastic slaters' cement colored to match the slate. Exposed nailheads are covered with the same cement.

WOOD SHINGLES AND SHAKES

Wood shingles may be cypress, redwood, or cedar. Most shingles used in the United States and Canada are produced from Western red cedar. The best trees are found in the coastal regions of British Columbia, Washington, and Oregon, where they grow as large as 16 ft in diameter. The size of the tree and its slow growth rate make it possible to produce shingles with a fine grain and relatively few knots, blemishes, or distorted grain. The moisture resistance of Western red cedar results from its natural preservative oils. The color ranges from yellow to brown.

Shingle Grades

At the sawmill cedar logs are cut into sections, or *bolts*, 16″, 18″, or 24″ long. The bolts are quartered and then requartered to produce choice vertical-grain blocks. The blocks are run through a shingle machine, which saws a tapered shingle with each pass of a power-driven carriage. An expert sawyer will turn the shingle block to obtain shingles having as nearly vertical grain as possible. If he encounters defects he cuts out that portion or places the shingle in the proper chute, where it will be carried to the sorting, grading, and bundling bins below.

Shingle grades have been established for each different

Fig. 9-15 Mission-tile roof. (*Pacific Clay Products; photo by Julius Shulman.*)

species of wood. Cypress shingles are graded as No. 1, bests, primes, and economy. Redwood shingles are graded as No. 1 and No. 2. Western red cedar shingles are graded as Nos. 1, 2, and 3. No. 1 shingles in all species include only heartwood and vertical grain. The lower grades contain progressively larger areas of flat grain and sapwood in the shingle.

The Red Cedar Shingle and Handsplit Shake Bureau has established grading rules for cedar shingles. Each bundle that is produced by a member company of the bureau is labeled as Certigrade, the bureau's trademark. The three grades are described in Table 9-2.

Shingle Coverage

Wood shingles are produced in standard lengths of 16″, 18″, and 24″. Individual shingles are usually of random widths, 3″ minimum and 14″ maximum, except No. 3 grade, which may have a minimum width of 2½″. Prefabricated hip and ridge units are available to match each length.

The thickness of shingles is measured across the butts. If five shingles were laid one on top of another, the total thickness would be 2 in. for 16″ shingles and 2¼ in. for 18″ shingles. If four 24″ shingles were laid one on top of another, the thickness would be 2 in. These thicknesses would be designated 5/2, 5/2¼, and 4/2, respectively. Shingles may be purchased green in some areas, but most have been kiln dried or air dried to reduce the moisture content. Kiln drying reduces the total four- or five-butt thicknesses by approximately ⅙ in.

Four bundles of shingles will cover one square (100 sq ft) at the recommended exposure. The allowed exposure is governed by local building codes. Table 9-3 shows the

TABLE 9-2 Red cedar shingle grades

GRADE	DESCRIPTION
Certigrade No. 1, blue label	Shingles are 100 percent heartwood, clear, vertical-grain, red cedar, and used for the highest-quality work. They lie flat and tight because of the edge grain and show minimum expansion and contraction with changes in moisture content.
Certigrade No. 2, red label	Shingles have no more than 1 in. of sapwood in the first 10 in. of the butt and no less than 10 in. of clear wood above the butt on 16″ shingles, 11 in. clear on 18″ shingles, and 16 in. clear on 24″ shingles. Flat grain is allowed. This grade will serve for roofing of secondary buildings and underlayment at eaves and under sidewall shingles.
Certigrade No. 3, black label	Wood must be clear not less than 6 in. above the butt on 16″ and 18″ shingles and not less than 10 in. on 24″ shingles. There are no limitations on amount of flat grain and sapwood. This grade is used where economy is the greatest factor.

coverage of single bundles and four-bundle squares for different exposures.

Shakes

Wood shakes are similar to shingles, except that they are split, rather than sawed, from 100 percent heartwood bolts. There is only one grade of red cedar shakes. Individual shakes are split from the bolt with a heavy steel-bladed

Fig. 9-16 A modern shingle house. (*Red Cedar Shingle and Hand Split Shake Bureau; photo by Hugh N. Stratford.*)

TABLE 9-3 Shingle coverage (number of square feet)

SHINGLE EXPOSURE, IN.	16″ SHINGLES		18″ SHINGLES		24″ SHINGLES	
	BUNDLE	SQUARE	BUNDLE	SQUARE	BUNDLE	SQUARE
3¾	18¾	75				
4	20					
4¼	21¼	85	19	77		
5	25	100	20	81½		
5½			25	100		
5¾					19¼	76¾
6					20	80
6½					21½	86½
6¾					22¼	89¾
7					23	93
7½					25	100

To determine the total number of bundles required:

1. Divide the roof area by the number of square feet covered by one four-bundle square for the shingle size and exposure to be used.
2. If special hip and ridge units are not specified, add quantities needed for cutting at hips and valleys, one square for each 100 linear feet of hips and valleys.
3. Add quantities needed for doubling first course at eave lines, one square for each 222 linear feet of 16″ shingles, 227 linear feet of 18″ shingles, and 167 linear feet of 24″ shingles.

By permission of the Red Cedar Shingle and Handsplit Shake Bureau.

Shingles

Sidewall Shakes

Split Shakes

Handsplit-&-Resawn
Tapersplit
Straight-split

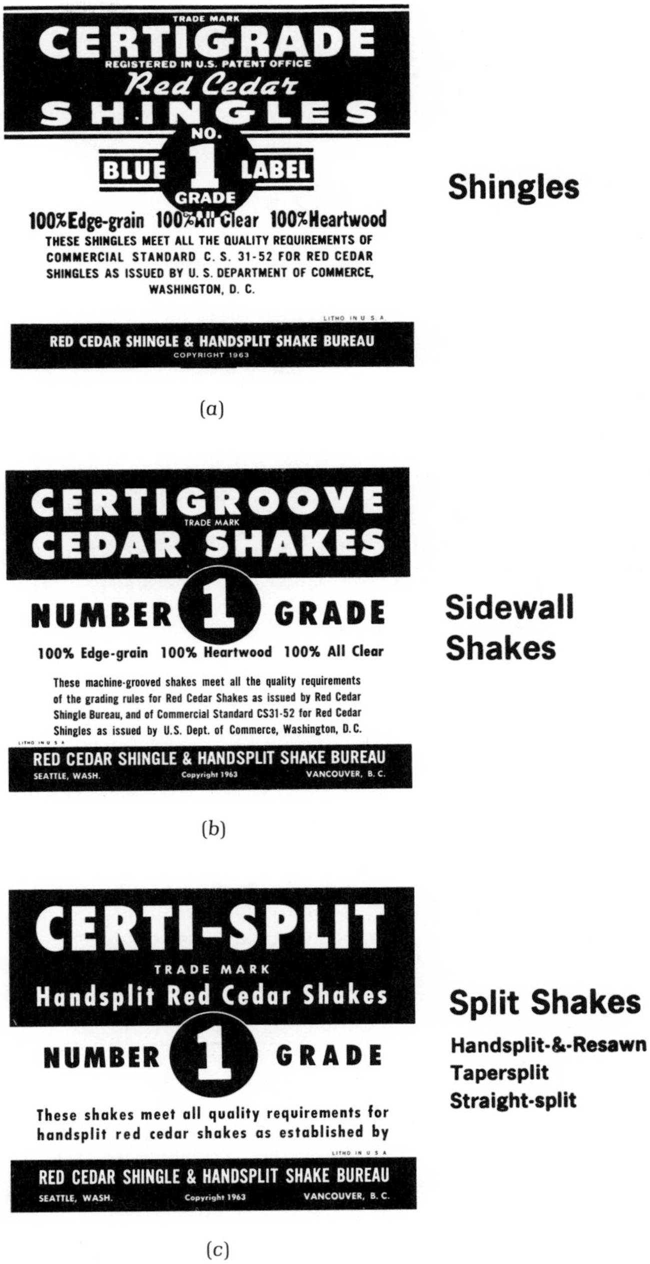

Fig. 9-17 Grade labels: (a) shingle; (b) side-wall shakes; (c) split shakes. (*By permission of the Red Cedar Shingle and Hand Split Shake Bureau.*)

tool called a *froe*. They are produced in lengths of 18″, 24″, and 32″. Coverage of each size is shown in Table 9-4. Shakes vary considerably in width and to some extent in thickness. Texture and color also vary from one shake to another, which gives character and warmth to the surface.

Shakes may be straight split, tapersplit, or handsplit and resawn. *Straight-split* shakes are split from the bolt to the desired thickness. In *tapersplit* shakes, the blocks are turned end for end after each split to produce the taper. *Handsplit-and-resawn* shakes are split into the desired thickness and then passed at an angle through a bandsaw. This produces a tapered shake that has a split face and a smooth-sawed back.

Installation of Shingles and Shakes

Shingles may be applied to roofs over solid or spaced sheathing, 1 × 3, 1 × 4, or 1 × 6 fir or pine strips laid horizontally at the same distance on center as the shingle exposure. Solid sheathing is sometimes covered with 15-lb roofing felt before the shingles are installed. Although the solid sheathing and felt make the roof more airtight and watertight, water that penetrates to the underside of the shingles cannot evaporate and will thus cause cupping and rotting. If a solid sheathing is desired under wood shingles, it is best to strip over it with 1 × 3 strips to allow air circulation under the shingles. Each shingle is nailed to the stripping or sheathing with only two nails to avoid splitting the shingle. A properly laid shingle roof has a minimum of three layers of shingles at all points on the roof.

Shakes may be applied to roofs of solid or spaced sheathing. Spaced sheathing usually is not separated more than 4 in. or more than the width of the sheathing board. In snow areas, on slopes of less than 8:12 solid sheathing

Fig. 9-18 Roofer fitting shakes at the ridge end of a course on a hip roof. Note that ends of black felt paper overlap at the ridge and lap upper ends of shakes. Rolls of 18-in.-wide paper are used for this application. (*By permission of the Red Cedar Shingle and Hand Split Shake Bureau.*)

and 15-lb felt is required as an underlayment. For lower slopes, two- or three-ply roof construction may be required under shakes. When shakes are applied over spaced sheathing, strips of 30-lb asphalt-saturated felt is laid, shingle fashion, between each row of shakes.

Fire-retardant Shingles and Shakes

Fire restrictions bar the use of untreated wood shingles and shakes in many areas. A recent innovation in roofing has been the development of wood shingles and shakes that have been pressure treated with a fire-retardant chemical. In 1968 these fire-retardant shingles were tested and accepted as a class C fire-retardant roof covering. In 1969 one roofing system was developed that is said to have a class B fire-retardant rating. This system uses fire-retardant red cedar shingles over a roof deck covered with a plastic-coated steel foil. Shingles are designed for exposure to all weather conditions.

MEMBRANE ROOFING

Several methods have been developed for applying roofing membranes either over a base of roofing felts or directly to roof decks. The materials may be brushed, rolled, or sprayed on to form a monolithic membrane that will follow any contour. They can be applied to horizontal as well as vertical surfaces and to hyperbolic paraboloids or any warped plane. Membranes may be reinforced with glass fiber for added strength or for surface texture. A wide range of colors is available in many of the systems.

Sprayed-on Asphalt Membranes

One company has developed a special gun with three nozzles that simultaneously delivers two sprays of emulsified asphalt and one of glass fibers which have been cut to predetermined length. The asphalt forms the protective layer and the glass fiber acts as reinforcement. The asphalts used in this system are specially blended to with-

TABLE 9-4 Coverage of Western red cedar handsplit shakes

SIZE AND TYPE	COURSES PER BUNDLE	BUNDLES PER SQUARE	NO. OF SHAKES PER SQUARE FOR VARIOUS WEATHER EXPOSURES											
			5½"	6½"	7"	7½"	8"	8½"	9"	10"	11"	11½'	13"	15"
Handsplit and resawn														
18" × ³⁄₈" to ³⁄₄"	10/10	4	55*	65	70	75	80†	85‡						
18" × ³⁄₄" to 1³⁄₄"	8/8	5	55*	65	70	75	80†	85‡						
24" × ½" to ³⁄₄"	10/10	4		65	70	75*	80	85	90	100†	110	115‡		
24" × ³⁄₄" to 1¼"	8/8	5		65	70	75*	80	85	90	100†	110	115‡		
32" × ³⁄₄" to 1¼"	6/7	6							90	100*	110	115	130†	150‡
24" × ½" to ⁵⁄₈"	10/10	4		65	70	75*	80	85	90	100†	110	115‡		
Tapersplit														
18" × ³⁄₈"	19 straight	5	65*	75	80	95	100‡							
Straight-Split														
24" × ³⁄₈"	16 straight	5		65	70	75*	80	85	90	100	110	115‡		

* Recommended maximum exposure for three-ply roof construction.
† Recommended maximum exposure for two-ply roof construction.
‡ Recommended maximum exposure for single-course wall construction.

By permission of the Red Cedar Shingle and Handsplit Shake Bureau.

stand the heat of the sun and are formulated to prevent sag on vertical surfaces.

The asphalt and reinforcing fiber is usually applied over one or more layers of asphalt-saturated felt or special glass fabric set in a specified asphalt cement. The thickness of film developed depends on the rate of application. Thicker membranes can be built up with repeated sprayings. Job requirements dictate the amount of glass reinforcement needed and the thickness of the membrane. Decorative or reflective coatings may be applied after the membrane has dried thoroughly.

Plastic Membranes

One of the more recent developments in the roofing field is the use of some of the new synthetic rubbers and vinyls to form roofing membranes. Silicone, Neoprene, Hypolon, and similar products are rolled or sprayed on the roof deck to form a membrane that has high resistance to sunlight, weathering, oxidation, and temperature extremes. The membranes may be developed in one application or in two or three coats to reach the desired thickness. The thickness of the membrane varies from 20 to 50 mils, depending on the system used. The complete membrane may weigh less than 20 lb/square. Most of these products are available in a wide range of colors. The color may be only in the final coating, or it may extend completely through the membrane.

Synthetic-rubber membranes have many advantages. They remain flexible at −65°F and can withstand temperatures of more than 300°F. Although they have a low water-absorption rate, they have high water-vapor permeability, permitting trapped moisture vapor to escape. This type of material has excellent adhesion to most surfaces, although most decks must be primed before application of the first layer of membrane material.

A variation of the plastic membrane is a synthetic-rubber-impregnated asbestos or glass sheet approximately 15 mils thick, coated on both sides with 20 mils of the same material. This sheet is cemented to the substrate with an emulsion-type rubber cement and then coated with one or two coats or liquid-solvent-type rubber and two color coats. A similar synthetic-rubber sheet is available for installation in a single layer, hot mopped with steep asphalt, or attached with cold adhesive.

METALS

Steel, aluminum, copper, lead, and various alloys and clad metals are used as roofing materials, as discussed in Chapters 6 and 7. Some are used as roof coverings, in either flat or corrugated sheets; others are used for flashings and other finishing materials. It is difficult in roofing construction to avoid contact between dissimilar metals. For this reason metals and fastenings must be carefully selected to avoid galvanic corrosion (see Chapter 7).

Fig. 9-19 Laying shakes over asphalt shingles. (*Red Cedar Shingle and Hand Split Shake Bureau; photo by Fred Milkie.*)

Corrugated Roofing

Corrugated sheets are widely used as roof coverings for industrial buildings, factories, and farms. The material often serves as an exposed ceiling as well as the roof covering. It can be installed with a minimum of skill and is relatively inexpensive.

Standard corrugated galvanized roofing sheets are produced with 2½-in. corrugations in 29-gauge or heavier sheets. The sheets are approximately 27½ in. wide and are commonly available in lengths of 5 to 12 ft, although special lengths are sometimes supplied. Standard sheets have corrugations 2½ in. deep and 4½ in. apart. *V-crimped roofing* is formed of two, three, or five longitudinal inverted-V crimps in the sides and centers of the sheets. Various modifications of the standard V-crimped sheets are used as roofing and siding.

Corrugated sheets are usually applied with a side lap of not less than 6 in. and an end lap of at least 1½ in. They may be nailed to wood sheathing, clipped to steel angles or channels, or spot welded to steel studs and purlins. Lead or Neoprene washers are sometimes used in attaching the corrugated roofing to structural framing members to compensate for the expansion and contraction of the sheets with changes in temperature.

Corrugated aluminum is widely used as a roofing material for room additions and screened porches. It is produced in several configurations, either uncoated or with colorful baked-enamel or porcelain-enamel finishes (see Chapter 7). Corrugated asbestos-cement sheets are also used as roofing. Asbestos-cement is a good insulator and

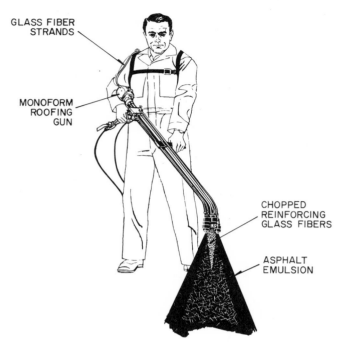

GLASS FIBER STRANDS

MONOFORM ROOFING GUN

CHOPPED REINFORCING GLASS FIBERS

ASPHALT EMULSION

Fig. 9-20 Asphalt roofing gun chops glass fibers to predetermined lengths. (*Flintkote Company, Pioneer Division.*)

does not cause condensation. It is durable, does not require painting, and is available in a wide variety of integral colors and plastic finishes.

Corrugated glass or plastic sheets may be installed in portions of the roof for light. Glass corrugated roofing material is usually ¼" thick, with wire embedded as reinforcement and as a safety factor if the glass is broken. Heavy translucent plastic sheets are sometimes used instead of glass where economy and light weight are desired. Glass sheets are not usually side lapped. Instead, the joint is covered with metal caps held in place by fasteners between the sheets. Premolded asphalt-impregnated strips are used to support the corrugated material over purlins.

Sheet-metal Roofing

Metal expands and contracts with changes in temperature, and a flat metal sheet rigidly fastened to a wood, concrete, or metal deck would buckle and split at the joints and seams. Not only must the size of sheet be limited, but the joints must allow for expansion and contraction and still remain watertight. Various seams have been devised for this purpose. With few exceptions, the seams used for any type of soft or annealed roofing sheet metal work in one of two ways: either they slide or they flex. The loose-

Fig. 9-21 Applying asphalt roofing with a monoform roofing gun to a folded plate roof. (*Flintkote Company, Pioneer Division.*)

lock seam is characteristic of the sliding types; the batten seam is characteristic of the flexing type.

FLAT-SEAM ROOF   Flat seams are commonly used on flat or slightly pitched roofs to form the horizontal joints between standing or batten seams. Flat seams are sometimes used in the covering of domes, towers, and warped surfaces, where small sheets can be fitted more easily to the curved or irregular surfaces. On domes, steeples, and steep slopes, where there is no danger of water collecting on the roof, the seams are left unsoldered and filled with a nonhardening mastic during installation. Individual sheets are held in place by clips nailed to the roof deck.

STANDING-SEAM ROOF   Standing seams are recommended for slopes of 3:12 or greater. Nailing strips must be provided under the standing seam if the roof deck is other than wood. The deck is covered with a layer of 15-lb asphalt-saturated felt. A smooth-surfaced building paper is usually applied over the roofing felt to prevent the felt and the metal roofing from bonding. This type of construction allows for expansion and contraction across narrow panels, and the loose-lock construction provides for lateral motion between rows of sheets.

BATTEN-SEAM ROOF   On roof areas with slopes of 3:12 or greater, where distinct lines are desired as a design feature, the batten-seam roof provides an excellent medium. The spacing and size of the battens may be varied to suit the architectural style, but the maximum distance between battens depends on the type and gauge of the material being used. Standard material widths should be chosen for minimum waste. Allowance for expansion of the metal roofing is made by slightly tapering the wood batten. The battens should be of cypress, redwood, cedar, or pressure-treated wood to resist termites or rot. Nails or screws must be compatible with the metal roofing or countersunk and sealed to prevent exposure to any electrolyte.

WEATHERPROOFING AND DRAINAGE

Expansion Joints

The expansion and contraction of building materials is an important consideration in design. Materials expand and contract at different rates. The total movement of materials and structures under different temperature conditions must be calculated in order to specify the exact width of expansion joints. Table 9-5 shows the coefficient of thermal expansion and the increase in length of the various construction materials for a temperature change of 100°F.

Roof surfaces are subjected to higher temperatures than wall or structural elements. The expanding roof slab moves faster and farther than the walls. If a large building is restrained in any way by an adjoining building or a

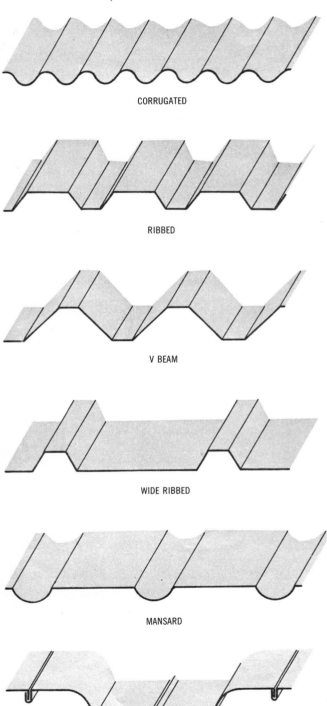

Fig. 9-22 Corrugated metal roofing and siding material. (*By permission of the Sheet Metal and Air Conditioning Contractors' National Association.*)

CORRUGATED

RIBBED

V BEAM

WIDE RIBBED

MANSARD

TYPICAL 12″ PANEL

TABLE 9-5 Linear expansion of building materials

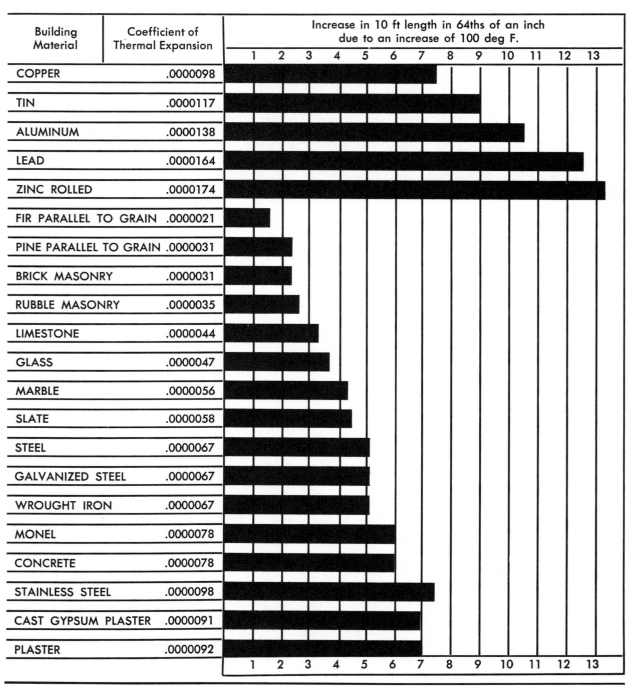

Building Material	Coefficient of Thermal Expansion	Increase in 10 ft length in 64ths of an inch due to an increase of 100 deg F.
COPPER	.0000098	
TIN	.0000117	
ALUMINUM	.0000138	
LEAD	.0000164	
ZINC ROLLED	.0000174	
FIR PARALLEL TO GRAIN	.0000021	
PINE PARALLEL TO GRAIN	.0000031	
BRICK MASONRY	.0000031	
RUBBLE MASONRY	.0000035	
LIMESTONE	.0000044	
GLASS	.0000047	
MARBLE	.0000056	
SLATE	.0000058	
STEEL	.0000067	
GALVANIZED STEEL	.0000067	
WROUGHT IRON	.0000067	
MONEL	.0000078	
CONCRETE	.0000078	
STAINLESS STEEL	.0000098	
CAST GYPSUM PLASTER	.0000091	
PLASTER	.0000092	

From the SMACNA Architectural Manual.

Fig. 9-23 Types of locks and seams used in sheet-metal work. (*By permission of the Sheet Metal and Air Conditioning Contractors' National Association.*)

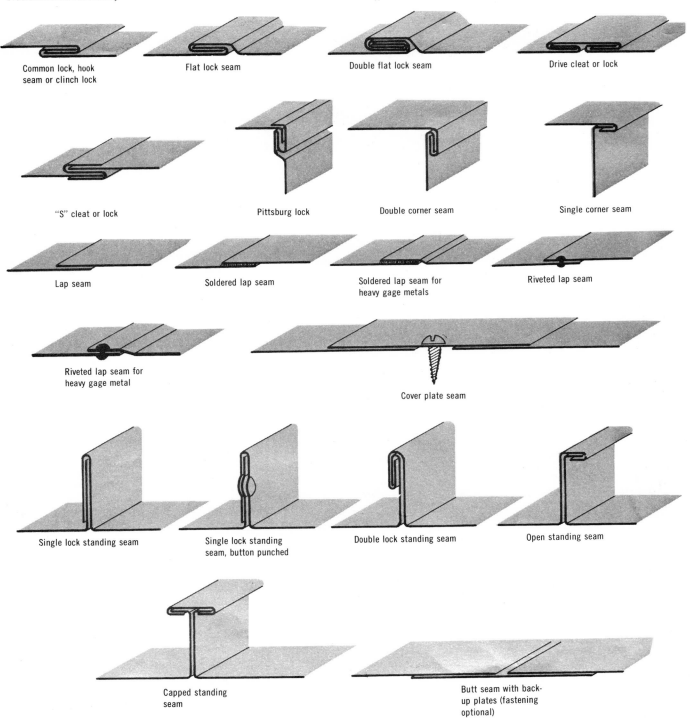

Common lock, hook seam or clinch lock

Flat lock seam

Double flat lock seam

Drive cleat or lock

"S" cleat or lock

Pittsburg lock

Double corner seam

Single corner seam

Lap seam

Soldered lap seam

Soldered lap seam for heavy gage metals

Riveted lap seam

Riveted lap seam for heavy gage metal

Cover plate seam

Single lock standing seam

Single lock standing seam, button punched

Double lock standing seam

Open standing seam

Capped standing seam

Butt seam with back-up plates (fastening optional)

Fig. 9-24 Standing-seam roof construction. (*By permission of the Sheet Metal and Air Conditioning Contractors' National Association.*)

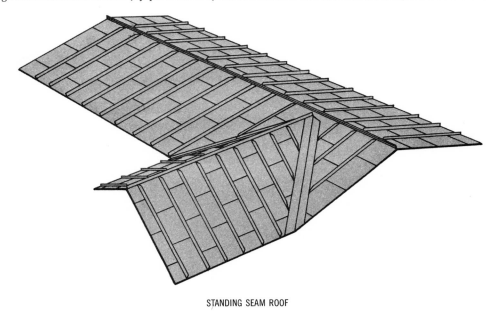

STANDING SEAM ROOF

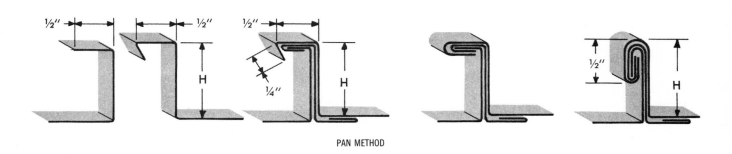

PAN METHOD

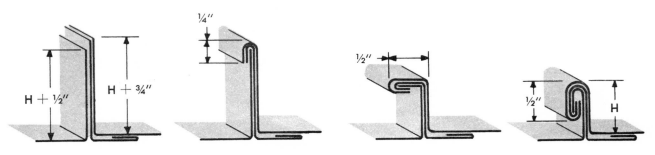

FIELD FORMED

portion of the same building with a different mass, allowances must be made for movement between the two units, with properly designed expansion joints to compensate for the different rates of expansion. When two materials with different rates of expansion are joined together and subjected to a change of temperature, stresses will be set up, causing the weaker material to fail. A masonry wall will expand approximately ³/₈ in. for every 100 ft of length with a winter-summer differential of 100°F. Expansion joints of a minimum of ¹/₂ in. must be provided every 100 feet. Aluminum will expand over 1¹/₂ in. in 100 ft during a temperature change of 100°F.

Large areas are frequently roofed in sections. Joints between these sections are subjected to continual expansion and contraction. Since these movements can cause leakage around the joints, roof expansion joints are usually installed on a *curb* or a *cant*. The expansion joint may be covered by sheet metal, prefabricated assemblies of sheet metal and Neoprene, or a similar flexible weather-resistant material held in place by a continuous metal receiver. Some prefabricated units are formed of metal flanges bonded adhesively and mechanically to either side of a strip of cured, calendered Neoprene. The resulting product is ready to be installed on a curb or cant according to conventional sheet-metal practices.

Openings left in concrete or masonry walls to take care of expansion and contraction must be provided with waterstops. These may consist of preformed copper or other sheet metal built into the structural wall spanning the opening. Premolded vinyl and synthetic-rubber shapes have been developed that are built into masonry walls or placed in the forms when the concrete wall is poured. These materials are abrasive resistant, and their high elasticity will accommodate anticipated movement within concrete or masonry structures. Metal expansion joints are usually *caulked* or sealed with a nonhardening mastic to provide soundproofing and insulation at the joint.

Expansion joints in floor slabs are similar, except that a flush walking surface must be provided. This is usually developed by installing a metal plate that rides on angles set in concrete. The plate is attached to one angle and is free to move on the other.

Flashing

Where roof surfaces meet a vertical wall, *flashing* is necessary to provide a waterproof joint. Flashing is an important factor in preventing the penetration of water into masonry walls or chimneys. Water that penetrates a masonry wall will flow downward through the masonry joints until it reaches a window, door, or other outlet. Poor flashing is probably responsible for more roof failures than any other single factor.

BUILT-UP AND FLAT METAL ROOFS   Flashing usually consists of heavy, flexible plastic sheets or strips of sheet metal, such as galvanized iron, aluminum, copper, zinc, or various alloys or clad metals. Flashing is made in an L shape to fit over the joint, with one leg extending up the wall and the other running across the surface of the roof. Water driven

Fig. 9-25 Titanaloy (zinc-copper-titanium alloy) batten-seam roof on Minas Department Store, Calumet City, Illinois, architects Schlossman, Bennett, and Dart. (*Matthiessen and Hegeler Zinc Company.*)

Fig. 9-26 Batten-seam roof construction. (*By permission of the Sheet Metal and Air Conditioning Contractors' National Association.*)

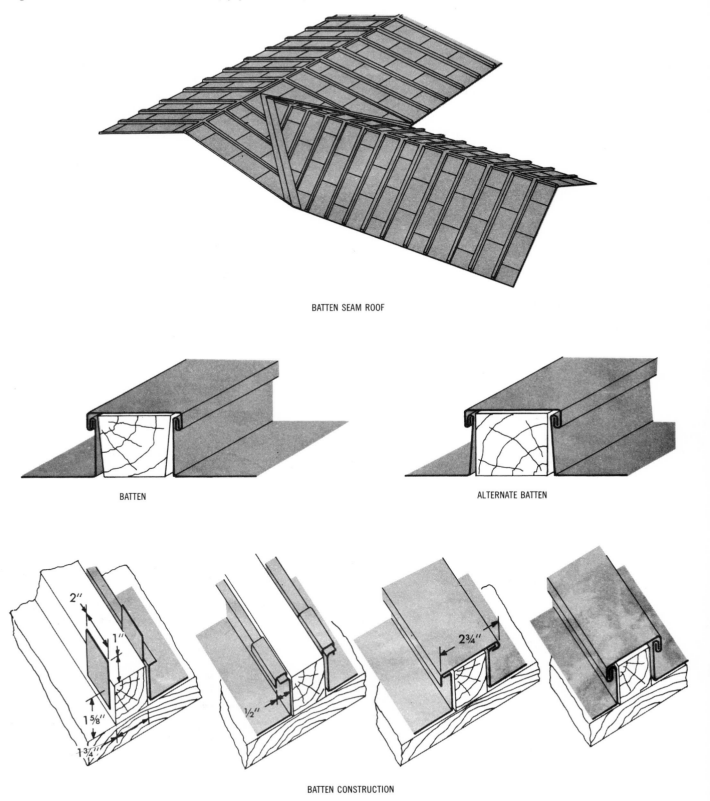

BATTEN SEAM ROOF

BATTEN

ALTERNATE BATTEN

BATTEN CONSTRUCTION

Fig. 9-27 Roof expansion joints. (*By permission of the Sheet Metal and Air Conditioning Contractors' National Association.*)

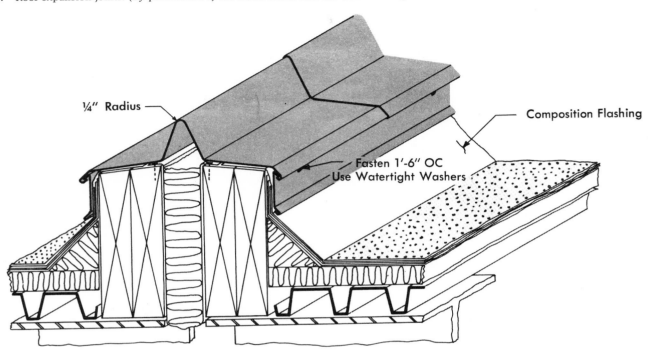

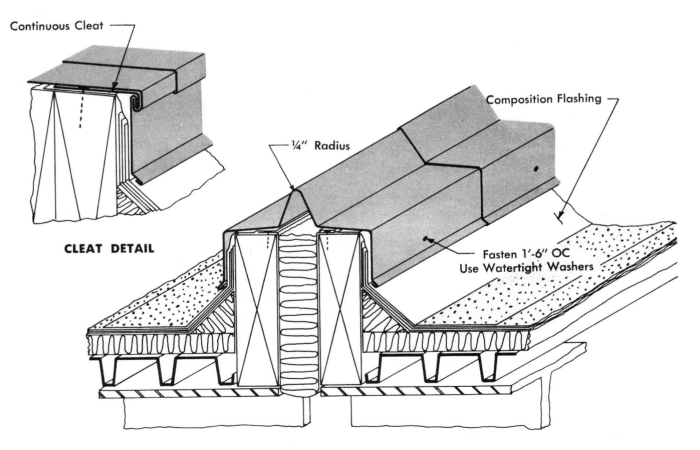

Fig. 9-28 Wall expansion joints. (By permission of the Sheet Metal and Air Conditioning Contractors' National Association.)

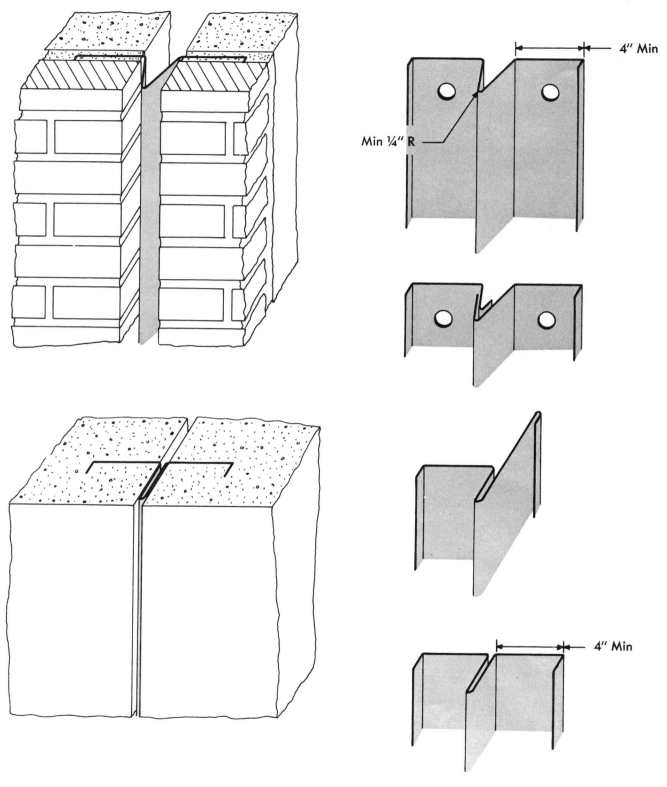

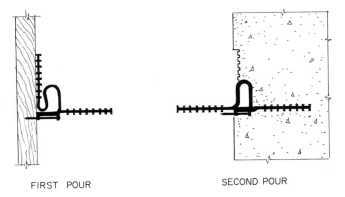

FIRST POUR   SECOND POUR

Fig. 9-29 Polyvinyl chloride (PVC) waterstops. For the first pour the waterstop is nailed to the form boards. For the second pour the form is removed, and the waterstop is released to its final position. (*Courtesy of R. W. Meadows.*)

against the vertical wall by wind is kept from running behind the flashing by *counterflashing* or *capflashing*. The counterflashing is embedded in horizontal mortar joints of masonry walls in a *raggle* or *reglet*, a groove cut or formed in a masonry or concrete wall to receive the upper edge of a flashing.

Built-up roofing is often carried across a triangular block to the wall to avoid the sharp right-angle bend at the wall surface. This triangular block is called a *cant*. Water may enter masonry walls at parapets above roofs. Masonry walls are protected by sheet metal, extruded metal, or concrete *copings* on top of the walls and by *through flashing* or sheet metal built into the walls.

SHINGLE, TILE, AND SLATE ROOFS   The angle between the higher portion of a chimney or other projection through a sloping roof is protected with a *saddle* or *cricket*, which diverts

Fig. 9-30 Building expansion joints at slabs. (*By permission of the Sheet Metal and Air Conditioning Contractors' National Association.*)

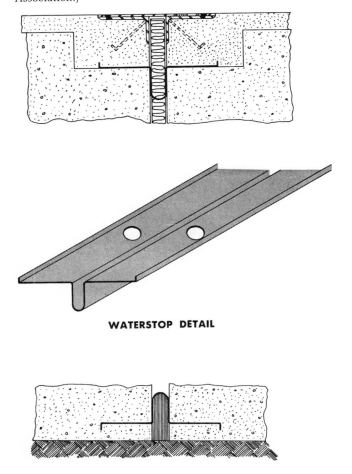

WATERSTOP DETAIL

Fig. 9-31 Parapet and through flashing. (*By permission of the Sheet Metal and Air Conditioning Contractors' National Association.*)

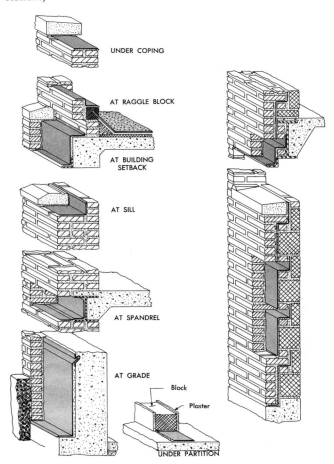

Fig. 9-32 Chimney flashing. (*By permission of the Sheet Metal and Air Conditioning Contractors' National Association.*)

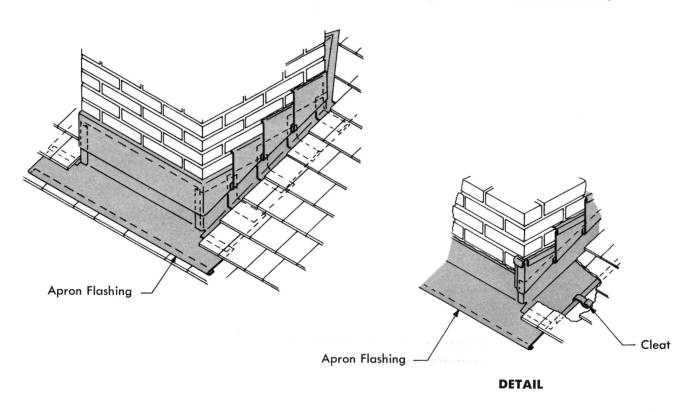

Apron Flashing

Apron Flashing

Cleat

DETAIL

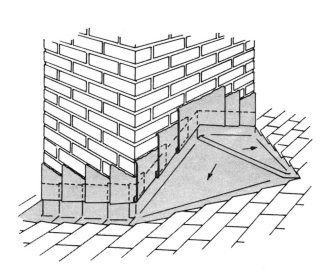

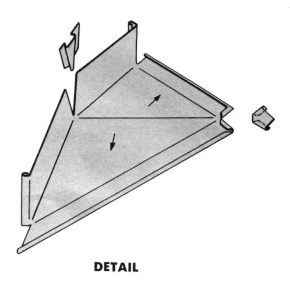

DETAIL

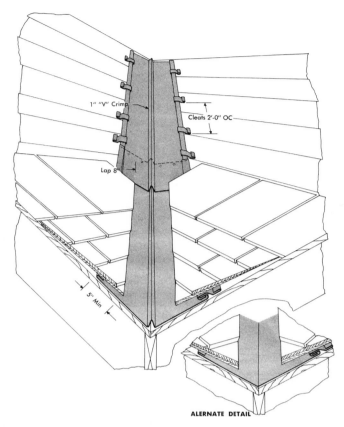

Fig. 9-33 Valley flashing. (*By permission of the Sheet Metal and Air Conditioning Contractors' National Association.*)

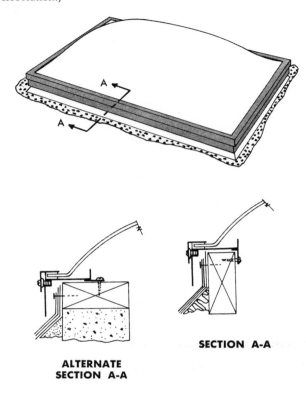

Fig. 9-34 Domed and flat plastic skylights. (*By permission of the Sheet Metal and Air Conditioning Contractors' National Association.*)

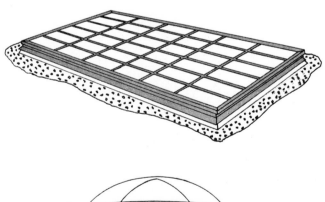

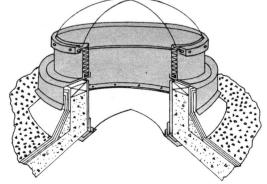

the water to either side of the chimney. The valley between two sloping roof surfaces is protected by *valley flashing*, which consists of sheet metal bent to fit the intersecting roof surfaces. The roofing material may meet at the roof intersections to form a *closed valley*, or it may be held back, exposing the valley flashing, to form an *open valley*.

Skylights and Scuttles

Openings through the roof, either for skylights or for access *scuttles*, are usually surrounded by curbs. The roofing material is carried up the side of the curb and over a *cant*. Flashing is provided under the roofing material, and counterflashing is carried down over it. Prefabricated metal curbs are available, ready for installation. Some manufacturers produce dome-shaped plastic skylights with counterflashing flanges to fit over the turned-up roofing material.

SKYLIGHTS Frames for flat skylights may be formed of sheet metal partially fabricated in the shop and completed on the job. Heavy sheet metal is used to form supporting

Fig. 9-35 Extruded-aluminum puttyless skylight. (*By permission of the Sheet Metal and Air Conditioning Contractors' National Association.*)

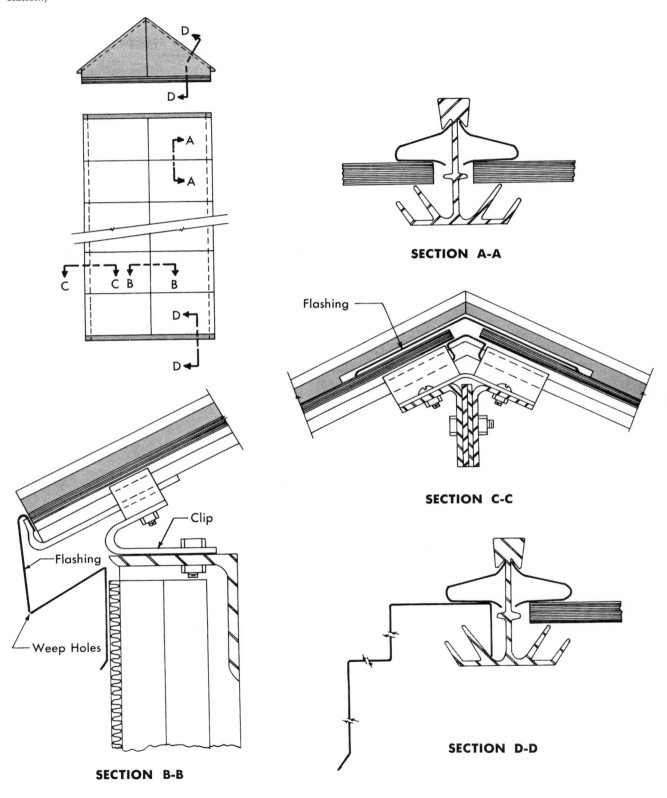

SECTION A-A

SECTION C-C

SECTION B-B

SECTION D-D

Fig. 9-36 Roof scuttle with heat and smoke hatch. (*Bilco Company.*)

angles for safety-glass lights. The lights are installed by glaziers and sealed with mastic. Channels are usually provided under each joint to take care of any water that might come through the sealing compound.

Puttyless skylights are manufactured with extruded aluminum frames, glazed with glass or plastic lights. The size of the extruded bars is governed by the length of the span and the type of material to be installed. The glass is held in place with continuous steel spring clips and aluminum extrusions, and channels are provided under the glass to carry out water that penetrates the joint.

ROOF SCUTTLES   The simplest form of roof access would be a metal pan fitting over a roof curb. However, most roof scuttles are prefabricated assemblies of sheet metal equipped with spring-loaded hinges, locking bars, and operating handles. The scuttle is placed over the opening and nailed or bolted to the roof deck through holes in the flanges. Roofing is built up to the flanges of the roof scuttle and is carried up the side under built-up counterflashing. Special types of roof scuttles, called *smoke scuttles*, are equipped with fusible links. In case of fire the links will melt, and the doors of the smoke scuttle will spring open to let out smoke and fumes from rooms below. Smoke scuttles are required in many public-assembly areas.

Gutters and Downspouts

Rainwater falling on a roof may cause no damage as it runs down the roof and drips off the eaves. However, it may be necessary or desirable to control the flow by collecting the water in *gutters* placed along the edge of the eaves. On flat roofs and roofs with parapet walls, roof drains are installed at low points of the roof. These drains are usually equipped with bronze strainers to keep leaves out of

the drain pipe. The roof drains are sometimes located in catch basins, or *sumps*. These are square sheet-metal receptacles built into the roof to assist in concentrating water at the drain. Where the drainpipe is carried down the inside of exterior walls or interior partitions, it is usually of cast iron and is constructed according to local plumbing codes. (For further information on roof drainage see Chapter 14.)

GUTTERS   Gutters may be built into the roof structure so that they are not visible from ground levels. Concealed gutters must be detailed and constructed with extreme care, since any leaks tend to go directly into the building. Expansion joints must be built into the metal lining to allow for movement of the structure.

Exposed gutters are fabricated in many sizes and shapes. The size is determined by roof-area calculations and the spacing of outlets. Shapes are classed as rectangular (including modified rectangular shapes), half-round, or *ogee*, sometimes called *crown-mold* gutters.

It is essential to provide expansion joints in all gutter

Fig. 9-37 Typical gutter shapes. (*By permission of the Sheet Metal and Air Conditioning Contractor's National Association.*)

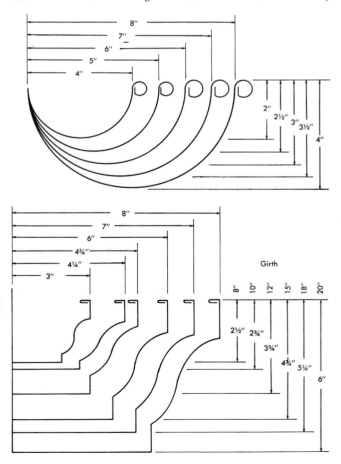

Fig. 9-38 Hanging gutter installations. (*By permission of the Sheet Metal and Air Conditioning Contractors' National Association.*)

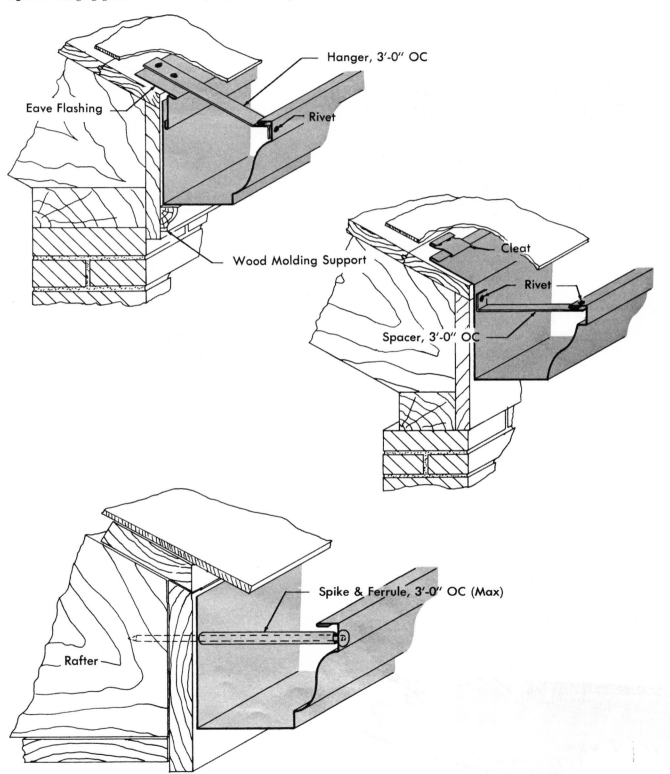

Fig. 9-39 Formed gravel stops and fascia design. (*By permission of the Sheet Metal and Air Conditioning Contractors' National Association.*)

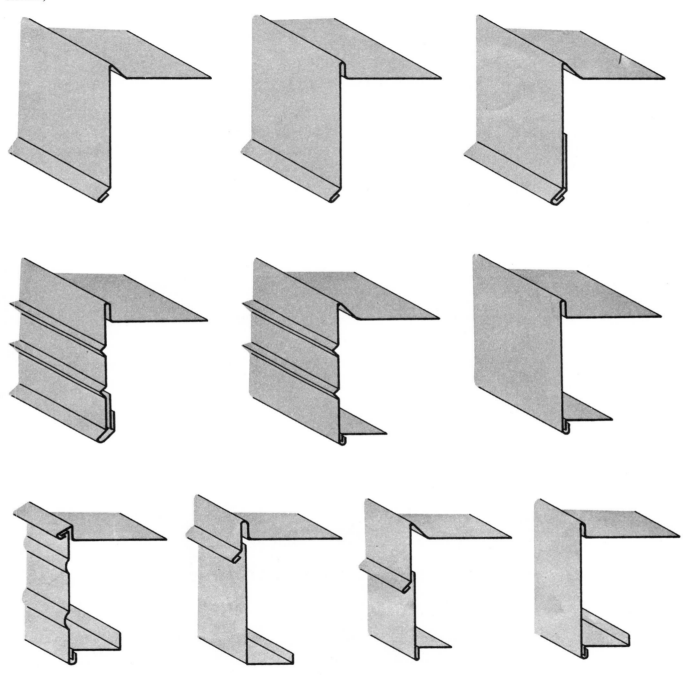

installation. Since the joints will act as dams, they must be located at the high point of the gutter. Gutters should slope a minimum of $1/16$ in./ft to allow for proper flow of water.

Gutters are usually hung from straps that continue under the roofing material or are fastened under a gravel stop. The type of hanger and the placement depends on appearance, expected life, ice or snow loading, the size of the gutter, and the amount of expansion expected.

DOWNSPOUTS Sheet-metal *downspouts*, sometimes called *leaders* or *conductors*, carry the water from the gutter to the ground either directly or through leaders and *conductor heads*. Conductor head and downspout are attached to the wall with sheet-metal leader straps. Water is carried away from the building foundation by *shoes* or *elbows*. Downspouts may be round or rectangular and either plain or corrugated. They must be at least 4 in. in diameter for half-round gutters and no less than 4 in. for square gutters. Downspouts larger than 4 in. will be needed for the larger-sized gutters.

Gravel Stops and Fascias

Gravel stops are used to contain the gravel on a built-up, gravel-surfaced roof. They also act as a transition member between the roof surface and the *fascia*. A fascia is a flat member or band covering the exposed eaves of a building. Gravel stops control damage caused by water drainage over the edge of the roof, and whenever possible, they should be installed on a raised curb. They may be formed of copper, galvanized steel, aluminum, stainless steel, and a number of alloys. A 4-in. flange is nailed to the roof deck or curb, and the roofing is carried over the flange.

The bottom edge of the gravel stop is carried down across the fascia and is bent out from it to form a *drip*. The bottom of the drip may be folded for additional stiffness. The bottom edge of a wide gravel stop may be fastened to the fascia with clips. It may also be connected to a sheet of the same metal to form a metal fascia, in any of several designs. Gravel stops and fascias must be provided with slip joints to allow for expansion. These joints would coincide with expansion joints in the wall and roof surfaces.

DAMPPROOFING AND WATERPROOFING

Dampproofing is a surface coating that may be applied by brush, spray, or roller to an underground or above-ground concrete or masonry wall. This type of coating is suitable for underground use only where there is no *hydrostatic pressure* from underground water. The deeper the structure is within the ground, the greater the hydrostatic pressure.

Waterproofing prevents the entrance of water that is under pressure by forming a continuous membrane around walls, through concrete footings, and under or within concrete floor slabs. Hydrostatic pressure will force water into the pores of masonry or concrete surfaces, where it can chemically attack cementitious materials and cause

Fig. 9-40 Installing a waterproofing membrane under a concrete slab. (*St. Regis Paper Company, Laminated and Coated Products Division.*)

Fig. 9-41 Spraying on asphalt-and-glass-fiber waterproofing membrane to basement walls. (*Flintkote Company, Pioneer Division.*)

them to deteriorate. Water penetrating deteriorating walls can cause reinforcing to fail. The freezing and thawing of entrapped water will cause concrete to spall and crack. Waterproofing includes dampproofing, but dampproofing does not serve the function of waterproofing.

Dampproofing

Many dampproofing systems have been formulated to prevent the penetration of surface moisture through masonry or concrete walls. The materials used must penetrate and fill the pores of the surface and must be sufficiently elastic to resist minor expansion and contraction. They may be applied by brush, roller, or spray or as prefabricated panels to either inside or outside of exterior walls. Such dampproofing materials include hot-applied and emulsified coal-tar pitch, hot-applied and cold-applied asphalt, emulsified asphalt combined with glass fibers, bentonite clays, butyl rubbers, silicones, vinyls, epoxy resins, cement-based aggregate coatings, and many proprietary products.

One of the most recently developed dampproofing materials is a metallic waterproofing, sometimes called *hydrolithic* or *ferrous waterproofing*. This consists of pulverized iron aggregate mixed with oxidizing agents. When the iron particles oxidize, or rust, they expand to $4\frac{1}{2}$ times their original size. This wedges them into the pores of the wall to create a relatively dense barrier that is impervious to the passage of water. The surface of concrete must be roughened by sandblasting to assure a good bond.

Fig. 9-42 Installing a vapor barrier for a cellular metal roof deck. (*St. Regis Paper Company, Laminated and Coated Products Division.*)

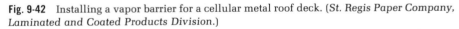

Waterproofing

To effectively prevent the entrance of water in any portion of a structure that is below grade, walls must be designed to resist lateral pressure and floors must be designed to resist upward thrust. Static water will exert a pressure of 62½ lb/sq ft of wall or floor surface plus 0.43 lb/sq in. for every foot below the groundwater table or the surface of seawater, rivers, or lakes. The waterproof membrane must prevent the water from entering pores and voids in the structure.

Whenever possible, a drainage system should be devised to reduce the hydrostatic pressure on basement walls. This may be in the form of open-joint drain tiles set in the excavation and covered with gravel. During construction water pressure must be removed from the outside of the basement walls until they attain their design strength. Some waterproofing membranes can be applied to wet or green concrete, whereas others cannot be applied until all moisture has left the structural wall. Because waterproofing membranes are ineffective unless they are intact, they must be protected during construction until backfill is complete. The backfill operation itself can sometimes puncture the membrane and destroy its value.

Waterproofing membranes are built up by the same methods used for built-up roofing. Rag, asbestos, or glass felts are hot-mopped with coal-tar pitch or asphalt or cold-mopped with emulsified asphalt or coal-tar pitch. Two to six layers of felt and three to seven moppings of bitumens may be necessary to resist hydrostatic pressure.

The deeper the structure, or the higher the hydrostatic head, the more layers of felt are needed. Manufacturers of asphaltic and coal-tar-pitch waterproofing materials publish tables with their recommendations for the number of plies necessary to resist different water pressures. Some manufacturers recommend a layer of rigid insulation board over the built-up membrane to protect it against the back-fill.

Plastic and synthetic-rubber waterproofing membranes include vinyls, butyl rubbers, Neoprene, polyvinyl chloride (PVC), and similar materials. The sheets are held tightly against the wall surface with special adhesives. The flexible sheets are easily installed and adjust to compaction and settling.

One manufacturer produces a synthetic-rubber sheet with ⅜-in.-high lugs on one side. The sheet is attached to the inside of concrete forms and on the bottom of excavations, with the lugs facing inward. When concrete is poured, the lugs are surrounded with concrete, so that the concrete walls and waterproofing membrane are an integral unit.

Prefabricated membranes are produced with a plastic or glass-fiber core between two layers of asphalt-impregnated felt. The outer surface is coated with finishing asphalt. This product is said to be particularly effective under conditions of excessive moisture and vapor. Another type of membrane is developed by simultaneously spraying cut-up glass fiber and asphalt to form a monolithic membrane. Sheet lead, joined by burning (welding), is

Fig. 9-43 Spraying an emulsified asphalt-and-glass-fiber waterproofing membrane on the inside of a concrete tank. Water level is lowered as membrane is applied, eliminating need for scaffolding. (*Flintkote Company, Pioneer Division.*)

also used as membrane waterproofing. It is placed under the slab and turned up the walls to make a continuous waterproof pan. Lead must be used with care, however, as green concrete will cause it to corrode. The lead membrane must be protected with a coating of asphaltum paint. Lead is particularly effective under outdoor pools.

Slab Dampproofing and Waterproofing

Slabs on grade, which are not subject to hydrostatic pressure, may be placed over 4 to 5 in. of granular fill. The granular fill tends to prevent water from being drawn up through the bottom of the slab by capillary action. A more positive waterstop is obtained by covering the granular fill with polyvinyl or butyl-rubber sheets after the side forms are in place. Reinforcing mesh is laid over the film, and the concrete is poured around the reinforcing. The danger of this type of construction is that the film is easily punctured by irregularities in the fill or during placement of the concrete. Where it is imperative that the structure remain waterproof, or where it will be subjected to a hydrostatic pressure, a structural slab is placed directly on the granular fill, finished, and allowed to cure. A waterproof membrane is then placed or built up on top of the structural slab in the same manner as for basement walls, and a 1½-to 2-in. finish slab is poured over the membrane.

THERMAL INSULATION

All materials resist the transfer of heat in direct proportion to their thicknesses. However, modern construction practices and the weight of materials limit the thicknesses of building materials that may economically be used. For this reason the loss of heat from buildings in winter and the gain of heat in summer is controlled by thermal insulation such as spun glass, foamed glass, vegetable fibers, mineral fibers, and certain foamed plastics. These materials may be pressed into boards, installed as loose blankets or batts, or blown in granular form into walls and ceilings.

Heat Transfer

The resistance of a material to the transfer of heat depends on its composition and physical characteristics. The *specific resistance R* or any material, however, varies directly with its thickness: a 2-in. thickness of a material will resist twice as much heat as a 1-in. thickness of the same material. Conversely, the amount of heat that will be *conducted* by that material *decreases* with thickness: a 2-in. thickness will conduct or transfer half as much heat as a 1-in. thickness. The *conductivity k* of a material is defined as the amount of heat it will conduct through one inch per unit of area. The amount of heat it will conduct through one square foot of surface area per unit of thickness is called its *conductance C*. Some manufacturers list the R value of their product, some list the k value, and some list the C value. Table 9-6 shows these values for some of the more common construction materials.

The actual heat loss through a structure, such as a wall or a floor, is measured in *British thermal units* (Btu). One Btu is the amount of heat needed to raise the temperature of one pound of water one degree Fahrenheit. In order to

Fig. 9-44 Blowing insulation. (*Premium Brand Insulation Group.*)

TABLE 9-6 Coefficients of heat transmission, values in Btu/hr/sq ft/°F

MATERIAL	CONDUC-TIVITY k	CONDUC-TANCE C	RESIS-TANCE R (1/C)
Air, inside			
Heat flow up		1.64	0.61
Heat flow horizontal		1.46	0.68
Heat flow down		1.08	0.92
Air, outside			
7½ mph		4.0	0.25
15 mph		6.0	0.17
Air, enclosed			
¾ in. or more vertical.		1.08	0.92
Insulation			
Blankets, batts, or loose fill,			
mineral or vegetable	0.27	3.75	
Rigid insulation board,			
wood or vegetable fiber	0.33	3.03	
Vermiculite	0.48	2.08	
Roofing			
Asbestos shingles		4.75	0.21
Asphalt shingles		2.27	0.45
Wood shingles		1.06	0.95
Built-up roofing		3.00	0.33
slate, ½"	10.00	20.00	0.05
Exterior materials			
Stucco, 1"	5.00	5.00	0.20
Wood siding, ¾"	0.80	1.02	0.98
Face brick, 4"	9.00	2.25	0.44
Common brick, 4"	5.00	1.25	0.80
Douglas fir, ¾"	0.80	0.48	2.08
Southern pine, 1½"	0.80	0.24	4.17
2"	0.80	0.18	5.56
3"	0.80	0.12	8.33
Concrete, sand and gravel	12.00	0.08	
Vermiculite, 1"	0.86	0.86	1.16
Stone	12.50		
Glass, ¼"	6.00		0.043
⅛"	6.00		0.021
Interior materials			
Gypsum lath and plaster		2.44	0.41
Metal lath and ¾" plaster		7.70	0.10
Vermiculite plaster, 1"	0.95	0.95	1.05
Plywood, ⅜"		2.10	0.46

find the heat loss in Btu's through a given structure, we must calculate the *total conductance U* of that structure. The *U factor* of a structure is the number of Btu's per hour that will flow through one square foot of the structure when there is a one-degree difference in temperature between the two sides. The higher the *U* factor of a structure, the more heat will be lost through it; the lower the *U* factor, the less heat will pass through — that is, the better its insulation properties. Tables that give the *k* and *C* values of construction materials usually include the *U* factor of

commonly used roof, wall, and floor constructions. These can be used to calculate the heat loss of a building.

Insulating Materials

Heat may be transferred by conduction, convection, and reflection. The conductivity of materials varies with their density. Materials such as aluminum, copper, and steel have a high conductivity. Construction materials such as concrete, building stone, and brick have lower conductivity than the metals but will still conduct considerable heat. Materials that have a low conductivity are considered *insulators*. Mineral wool, vegetable and wood fiber, asbestos, glass fiber, cork, and several other materials fall into this category.

Moving air transmits heat by convection. However, still air has a very high insulating value (see Table 9-6). Thus air enclosed in cellular materials such as foamed glass or plastic serves as an insulator. A ¾-in. enclosed air space has better insulating value than 1 in. of solid oak or 4 in. of solid concrete. Materials with entirely closed air cells make better insulators than a pressed fibrous material.

Insulation may also be surfaced with materials that reflect heat, such as aluminum foil. Aluminum is an excellent conductor of heat. However, 95 percent of the heat that reaches a bright aluminum-foil surface through an air space will be reflected back into the air space. For aluminum or other reflective insulations to be effective, there must be an air space of at least ¾ in. on one side of the foil. An air space on both sides of a reflective foil increases the insulating value.

VAPOR BARRIERS   The fact that warm air carries more moisture than cool air complicates the problem of insulation. When warm air is cooled, some of this moisture condenses. Thus when air from a heated room comes in contact with the colder exterior wall, moisture will condense inside the wall structure unless it can escape. Since moisture inside a wall can damage the structure or destroy the value of the insulation, the warm air must be kept from reaching the colder side by airtight *vapor barriers* on one side of the insulation. The vapor barrier must be placed on the warm side of the structure to block the entry of moisture-laden air. The opposite side of the insulating material must be allowed to "breathe," so that any moisture that does get inside can pass through.

RIGID INSULATION   Pressed boards of wood fiber, cane fiber, mineral wool, cork, glass fiber, foamed glass, and foamed plastics are used as rigid insulation. These boards serve the dual purposes of insulation and strengthening of exterior walls. They may be impregnated with asphalt products to make them water resistant. Many have vapor barriers of kraft paper or metal foil laminated to one or both sides. Rigid insulation can be used under built-up roofing. Some boards are graded in thickness to provide a sloping deck for water drainage. Rigid structural sandwich boards can be obtained that combine roof sheathing, insulation, and finished ceiling in one composite board.

BLANKET OR BATT INSULATION Loose fibers of glass, rock wool, or mineral wool are formed into blankets and enclosed in kraft paper to form a low-density insulating material. If the material is produced in rolls, which may be 30 to 80 ft long, it is termed *blanket insulation*. If it is cut into 2′, 4′, or 8′ lengths, it is called *batt blanket* or *batt*. Batts are produced for installation between wood studs and ceiling joists.

Some blankets are encased in waterproof kraft paper on one side as a vapor barrier, with perforated paper on the reverse side. Batts and blankets are also produced with foil vapor barriers on one side. It is important that these blankets be installed with the vapor barrier facing the warm side of the construction.

Blankets and batts are produced in widths that correspond to the normal spacing of wall studs, ceiling joists, and floor joists. The blankets have flanges of paper on both edges so that they can be nailed or stapled between studs or joists. Blankets or batts can be obtained in several thicknesses. Product catalogs of the various manufacturers indicate the R or C value of each thickness.

BLOWN OR POURED INSULATION Several types of loose insulation, such as perlite, vermiculite, and glass fiber, are blown between framing members through holes left or drilled in the walls. They may be poured or blown between the ceiling joists to any desired thickness after the

Fig. 9-46 Installing foil-covered insulation batts in a residence.

Fig. 9-45 Blown insulation in attic space. (*Premium Brand Insulation Group.*)

ceiling below has been finished. Independent vapor barriers must be provided with this type of insulation.

REFLECTIVE INSULATION There are several types of reflective insulation. Aluminum-backed gypsum-plaster lath or wallboard is available for interior walls. The aluminum foil acts as a vapor barrier on the warm side of the wall in winter and acts as reflective insulation in the summer. Aluminum can be laminated to one or both sides of heavy kraft paper. When one layer of this laminated product is installed in the center of a wall, with air spaces on both sides, it acts as reflective insulation. Two layers with an air space between them greatly increases the insulating value. Accordion-type insulation of foil in conjunction with waterproof paper, is manufactured for use between wood studs or joists. When it is stapled between studs the material fans out, forming one or two dead air spaces between several layers of aluminum foil. This type of insulation can be used as a combination vapor seal and reflective insulation.

QUESTIONS

1. What are two basic considerations in the selection of roofing materials?

2. What type of roof deck is recommended under wood shingles?

3. What is the difference between pitch and slope?

4. Describe two types of *bitumen*.

5. List the advantages and limitations of asphalt as a roofing surface.

6. List the advantages and limitations of coal-tar pitch as a roofing surface.

7. What is a *square* of roofing?

8. What does the designation 15-lb felt mean?

9. Outline the steps in applying a built-up roof.

10. Describe two methods of holding down the tabs of asphalt shingles.

11. List the advantages and disadvantages of asbestos-cement shingles.

12. Sketch and name four types of clay roofing tiles.

13. What are the advantages and limitations of concrete roofing tile?

14. How are slates attached to the roof deck?

15. What type of grain do the best grades of wood shingles usually have?

16. What are the standard sizes of red cedar shingles?

17. How is the thickness of wood shingles measured?

18. How many bundles of 18 in. shingles, laid 4½ in. to weather, would be needed to cover 1540 sq ft of roof surface?

19. How do wood shakes differ from shingles?

20. What is membrane roofing?

21. Explain the principle of galvanic action.

22. Sketch a roof expansion joint.

23. What would be the linear expansion of a 300-ft brick wall during a temperature change of 50°F?

24. Define the following words: raggle, cant, counterflashing, coping.

25. What is a fascia?

26. What is the difference between dampproofing and waterproofing?

27. Define the term *hydrostatic head*.

28. Describe the process of applying a built-up waterproofing membrane to a basement wall.

29. Define the following terms in relation to heat transfer: *k, C, R.*

REFERENCES FOR FURTHER STUDY

Asphalt Roofing Manufacturers' Association: 727 Third Avenue, New York, N.Y., 10017. "Manufacture, Selection and Application of Asphalt Roofing and Siding Products," 1964.

Callender, John Hancock: "Time-Saver Standards," 4th ed., McGraw-Hill, New York, 1966.

Construction Specifications Institute: Suite 300, 1150 17th Street, N.W., Washington, D.C., 20036. "A Special Report on Built-up Roofings," *The Construction Specifier*, fall 1957. "Specifying Metallic Waterproofing," Document 701. "Specifying Building Insulation: Fibrous and Reflective," Document 07201. "Bulk Sealants Used in Building Joints," Document 07M901. "Specifying Dampproofing Silicone," Document 07170. "Roofing: Steep Asphalt and Coal-tar Pitch," Document 07M510.

Copper Development Association: 405 Lexington Avenue, New York, N.Y., 10017. *Contemporary Copper*, a periodical.

Dow Chemical Company: Midland, Mich., 48640. "Permanent Insulation of Buildings," 1968.

GACO Western, Inc.: P.O. Box 698, Tukila Station, Seattle, Wash., 98168. "Neoprene-Hypalon Elastromeric Roofing Systems," 1968.

Insulating Board Institute: Chicago, Ill., 60602. "Fundamentals of Building Insulation."

Johns-Manville: 22 East 40th Street, New York, N.Y., 10016. "What You Should Know about Your Roof."

Koppers Company: 612 Chatham Center, Pittsburg, Pa., 15219. "Waterproofing and Dampproofing," 1969.

Lead Industries Association: 292 Madison Avenue, New York, N.Y., 10017.

National Mineral Wool Insulation Association: New York, N.Y., 10020. "Standard of Mineral Wool Building Insulation," "Mineral Wool Insulation and the All Weather Comfort Standard."

Owens-Corning Fiberglas Corporation: 717 Fifth Avenue, New York, N.Y., 10022. "Foamglas Cellular Glass Insulation," 1968.

The Producers' Council: 1717 Massachusetts Avenue, N.W., Washington, D.C., 20036. "Handbook of Roofing," 1969.

Red Cedar Shingle and Handsplit Shake Bureau: 5510 White Building, Seattle, Wash., 98101. "Certigrade Handbook of Red Cedar Shingles." "Certi-split Manual of Handsplit Red Cedar Shakes."

Roofing Industry Trust: 520 South Virgil Avenue, Los Angeles, Calif., 90005. *R.I.T. Report*, a periodical. "Roofing Conditions in Southern California," 1966.

Sheet Metal and Air Conditioning Contractors' Association: 1161 North Kent Street, Arlington, Va., 22209. "A Manual for the Specification of Sheet Metal and Related Work," 1965. "Architectural Sheet Metal Manual," 1969.

Sheet Metal Industry Fund of Los Angeles: 1830 West Eighth Street, Suite 114, Los Angeles, Calif. 90057.

FLOOR
AND
WALL
COVERINGS
10

FLOOR COVERINGS

Many types of floor coverings are used as wearing surfaces over structural concrete slabs, steel decks, or wood subfloors. They may be thin membranes that contribute little or no strength to the floor system or thicker materials that are essential to the strength of the building. Thin floor coverings are sheet materials such as linoleum, plastic, rubber, cork, asphalt, vinyl, and wood-veneer tiles. Floors may be finished with thin films of plastic applied to the subfloor as a liquid or paste. Terrazzo floors are applied to rigid subfloors and finished in place. Ceramic tile, slate, and marble floors are set in beds of concrete or mastic. Terrazzo, tile, and stone floors contribute some structural strength. Concrete and wood flooring may be either structural or nonstructural.

The first consideration in selecting a flooring type is moisture. Some types of flooring are adversely affected by moisture, either coming up through the subfloor or settling on the surface, as is likely in bathrooms and kitchens, around laundry equipment, and in similar installation. The second criterion is the amount and type of wear to which the surface will be subjected. Flooring products vary in their ability to withstand harsh treatment, foot traffic, wheeled traffic, or exposure to chemicals. Cost of materials, installation, maintenance, and expected service life must be considered. After these practical factors have been carefully weighed, visual and esthetic considerations such as color, texture, resilience, and sound-absorbing qualities must be considered.

Undoubtedly the first floor covering was packed earth or clay, used to level the natural rock bottoms of caves. The ancient Egyptians used squared sandstone blocks as structural and finish flooring for their temples and tombs. Precisely cut and set marble slabs were used as flooring in Greek temples.

The first decorative floorings were developed by the Romans. Their mosaic floors of small marble chips set in cement have lasted through the centuries. Builders of the Byzantine and the later Moslem Empires carried this form of construction to its highest point when they paved, not only floors, but columns, walls, and the underside of domes with colorful marble and glass mosaics. Although wood was used from ancient times as a combination structural and finish flooring material for residences, it was not until the development of wire nails that it became the major flooring material. Resilient flooring such as linoleum, plastic sheet, tile, and carpeting have now replaced much wood flooring.

WOOD FLOORING

Woods used for finished flooring must have hard, dense surfaces to withstand heavy wear and abrasion. Both hardwoods and softwoods are used for flooring. However, certain hardwoods, because of their resistance to wear and indentation, are more often used for this purpose. Wood for finished flooring must be selected carefully for color, texture, freedom from defects, and grain. All wood flooring is carefully kiln dried, and when it is unfinished, it must be stored in locations where the moisture content can be controlled. Wood flooring requires a protective coating such as a filler, sealer, varnish, lacquer, shellac, or wax. Hardwood flooring can be obtained either unfinished or prefinished.

Softwood Flooring

The softwoods most commonly used for flooring are yellow pine, douglas fir, western hemlock, and larch. Some redwood, cedar, cypress, and eastern white pine are used in areas where these woods are native. Softwood finish flooring should always be vertical grain to resist splintering and warp. It can be obtained as strip flooring or as end-grain blocks for use as industrial floors.

Strip flooring is manufactured in several sizes and thicknesses. The most common size used in residences and offices is $1'' \times 5''$ nominal size; the actual dimensions are $^{25}/_{32}'' \times 4^{1}/_{4}''$. The long edges of the flooring are tongue and groove or side matched to provide tight joints. Some softwood is tongue-and-grooved to provide end-matched flooring. The underside of most softwood flooring is *ploughed*, or hollowed out, to minimize warping and cupping. Special types of strip flooring are produced for use in heavy timber construction, where it may span 8 to 10 ft between girders or beams. This flooring may be $2''$ to $4''$ thick and has special matched tongues and grooves or splines cut into the sides.

Wood blocks of yellow pine, douglas fir, or redwood may be used for industrial flooring. These blocks are laid like bricks, in pitch or asphalt, with the end grain showing. The end grain of the blocks makes an excellent floor where the traffic is heavy, or where a nonsparking, dustfree flooring is desired. The joints between the blocks are filled with asphalt or pitch, and a thin layer of asphalt or pitch is left on the surface. This layer seals any voids in the end grain of the blocks and gradually wears off with use. When the blocks have been set in asphalt or pitch, expansion joints must be left around the perimeter of the floor. Wood-block

Fig. 10-1 First-century Roman marble mosaic floor, Island of Delos, Greece.

flooring can be obtained in sizes ranging from $2''$ to $4''$ in width, $3^{1}/_{2}''$ to $9''$ in length, and $1^{1}/_{2}''$ to $4''$ in thickness.

Hardwood Flooring

The hardwood most commonly used for flooring is oak, because of its beauty of grain, strength, and durability. Both red oak and white oak are used for flooring. The difference between them is mainly one of color; both follow the same grading rules, established by the National Oak Flooring Manufacturers' Association. Oak flooring may be obtained either flat-sawed or quarter-sawed. Quarter-sawing brings out the characteristic grain and produces the best quality of flooring. Flat-sawed flooring shows a more prominent and varied grain pattern.

Northern hard maple is a smooth, durable wood that is widely used where wear is particularly important. The grain of maple flooring is not as interesting as that of oak, but in areas where a smooth, highly polished surface is desired, such as dance floors, gymnasiums, and assembly halls, maple makes an excellent floor. Grade rules for maple flooring have been established by Maple Flooring Manufacturers' Association.

Other hardwoods used as finish flooring are beech,

birch, pecan, and hickory. Beech and birch, although somewhat darker, with a more prominent grain, are produced under the same grading rules as maple. Walnut, cherry, teak, and other hardwoods are occasionally used as flooring.

Hardwood flooring is produced as strip flooring and as thin blocks.

STRIP FLOORING Strip flooring can be obtained with square edges, side matched, or side matched and end matched. Side-matched strips have tongue-and-groove sides and square ends. Side- and end-matched strip flooring are tongue and grooved at both ends. Most hardwood strip flooring is relieved, or hollowed, on the back. Strip flooring is most commonly produced in thicknesses of $3/8''$, $1/2''$, or $25/32''$ and widths of $1\frac{1}{2}''$, $2''$, $2\frac{1}{4}''$, and $3\frac{1}{4}''$. These nominal sizes are not necessarily the actual dimensions of the strips. Sometimes the actual thickness of the hardwood flooring is $1/32$ in. less than the nominal size measured across the face, excluding the tongue. Strip hardwood flooring is graded according to characteristics and number of defects. The grade rules also define the average length of the individual strips in each bundle. The higher grades are made up of the longer strips, while the lower grades allow more shorts, or short pieces, in each bundle.

Strip flooring may be obtained either unfinished or prefinished. Unfinished flooring is usually supplied with square, tight fitting edges that form a smooth, tight joint when finished. Prefinished flooring usually is furnished with a more or less prominent V joint on the edges and ends of the strips. It is finished and waxed at the factory and is ready for use as soon as it is laid. Prefinished flooring is available as an imitation of plank flooring, or random-width strips. Other types have imitation pegs of contrasting hardwood or spline-shaped inserts. Prefinished flooring can be obtained in a variety of finishes and surfaces.

THIN-BLOCK FLOORING Solid hardwood, in $9'' \times 9''$ or $12'' \times 12''$ blocks $5/16''$ or $1/2''$ thick, are used to produce a *parquet floor*, patterns formed by alternating grain direction, contrasting woods, or combinations of blocks and strips. These squares are available in white oak, maple, American walnut, mahogany, cherry, teak, and several other hardwoods. Laminated veneer blocks are also produced. Short strips of hardwood, joined together into blocks with metal splines, are available in many hardwoods. Most thin-block flooring is produced in prefinished units, either with square edges or tongue-and-groove matched edges. The blocks may be nailed to the subfloor or set in mastic. Most prefinished flooring materials are treated to resist the attack of fungi and insects.

CUSHIONED FLOORING Special types of floors and flooring have been developed for gymnasiums, dance floors, auditorium floors, and other locations where some cushioning is desired. This flooring is produced in thicknesses of $1\frac{1}{4}''$ to $2\frac{1}{2}''$. Some types are square edges, some tongue and grooved, and some shaped to be joined together with steel splines. Most cushioned floorings are designed for installation over concrete subfloors, but they can usually be installed over any firm, level surface.

Cushioned hardwood floors are usually installed on a cushion of cork or other resilient material or on *sleepers* set on rubber or synthetic-rubber pads. Resilient cushioned floors in gymnasiums are said to prevent sore leg muscles and protect the feet of athletes. The additional thickness and resiliency lead to longer wear with less maintenance.

RESILIENT FLOORING

Resilient floor coverings include a wide variety of dense, nonabsorbent sheet materials laid, either as individual tiles or as large sheets, over properly prepared subfloors. These materials have varying abilities to give under impact loads and recover their original shape after the load is removed.

The selection among the various materials depends on cost, required resilience for safety and acoustical properties, resistance to moisture, ease of maintenance, thermal conductivity, light reflection, and appearance. The location of the floor, whether it is to be suspended above grade, on grade, or below grade, is an extremely important factor. The life of a flooring material must be considered not only in terms of the physical life of the material, but in terms of how long the flooring will present an acceptable appearance.

New materials and adaptations of old materials and new patterns, colors, and sizes of resilient flooring are introduced on the market constantly. The designer must always be sure that materials selected are still available or are the best for the job at hand.

Linoleum

Linoleum was developed in England about 100 years ago and was the only type of resilient flooring material available for many years. It consists of a blended and cured composition of linseed oil, resin binders, pigments, and fillers, bonded to a backing of asphalt-saturated rag felt. Hot linseed oil is oxidized in closed containers until it forms into a jellylike mass. Binders, fillers, and pigments are mixed into the oxidized linseed oil and spread in thin sheets onto felt or burlap backing. The linoleum is then seasoned in ovens for 2 to 4 weeks to set the material. After seasoning it is given several coats of lacquer for greater stain and spot resistance.

Linoleum is available in plain or marbleized colors and with inlaid, textured, or embossed patterns, either in colorful designs or to simulate stone, wood, or tile. Sheet linoleum is manufactured in rolls $72''$ wide and 42 to 90 ft long.

Linoleum tiles, either $9'' \times 9''$ or $12'' \times 12''$, are available in the same patterns as sheet linoleum. Feature strips and shapes are fabricated from sheet linoleum for special effects.

Three thicknesses are generally available: a $1/16''$ light-gauge service weight, a 0.090'' standard gauge, and a $1/8''$ heavy gauge. Light- and standard-gauge linoleums are usually furnished with an asphalt impregnated backing; heavy-gauge linoleum is manufactured with a burlap backing. Light and standard gauge linoleum is suitable for residences and light commercial construction. They are used as countertops and work tables for light work. A special standard-gauge linoleum is produced for use as a surface for drafting tables. Heavy-gauge linoleum is used for heavy commercial applications. Battleship linoleum is a special dark-colored, heavy linoleum with a burlap backing.

Linoleum has good resistance to wear. The designs and colors in inlaid linoleum usually extend completely through to the backing and will maintain their appearance through the life of the floor. However, linoleum is easily damaged by alkali cleaning solutions. It can only be installed on floors not in contact with the earth.

Asphalt Tile

Asphalt tile consists of asbestos fibers, fillers, and pigments bonded with asphaltic or resinous binders. Asphaltic binders of natural asphalts mined in Utah and Colorado are used in the darker colors of asphalt tile. The lighter colors are made with thermoplastic resinous binders. The price of asphalt tile depends on the color, as shown in Table 10-1.

Most asphalt tiles are produced in a marbleized pattern. This pattern runs completely through the tile. Some asphalt tile is patterned to simulate cork or terrazzo. However these tiles are recommended for light use only, as the pattern does not penetrate the full thickness of the tile and is subject to wear under heavy traffic. Standard asphalt tiles are $1/8''$ thick $9'' \times 9''$ square. On special large-quantity orders $3/16''$ thick $12'' \times 12''$ tiles are available. Some manufacturers produce a grease-resistant asphalt tile for use where animal or vegetable oils are likely to be present; however, this type of tile has generally been replaced with vinyl-asbestos tile, which is inherently grease resistant.

TABLE 10-1 Asphalt-tile groups

GROUP	DESCRIPTION
B	Dark colors, lowest cost
C	Medium colors
Special patterns	Cork, terrazzo, decorative inserts
D	Light colors
Grease resistant	Highest cost

Asphalt tile is one of the least expensive of the resilient floorings. It is stained and softened by mineral oils and animal fats. The individual tiles are brittle and have poor recovery from indentation. However, it is one of the few types of resilient floorings that can be installed on a concrete slab below grade or in contact with water.

Vinyl

Vinyl floor coverings consist of mineral fillers, stabilizers, and pigments in a polyvinyl chloride (PVC) resin binder. The colorless resin permits a wider range of colors than those used in asphalt tile. Homogeneous vinyl tile may be filled or unfilled. *Unfilled vinyl* consists of an underlayment of decorative granules or pigments covered with a wearing surface of clear vinyl. The clear vinyl surface offers excellent resistance to wear and abrasion. *Filled vinyl* consists of particles or chips of vinyl sheets embedded in clear vinyl. The vinyl chips of various colors and shapes are spread over a clear vinyl base and bonded to it under heat and pressure. Additional vinyl coatings may be applied over the chips to form a superior wearing surface.

VINYL TILE   Vinyl tile may be homogeneous vinyl or backed vinyl. Backed vinyl tile is basically a vinyl sheet backed with asphalt-saturated felt and then cut into tile-sized units. Vinyl tiles are produced to simulate the color and texture of brick, quarry tile, wood parquet, and marble. Vinyl tiles are produced in $9'' \times 9''$ and $12'' \times 12''$ squares in standard thicknesses of $1/16''$, 0.080'', $3/32''$, and $1/8''$. Some manufacturers produce a wood-grained vinyl tile in sizes of $4'' \times 36''$ to simulate hardwood flooring. Feature decorator strips in solid colors are offered in $1/4''$, $1/2''$, and $1''$ widths, with other sizes available on special order.

SHEET VINYL   Sheet vinyl consists of a filled or unfilled vinyl wearing surface over an asphalt, rubber, or vinyl foam backing. Cushioned vinyl flooring consists of a heavy-duty layer of vinyl as a wearing surface and an underlayment of foamed vinyl. This produces a resilient flooring material with remarkable underfoot comfort and superior sound-absorption qualities.

Sheet vinyl is regularly manufactured in rolls 72'' wide and 42 to 100 ft long. The thickness of the sheet varies greatly, depending on the type of backing and the manufacturer. Vinyl products can be installed on any type of surface. Some of the translucent unfilled vinyls must be set with light-colored or clear adhesives. They have excellent resistance to grease, alkali, and stains; however, they are generally soft and subject to abrasion and indentation. Sheet vinyl is recommended only for installation above grade.

VINYL-ASBESTOS TILE   Vinyl asbestos is a versatile flooring material with a high resistance to abrasion and with lasting appearance. It requires little maintenance and can be installed above grade, on grade, or below grade. Vinyl-asbestos tile consists of blended compositions of asbestos fibers, vinyls, plasticizers, color pigments, and fillers formed into thin sheets under heat and pressure. The thin sheets, without backing, are cut into tiles.

Tiles are available in $9'' \times 9''$ squares in standard thicknesses of $1/16''$, $3/32''$, and $1/8''$. Some patterns are available in $12'' \times 12''$ squares. Vinyl-asbestos tile can be obtained

Fig. 10-2 Custom-designed vinyl-asbestos floor. (*Azrock Floor Products.*)

in many marbleized patterns which run completely through the tile. Textured tiles are produced to represent stone, travertine marble, wood, and exposed-aggregate concrete. Solid colors and accent strips in $1/2''$, $1''$, and $2''$ widths are available for special effects.

Vinyl-asbestos tile is semiflexible and must be installed over a rigid subfloor. It has excellent resistance to grease, oil, alkalis, and mild acids. It is generally quieter under foot than asphalt tile, and in many installations can be maintained for extended periods without waxing.

Rubber Tile

Rubber tile is produced from natural, reclaimed, or synthetic rubber. Mineral fillers and pigments are added to produce a limited range of colors and marbleized patterns. Several manufacturers produce embossed tiles for a textured finish. Standard sizes of rubber tile are $9'' \times 9''$ and $12'' \times 12''$, although some patterns are available in sizes of $18'' \times 36''$ and $36'' \times 36''$. Standard thicknesses are 0.080'', $1/8''$, and $1/16''$.

Rubber-tile floors are resilient under foot and have good resistance to indentation. Resistance to grease and

vegetable oil varies with the manufacturer. Most rubber tile is softened by petroleum derivitives. Rubber tile requires more maintenance than many other resilient floorings. Occasional buffing with steel wool and heavy waxing is required to maintain a high gloss. Rubber tile is not recommended for application on concrete slabs in contact with earth unless special sealers and adhesives are used.

Cork Tile

Cork tile consists of cork granules combined with a suitable thermosetting binder. The cork particles are subjected to a high compressive load and heat to form a smooth wearing surface. The top surface of the tile may be given a plastic coating to improve the wearing surface and develop a gloss.

Standard sizes are $6'' \times 6''$ and $12'' \times 12''$. Thicknesses range from $1/8''$ to $1/2''$, depending on the region and the manufacturer. The tile may be produced with square edges or beveled edges.

Cork-tile floors are particularly valuable where underfoot comfort and quietness are of paramount importance. However, their poor resistance to wear and impact loads make them extremely difficult to maintain. Cork tile is very susceptible to grease, alkalis, and stains. Cork tile must be kept covered with a heavy coat of wax. If the protective plastic coating is worn off, it cannot be successfully replaced after installation. Cork-tile floors should be used only above grade.

Bases and Accessories

Bases form a transition between the horizontal plane of the floor and the vertical plane of the wall. They may be straight bases, which form a sharp angle of almost 90° at the intersecting corner, or cove bases, which form a rounded transition between the two planes. There are several types of cove bases. *Butt cove base* is a rubber or vinyl base, in heights of $2\frac{1}{2}''$, $4''$, or $6''$, with a molded cove formed at the bottom. It is designed to butt to $1/8''$-thick resilient flooring. This provides a smooth, easy-to-clean joint between the base and the floor. *Top-set base*, in solid colors of vinyl or rubber, is installed on top of resilient flooring to form a functional or decorative intersection between the floor and wall. The top is tapered to form a tight joint with the wall surface, and the bottom is molded to form a slight cove at the intersection of the base and floor tile. Interior and external corners are premolded to assure tight joins. Some types of highly flexible vinyl top-set bases may be formed around external corners with the application of heat. Top-set bases are produced in heights of $2\frac{1}{2}''$, $4''$, and $6''$. *Flash cove base* is a combination border and coved base, usually of the same material as the resilient flooring. It may be in contrasting color or of the same color and pattern as sheet vinyl to form an integral border. Since the material is flexible, the cove at the junction of the horizontal and vertical surfaces must be backed by a structural fillet.

Special accessory shapes are produced for use with resilient floorings. Stair treads of rubber or vinyl come in many widths and surface textures. The treads may be smooth, ribbed, or impregnated with abrasives to provide a nonskid surface. Edge strips, threshholds, and carpet bars are available as transitions from one type of flooring to another.

SEAMLESS RESILIENT FLOORING

Seamless floorings composed of marble chips or various mineral fibers mixed with oxychlorides have been used for many years.

In the last decade many seamless resilient-flooring systems have been developed, consisting of plastic chips in a clear or pigmented resin, applied in liquid form. These materials produce a seamless surface that is easier to clean, requires considerably less maintenance, and has a higher resistance to abrasion, indentation, chemicals, and stain than other resilient floors. However, there are limitations to most of the systems that have been developed.

The most common system employs prime coats of epoxies and finish coats of urethane. Plastic chips are broadcast into the wet surface of a prime coat. Additional coatings of resins and plastic chips are applied until the prime coating is completely covered. The surface is allowed to dry and then sanded lightly, and several urethane glaze coats are applied as a wearing surface. The entire coating is 35 to 60 mils thick and has a textured

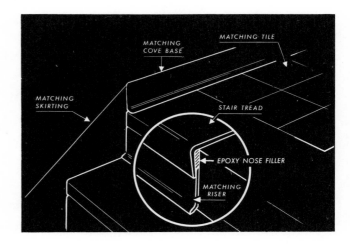

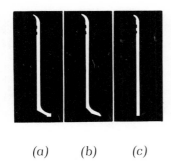

Fig. 10-3   Resilient-flooring bases. (*By permission of the Burke Rubber Company.*)

(a)   (b)   (c)

a. BUTT-COVE BASE

b. TOP-SET COVE BASE

c. CARPET BASE

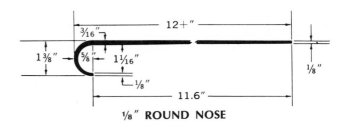

1/8" ROUND NOSE

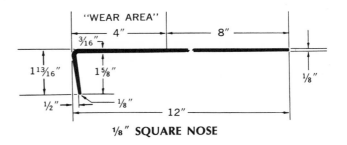

1/8" SQUARE NOSE

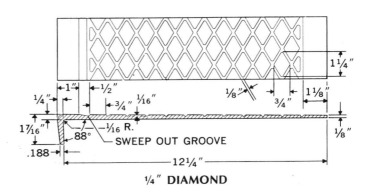

1/4" DIAMOND

Fig. 10-4   Stair treads. Square-nose 1/4-in. tread has same dimensions as 1/8 in., but thickness is uniform instead of tapered. (*By permission of the Burke Rubber Company.*)

"orange-peel" surface. The appearance and life of this flooring is dependent on constant maintenance and the application of additional glaze coats before any portions have been worn through to the plastic chips. For exterior applications, special urethanes must be used. This seamless flooring is subject to delamination of the flooring from the substrate if proper preparation and application procedures are not followed. Hydrostatic pressure, developed by the penetration of water through concrete slabs, will also cause delamination.

Another system is composed of epoxies throughout. It consists of a base coat 20 to 30 mils thick, into which plastic chips are broadcast. The base coat is allowed to dry, and is sanded lightly, and one or two coats of clear epoxy compounds are applied as a finish. Epoxy compounds that do not yellow or deteriorate in the sun permit exterior applications of the product. Epoxies have good adhesion to concrete; however, the substrate must be completely free from contamination. The floor must be reglazed periodically or heavily waxed to prevent wear in traffic patterns.

A recently developed system, not yet thoroughly field tested, consists of plastic chips in a base coat of acrylic, vinyl, or urethane water emulsion. The wet base coat is covered with plastic chips and allowed to dry, and one or

two coats of urethane are usually applied as a wearing surface.

The fourth type of seamless flooring consists of a polyester containing colored marble fines. The combination is poured onto the floor to form an ⅛-in. marbleized film. Application of this material requires considerable skill to achieve a realistic marble effect.

TERRAZZO

For centuries a form of mosaic flooring was produced by embedding small pieces of marble in mortar and polishing the surface. The Greeks used regularly shaped stones, marble, gems, and ceramic shapes set in gypsum as decorative flooring. Stones of regular and irregular shape were set in concrete and hand polished by the Romans in making decorative floors. Terrazzo as we know it today was not produced until after the development of portland cement in the eighteenth century. The word *terrazzo* is derived from the Italian word *terrassa*, meaning terrace. The National Terrazzo and Mosaic Association defines terrazzo as "a composition material, poured in place or precast, which is used for floor and wall treatment. It consists of marble chips, seeded or unseeded, with a binder or *matrix*

Fig. 10-5 Terrazzo floor in the People's Bank, Bellville, New Jersey, architect Neil J. Convery. (*National Terrazzo and Mosaic Association, Inc.*)

that is cementitious, noncementitious, or a combination of both." Terrazzo is poured, cured, and then ground, polished, or otherwise finished.

Types of Terrazzo Toppings

Marble is broadly defined in modern usage as any rock capable of being ground and taking a polish. There are hundreds of marbles that are used in terrazzo floorings. The marble is carefully quarried and selected to eliminate off-color or contaminated material. It is then crushed to eliminate flat flakes or slivers and sized to yield uniform chips for use in terrazzo. The wide range of colors may be combined to produce a great many colors and textures. Marble producers have established standards regulating the size of chips as shown in Table 10-2.

TABLE 10-2 Standard sizes of terrazzo chips

GAUGE	PASSES SCREEN, MAX. DIAM., IN.	RETAINED ON SCREEN, MIN. DIAM., IN.
0	1/8	1/16
1	1/4	1/8
2	3/8	1/4
3	1/2	3/8
4	5/8	1/2
5	3/4	5/8
6	7/8	3/4
7	1	7/8
8	1 1/8	1

Both standard grey cement and white cement are used in the installation of terrazzo. White portland cement is produced by careful selection of raw materials and greater color control during manufacture. It offers a clearer matrix for the colored marble chips and also lends itself to coloring by mineral pigments.

Terrazzo topping consists of two parts of selected marble granules, one part of portland cement, and not over 5 1/2 gal of water per sack of cement. The dry ingredients are mixed first. Colors are weighed and added dry to the mix. The water is then added and mixed in thoroughly.

The overall color and texture of terrazzo toppings depends on the size of marble granules, the percentage of each color used, and color of the cement matrix. The National Terrazzo and Mosaic Association publishes a handbook of color plates as a guide in selecting colors and finishes. These color plates show the finished appearance and the percentage of each color of marble and pigment used to produce it. The customary sizes of marble used for toppings are shown in Table 10-3.

TABLE 10-3 Marble toppings

TOPPING	COMPOSITION
Standard	Equal parts of 1- and 2-gauge chips of the same or different marbles
Intermediate	Varying percentages of gauges 1 to 5 or 6 to 8
Venetian	Larger chips than for intermediate topping

In *washed*, or *rustic*, *terrazzo* marble, quartz, quartzite, onyx, or granite chips may be used with either a white or a colored matrix. Instead of being ground and polished, the flooring is washed with water or acid to expose a pebbled surface. Abrasive toppings are developed by the

Fig. 10-6 Terrazzo color plates. (*National Terrazzo and Mosaic Association, Inc.*)

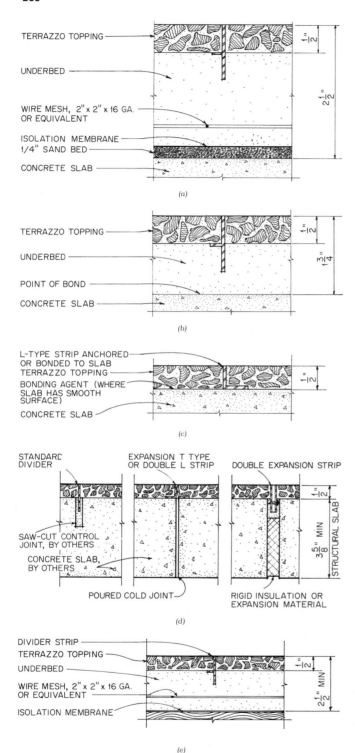

Fig. 10-7 Sections through terrazzo floors: (*a*) sand-cushion terrazzo; (*b*) terrazzo bonded to concrete; (*c*) terrazzo bonded to concrete with adhesive; (*d*) monolithic terrazzo; (*e*) terrazzo over wood, all conduit or pipe below terrazzo topping. (*By permission of the National Terrazzo and Mosaic Association, Inc.*)

addition of abrasives such as aluminum oxide to present a nonskid surface. *Conductive terrazzo* is used in hospital operating rooms to provide a floor that will ground the static electricity generated between persons and equipment. This lessens the danger of explosions of pure oxygen and anesthetics. Acetylene carbon black is mixed with the topping to provide a path for static electricity.

Divider Strips

Terrazzo floors are divided into panels by divider strips. The strips are installed to localize setting shrinkage of the topping and to control cracks caused by structural movement. They are located at points at which fractures would be likely if and when movement occurs. They are also used to separate panels of different colors. Panel size and shape is governed by room size and shape. Panels of 16 to 36 in. are common in lobbies and public places subject to heavy traffic. In offices and areas of moderate traffic panels may be from 25 to 50 in. Dividers are also used to separate different colors and to develop decorative patterns in large floor areas.

Dividers are most commonly made of half-hard brass, white alloy zinc (99 percent zinc), or colored plastic. The exposed face of divider strips ranges from 20 gauge to 1/8 in. or thicker. Dividers of 1/8 in. or thicker taper down to a thinner bottom portion. Dividers are usually 1 1/4 in. deep; however, 1 1/2-in. deep dividers are recommended for venetian terrazzo. Special expansion joints are produced for large areas.

Installation of Terrazzo

A terrazzo topping approximately 5/8 in. thick is placed over an underbed of concrete. Where structural movement is anticipated, a sand cushion, or floating underbed, is used. It consists of a 1/4-in. layer of sand on the structural member, covered with a layer of waterproof paper and reinforcing wire mesh. A 2 1/8-in. concrete slab is poured over the waterproof paper and the divider strips are embedded, with 5/8 in. left exposed for the topping. The total thickness of sand-cushion terrazzo, from the structural slab to the finish floor, is 3 in.

Bonded concrete underbeds are used for general areas where movement is not likely to occur, as in swimming pool decks, corridors, and walks. The base slab is coated with a neat coat of portland cement to ensure a good bond; a 1 1/8-in. underbase is poured, and the divider strips installed. The total thickness of the terrazzo is 1 3/4 in. Terrazzo toppings may also be monolithic with the structural slab. The divider strips must be placed when the slab is poured, with 5/8 in. left for the finish topping.

The underbed is coated with a thin layer of cement grout of the same composition and color as the cement that will be applied in the topping. The topping is placed in the panels formed by the divider strips, and sprinkled with chips of the same composition and percentages as the topping. The surface is compacted by heavy rollers until much of the water has been removed, and the surface is then troweled to expose the divider strips. The floors are carefully cured for at least 6 days.

When the floor has cured, it is ready for grinding and polishing. The floor is flooded with water and machine ground with abrasive stones. After the initial grinding a light grout of cement is applied to fill all voids. The floor is then ground until it is level and shows approximately 70 percent marble chips. After the final grinding, the floor is thoroughly cleaned and given a seal coat. It is then machine buffed to bring out color and luster of the marble chips and cement matrix.

Terrazzo may also be used as a wainscot extending up walls. A precast terrazzo cove base may be used at the intersection of horizontal and vertical surfaces, or an integral cove may be formed by the topping. Divider strips are installed in the wall underbed. The minimum thick-

ness for wainscots is 1 in., with a terrazzo topping of no less than $3/8$ in.

Precast Terrazzo

Precast terrazzo steps, risers, and other special shapes are available. The stair treads are usually $1\frac{1}{2}$ to 2 in. thick, with rounded or shaped edges. The steps are either set in $3/4$-in. underbeds or attached to steel stringers and steel plates. They are factory fabricated in waterproof molds. The terrazzo topping is compacted by vibration or compression and ground smooth.

Thin-set Terrazzo

Several thin-set terrazzo systems have been developed which use epoxies, polyesters, or latex as a matrix for the marble chips. These materials are bonded directly to the

Fig. 10-8 Inspecting dry-pressed tile bisque before firing. (*Interpace Corporation; Gaskins Creative Communications.*)

Fig. 10-9 Ceramic tile entering a tunnel kiln for firing glaze. (*Interpace Corporation.*)

structural slab, thereby eliminating the 1½- to 2⅛-in. underbed necessary with portland cement terrazzo. This reduces the weight, eliminates the need for depressing the slab to allow for the underbed, and shortens the setting time from 6 days to less than 24 hr with some products. Thin-set systems are usually ¼ to ⅝ in. thick. The thinner systems do not require divider strips except in locations where movement or stress is anticipated, as around columns and over beams.

All the thin-set systems are proprietary systems, and the manufacturer's instructions must be followed implicitly. Substrates must be cleaned carefully and prepared properly, or delamination will result. There are three basic types available. One is a standard portland cement topping mix, bonded to a substrate with polysulfides, vinyls, Neoprenes, or epoxies. The topping is usually ⅝ in. thick, placed between dividers that have been set in adhesive. The second type contains admixtures of vinyl or acrylic emulsions in the portland cement topping. The topping is laid ¼ in. thick over a substrate that has been coated with a bonding agent. The plastic admixtures give the topping greater tensile and flexural strength. A third type consists of marble chips held in a matrix of epoxy, Neoprene, or polyester, which can be installed as thin as ³⁄₁₆ in. The

plastic replaces the portland cement and produces a topping that has extremely high strength.

Magnesium oxychloride cement, sometimes called *magnesite*, and limestone fines and pigments, are combined with inert fillers to produce a material that hardens like portland cement concrete. A magnesium chloride solution and a dry-mix magnesium oxide, plus fillers and fine aggregates, are mixed to a paste ready to spread on the subfloor. It is usually applied ½ in. thick, and the surface is ground to simulate marble.

Oxychloride flooring can be applied over any type of structurally sound subfloor. It is not recommended for locations which are constantly wet or subject to hydrostatic pressure. However, it has been used successfully in southern California as a flooring for wood balconies and decks.

WALL AND FLOOR TILE

The word *tile* is derived from the Roman word *tegula*, meaning cover. Tiles of clay, cement, marble, or glass are used as floor and wall coverings. Structural and nonstructural hollow tile units are widely used in wall construction (see Chapter 4).

Ceramic Tile

The art of making ceramic tile is as old as civilization. Over 5000 years ago the Sumerians and the Babylonians produced brilliantly glazed tiles to protect the sun-dried bricks of their temples and palaces. One of the most interesting of these is a small temple erected about 3200 B.C. in the city of Erech in ancient Sumeria (now Iraq). The clay walls are decorated in a zigzag pattern of colorful tile mosaics in black, red, and white. The individual tiles are actually clay cones inserted into the walls, with only their round bases protruding. At one side of the temple stands a row of massive columns decorated with the same mosaics. Nothing is left of the Tower of Babel, built by Nebuchadnezzar. The Greek historian Herodotus, who visited the site in the fifth century B.C., described it as a wondrous building of seven levels, each faced with a different color of baked brick. On top was a shrine covered with brilliant blue glazed tile. Inside was a solid gold couch and table for the deity when he came down to earth.

The Persians, who conquered Babylon in 539 B.C., further developed the art of tile making by the use of rich glazes in reds, yellows, and blues. Moslems from the Arabian deserts conquered the Persians in 623 A.D. and adopted the use of glazed tiles for their palaces and mosques. As the Ottoman Empire spread, the skills of tile making were carried up into Spain. The tradition of beautiful tile work of Spain and Portugal was brought to the New World, where it has continued to flourish.

Ceramic tiles may be glazed or unglazed. They range in size from ⅜″ × ⅜″ mosaic tiles to 16″ × 18″ units and are produced with various physical properties and surface finishes.

Glazed Wall Tile

Most glazed ceramic tiles for interior use are produced by the *dust-press process*. A mixture of damp white-burning clays and other ceramic materials are forced into steel dies under heavy pressure. After pressing, the tile is inspected for smoothness, size, and imperfections. It may then be fired at a high temperature to form a *bisque*, a tile ready to be glazed. A glaze of ceramic materials and mineral pigments is sprayed on the bisque, and a second firing, at a lower temperature, fuses the glaze to the bisque. Some glazed tiles are produced with a single firing. In this process the tile is pressed, allowed to cure, given a coat of glaze, and then fired in the kiln.

Tiles are also made by extrusion, a slush-mold process, or a ram-press process. In the *extrusion process* the clay is mixed to the consistency of thick mud and forced through a die. The machine cuts the clay to proper lengths as it comes from the die. In the *slush-mold process* a wet mixture of clay is poured into molds and allowed to set. The tiles are then removed from the molds, glazed, and fired in a kiln. In the *ram-press process* tiles are formed between two steel dies. This method produces larger tiles of any shape or surface texture. The tiles are glazed and fired in the same manner as dust-pressed tile.

BODIES   Tiles are generally classified in terms of the amount of water they will absorb as impervious, vitreous, semi-vitreous, or nonvitreous. *Impervious tile*, the most dense tile produced, has a moisture absorption of less than 0.5 percent of its own weight. It is usually manufactured only on special order. *Vitreous tile* has a moisture absorption of less than 3 percent. *Semivitreous tile* has a water absorption of 3 to 7 percent. *Nonvitreous tile* has a water absorption of over 7 percent of its weight. Tiles used for exterior applications are generally vitreous or semi-vitreous. Nonvitreous tiles are suitable for interior use, where they will not be subject to impact or freezing and thawing conditions.

FINISHES   Glazed ceramic tiles may be finished with a highly reflective bright glaze, a matte glaze, with little or no sheen, or any of several intermediate satin finishes. Any color or shade can be produced, either plain or with a spotted, textured, mottled, rippled, or stippled surface.

Contoured or sculptured tiles offer opportunities for special decorative effects, either as accents or combined to form a textured wall. Picture tile, produced by a silk-screen process, may be also used as decorative accents, either singly or with two or more designs combined to form a panel. Some manufacturers can provide tile featuring emblems or other custom designs, hand painted or silk screened to order.

Tiles with special glazes are produced for use in areas subject to abrasive action or heavy wear, such as kitchen countertops and bathroom floors. These harder glazes are generally fired at higher temperatures and provide a finish that resists scratches and is not affected by direct contact with hot pots or household cleansers. Special glazed tiles are also produced for exterior use. These tiles will withstand freezing and thawing. They have a dense body and a durable glaze that resist abrasion and wear.

Faience tiles are surfaced with highly colored glazes simulating the renowned hand-crafted tiles produced during the Middle Ages in the Italian town of Faenza. They are either formed by hand in molds or cut from a ribbon of clay as it is forced through a die. They are produced with variations in edge, face, size, and glaze which give them a hand-crafted appearance.

SIZES AND SHAPES   Glazed tiles are usually produced in sizes of $4\frac{1}{4}'' \times 4\frac{1}{4}''$, $4\frac{1}{4}'' \times 6''$, and $6'' \times 6''$. Other sizes produced by some manufacturers are $1\frac{3}{8}'' \times 1\frac{3}{8}''$, $2'' \times 2''$, $3'' \times 3''$, $3'' \times 6''$, $6'' \times 9''$, $8'' \times 8''$, and $12'' \times 12''$. Hexagonal and octagonal tile in $3''$ and $4\frac{1}{4}''$ units are produced in a limited number of colors and glazes. Glazed interior tile are produced with straight grooves, scored or cut into the surface, to simulate the smaller glazed mosaic tile.

Most glazed tiles are $\frac{5}{16}''$ thick. Faience tiles vary in thickness according to the manufacturer from $\frac{7}{16}''$ to $\frac{3}{4}''$. Tiles may be produced with a square edge, so that each

Fig. 10-10   Sculptured-tile wall. (*Ceramic Tile Institute.*)

tile is installed flush with the adjoining tile, or with a cushion edge, which allows the grout joint to be below the wearing surface of the tile. Tiles may have *space lugs* on all four edges to assure a uniform grout joint of 3/64 in. between tiles.

Glazed trimmers, caps, end pieces, inside and outside corners, and special bullnose corners for use with thin-set methods are produced for borders and finish edges.

Glazed tiles are graded as standards or seconds on the basis of warpage and surface blemishes. Uniformity of color, texture, finish, and size are considered. Seconds have minor blemishes and variations not permissible in standard grade.

Mosaic Tile

CERAMIC MOSAIC   Tiles less than 6 sq in. in surface area and approximately 1/4 in. thick are usually classed as mosaic tiles. They may be glazed or unglazed. These tiles are impervious to water and have a dense body. There are two distinct types of ceramic mosaic tile: porcelain type or natural-clay type. *Porcelain types* are made by the dust-press method from a carefully proportioned blend of ceramic materials with a vitreous (glasslike) body which is resistant to freezing and thawing and to abrasive wear. A

wide range of colors is obtained by adding mineral pigments to the mix, so that the color goes all the way through the tile. The surface may be mottled, textured, or glazed. *Natural-clay types* are made of natural clays or shales, which produce a strong, long wearing body with a slightly textured surface. The color range of natural-clay tile is generally limited to the natural colors of the clays, although some color variations may be obtained by the addition of mineral oxides and dyes.

Both types of ceramic mosaics are suitable for walls, floors, and countertops, both inside and outside. Unglazed tiles are produced in either square-edged or cushion-edged types, depending on the manufacturer. The usual sizes are 1″ × 1″, 1″ × 2″, 2″ × 2″, 2″ hexagonal, and 1 3/16″ round.

Ceramic mosaic tiles are usually mounted, face down, on paper sheets about 1 by 2 ft. The sheet may contain tiles all of one type or patterns of different sizes and colors. Manufacturers publish suggested color and texture patterns as a guide in the selection of ceramic mosaics.

GLASS MOSAIC   Venetian glass mosaics consist of small pieces of molded glass (tesserae), 5/8″ × 5/8″ to 1 3/16″ × 1 3/16″ in size, combined to form textured panels or custom-designed walls, facings, bars, or tabletops. Most glass mosaic tiles are imported from Italy, although some are

Fig. 10-11   Hand-painted-tile panel at Disneyland, Anaheim, California. (*Produced by Interpace Corporation; courtesy of the Ceramic Tile Institute.*)

produced in Spain, Mexico, and Japan. Venetian glass is poured in waffle-type molds and allowed to cool. The pieces are then broken into individual *tessera* approximately ³/₁₆″ thick and are usually mounted face down on 12½″ × 12½″ sheets of paper.

Glass mosaic tiles come in a wide range of colors. Prices of different colors vary widely. Glass tile with pure gold used as a pigment can be extremely expensive, whereas other pigments are quite inexpensive. Tile may be assembled on sheets in the pattern in which it is to be installed. Glass tesserae may be individually cut, fit, and mounted, face down, on heavy paper to form mosaic murals. The sheets are then cut in sections, to be fitted together on the wall by the tilesetter. After the setting bed has hardened, the paper is removed from the tile face, revealing the design.

Another type of glass mosaic, called *Byzantine* or *smalti mosaic,* is produced from glass tile roughly ³/₈″ × ⁵/₈″ thick. Smalti tiles come in many colors and are hand cut to form murals, geometric designs, and interesting surface textures.

Quarry Tile

Quarry tile, usually an unglazed tile, is made from graded shapes and selected clays that produce an unusually strong, long-wearing surface. It is used primarily as flooring in residential construction and commercial buildings such as food-processing plants. The ease of maintenance and lasting qualities of quarry tile make it a preferred

Fig. 10-13 Ceramic mosaics set in quarry tile floor. (*Ceramic Tile Institute.*)

material for floor areas subject to heavy foot traffic and abrasion. It is also excellent for use on walls and countertops, where it will withstand impact from equipment and containers.

Quarry tile is manufactured by both dust-press and extrusion processes. The colors, produced by the natural clays and shales, range from reds through golds and buffs and from blacks and browns through greys. A paraglazed quarry tile is also produced in rich greys, greens, and browns. Quarry tile is produced with several surface patterns for special design effects. Tiles are available with indented designs glazed and the wearing surface unglazed. Such combinations provide unlimited possibilities for special effects.

Quarry tiles may be ground to size after firing. The larger sizes generally exhibit some warpage and surface irregularities. Tiles are produced in several thicknesses, from ¼″ up to 1½″, depending on their size. They are manufactured in squares, rectangles, and various geometric shapes. Table 10-4 illustrates the most common sizes and thicknesses.

Fig. 10-12 Modular breakdown of a 6″ × 6″ tile. (*By permission of the Ceramic Tile Institute.*)

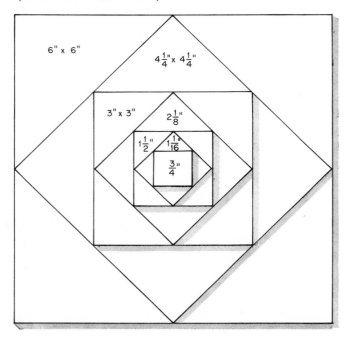

Fig. 10-14   Ceramic-mosaic panel. (*Mosaic Tile Company.*)

TABLE 10-4   Sizes and thicknesses of quarry tile

SIZE	THICKNESS, IN.
1″ × 1″	¼
Small geometric shapes	⅜
Large geometric shapes	½
2¾″ × 2¾″, 4″ × 4″	½
3⅞″ × 8″, 6″ × 6″	½, ¾
2¼″ × 8″, 3⅞″ × 8″	¾
6″ × 9″, 9″ × 9″	¾
3⅞″ × 8″	1
4″ × 8″	1⅜
4″ × 8″	1½

Special *paver tiles* are generally made of the same material as quarry tile, but they are thicker. They are available with either a smooth or a nonslip surface in 6″ × 6″ units ½″ thick. Paver tiles are used for heavy-duty floors in power plants, packing houses, and dairies. They are also used as fireplace hearths, stairs, and exterior walks in residences.

Cement Tile

Cement tiles, made of portland cement, aggregate, and mineral pigment, are cast in molds and compacted by vibration. They may be obtained in plain colors, mottled finishes, or patterns. The face may be left as cast or highly polished. Tiles are produced with ground faces and exposed colored aggregate resembling terrazzo. Exposed-aggregate tiles are manufactured by coating the form with a retarder. When the body of the tile has taken its initial set, the tile is removed from the mold, and the fines are washed or brushed from around the surface aggregate to expose the aggregate.

Cement tiles are produced in nominal sizes of 9″ × 9″ and 12″ × 12″, ¾″ thick, and 18″ × 18″, 1¼″ thick. The edges are usually square. When the tile is used as flooring, the joints are usually 1/16 in., although joints as wide as ½ in. are sometimes used for the larger units.

Tile Inserts and Accessories

Inserts in tile walls are installed by the tilesetter. These include soap dishes, grab bars, towel bars, paper holders, concealed lavatory units, and similar accessories. They may be of china, chrome-plated brass, or steel. Inserts to be installed in tilework are generally designed to fit into a particular module; standard modules are 6″ × 6″, 6″ × 3″, 4¼″ × 4¼″, or 4¼″ × 6″.

TILESETTING

Grout

Grout is a strong, cementitious material used for filling the joints between tile. Several types of grout are used for this purpose. *Portland cement grout* is composed of grey or white portland cement mixed with water to a creamy consistency and forced between the joints from the outside. This type of grout tends to show unevenness in color owing to variations in the depth of the bed and porosity of the surface. Commercial grouts are produced by a number of manufacturers. Some consist of white portland cement mixed with titanium dioxide to produce a uniformly white joint. Others are colored to match or contrast with particular tile colors. Nonstaining grouts of epoxy resin have been developed for use in locations subject to excessive staining action. They are particularly valuable where an acid- or alkali-resistant floor is needed. Flexible grouts, latex rubbers specially compounded for mixing with portland cement grout, are available for use where movement in the underlying structure is anticipated. These products require strict adherence to the manufacturers' instructions.

Mortar

Four basic methods have been developed for the setting of tile. Each of these methods has features that make it particularly valuable for specific installations. New methods developed within the last twenty years have not only increased the versatility of tile as a wall- and floor-surfacing material, but have reduced the cost of tile installations.

PORTLAND CEMENT MORTAR   The conventional mortar for setting tile consists of one part of portland cement to five parts of sand for floors and one part of cement, six parts of sand, and up to one part of hydrated lime for walls. The tile is set over a setting bed, or *float coat*, of portland cement mortar placed 1¼ in. thick on floors and ¾ in. thick on walls. If the setting bed is applied over wood studs, it is reinforced with metal lath, and the studs are protected with waterproof building paper. In wood-stud construction the setting bed is applied over a scratch coat of portland cement plaster.

The setting bed is screeded level and plumbed to proper plane. Only enough wall or floor area is covered with the setting bed to allow the tile to be pressed into true alignment. A bond coat of neat portland cement paste, 1/32 to 1/16 in. thick, is applied over the setting bed while it is still wet. Tiles that have been soaked in water for at least a half-hour are then pressed, or *beat*, into the bond coat. After curing, the tile is grouted with portland cement or other grout.

DRY-SET MORTAR   Portland cement mortars with water-retentive additives may be spread as thin as 3/32 in. over a pre-leveled deck or wall. The mortar is applied with a notched trowel to a suitable backing. This method eliminates the need for soaking the tile and its backing before installation. Dry-set mortar should never be applied directly to gypsum plaster, masonite, or wood.

ORGANIC ADHESIVES   Solvent-base latex adhesives are produced which are ready for use without the addition of liquids and cure by evaporation. They are applied with a notched trowel to properly prepared surfaces. As with other thin-set methods, the underbed must be perfectly true. Any irregularities in the surface of the underbed will be reflected in the tile surface. Priming is recommended for most surfaces. This method is generally not suitable for wet areas such as kitchens, bathrooms, and showers or in areas subject to heavy traffic. The tile must not be grouted until the solvent in the adhesive has been allowed to evaporate. Some organic adhesives are toxic and inflammable and must be handled with care.

Fig. 10-15   Glass-mosaic panel at LLoret De La Mar, Costa Brava, Spain.

EPOXY MORTAR   Epoxy resins, mixed on the job with a resin hardener, are used where a high bond strength or resistance to acids is important. This mortar is applied in a smooth, thin layer and will bond to either wet or dry surfaces. The mortar must be applied and the tile set within a given time after the resin and hardener have been mixed. The *pot life* of the material after it is mixed, its adhesive qualities and chemical resistance, and application methods vary with the manufacturer. The manufacturers' instructions must be followed carefully.

FURAN MORTAR   Furan mortar consists of furan resin and hardener similar to the two-part epozy system. The properties vary with the manufacturer.

WALL COVERINGS

Wall coverings, applied to interior or exterior structural walls as a final finish, are supplied prefinished or unfinished in either roll or sheet form. Such materials include porcelain-enameled metal panels, flexible wood veneer,

Fig. 10-16   Setting glass-mosaic tile. (*By permission of the Ceramic Tile Institute.*)

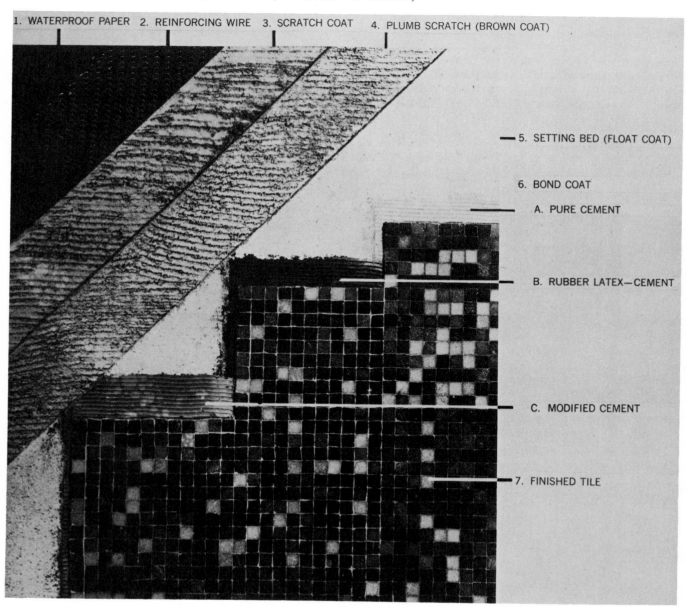

1. WATERPROOF PAPER   2. REINFORCING WIRE   3. SCRATCH COAT   4. PLUMB SCRATCH (BROWN COAT)

5. SETTING BED (FLOAT COAT)

6. BOND COAT

A. PURE CEMENT

B. RUBBER LATEX—CEMENT

C. MODIFIED CEMENT

7. FINISHED TILE

plastic-laminate paneling, and vinyl plastics either as a monolithic vinyl covering or bonded to cloth or paper backing.

Porcelain-enameled Metal

Porcelain-enameled metal sheets are used for both interior and exterior walls. The porcelain enamel consists of low-temperature-softening glass fused to aluminum or steel sheets. Porcelain-enameled sheets are produced in a wide variety of colors and textures. Facing panels are produced of porcelain enamel over textured aluminum. The finish coating resembles a smooth uniform layer of colored, opaque glass and has the same abrasion and corrosion resistance as glass.

Porcelain-enameled sheets are used for fascias, column covers, spandrels, mullion covers, and entrance facings. The glass-hard enamel surface makes them particularly suitable where wind-blown dust, corrosive atmospheres, or salt sprays are anticipated. The panels may be attached to the structural members with self-tapping screws or backed with insulation for use in curtain-wall construction. Porcelain-enameled sheets may be bonded to cement-asbestos boards to ensure maximum flatness for exterior application.

Flexible Wood Veneer

Thin-sliced hardwoods (0.012 in. or less) are bonded to a backing to produce wall coverings that are similar to wallpaper. The thin wood veneer is treated to make it flexible. It can be bent around corners parallel to the grain and fit to curved surfaces. The backing may be paper or woven cotton cloth. Matched veneer panels or random panels in several selected hardwoods are available. The surface of the wood veneer may be unfinished or prefinished.

Flexible wood-veneer sheets are usually produced in 24″ widths up to 12 ft long, depending on the type of wood. End-matched sheets are available for walls of 30 ft or more in height. Flexible wood veneer may be applied to an

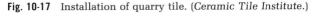

Fig. 10-17 Installation of quarry tile. (*Ceramic Tile Institute.*)

incombustible surface with a special adhesive, for use where building or fire regulations do not allow solid wood or plywood paneling.

The surface to which the material is applied must be perfect; as the veneer is very thin, any surface irregularities will be reflected in the veneered surface.

Vinyl Wall Coverings

Vinyl wall coverings consist of a coating of polyvinyl chloride resins, pigments, stabilizers, and plasticizers fused to a dimensionally stable, preshrunk cotton backing. A clear vinyl surface sheet may be placed over the base sheet and fused by heat and pressure. This produces a tough flexible material which can be applied by standard wallpaper-hanging techniques and provides permanent protection with low upkeep and assured fire resistance. Vinyl wall coverings with a clear coating of vinyl-fluoride resins are particularly effective in hospitals and restaurants because of the ease of cleaning. They are also widely used in schools, since ballpoint ink, lipstick, shoe polish, and crayons wipe off easily. Sheets are available in widths of 24″, 48″, and 50″ and lengths ranging from 6 to 35 yards. Vinyl coverings are produced in a wide

Fig. 10-19 Decorative inserts in tile walls. (*Ceramic Tile Institute.*)

Fig. 10-18 Cement-tile paving. (*Ceramic Tile Institute.*)

range of colors and textures. Many patterns have been developed to simulate fabric textures, grass cloths, straw, wood grains, and various sculptured effects.

Most vinyl coverings are backed with tightly woven, preshrunk, cotton. However, nonwoven fiberglass, asbestos, or other materials may be used for greater flexibility or to meet certain physical requirements. Three weights are generally available: light duty (7 oz/sq ft), medium duty (13 oz/sq ft), and heavy duty (22 oz/sq ft). Light-duty materials are suitable for walls not subject to heavy wear. Medium-duty types are used in areas subject to moderate wear, such as offices, reception rooms, and dining rooms. The heavy-duty materials are placed in locations subject to heavy wear, such as school corridors, gymnasiums, and service areas. Backings may be either

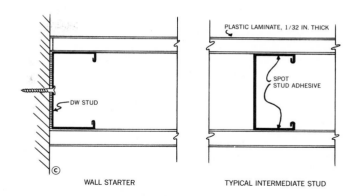

Fig. 10-21 Construction of plastic-laminate covered partitions. (*By permission of Wilson Art.*)

Fig. 10-20 Installation of ceramic tile with portland cement mortar: (*a*) tile over wood or steel studs with plaster above wainscot; (*b*) tile over wood or steel studs with solid covered backing; (*c*) tile over solid-wall construction with plaster above wainscot; (*d*) tile over solid-wall construction without plaster above wainscot; (*e*) tile over heavy-gauge steel. (*By permission of the Ceramic Tile Institute.*)

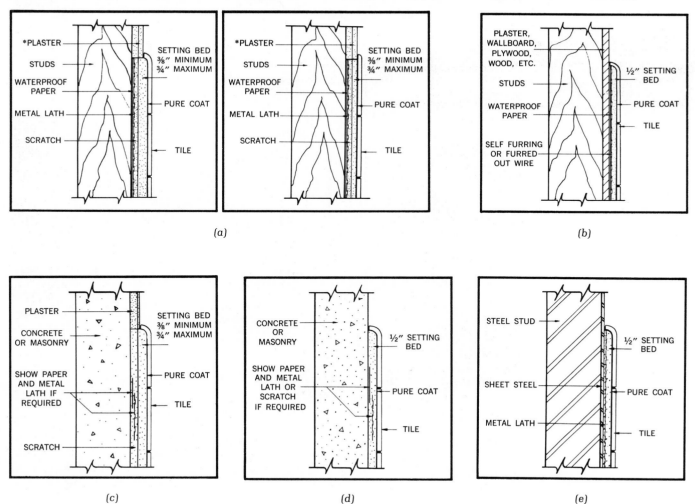

untreated or treated with a mildew-resistant chemical. Vinyl wall coverings are also classified for fire hazard on the basis of flame spread, fuel contributed, and smoke developed under laboratory test conditions. Many building codes require vinyl-coated wall coverings to meet specific ratings for certain installations. Manufacturers should be able to furnish laboratory reports showing that their products meet these requirements.

Vinyl coverings are applied with the joints butted, as the material will not stick to itself. Joints are never made at corners where they might be subject to tearing. They are applied with the adhesive recommended by the manu-

Fig. 10-22 Plastic-laminate paneling formulated for exterior use, Formica Plant, Roseville, California, architect A. Reasoner. (*By permission of the Formica Corporation.*)

facturer. Any type of rigid, smooth surface is suitable for application. Priming with a material recommended by the manufacturer may be necessary on some surfaces.

Plastic-surfaced Paneling

Plastic-surfaced paneling is produced in many colors, textures, and simulated wood grains. Hardboard panels, some grooved to simulate wood paneling, are printed and textured, then given a vinyl coating. Panels of ⅛″ hardboard are intended for adhesive installation; ¼″ panels are installed like wood paneling. Vinyl-surfaced gypsumboard panels, both ⅜″ and ½″, are produced as interior wall paneling.

High-pressure melemine plastic laminates, which have been used for years as kitchen countertops and bathroom pullmans, are being used increasingly as wall surfacing in both residential and commercial buildings because of their ease of maintenance and design versatility. They are produced in a wide range of wood-grain patterns, solid colors, and textures. Silk-screened designs can also be produced on special order.

The plastic surfacing is laminated to sheets of ⅜″ particleboard which is backed by a 0.20-in. stabilizing laminate. One type of paneling consists of a high-pressure laminate backed with polystyrene foam. The foam backing is intended to crush slightly when the paneling is installed, so that it accommodates surface irregularities. The panels are usually fabricated in 16″ and 24″ widths and 8-, 10-, or 12-ft lengths. The total thickness of the paneling is ⁷⁄₁₆″, although ½″, ¾″, and 1″ thicknesses are available on special order.

Laminate paneling is usually installed over 1 × 3 stripping applied horizontally 16 in. on center. The air space behind the paneling increases the sound-deadening qualities of the wall. Matching moldings are produced as caps for wainscoting, bases, and trim. Individual panels are joined with metal splines, which may be concealed in some systems. Metal strips are produced to form inside and outside corners. One manufacturer produces paneling that provides flush joints between the sheets by means of a special tongue and groove.

QUESTIONS

1. What are five factors that influence the selection of flooring materials?

2. What are the characteristics of high-quality wood flooring?

3. Describe five types of hardwood used for flooring.

4. Describe four types of resilient flooring and give the advantages and limitations of each.

5. What type of resilient flooring would you recommend for installation on: (a) concrete slabs below grade? (b) concrete slabs on grade? (c) concrete slabs above grade?

6. What are the advantages of oxychloride flooring?

7. How are seamless resilient floorings applied?

8. How is terrazzo installed?

9. What are the limitations of terrazzo flooring?

10. Describe the manufacture of glazed ceramic tile.

11. What is vitreous tile?

12. What are the common sizes of glazed wall tile?

13. Describe the process of installing ceramic mosaic tile.

14. What is the difference between square-edge and cushion-edge tile?

15. How are glass mosaics set?

16. What is quarry tile, and where is it used?

17. What is the difference between grout and mortar?

18. Describe four methods of setting ceramic tile.

19. What is faience tile, and where might it be used?

20. Compare glazed and unglazed ceramic tile.

21. What factors must be considered in selecting wall coverings?

22. Describe flexible wood-veneer wall coverings.

23. Describe three types of vinyl wall coverings and where each would be used.

24. What is meant by flame spread?

25. Give the trade names of four types of high-pressure melamine plastic laminates.

REFERENCES FOR FURTHER STUDY

Almy, Richard: "Vinyl Flooring," The *Construction Specifier*, January 1961, p. 38.

Armstrong Cork Company: 97200 Flair Drive, El Monte, Calif., 91734. "Floors: Technical Data," 1968.

Asphalt and Vinyl Tile Institute: "Resilient Floorings," *The Construction Specifier*, October 1968, p. 37.

Callender, John Hancock: "Time-Saver Standards," 4th ed., McGraw-Hill, New York, 1966.

Ceramic Tile Institute: 3415 West Eighth Street, Los Angeles, Calif., 90005. "Standard Specifications for Installation of Ceramic Tile," 1961.

Construction Specifications Institute: Suite 300, 1150 17th Street, N.W., Washington, D.C., 20036. "Specifying Wood Flooring: Parquet Adhesively Applied," 1968. "Specifying Tile: Ceramic," 1966. "Specifying Resilient Flooring," 1965. "Specifying Portland Cement Terrazzo: Cast in Place Floors," 1967. "Specifying

Vinyl-coated Fabric," 1969. "An Introduction to Carpet," 1969.

Construction Specifications Institute, Los Angeles Chapter: P.O. Box 65756, Los Angeles, Calif., 90065. "Specifying Quarry Tile," 1966. "Inspectors' Checklist for Ceramic, Glass and Marble Tile," 1965. "Specifying Vitreous Wall Coatings," 1965.

Georgia-Pacific Corporation: P.O. Box 311, Portland, Ore., 97207. "Georgia-Pacific Building Products," 1968.

Hornbostel, Caleb: "Materials for Architecture," Reinhold, New York, 1961.

International Pipe and Ceramics Corporation: 2901 Los Feliz Boulevard, Los Angeles, Calif., 90039. "Gladding, McBean Building Products," 1962.

Merritt, Frederick S.: "Building Construction Handbook," McGraw-Hill, New York, 1958.

National Terrazzo and Mosaic Association: 1901 Fort Myer Drive, Arlington, Va., 22209. "Terrazzo Catalog," 1966; "Terrazzo, Specifications Details, Technical Data," 1966.

Schmidt, John L.: "A Handbook of Homebuilding Design and Construction," McGraw-Hill, New York, 1966.

Tile Council of America, Inc.: 800 Second Avenue, New York, N.Y., 10017. "1969 Handbook for Ceramic Tile Installation." "Highlights of Tile Technical Progress," 1962.

DOORS

Many types of exterior doors are available to provide access, protection, safety, and privacy. Interior doors control the passage of sound and separate interior living spaces. They may be used to conceal storage areas or as movable partitions to provide flexible interior areas. Sliding metal- or wood-framed glass doors are used to connect indoor and outdoor spaces visually as a means to indoor-outdoor living.

Because of its ease of workability and its availability, wood soon followed hanging animal hides as a material for doors. However, since wood tends to warp, solid wood slabs were soon replaced by doors made of many pieces of solid wood joined together by ingenious methods. The familiar paneled doors were developed in an attempt to hide as many joints as possible. The mass production of plywood after World War II brought about the substitution of thin plywood for door panels. The use of plywood skins over wood frameworks has led to the widespread use of the *flush door*. Flush doors account for almost three-fourths of the doors produced in the United States.

Wood, metal, plastics, glass, and various combinations of these materials are used in the manufacture of doors. The selection of door type or material depends not only on the degree of protection or privacy desired, but on such factors as architectural compatibility, esthetics, psychological effect, fire resistance, and cost. Doors may be hinged at the side to open and shut in one direction or they may be double-acting doors, which swing both ways. They may be hinged at the top to swing up or at the bottom to swing down. They may be hung on tracks or rest on rollers to slide past each other horizontally or disappear into pockets. They may consist of leaves hinged to fold against each other or be set on pivots to revolve around a vertical axis in the center of an opening.

Door Frames

The portion of a doorway against which a door swings and to which it is hinged is known as the *door frame*. This consists of two side pieces called *jambs* and an overhead piece

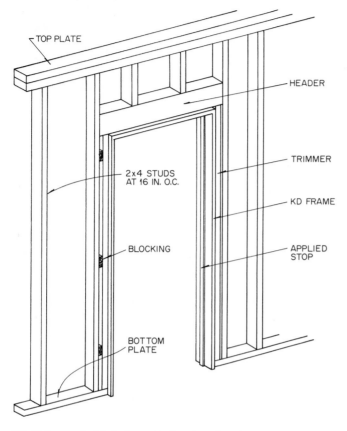

Fig. 11-1 Typical interior swinging-door framing.

Labels on figure: TOP PLATE, HEADER, 2×4 STUDS AT 16 IN. O.C., TRIMMER, KD FRAME, BLOCKING, APPLIED STOP, BOTTOM PLATE

to carry the load of the wall above the opening. In masonry walls door frames may be fastened to the walls by metal anchors built into the masonry. Wood frames, called *bucks*, may be built into masonry walls to form an anchorage for door frames. The joints between the frame and wall are covered with *casing* or *trim*.

Framed glass openings over doors are called *transoms*. The framing member between the top of the door and the opening above is referred to as the *transom bar*. The glazed opening may be included as part of the door frame or it may be framed separately. Framed glass openings at the side of a door are called *side-lights*.

Door Swings and Sizes

The most common type of door is the *swinging door*, classed as either right hand or left hand, depending on which side is hinged. If a person is standing on the outside of an exterior door, the corridor side of an interior door, or the room side of a closet door, and the *hinges* are on the left-hand side, the door is said to be a *left-hand door*. For a door to swing freely in an opening, the vertical edge

Fig. 11-2 Interior door casing and trim. PS 32-70, hinged interior door units. (*U.S. Department of Commerce.*)

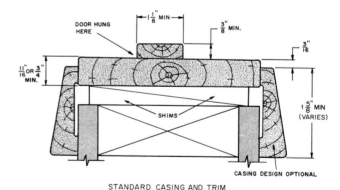

STANDARD CASING AND TRIM

ADJUSTABLE CASING AND TRIM

called a *head*. Exterior wood doors usually have a horizontal piece of hardwood at the bottom of the opening called a *sill*. A *threshold*, a thin, shaped wood or metal strip, is used to cover the joint between the sill and the flooring material at exterior doors, to provide clearance allowing the door to swing, or to provide a reasonably weathertight seal at the bottom of the door.

The bottom of the door may be equipped with a length of hooked metal that engages with a specially shaped threshold to provide a weatherstripped door. Metal thresholds are available with flexible synthetic rubber tubes that press tightly against the bottom of the door to seal out water and cold air.

Door frames may be delivered to the job knocked-down or subassembled and ready for installation. Interior wood door frames are usually manufactured from 3/4″ material; exterior door frames are milled from thicker material. The *door stop*, a projection or strip against which the door closes, is usually applied to interior door frames after they have been installed and plumbed. The stop on exterior door frames is usually an integral part of the frame. This is called a *rebated* or *rabbeted frame*. Door frames set in wood stud walls are usually stiffened by a *trimmer* on both sides of the opening. The trimmer in turn supports a *header*

opposite the hinges must be beveled slightly. On a left-hand door that swings away from the viewer, a *left-hand regular bevel* is used; if the door opens toward the viewer it has a *left-hand reverse bevel*. Similarly, if the hinges are on the right and the door swings toward the viewer, it has a *right-hand reverse bevel*.

A door that swings both ways through an opening is called a *double-acting door*. Two doors that are hinged on opposite sides of a doorway and open from the center are referred to as *double doors*; such doors are frequently double acting. One leaf of a double door may be equipped with an *astragal*, an extended lip that fits over the crack between the two doors. A *Dutch door* is one that is cut and hinged so that top and bottom portions open and close independently.

Interior doors are produced in standard widths of 2'-0", 2'-4", 2'-6", and 2'-8". Interior doors through which furniture must be moved should be at least, 2'-6", and preferably 2'-8". Exterior secondary doors are usually 2'-6" or 2'-8", and entrance doors 3'-0", 3'-6", or 4'-0". The standard door height is 6'-8", although doors are sometimes produced in heights of 7'-0" and may be ordered up to 8'-0". Interior doors are usually 1⅜" thick, and exterior doors are usually 1¾"; exterior doors 2" and 2¼" thick are available on special order. Storm doors and screen doors are usually 1⅛" thick.

WOOD DOORS

Wood doors may be either hollow-core or solid-core construction. Solid-core doors are used as exterior doors, in locations where extremely heavy service is anticipated, or where additional fireproofing is desired, as with doors into garages or heater rooms. Hollow-core doors are used only for interior applications. Wood doors are classified according to method of construction as *panel doors* or *flush doors*.

Panel Doors

A panel door, or stile-and-rail door, consists of vertical members called *stiles* and horizontal members called *rails* which enclose panels of solid wood, plywood, louvers, or glass. The stiles are vertical members extending the full height at each side of the door. The vertical member at the hinged side of the door is called the *hinge* or *hanging stile*, and the one to which the latch, lock, or push is attached is called the *closing* or *lock stile*. Three rails run across the full width of the door between the stiles: the top rail, the intermediate or *lock rail*, and the bottom rail. Additional vertical or horizontal members, called *muntins*, may divide the door into any number of panels. The rails, stiles, and muntins may be assembled with either glued dowels or mortise-and-tenon joints.

Panel doors in which one or more panels are glass are classed as *sash doors*. Fully glazed panel doors, with only a top and a bottom rail and with or without horizontal or vertical muntins are referred to as *casement doors* or *French doors*. *Storm doors* are lightly constructed glazed doors for use in conjunction with exterior doors to improve weather resistance in cold climates. *Combination doors* consist of interchangeable or hinged glass and screen panels to fit into sash doors.

Flush Doors

Flush doors are usually made up of sheets of thin veneer over a solid core of wood, particleboard, or fiberboard; or over a hollow-core grid of paper, wood strips, or plastics. The veneer faces act as stressed-skin panels and tend to stabilize the door against warping. The face veneer may be of ungraded hardwood suitable for a plain finish or selected hardwood suitable for a natural finish. The appearance of flush doors may be enhanced by the application of plant-on decorative panels. Several patterns are marketed for home craftsmen. Both hollow-core and solid-core doors usually have solid internal rails and stiles so that hinges and other hardware may be set in solid wood.

Fig. 11-3 Typical exterior swinging-door framing.

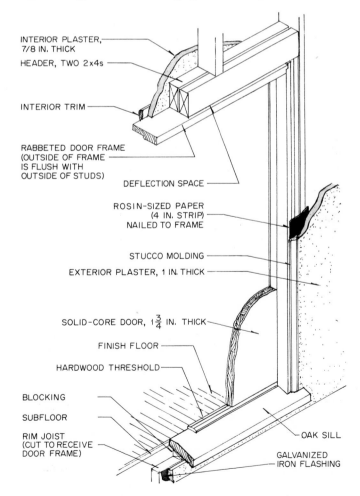

INTERIOR PLASTER,
7/8 IN. THICK

HEADER, TWO 2x4s

INTERIOR TRIM

RABBETED DOOR FRAME
(OUTSIDE OF FRAME
IS FLUSH WITH
OUTSIDE OF STUDS)

DEFLECTION SPACE

ROSIN-SIZED PAPER
(4 IN. STRIP)
NAILED TO FRAME

STUCCO MOLDING

EXTERIOR PLASTER, 1 IN. THICK

SOLID-CORE DOOR, 1¾ IN. THICK

FINISH FLOOR

HARDWOOD THRESHOLD

BLOCKING

SUBFLOOR

RIM JOIST
(CUT TO RECEIVE
DOOR FRAME)

OAK SILL

GALVANIZED
IRON FLASHING

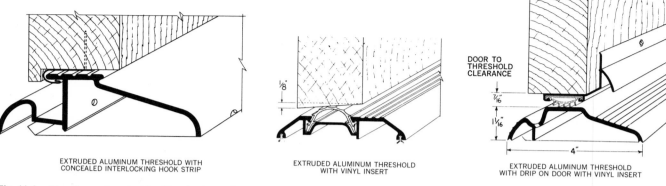

EXTRUDED ALUMINUM THRESHOLD WITH
CONCEALED INTERLOCKING HOOK STRIP

EXTRUDED ALUMINUM THRESHOLD
WITH VINYL INSERT

EXTRUDED ALUMINUM THRESHOLD
WITH DRIP ON DOOR WITH VINYL INSERT

Fig. 11-4 Aluminum thresholds. (*Pemko Manufacturing Company.*)

SOLID-CORE DOORS   Two types of solid wood cores are widely used in flush-door construction. The first type, called a *continuous-block, strip,* or *wood-stave core,* consists of low-density wood blocks or strips which are glued together in adjacent vertical rows, with the end joints staggered. This is the most economical type of solid core. However, it is subject to excessive expansion and contraction unless it is sealed with an impervious skin such as a plastic laminate. The second type is the stile-and-rail core, in which blocks are glued up as panels inside the stiles and rails. This type of core is highly resistant to warpage and is more dimensionally stable than the continuous-block core.

In addition to the solid lumber cores, there are two types of composition solid cores. *Mineral cores* consist of inert mineral fibers bonded into rigid panels. The panels are framed within wood rails and stiles, resulting in a core that is light in weight and little affected by moisture. Because of its low density, this type of door should not be used where sound control is important. *Particleboard cores,* consisting of wood chips or vegetable fibers mixed with resins or other binders, are also formed under heat and pressure into solid panels. This type of core requires a solid-perimeter frame. Since particleboard has no grain direction, it provides exceptional dimensional stability and freedom from warpage. Because of its low screw-holding ability, it is usually desirable to install wood blocks in the core at locations where hardware will be attached.

HOLLOW-CORE DOORS   The American Woodwork Institute outlines standards and describes construction procedures for hollow-core doors in AWI Bulletin 5, as shown in Table 11-1.

GRADES OF FACE VENEER   The National Woodwork Manufacturers' Association (NWMA I.S. 1-66) and the U.S. Department of Commerce (CS-171-58 and CS-35-61) have established standards for flush doors on the basis of their ability to withstand weather and water. Type I doors are manufactured with *waterproof* glues and are suitable for exterior use. Type II doors are produced with *water-resistant* glues and are suitable for interior use only. The hardwood face panels are also graded according to grain, color, and type of finish for which they are suitable, as shown in Table 11-2.

Fig. 11-5 Door swings.

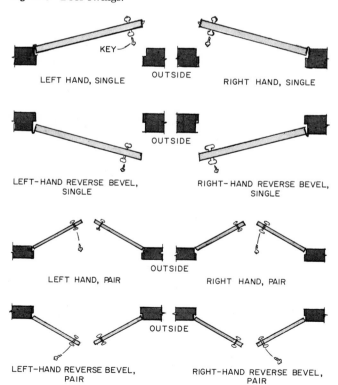

LEFT HAND, SINGLE

KEY

OUTSIDE

RIGHT HAND, SINGLE

LEFT-HAND REVERSE BEVEL,
SINGLE

OUTSIDE

RIGHT-HAND REVERSE BEVEL,
SINGLE

LEFT HAND, PAIR

OUTSIDE

RIGHT HAND, PAIR

LEFT-HAND REVERSE BEVEL,
PAIR

OUTSIDE

RIGHT-HAND REVERSE BEVEL,
PAIR

TABLE 11-1 Grades of hollow-core doors

GRADE	DESCRIPTION
Premium or institutional grade	Core composed of strips of wood, wood derivatives, or insulation board, usually placed in geometric patterns as an interlocking grid. This core is framed with solid wood rails and stiles and has solid wood blocks for hardware installation. It is reasonably stable but must be used with caution where extreme changes in humidity are likely.
Custom grade	Cores are similar to premium grade, except the rails and stiles are thinner.
Economy grade	Cores such as honeycombs made of resin-impregnated kraft paper or thin wood spirals spanning from face to face of the exterior panels; edging and blocking the same as for custom grade. Core material may be any one of several types, and quality varies widely, depending on type of core.
Hollow-core composition core	Core is similar to solid particleboard core, except that it is molded with tubular cores in the material.

By permission of the American Woodwork Institute.

OPENINGS IN FLUSH DOORS Openings may be provided in flush doors for the installation of glass panels or louvers. Openings in exterior flush doors subject to weather are usually lined with a hardwood molding that extends through the door and is turned down over the outside face to form a drip. Thin metal flashing may be inserted under the exterior removable molding which holds the glass. Moveable glass louvers may be installed in openings for ventilation as well as light.

TABLE 11-2 Grades of face veneer for flush doors

GRADE	DESCRIPTION
Specialty	Specially matched veneer characteristics, for use in connection with hardwood wall paneling or for special effects.
Premium	Veneers smoothly cut and free of defects, intended to receive a natural finish. If the veneer face consists of more than one piece, the pieces are approximately the same width and are matched for color and grain at the veneer joint.
Good	Veneers similar to those of premium grade, except not matched in color or grain. Usually satisfactory when stained before the final finish.
Sound	Intended for painted finish; allows any defect that will not be visible after two coats of paint have been applied.

Fig. 11-6 Types of solid-core doors.

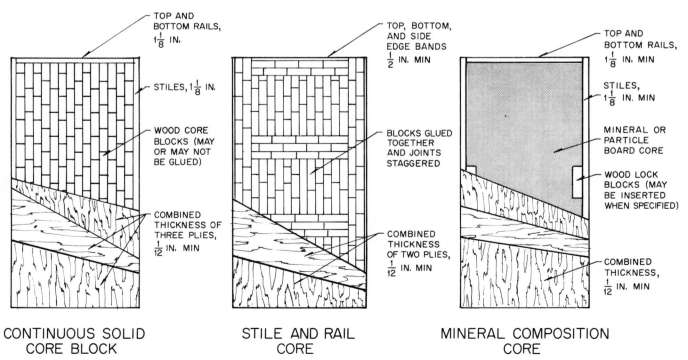

CONTINUOUS SOLID CORE BLOCK

STILE AND RAIL CORE

MINERAL COMPOSITION CORE

Louver Doors

Full louver doors consist of horizontal wood slats within a stile-and-rail frame. The louvers may be beveled flat slats, rounded-edge slats or V-shaped slats classified as *sightproof* louvers. Some building codes require louvers at the top and bottom of doors to gas water-heater compartments. Louvers may be installed in the bottom portion of doors to act as return air passages for air-conditioned spaces. Louver doors are useful for interior locations where sound privacy is not required and for closet and laundry-area doors where ventilation and dissipation of moisture is important.

Laminated-plastic-clad Doors

Both hollow-core and solid-core flush doors covered in high-pressure melamine laminates such as Formica are precision manufactured to fit specific openings. The plastic laminate is applied to both faces of the door and to both vertical edges. Cutouts for hinges and door-operating hardware are usually made at the factory from manufacturers' templates. Cutouts and view panels are installed in hardwood molding applied before delivery. The plastic-laminate covering comes in a wide variety of solid colors and in many wood-grain patterns. The surface may have a matte finish or a bright smooth finish for easy cleaning.

Plastic-laminate-clad doors offer good resistance to impact and abrasion and usually do not need refinishing for the life of the building. The surface resists staining and can be cleaned with soap and water or detergents. The cost of this type of door is comparable with that of solid

wood types and metal doors, as no finishing is required and the speed of installation greatly reduces the job labor costs. The dimensional stability of the door is improved because of the impervious nature of the plastic laminate face. However, because of the dissimilarity of the plastic-laminate face and the core, plastic-laminate-covered doors tend to warp if they are not completely sealed. They are not recommended for use in direct sun. Although they have high resistance to abrasion and impact, once they have been damaged, they must usually be returned to the factory, where proper equipment and tools are available to repair the surface.

SLIDING AND FOLDING DOORS

Sliding Wood Doors

Horizontal-sliding wood doors are usually hung on overhead tracks and operated on steel or nylon rollers. The overhead tracks may be attached to the surface of a framed opening and concealed with wood or metal trim, or the track may be mounted in such a way that the bottom of the track is flush with the ceiling. Sliding doors may be mounted on rollers operating in floor tracks. The more common method is to provide floor guides to prevent the door from swinging.

POCKET SLIDING DOORS If a single door is used to close an opening, it must slide into a pocket built into the wall. Door pockets are built into wood stud walls during construction. *Bi-parting doors* slide into pockets at both sides

Fig. 11-7 Types of hollow-core doors.

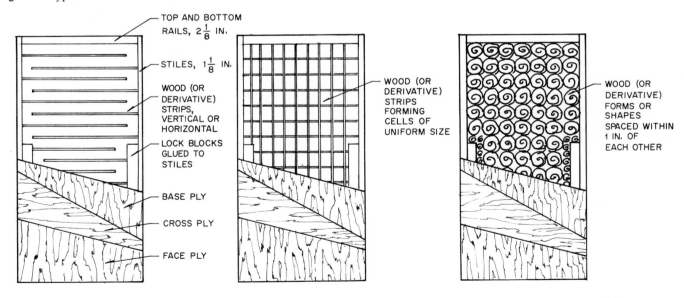

HOLLOW LADDER CORE   HOLLOW CELLULAR CORE   HOLLOW IMPLANTED CORE

of the opening. Pocket sliding doors are installed where they will usually remain either open or closed. Sliding doors have generally been replaced by swinging doors for passageways.

BYPASS SLIDING DOORS   Two or more doors may be hung on parallel tracks as *bypassing doors*. Tracks are available to accommodate doors from ¾″ to 1⅜″ thick. For wide openings, multitrack installations permit the stacking of doors at one side or both sides of an opening. Pockets may be provided at one or both sides to completely conceal the doors when they are in the open position. Bypass sliding doors are widely used as visual screens for wardrobes and closets. Lightweight decorative screens, similar to the Japanese sliding paper screens called *shoji*, are used as sliding walls or room dividers. Sheets of decorative translucent plastic may be set into the wood frames. Most such movable screens do not require a floor track and can be concealed in wall pockets when not in use.

Bypass sliding doors may be covered with fabric or wallpaper to match the decor of a room. Several manufacturers produce aluminum-framed particleboard door panels that may be left natural, painted, or wallpapered. The aluminum frame may be anodized or colored to match the hardware in the room. The metal frame stiffens the sliding door and helps prevent warping.

Two or more bypassing doors covered with mirrors can form a mirror wall that increases the apparent size of the room. The mirrors are installed on wardrobe doors in metal frames. The doors are usually custom made completely finished and ready for installation.

Folding Doors

Folding doors are hung from overhead tracks with nylon rollers similar to those used on sliding doors. They may or may not require a floor track or guides. They can be used as wardrobe doors or as space dividers. The door leaves are hung under the nylon carriers on pivots to allow the leaves to turn independently. Adjusting devices on the folding-door hardware permit perfect fit despite out-of-plumb openings.

The folding-door leaves may be ⅜″ or ½″ thick and from 3½ to 12 in. wide. They may be of solid wood, plywood, vinyl-covered plywood, or hardwood veneers over particleboard cores. The leaves on most folding doors are hinged with extruded vinyl strips. One manufacturer produces a folding wood door that is tied together with steel springs running horizontally through the door. The door can be disassembled for repair or replacement of damaged panels. Folding doors or partitions may be hung as single units attached to one side of an opening, or a pair may be installed to part in the center of the opening and stack against opposite jambs. A single door unit may be installed as a floating door, capable of being opened in either direction. Curved tracks and switching arrangements may be used to provide a group of flexible irregular spaces.

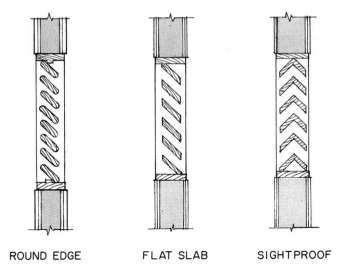

ROUND EDGE   FLAT SLAB   SIGHTPROOF

Fig. 11-8 Louver types.

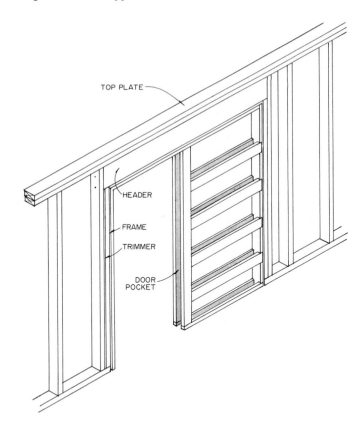

Fig. 11-9 Framing for pocket door in wood stud wall.

The *stack size*, the space taken up by a folding door in its folded position, must be considered when calculating the opening size. The width of the stack will vary from 4½ to 14 in., depending on the manufacturer. The door will extend into the opening approximately 1¼ to 1½ in. per

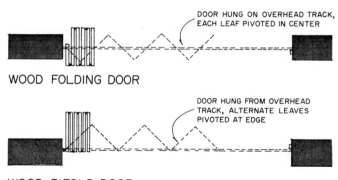

WOOD FOLDING DOOR

DOOR HUNG ON OVERHEAD TRACK,
EACH LEAF PIVOTED IN CENTER

WOOD BIFOLD DOOR

DOOR HUNG FROM OVERHEAD
TRACK, ALTERNATE LEAVES
PIVOTED AT EDGE

WOOD FOLDING DOOR IN POCKET

FABRIC COVERED ACCORDION DOOR

Fig. 11-10 Types of folding doors. The doors shown may be installed as single doors or used as a pair to close larger openings.

foot of opening plus 3 to 4 in. for the end post. Folding doors may be stacked in a recessed area or pocket to provide a full-width opening.

BIFOLD DOORS   If each leaf of the folding door is hinged at the center, they will stack evenly between rooms. If the leaves are attached to the carrier at alternate corners, the stack will extend out into only one room. This is called a *bifold door.* Bifold doors are particularly useful for wardrobes and storage areas, since in their folded position they do not extend into the storage space. The width of each leaf of a bifold door depends on the size of the opening. The leaves may be hinged on one side or be installed as biparting doors. The leaves of bifold doors are usually wider than those of other types of folding doors. Bifold doors are available with flush, paneled, veneered, and fabric-covered leaves in thicknesses of $5/8''$ to $1\,3/8''$. They may also be produced from metal for use as wardrobe doors.

ACCORDION DOORS   Accordion doors consist of a framework of steel covered with a vinyl-coated fabric in a wide range of colors and textures. The steel inner frame is a series of

vertical rods with double hinges at the top and bottom, arranged in such a manner that when the door opens or closes it resembles an accordion. Accordion doors stack in approximately the same space as wood folding doors Lead-filled vinyl blankets may be used under the outer vinyl finish to provide additional soundproofing. Sweep strips at the top and bottom of the door help to control the passage of sound.

Sliding Glass Doors

In contemporary residences and modern office buildings glass areas have increased until entire walls of glass are being demanded. Movable walls of glass are provided to allow for indoor-outdoor living. Solid interior walls penetrating and surrounding exterior gardens increase the apparent size of rooms and visually tend to bring the garden inside. Screened sliding glass doors may be used as replacement for windows for light and ventilation.

The earliest sliding glass doors were set in a wood frame. Such doors are still produced for those who feel that the softness and beauty of natural wood outweighs the advantages of rigid metal frames. Steel-framed glass doors and windows came into general commercial use in the late 1920s. These were utilized for residential applications by forward-looking architects such as Richard Neutra. The use of aluminum extrusions as framing members for sliding glass doors has dominated the field in recent years. Over 50 percent of all sliding glass doors are now made with aluminum framing members that have been forced through dies, or extruded, into intricate shapes. These aluminum extrusions are fitted and assembled in the factory to modular sizes. Sliding glass doors are usually equipped with screens that are designed to be on either the outside or the inside of the glass door, depending on the manufacturer.

The doors and frames are delivered to the job site either glazed or unglazed. Glass doors may be glazed with $3/16''$ or $1/4''$ glass, depending on the size. Building codes may require the installation of safety glass or tempered glass to reduce the possibility of accident. Some doors may be glazed with double layers of glass to reduce the heat loss through large areas of glass. The glass is held in place with vinyl strips placed in the frame on both sides of the glass. In some areas it is required, and in other areas it is desirable, to apply decals to the glass surface to lessen the chance of accidental collision with the transparent glass and subsequent injury. Tinted or darkened glass may be used to reduce glare.

The simplest type of sliding door consists of one sliding panel and one fixed panel. Other types include three-panel doors in which one, two, or all three panels slide. Four-panel doors may be arranged so that the two center sections slide to provide an opening in the center, or the two end panels may slide to the center. Sliding doors can be obtained with as many as eight panels, of which the center six will slide to the outside to provide an extremely large opening. The type of door selected depends on the size of the opening and the kind of access desired. The size of individual leaves depends on the manufacturer; however, sliding glass doors are seldom manufactured with leaves wider than 5 ft.

Sliding glass doors are identified with an X to indicate movable sections and an O to indicate fixed sections. The door is identified as viewed from the outside. Thus an OX door consists of two leaves which, when viewed from the outside, consists of a fixed section on the left and a movable section on the right. An OXXO door consists of biparting doors flanked by two fixed sections. The active or movable section of sliding doors is usually located on the inside for ease of operation. Sliding screen panels corresponding to the active doors may be installed either on the inside or the outside depending on the manufacturer.

Sliding-door heights vary with the manufacturer. They may be produced in standard nominal heights of 6'-8", 6'-10", and 8'-0". Custom-built doors can be obtained on special order up to 10 or 12 ft in height. The actual dimensions may vary as much as 1½ in. from these nominal sizes. The manufacturer's catalog must be checked for the exact dimensions. Two-panel doors are usually available for 6'-0", 8'-0", and 10'-0" openings; three-panel doors for 9'-0", 12'-0", and 15'-0" openings; and four-panel doors for 12'-0", 16'-0", and 20'-0" openings. Some manufacturers will produce doors on special order consisting of any number of sizes and sliding panels to fulfill special requirements.

Frames for sliding glass doors are produced in several thicknesses for use in different types of construction. Door units 3⅝" thick are manufactured for use in wood-stud construction. These door frames may have nailing fins so that they can be nailed directly to the outside of wood studs. Some door frames have integral aluminum moldings to receive siding or stucco. Multiple-track frames vary in width, depending on the thickness of the individual doors and the number of active leaves.

Sliding glass doors roll on nylon, steel, or brass rollers. The tracks on which the movable sections roll may be an integral part of the aluminum door frame or, in the better doors, they may be stainless steel inserts. The movable leaves of sliding doors are equipped with woven silicone-coated wool or nylon pile weatherstripping at the jambs, sill, locking rails, and meeting rails. The weatherstripping helps prevent aluminum-to-aluminum contact and provides protection against penetration of water and air. Most manufacturers provide a choice of several types of handles and locking devices. Rolling screens may consist of aluminum frames holding galvanized-steel, copper, aluminum, or glass-fiber screens.

The aluminum frames are finished in several ways. The most inexpensive finish is a mill finish; however, most aluminum frames are anodized. This process provides a protective oxide covering the surface to resist corrosion. Colored frames may be produced by special anodizing processes. Special hard coatings are produced for areas

subject to salt sprays or atmospheres high in alkali. Finishes for nonferrous metals were discussed in Chapter 7.

METAL AND METAL-COVERED DOORS

Hollow Steel Doors

Hollow steel doors and frames, called *hollow metalwork*, combine esthetics with practicality. Hollow steel doors can be used in practically any type of opening. Steel frames are produced in various depths to fit most wall conditions. Hollow steel doors are produced with factory-applied

Fig. 11-11 Standard sizes and nomenclature for sliding glass doors. (*By permission of the Architectural Aluminum Manufacturers' Association.*)

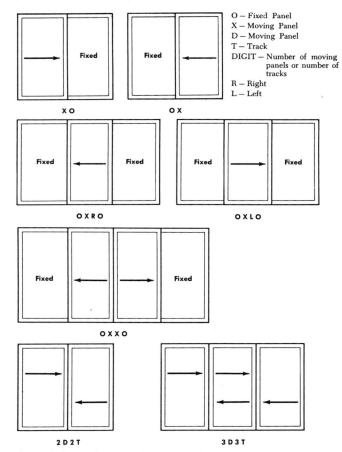

The standard nominal sizes of sliding glass doors are derived from width modules of 3', 4' and 5' with heights being nominally 6'9" and 8'0". Manufacturer's literature should be consulted for exact sizes and availability of panel arrangements. Exact dimension of sliding doors are governed by standard glass sizes which are 34" x 76"   34" x 92"

46" x 76"   46" x 92"

58" x 76"   58" x 92"

Sliding door arrangements, locks, handles, and accessories are determined as viewed from the outside looking in.

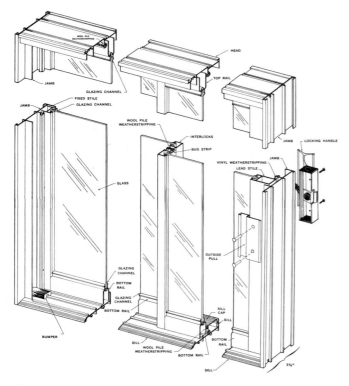

Fig. 11-12 Isometric view of typical sliding glass doors. (*By permission of the International Window Corporation.*)

baked-enamel finishes on smooth or textured steel, or applied vinyl fabrics which are available in wood grains or in a variety of patterns.

Some doors are given a protective coating of zinc, either hot-dip galvanized or electrolytically deposited, before the final finish is applied. Hollow doors have internal steel reinforcements at hardware points. The hardware is usually attached with self-tapping screws into predrilled holes. Hollow steel doors may have louvers or glass view panels installed at the factory.

The internal construction of hollow metal doors varies with the manufacturer, but there are two basic construction methods. In the first, horizontal and vertical steel members are welded to the inside of the face panels, and sound-deadening material is applied to both inside faces so that the doors will not have a metallic sound when closing. In the second method paper honeycomb, polyurethane, polystyrene, or solid mineral cores are bonded to both face sheets. This type of construction needs no sound deadening material. Hollow metal doors are manufactured with extreme accuracy, to fit particular metal frames, and are usually delivered to the job site as a complete assembly with all hardware prefitted. Doors from one manufacturer will seldom fit frames produced by others.

The Steel Door Institute has established standard steel-door categories as shown in Table 11-3.

The selection of the proper door is based on two criteria: frequency of use and resistance to impact. Many doors remain either open or closed most of the time. The less-expensive Type I or Type II are suitable for these openings. Doors for areas of high-frequency operation should be of the heavier construction. Doors in high-impact areas must be Type III.

All three weights may be of seamless, full-flush, flush-panel, or industrial-tube construction. *Seamless doors* have no visible seams on the face or edges. Necessary edge seams are welded and ground smooth. *Full-flush doors* have no visible seams on the face but may have visible seams on the vertical edges. *Flush-panel doors* may be either stile and panel or stile and rail. These doors have visible seams where the panels meet the rails or stiles. Flush-panel doors are considered flush doors, in that the panels are not recessed by more than the thickness of the metal. *Industrial-tube doors* are stile-and-rail doors having recessed panels of two sheets of 18-gauge separated by resilient material or one sheet of 16-gauge steel.

Steel frames for metal doors must be rigid and present a trim appearance when erected. They may be delivered to the job knocked down or welded and braced for installa-

Fig. 11-13 Steel-door types and construction. (*By permission of the Steel Door Institute.*)

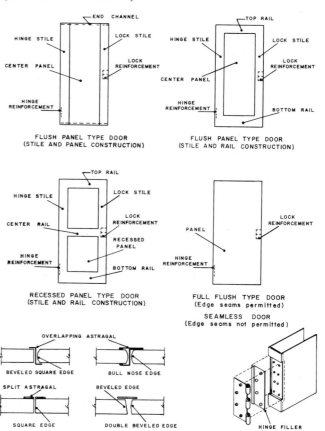

TABLE 11-3 Standard steel-door categories

TYPE	DESCRIPTION
I. Standard duty	Doors may be 1⅜″ or 1¾″ thick with face panels of 20-gauge cold-rolled, hot-rolled, or pickled and oiled steel. Seamless doors with solid structural mineral cores may have 22-gauge face panels.
II. Heavy-duty	Doors are 1¾″ thick with face panels of 18-gauge steel. Doors with solid mineral cores may have 20-gauge face panels.
III. Extra-heavy duty	Doors are 1¾″ thick with face panels of 16-gauge steel. Seamless doors with solid mineral cores may have 18-gauge face panels. Doors with stile-and-rail or industrial-tube construction have 16-gauge stiles and rails and 18-gauge panels.

tion. Both the door and frame must be prepared to receive locks, strikes, pushplates, and hinges. Most door frames are provided with slip-in anchors intended for field installation. The inside of the frame is rigidly braced and erected before the wall is built. Anchors designed to fit the particular wall construction are slipped into the frame. Three anchors are usually installed on each jamb, positioned to coincide with the hinges and latch. With certain types of metal fire doors the anchors must be welded to the frame.

Fire Doors

Building codes require certain passageways to be closed with *fire assemblies* which consist of a fire door, fire win-

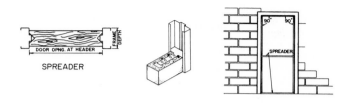

MASONRY CONSTRUCTION

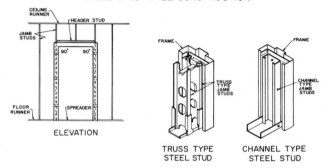

STEEL STUD WALL CONSTRUCTION

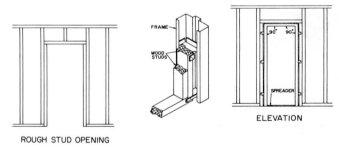

WOOD STUD CONSTRUCTION

Fig. 11-15 Steel door-frame installations. (*By permission of the Steel Door Institute.*)

dow, or fire shutter and all hardware, anchorage, door frames, and sills. All three of the parts must be labeled or listed and must be used together in order to ensure proper fire protection.

The Underwriters' Laboratories label is the most widely recognized label. The labels are attached to the underside or edge of the door. Certain fire doors, frames, and hardware assemblies are classified as *fire-assembly automatic*. These are assemblies that may remain in the open position and will close automatically with a given rise in temperature or if they are subjected to smoke or the products of combustion.

Fire doors are rated A through E, indicating the length of time the door should resist the spread of fire. These designations are coordinated with various types of wall construction as shown in Table 11-4.

Many different fire doors have been developed to meet the requirements of architects, owners, and insurance

Fig. 11-14 Standard nomenclature for hollow metal doors. (*By permission of the Steel Door Institute.*)

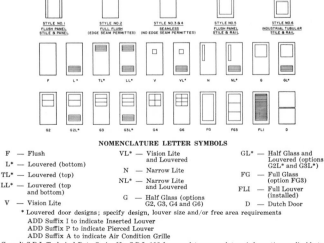

NOMENCLATURE LETTER SYMBOLS

F — Flush
L* — Louvered (bottom)
TL* — Louvered (top)
LL* — Louvered (top and bottom)
V — Vision Lite

VL* — Vision Lite and Louvered
N — Narrow Lite
NL* — Narrow Lite and Louvered
G — Half Glass (options G2, G3, G4 and G6)

GL* — Half Glass and Louvered (options G2L* and G3L*)
FG — Full Glass (option FG3)
FLI — Full Louver (installed)
D — Dutch Door

* Louvered door designs; specify design, louver size and/or free area requirements
ADD Suffix I to indicate Inserted Louver
ADD Suffix P to indicate Pierced Louver
ADD Suffix A to indicate Air Condition Grille
Consult S.D.I. Technical Data Series No. S.D.I. 106 for complete nomenclature information applicable to Standard Steel Doors.

TABLE 11-4   Size, ratings, and method of operation of fire doors*

TYPE, METHOD OF OPERATION(AND MAX SIZE OPENING	RATING AND CLASS OPENING	MAX EXPOSED GLASS AREA
COMPOSITE — wood (flush)		
Swinging Single		
4'0" x 10'0"	1½ hrs. (B)	100 sq. in. per door
4'0" x 10'0"	1 hr. (B)	100 sq. in. per door
4'0" x 8'0"	¾ hr. (C)	1200 sq. in. per door
4'0" x 10'0"	¾ hr. (C)	100 sq. in. per door
Swinging in Pairs		
6'0" x 7'2"	1 hr. (B)	100 sq. in. per door
6'0" x 7'2"	¾ hr. (C)	100 sq. in. per door
COMPOSITE — plastic (flush)		
Swinging Single		
4'0" x 7'2"	1½ hrs. (B)	100 sq. in. per door
4'0" x 7'2"	1 hr. (B)	100 sq. in. per door
4'0" x 7'0"	¾ hr. (C)	1200 sq. in. per door
COMPOSITE — steel (flush)		
Swinging Single		
4'0" x 8'0"	3 hrs. (A)	None
Swinging in Pairs		
8'0" x 7'6"	3 hrs. (A)	None
Swinging Single	1½ hrs. (B)	100 sq. in. per door
4'0" x 8'0"	¾ hr. (C)	1296 sq. in. per light
Swinging in Pairs	1½ hrs. (D)	None
8'0" x 7'6"	¾ hr. (E)	720 sq. in. per light
Horizontal sliding single and center parting,	3 hrs. (A)	None
120 sq. ft. with	1½ hrs. (B)	100 sq. in. per door
maximum dimensions 12'0"	¾ hr. (C)	100 sq. in. per door
Sliding (pass. elevator)	1½ hrs. (B)	None
4'0" x 7'0"	¾ hr. (C)	None
Counter-balanced (freight)	1½ hrs. (B)	100 sq. in. per opening
8'0" x 10'0"		
Counter-balanced (dumb-waiter)	1 hr. (B)	100 sq. in. per opening
4'0" x 5'9"		
HOLLOW METAL — (flush or panel)		
	3 hrs. (A)	None
Swinging Single	1½ hrs. (B)	100 sq. in. per door
4'0" x 10'0"	¾ hr. (C)	1296 sq. in. per light
Swinging in Pairs	1½ hrs. (D)	None
8'0" x 10'0"	¾ hr. (E)	720 sq. in. per light
Sliding (pass. elevator)	1½ hrs. (B)	100 sq. in. per opening
8'0" x 8'0"	¾ hr. (C)	1296 sq. in. per light
Horizontal sliding single and center parting,	3 hrs. (A)	None
120 sq. ft. with maximum	1½ hrs. (B)	100 sq. in. per door
mum dimensions 12'0"	¾ hr. (C)	100 sq. in. per door
HOLLOW METAL — (flush)		
Counter-balanced (freight)	1½ hrs. (B)	100 sq. in. per opening
8'0" x 10'0"		
Counter-balanced (dumb-waiter)	1 hr. (B)	100 sq. in. per opening
4'0" x 5'9"	1½ hrs. (B)	100 sq. in. per opening
Swinging (intake chute)	1½ hrs. (B)	None
24" x 24"	1 hr. (B)	None
Swinging (discharge chute)	1½ hrs. (B)	None
28" x 36"	1 hr. (B)	None
METAL CLAD — (KALAMEIN) (panel)		
Swinging Single	1½ hrs. (B)	100 sq. in. per door
4'0" x 8'0"	¾ hr. (C)	1296 sq. in. per light
Swinging in Pairs	1½ hrs. (D)	None
8'0" x 8'0"	¾ hr. (E)	720 sq. in. per light
METAL CLAD — (KALAMEIN) (flush)		
Swinging Single	1½ hrs. (B)	100 sq. in. per door
3'9" x 7'6"	¾ hr. (C)	1296 sq. in. per light
Swinging in Pairs	1½ hrs. (D)	None
7'6" x 7'6"	¾ hr. (E)	720 sq. in. per light
STEEL — (plate)		
Counter-balanced (freight)	1½ hrs. (B)	100 sq. in. per opening
8'0" x 10'0"		

TYPE, METHOD OF OPERATION, AND MAX SIZE OPENING	RATING AND CLASS OPENING	MAX EXPOSED GLASS AREA
Counter-balanced (dumb-waiter)	1 hr. (B)	100 sq. in. per opening
4'0" x 5'9"	1½ hrs. (B)	100 sq. in. per opening
TIN CLAD — (3 ply)		
Sliding Single		
120 sq. ft. with maximum dimension 12'0"		
Sliding Center Parting		
120 sq. ft. with maximum dimension 12'0"	3 hrs. (A)	None
	1½ hrs. (B)	100 sq. in. per door
Sliding Vertical	¾ hr. (C)	1296 sq. in. per light
80 sq. ft. with maximum dimension 10'0"	1½ hrs. (D)	None
	¾ hr. (E)	720 sq. in. per light
Swinging Single		
6'0" x 12'0"		
Swinging in Pairs		
10'0" x 12'0"		
TIN CLAD — (2 ply)		
Sliding Single		
80 sq. ft. with maximum dimension 10'0"	1½ hrs. (B)	100 sq. in. per door
	¾ hr. (C)	1296 sq. in. per light
Swinging Single	1½ hrs. (D)	None
4'0" x 10'0"	¾ hr. (E)	720 sq. in. per light
Swinging in Pairs		
8'0" x 10'0"		
Counter-balanced (freight)	1½ hrs. (B)	100 sq. in. per opening
8'0" x 10'0"		
METAL CLAD — (KALAMEIN) (flush or panel)		
Counter-balanced (freight)	1½ hrs. (B)	100 sq. in. per opening
8'0" x 10'0"		
SHEET METAL — (corrugated or flush)		
Sliding Single		
120 sq. ft. with maximum dimension 12'0"		
Sliding Center Parting		
120 sq. ft. with maximum dimension 12'0"	3 hrs. (A)	None
	1½ hrs. (B)	100 sq. in. per door
Sliding Vertical	¾ hr. (C)	1296 sq. in. per light
80 sq. ft. with maximum dimension 10'0"	1½ hrs. (D)	None
	¾ hr. (E)	720 sq. in. per light
Swinging Single		
6'0" x 12'0"		
Swinging in Pairs		
10'0" x 12'0"		
Counter-balanced (freight)	1½ hrs. (B)	100 sq. in. per opening
8'0" x 10'0"		
SHEET METAL — (panel)		
Swinging Single	1½ hrs. (B)	100 sq. in. per door
4'0" x 8'0"	¾ hr. (C)	1296 sq. in. per light
Swinging in Pairs	1½ hrs. (D)	None
8'0" x 8'0"	¾ hr. (E)	720 sq. in. per light
STEEL — (interlocking slats)		
Rolling	3 hrs. (A)	None
120 sq. ft. with	1½ hrs. (B)	None
maximum dimension 12'0"	¾ hr. (C)	None
	1½ hrs. (D)	None

*Reproduced by permission from the Standard for Fire Doors and Windows, 1970 ed.; copyright, National Fire Protection Association, Boston, Mass.

companies. New types are being developed as needs arise. The Underwriters' Laboratories publishes a "Building Materials List" that describes all approved products. Bi-monthly supplements list the latest improvements and new products tested and approved.

Doors, usually 1¾″ thick, consisting of sheet-metal facings bonded or attached to kiln-dried wood cores, are commonly called *kalamein doors*. Joints in the metal facing are locked, recessed, and ground, with all the seams soldered. The sheet metal is usually furniture steel, which may or may not be galvanized. Panel doors are similar to paneled wood doors. The panels may be cement-asbestos board with the metal facings glued to the core. This type of door offers maximum fire resistance. Flush doors, for use where additional fireproofing is needed, may have sheets of asbestos bonded to the core and the steel sheet applied to the face. These doors must be installed in metal frames if they are to act as fire doors.

Special-purpose Doors

There are many types of special-purpose doors such as doors for aircraft hangars, gymnasium and auditorium doors and partitions, and service and loading-dock doors, which often have to be designed for specific projects. Garage doors for residences differ from one part of the country to another. Roll-up doors composed of several panels are used in some areas, and pivoted overhead doors are favored in other locations. Metal service doors and grilles are widely used in commercial construction. These doors, either hand powered or electrically operated, are widely used as fire doors and as security doors.

In some parts of the country revolving glass doors are used to exclude cold air and to conserve heat in building lobbies. The doors are usually arranged so that in milder weather the revolving-door portion can be moved out of the way. Most revolving doors also are equipped with a device that allows all the leaves to fold outward if pressure is applied to two leaves in opposite directions. This allows the openings to serve as an emergency exit.

WINDOWS

Openings in walls to provide natural light, ventilation, or views are classed as windows. The first glass windows were fixed in crude wood frames. Progressive builders combined more and more small pieces of glass to fill larger openings. The development of stained glass added further uses to windows. In addition to letting in needed light to the interiors of great cathedrals, they presented stories of the gospel to the unlettered general populace. The brilliantly colored stained-glass windows of the great Gothic cathedrals are still an inspiration in our modern world.

The development of movable *sash*, a system of one or more panes of glass in a movable frame of wood or metal, provided a means of ventilation as well as natural light.

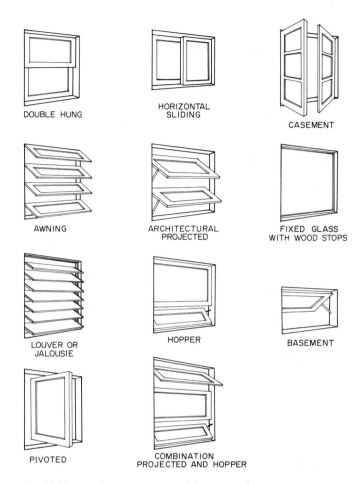

Fig. 11-16 Window types (viewed from outside).

The top member of a sash is called the *top rail* and the bottom member is called the *bottom rail;* the vertical side members are termed *stiles*. If the window consists of two sashes, one above the other, the adjacent horizontal rails are called *meeting rails*. If the two sashes are placed side by side and slide in a horizontal plane, the adjacent stiles are *meeting stiles*. The individual sheets of glass within a sash are called *panes* or *lights*, divided by horizontal or vertical *muntins*.

The window frame consists of the members forming the perimeter or frame of the window. The frame is attached to the structural framing of the surrounding wall. The horizontal member at the top of the frame is the *head;* the vertical side members are the *jambs;* and the horizontal member at the bottom of the frame is the *sill*.

Wood Windows

Windows are classified by their method of operation, regardless of the materials from which they are made. The glass areas may be subdivided in several ways in each sash.

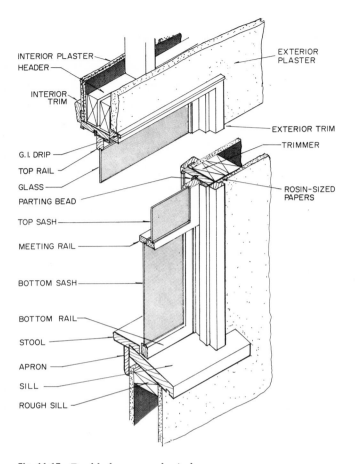

INTERIOR PLASTER
HEADER
INTERIOR TRIM
G.I. DRIP
TOP RAIL
GLASS
PARTING BEAD
TOP SASH
MEETING RAIL
BOTTOM SASH
BOTTOM RAIL
STOOL
APRON
SILL
ROUGH SILL
EXTERIOR PLASTER
EXTERIOR TRIM
TRIMMER
ROSIN-SIZED PAPERS

Fig. 11-17 Double-hung wood windows.

DOUBLE-HUNG WINDOWS

The double-hung window consists of two sashes, both of which slide vertically. Each sash is attached to a weight or spring balance to assist in raising the individual sash. The earliest type of sash balance consisted of cast-iron weights, called *sash weights*, hung on rope or chain over a pulley at the top of the window frame. The sash weight moves up and down in a pocket beside the stile. Sash weights have been largely superseded by *sash balances*, coiled springs either at the top of the frame or mortised into the jambs. Sash balances are produced with varying degrees of tension to take care of windows of various sizes and weights. Some windows require one balance and others require two.

Double-hung and horizontal sliding windows are usually equipped with cam-action *sash locks*. These sash locks draw the two sashes together at the meeting rails or stiles and force the sash against the weatherstripping. The bottom rail of the lower sash is equipped with a *sash lift* to assist in raising the lower sash.

Windows to be installed in wood-frame construction are usually delivered to the job site assembled and ready for installation. The exterior trim, stucco mold, and a 4-in.

strip of kraft-paper *flashing* is in place when the frame is delivered. The *parting strip* and *window stop* are left loose to allow for installation of the sash. The *interior trim*, *stool*, and *apron* are applied after the frame is installed. The entire window frame with the sash prefitted may be provided as a unit, or the sash may be fitted to the frame after installation.

One manufacturer produces wood windows with exposed exterior members of the frame and all wood portions of the sash sealed with a rigid vinyl covering. The vinyl covering helps to eliminate the swelling and sticking of wood double-hung windows. Vinyl strips are provided as weatherstripping at the head, meeting rails, and sills in some types of windows. Metal weatherstripping at the jambs, meeting rails, and sills are provided in some windows. Proper weatherstripping of double-hung windows will reduce air infiltration anywhere from 50 to 85 percent.

Wood or metal-framed screens are usually installed on the outside of the sash. Storm sash, which consist of single panes of glass frames in wood or metal, can replace screens in cold weather. The need for storm sash is eliminated if the window is glazed with two layers of glass with an air

Fig. 11-18 Double-hung windows for residential installations. (*By permission of the Architectural Aluminum Manufacturers' Association.*)

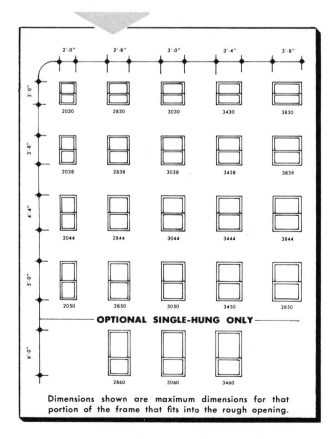

2'-0"   2'-8"   3'-0"   3'-4"   3'-8"

3'-0"

2030   2830   3030   3430   3830

3'-8"

2038   2838   3038   3438   3838

4'-4"

2044   2844   3044   3444   3844

5'-0"

2050   2850   3050   3450   3850

OPTIONAL SINGLE-HUNG ONLY

6'-0"

2860   3060   3460

Dimensions shown are maximum dimensions for that portion of the frame that fits into the rough opening.

space between the glass panes. Roll screens, which disappear into pockets at the head of the frame, may replace the removable screen.

Wood double-hung windows are usually manufactured in sizes that can be coordinated with modular brick masonry. The sash opening, or the dimension inside the frame, is usually in 4-in. increments from 2'-0" to 4'-0" in width, and from 3'-0" to 6'-0" in height. The rough openings, or the masonry openings, necessary for given window sizes are detailed in manufacturers' catalogs. Double-hung windows larger than this tend to be unmanageable. If wider openings are desired, individual windows must be installed side by side. Windows installed side by side are said to be separated by a *mullion*. In calculating the ventilation provided by a double-hung window, it is important to note that only 50 percent of the window is available for ventilation.

HORIZONTAL SLIDING WINDOWS Windows with two or more sashes that slide horizontally are called *horizontal sliding* or *gliding windows*. If the window consists of two sashes, usually only one slides. If it consists of three sashes, the two outer ones will slide toward the middle to provide ventilation on both sides of a fixed picture window. The sliding units usually glide or roll on a plastic-faced metal track. Plastic guides are used to stabilize the top of the window. Some horizontal sliding windows are designed so that the individual sashes can easily be removed for cleaning. Screens may cover the entire window opening or only the operating sash. Some manufacturers produce interchangeable full-sized screens and storm sash. Horizontal sliding sash may be glazed with double panes of glass to provide further insulation. Horizontal wood sliding windows range from 2'-0" to 4'-6" in height and from 3'-0" to 6'-0" in width.

CASEMENT WINDOWS Casement windows consist of one or more sashes hinged at the sides to swing in or out. If they

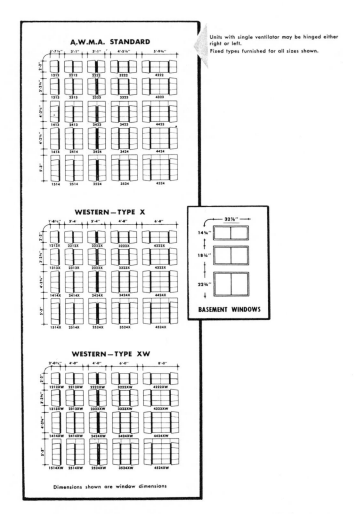

Fig. 11-20 Casement windows for residential installations. (*By permission of the Architectural Aluminum Manufacturers' Association.*)

Fig. 11-19 Horizontal sliding windows for residential installations. (*By permission of the Architectural Aluminum Manufacturers' Association.*)

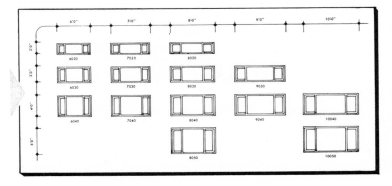

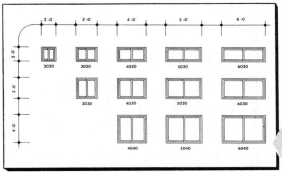

are designed to swing out from the building, they are called *outswinging casements*. In most wood casement windows with two sashes, both usually swing. Inswinging casements were used widely in the 1930s; however, they are seldom used now because of the difficulty of making them watertight and the problem of hanging drapes on the inside of the window. Care must be taken that outswinging casements do not swing over walks or passageways where they could act as an obstruction when open.

A fixed light may be included as a picture window between two single outswinging casements. The picture window and the casement windows are then separated by mullions. A pair of casement windows may close on a mullion or close against themselves. If the windows close upon themselves, an astragal is usually provided to cover the joint between the meeting rails and make a more watertight closure. Casement windows may be operated with

Fig. 11-21 Casement windows for commercial and monument installations. (*By permission of the Architectural Aluminum Manufacturers' Association.*)

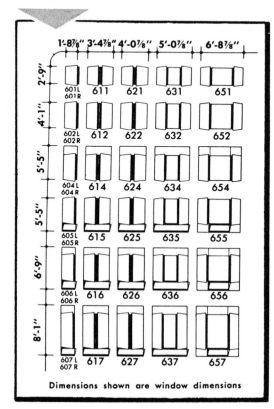

Horizontal and/or vertical muntins may be added if desired, provided they are based on 20" or 24" bar centers for width and 16" bar centers for height.

Fixed light may be provided at sill in place of sill vents.

Fixed types furnished for all sizes shown.

Dimensions shown are window dimensions

sash locks attached to the meeting stiles of the casement or by cranks attached to the sill. A crank, either removable or fixed in place, may be provided for each sash, or one crank may operate both simultaneously. Screens are placed on the inside of the sash on outswinging casements.

Wood casement windows have several disadvantages. If they are not treated with perservatives during manufacture and are not constantly maintained, they tend to warp and become difficult to close tightly.

Casement windows are usually constructed of 1⅜" pine. Sizes vary with the manufacturer. Single units can usually be obtained in 1'-0", 1'-6", and 2'-0" widths. Double units are generally produced in 3'-0" and 4'-0" widths. Many different widths may be obtained by combining fixed picture windows with one or more outswinging casements.

AWNING WINDOWS   Awning windows consist of one or more outswinging sashes hinged at the top. Awning windows are often combined with other types of sash, such as fixed or casement sash. They may be stacked vertically, each in its own frame, or they may be installed in a single frame and close on themselves. Awning windows may be opened and closed individually with hand pulls located on the bottom rail of each sash, or they may be joined in such a way that a vertical bank opens simultaneously with a single pull or crank.

Awning windows offer some rain protection when they are partly open. Like casement windows, they must be kept from projecting over walks and passageways. A modified type of awning window which projects inside when opened is classed as a *basement window*. This type of window is used for less demanding installations, such as basement walls of masonry or concrete.

HOPPER WINDOWS   Hopper windows are like awning windows, except they are hinged at the bottom and swing inward. They may actually be inverted awning-type windows with a slight modification in weatherstripping and operating hardware. Hopper windows are often combined with fixed panels or casement windows. The hopper is installed at the bottom, either in a combination frame or in a separate frame. Hopper windows allow complete ventilation with a minimum of draft, as the incoming air is diverted upward to miss the occupants of the room. One manufacturer produces a combination window consisting of an awning sash at the top, a fixed sash in the center, and a hopper sash at the bottom. Incoming air would thus come in at the bottom and be exhausted at the top without creating drafts in the room.

Metal Windows

The most common metals used in the construction of windows and frames are aluminum, steel, and stainless steel. Bronze is sometimes used for monumental and decorative windows. Metal windows are made in a wide variety of types. Wood windows provide good insulation and are inexpensive, but they tend to swell and shrink with changes in moisture. Metal windows have more strength and rigidity, but they offer poor insulation and are subject to the condensation of moisture on their inner surfaces. Although steel windows are stronger than aluminum, they must be painted and maintained. Stainless-steel windows do not have to be painted and are strong; however, their higher cost limits their use.

ALUMINUM WINDOWS   Aluminum windows are made from aluminum-alloy sections that have been formed by extrusion. This process consists of forcing a bar of aluminum through a steel die to produce sections of the desired shape and size. The most commonly used alloy for all types of aluminum windows is 6063-T5. A stronger-tempered alloy, 6063-T6, is used where a thinner section or a harder surface is desired. The thickness of metal is approximately $1/16''$ for residential windows, $5/64''$ for most commercial windows, and $5/32''$ for large-size or monumental windows. Aluminum windows are usually given an etched and lacquered finish. If the window is to be exposed to salt spray or industrial atmospheres, an anodized finish may be used. Special colored hard finishes may be applied at additional cost (for further information on aluminum alloys and finishes see Chapter 7).

The joints in aluminum windows and frames are either welded or fastened mechanically. Projected or casement windows are usually welded. Hardware, fasteners, or anchors of aluminum windows must be of metals that are compatible with aluminum, such as nonmagnetic stainless steel, aluminum, or cadmium-plated steel. Weatherstripping, whether it is woven fabric, plastic, or metallic, must also be compatible with aluminum. Contact between moving parts is avoided by the use of spring weatherstripping or nylon-pile strips.

Protective coatings are usually factory applied to aluminum windows and frames to protect them from construction abuse. Plaster droppings are very injurious to most aluminum finishes. Water-white methacrylate-type lacquers are usually used as protective coatings against plaster. When aluminum frames are to be in contact with steel, zinc chromate or an alkali-resistant primer is used on the steel. A wood preservative should be applied to wood before the installation of aluminum frames.

Aluminum windows are produced in three basic grades: *residential*, *commercial*, and *monumental*. The Architectural Aluminum Manufacturers' Association has established standard sizes and construction requirements for each of these grades. Windows conforming to each of these grades are tested for water leakage, wind load, structural strength, and air infiltration.

Aluminum windows are manufactured for various types of installations. Some are equipped with fins to fit on the outside of a rough frame in wood-stud construction. Others have special fins that can be incorporated in masonry veneer or solid masonry buildings. Manufacturers' cata-

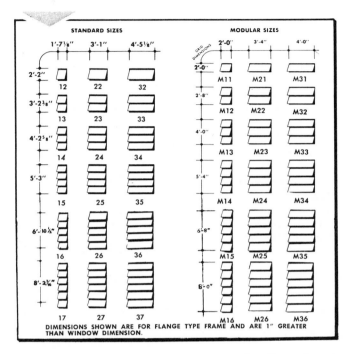

Fig. 11-22 Awning windows for commercial and residential installations. (*By permission of the Architectural Aluminum Manufacturers' Association.*)

logs give details of installation, actual dimensions, and rough-opening sizes.

STEEL WINDOWS   Steel windows are manufactured of hot-rolled sections or cold-formed strip steel. The grade is based on the thickness of the individual sections, or the weight of the outside frame and the ventilator sections in pounds per linear foot. The two basic grades are *residential* and *intermediate*. Intermediate windows are better constructed of heavier materials. Heavy-duty intermediate windows are manufactured to fit special conditions, such as extremely large windows that may be subject to hurricane-force winds.

Steel windows are usually furnished with a shop finish, applied by cleaning the steel assembly in a hot alkali bath and dipping or spraying a coat of primer. The best types of prime coat are baked on at a temperature of 300°F or more. Some windows are hot-dip or electrolytically galvanized before they are primed. One manufacturer provides windows with a polyvinyl chloride corrosion-resistant coating which supposedly will not crack, chip, chalk, blister, or peel, so that the window need not be painted. Most steel windows, however, must be painted regularly to avoid deterioration and rust streaks on adjacent surfaces.

Residential casement and picture windows are fabricated from hot-rolled structural steel sections having a minimum depth of 1″ and a weight of 2 lb per linear foot.

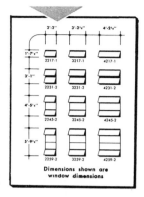

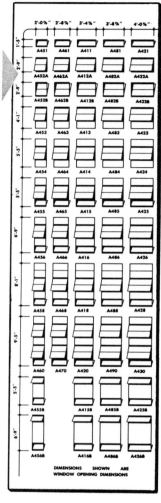

Fig. 11-23 Projected windows for commercial and residential installations. (*By permission of the Architectural Aluminum Manufacturers' Association.*)

Security windows consist of a rigid frame and muntins that form a continuous fixed grill. Ventilators projecting into the room are used for warehouses, stores, and factories to prevent forced entry.

STAINLESS-STEEL WINDOWS   In recent years automated fabrication techniques and improved design have widened the use of stainless steel for windows in institutional and commercial buildings. Although the initial cost for material and assemblies is usually higher than for steel and aluminum, the longevity, strength, and ease of maintenance of stainless steel have made it increasingly popular for quality installations.

Most stainless-steel windows are fabricated from 20-gauge type 302 stainless steel. The frames and movable sash are constructed of roll-formed tubular sections. Most stainless-steel windows are presently custom made to fit particular applications.

Jalousie Windows

Jalousie windows, sometimes called *louver windows*, consist of strips of glass, $3/16''$ to $7/32''$ thick and from $3''$ to $4\frac{1}{2}''$ wide. Each leaf of glass is pivoted in the center so that the leaves close tightly against each other or open into a horizontal position for complete ventilation. Screens are usually mounted on the outside. Single windows are limited to 42 in.; however, wider windows can be developed by installing vertical metal joiners or mullions.

Jalousie windows can be obtained prefit in aluminum frames, or as strip hardware that can be installed in any opening. Strip hardware is screwed to stiles of wooden frames. This type of hardware is particularly useful in remodeling, where old windows are removed from the frame and the strip hardware is installed. All edges of the louver glass are ground. Glazing is accomplished by inserting the glass leaves into hardware clips. Clear glass can be installed for view panels or obscure glass can be used where privacy is desired.

Window Walls

Window walls are nonstructural, continuous facings consisting of combinations of windows, panels, and mullions filling the space between the structural elements. They are generally one story in height, installed between the floor and ceiling slabs. The individual components of the window wall are usually set in a modular framework of aluminum or steel tubes or shapes. Doors may be either swinging or sliding glass doors. Insulating panels of many materials may be set between the metal framing members. Windows may be fixed, casement, sliding, pivoted, or projected to fit many situations.

GLAZED WALLS

Glazed openings in interior partitions are considered *borrowed lights*. If the openings are in wood stud parti-

The largest ventilator is $1'$-$11\frac{1}{2}''$ wide by $4'$-$\frac{3}{8}''$ high. Residential casements may be either crank operated or manually operated with friction hinges. If the window is manually operated, a sliding wicket must be provided for inside mounted screens to give access to the operating handle. Residential double-hung windows are made from cold-formed strip steel galvanized before forming. The maximum size is $4'$-$0''$ by $7'$-$0''$.

Intermediate-grade windows are made in a number of types for a wide range of uses. Projected, casement, and combination windows are produced, consisting of hopper or projected vents combined with either fixed sash or casement windows. Classroom windows, a recent development in steel windows, usually combine a large clear fixed sash with a small ventilating hopper window underneath.

tions, the fixed glass is usually set in wood stops. In movable partitions and metal partitions the glass is usually set in metal frames.

Curtain Walls

A curtain wall is defined by the National Association of Architectural Metal Manufacturers as: "An exterior building wall which carries no floor or roof loads and which may consist principally of metal or of a combination of metal, glass and other surfacing materials supported in a metal framework." Metal curtain walls are attached to the exterior of the building frame by clips or anchors forming a continuous curtain. The framework may be aluminum, steel, stainless steel, or bronze. A large portion of the wall may be sheathed in metal, or only a minimum amount of metal may be used to support panels of aluminum, porcelain-enameled steel, or sandwich panels of insulating materials between metallic or composition face panels. Many types of glass are used in curtain-wall construction. Clear or colored glass may be used as view panels; opaque structural glass may be used as paneling in custom and prefabricated curtain walls. Many buildings consist of curtains of glass with only a minimum of exposed metal. Curtain walls may consist of precast concrete or masonry panels with fixed or movable windows.

Metal curtain walls are classified as stick systems, stick-and-panel systems, or panel systems, according to the method of fabrication and installation of window-wall components. *Stick systems* are generally shipped knocked down, to be assembled in place. Mullions, rails, panels, and glass are usually prefabricated and prefitted and are installed piece by piece to form the wall. This system involves the handling of many small and relatively lightweight sections. *Stick-and-panel systems* consist of vertical grid members which are installed first. Subassemblies of mullions, panels, and glass are then installed in the grid to form the finished wall. *Panel systems* consist of preassembled panels, one or more stories in height, which are anchored to the structural frame to form the entire envelope of the building, with the addition of few, if any, other parts. The panels may consist of only the exterior panels, metal framing, and glass, or they may include insulation and the interior finish of the wall.

Curtain walls may not have to support floor and roof loads, but they must withstand wind loads that vary in intensity in various parts of the country. The wind load also varies with the height above the ground. Allowance must also be made for movement of the structural frame as a result of wind or seismic forces. In addition, temperature differences between the inside and the outside of the building will cause unequal expansion and develop stresses in the curtain wall. Outside temperatures may vary as much as 100° while interior temperatures remain essentially the same. An exposed aluminum member 100 ft long will expand or contract nearly 1½ in. during a temperature change of 100°F. If some of the components

of the system are absorptive materials, they will swell and contract with changes of humidity or moisture. The curtain-wall system must be flexible enough to accommodate all this movement, or it will buckle and collapse.

Joint design is the most difficult problem in curtain walls. If large panels are factory fabricated and erected as units, the only movement should be between the units. However, the movement in any unit is proportional to its size. As the amount of movement increases, the possible penetration of water becomes greater. The more separate units are installed, the greater number of joints must be waterproofed.

When the wall is composed of a grid made of vertical mullions and horizontal framing members, horizontal movement is provided for at each mullion. One method of providing for this movement is *split mullion*, two channel-shaped sections that slide in relation to each other. A *batten mullion*, in which inner and outer members are clamped to the inner and outer surfaces of the panels, permits the panel to expand and contract between the two sections of the mullion. The joint is sealed with a nonhardening mastic. A *bellow mullion* is constructed of lightweight metal that will flex when the panels expand and contract. A *structural gasket* of flexible material may be employed to hold the panel in place and allow for the movement of the panel and mullions. Vertical expansion is usually provided by a slip joint at each floor, or in two-story units at alternate floors. Other aspects of curtain walls are discussed in Chapters 7 and 12.

BUILDERS' HARDWARE

Builders' hardware includes a wide variety of metal and plastic fastenings and devices ordinarily used in building construction. Although these devices may only represent 1½ to 2 percent of the cost of a building, they include all concealed metal fasteners and the operative and decorative hardware for the proper operation of doors, windows, and cabinets which provide for the safe use of building, the security of its contents, and the stability of its operation. By common usage, builders' hardware is usually classified as rough hardware and finishing hardware.

In general *rough hardware* consists of utility items which are not usually visible in the finished building. This includes such items as nails, bolts, framing anchors, anchor bolts, straps, expansion bolts, sash balances, steel channels or angles at sills, coal chutes, ash-pit doors, fireplace dampers, and various other devices that go into the basic structure of a building. Various types of rough hardware have been discussed in other chapters.

Finishing hardware designate the locks, hinges, operating devices, and other metallic trimmings used on buildings for protective and decorative purposes. Bath accessories such as towel bars, paper holders, and curtain track or shower and bath inclosures are usually not considered builders' finishing hardware. In view of the wide variety of types, styles, materials, and finishes and the constant changes in finishing hardware, most designers prefer to call in a manufacturers' representative or a hardware consultant to assist them in the selection of these items.

Many hardware consultants belong to the American Society of Architectural Hardware Consultants. The members of this organization subscribe to a strict code of ethics and can advise on the selection of stock items for each particular use. The consultant's services are often available without charge, since in most cases he is a manufacturers' representative.

Finishing hardware may be fabricated of cast iron, steel, brass, bronze, aluminum, and many other metals. The finished products may be prime coated to receive a painted finish or polished and lacquered. In ordering finishing hardware the final finish must be specified. Each manufacturer has his own standard finishes, which usually conform to federal government standards, and most will provide special finishes on order. Table 11-5 lists the most commonly used finishes and their designations.

Fig. 11-24   Types of hinges.

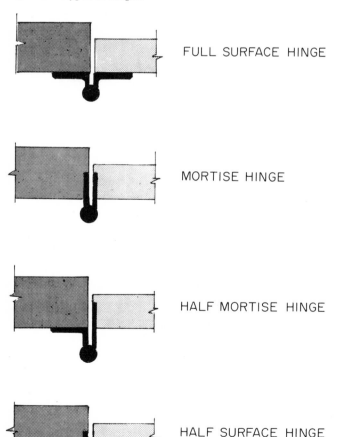

FULL SURFACE HINGE

MORTISE HINGE

HALF MORTISE HINGE

HALF SURFACE HINGE

TABLE 11-5   U.S. standard finishes for builders' hardware

SYMBOL	DESIGNATION	DESCRIPTION
USP	Primed	Cleaned and primed
US1B	Bright japanned	Baked-on Japan varnish
US1D	Dead black	No gloss, Japan varnish
US2C	Cadmium plated	Electroplated iron and steel
US2G	Zinc	Electroplated steel
US2H	Zinc	Hot-dip-galvanized steel
US3	Polished brass	Polished and lacquered solid brass or brass-plated iron or steel
US4	Dull brass, satin finish, lacquered	Etched or brush finished and lacquered
US9	Polished bronze, lacquered	Polished and lacquered solid bronze or bronze-plated iron or steel
US9A	Polished bronze, no lacquer	Polished solid bronze or bronze-plated iron or steel
US10	Dull bronze, satin finish, lacquered	Etched or brush finished and lacquered
US10NL	Dull bronze, no lacquer	Etched or brushed finish
US10B	Oiled rubbed bronze	Rubbed with oil and abrasives
US11	Oxidized relieved bronze	Dull bronze highlights buffed onto a textured dark surface
US14	Polished nickel	Nickel-plated iron, steel, brass, or bronze, buffed
US15	Dull nickel	Etched nickel plating
US17A	Old iron	Black nickel plating over sanded brass
US19	Flat black	Flat black coating on sanded brass
US26	Polished chromium	Chromium-plated iron, steel, brass, or bronze, buffed
US26D	Dull chromium	Chromium-plated brass or bronze, buffed
US27	Satin finish aluminum	Matte-finish aluminum, lacquered
US28	Silver satin finish aluminum	Silver-anodized aluminum, satin finish, no lacquer
US28B	Black satin finish aluminum	Black-anodized aluminum, satin finish, no lacquer
US32	Bright stainless steel	Polished stainless steel, no lacquer
US32D	Dull stainless steel	Matte-finish stainless steel, no lacquer

Door Hinges

A hinge is a device that permits a door, window, or panel to turn or swing. It consists of two leaves which pivot on a pin inserted through a barrel or *knuckles*. Hinges may be exposed, semiconcealed, or concealed. Exposed hinges mounted on the face of the door are called *surface, strap,* or *butterfly hinges*. Concealed hinges that consist of one pin extending from the top of the door into the head of the door frame and another pin extending from the bottom of the door into the sill, are called *pin* or *pivot hinges*. Hinges installed on the edge of a door between the door and the stile are *butt hinges*.

BUTT HINGES   The leaves of butt hinges, or butts, cannot be wider than the thickness of the door. The pin and knuckle must extend past the face of the door to obtain clearance for the door to swing. When extremely heavy trim is used around the door frame or the frame is exceptionally wide, *long-throw butts* must be used to obtain clearance. On this type of butt a portion of the leaves do extend past the door surface. Butts are usually mortised into the edges of the door and frame to fit flush with the edges. They are shaped to allow the door to close without binding. On metal doors a half-mortise hinge may be used, with one leaf mortised into the frame and the other applied to the surface of the door.

Olive-knuckle butts are used where appearance is of primary importance. When the door is closed, only the knuckle, shaped like an olive, is visible. This type of butt is a loose-joint hinge which can be separated by lifting the door. Butt hinges may be obtained as friction hinges, which will hold a door in any open position. These are widely used in hospitals. Spring hinges are used to automatically close doors. These hinges may be single acting or double acting. Double-acting spring hinges are widely used on restaurant service doors. *Template hardware* is made to a master template so that each piece and all hole spacing is located to match predrilled holes in metal doors and frames.

For thicker or heavier doors or doors receiving high-frequency service, *ball-bearing butts* are generally used. It is also customary to use a ball-bearing butt when door closers are used. This type of hinge has ball bearings in stainless steel cups which nest in the top and bottom of the center knuckle. Two-bearing or four-bearing hinges are obtainable. The selection depends on the type of use expected. The ball-bearing race of this type of hinge usually projects somewhat from the knuckles, although in some of the newer types it is flush.

The most commonly used sizes of butts are $3\frac{1}{2}'' \times 3\frac{1}{2}''$, $4'' \times 4''$, $4\frac{1}{2}'' \times 4\frac{1}{2}''$, and $5'' \times 5''$ (measured with the leaves extended). The length of the hinge is usually the same as the width; although $4\frac{1}{2}'' \times 4''$, $5'' \times 4\frac{1}{4}''$, $5'' \times 4\frac{1}{2}''$ hinges are used as long-throw butts. Two hinges are usually installed on interior doors, and three hinges are recommended for exterior doors. The top hinge is normally located 5 in. from the top of the door and the bottom hinge 10 in. above the floor. If a third hinge is used, it is centered between the top and bottom hinges.

Hinges may be made of brass, bronze, steel, stainless steel, or chromium-plated steel or brass. With brass or bronze hinges, hardened steel bushings are sometimes included in the knuckles surrounding the pin to reduce

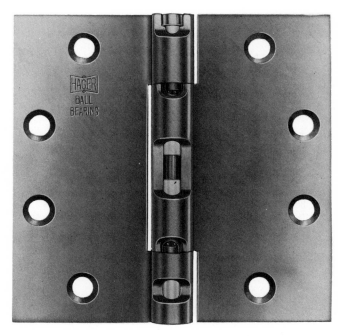

Fig. 11-25   Section through a ball-bearing butt hinge. (*By permission of the Hager Hinge Company.*)

wear. One manufacturer produces a hinge with a nylon-encased pin for improved lateral stability. *Oilite* bearing hinges are equipped with oil-impregnated brass bearings between the knuckles to reduce friction.

HINGE PINS   Hinges may pivot on either loose pins or tight pins. The ordinary *loose pin* slips out of the barrel so that the leaves can be installed separately on the jamb and door. The door can be removed easily by removing the pin. The disadvantage of this type of pin is that the twisting motion of the door as it is opened and closed may cause the pin to work up in the barrel. Nonrising loose pins have been developed that have the advantages of the loose pin but overcome the climbing action in various ways, depending on the manufacturer. Nonremovable loose pins have been developed for outswinging exterior doors, which have the hinge barrel on the outside of the door. The pin is held in place by a set screw that can be reached only when the door is open. Without this feature a locked exterior door could be removed simply be removing the pin.

A *tight pin*, sometimes called a *fast pin*, is securely fastened at the factory in such a way that the leaves cannot be separated without destroying the hinge. This type of hinge is usually used in hospitals, asylums, and other locations where security is paramount. The hinge is difficult to install, as the door must be blocked into position as the hinges are installed.

The heads of hinge pins are made in several shapes. The most common type is the flat-button tip, which is usually furnished if not otherwise specified. Flush tips are usually furnished when tight-pin hinges are used. Round tips, oval tips, cone tips, hospital tips, and others are produced by various manufacturers.

Door-control Devices

Devices that control the swing of a door include items such as door closers, automatic door openers, door stops, door holders, push plates, panic hardware, and similar devices. Selection of the proper device from among the hundreds of items available usually requires the assistance of an expert in the field.

DOOR CLOSERS   There are several types of door closers that combine a spring for closing and a compression chamber in which the liquid or air escapes slowly, thus retarding the closing action to prevent the slamming of the door. The closer may be mounted to the top of the door, to the door

frame, inside the door, or in the floor. A self-releasing device may be installed in connection with the door closer to release the door automatically when fire is detected by a flame or smoke detector. Automatic door openers, mounted in the top of the frame or in the floor, operate on the same principle as the door closer.

The traditional surface-mounted door closer is usually mounted on the top of the door, with the lever arm attached to the head of the frame. The holder may be bracket mounted on the frame, with the arm attached to the door. This type of holder is rugged and easy to adjust; however, the trend is toward the more compact models or the semiconcealed or concealed types of closers. Semiconcealed door closers are partly mortised into the top of the door, with a double lever arm exposed. Overhead closers may be fully concealed in the door or in the frame. This type is effective on metal frames or doors. The action is similar to the surface-mounted units, except that a single lever

Fig. 11-26   Traditional door closer. (*LCN Closers.*)

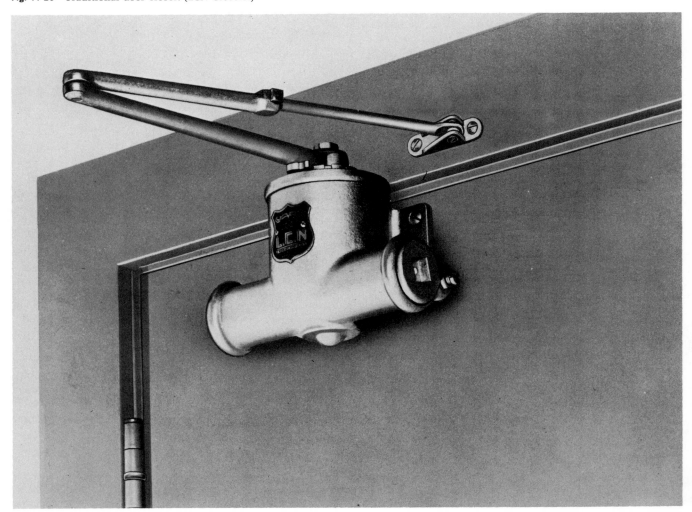

arm is usually needed. Concealed overhead door closers are usually more difficult to adjust than the surface-mounted models, but since they are enclosed, they are less likely to be affected by dust.

Two types of floor closers, sometimes called *floor checks*, are produced. One type, used with butt-hinged doors, is similar in operation to the overhead closer, and the other is a combination pin hinge and closer. Floor closers require a depression in the floor for installation. This presents problems with concrete and terrazzo floors. The opening for the closer must be accurately blocked out before the slab is poured, and forms must be placed for the necessary depression. Often a contractor will pour the slab and then cut the required hole, which also involves additional expense. Floor hinges and closers are subject to abuse from dirt and floor cleaning operations.

Another consideration is the expected swing of the door. Certain types of closers allow the door to swing back a full 180°, but others allow swings of only 100°. Some closers are equipped with stops to hold the door at fixed points in its swing.

DOOR HOLDERS AND STRIKES Doors may be equipped with overhead door holders or stay to limit the door swing and provide a holding mechanism. Door stops may also be attached to the floor or wall to prevent the door from swinging into a wall or permanent obstruction. Some types have a hook or latch to hold the door open.

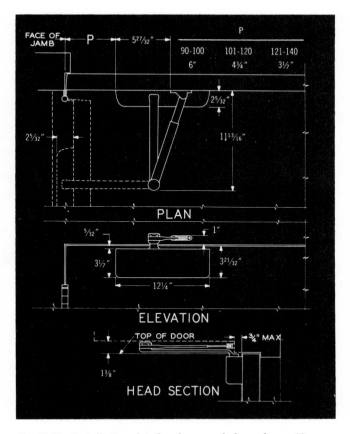

Fig. 11-28 Installation details of exposed door closer. (*By permission of LCN Closers.*)

Fig. 11-27 Exposed door closer. (*By permission of LCN Closers.*)

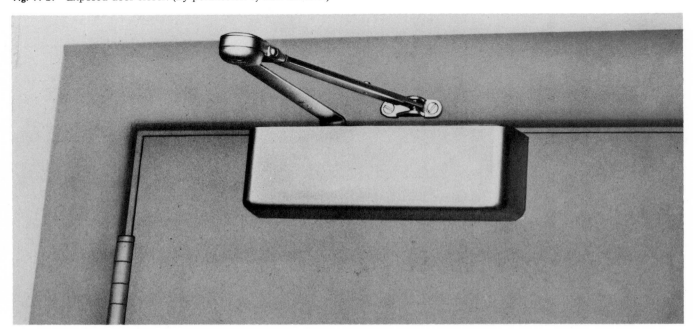

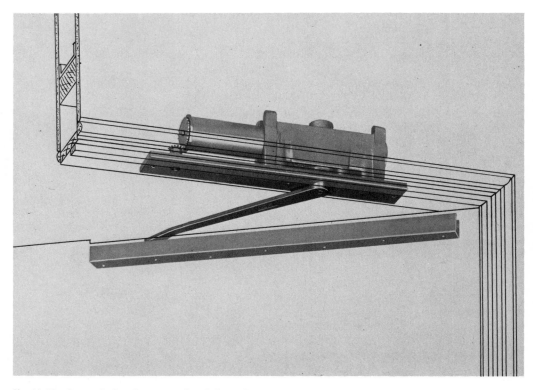

Fig. 11-29 Concealed-in-frame overhead door closer. (*By permission of LCN Closers.*)

Fig. 11-30 Installation details of concealed-in-frame overhead door closer. (*By permission of LCN Closers.*)

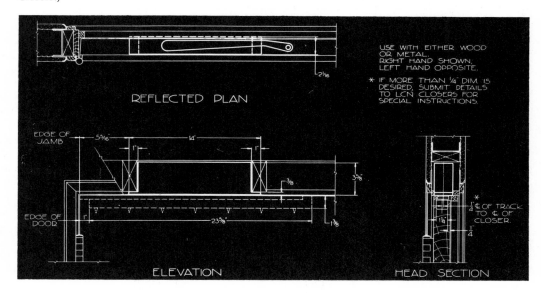

PANIC DEVICES   Most building codes and fire regulations require *panic bars* on exit doors from assembly areas, restaurants, schools, and other public buildings. These are horizontal bars, placed at latch height, which will open one or more doors when pressure is exerted. Most codes specify that panic devices cannot be locked in any manner to prevent their being opened from the inside. Doors with panic hardware have various types of locking arrangements to control entry from outside the building. If the door, or pair of doors, form part of a fire-door assembly, only devices that have been approved and rated by one of several testing laboratories will be accepted. For example, hardware applied to a 3-hr fire door must hold the door latched for a period of three hours with the temperature in the testing furnace at 1900°F.

One type of panic device is based on a center latch bolt. When the panic bar is depressed, it activates a rim lock which releases the door. This type may be used with a single door or a pair of doors. If a pair of doors act as fire doors, the active door must have an astragal or extension to cover the crack between the two doors. An alternative is a removable mullion, which allows the pair of doors to be locked separately and seals the crack between them.

A second type of panic hardware operates by means of a vertical rod mounted on the surface or inside of the door. When the panic bar is depressed, vertical rods extending above and below the actuating hardware retract

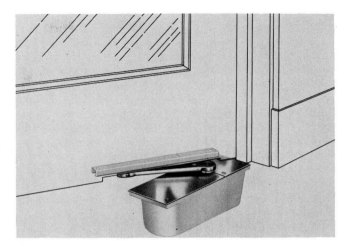

Fig. 11-32   Concealed-in-floor closer. (*By permission of LCN Closers.*)

bolts (latches) at the top and bottom of the door. Vertical-rod hardware offers positive locking at both the top and bottom of the door. This type of hardware is often used on the inactive door in a pair of doors, with a center latch bolt on the active door.

Latches and Locks

The function of latches and locks is to hold doors in a closed position. This is accomplished by bolts which operate in various ways. A *dead bolt* is a square-ended locking bolt that is extended and retracted by means of a thumb turn or a key. A *latch bolt* is a beveled bolt held in an extended position by a spring and pushed in by contact with the strike plate or retracted by means of a thumbpiece, lever, or knob. A *night latch*, which is an auxiliary to the regular door lock, has a spring latch bolt operated from the outside by a key and from the inside by a thumbpiece.

A *lockset* is the complete set of all the parts necessary to operate the latch bolt, including the latch bolt, lock, keys, knobs, roses, escutchens, strikes, and fastenings. The *rose* is the round base trim of a knob or lever used for attaching the lockset to the door and containing a socket to support and guide the shank of the knob. An *escutchen* is the decorative plate that is usually placed under the rose. It may be round, square, rectangular, or irregular in shape and either solid or pierced in a decorative pattern. The escutchen may be elongated to cover a lock case containing a knob bushing and a separate cylinder lock.

SURFACE LOCKS AND LATCHES   Locks and latches attached to the surface of a door without mortising are called *rim locks* or *rim latches*. Both the case and the strike are mounted on the face of the door. This type of installation is seldom

Fig. 11-31   Installation details of concealed-in-door overhead door closer. (*By permission of LCN Closers.*)

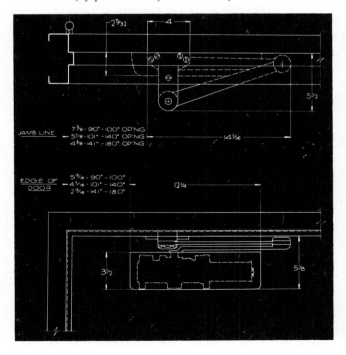

used in new construction. It may occasionally be used in remodeling or as a night latch after the door and hardware have been installed and is sometimes used for locked gates.

MORTISE LOCKS   One of the first types of concealed lock was the *mortise lock*, which is mortised into the edge of the door. The large mortise area and accurate fitting necessary to install mortise locks in wood doors tends to limit their use. When they are to be installed in hollow metal doors, the opening can be easily cut to template during fabrication. However, the door manufacturer must know exactly which lock will be installed before he starts fabrication. The size and accessibility of the case of a mortise lock allow for the greatest number of key and latch functions.

One advantage of the mortise lock is that it uses an easily removable *pin-tumbler cylinder*. The pin-tumbler cylinder contains a key-control mechanism, a rotating spindle or plug, and a cam for actuating the bolt. It is a separate mechanism from the lock proper, but it is screwed into threads in the lock body. The standard cylinder for doors or mortise locks is 1⅛ in. in diameter.

The plug of a cylinder lock has a slot, or *keyway*, formed so that only keys with a matching configuration can be inserted. Several matching holes are drilled into the plug and cylinder at right angles to the cylinder, and a small phosphor-bronze coiled spring and two pins, or tumblers are inserted in each hole to prevent rotation of

the plug except when it is operated by the proper key. The pins vary in length, and when a key is inserted in the slot, each set of pins is lifted a distance corresponding to the notches, or *bitting*, of the key. When the proper key is inserted, each notch pushes its corresponding pins just far enough back into the shell to bring them exactly to the outside edge of the plug. The plug will then turn freely and the latch can be retracted.

A standard cylinder has at least five tumblers, although more may be used. The more tumblers used in a lock, the more different keys it can be set for. By correlating variations in the section of the milled keyway with adjustment of tumblers, a large number of key changes are possible. One manufacturer produces a key with a shank that is roughly hexagonal, having depressions drilled in any or all of the six sides. As the key is inserted into the specially made plug, pins drop into the depressions to release the tumblers. With this type of cylinder it would be possible, theoretically, to have as many as 36 tumblers, which would allow an almost infinite number of key changes. Cylinders are produced in three general types: mortise cylinders, for use with mortise locks, rim cylinders for use with rim locks, and knob cylinders for use with key-in-knob locks.

BORED-IN LOCKS   Bored-in locksets may be either a tubular or a cylindrical type. Both types require a horizontal hole bored into the edge of the door intersected by a second horizontal hole bored from one face of the door to the other.

Fig. 11-33   Installation details of concealed-in-floor closer. (*By permission of LCN Closers.*)

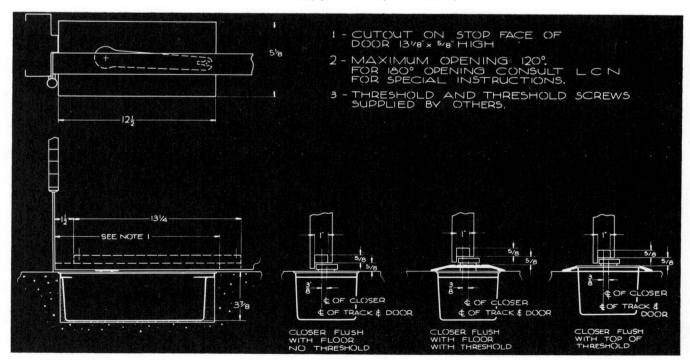

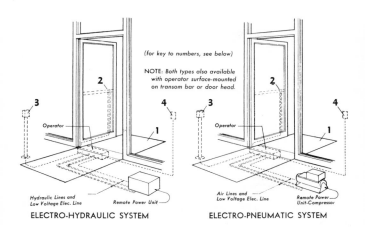

(for key to numbers, see below)

NOTE: Both types also available with operator surface-mounted on transom bar or door head.

ELECTRO-HYDRAULIC SYSTEM

ELECTRO-PNEUMATIC SYSTEM

Operator

Hydraulic Lines and Low Voltage Elec. Line

Remote Power Unit

Air Lines and Low Voltage Elec. Line

Remote Power Unit-Compressor

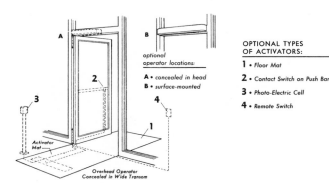

optional operator locations:

A • concealed in head

B • surface-mounted

Activator Mat

Overhead Operator Concealed in Wide Transom

ELECTRO-MECHANICAL SYSTEMS

OPTIONAL TYPES OF ACTIVATORS:

1 • Floor Mat

2 • Contact Switch on Push Bar

3 • Photo-Electric Cell

4 • Remote Switch

Fig. 11-34 Automatic door operators. (*By permission of the National Association of Architectural Metal Manufacturers.*)

Fig. 11-35 Door catch and strike. (*Glynn-Johnson Corporation.*)

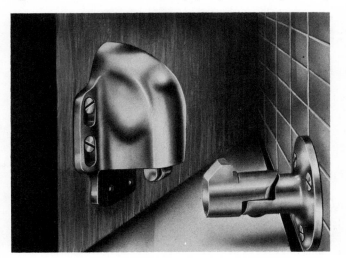

Fig. 11-36 Panic device. Surface-mounted vertical rod and mortise lock combination on double doors. (*Von Duprin, Inc.*)

Fig. 11-37 Mortise lock. (*Von Duprin, Inc.*)

Fig. 11-38 Strike for mortise lock. (*By permission of Von Duprin, Inc.*)

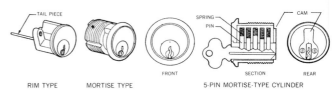

Fig. 11-39 Cylinder locks. (*By permission of the National Association of Architectural Metal Manufacturers.*)

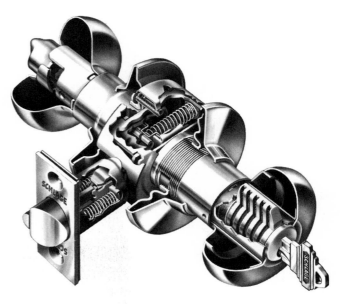

Fig. 11-40 Key-in-knob cylinder lockset. (*By permission of the Schlage Lock Company.*)

Cylindrical locksets require a considerably larger hole through the door than tubular locksets. They have a cylindrical case that fits over the smaller latch-bolt case. Both types may have either plain knobs or a cylinder lock inside the knob.

The usual *backset* for bored-in locks, the distance the knob is set back from the edge of the door, is 2⅜″ or 2¾″. If a larger backset is desired to accommodate large decorative escutchens or for design reasons, an extension link may be joined to the latch to increase the backset to 5″, 7″, 10″ or 18″.

UNIT LOCKS These are complete factory-assembled locksets that are installed in a notch cut in the edge of a door. They are rigid units that can be simply slid into the notch. The adjustments that would be required for other types of locksets are eliminated. They are produced for doors 1⅜″, 1¾″, and up to 3″ thick. They are also produced with backsets of 2¾″ and 3¾″.

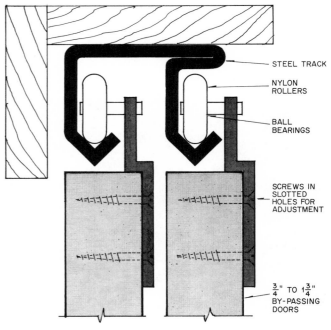

Fig. 11-41 Sliding-door hardware.

Sliding-door Hardware

Since most sliding doors are top hung, the size of the track and rolling devices needed to support and guide them varies with the weight as well as the arrangement of the doors. Sliding doors may or may not have guides or rollers on the floor. Special pulls and locks must be supplied for pocket and bypass doors.

OVERHEAD TRACKS Overhead tracks may be made from aluminum extrusions or formed steel sheet. For a single sliding (pocket) door a single track is used. For bypassing doors either two single tracks or a double track may be used. Wheels are usually nylon, with Teflon or steel ball bearings. Several high-quality carriers consist of hangers supported by twin rows of hardened steel ball bearings rolling in machined slots. This type of hanger will support loads of 300 lb or more. The doors may be hung from brackets mounted to either the top or the side. Thinner

doors require a side mounting. Where doors may be approached from both sides, brackets are attached to the top of the door.

Folding doors use similar types of tracks and carriers. The hanger is made in such a way the door can pivot as well as slide.

PULLS, LATCHES, AND LOCKS Bypassing doors require flush pulls. The pull may be mortised into the side of the door. Small round flush pulls are sometimes called *finger pulls*. Pocket doors need an edge pull, mortised into the edge of the door. Locks and latches made especially for sliding doors are manufactured in a wide range of types.

CABINET HARDWARE

Cabinet hardware includes all hinges, pivots, knobs, pulls, and catches necessary for cabinetwork. It also includes

Fig. 11-42 Cabinet doors and drawers: (a) lipped, (b) flush, and (c) overlay.

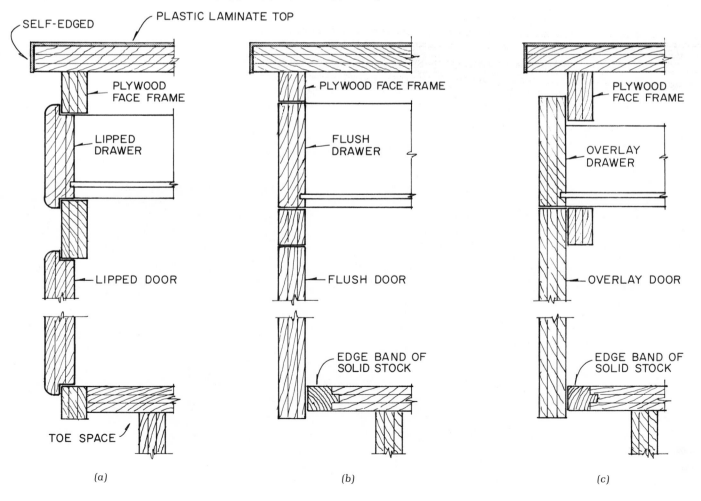

(a)   (b)   (c)

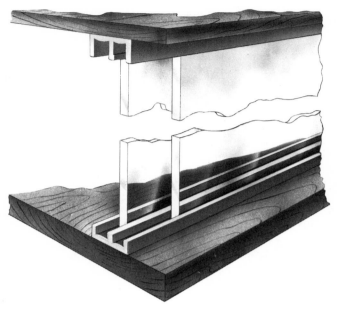

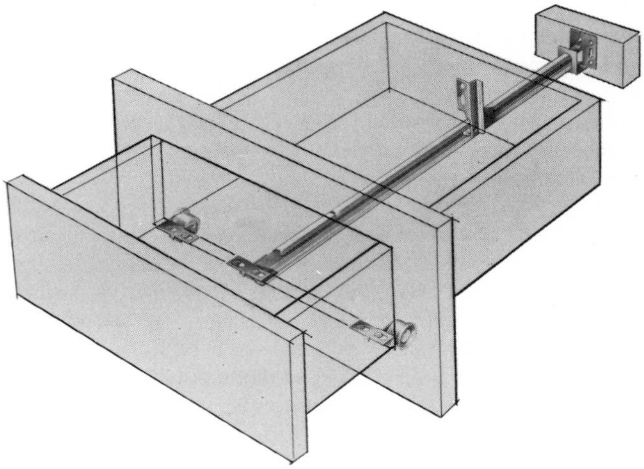

Fig. 11-45 Center-mounted drawer guides. (*By permission of the Knape and Vogt Manufacturing Company.*)

Fig. 11-43 Sliding-cabinet-door guide. (*By permission of the Knape and Vogt Manufacturing Company.*)

Fig. 11-44 Extension side drawer guides. (*By permission of the Knape and Vogt Manufacturing Company.*)

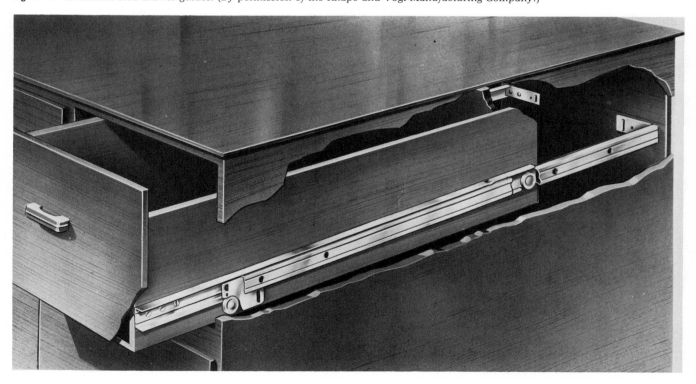

such items as rotating metal shelves to fit into corners of base cabinets (lazy susans), adjustable shelf brackets, drawer guides, metal vegetable bins, linings for sugar and flour bins, and many other metal products that may be installed in or on cabinets. However, it does not include such items as metal sinks, range and oven hoods, and appliances. Hardware for wardrobe and storage-area doors is sometimes considered cabinet hardware. Visible cabinet hardware, or visible portions of cabinet hardware, may be obtained in various finishes (see Table 11-5). Thousands of different items and varieties are marketed, and only a general description of the most common types and styles is possible here.

There are four basic types of cabinet construction, designated by the manner in which the doors are fitted, guided, or hinged. Openings in cabinets may close with sliding panels, lipped doors, flush doors, or overlay doors. Each requires a specific type of hardware. Sliding panels usually slide in rectangular grooves milled into wooden guides. In better types of construction these grooves may be faced with nylon or other plastic. In top-quality construction the panels may move on ball-bearing rollers. The remaining types of doors require hinges.

CABINET HINGES   Cabinet doors may be mounted with surface hinges, semiconcealed hinges, pin hinges, or invisible hinges. *Surface hinges* are applied to the surface of the stile and the door. When this type of hinge is used, it is usually treated as a decorative feature of the cabinetwork. One common style is the HL hinge, so-called because of its shape, which is usually furnished in a dull hammered black finish. *Semiconcealed hinges* consist of a surface-mounted leaf that is applied to the stile and a leaf that is bent to fit the back of the cabinet door. *Pin hinges* are attached to the back of the door and the inside of the stile or rail. *Invisible hinges* are mortised into the edges of the stile and rail so that they are completely concealed.

CATCHES AND PULLS   The simplest type of cabinet catch consists of a screw with a special type of head that is attached to the inside of the door, which engages a spring or spring-loaded nylon rollers when the door is closed. In higher-quality cabinet construction, a magnetic catch is used to hold the door tightly against the face frame of the cabinet.

There are literally hundreds of types and styles of cabinet pulls or knobs. These pulls or knobs may be obtained in aluminum, brass, bronze, wrought iron, steel, wood, plastic, or ceramic materials.

DRAWER GLIDES   The simplest type of drawer glide consists of a wood guide at the bottom of the drawer. In quality construction, metal tracks and nylon rollers are used. These are sometimes referred to as extension drawer slides. They may be installed on both sides of the drawer, on the bottom of the drawer, or on top of the drawer, depending on the manufacturer or the type of use expected.

MISCELLANEOUS CABINET HARDWARE   Adjustable-shelf hardware, metal towel hangers, metal pot hangers, and other miscellaneous cabinet hardware vary from manufacturer to manufacturer. A number of types of ventilated vegetable-storage bins and flour and sugar containers are produced to be built into cabinets. Spice racks, pull-out shelves for mixers or blenders, and many other specialty items are often available.

QUESTIONS

1. Describe a flush hollow-core door.

2. Describe a flush solid-core door.

3. What are the differences between an interior wood door frame and an exterior wood door frame?

4. What size would you recommend for a bedroom door? Why?

5. Why is a door beveled?

6. Describe three types of solid-core doors and the advantages of each.

7. What is the difference between a right-hand door and a left-hand door?

8. What type and grade of door would you specify for a painted closet door?

9. What are the advantages and limitations of a plastic-laminate-clad door?

10. Describe four types of wardrobe doors.

11. What type and thickness of glass would you specify for a sliding glass door in a residence in your area?

12. Describe an OXO sliding door.

13. Where would a hollow metal door be used?

14. What is the significance of a UL label on doors?

15. Name the parts of a wood double-hung window.

16. What are some of the disadvantages of wood casement windows?

17. Describe a jalousie window.

18. What is the difference between a window wall and a curtain wall?

19. List 10 items that would be considered rough hardware.

20. What is the difference between rough hardware and finishing hardware?

21. What are the type of lockset and finish designation on the door of the room in which you are now located?

22. Describe an olive-knuckle butt.

23. Describe the operation of a cylinder lock.

24. What is the purpose of a panic device, and how does it operate?

25. What is an escutchen?

26. What are the differences between a tubular lockset and a cylindrical lockset?

27. What type of catch would you install on quality cabinetwork?

28. Describe a semiconcealed cabinet hinge.

REFERENCES FOR FURTHER STUDY

American National Standards Institute: 1430 Broadway, New York, N.Y., 10018. "Nomenclature for Steel Doors and Steel Frames," A123.1, 1967.

Architectural Aluminum Manufacturers' Association: 35 East Wacker Drive, Chicago, Ill., 60601. "Specifications for Aluminum Windows," 1970.

Brownell, Adon H.: "Hardware Age Builders' Hardware Handbook," Chilton Company, Book Division, Philadelphia, 1956.

Builders' Hardware Manufacturers' Association: 60 East 42d Street, New York, N.Y., 10017. "Basic Builders' Hardware," 1969. "Abbreviations and Symbols Used in Builders' Hardware Schedules and Specifications," 1961. "Hardware for Labeled Fire Doors," 1970. "Standardization of Terms and Nomenclature of Keying," 1969. "Hardware for Schools," 1966. "Hardware for Hospitals," 1965.

Callender, John Hancock: "Time-saver Standards," 4th ed., McGraw-Hill, New York, 1966.

Construction Specifications Institute: Suite 300, 1150 17th Street, N.W., Washington, D.C., 20036. "Builders' Finishing Hardware," 1961. "Specifying Custom Hollow Metal Work," 1970.

Haswell, William S.: "Finish Hardware Mysteries Dispelled," The *Construction Specifier*, July 1970, p. 27.

Huntington, Whitney Clark: "Building Construction," 3d ed., Wiley, New York, 1963.

National Woodwork Manufacturers' Association: 400 West Madison Street, Chicago, Ill., 60606. "Industry Standard for Wood Window Units," I.S.2-69, 1969.

Underwriters' Laboratories: 207 East Ohio Street, Chicago, Ill. "Tin-clad Fire Doors," UL 10(a), 1968. "Fire Door Frames," UL 63, 1968. "Building Materials List," 1970.

Weyerhaeuser Company, Box B, Tacoma, Wash., 98401. "Architectural Wood Doors," 1970.

Woodwork Institute of California: 1833 Broadway, Fresno, Calif, "Manual of Millwork," 1969.

GLASS

~~Glass is a supercooled liquid,~~ one that is ~~physically solid but uncrystallized~~, which has sufficient *viscosity* to prevent the formation of crystals. It is a thermoplastic material (~~it melts~~) that can be shaped at temperatures above ~~2300°F~~. In its molten state glass is a chemical compound, but if it is held too long in its molten state, the various chemicals tend to crystallize. If it is allowed to cool too slowly, the compounds will crystallize out of the solution. When crystallization takes place, the glass could be said to be "frozen." To avoid this condition glass is carried through the crystallization temperature as quickly as possible, so that it will form an amorphous (uncrystallized) solid characterized by ~~hardness, brittleness, transparency, and chemical inertness~~.

Composition

The basic materials used in the manufacture of glass for construction purposes are sand ~~(silica)~~, soda ~~(sodium oxide)~~, and ~~lime~~ (calcium oxide), with the addition or substitution of various other chemicals to modify the characteristics of the resultant glass products.

Sand is a material that has been broken down from stone by the action of streams, rivers, or oceans. The sand found along stream beds or on the seashore is seldom suitable for glassmaking because of its impurities. However, throughout the ages sand deposits have been solidified into sandstone, which has been subjected to the action of rain and surface water to wash away most impurities. Consequently, most sandstone consists of nearly pure silica. For high-grade plate and sheet glass, a sand that is 99.9 percent silica and contains no more than 0.05 percent iron oxide is required.

Extremely high temperatures are needed to convert silica into glass without the presence of fluxes. Fluxes such as soda permit silica to melt at a much lower temperature. The soda used in glassmaking is closely related to common baking soda or bicarbonate of soda. It is usually derived from sodium carbonate (Na_2CO) or sodium sulfate (Na_2SO), although common table salt or the salt in sea water (NaCL) is occasionally used. Many other salts are used to impart certain qualities or improve workability.

The introduction of lime, in the form of limestone, to the glass batch results in the forming of a soda-lime-silicate or a silicone-sodium-calcium type of glass. Lime makes the glass batch easier to work, shortens the working time, and improves the weathering qualities of the glass.

Chemical and Physical Properties

The physical properties of glass vary widely, depending on its chemical composition. Its thermal expansion is increased by the addition of sodium (Na) and potassium (K). Boron (B) tends to reduce the thermal expansion. Lead (Pb) increases the brilliancy of glass. Iron (Fe) is usually present in glass batches as an impurity. Iron may be added to glass to produce aquamarine coloring. Over 41 different chemical elements are used in the manufacture of glass. Dynamic progress is being made in the glass industry today through research and development, not only in developing new compounds, but also in creating new methods of manufacture involving completely new concepts in mass production.

Glass is classed as a ceramic material (any product made from earth by the agency of fire). Ceramic materials, such as clays used in the production of brick and tile, are shaped cold and then fired to produce the required product. Glass is shaped at extremely high temperatures and allowed to cool. It can again be made plastic or even molten by the further application of heat.

Glass is impervious to most acids except hydrofluoric acid. It is damaged by alkaline solutions. The runoff alkali from masonry or concrete structures can stain or etch the glass. The alkali in most soap, if in contact with a glass surface for a period of time, will etch glass sufficiently that it cannot be restored to its original brilliance regardless of the rubbing and polishing. Glass is also slowly dissolved by water.

Regular window and plate glass exclude most of the ultraviolet light that has a therapeutic value. The addition of tin to the glass batch somewhat improves the transmission of ultraviolet light. Regular clear sheet glass or plate glass will transmit 75 to 90 percent of the solar energy that strikes it. The addition of controlled quantities of ferrous oxide (iron rust) to glass will reduce the solar radiation. Tinted and reflective glasses reduce the transmission of light, heat, and glare.

Unlike most ductile materials (those capable of being drawn out or worked), glass does not have a clearly defined tensile strength. A group of identical glass specimens may exhibit a wide range of strengths when tested. Individual glass fibers may have a tensile strength of 1,500,000 psi, whereas 1 sq in. of glass has a strength of only 6000 psi. The surface quality and the size of individual lights (panes of glass) greatly affect the breaking-stress level. Large lights usually break at somewhat lower levels than small lights. A light of annealed glass, glass which has been stress relieved during manufacture by cooling under controlled conditions, will fail at some surface variation that may be undetectable before the break occurs. The coefficient of expansion of glass varies from 0.00000056 to 0.00000140.

Early Methods of Glassmaking

The use of glass dates back to the caveman. Obsidian, the product of volcanic fires which fused the necessary elements into great masses of black glass, is found throughout the world. Primitive man discovered that this material could be broken into sharp, elongated pieces for use as arrowheads, spearheads, scrapers, and knives. Where and when man discovered the process of fusing the basic elements of glass is not known. From the hieroglyphics in Egyptian tombs we know that glassmaking had become a stable industry by 1500 B.C.

Pliny the Elder, a Roman historian (23–79 A.D.), relates that the process of making glass was discovered by a group of Phoenician mariners. According to Pliny, they were huddled together on the sandy shore of a river in Syria preparing their evening meal and had used lumps of natron (soda, Na), carried as ballast in their ship, to support their cooking pot. The heat of the fire, aided by the fluxing action of soda, melted and fused the sand (silica), and in the dying embers of their fires the mariners discovered the first man-made glass.

The invention of the blowpipe, attributed to the Phoenicians around 300 B.C., made it possible to shape glass articles. The blowpipe, in essentially the same form, has been used for 2000 years to produce hollow vessels, globes, vases, and many other types of glassware. It consists of a long metal tube. One end of the tube is dipped into a batch of molten glass, and a blob of glass, which immediately begins to solidify is lowered into a mold. By blowing through the tube, the glassblower forces the glass against the side of the mold.

The Romans developed the process of rolling out glass into thin sheets, which were broken or cut into small pieces (tesserae) for glass mosaics. Small sheets of semiopaque glass were also used to close openings in walls, the first use of glass as a window. The first relatively clear glass was produced in Venice about 1000 A.D. Glass used for windows was blown into cylindrical shapes, and the cylinder was cut while it was hot and flattened on a smooth surface. The sizes and quality of glass produced by this method was extremely limited.

In 1688, in France, Louis Lucas de Nehou developed a method of casting plate glass. The large polished plates made excellent mirrors, and after Louis XIV installed hundreds of them in the Hall of Mirrors at Versailles Palace and in all of his coaches, mirrors became the rage of Europe. This fad soon spread to America. The first glass factory in America was established in Jamestown in 1608; however, this operation was discontinued after seven years of intermittent operation. Other small factories were established through the colonies to manufacture beads for trade with the Indians and handmade bottles and containers. The first real glassworks was established at Wisterberg, New Jersey, by Casper Wister. The glass he produced was fashioned into heavy-bodied glassware, now known as *Wister glass,* which is widely sought by lovers of antiques.

The first window glass in the United States was produced by the ancient method of glass blowing. Around 1800 a window glass called *crown glass* was produced. This process, which originated in Europe, consisted of gathering a blob of glass on the end of a blowpipe and blowing it into a sphere. An iron rod called a *punty* was attached to the sphere opposite the blowpipe, and the blowpipe was removed, leaving a large opening in the sphere. The glass was reheated and the punty was spun so that the glass flattened out into a disk. The disks were then cut into small, relatively flat panes for use in glazing. The center of the disk, where the punty had been attached, was called *bullseye glass* and is still highly prized for its decorative value.

SHEET GLASS

Sheet glass was first produced on a large scale by a hand process. A blob of glass was gathered on the end of a blowpipe, blown into a sphere, and lowered into a furnace, where it was kept in a plastic state. The blower maintained air pressure on the globe while swinging it like a pendulum in a pit (called the "glory hole") below the working floor. The weight of the glass caused the sphere to elongate into a cylinder approximately 6 ft long and 20 in. in diameter. The ends of the cylinder were cut off, the cylinder was split longitudinally, and the glass was reintroduced into a furnace with a flat clay bottom. As the glass softened, the operator unfolded it and ironed it into a relatively flat sheet with a heavy wood flattening block. The resulting glass sheet was uneven in thickness and disfigured by sand marks, burn marks, and marks of the flattening tool.

The hand process evolved into a machine process which used compressed air to produce cylinders up to 40 ft long and 40 in. in diameter. The cylinders were cut and flattened by the same method in the hand process. Machine-blown glass was of higher quality and was more uniform in thickness, although many of the defects of hand-processed glass were still evident.

Fourcault Process

Another development in the production of sheet or window glass was the invention in Belgium of the Fourcault process, in which a continuous sheet of glass is drawn out through a slot in a water-cooled boat floating on a pool of molten glass. As the semicooled glass is extruded through the slot, clamps are attached to it and it is drawn vertically between asbestos-covered rollers through a metal casing called a *lehr.* As the glass travels up through the lehr, it is slowly cooled, or annealed. At the top of the drawing machine it is cut into sheets of the desired length, inspected for defects, and trimmed to final size.

TABLE 12-1 Load table

Elev. above Grade "h" (Ft.)	70 MPH				80 MPH				90 MPH				100 MPH				110 MPH				120 MPH			
	VP†	DP	STP	WTP	VP	DP	STP	WTP	VP	DP	STP	WTP	VP	DP	STP	WTP	VP	DP	STP	WTP	VP	DP	STP	WTP
5	7.5	8.3	(12.4)	(.83)	9.8	10.8	(16.2)	(1.08)	12.4	13.6	20.5	(1.36)	15.3	16.8	25.2	(1.68)	18.6	20.5	30.7	(2.05)	22.1	24.3	36.5	(2.43)
10	9.2	10.1	(15.2)	(1.01)	12.0	13.2	(19.8)	(1.32)	15.2	16.7	25.1	(1.67)	18.7	20.6	30.9	(2.06)	22.6	24.9	37.3	(2.49)	26.9	29.6	44.4	2.96
15	10.3	11.3	(16.0)	(1.13)	13.4	14.7	22.1	(1.47)	17.0	18.7	28.1	(1.87)	21.0	23.1	34.7	(2.31)	25.4	27.9	41.9	(2.79)	30.2	33.2	49.8	3.32
20	11.2	12.3	(18.5)	(1.23)	14.6	16.1	24.1	(1.61)	18.5	20.4	30.5	(2.04)	22.8	25.1	37.6	(2.51)	27.6	30.4	45.5	3.04	32.8	36.1	54.1	3.61
25	11.9	13.1	(19.6)	(1.31)	15.6	17.2	25.7	(1.72)	19.7	21.7	32.5	(2.17)	24.3	26.7	40.1	(2.67)	29.4	32.3	48.5	3.23	35.0	38.5	57.8	3.85
30	12.5	13.8	20.6	(1.38)	16.4	18.0	27.1	(1.80)	20.7	22.8	34.2	(2.28)	25.6	28.2	42.2	(2.82)	31.0	34.1	51.2	3.41	36.9	40.6	60.9	4.06
37½	13.4	14.7	22.1	(1.47)	17.5	19.3	28.9	(1.93)	22.1	24.3	36.5	(2.43)	27.3	30.0	45.0	3.00	33.0	36.3	54.5	3.63	39.3	43.2	64.8	4.32
45	14.1	15.5	23.3	(1.55)	18.4	20.2	30.4	(2.02)	23.3	25.6	38.4	(2.56)	28.7	31.6	47.4	3.16	34.8	38.3	57.4	3.83	41.4	45.5	68.3	4.55
55	14.9	16.4	24.6	(1.64)	19.5	21.5	32.2	(2.15)	24.7	27.2	40.8	(2.72)	30.4	33.4	50.2	3.34	36.8	40.5	60.7	4.05	43.8	48.2	72.8	4.82
100	17.7	19.5	29.2	(1.95)	23.1	25.4	38.1	(2.54)	29.3	32.2	48.3	3.22	36.1	39.7	59.6	3.97	43.7	48.1	72.1	4.81	52.0	57.2	85.8	5.72
125	18.9	20.8	31.2	(2.08)	24.6	27.1	40.6	(2.71)	31.2	34.3	51.5	3.43	38.5	42.4	63.5	4.24	46.6	51.3	76.9	5.13	55.4	60.9	91.4	6.09
200	21.6	23.8	35.6	(2.38)	28.2	31.0	46.5	3.10	35.7	39.3	58.9	3.93	44.0	48.4	72.6	4.84	53.3	58.6	87.9	5.86	63.4	69.7	104.6	6.97
250	23.0	25.3	38.0	(2.53)	30.0	33.0	49.5	3.30	38.0	41.8	62.7	4.18	46.9	51.6	77.4	5.16	56.8	62.5	93.7	6.25	67.6	74.4	111.5	7.44
300	24.2	26.6	39.9	(2.66)	31.6	34.8	52.1	3.48	40.0	44.0	66.0	4.40	49.4	54.3	81.5	5.43	59.8	65.8	98.7	6.58	71.2	78.3	117.5	7.83
375	25.8	28.4	42.6	(2.84)	33.7	37.1	55.6	3.71	42.7	47.0	70.5	4.70	52.7	58.0	87.0	5.80	63.8	70.2	105.3	7.02	75.9	83.5	125.2	8.35
450	27.2	29.9	44.9	2.99	35.5	39.1	58.6	3.91	45.0	49.5	74.3	4.95	55.5	61.1	91.6	6.11	67.2	73.9	110.9	7.39	79.9	87.9	131.8	8.79
550	28.8	31.7	47.5	3.17	37.6	41.4	62.0	4.14	47.6	52.4	78.5	5.24	58.8	64.7	97.1	6.47	71.1	78.2	117.3	7.82	84.6	93.1	139.6	9.31
650	30.2	33.2	49.8	3.32	39.4	43.3	65.0	4.33	49.9	54.9	82.3	5.49	61.6	67.8	101.6	6.78	74.6	82.1	123.1	8.21	88.8	97.7	146.5	9.77
750	31.5	34.7	52.0	3.47	41.1	45.2	67.8	4.52	52.0	57.2	85.8	5.72	64.2	70.6	105.9	7.06	77.7	85.5	128.2	8.55	92.5	101.8	152.7	10.18
1000	34.2	37.6	56.4	3.76	44.6	49.1	73.6	4.91	56.5	62.2	93.2	6.22	69.7	76.7	115.0	7.67	84.4	92.8	139.3	9.28	100.4	110.4	165.6	11.04
Over 1000	REQUIRES SPECIAL CONSIDERATION																							

* Wind velocity—30 ft. elev.—from map

† VP = velocity pressure; the uniform load exerted by the wind on doors or windows

DP = design pressure; allows for wind gusts and building shape, corresponds to loads published in building codes

STP = structural test pressure; obtained by multiplying DP by a safety factor

WTP = water test pressure; used for testing resistance to water leakage

By permission of the National Association of Architectural Metal Manufacturers.

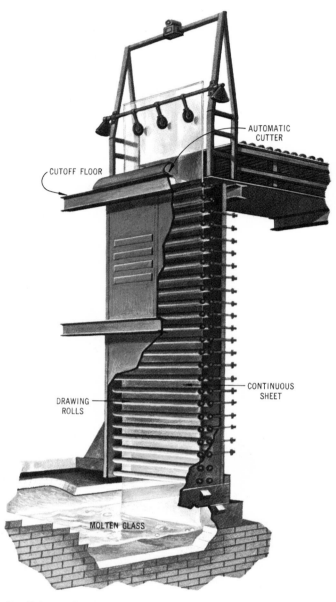

AUTOMATIC
CUTTER

CUTOFF FLOOR

CONTINUOUS
SHEET

DRAWING
ROLLS

MOLTEN GLASS

Fig. 12-1 Production of sheet glass with the Pennvernon draw machine. (*By permission of PPG Industries.*)

Glass is drawn from the bath at 1400°F. At 1200°F it is still viscous and continues to stretch. Between 1200 and 1100°F it becomes rigid. As the glass sheet is drawn from the molten bath, the heat of the molten glass in the furnace polishes the surface. Further finishing or polishing is unnecessary. The glass is said to be *flame polished* or *fire finished*.

Most drawing furnaces are of the gas-fired *regenerative* type. Hot gases flow across the surface of the glass in the hearth, with the direction of flow reversed at regular inter-

vals. Most of the heat of the exhaust gases is absorbed as they pass through a honeycomb of refractory brick on their way to the exhaust stack. When the flow is reversed, this heat is recovered by combustion gases entering the furnace. The basin of the furnace is kept constantly full of molten glass (2000 tons). Sand, soda ash, limestone, carbon, dolomite, and crushed glass, called *cullet*, are carefully weighed, mixed, and fed continuously into the fired end of the furnace. As the batch is fed into one end of the furnace, a corresponding amount of glass is drawn out at the other end. As the glass flows from the fired end of the furnace, residual air bubbles rise to the surface, and by the time the glass reaches the drawing end of the furnace, it is fully homogeneous and refined.

In one modification of the Fourcault process, called the Pennvernon process, a horizontal clay bar is submerged several inches below the surface of the molten glass and the glass sheet is drawn from a point directly above the bar. The draw is started by submerging a steel frame supporting taut wires into the molten glass as a *bait*. When the bait is raised, a sheet of glass follows it and continues to be generated as the bait passes between asbestos-covered rollers. By the time the glass reaches the rollers, it is sufficiently hard to be drawn upward by the pressure between them. The bait, which is no longer needed, is removed at the top of the drawing machine, about 30 ft above the furnace. The glass comes from the bath in a relatively thick mass. The speed of the draw determines the final thickness of the sheet; the slower the draw, the thicker the sheet.

Colburn Process

Another method of producing window glass, known as the ~~Colburn process~~, was developed soon after the Fourcault process. In this process the glass is drawn up from a shallow furnace through a drawing trough at the surface of the molten glass. After traveling vertically for about 24 in., the continuous ribbon of viscous glass is bent over a roller and conveyed through a horizontal lehr, where it is annealed. This process will produce a glass ribbon of unlimited length. Both processes, or modifications of them, are in use today.

All sheet glass has some inherent distortion, or waves, in one direction as a result of waves introduced by the drawing process. Modern techniques have reduced the waves to a minimum; however, sheet glass should always be installed with the waves in a horizontal direction to minimize distortion of persons and objects moving past a window.

Sizes and Grades

Sheet glass is produced in a number of thicknesses, but only $3/32''$ ~~and~~ $1/8''$ sheet are commonly used as window glass. These thicknesses are designated, respectively, as ~~single strength~~ (SS) and ~~double strength~~ (DS). Thick sheet

TABLE 12-2 Weight and maximum sizes of sheet glass

THICKNESS, IN.	WEIGHT, OZ/SQ FT	MAX. SIZE, IN.
Window glass		
SS $^3/_{32}$	19	40 × 50
DS $^1/_8$	26	60 × 80
Thick sheet glass		
$^3/_{16}$	40	120 × 84
$^7/_{32}$	45	120 × 84
$^1/_4$	52	120 × 84
$^3/_8$	77	160 × 84
$^7/_{16}$*	86	60 × 84

*Used for glass shelving and table tops.

glass, manufactured by the same method as window glass, is used in openings which exceed window-glass size recommendations. This glass is sometimes, improperly, called crystal, crystal sheet, or semiplate. Table 12-2 lists the thicknesses, weight per foot, and recommended maximum sizes of sheet glass.

The maximum size of glass that may be used in a particular location is governed to a great extent by the wind load. Wind velocities, and consequently wind pressures, increase with height above the ground. Various building codes specify the maximum allowable areas of glass for wind loads (in pounds per square foot). The appropriate design wind load is determined from a U.S. Weather Bureau wind-velocity map and tables which give the increase in wind load at various heights above grade in different sections of the country. The proper type and thickness of glass for a given location can then be established from manufacturers' literature or building-code tables.

Glass is graded according to its intended use. Each grade permits certain defects in a given area of glass. Federal specification DD-G-451c identifies specific defects as shown in Table 12-3 and establishes grades for sheet glass as shown in Table 12-4.

PLATE GLASS

Plate glass is the same type of glass as sheet glass. It is not the thickness, composition, or strength that distinguish it, but the surface treatment. The brilliant surface of sheet glass is imparted by the action of heat on the surface of the glass as it is drawn from the furnace, and no further treatment is necessary; plate glass must be ground and polished after it is cast or extruded from the furnace and cooled.

Fig. 12-2 Map of fastest wind velocity (mph) at 30 ft above the ground, 50-year occurrence, from U.S. Weather Bureau data. (*By permission of the National Association of Architectural Metal Manufacturers.*)

WIND VELOCITY MAP   U.S. Weather Bureau

TABLE 12-3 Defects in glass

DEFECT	DESCRIPTION
Crush	Light pitting resulting in a dull grey appearance over the area
Digs	Deep, short scratches
Dirt	A small particle of foreign matter embedded in the glass
Gaseous inclusions	Round or elongated bubbles in the glass
Knot	A transparent area of incompletely assimilated glass having an irregular knotty or tangled appearance
Lines	Fine cords or strings, usually on the surface
Open gaseous inclusions	Bubbles at the surface which are open, leaving a cavity in the finished surface
Process surface defects	In plate glass, very fine pits and cracks left by the grinding and polishing process, called *short finish*; in float glass, foreign particles left by the float
Ream	Inclusions within the glass of layers or strings of glass which are not homogeneous with the main body of the glass
Rub	An abraded surface area with a frosted appearance
Scratch	Any marking or tearing of the surface appearing as though it had been produced by a sharp edge
Smoke	Streaked areas appearing as slight discolorations
Stone	Any crystalline inclusion embedded in the glass
Strings	Transparent lines appearing as if threads of glass had been incorporated into the sheets
Wave	Distortion introduced by the extrusion process

By permission of the General Services Administration.

TABLE 12-4 Grades of sheet glass

GRADE	USE
AA	For uses where superior quality is required
A	For selected glazing
B	For general glazing
Silvering quality A	For silvering mirror applications, seldom used for glazing
Silvering quality B	For mirror applications, seldom used for glazing
Greenhouse quality	For greenhouse glazing or similar applications, where appearance is not critical

The first plate glass was cast on large cast-iron tables and rolled roughly to thickness while it was still in plastic form. The hardened sheet was then set in plaster of paris on a heavy revolving table, where multiple polishing heads ground the surface flat, first with sand and then with emery. The surface was then polished with soft felt pads and jewelers' rouge. After one side of the plate was polished, the glass was turned over and the entire process was repeated for the other side.

Most plate glass is now produced in a shallow furnace by a continuous process. The raw materials are fed into the melting end of the furnace, and as the glass flows to the working end, it is melted and refined. At the working end of the furnace the molten glass has been cooled to 2100°F. At this point it is fed by gravity between a pair of heavy water-cooled rollers which are adjusted to control the thickness of the sheet and cool it to working temperatures. The glass ribbon flows down inclined rollers, where it cools to about 1500°F. From the rollers it proceeds into an open-ended metal lehr approximately 400 ft long, where it is slowly cooled to relieve any stress that may have built up in the surfaces. When it emerges from the lehr, it is cut into lengths and passed to the grinding machines, where it is ground and polished.

Twin-ground Plate Glass

In the twin grinding process the glass passes from the end of the lehr in a continuous ribbon about 100 in. wide to twin grinding machines, which grind both sides of the glass simultaneously. The grinding is done by iron disks approximately 10 ft in diameter, with a mixture of sand and water as an abrasive compound. Glass produced by this method is known as *twin-ground plate glass*. Twin-ground plate glass is distinguished by its parallel, uniform surfaces. At the end of the grinding line, the glass is inspected for flaws, cut into sheets, and passed on to polishing machines where it is given a final polish.

Sizes and Grades of Plate Glass

Plate glass is produced in thicknesses from 1/8″ to 1¼″. The maximum-size sheet for different thicknesses varies with

TABLE 12-5 Typical plate-glass sizes

THICKNESS, IN.	MAX. SHEET SIZE PRODUCED, IN.		
	AMERICAN SAINT GOBAIN	LIBBY-OWENS-FORD	PPG INDUSTRIES
1/8	130 × 80	72 × 74	76 × 128
1/4	130 × 240	142 × 170	126 × 226
5/16	130 × 240	120 × 170	127 × 226
3/8	130 × 240	96 × 120	125 × 281
1/2	130 × 240	96 × 120	125 × 281
5/8	—	72 × 120	—
3/4	130 × 240	72 × 120	120 × 280
7/8	—	72 × 120	—
1	—	—	74 × 148
1¼	—	—	74 × 128

the manufacturer. Generally, ¼″ plate glass is available in a wide range of sizes from distributors throughout the country. Other thicknesses are usually stocked in metropolitan areas. Extremely thick plate glass is usually made only on special order.

Table 12-5 indicates the sizes available from three domestic producers in 1969 (larger sizes may be available on special order).

Federal specification DD-G-451c grades plate glass as *silvering quality,* suitable for silvering and mirror applications; *mirror glazing quality,* intended for mirrors; and *glazing quality,* intended for glazing windows and doors, and for furniture, shelves, and portlights.

The first step in the production of polished plate results in *rough plate,* which has a pleasant textured translucence. It offers relatively high light transmission with good obscurity for use in interior partitions where both light and privacy are required. Rough plate is available in thickness of ⁹/₃₂″, with both sides rough, or ¹⁷/₆₄″, with one side polished and one side rough.

Fig. 12-3 A line of continuous polishers grinding and polishing plate glass. (*By permission of PPG Industries.*)

Float Glass

In 1959 another process of manufacturing flat glass was developed in England by Pilkington Brothers. This glass, called ~~float glass~~, is produced in the United States by several manufacturers. Float glass is a ~~flat glass~~ of controlled thickness with a ~~nearly optically true surface~~ that is ~~fire-polished and does not need to be ground or polished.~~

The furnace in which it is produced is similar to that used for plate glass. ~~Raw materials are fed into one end~~ of the furnace, and ~~refined glass emerges from the other end~~ in a continuous horizontal ribbon that flows onto a bed of molten tin. As the glass ribbon passes over the molten tin, heat is applied from the top to melt out any irregularities in the upper surface. Since gravity keeps the molten tin perfectly flat, the result is a perfectly flat sheet with a fire-finished surface. As the glass passes over the molten metal, it is cooled and hardened sufficiently to be withdrawn on a series of rollers and fed into a lehr, where it is annealed. After leaving the lehr, it is cut to length, inspected, and packed for shipment.

A ~~float-glass line~~ is usually ~~run continuously~~ day and night. In a single year a float line will produce a ribbon of glass 130 in. wide and 1500 miles long. Once the process is started, it will run for three to five years, or until the furnace liner must be replaced.

Float glass is currently produced in thicknesses of $\frac{1}{8}''$ and $\frac{1}{4}''$ in glazing-quality sheets up to $72'' \times 120''$. It is interchangeable with plate glass for most applications.

Surface-modified Float Glass

The inventor of float glass has recently developed a process of surface modification to produce glass in several grey-bronze hues for use as ~~heat-absorbing~~ or ~~glare-reducing glasses.~~ While the glass is passing over the molten tin, an electrochemical process ~~drives fine metallic particles into the glass.~~ The metallic particles are concentrated immediately below the surface, where they are impervious to abrasion.

This process should greatly ~~reduce the cost of tinted glass.~~ Since the surface modification takes place in the float line, it is not necessary to add special ingredients to the melt. Thus changes from tinted float glass back to clear glass can be effected in minutes without shutting down the float process, so that small quantities of special glass can be produced with no loss of time.

SAFETY GLASS

The fragile nature of glass is a serious drawback in large exposed glazed areas. Broken glass is a public hazard. Large clear-glass sliding doors in residences are subject to breakage by small children with wheeled toys. Many persons have been seriously injured by falling against shower and bath enclosures of annealed glass. Some building codes require safety glass or glazing materials for such installations. Security in stores, schools, and other public buildings is also increased by the installation of shatter-

Fig. 12-4 Flow chart for the production of float glass. (*By permission of PPG Industries.*)

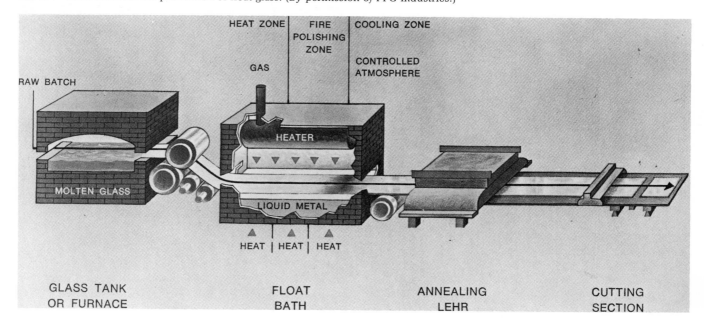

proof glass, which can be penetrated only with special equipment.

Three types of glass may be used to enhance the safety of buildings: tempered glass, laminated glass, and wired glass.

Tempered Glass

Tempered glass is produced by heating annealed glass almost to the melting point and then chilling it rapidly. This process creates a thin skin of glass on both surfaces that is under high compression, placing the center of the glass under extremely high tension. Fully tempered glass is three to five times as strong as annealed glass. Sheet glass, plate glass, float glass, tinted glass, and heat-absorbing glass may be tempered. Tempered glass is breakable. However, when the thin skin is pierced, the entire sheet usually disintegrates into small, pebblelike particles instead of sharp, daggerlike slivers. Heat-strengthened glass is slightly tempered, so that it is approximately twice as strong as regular glass. When it breaks, it has a fracture pattern similar to that of annealed glass.

Any type of heat treatment leaves a specific strain pattern in the glass. This pattern is usually not visible to the naked eye, although it can be seen under polarized light or through polarized glasses. When the strain pattern does show, it appears in iridescent colors. All tempered glass has some iridescence. Tempered glass, by nature of the tempering process, connot be made as flat as annealed sheet glass. In general, this defect is slight depending on the thickness, the length of the sheet, and other factors.

Tempered glass cannot be cut, ground, chipped, drilled, or refabricated in any way after it has been tempered. There are also special limitations on the placement, size, and configurations of holes, notches, and other necessary cutouts. Since tempered glass cannot be cut on the site, the exact size required and any special features must be specified when ordering. Tempered glass should not be regarded as a fire-retardant material, although it will withstand temperatures up to 500°F for a considerable length of time without serious loss of temper. If tempered glass is to be sandblasted, the sandblasting must be done before the glass is tempered. Tempered glass with large sandblasted decorations on one or both sides cannot be expected to meet the tests of smooth tempered glass.

Laminated Glass

This type of safety glass is made by sandwiching a layer of polyvinyl butyral between two or more lights of sheet or plate glass. The glass and plastic are bonded into a single unit with heat and pressure. The elasticity of the plastic acts to cushion any blow to the laminated unit. If the impact is sufficient to break the glass, the plastic sheet holds the small, sharp pieces firmly in place.

The type, number of laminations, and thickness of laminated glass units vary with the manufacturer and

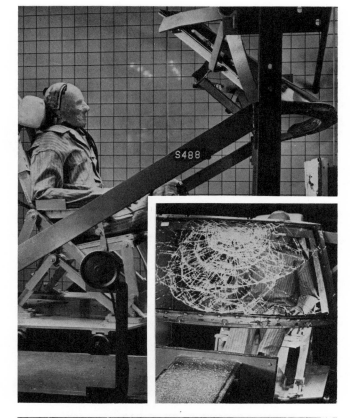

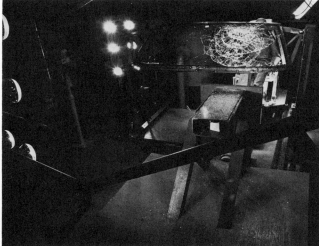

Fig. 12-5 Testing laminated safety glass. (*By permission of PPG Industries.*)

with specific design criteria. The maximum size of laminated sheet glass is 15 sq ft. Laminated plate is available in sizes of 66″ × 120″ or 72″ × 138″, depending on the manufacturer. Tinted and coated glass may be incorporated into laminated units. Some coatings used to produce reflective glass will not withstand abrasion and are protected by lamination to another piece of glass.

Bullet-resistant glass consists of three or more pieces of polished plate with sheets of clear, tough plastic material between each layer. Bullet-resisting glass is usually clear, and in many cases cannot be detected without close inspection. It is used for glazing bank-teller cages and jewelry-store display cases. Bullet-resistant glass is produced in thicknesses of ³/₄" to 3" to resist the impact of low-, medium-, and high-powered firearms. Some 3" glass of this type will resist the impact of a 50-caliber armorpiercing bullet fired at point-blank range.

Wired Glass

The search for fire-resistant materials led to the development of wired glass. Wired glass is produced by feeding wire mesh into the center of molten glass as it is passed through a pair of rollers. To be given a fire rating the mesh must be at least 25-gauge wire, with openings no larger than 1¹/₈ in., and the glass must be no less than ¹/₄". The mesh may be welded or twisted wire in a hexagonal, diamond-shaped, square, or rectangular pattern. The use of diamond-shaped or square welded wire mesh has overcome the "chicken-wire" appearance of twisted wire mesh. Wired glass may be acid etched or sandblasted on one or both sides to soften the light or provide privacy. It may be obtained with a pattern on one or both sides.

For wired glass to be approved as a fire-retardant material, it must pass stringent Underwriters' Laboratories tests. The tests consist of glazing several openings in a removable wall of a gas-fired furnace with the wired glass. The temperature inside the furnace is raised to approximately 1600°F in 45 minutes and is held at this temperature for an additional 15 minutes. At this point the furnace wall containing the wired-glass openings is moved aside, and the glass is subjected to a 1¹/₈-in. stream of water from a fire hose, applied at a pressure of 35 to 40 lb. The glass must remain in the sash substantially unchanged except for cracking due to thermal shock.

The maximum size of wired glass varies with the manufacturer from 60" × 144" to 72" × 130". The size of individual lights in fire doors is limited to 1296 sq in., or 54 in. in either direction, for a C rating (³/₄ hr); 720 sq in., or 54 in. in height and 48 in. in width, for an E rating (³/₄ hr); and 10 sq in., with neither length nor width to exceed 12 in., for a B rating (1¹/₂ hr).

Wired glass may be used in any situation where flying glass would be dangerous. Skylights are usually glazed with wired glass. Wired glass is approved by the FHA and most building codes for shower and bath enclosures and sliding glass doors. It may also be used as a burglarproofing material. The incorporation of wire in glass does not make it more resistant to breakage. In fact the wires may contribute to breakage by developing thermal stress in the glass. However, the wires help prevent penetration after the glass is broken and tend to keep the broken pieces in place. They also make a strong, clean edge extremely difficult to achieve.

TINTED AND COATED GLASS

The properties of glass can be controlled by adding various metallic oxides or by coating one side with metallic films, oxides, or paint. The tints and coatings will filter light, conduct electricity, reflect heat and light, reduce the reflection of light, or impart brilliant colors and decorative effects. Both inorganic and organic materials may be used as films.

Heat-absorbing and Glare-reducing Glass

Glass designed to absorb a portion of the solar energy that reaches it is termed heat-absorbing or glare-reducing glass. The chemical composition of the glass has been altered to produce these qualities. This type of glass can be selected with performance characteristics to accommodate varying conditions of climate, orientation, and building site. The glass may be given a bronze tint that blends with a variety of architectural metals or a blue-green tint that contrasts with masonry and other building materials.

HEAT-ABSORBING GLASS   Some heat-absorbing glasses contain controlled quantities of ferrous oxide, resulting in blue-green glasses that absorb a high percentage of radiant energy. The lower light transmission of this type of glass offers a pleasing color and provides a moderate reduction of glare and brightness. Blue-green glass permits the maximum transmission of that portion of the spectrum most restful to the eyes, blue-green and yellow.

Heat-absorbing glass dissipates much of the heat it absorbs, but some of the heat is retained by the glass. Thus heat-absorbing glass may become much hotter than ordinary plate glass. Because of its higher rate of expansion, it requires careful cutting, handling, and glazing. Sudden heating or cooling may induce edge stresses which can result in failure if edges are improperly cut or are damaged. Large lights that are partially shaded or heavily draped are subject to higher working stresses and require special design consideration.

GLARE-REDUCING GLASS   Glare-reducing glass is white translucent glass or sheet or plate with a blue-green, grey, or bronze tint. The lower light transmission and pleasing color of blue-green glass provide only a moderate reduction of glare and brightness. For example, a ¹/₈" sheet will transmit 63 percent of the light and a ¹/₄" sheet will transmit 52 percent. Although the bronze tints are used principally for reducing heat transfer, they also impart a subtle richness to outdoor objects without noticeably changing their color.

Grey-tinted glass is offered in a wide range of light transmittance. Both window glass and heavy sheet glass are available, with light transmittances from 14 to 61 percent of the visible light. Graylite 14, a product of PPG Industries, transmits only 45 percent of the solar energy and so also qualifies as a heat-absorbing glass. The neutral tint provides minimum distortion of colors viewed from either the outside or the inside. The properties of Pennvernon, a grey-tinted sheet produced by PPG Industries, are shown in Table 12-6.

White translucent glasses are effective in reducing glare. They may diffuse direct sunlight as much as 95 percent and still transmit an abundance of diffused light. Translucent glass can provide glare reduction during the day and act as a glowing light source at night. Huewhite, a milk-white translucent glass produced by American Saint Gobain, is available in thicknesses of ¼" and ⁵⁄₁₆". The maximum size produced is 48" × 132".

TABLE 12-6 Properties of Pennvernon, July 21, 4:00 P.M., 40°N., west elevation

TYPE	THICKNESS, IN.	MAX. SIZE, IN.	VISIBLE LIGHT TRANS., PERCENT	MAX. HEAT GAIN Btu/(HR)(SQ FT)
Clear single strength	³⁄₃₂	40 × 50	90	220
Graylite 45 heavy sheet	³⁄₁₆	120 × 84	45	195
Graylite 31 window glass	⅛	60 × 84	31	170
Graylite 14 heavy sheet	⁷⁄₃₂	60 × 84	14	150

Reflective Coatings

Coatings to change the optical characteristics of glass are applied by the sprayer-vacuum process. Particles of coating substance are suspended on a flat plate, and the plate and the glass are placed in a chamber from which practically all air is removed. When a virtual vacuum has been achieved, an electric current is run through the flat plate, and the molecules of the coating substance bombard the glass surface with the speed of light. The coating becomes an integral part of the glass surface and is relatively resistant to damage; however, nonabrasive cleaners must be used. This type of coating process tends to heat strengthen the glass to the point that it cannot be cut or altered after coating.

The thickness of the coating on glass can be controlled to within millionths of an inch. The technique is so exact that visible light can be broken down into separate colors. Vacuum-coated filter lenses in television cameras can be used to separate the image into three distinct colors, so that each lens transmits one color and reflects the other two.

ARCHITECTURAL GLASS Most reflective glass used in architecture is ¼" plate glass with coatings that reflect heat

and light from the surface. This type of glass is sometimes called *mirror glass,* because it is actually a one-way mirror. Reflective glass may be installed with the coated face inside or outside. Since the coating reflects the heat and light, it conducts less heat than heat-absorbing glass. These qualities help reduce air-conditioning and heat requirements.

Reflective glass is opaque from the side facing the light. Thus it is translucent from the inside during the day and translucent from the outside at night. The reflectivity of this type of glass can also be an important consideration in exterior design. A building clad in reflective glass will reflect outdoor sculptural elements and change with the movement of passing people and vehicles. On grey days it will be grey, and on sunny days it will reflect the blue of the sky and the white of the clouds. The facade of a

Fig. 12-6 Typical values of heat transmission through glass: (a) ¼" clear plate glass; (b) 50 percent grey heat-absorbing glass; (c) 10 percent grey heat-absorbing glass.

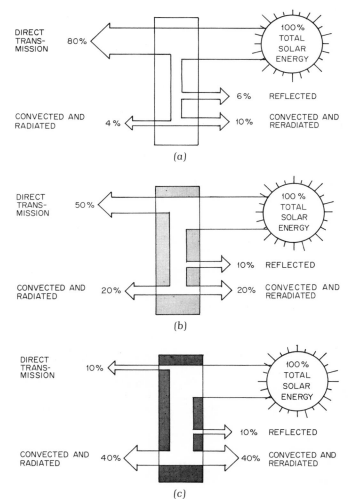

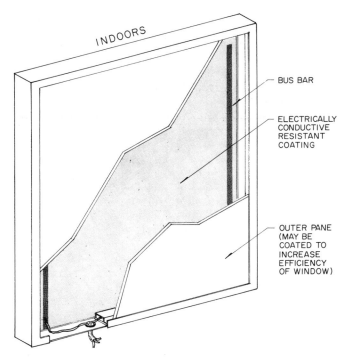

Fig. 12-7 Electrically conductive glass unit.

reflective glass building changes with the movement of passing people and vehicles.

Reflective coatings may be applied to clear or tinted sheets of plate or float glass. The coatings may be laminated between two sheets of glass. The delicate metallic coating is then permanently protected from the elements and cannot be damaged by cleaning compounds. The exterior sheet of glass may be tinted to further reduce glare and heat transmittance. Reflective glass may also be combined with plain glass in double-glazed units.

TRANSPARENT MIRRORS   The glass used for observation windows in supermarkets, department stores, and institutions is similar to architectural reflective glass. The most widely used type is clear or tinted plate glass with a special chrome alloy vacuum deposited on one side. The chrome coating is opaque, but it is so thin that very small spaces of uncoated glass are uniformly distributed over the entire surface. Thus it is transparent from the dark side and forms a mirror on the brighter side. The glass is always installed with the coated surface facing the area to be observed.

Any clear glass with low transmission characteristics acts as a transparent mirror if there is a ten-to-one lighting differential between the subject room and the observation room. This effect is noticeable with clear windows in a brightly lit room at night. However, since some light is usually desirable in observation rooms, the use of coated glass provides more latitude. It is usually desirable to use

dull, subdued colors in the observation rooms and bright light-colored walls and ceiling in the subject room.

Transparent mirror coatings can be used in laminated units. The surface coating may be as hard as the glass itself. However, it can be scratched by bumping or scraped by animals, children, or furniture, and once the coating is scratched, the effectiveness of the mirror is greatly reduced. An additional pane of glass laminated to the coated surface reduces the reflectivity of the mirror to some extent, but the added protection may be worthwhile.

Nonreflective Coatings

The reflectivity of glass can also be reduced by coatings. Nonreflective glass is used on aircraft instrument panels, in framing pictures, and in other situations where it is desirable to reduce extraneous reflections from natural or artificial light sources. The coatings disperse reflections and increase the light transmission to almost 99 percent.

The standard nonreflective coating is magnesium fluoride. This coating produces the bluish tint on binoculars, telescopes, and eyeglasses.

Electrically Conductive Coatings

Glass is commonly used in electrical installations as an insulating material. However, a transparent metallic oxide coating has recently been developed that conducts electricity. The principal use of transparent electrically conductive glass is for heating windows of automobiles, planes, and other vehicles as a defogging device.

The transparent films may be produced by spraying glass that has been heated to 900 to 1300°F with a solution of metallic tin salts. They may also be applied by the vacuum-deposition system. The thickness of the coatings will vary from 15 to 20 millionths of an inch, depending on the resistance desired. The film is as durable as glass, but harsh abrasives must not be used in cleaning.

Glass with a conductive coating can be used as a lighting element if it is coated with a thin film of phosphor. Films have been developed that glow with a green, yellow, or blue light. PPG Industries has developed a special glass window unit that may be used as a heat source in buildings. The unit is double glazed, with an outer layer of light- and heat-reflective glass and an inner pane of conductive-coated glass separated by a 1/2-in. air space. The coated side faces the enclosed air space and so is protected from damage. The outer reflective pane tends to reflect heat in the summer, and the inner conductive pane can be maintained at the temperature of the room to prevent heat loss. Electric current is carried to the glass coating by two bus bars located at opposite sides of the unit and generates heat as it passes through the conductive coating.

Spandrel Glass

The horizontal structural members between rows of windows in successive stories on a multistory building are called *spandrels*. Spandrel glass is designed as an external opaque covering for back-up walls or structural elements. The base material may be polished plate glass, float glass, or rolled textured glass. An opaque coating of fired ceramic enamel is applied to the back of the glass sheet and becomes an integral part of the glass. The glass is heat strengthened during this process, which provides additional protection against breakage. Opaque glass spandrels, available in a wide variety of colors, can be combined with tinted vision glass or with other materials. The meeting line between vision glass and spandrel glass can be made unobtrusive for continuity of design in a glass-walled building. The hard, nonporous, polished surface of spandrel glass protects the colored ceramic coating and ensures permanent colorfastness.

Spandrel glass is usually installed by the contractor who handles the rest of the glazing. Since it is heat strengthened, it cannot be cut, drilled, or otherwise fabricated on the job site. It must be manufactured to the exact size and shape of each opening. One manufacturer recommends at least ½ in. of air space behind the glass as protection against the possible condensation of moisture between the glass and the backing. Other manufacturers produce spandrel glass with a factory-applied layer of fiberglass insulation protected by an aluminum vapor barrier on the interior color surface.

Double-glazed Units

The increasing demand for weather-conditioned buildings has led to the development of many different types of double-glazed units, sometimes referred to as *insulating glass*. These units consist of two or more sheets of glass separated by an air space. The air between the sheets of glass is dehydrated at atmospheric pressure by means of a *dessicant*, or drying agent, or a dry gas is forced between the sheets to remove any moisture that is held in the air. The unit is then sealed to keep out further moisture that may condense between the glass sheets under varying temperatures and humidities. Double-glazed units vary in overall thickness from ½ to 1 in. Air spaces vary from ¼ to ½ in. The glass may be clear sheet glass, polished plate, float glass, tinted glass, glare-reducing glass, heat-absorbing glass, or laminated glass. The two sheets of glass are generally the same thickness, although one manufacturer produces a sound-insulation unit which consists of two sheets of glass of different thicknesses. The two sheets vibrate at different frequencies, which tends to reduce sound transmission.

Insulating glass helps overcome the problem of condensation, which usually occurs on the inside of single sheets as a result of the higher humidity in a warm room. The light transmission of a clear insulating unit of sheet or plate is little different from that of a single sheet, but clear insulating glass can reduce the transmission of heat by almost half.

Double-glazed units may be constructed as organically sealed nonrigid units, which employ some sort of spacer, a dessicant to remove moisture from between the glass sheets, and an organic sealant, or as inorganically sealed rigid units, in which the glass sheets are either fused together at the edges or separated by metal spacers rigidly bonded to each sheet of glass.

Organically sealed units are sealed with synthetic rubber (polysulfide), epoxies, or extruded sealants. The units are completely factory assembled, ready for installation. Some are available with metal edge protection.

Fig. 12-8 Types of double-glazed units.

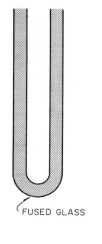
FUSED GLASS

GLASS-EDGE SEAL

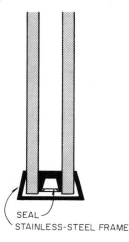
SEAL
STAINLESS-STEEL FRAME

METAL-EDGE SEAL

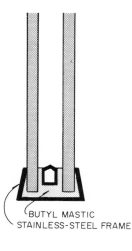
BUTYL MASTIC
STAINLESS-STEEL FRAME

BUTYL SEAL

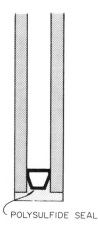
POLYSULFIDE SEAL

POLYSULFIDE SEAL

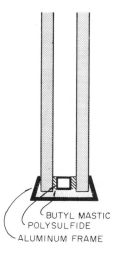
BUTYL MASTIC
POLYSULFIDE
ALUMINUM FRAME

POLYSULFIDE-BUTYL SEAL

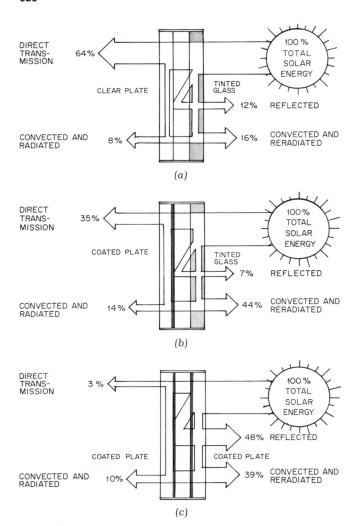

Fig. 12-9 Typical values for transfer of solar energy through double-glazed window units: (a) tinted glass and clear plate; (b) tinted glass and coated plate; (c) two panes of coated plate.

Glass-sealed units consist of two sheets of single- or double-strength window glass separated by a ³/₁₆-in. dehydrated air space. The edges are fused by a process that produces a hermetically sealed air space between the sheets. Glass-sealed units are not recommended for installation at altitudes above 4000 ft, since the difference in air pressure at higher altitudes can cause them to fail. They are produced in overall thicknesses of ³/₈″, ⁷/₁₆″, and ¹/₂″ and are used primarily for residences and for smaller openings in commercial buildings. Because of the high stresses that can develop during the fusing and cooling processes, similar types of glass must be used for both sheets.

Metal-sealed units consisting of two sheets of ¹/₈″, ³/₁₆″, or ¹/₄″ glass with ¹/₄-in. or ¹/₂-in. air spaces are produced for glazing larger openings. The sheets are held apart by metal spacers, and the air spaces are hermetically

sealed with a permanent metal-to-glass bond. Overall thicknesses range from ⁷/₃₂″ to 1¹/₁₆″, depending on the thickness of the glass and the air space. The unit is usually surrounded with an aluminum or stainless-steel frame to provide greater ease in handling and to minimize the chance for edge chipping during installation. Some units contain a breather system to reduce visual distortion due to temperature or barometric changes. The metal used as a spacer must have the same coefficient of expansion as the glass, or strains will develop in the glass during extreme temperature changes.

Both organically sealed and inorganically sealed units are available in a large number of standard sizes. Other sizes within the manufacturer's established maximums are available on special order, although nonstandard sizes generally involve higher cost, longer delivery time, and a minimum order for each size of unit.

Special insulating-glass units are produced with an outer pane of heat-absorbing tinted glass and an inner pane of clear glass. The combination of reduced heat gain and insulating qualities make these units particularly valuable in air-conditioned buildings. This type of unit permits the use of larger areas of glass, even in areas with severe winter or summer temperatures.

Patterned Glass

The primary functions of patterned glass, sometimes called *figured glass* or *rolled patterned glass*, are the diffusion of light, decoration, and privacy. By means of patterned glass, rooms can be adequately daylighted far from windows. Small skylights can furnish diffused light over a wide area. Interior screens or partitions will afford any degree of privacy desired as well as decoration.

Patterned glass is produced by a method similar to that for plate glass. The glass is drawn horizontally from a furnace through rollers. The rollers are incised with a pattern or texture, and as the glass passes between them, the pattern is impressed on either one or both surfaces. Patterned glass may be colorless or tinted and is produced in many patterns and textures, with varying degrees of transparency. Glass that is relatively transparent from one side and diffuses the image from the other side is frequently used for tub and shower enclosures. Translucent wired glass is produced in patterns similar to standard patterned glass. In addition to the light-diffusing characteristics of patterned glass, it provides approved fire and breakage protection.

Stained Glass

The art of making and installing stained glass, sometimes called *art glass* or *cathedral glass*, dates back at least a thousand years. With the development of Gothic architecture around the beginning of the twelfth century, the windows of the great cathedrals became virtually walls of magnificent stained-glass murals, a major color and inspirational factor of the cathedral. It has been said that the making of stained glass to match that of the Middle Ages is a lost art. However, stained-glass windows of equal beauty are used in many modern churches, commercial buildings, and even residences.

A stained-glass window consists of a mosaic of translucent, colored glass. The colors are produced by adding metallic oxides to the glass while it is in a molten state. The colored glass is cut and fit into place according to the artist's "cartoon," and ceramic or metallic pigments are applied to complete the design. These pigments are fired so that they become an integral part of the glass.

LEADED GLASS   Stained-glass windows are sometimes termed *leaded glass*. Leaded glass, however, actually refers to the method of installation rather than the type of glass. After the colored glass has been cut to shape, painted, and fired, the pieces are glazed in H-shaped lead sections called *cames*. The H sections are shaped and spread to receive the glass. When the entire window has been assembled, the open legs of the lead sections are pressed tight against the glass and the joints are secured by soldering.

FACETED GLASS   The color and richness of stained glass is also provided by faceted colored glass. Slabs of colored glass an inch or more thick are cut and chipped, or *faceted*, to reflect and disperse rays of colored light. Varying degrees of translucency, transparency, and opacity are obtained, depending on the technique. Faceted stained glass is usually set in concrete. Entire walls can be designed which consist of glass in combination with a filigree of stone or concrete. This type of glass provides a dimension and depth not possible with the thinner stained glass.

MIRRORS

Early mirrors were made by applying a liquid alloy of mercury and tin to the back of glass. Around 1865 a French chemist developed a method of chemically applying pure metallic silver to glass. Most commercial mirrors are still made by modifications of this process. Vacuum-deposited aluminum is frequently used on glass for *front-surface mirrors*, used in precision optical and projection equipment for durability and freedom from *ghosts*. Ghost in a back-silvered mirror are caused by the light reflected from the front surface of the glass back to the silvered surface, where it is rereflected as a second image.

Glass for Mirrors

Mirrors are made from window glass, sheet glass, plate glass, or float glass. The best mirrors are made from polished plate glass and the most inexpensive ones are made from sheet glass or window glass. Sheet glass suitable for mirrors is graded as silvering quality A or B. Mirrors made of sheet glass have the inherent waves of all sheet glass. Float or plate glass for mirrors may be silvering quality,

mirror-glazing quality, or glazing quality. Silvering quality is used in those applications requiring the highest-quality glass. It is usually produced only in ¼" thickness. Mirror-glazing quality is exceptionally free of defects and surface imperfections. Many manufacturers produce mirrors of glazing-quality plate which, to all appearances, are as good as those of silvering-quality plate.

Silvering

There are several methods of depositing a coating of silver to the back of a mirror, but the silver solution is approximately the same for all methods. Silver nitrate is dissolved in chemically pure water, and ammonia is added to this solution. The silver nitrate is changed to silver hydroxide, which is suspended in the solution. For metallic silver to be deposited on the glass a reducing agent is necessary. The silvering solution and reducing agent are usually

Fig. 12-10   Modern stained-glass window by Roger Darricarrere, in concrete window wall 45 ft high by 25 ft wide, St. Mel's Catholic Church, Woodland Hills, California, architect J. Earl Trudeau.

Fig. 12-11 Screen of faceted stained glass up to 3 in. thick, by Roger Darricarrere for Equitable Savings building, Palo Alto, California, architects, Kurt Meyer & Associates.

brought together at the spray nozzle. The silvering process may be completed in 30 sec or may take as long as an hour.

Gold mirrors are sometimes used for decorative purposes. Pure metallic gold is deposited from a solution by the action of reducing agents, as in silvering. Gold films are usually so thin that it is possible to see through the mirror before a backing has been applied.

Aluminum or chromium may be deposited by the same method used in the manufacture of reflective glass. The reflective coating is electrically deposited in a near vacuum. The 200-in. mirror in the Mt. Palomar observatory in California is coated with an aluminum-magnesium film. Some mirrors may be coated with hard quartz to increase durability.

Backing

The silver film on the back of commercial mirrors must be protected from scratches and from atmospheric damage. Pinholes in the film will allow water vapor to penetrate the reflecting surface and tarnish the silver. The minimum

protection for inexpensive mirrors is a coat of shellac covered with a single coat of special mirror-backing paint. The backing on better mirrors consists of a double coating of silver covered by an electrolytically or galvanically deposited film of copper. A copper-backed mirror can be expected to have a life several times that of one not so protected.

Federal specifications DD-M 411 designate testing procedures and requirements for mirror backing. These specifications set forth the number of hours a backing must stand up under a salt-spray test without becoming spotted or deteriorating. The highest-quality backings must withstand the salt spray for as long as 300 hr and is required for mirrors to be installed in Navy ships. Other tests are less severe and are used for mirrors that will be installed under ordinary building conditions.

Installation

Unframed mirrors with beveled or polished edges may be installed with mastic if proper precautions are taken. Special mastics that will not bleed through the backing paint must be used. Durable mirror backings are available for mirrors to be applied adhesively. The wall surface upon which the mirror is to be mounted must be thoroughly primed and sealed, and the mastic must be applied in 6-in. round spots that cover no more than 25 percent of the mirror area. For best results a $\frac{1}{8}$-in. space between the mirror and the wall should be left for air circulation, to prevent condensation from forming on the back of the mirror. The bottom of the mirror should be supported in a metal channel. Weep holes are included in the channel to allow any moisture condensing on the back of the mirror to drain off.

Unframed mirrors may be installed with *rosettes*, decorative-headed screws that are inserted through holes drilled in the mirror. The mirror is held away from the wall with lead washers. A rubber or plastic sleeve is inserted in the hole drilled in the mirror, and felt is placed under the washer. Some mirrors are factory installed in formed or extruded metal frames with masking tape or plastic-foam tape used to avoid vibration or chatter. The better grades of framed mirrors have a galvanized back to protect the backing paint.

PLASTIC GLAZING MATERIALS

The term *plastic* designates a variety of synthetic materials which can be shaped by flow at some point in its manufacture. The first translucent plastic was celluloid, produced in the United States in 1870. Celluloid was first used for side curtains in automobiles. Since then a number of clear and translucent plastic products have come into increasing use as light-diffusing devices, in interior partitions, in lighting fixtures, and in the glazing of window openings. The most commonly used plastic products consist of acrylic, vinyl, polyester, polystyrene, and poly-carbonate plastics either translucent, clear, plain, or reinforced with glass fibers.

Corrugated Plastic Panels

Corrugated translucent plastic sheets are manufactured for use with corrugated metal sheets (see Chapters 7 and 9). This material can be used in skylights and light-diffusing openings in industrial buildings. The dimensions of the corrugations are usually coordinated with standard metal corrugations. The sealing and closing strips used on corrugated metal can usually be used in attaching corrugated plastic.

Corrugated plastic panels are usually attached to structures with self-tapping screws or annular-ring nails. A sealant washer of Neoprene is usually installed under the head of the nail. The sides of adjoining panels are lapped one full corrugations and joined with aluminum or stainless-steel machine screws, washers, and nuts. The screws are surrounded with Neoprene jackets that expand into drilled holes for a waterproof seal. End joints are lapped a minimum of 6 in. and sealed with either a clear or opaque nonhardening mastic.

Plastic Glazing Panels

The only two types of plastic suitable for exterior glazing are acrylic and polycarbonate sheets. Acrylic sheets such as Plexiglas, manufactured by Rohm Hass, and Acrylite, produced by American Cyanamid, are available in clear sheets and in many colors, ranging from virtually no light transmittance to 92 percent light transmittance. Acrylic sheet will withstand seven to sixteen times the impact of double-strength window glass and nearly twice that of a comparable thickness of tempered glass. However, it tends to be brittle and is subject to scratching. It is classed as slow burning. Most plastic sheet has three times the coefficient of expansion of aluminum and eight times that of glass. Special frames must be used for installations subject to extremes of weather.

Polycarbonate sheets such as Merlon, produced by Mobay Chemical Company, and Lexon, produced by General Electric, have a strength factor four times that of acrylic sheets. However, they have a relatively short life, and at the present time their high cost limits their use.

GLAZING

Glazing refers to the installation of glass in prepared openings of windows, doors, partitions, and curtain walls. Glass may be held in place with glazier's points, spring clips, or flexible glazing beads. Glass is kept from contact with the frame with various types of shims. Putty, sealants, or various types of caulking compounds are applied to make a weathertight joint between the glass and the frame.

Fig. 12-12 Windows glazed with shatter-resistant Acrylite cast-acrylic sheet in Duke Power Company's Marshall plant, Terrell, North Carolina. (*American Cyanamid Company, Plastics Division.*)

Fig. 12-13 Windows glazed with Lexan polycarbonate sheets in Public School 36, New York City. (*General Electric Company, Plastics Division.*)

Glazing Wood Sash

Most wood sash is ~~face glazed~~. The glass is installed in *rabbets,* or rebates, consisting of L-shaped recesses cut into the sash or frame to receive and support panes of glass. The glass is held tightly against the frame by *glazier's points,* triangular pieces of zinc or galvanized steel driven into the rabbet. The rabbet is then filled with putty. The putty is pressed firmly against the glass and beveled back against the wood frame with a putty knife. A priming paint is essential in glazing wood sash. The priming seals the pores of the wood preventing the loss of oil from putty. Wood frames are usually glazed from the outside.

Wood-sash putty is generally made with linseed oil and a pigment. Some putties contain soybean oil as a drying agent. Putty should not be painted until it is thoroughly set. A bead of putty or glazing compound is applied between the glass and the frame, as a *bedding.* The bedding is usually applied to the frame before the glass is set. *Back puttying* is then used to force putty into spaces that may have been left between the frame and the glass.

The glass may be set in wood sash or openings in wood-frame construction by *wood-stop glazing.* In this type of glazing, the rabbet is covered with a thin layer of putty or bedding compound, and the glass is pressed or bedded into it. Wood stops are then nailed to the sash to hold the glass in place. These wood stops are usually cut and fit by the carpenter and tacked lightly in place for installation by the glazier after the glass has been set.

Glazing Metal Windows and Doors

~~Glass set in metal frames must be held from any contact with metal.~~ This may be accomplished by applying a setting bed of metal-sash putty or glazing compound. Metal-sash putty differs from wood-sash putty in that it is formulated to adhere to a nonporous surface. Elastic glazing compounds may be used in place of putty. These com-

pounds are produced from processed oils and pigments and will remain plastic and resilient over a longer period than putty. A skin quickly forms over the outside of the compound after it is placed, while the interior remains soft. This type of glazing compound is used in windows or doors subject to twisting or vibration. It may be painted as soon as the surface has formed.

For large panes of glass, *setting blocks* may be placed between the glass edges and the frame to maintain proper spacing of the glass in the openings. The blocks may be of wood, lead, Neoprene, or some flexible material. For large openings flexible shims must be set between the face of the glass and the glazing channel to allow for movement. Plastics and heat-absorbing or reflective glass require more clearance to allow for greater expansion. The shims may be in the form of a continuous tape of a butyl-rubber-based compound, which has been extruded into a soft, tacky ready-to-use tape that adheres to any clean, dry surface. The tape is applied to the frame and the glass-holding stop before the glass is placed in the frame. Under compression, the tape also serves as a sealant.

Glass may be held in place in the frame by spring clips, inserted in holes in the metal frame, or continuous angles or stops, attached to the frame with screws or with snap-on spring clips. The frames of metal windows are shaped either for outside glazing or inside glazing.

Flush Glazing

Sometimes openings are flush glazed. This method consists of inserting the glass in channels with no removable stops. The channels must be deep and wide enough to allow the glazier to install the glass. It may be part of a metal tube, a cut in a wood structural member, or a formed reglet in a concrete or masonry structure. Glazing compound, used to seal the glass after installation, is kept flush with the face of the metal tube or surface.

Fig. 12-14 Types of wood-sash glazing.

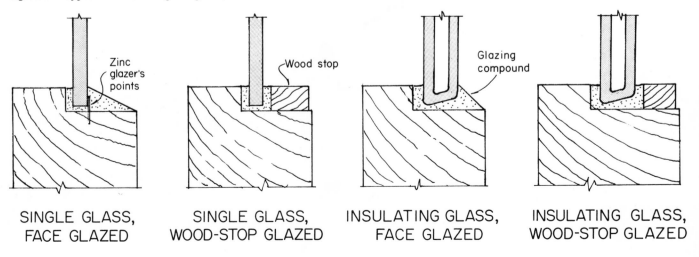

SINGLE GLASS, FACE GLAZED
SINGLE GLASS, WOOD-STOP GLAZED
INSULATING GLASS, FACE GLAZED
INSULATING GLASS, WOOD-STOP GLAZED

Sealants

After the glass is positioned in an opening and held in place, the joint between the glass and the frame must be sealed against moisture. The sealant may be a material that is formed on the job or it may be a preformed joint sealer made of natural or synthetic rubber or plastic. Some sealants are in liquid form and are poured into the joints. Others are in a mastic form and are applied with a caulking gun.

ONE-PART SEALANTS Premixed sealants with polysulfide, silicone, or urethane bases are usually applied with a caulking gun. They undergo a chemical reaction at room temperatures. These chemically curing one-part sealants generally exhibit rubberlike qualities for many years after they are cured. Some require priming of all glass or metal surfaces for proper adhesion; others will adhere directly to glass or metal. *Polysulfides* offer good resistance to most solvents and fuels. *Silicones* provide a flexible seal that continues to function over a wide temperature range. *Urethanes* provide a seal that is resistant to abrasion and most chemicals.

SOLVENT-RELEASE SEALANTS This type of sealant does not change chemically while setting to a flexible or semirigid state. The set results from evaporation of the solvent from the compound. Many sealants of this type shrink and harden on drying, which limits their usefulness. Their properties vary widely, from compounds that remain soft and pliable to those that become hard and brittle with time.

TWO-PART SEALANTS Chemically curing two-part resilient sealants offer the advantage of quick curing (usually in a matter of hours). They generally consist of a polysulfide or urethane base plus a catalyst. The base material and catalyst are packaged in separate containers, and the catalyst is added to the base materials as it is needed. Once the two have been mixed they must be applied within a definite time limit. This limit, known as *pot-life*, varies with the composition of the materials, and the manufacturer's directions must be followed closely.

Two-part polysulfide and urethane sealants may be mixed, packed in containers, and quick frozen at temperatures of −40°F. The cartons are maintained at temperatures of −20°F until ready for use and are then allowed to thaw to room temperature on the job site.

Two-part curing sealants are available in a wide range of hardnesses. The softest types are used where maximum movement and a minimum of strain is expected. A medium grade is produced for applications subject to vibration and movement. In applications where a high resistance to abrasion is desired, the hardest type is used.

PREFORMED RESILIENT SEALANTS Flexible, premolded sealants are fabricated from both natural and synthetic rubber, polyvinyl chloride, or other plastics. They are produced

REPRESENTATIVE EXAMPLES OF WET GLAZING ARE SHOWN IN THE FOLLOWING SKETCHES

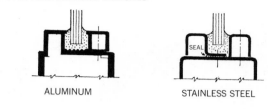

ALUMINUM STAINLESS STEEL

ALUMINUM ALUMINUM STAINLESS STEEL

REPRESENTATIVE EXAMPLES OF DRY GLAZING DETAILS ARE SHOWN IN THESE DRAWINGS

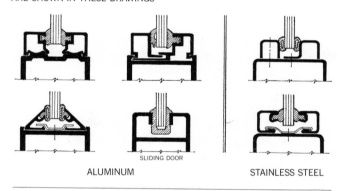

ALUMINUM STAINLESS STEEL

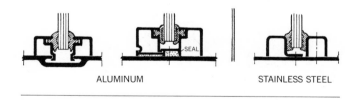

ALUMINUM STAINLESS STEEL

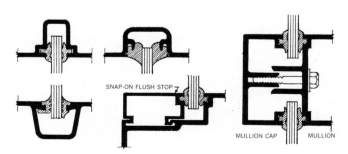

Fig. 12-15 Types of metal-sash glazing.

(a)

(c)

(b)

(d)

Fig. 12-16 Shell One Plaza Building, Houston, Texas, architects Skidmore, Owings, Merrill and Wilson, Morris Crain and Anderson: (a) installation of structural gasket in frame; (b) installing glass in gasket; (c) insertion of filler strip; (d) completed installation. (*F. H. Maloney Company; E. I. DuPont Corporation.*)

as tapes, ribbons, beads, or extruded shapes. Preformed sealants may be used in glazing applications as primary seals, shims, spacers, or secondary seals in combination with primary bulk sealers. Many patented extruded shapes are available for glazing. These may be in a raw state (sticky and rubbery) or vulcanized. Some tapes and shapes are reinforced with twine or rubber to minimize plastic flow when the material is being installed or is in use. The tapes are usually installed on one side before the glass is set. The extruded shapes and beads are rolled in with special tools after the glass is in place and secured.

PREFORMED STRUCTURAL GASKETS Structural gaskets usually consist of natural or synthetic vulcanized rubber. Neoprene is widely used because of its ability to spring back after a load has been removed. Integral locking strips, termed *zipper strips*, are used to force the gasket against the glass and the frame. No other sealant or holding device is needed. Structural gaskets must be formed to exact dimensions and the corners vulcanized to form the gasket into one integral unit. Gaskets installed during cold weather must be heated for ease of application.

QUESTIONS

1. What is the structural form of glass?

2. How is glass made?

3. What are the properties of glass?

4. Discuss the strength of glass.

5. Describe the process of manufacturing sheet glass.

6. What is flame-polished glass?

7. What are the standard thicknesses of sheet glass, and where would each be used?

8. What wind load would you use in designing the glass for a new building 80 ft high, to be built next to the one in which you are now working?

9. What produces waves in sheet glass, and how do they affect glazing?

10. Describe the process of manufacturing plate glass.

11. Describe three grades of plate glass.

12. Describe the manufacture of float glass.

13. Describe tempered glass and list six places it could be used.

14. How is tempered glass fabricated?

15. How is laminated glass made?

16. Where is wired-glass used?

17. What imparts special properties to heat-absorbing and glare-reducing glasses?

18. Where can reflective glass be used effectively?

19. Where are transparent mirrors used?

20. Describe three types of insulating-glass units.

21. How are stained-glass windows usually installed?

22. Describe the process of silvering a high-quality mirror.

23. Describe the process of glazing a wood-framed window.

24. What is a sealant, and where is it used?

25. Describe the installation of a structural gasket.

REFERENCES FOR FURTHER STUDY

American Saint Gobain Corporation: P.O. Box 929, Kingsport, Tenn., 37662. "Glass Index," 1970. *Creative Ideas in Glass*, a quarterly.

Callender, John Hancock: "Time-saver Standards," 4th ed., McGraw-Hill, New York, 1966.

Flat Glass Marketing Association: 726 Mt. Moriah, Suite 105, Memphis, Tenn., 38117. *U.S. Glass, Metal, & Glazing*, a periodical.

Hornbostel, Caleb: "Materials for Architecture," Reinhold, New York, 1963.

Libbey-Owens-Ford Glass Company: 811 Madison Avenue, Toledo, Ohio, 43624. "Glass for Construction," 1970.

Mississippi Glass Company: 88 Angelica Street, St. Louis, Mo., 63147. "Rolled, Figured and Wired Glass," 1970.

PPG Industries: 1 Gateway Center, Pittsburgh, Pa., 15222. "Glass Manual," 1946. "Glass Products," 1970. *PPG Construction News*, a periodical.

Richards, John Noble: "An Architect Looks at the Possibilities of Glass in the Future," *U.S. Glass Metal & Glazing*, June 1966.

PAINT
AND
FINISHES
13

PROPERTIES OF PAINT

Paint consists of white or colored solids suspended in a liquid, which, when applied to a suitable surface, generally forms a continuous solid film by oxidation or evaporation. The finely divided solid particles used in paint are known as *pigments*. The liquid portion of paint is known as the *vehicle* or *medium*. The vehicle includes *binders* to hold the pigment in place, *driers* to speed the formation of the film, *stabilizers*, and *emulsifiers* to improve the working qualities, and volatile substances such as *solvents* or *thinners*, which evaporate and leave a solid film. The type of thinner or solvent used determines whether a material is classed as a paint or a lacquer. An *oil-based paint* is thinned with turpentine or mineral spirits; a *lacquer* is thinned with acetates, ketones, or alcohols; and a *water-based paint* is thinned with water. A wide variety of pigmented paints, clear coatings, and stains have been developed to suit particular purposes.

Gloss

The ability of a surface to reflect light, its brightness or luster, is spoken of as *gloss*. The higher the reflectivity of a surface, the higher the gloss. The gloss of a painted surface can be judged by actual measurements of its reflectivity. However, the designation of a particular painted surface as *gloss, semigloss, eggshell gloss, eggshell flat, matte, or flat* often depends on the judgment of the person who examines and rates its qualities.

The instrument used in testing the gloss, or *specular gloss,* of a paint sample consists of an incandescent light source, a device for locating the painted surface, and a receptor located to receive the required pyramid of rays reflected by the specimen. Federal Test Method Standard No. 141a describes the instruments to be used and the standard against which the sample is to be judged. The primary working standard is polished black glass. A ray of light is directed on the surface of the black glass (at a specified angle of 85°, 60°, or 45°), the amount of light reflected back to a meter is recorded, and the meter is adjusted to read 100. The black glass is then replaced by the sample to be tested, and its specular gloss is measured against this standard (a reading of 0 would indicate that no light is reflected from the sample). The standard designations for painted surfaces, based on federal standard No. 141a, are shown in Table 13-1.

TABLE 13-1 Federal standard of specular gloss

DESIGNATION	STANDARD
Flat (or matte)	Practically free of sheen even when viewed from oblique angles; usually less than 15° on 85° meter
Eggshell flat	Usually 10 to 15° on 60° meter
Eggshell gloss	Usually 15 to 30° on 60° meter
Semigloss	Usually from 30 to 70° on 60° meter
Full gloss	Smooth, almost mirrorlike surface when viewed from all angles; usually above 70° on 60° meter

The gloss of a paint depends to a great extent on the composition of the vehicle. Generally, the lower the pigment content, the higher the gloss. All paints lose gloss with time, and this factor must be taken into consideration in comparing one paint with another.

Paint selection depends on where the paint is to be used and the type of surface to which it is to be applied. For exterior surfaces the type of environment is the chief consideration. In rural areas painted surfaces must resist sunlight, rainfall, heat, and cold. In industrial environments, chemical fumes, smog, and other contaminants must be considered. For example, sulfur fumes will darken any paint that contains lead pigments. Sea breezes carry salt-laden air that will corrode metal surfaces, and paints with special rust inhibitors must be used in these areas. In interior areas the problem is simply to keep the color and gloss as long as possible. Bathrooms must have finishes that will resist water or steam. Kitchen walls and ceilings require paints that can be washed repeatedly to remove grease and soot stains.

Hiding Power

The opacity, or hiding power, of a paint depends on its ability to reflect ultraviolet rays of light. The ability of a paint coating to reflect these rays is measured by its *refractive index*, the ratio of the amount of light that hits the surface to the amount of light that is reflected. The higher the refractive index of a material, the more light or heat will be reflected from the surface. The hiding power of paint depends on the amount of difference between the refractive index of the pigment and that of the vehicle. A large difference between the two gives the paint good hiding power. As the difference decreases, the paint becomes less opaque. The refractive index of white lead is 1.95 and that of titanium dioxide is 2.70; most vehicles have an index of about 1.50. Thus titanium dioxide produces much better hiding power than white lead.

Another factor affecting the hiding power of paint is the size and shape of the pigment particles. Rounded particles impart the greatest density, needle-shaped particles produce a high-strength film, and platelike particles produce a film that is less permeable to moisture. Within limits, the

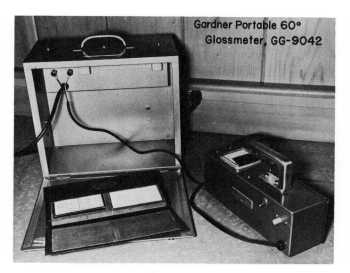

Fig. 13-1 Portable specular glossmeter. (*Gardener Laboratory, Inc.*)

finer the pigment is ground, the greater its hiding power. Fine grinding is necessary to provide smoothness in the paint film. The particle size of the pigment used in most paint ranges from 0.0001 to 0.006 mm.

Chalking

The usual effect of weathering and exposure to sunlight is reduction of gloss in a paint film, followed by chalking. As the film loses its gloss, the pigment wears away in a fine powdery substance. A reasonable amount of chalking is desirable for several reasons. As a painted surface ages, it collects dirt and changes color. When chalking occurs, the rain washes off the dirt along with the chalking. This self-cleaning action eventually produces a full surface that is best for adhesion of new paint. When no chalking occurs, the thickness built up with successive coats of paint causes the coatings to crack and scale.

Paint Coats

A *coat* consists of a single application of paint, varnish, or lacquer applied to a surface to form a properly distributed film when dry. A paint system usually consists of a number of coats, separately applied at suitable intervals to allow for drying. With certain types of material it is possible to build up paint systems of adequate thickness and opacity by a more or less continuous process of application, as in wet-on-wet spraying. In this case no part of the system can be defined as a separate coat in the above sense. In general, however, terms used to designate various coats in a paint system are defined as shown in Table 13-2.

The thickness of a coating is designated in mils, or thousandths of an inch. Thus a coating of 6 mils has a

TABLE 13-2 Types of coat

COAT	DESCRIPTION
Full coat	As thick a coat of paint, varnish, or lacquer as can be applied in any one operation consistent with the production of a final film of uniform appearance, satisfactory hardness, and wearing qualities.
Glaze coat	A translucent or semitransparent coating, sometimes colored, used either as an intermediate or as the final coat in a paint system. It is frequently applied with the objective of modifying but not obscuring the ground color.
Ground coat	A coat of paint having good opacity which is applied before a glaze coat. The final color effect depends on the mutual influence of the ground coat and the glaze coat.
Mist coat	A very thin coat applied by spraying, more particularly in connection with cellulose lacquers. In some cases it may form a fogged coat of continuous film. Also, a thin coat of volatile thinners, with or without a small amount of lacquer, which is sometimes sprayed over a dry lacquer film to improve smoothness and luster.

thickness of $^6/_{1000}$, or 0.006 in. A coating of 15.6 mils is approximately $^1/_{64}$ in. thick. Paint films vary from 0.5 mils for prime coats on metal to 22 mils for industrial-maintenance coatings. As a coating dries it becomes thinner, so the thickness must be specified as either *wet-film thickness* or *dry-film thickness*.

Fig. 13-2 Wet-film-thickness gauge. (*By permission of the Nordson Corporation.*)

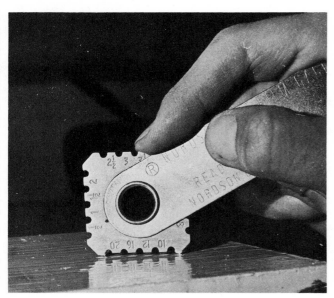

A positive means of determining coverage is with a *wet-film-thickness gauge*. This gauge measures the thickness of the freshly applied film, and the corresponding coverage, in square feet per gallon, is calculated from the relation between thickness and coverage. Some manufacturers give the coverage of their product in square feet and others give the wet- or dry-film thicknesses.

The dry-film thicknesses corresponding to required coverages for the various types of paints are obtained experimentally. There is no way of calculating the dry-film thicknesses that will result from a particular coverage unless the exact formulation of the paint is known, since the computation involves the percentage of nonvolatile solids in the paint. However, dry-film-thickness gauges are available either as self-contained pocket-sized units or units operated on 115-volts alternating current. For most paint systems on ferrous metalwork, these gauges are quite accurate. The instrument is calibrated for each thickness and composition of metal. When it is placed on the metal to be tested, it will read the dry-film thickness in mils. It is very difficult, and usually unnecessary, to measure the dry-film thickness of paint on wood, concrete, and plaster surfaces.

PIGMENTS

Paint pigments consist of finely divided natural or synthetic solids. They may be either organic or inorganic in origin. Pigments were originally employed solely to impart color and hiding power. However, they also influence many other properties of paint. Paint is seldom composed of a single pigment. The selection and proportioning of pigments for different colors, to be applied on different surfaces and to withstand various environments, is directed by the paint chemist. Combinations must be considered in terms of their effects on settling, sagging, workability, stability after exposure, and the ability to protect organic vehicle binders from the damaging rays of the sun.

Fading and color change in paint result largely from instability of pigments. Pigment stability is particularly important in paints designed for exposure to sunlight, industrial fumes, and smog. Some pigments act to improve paints through their ability to form stable reaction products with vehicle ingredients; for example, certain lead and zinc pigments combine with drying oils to contribute hardness to the paint film. The amount of pigment in paint may be as low as 5 percent by weight in some vinyl-resin paints and as high as 80 percent in some lead and oil paints.

The pigments used to impart color to exterior and interior paints include mineral and earth colors, which are obtained from natural mineral deposits, and chemical colors, produced by various chemical reactions. Vegetable colors, extracted from normal or decayed matter, and animal colors, derived from burned bones, are seldom used in the paint industry.

White Pigments

The major function of opaque white pigments is to hide the surface. However, they are also used in combination with colored pigments to produce the many tints, values, or tones of modern finishes. Clear or transparent coatings seldom contain white pigments.

WHITE LEAD   The oldest known white pigment is white lead. It is mentioned in literature as early as 430 B.C. White lead, by itself, will produce a durable exterior paint. The term *lead,* when applied to paint pigments, does not necessarily denote pulverized metals, but includes such chemical compounds as lead carbonate, lead sulfate, or combinations of the two. Several processes are used in the manufacture of white lead for the painting industry.

Basic lead carbonate, a widely used white pigment, is a compound of metallic lead, acetic acid (vinegar), and carbon dioxide gas. One method of production, called "the old Dutch process," consists of casting the lead into perforated sheets, which are put in earthenware jars containing acetic acid. Layers of *tanbark,* the bark of certain trees used in tanning animal hides, are placed between the earthenware jars. The jars are kept in a sealed room for several months until the lead is reduced to a fine white powder by the action of carbon dioxide, caused by fermentation of the tanbark.

Basic sulfate white lead is obtained by fuming, or burning, lead sulfide ores. The result is a very fine, white powder with a high degree of opacity. When used alone, it chalks more freely than basic lead carbonate.

White lead, both basic lead carbonate and basic lead sulfate, is widely used as a white pigment, although it has been replaced in many instances by new products. It has good hiding power, and because of its gradual chalking, it leaves a good surface for repainting. However, it tends to darken on exposure to several types of industrial fumes. The fumes from white lead paint are poisonous, and it should be used only for exterior applications or well-ventilated interior locations.

ZINC OXIDE   Zinc pigments have been used for many years in the painting industry. The most widely used form is zinc oxide, which is an extremely white pigment. When it is used in combination with white lead, it produces greater hardness, elasticity, and better resistance to chalking. Zinc oxide has better color retention and is less likely to yellow than some other pigments, However, if more than 20 percent zinc oxide is used in the pigment of exterior paint, the coating tends to check and peel.

LEADED ZINC   Most of the zinc ore mined in the United States contains some lead in the form of lead sulfide. Lead sulfide is the basis for lead sulfate, which, when united with zinc oxide, is known as *leaded zinc.* Leaded zincs have slightly better hiding power than white lead and are widely used in combination with other pigments.

Fig. 13-3   Self-contained dry-film-thickness gauge. (*By permission of the Nordson Corporation.*)

TITANIUM DIOXIDE   One of the most valuable white pigments is titanium dioxide, which is produced in several forms. Titanium dioxide, which has been called the whitest of whites, is produced from an ore called *ilemite,* found chiefly in India. After impurities such as iron have been removed from ilemite, an extremely white powdered pigment with a high refractive index and high density is produced. The high refractive index of titanium dioxide gives it great hiding power. For this reason titanium dioxide is not only valuable to the paint industry, but is in great demand for making white paper products and coated fabrics.

EXTENDERS   Most pigmented paints contain fillers of white or colorless mineral pigments termed *extenders.* They may contribute little to hiding power because of their low refractive index, but they have useful stabilizing characteristics. Extenders that are high in oil-absorption properties minimize the settling of pigments. They are helpful in controlling gloss and in adjusting consistency and workability, and if they are properly incorporated into a paint formula, they add durability. Commonly used extenders are aluminum silicate, magnesium silicate, natural barium sulfate, synthetic barium sulfate, barium carbonate, calcium carbonate, and mica.

Earth Colors

The most widely used earth colors in the paint industry are the ochres, raw and burnt sienna, and raw and burnt umber. These earth colors are the oldest known pigments. *Ochre,* which owes its color to certain iron compounds, is one of the most widely used yellow earth pigments in the paint industry. *Sienna,* an ore with a high iron content, is imported from a section of Italy surrounding the town of Sienna. *Raw sienna* is used as a tinting material in the production of ivories and buffs and as a glaze to produce a deep, rich yellow. *Burnt sienna* is obtained by roasting raw sienna. This results in a reddish-brown pigment that is valuable for both tinting and glazing. *Umber* is similar to sienna, except that it has a higher percentage of manganese dioxide, which gives it a darker greyish-brown color. Some of the best grades of umber come from Turkey. *Raw umber* varies widely in chemical properties and color tone, as do all natural earth colors. Used with white, it produces grey tints with an olive-green tone. *Burnt umber*, produced by roasting raw umber, is a deep, rich, reddish brown.

Chemical Colors

There are many chemical colors that have been used for centuries. Others are relatively new to the paint industry, and more are developed each year.

YELLOWS   Some of the more widely used yellows are the *chrome yellows*, which range from lemon yellow through the oranges. They are formed by combining chemically pure chromate salts and lead salts. The manufacturing process can be closely controlled to produce exact colors. Chemically pure basic lead chromate produces an exceptionally durable *chrome scarlet* sometimes referred to as "international orange." This pigment is the accepted international standard for the coating of obstructions to navigation such as bridges or high towers.

GREENS   Most green pigments are prepared chemically. Some green earths are used, but they vary greatly in their ability to withstand weathering. *Chrome greens*, formed by combining chrome yellow and iron blue, are produced in light, medium, and dark shades. Chrome greens produce clear bright colors, but they are somewhat subject to fading on exposure to weather. Chemically pure *chromium oxide green* is an extremely stable chemical compound that is less subject to fading than the chrome greens. However, the tints made with this pigment do not have the brilliance of chrome greens and tend to produce slightly greyed tones.

BLUES   In years past the best blue pigment was obtained by grinding the rare stone *lapis lazuli*, which produced a rich blue known as *ultramarine* (literally, bluer than blue). Most blue pigments used today are artificially produced. The two principal types are *soda ultramarine*, which has a deep violet cast, and *sulfate ultramarine*, which shows a greenish tinge. *Cobalt blue* is usually an ultramarine toned with cobalt to produce a blue-green. *Prussian blue*, a chemically pure iron compound known as ferric ferrocyanide, is one of the most valuable of the blue pigments. Its tinting strength is greater than most blue pigments, and it is fairly permanent. The pigment is produced under carefully controlled conditions, from a light to a dark tone.

Phthalocyanine blue, an organic pigment made from phthalic anhydride, is described by paint chemists as the greatest advance in pigments in the last 200 years. This amazing chemical is important not only in paint, but in the production of alkyd resins, nonflash smokeless powder, and insect repellents. The pigment is used widely for making light blue and green tints from white. It is outstanding in color retention and produces clean bright tones. It is usually used where color retention on long exposure is important.

Sublimed blue lead is rarely used as a color pigment in paints, but it is used in some metal-protection applications. It is produced by subliming litharge to a gaseous state and recondensing it to a solid.

REDS   Red pigments are generally either *iron oxide* (ferric oxide) or reds produced from organic compounds. Iron oxide pigments vary in color and nature, depending on the quantity and nature of the remaining components. They include such colors as *Venetian red*, *Indian red*, and *Tuscan red*. *Rose lake* is a brilliant, fairly transparent color consisting of a mineral base colored by an organic dye. Since it tends to fade, it is not recommended for exterior use.

Red lead is not usually used as a color pigment, but it is widely used as a priming coat for metal surfaces. It is produced from litharge (lead monoxide) as an orange-red powder and is available in dry, paste, or paint form.

Toluidine red is an organic pigment produced from coal tar. It does not mix well with other pigments for tinting and is insoluble in most paint vehicles. However, it is very permanent when used alone and is widely used in the painting of signs and vehicles to produce a vermillion color. *Permanent red* is produced by compounding an analine dye with a suitable base pigment. This pigment is not used for tinting, but produces a relatively permanent color when used alone.

BLACKS   The most widely used black pigment is *lampblack*, produced by the imperfect combustion of coal-tar oils. It consists of very finely divided pure unburned carbon. Although lampblack is not the blackest of the black pigments, it is very useful in toning down or greying various tints. A small amount of lampblack added to white produces a clear grey with a bluish tint. *Carbon black* is extracted from carbon smoke. It produces some of the densest blacks, but is not widely used in tinting. *Bone black* is the result of carbonizing or burning of animal or vegetable matter.

VEHICLES

The function of the vehicle, the liquid portion of paint, is to carry the pigment and bind it in a film. The vehicle consists of volatile solvents and thinners which facilitate application and a nonvolatile *binder*, which remains as an integral part of the paint film to bind the pigment particles together. It is the binder that determines adhesion of the film to the surface, as well as the protective qualities and durability of the paint. A vehicle suitable for exterior surfaces may not be suitable for interior surfaces.

Most binders consist of *drying oils*, *resins*, or a mixture of the two. In connection with paint, *drying* refers not only to evaporation of volatile material, but also to the setting or hardening process that occurs when certain oils are exposed in thin films to the atmosphere. The drying in this case results not from evaporation, but from *oxidation*, the absorption of oxygen from the air, and *polymerization*, the combination of molecules within the oil.

Blends of drying oils and natural resins are classed as *oleoresins*. Great progress has been made in the paint industry in the modification of natural drying oil, such as linseed oil, and the development of synthetic resins.

Natural Drying Oils

LINSEED OIL   This oil is produced by crushing the seed of the flax plant. When it is filtered and allowed to stand for several months, it becomes a clear, translucent, amber material called *raw linseed oil*. Raw linseed oil has a tendency to yellow with age, but it forms a tough, elastic, durable coating in paints. Linseed oil is classed as a slow-drying oil, and like other drying oils, it oxidizes on exposure to form a hard protective film. Raw linseed oil is used where slow drying is not objectionable and wetting ability is important, as in some priming paints for exterior wood surfaces.

Raw linseed oil heated to a temperature of 360°F and then cooled is called *boiled linseed oil* (although it is not actually boiled). During the heating process *siccatives*, or driers, are added to the oil to increase its speed of drying. Although the speed of drying may be increased as much as four times, there is a corresponding loss in durability, elasticity, and penetration. Boiled linseed oil is generally limited to interior paints.

If raw linseed is heated to temperatures of 500 to 600°F, it becomes polymerized and forms *heat-bodied oil*, or simply *bodied oil*. The heating process causes two of the molecules of the linseed oil to combine to form a thick, highly viscous oil. This is light in color, dries faster than boiled oil, and is more water resistant. The film yellows with age and whitens when it is submerged in water.

TALL OIL   Tall oil is a by-product of the manufacture of paper from pine trees by the sulfate process. Distilled tall oil is blended with other oleoresinous vehicles or alkyds in the production of interior gloss enamels or interior flat wall paints. It is blended with semidrying oils such as soybean oil and fish oil as a metal primer.

TUNG OIL   Tung oil, pressed from the fruit of the tung tree, has been used as a waterproofing material for centuries by the Chinese. During the last twenty years no tung oil has been imported from China, but many tung trees are now grown in our Southern states. Although tung oil has been replaced to a certain extent by the new synthetics, it is still used in quick-drying oil-based paints. It is faster drying, more resistant to water, and more durable than linseed oil, but not so elastic. It is generally used with other drying oils as varnish.

SOYBEAN OIL   Soybean oil has been used in its natural state as a semidrying oil since the 1930s, intermediate in character between nondrying oils and slow-drying linseed oil. Modern research has developed soybean oils of improved drying qualities which, because of their nonyellowing qualities, are widely used for gleaming white baked finishes on modern appliances. Soybean oils are used extensively in varnish and enamel vehicles. Improved soybean oils are usually produced by a polymerization process similar to that used to produce heat-bodied linseed oil. Oil-based exterior house paints formulated from improved soybean oil have excellent weathering qualities. With further heat treatment and chemical modification these oils are used for alkyd exterior house paints.

CASTOR OIL   Dehydrated castor oil is used in a variety of paints and varnishes. It is made from castor oil, itself a drying oil, and acquires further drying properties through a change in its chemical structure as the result of the removal of water molecules. Because of its nonyellowing characteristics, it is used in special preparations for interior paints where color maintenance is necessary. It is also useful in the formulation of special baked varnishes, usually in combination with a synthetic resin.

PERILLA OIL   This oil is obtained from the seeds of a plant cultivated in Asia, and is used to some extent as a substitute for linseed oil.

OITICICA OIL   This oil is obtained from a Brazilian nut tree. It is used in the manufacture of varnishes and enamels.

FISH OIL   Oils extracted from tuna, shark, or menhaden are used in some paints and varnishes. When used alone, these oils are generally slow drying and tacky and tend to yellow with age. Paints made with fish oils are useful for coating smokestacks and other hot surfaces, where a hard coating would become brittle. By careful processing, certain fish-oil fractions can be produced that have very good drying properties. They have also been combined with certain resins to produce superior coatings.

Natural Resins

The natural resins used in paint vehicles are hard, glossy substances distilled from animal or vegetable matter. Most natural resins are obtained as exudations of living trees. *Rosin*, a by-product of the distillation of turpentine, is used as a binder in dark clear coatings. *Copal* and *dammar* are natural resinous exudations from trees found in the Philippines, Africa, and the East Indies. These resins are responsible for the beautiful, clear finishes on fine furniture and stringed instruments. *Shellac* is made from resin produced by an insect in India, Thailand, and Indonesia.

The natural resins are flammable, nonconductive of electricity, and fracture with a sharp line when they have hardened. Natural resins are soluble in turpentine and mineral spirits, but not in water.

Synthetic Resins

Many new synthetic resins (manufactured) are being used in the coating industry. Synthetic resins have steadily grown in favor because the close control possible during their manufacture results in consistent properties, which in turn allows paint manufacturers to produce materials with uniform and generally superior properties. Curability, waterproofness, toughness, resistance to chemicals, and strength of coatings have been greatly improved by their use. Synthetic resins may be used alone or in combination with drying oils as *oleoresins*.

Alkyds

Alkyds are produced from the same chemical as the pigment phthalocyanine blue. They are probably the most versatile of the synthetic resins used in the paint industry. Alkyd paints are made by combining the synthetic resin with various drying oils, such as linseed oil, tung oil, or soybean oil. These paints can be formulated with extremely high concentrations of pigment to give better hiding power, thus producing the so-called one-coat paints. The self-healing properties of alkyd paints make primers and undercoats unnecessary on many surfaces. They are produced for both interior and exterior applications, from a flat finish to a high gloss. The exterior formulations have good weather resistance and gloss retention. The film is tough and is more resistant to ultraviolet rays than that of any other paint.

Alkyd paints darken slightly with age, but not as much as oil- or varnish-based paints. Alkyd-oil preparations formulated as flat interior paints have limited resistance to grease stains, abrasion, and scrubbing, and thus limited washability. These paints are sensitive to free alkali in insufficiently cured masonry or plaster surfaces, which sometimes results in peeling.

The addition of chlorinated paraffin, produced by distillation of wood, coal, petroleum, and similar products, to alkyd produces a vehicle with the positive features of both alkyds and linseed oil. Paints produced with this type of vehicle have excellent color retention, outstanding resistance to fumes, superior gloss retention, and improved flexibility. It may be used on bare wood without a primer.

Vinyl Resins and Latexes

Latex originally referred to a natural-rubber emulsion, natural rubber held in suspension in water. It is now applied to emulsions of various synthetic resins. Vinyl resins are produced chemically by building up a large molecule from a number of smaller molecules by direct linkage, without eliminating water or other by-products. This group of vehicles includes several resins. They are sometimes formulated as resin-emulsion or vinyl-emulsion paints, which are thinned with water. Since they contain no flammable solvents, latex-emulsion paints present no flammability hazard in storage or application. They dry rapidly with a minimum of odor. The most common types are styrene-butadiene, polyvinyl acetate (PVA), and acrylic.

STYRENE-BUTADIENE This resin is produced by combining butadiene and styrene, the same ingredients used in synthetic rubber. One of its greatest advantages is its resistance to the alkali found in all types of masonry construction, which makes it an effective masonry paint. The film forms with minute pores which allow the coating to breathe, so that water vapor trapped behind the coating can escape without forming blisters. When properly formulated, this material produces an interior paint that does not darken with age, resists abrasion, can easily be patched, and is washable. It does, however, give a thinner film than alkyds and oil-based paints.

POLYVINYL ACETATE This vinyl emulsion is widely used as an interior paint and as exterior paint for masonry surfaces. It does not yellow with age and is highly resistant to alkali, salt air, chemical contamination, smog, and sunlight. It is a breather type of coating which will allow trapped air to escape and still be water repellent. It cannot be used on unprimed ferrous metal.

ACRYLIC OR VINYL ACRYLIC Many forms of this polymer can be created from the basic material (methyl methacrylate or acrylic acid), ranging from a soft, tacky substance to a hard, brittle coating. Some acrylic paints are not emulsions, but are thinned with solvents manufactured from coal tar or petroleum, such as toluol or xylol. A plasticizer is usually added to the vehicle to improve flexibility. Acrylic paints do not oxidize to form a film. Many types dry in 20 minutes, making it easy to apply two coats in one day. They do not darken and are easily patched. The film is flexible and has excellent gloss and color retention. It is resistant to industrial fumes, mild chemical atmospheres, and alkali and will not support mildew growth.

Acrylics generally have poor hiding power and must be applied in thicker coatings for complete hiding of substrate. When acrylic-emulsion paints are applied to exterior surfaces in hot weather, it is advisable to wet the surface before applying the paint. These paints cannot be used over metal surfaces without a suitable primer.

Some metal-finishing systems have been developed that include a rust inhibitor for use as a primer coat. These coatings are emulsions and are thinned with water. The absence of solvents makes them safe to use in enclosed areas and in areas of high fire danger, where solvents cannot be used.

COPOLYMER LATEX   This type of latex is produced by adding a small amount of modifying resin to a basic resin such as polyvinyl acetate. The resin is polymerized into the latex at the time of manufacture. The modification produces a harder, tougher, more flexible surface film than the original latex. This vehicle produces an oil-free, stable emulsion paint to form flat and satin sheens on interior surfaces. The film does not darken with age like most alkyds, and so it can be patched without showing color change. The coating is not affected by alkali in masonry and has good washability. This type of paint has less pigment concentration than alkyds, and two coats are usually required to obtain the same hiding power.

Phenolic Resins

Phenolic resins, often called *varnish resins,* are produced from formaldehyde and phenol and are thinned with solvent. Phenolic coatings are nonoxidizing materials which dry entirely by solvent evaporation to form a tough, flexible coating on surfaces such as metal, wood, gypsum wallboard, plaster, and concrete. The coatings can be formulated to dry hard enough to handle or recoat in five minutes. They make effective primers for rough or smooth surfaces and are used extensively as filling and caulking compounds, as traffic paints, and for nonskid floorings.

Some phenolic coatings are of the two part type and must be mixed with a catalyst, sometimes termed an accelerator, hardener, or curing agent, at the time of application. They harden or set as a result of chemical reaction. This type of coating is used for special conditions in the chemical and petroleum industries, where resistance to extreme chemical exposure is required.

Alkyd resins modified with phenolic resins penetrate rusted surfaces; ground with rust-inhibitive pigments such as red lead, zinc chromate, or iron oxide, they make excellent primers for steel. A durable-gloss synthetic enamel is produced for exterior and interior protection of steel or aluminum. Mixed with aluminum paint, this enamel provides a durable one-coat finish with high reflective values.

Polyester Resins

Several types of resins are formed by the reaction of a polybasic acid with polyhydric alcohols to form esters. The product of the reaction is dissolved in a solvent to form a fluid which can be pigmented and stored until ready for use. The product is reactivated for application by a catalyst or heat. Once the catalyst has been added to the basic resin, the material has a limited pot life.

Polyester paints are nontoxic and odorless after proper curing. The film is nonporous and will not support the growth of bacteria. These paints may be applied to metals, wood, concrete, plaster, and plastics. Finishes range from dead flat to high gloss.

Epoxy Resins

Since their introduction in the 1940s, epoxy resins have matured into sophisticated materials capable of meeting the new demands generated by recent technological advances. Approximately 50 percent of the epoxy resins produced are compounded into protective coatings. Epoxies are thermosetting materials; they become permanently rigid with the application of heat. The most common epoxies are produced by reacting an epichlorohydrin and polyhydroxy compound in the presence of a catalyst. The resins produced may be varied from a low-viscosity fluid to a high-melting-point solid.

Epoxy coatings are used where they must withstand extreme abuse, as in public restrooms, cold-storage and chemical plants, refineries, and laboratories. They are characterized by exceptional adhesion, and their resistance to chemicals makes them especially suited where various alkali, acids, and chemicals are apt to splash or splatter and cannot be cleaned up at once.

Epoxy resins are valuable in formulating materials for painting, repairing, and maintenance of masonry materials. They offer maximum resistance to efflorescence and hydrostatic pressure. These coatings are classed as solventless coatings; they do not harden by the evaporation of solvents. This permits a large buildup in a single coat, which minimizes pinholes and other surface defects and eliminates solvent vapors. Epoxy coatings chalk and fade rapidly on exterior surfaces, but without any damage to the film integrity.

EPOXY ESTERS   Several types of finishes are produced as one-part epoxy esters. Although one-part epoxy-ester coatings exhibit poorer chemical resistance than the two-part system, they still have better resistance than alkyds and other oil-based coatings.

EPOXY POLYESTER   This two-part system is a recent development for use as interior or exterior coating. It combines the physical toughness, adhesion, and chemical resistance of epoxy with the color retention of polyester compounds. The high density of solids produces a tilelike film of 6 to 8 mils dry thickness in one coating. Coatings can be formulated to produce sheens from eggshell to full gloss and have greater stain resistance than most other finishes.

Silicones

A large group of chemical compounds has been developed in recent years which consist of resins, clear fluids, and synthetic rubbers. These compounds are produced from quartz rock (sodium silicate, similar to common beach sand). Silicones have great resistance to heat and moisture.

Silicone resins are used in pigmented paints formulated to withstand high temperatures. Paints made with aluminum and silicone resins will withstand temperatures of over 1200°F and are used for smokestacks, household heaters, and other applications where resistance to heat is important. At extremely high temperatures the binder is actually destroyed, but a fusion product of the base metal, silicone resin, and aluminum pigment results. The ultimate performance of high-temperature coatings on metal is in direct proportion to surface preparation.

Chlorinated Rubber

When combined with suitable resins for adhesion and gloss and plasticizers for flexibility, chlorinated rubber makes a useful vehicle for pigmented paints. These paints are solvent thinned. The coatings have excellent resistance to acid, alkalis, and some salt-air or salt-water exposure. They are suitable for use on interior or exterior metal or masonry surfaces. The coating forms one of the best moisture and vapor barriers that can be used on plaster and masonry surfaces. Chlorinated-rubber-base paints are available as swimming-pool paints and are used extensively on basement walls and in sewage-disposal plants. They have unusually good abrasion and wearing qualities for floors. Chlorinated rubber coatings are not recommended for wood surfaces. They will soften and deteriorate in contact with animal or vegetable fats or oils.

SOLVENTS

The volatile portion of the vehicle includes not only liquids that actually dissolve nonvolatile ingredients of the vehicle, but also the thinners that act as suspending agents. The water in latex paints is merely a thinner; it does not dissolve the ingredients. Solvents are introduced into paint to increase the fluidity to a point where it can readily be applied by brushing, rolling, or spraying. They volatilize, or evaporate, during drying, and do not become a part of the film. Solvents affect consistency, leveling, drying, and even adhesion and durability.

Turpentine

The use of turpentine dates back to 2000 B.C., when it was used by the ancient Egyptians. It was rediscovered early in the seventeenth century and was one of the first exports from Jamestown in the American colonies. It was classed as "naval stores" because of its use in the maritime industry, in the form of *rosin*, as a waterproofing material for ships.

Gum turpentine is obtained from living pine trees or fossilized pine trees. The turpentine from living trees is obtained by tapping the trees in a manner similar to that used in extracting natural rubber. The raw material is then distilled to produce turpentine, leaving a residue of rosin. *Steam-distilled turpentine* is produced from ground up stumps of pine trees. The turpentine is extracted from the ground wood pulp by steam. *Destructively distilled turpentine* is produced by roasting ground pine stumps in a still and catching the vapor. This vapor is distilled to produce turpentine. *Sulfate wood turpentine* is a by-product in the manufacture of paper by the sulphate process. This is the strongest of the turpentines with a more pungent odor.

Mineral Spirits and VM and P Naphthas

Varnish makers' and painters' naphthas, always referred to by their initials as VM and P naphthas, are petroleum products midway between kerosene and gasoline. The drying rate of naphthas varies considerably. Some dry faster than turpentine, and others dry more slowly. Special types of mineral spirits, classed as low-odor or odorless, are a by-product from the production of gasoline. The aromatic portions of the mineral spirits have been removed. These solvents are used in odorless solvent-thinned paints.

BENZINE This solvent, produced from petroleum, is used as a thinner in spray painting. Its rapid rate of evaporation makes it extremely difficult to use for brushing. The material is highly flammable and has a low solvent power. It is sometimes used as a dilutant in lacquers. Benzine should not be confused with benzene, which is a coal-tar distillate.

BENZOL Benzol (benzene) is a very light coal-tar distillate which acts as a powerful solvent for many materials. It is very toxic and must be used only in well-ventilated spaces. It is highly flammable. Because of its high solvent power, it is used principally in varnish and paint removers.

TOLUOL Toluol (toluene, methyl benzene) is obtained as a by-product in the production of coke from coal or is extracted from coal tar. It resembles benzene, but has a distinctive odor. Although toluol is not as toxic or flammable as benzol, it must be used with care. It is used as a dilutant in lacquers, along with other solvents.

XYLOL Xylol (xylene) resembles benzene and tuluol, but has a slower solvent action. It is used as an ingredient in synthetic enamels and lacquers. It is the product of the distillation of coal tar or petroleum.

SOLVENT NAPHTHA High-flash, or aromatic, naphtha is an extremely volatile solvent used principally in lacquers and synthetic baking enamels. It is a *hydrocarbon*, a solvent derived from coal tar and petrolem containing carbon and hydrogen.

ACETATES The acetates are a group of esters formed by combining various alcohols with acetic acid and are generally used as lacquer solvents. There are many possible chemical compounds; the principal ones used as solvents are *ethyl acetate*, combined with alcohol for lacquer; *butyl acetate*, a slow-working lacquer solvent; *propyl acetate*, a medium-fast lacquer solvent; *isopropyl acetate,* a fast lacquer solvent; and amyl acetate, one of the slowest lacquer solvents.

KETONES   The ketones are produced by oxidizing alcohols and natural gas. They are extremely hazardous to use, but are valuable in the formulation of synthetic enamels and lacquers. Certain vinyl and chlorinated-rubber coatings are soluble only in ketone. Some ketones will mix with water. The most commonly used ketones are *acetone,* a very strong, fast solvent used in paint removers and as a super-fast lacquer solvent; *methyl ethyl ketone,* a good solvent for lacquers, synthetic-resin products, and some epoxy coatings; *methyl isobutyl ketone,* a medium-fast solvent for lacquers and synthetic resins; and *cyclohexanone,* a slow solvent used for lacquers, vinyls, and polyvinyl-acetate systems.

Alcohols and Alcohol Derivatives

The alcohols are a family of organic compounds and are noticeably different in the products they will dissolve. Some will mix with water; others dissolve gums and resins not soluble in the hydrocarbon solvents.

ALCOHOLS   The chief use of alcohol as a solvent is in shellac. The alcohols most frequently used in the paint industry are *methyl alcohol* (methanol, wood alcohol), an excellent solvent for shellac but very hazardous when in contact with the skin or inhaled; *ethyl alcohol,* widely used in commercial lacquer solvents; *propyl alcohol,* usually used in special sealers; *butyl alcohol,* used as a lacquer solvent; and *amyl alcohol,* a slow lacquer solvent.

LATEX-EMULSION SOLVENTS   In latex-emulsion paints, water is not a solvent, but a dilutant. These paints would have a viscosity similar to that of water if thickeners were not added to make them workable. The latex particles are never dissolved; the water acts simply as a carrying agent. The proper solvents must be carefully selected and blended as required for the different resins and drying oils.

Synthetic-resin Solvents

Many modern coatings are based on synthetic resins which often require strong solvents. The selection of the proper solvent for a particular painting system is based on several factors. Table 13-3 lists the standard solvents used in the coating industry.

Driers

Driers are used in some types of paint to promote the absorption of oxygen. They are usually chemical compounds produced from the metallic salts of cobalt, lead, manganese, iron, zinc, and calcium. Most paints achieve their final film-forming properties and hardness through the

TABLE 13-3 End-use applications of solvents

RESIN	SOLVENT
Nitrocellulose	Ketones
Ethyl Cellulose	Acetates
Cellulose Acetate	Glycol Ether
Butyrate	Nitroparaffins
Acrylics	Ketones
	Acetates
	Glycol ethers
	Chlorinated hydrocarbons
	Nitroparaffins
Vinyl chloride–acetate copolymers	Ketones
	Acetates
	Nitroparaffins
Phenolics	Alcohols
	Glycol ethers
Urea formaldehyde	Alcohols
Melamine formaldehyde	Alcohols/aromatics
Epoxies	Ketones
	Acetates
	Glycol ethers
	Chlorinated hydrocarbons
	Nitroparaffins
Urethanes	Ketones
	Acetates
Silicones	Alcohols
Latex	Glycol ethers

process of oxidation. The addition of driers to the paint formulation results in increased oxygen absorption, thus hastening the curing process.

CLEAR COATINGS AND STAINS

Varnish, sealers, lacquer, shellac, and wax polish have for years been the standard clear coatings used in the paint industry. Linseed oil may be considered a clear coating, since it is sometimes used alone as such. New types of synthetic resins, such as the polyurethanes, are continually being developed to take the place of the time-tested formulations. Clear coatings generally do not have the durability of pigmented coatings in outside exposure because they do not give the protection against sunlight afforded by pigmentation. They are used primarily to beautify and protect surfaces without obscuring their natural appearance.

Varnish

Varnishes are any of several homogeneous mixtures of resin, drying oils, driers, and solvents. Varnish is manufactured by heat polymerization of the oils in combination with the resins, with the solvents and driers added after the cooked ingredients have partially cooled. The resins may be fossil gums, natural resins, or some of the synthetic resins. Varnish dries by evaporation of the solvent, followed by oxidation and polymerization of the drying oils and resins. Varnish is commonly used as the vehicle in pigmented paints of the quick-drying smooth-leveling type. *Enamel* is a special type of paint made with varnish as the vehicle.

The types of oil and resin and the ratio of oil to resin are the principal factors governing the properties of varnish. It is generally considered that the oils in the finish coating contribute to elasticity and the resins to hardness. The oil-to-resin ratio of varnish, expressed as the number of gallons of oil that are combined with 100 pounds of resin, is commonly referred to as the *length* of the varnish. Thus if 50 gal of oil are used with 100 lb of resin, the varnish has a 50-gal length. Varnish containing less than 20 gal of oil per 100 lb of resin is usually classed as *short-oil varnish;* a *medium-oil varnish* contains 20 to 30 gal, and a *long-oil varnish* is one in which 30 gal or more are used. Short-oil varnishes are used primarily for hardness, a high degree of impermeability, or resistance to alcohols, alkalis, or acids, where elasticity of the film is relatively unimportant.

Varnishes for exterior exposure are usually of long-oil formulation because of the benefits of drying oil in providing elasticity and resistance to weathering. *Spar varnish*, a high grade exterior varnish originally formulated for use on the wooden spars on sailing ships, is a varnish of this type. Recently, however, phenolic-resins medium-oil varnishes have been formulated which provide increased moisture resistance without sacrifice of sunlight resistance. Spar varnish should be used with care for interior applications, as it is likely to be sticky in warm weather. Short-oil varnishes produce hard brittle films that have less durability and water resistance than spar varnish; however, they are widely used as rubbing varnishes for highly polished furniture finishes and alcohol-resistant finishes on bar tops.

Lacquer

The term *lacquer* is frequently applied to nearly any coating that dries quickly and solely by evaporation of solvent. It is limited here to coatings with nitrocellulose as the basic nonvolatile constituent. Lacquer is characterized by very rapid drying and a distinctive odor. Both result from the use of low-boiling highly volatile acetates, ketones, and alcohols as solvents. Resins, plasticizers, and reacted drying oils may be added to improve adhesion and elasticity. Colored lacquers contain pigment similar to those used in oil-based pigmented paints.

Lacquers dry *tack-free*, or no longer sticky, in 5 to 15 minutes and form a firm film in 30 minutes to four hours. They are usually formulated as either brushing lacquers or spraying lacquers. The spraying lacquers dry too rapidly for brush application. Clear lacquers are used where thin, colorless, tough films are desired. They are not generally considered as durable as high-grade varnishes on exposure to sunlight and moisture. Lacquer with a high solids content will give a lasting smooth finish to stained or natural wood.

Shellac

Technically, shellac is a solid, the flaked form of refined lac resin, and the solution is a *shellac varnish*. Lac is refined from a secretion deposited on trees by the insect *Tachardia lacca*, native to India and the Malay Peninsula. The natural color of lac resin is amber, which produces *orange shellac*. The resin is bleached to produce *white shellac*, which is considerably lighter than orange shellac, but still has some color.

Shellac is furnished as a solution in denatured alcohol. It comes in various *cuts* which indicate the amount of resin per gallon of denatured alcohol. The most commonly used cuts are 4-, 4½-, and 5-lb cuts, which cover the range of light-, medium-, and heavy-bodied materials. Shellac is often used as a liquid filler and sealer on furniture and paneling under clear varnish finishes. Mixed with linseed oil and wax, it is applied to fine furniture as a hand-rubbed finish called *French polish*. Shellac is also used to seal knots and pitch streaks in lumber prior to painting, to prime "hot spots" in plaster, to seal bituminous coatings preparatory to application of decorative paints, and to prime certain types of walls for the application of ceramic, metal, or plastic wall tile.

Silicone

Combined with oil and certain solvents in proportions of 3½ to 5 percent, silicone acts as a colorless water-repellent coating for new brick and concrete masonry units. It is also used on porous concrete to prevent staining and is said to protect the surface up to 10 years. Silicone is sometimes referred to as a "waterproofing" material; however, it is more properly termed a water *repellent*. It sets up a surface tension which causes water to bead on the surface and roll off. The material may bridge microscopic openings in masonry walls, but to be effective as a water repellent it must be applied over a filler which closes pores and cracks in the masonry surface. The oils and waxes usually combined with silicone coatings may cause paint applied over such a surface to blister and peel. A silicone coating must be completely removed with a strong solvent before the surface can be satisfactorily painted. Silicone coatings should not be used on limestone or similar light-colored stones.

Polyurethane

The polyurethane resins are a group of nitrogen-bearing chemical reactants used in the production of clear or pigmented coatings. Oil-modified polyurethane resins consist of combinations of polyurethane, alkyd, soybean, and linseed oil. These compounds may be formulated for use as clear exterior or interior coatings for wood or as pigmented floor enamels. They provide better color and gloss retention and better abrasion resistance than regular varnishes. They are outstanding as a concrete floor finish, where heavy traffic wears through an alkyd finish in a short time. The application of polyurethane finishes is extremely critical. The surface must be absolutely clean and free from moisture for proper adhesion.

One-part polyurethane coatings cure by reaction with atmospheric moisture and must be installed when the humidity is between 30 and 90 percent to avoid incomplete cure or bubbling of the surface film. They are not recommended for application over enamels, lacquers, shellac, vinyl sealers, or paste wood fillers. Clear polyurethane finishes have been developed for gymnasium and dance floors, where a high degree of resistance to wear and abrasion is needed.

Wax Polish

Wax is seldom used alone, but it is widely used to beautify and protect other clear finishes. Two general types are available: one with mineral spirits or a similar organic solvent, and one in which the wax is emulsified with water for fluidity. The most commonly used waxes are carnauba wax, beeswax, ceresin wax. *Carnauba wax*, from Brazilian carnauba palm, is one of the highest grades of wax. Frequently waxes are modified with resins or oils; for example, shellac resin is often added to floor wax to impart nonslip properties. Emulsion-type waxes can be used on asphalt and rubber tile floors, which are adversely affected by other solvents. Emulsion-type waxes dry with some gloss and do not need polishing. These waxes are sometimes called self-polishing waxes.

Stains

Stains are a variety of pigmented paint in that they are composed of pigment and vehicle. They have a low pigment content which will not obscure the natural grain of the wood to which they are applied. They are used to modify the color or bring out the grain in fine woods. A clear coating is usually applied over the stain as a protective finish. Analine dye, a derivative of coal tar, is the basis of many stains. There are three types of stains: water stains (or acid stains), oil stains, and spirit stains.

WATER AND SPIRIT STAINS   These stains have an analine dye as the coloring agent. Water stains are applied over wet wood. Both water and spirit stains require some skill in application, as the stain penetrates the wood immediately and it is extremely difficult to obtain a uniform color.

OIL STAIN   The viscosity of oil stains is low, and they have high penetrating powers. The vehicle consists of drying oils and solvents. Oil stains may be applied with cheese-cloth pads and wiped to produce a finish that hides irregularities in grain or colors. The most common oil stains are based on linseed oil or tung oil. These types must set at least 24 hours before being varnished and 48 hours before being lacquered. New types of oil stains have been developed that use an alkyd-resin vehicle. These may be varnished over in 4 to 6 hours and lacquered in 24 hours.

SHINGLE STAINS   Some stains contain a high proportion of highly refined creosote oil which protects the wood against decay and insects. This type of stain is often called *shingle stain*. Heavy-bodied oil stains are produced for use on exterior woodwork, horizontal and vertical siding, and rough wood shingles and shakes. Stain is usually preferable to paint for wood shingles, because it does not form a tight film and thus permits breathing for better drying after rains and snowfall. The heavy-bodied oil stains have considerable hiding power and can be used over old weather-beaten wood as well as new shingles or siding. They are available in many distinctive shades that will not crack, peel, or blister.

VARNISH STAINS   Mixtures of oil stain and varnish have been developed with the idea of performing two jobs at once. They must be applied with extreme care to obtain an even color distribution. They could properly be called translucent pigmented paints.

PRIMERS AND SEALERS

The first of two or more coats of a paint, varnish, or lacquer system is called the primer. *Back priming* consists of applying a coat of paint to the back of woodwork and exterior siding to prevent moisture from entering the wood causing the grain to swell or the wood to warp because of uneven moisture on the exposed face and the hidden face. Primers used on steel usually contain a rust-inhibiting agent.

Wood Primers

The primer for wood may be simply a thinned-down coat of paint that is being used on the job, or it may be a specially formulated material with mildew inhibitors, fungicides, or sealants to stop pitch or oil in the wood surface from penetrating the final finish. Sealers may be needed on plaster that has not cured properly or has hot spots that may bleed through. It is sometimes necessary to prime painted surfaces when a different type of paint is to be applied.

Undercoaters are a special type of primer which has sealing qualities and is pigmented to hide the substrate and to provide a smoother surface for the finish coats.

Aluminum primers are especially valuable on resinous timber or timber which has been treated with oil-soluble wood preservatives. These primers contain a proportion of aluminum pigment. They should be distinguished from *aluminum paints,* in which the aluminum is designed to float to the top of the film and give a metallic brilliance, a feature undesirable in a primer.

Ferrous-metal Primers

At one time red lead was universally used as an anti-corrosive coating for iron and steel. The red lead coating forms a barrier between the corroding environment and the metal. Zinc chromate has also been found to be an excellent pigment for metal primers. Today a large variety of primers are available for protection against various exposure conditions. No one primer is a cure-all. Although the condition of exposure is the most important criterion in choosing a primer for iron and steel, there are other factors involved, such as type of structure, accessibility for maintenance painting, and job conditions.

Several types of vehicles are used in metal-priming paints. Linseed oil, although it is slow drying, is especially suitable where it is impracticable to provide a perfectly cleaned surface, because it is characteristically a good wetting vehicle and will bond well where most synthetic vehicles will not. Alkyd vehicles are quick drying and very durable in ordinary atmospheric conditions. Phenolic vehicles, which are also quick drying, are preferable where exposed metalwork will be subject to excessive moisture. Both alkyd- and phenolic-vehicle paints require a very clean surface to be effective.

Etching Primers

Etching or wash primers are generally two-part systems. The mixed paint contains carefully balanced proportions of an inhibiting chromate pigment, phosphoric acid, and a synthetic-resin binder in an alcohol solvent. On clean, light alloys or ferrous and many nonferrous surfaces, they give excellent adhesion, partly through chemical etching of the substrate. They produce a corrosion-inhibiting film which is a very good base for subsequent coats of paint. Although these materials are referred to as primers, the films are so thin that it is better to consider them as etching solutions and, where maximum protection is required, to follow them with a more orthodox type of primer.

Galvanized-metal Primers

Galvanized iron is one of the most difficult metals to prime properly. The galvanizing process forms a hard, dense surface that paint cannot penetrate. Most primers contain portland cement or zinc compounds. When these primers are used, the surface must be cleaned thoroughly of dirt and grease and usually etched with a dilute acid to provide some tooth for the coating. New types of galvanized-iron primers or portland cement and alkyd resins have been developed that may be applied without an acid treatment.

SPECIAL-PURPOSE PAINTS

Bituminous Paints

These paints consist essentially of natural bitumens dissolved in organic solvents. The bitumens may be either coal tar or asphaltic products. They may or may not contain softening agents, pigments, synthetic resins, and inorganic fillers. They are usually black or dark in color. In general, paints made from asphalt and coal tar are not well suited to atmospheric exposure because of the effects of air, heat, and sunlight in producing early embrittlement in relatively thin films of these materials. However, considerable improvement in this respect has been made in recent years through careful selection of materials. *Coal-tar enamel,* sometimes called *pipeline enamel,* is applied in conjunction with heat to pipes that will be installed underground, where they will be subjected to few and moderate variations of temperature.

COAL-TAR PAINTS   A cold-applied bituminous coating material has been developed by liquefying coal-tar pitch, heating, and then combining it with solvents, fillers, and other constituents. The solvent must be a coal-tar distillation product, such as xylol or coal-tar naphtha. Coal-tar-pitch materials may be combined with synthetic resins, such as epoxies, polyurethanes, and polyvinyl chlorides, to produce coating materials that provide better protection for metalwork submerged in fresh water than do some paints based on a single resin.

COAL-TAR EMULSIONS   The principal difference in composition between coal-tar emulsions and cold-applied coal-tar paint is that water, rather than coal-tar distillates, is used as the dispersing medium. Emulsions have certain advantages over solvent-thinned paints. They will adhere satisfactorily to damp surfaces and are practically odorless. They also have better resistance to sunlight.

ASPHALT PAINTS   Coatings derived from petroleum are available as enamels, cold-applied paints, and emulsions. They are generally considered to be more resistant to moisture penetration than the corresponding coal-tar products. As a rule, they are less susceptible to temperature extremes.

Luminous Paints

Luminous coatings contain substances that give off light. These substances should not be confused with a painted surface that simply reflects light. Their luminescence may be a result of florescence, phosphorescence, or radioactivity. Luminous paints are used on warning signs or obstructions to be viewed in dim light.

FLUORESCENT PAINTS   Fluorescent paints contain pigments which absorb energy from the blue or ultraviolet end of the spectrum and reemit it as light in the visible wavelengths. Fluorescent paints cease to glow when the activating source is removed.

PHOSPHORESCENT PAINTS Phosphorescent paints contain phosphors which absorb energy at one wavelength and emit it over a period of time as light at a longer wavelength in the visible spectrum. They differ from fluorescent paints in that they continue to glow after the stimulating source has been removed.

RADIOACTIVE PAINTS Radioactive paints are self-luminous. Normally these paints contain radioactive compounds which permanently activate the phosphor by radioactive rays, so that it continuously emits light in the visible spectrum.

Fire-retardant and Fire-resistant Paints

Several paints or paint systems have recently been developed to retard or resist the spread of fire. Fire-retardant paints will burn, but by themselves they will not support combustion. The film retards the spread of flame but does not protect the surface underneath. Flat or semigloss paints with alkyd vehicles are of this type because of their high pigment volume.

Fire-resistant paints will not burn. They protect the surface by puffing up and forming an insulating blanket for the flammable substrate. These paints may have the disadvantages of higher cost, limited color selection, and poor washability, and they tend to release toxic gases when subjected to high temperature.

QUESTIONS

1. How is gloss measured?
2. What is the major factor in the fading and color change in paints?
3. What determines the hiding power of a paint?
4. How is the thickness of a paint coating measured?
5. What are the basic types of ingredients in a paint system?
6. What are the functions of pigments in paints?
7. What is a vehicle?
8. Describe two types of white lead.
9. What is the function of an extender?
10. Describe five types of blue pigment.
11. What is a polymerized oil?
12. What is tall oil?

13. What are the differences between a natural resin and a synthetic resin?
14. What is the composition of alkyd paints, and where are they generally used?
15. What is PVA, and where is it used?
16. What is a latex paint?
17. What is an epoxy?
18. What is the difference between benzine and benzene?
19. What is an enamel?
20. What is varnish?
21. What material would you specify to be applied to a masonry wall to make it water resistant?
22. Where would you recommend the use of a polyurethane coating?
23. What is the composition of shellac?
24. What is a spirit stain?
25. Describe three types of primer to be used on structural steel.

REFERENCES FOR FURTHER STUDY

American Society for Testing and Materials: 1916 Race Street, Philadelphia, Pa., 19103. "Terms Relating to Paint, Varnish, Lacquer, and Related Products," ASTM D16, 1959.
Close, Lewis E.: "The Value of Complete and Precise Painting Specifications," *The Construction Specifier*, November 1960.
Construction Specifications Institute: Suite 300, 1150 17th Street, N.W., Washington, D.C., 20036. "Paint, Painting and Finishing," 1963. "Specifying Dampproofing Silicone," 1968.
General Services Administration: U.S. Government Printing Office, Washington, D.C., 20402. "Paint, Varnish, Lacquer, and Related Materials: Methods of Inspection, Sampling, and Testing," Standard 141a, 1965.
Maslow, Philip: "Epoxy-based Masonry Materials," *The Construction Specifier*, February 1960.
National Bureau of Standards: U.S. Government Printing Office, Washington, D.C., 20402. "Organic Coatings: Properties, Selection, and Use," 1968.
National Paint, Varnish and Lacquer Association, Inc.: 1500 Rhode Island Avenue, N.W., Washington, D.C., 20005. "The Selection of Paint," circ. 796, 1967.
Painting and Decorating Contractors of America: 2625 West Peterson Avenue, Chicago, Ill., 60645. "Painting and Decorating Craftsman's Manual and Textbook," 1961.
Pickett, C. F.: "Why Paint Specifications," *The Construction Specifier*, fall 1958.

Steel Structures Painting Council: 4400 Fifth Avenue, Pittsburgh, Pa., 15213. "Steel Structures Painting Manual," vols. I and II, 1966.

U.S. Bureau of Reclamation: U.S. Government Printing Office, Washington, D.C., 20402. "Paint Manual," 1966.

"New Construction and Maintenance, Engineers' Manual," 1961.

U.S. Department of the Army: U.S. Government Printing Office, Washington, D.C., 20402. "Manual, Paints, and Protective Coatings," TM5-618, 1969.

THE MECHANICAL TRADES

The mechanical section of a set of building specifications deals with plumbing, heating, and air-conditioning systems. The systems are usually designed by a mechanical engineer and installed under the direction of a plumbing contractor or a heating and air-conditioning contractor. A plumbing system includes all water supplies and distribution pipes, soil and waste piping and devices, drainage and vent piping, gas or fuel-oil piping, water-heating devices and storage tanks, and all plumbing fixtures and traps. It may also include the distribution of chilled-water, oxygen, nitrous oxide, compressed-air, or vacuum lines. Plumbing systems are covered by codes such as the "Uniform Plumbing Code," published by the International Association of Plumbing and Mechanical Officials. The installation of heating, ventilating, comfort conditioning, refrigeration systems, and miscellaneous heat-producing devices is covered by a mechanical code such as the "Uniform Mechanical Code," published jointly by the International Association of Plumbing and Mechanical Officials and the International Conference of Building Officials.

WATER-DISTRIBUTION SYSTEMS

The Uniform Plumbing Code specifies that each plumbing fixture shall be provided with an adequate supply of *potable*, or drinkable, running water. The water must be piped to the fixture in an approved manner so arranged to keep it in a clean and sanitary condition. Care must be taken that unclean, used, polluted, or contaminated water or solids cannot enter the potable-water system. Any arrangement of piping or connections that allows such contamination is called a *cross-connection*. Cross connections allow sewage to be drawn into the potable-water mains when a difference in pressure or vacuum develops in the public or private water-distribution system. A cross connection would exist when the piping or fixtures were so connected or placed as to allow the waste system to siphon into the potable-water system. This may be prevented by the use of *backflow* or *check valves* that allow the water to flow in only one direction. An *air gap or air break*, which consists of a vertical separation between any pipe or faucet conveying water to a tank or fixture receptor and the flood-level rim of the receptacle, will also prevent the backflow of contaminated water. Local codes govern the air gap

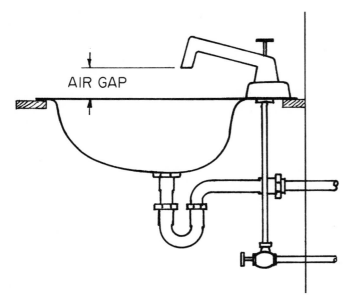

Fig. 14-1 Air gap in plumbing fixture.

Fig. 14-2 Typical residential water-supply system.

requirement for each type of plumbing fixture installation.

Valves and fittings used in residential or light construction are usually rated to operate satisfactorily up to a given water pressure. Higher pressures lead to shortened life of valves and washers in plumbing fixtures. Where local water pressure in the main or other source of supply exceeds a given pressure, a *pressure regulator* must be inserted in the line to reduce this pressure. Whenever the local water pressure is insufficient to provide pressure of at least 15 psi to the building supply main, a pump and tank must be provided to increase the pressure. In calculating the pressure, friction in the piping and other pressure losses must be taken into consideration. The required sizes of pipe for given length of run and height above the main water supply system are specified by local plumbing codes.

Water Demand

The size of the water meter and of each pipe carrying water from the meter to the fixture is based on the *water demand*

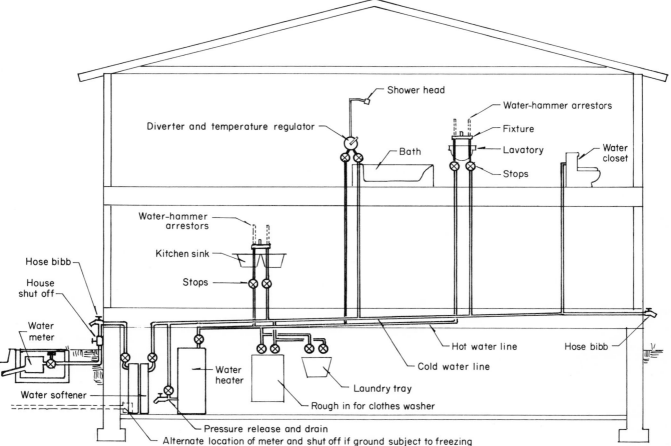

of that fixture or group of fixtures. The total water demand is represented in fixture units. The size of pipe required by each type of fixture is governed by local plumbing codes. Tables 14-1 and 14-2 are examples of tables used to determine meter and pipe sizes.

To determine the proper pipe size for a water-supply system, the number of fixture units is determined from Table 14-1. The length of supply piping to the most distant fixture and the difference in elevation between the meter and the highest fixture outlet are calculated, with $1/2$ lb of pressure subtracted for each foot of difference in elevation between the source and the highest fixture. The pressure at the street main or water source is then determined (100 psi is the maximum pressure that can be used in calculations). In localities where there may be wide pressure fluctuations, consider the minimum pressure to be expected during heavy water use. Add the equivalent fixture units, as determined by Table 14-1, and calculate the pressure range available, subtracting the pressure loss due to elevation above the source. Follow the vertical column under the length of feet in the pipe runs for a par-

ticular pressure down to the number of fixture units involved. The side of the meter, the supply line to the building, and the required size of branch lines will be found in the two left-hand columns.

Water Softeners

The hardness of water varies greatly with different localities. Water containing salts of calcium and magnesium in quantities of over 5 grains/gal is classed as *hard water*. Salts in this amount not only make washing difficult, but also tend to clog pipes. The most common method of removing these salts from domestic water supplies is through water softeners.

One method of water softening is the *zeolite process*. The water is passed through a bed of zeolite, which takes up the calcium and magnesium. The zeolite bed must be regenerated periodically with common salt. Domestic water-softener systems usually consist of twin tanks, one containing the bed of zeolite and a sand-and-gravel filter and the other containing the salt for the rejuvenation of the

TABLE 14-1 Equivalent fixture units (includes combined hot and cold water demand)

FIXTURE	NUMBER OF FIXTURE UNITS	
	PRIVATE USE	PUBLIC USE
Bar sink	1	2
Bathtub (with or without shower over)	2	4
Dental unit or cuspidor	—	1
Drinking fountain (each head)	—	1
Hose bibb or sill cock (standard type)	3	5
House trailer (each)	6	6
Laundry tub or clotheswasher (each pair of faucets)	2	4
Lavatory	1	2
Lavatory (dental)	1	1
Lawn sprinklers (standard type, each head)	1	1
Shower (each head)	2	4
Sink (bar)	1	2
Sink or dishwasher	2	4
Sink (flushing rim, clinic)	—	10
Sink (washup, each set of faucets)	—	2
Sink (washup, circular spray)	—	4
Urinal (pedestal or similar type)	—	10
Urinal (stall)	—	5
Urinal (wall)	—	5
Urinal (flush tank)	—	3
Water closet (flush tank)	3	5
Water closet (flushometer valve)	6	10
Water supply outlets for items not listed above shall be computed at their maximum demand, but in no case less than:		
$3/8$ in.	1	2
$1/2$ in.	2	4
$3/4$ in.	3	6
1 in.	6	10

From Uniform Plumbing Code, 1967 ed.; by permission of the International Association of Plumbing and Mechanical Officials.

water-softening bed. The two tanks are usually connected into the water-supply system with flexible hoses and couplings for ease of replacement. Rejuvenation may be either manual or automatically controlled by a meter and valve on the softened-water line.

Hot-water Systems

The simplest form of hot-water piping is a noncirculating system, in which hot water (maximum temperature 140°F) is taken off the top of the water heater or hot-water storage tank and piped through a series of risers to the individual fixtures. This system requires a temperature-operated pressure-relief valve, which will open in case the water gets too hot and there is a possibility of excess pressure developing in the system. If the pressure-relief valve is located within the building, it must be connected to a drain. A *check valve*, which allows water to flow in only one direction, must be installed on the cold-water side of the water heater to prevent hot water from entering the cold-water supply lines.

Noncirculating systems are relatively inexpensive to install and are usually satisfactory in small residences. However, in larger residences or systems, a circulating

TABLE 14-2 Fixture unit table for determining water pipe and meter sizes for flush tank systems

METER AND STREET SERVICE, IN.	BUILDING SUPPLY AND BRANCHES, IN.	MAXIMUM ALLOWABLE LENGTH, FT					
		40	60	80	100	150	200
Pressure range, 30 to 45 psi							
3/4	1/2	6	5	4	4	3	2
3/4	3/4	18	16	14	12	9	6
3/4	1	29	25	23	21	17	15
1	1	36	31	27	25	20	17
1	1 1/4	54	47	42	38	32	28
1 1/2	1 1/4	90	68	57	48	38	32
1 1/2	1 1/2	151	124	105	91	70	57
2	1 1/2	210	162	132	110	80	64
1 1/2	2	220	205	190	176	155	138
2	2	372	329	292	265	217	185
2	2 1/2	445	418	390	370	330	300
Pressure range, 46 to 60 psi							
3/4	1/2*	9	8	7	6	5	4
3/4	3/4	27	23	19	17	14	11
3/4	1	44	40	36	33	28	23
1	1	60	47	41	36	30	25
1	1 1/4	102	87	76	67	52	44
1 1/2	1 1/4	168	130	106	89	66	52
1 1/2	1 1/2	270	225	193	167	128	105
2	1 1/2	360	290	242	204	150	117
1 1/2	2	380	360	340	318	272	240
2	2	570	510	470	430	368	318
2	2 1/2	680	640	610	580	535	500
Pressure range, over 60 psi							
3/4	1/2*	11	9	8	7	6	5
3/4	3/4	34	28	24	22	17	13
3/4	1	63	53	47	42	35	30
1	1	87	66	55	48	38	32
1	1 1/4	140	126	108	96	74	62
1 1/2	1 1/4	237	183	150	127	93	74
1 1/2	1 1/2	366	311	273	240	186	154
2	1 1/2	490	395	333	275	220	170
1 1/2	2	380†	380†	380†	380†	370	335
2	2	690†	670	610	560	478	420
2	2 1/2	690†	690†	690†	690†	690†	650

*Building supply, 3/4″ minimum.
†Maximum allowable load on meter.

From Uniform Plumbing Code, 1967 ed.; by permission of the International Association of Plumbing and Mechanical Officials.

type of system is needed. A circulating system has return lines which hook back from each fixture or group of fixtures to the hot-water supply line. A circulating hot-water system will give almost instantaneous hot water to any fixture. When a faucet is opened, hot water is drawn from the hot-water line, thus stimulating flow of the water in the return lines to the water heater where it can be reheated. To ensure a constant supply of hot water, it may be necessary to install a circulating pump to maintain hot water at all fixtures. Insulation of piping in the hot-water system increases the efficiency of the system.

Consumption of hot water is usually figured as one-third that of cold water. Heater capacities and storage-tank sizes are based on the maximum probable hourly demand for hot water. Instantaneous water heaters, which do not require a storage tank, can supply this demand if the use is relatively constant. However, if the demand varies widely, it is necessary to have a storage tank that will furnish the required hot water at peak periods of use.

Water-heating devices, with the storage tank as either an integral part of the heating element or a separate unit, are rated on the basis of *storage capacity* and *recovery time*. The demands on the system and economic factors govern the selection of a heater with a large storage tank and a slow recovery rate or one with a small storage tank and a high recovery rate. In general, the less uniform the demand for hot water, the greater storage capacity is needed.

The heating medium may be steam or hot-water coils immersed in the water tank. This type of water heater is usually limited to those buildings which use steam or hot water for general heating. Electric water heaters are popular in those areas where cheap electric power is available. Electric water heaters tend to be more bulky and have a slower rate of recovery. Gas water heaters have become increasingly popular for both domestic and commercial installations. The location, venting, and safety regulations for water-heating appliances are governed by local codes.

Water-hammer Arrestors

Water hammer refers to the destructive forces, pounding noises, and vibration which develop in a piping system when the liquid flowing through a pipe line at a given pressure and velocity is stopped abruptly by a closing valve. The momentary pressure suddenly created in the line may be four times the operating pressure. When water hammer occurs, a high-pressure shock wave travels back and forth within the piping system until its energy has been expended in friction loss and expansion of the material of the piping system. This action accounts for the noise and vibration in pipes. Excessive surge pressure such as this may be prevented by arresting devices in the system.

Capped-pipe air chambers have been utilized as water-hammer arrestors for years, and when properly sized, they provide a temporary means of protection. The entrapped air in the capped pipe acts as a cushion to relieve the pressure waves. However, the air in a capped-pipe air chamber gradually dissipates, and there must be some means of replenishing it if the arrestor is to continue to

Fig. 14-3 Water-hammer arrestors: (a) compressed-air-filled metal bellows compresses as shock waves travel along pipe; (b) cylinder is charged to a predetermined design pressure, based on pressure in the pipe system. When a valve closes quickly, flow in the line is diverted into the cylinder, and the spherical piston moved up into the cylinder, absorbing the shock wave. (*By permission of Zurn Industries, Inc.*)

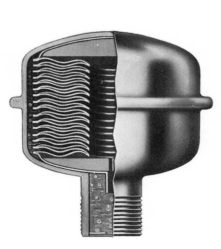

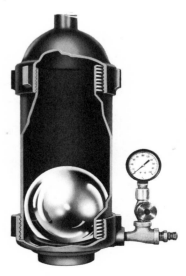

(a)   (b)

operate. The air chamber must be located in an accessible area, where it can be drained periodically by valves and petcocks.

Commercially produced water-hammer arrestors are available which provide permanent protection. They are designed so that the water in the piping system does not come in contact with the air cushion in the arrestor, and once they are installed they require no maintenance. For an air chamber or water-hammer arrestor to control shock, it must be of sufficient size or capacity to control the maximum shocks occurring in a line to a safe limit of pressure. The size is governed by the length of pipe, the velocity of flow, and the pressure in the line. The proper size of water-hammer can be determined from "Water Hammer Arrestors," PDI-WH 201, published by the Plumbing and Drainage Institute.

The location of water-hammer arrestors depends on the system. On single-branch fixture lines the arrestor should be placed immediately upstream of the fixture valve. On multiple-fixture branch lines the best location is in the branch line supplying the fixture group, between the last two fixture-supply pipes.

WATER-SUPPLY PIPING

Water-supply pipe and fittings may be of brass, copper, cast iron, malleable iron, galvanized wrought iron, galvanized steel, lead, or one of several types of plastic. In some areas asbestos-cement pipe may be used for water-distribution systems outside a building. All fittings used in a water-supply system, except valves and similar devices, must be of a like material. Cast-iron fittings smaller than 2 in. and all malleable-iron fittings must be galvanized. Valves 2 in. or smaller must be brass, and valves over 2 in. must have a cast-brass body.

TABLE 14-3 Dimensions, weights, and test pressures of standard weight pipe

standard pipe size dimensions				pressure, allowable* internal, psi at 100 F.				weight lb/ft	
pipe size, in.		wall in.	i.d. area sq. in.	threaded ends		plain ends†			
nominal	o.d. (actual)			Red Brass	Copper	Red Brass	Copper	Red Brass	Copper
⅛	.405	.062	.062	370	280	2640	1980	0.253	0.259
¼	.540	.082	.110	870	650	2610	1960	0.447	0.457
⅜	.675	.090	.192	890	670	2280	1710	0.627	0.641
½	.840	.107	.307	900	670	2160	1620	0.934	0.955
¾	1.050	.114	.531	810	610	1800	1350	1.27	1.30
1	1.315	.126	.887	630	480	1580	1190	1.78	1.82
1¼	1.660	.146	1.47	690	520	1440	1080	2.63	2.69
1½	1.900	.150	2.01	630	480	1280	960	3.13	3.20
2	2.375	.156	3.34	540	410	1050	790	4.12	4.21
2½	2.875	.187	4.91	450	340	1040	780	5.99	6.12
3	3.500	.219	7.37	510	380	1000	750	8.56	8.75
3½	4.000	.250	9.62	570	430	1000	750	11.2	11.4
4	4.500	.250	12.6	510	380	880	660	12.7	12.9
5	5.562	.250	20.1	410	310	710	540	15.8	16.2
6	6.625	.250	29.5	340	260	600	450	19.0	19.4

length: 12 feet

specification compliance:

Red Brass Pipe—
Federal Standard: WW-P-351, grade A
ASTM: B43 (Red Brass)

Copper Pipe—
Federal Standard: WW-P-377
ASTM: B42

temp	coefficient	
F	Red Brass Pipe	Copper Pipe
200	1.0	.91
300	.87	.78
400	.38	.50

* plain ends for use with welded, brazed, or solder-type fittings.

†for allowable internal pressure (approximate) at higher temperatures, multiply value in the table by proper coefficient

Galvanized Steel Pipe and Fittings

Galvanized steel pipe has great strength, dimensional stability, and long service life. The inherent strength of steel provides high safety factors and economy of materials, and the galvanized coating, both within and without, protects the piping from corrosion and damage. Galvanized pipe used in water-distribution systems is joined with screwed, galvanized fittings which are available in a wide variety of types. Steel pipe is produced in three grades of wall thickness. *Standard-weight pipe*, normally used in domestic water systems, is available in sizes of 1/8″ to 6″. It is usually furnished with threaded ends and couplings. *Extra-strong pipe* comes in sizes of 1/8″ to 12″ and may be furnished with threaded or plain ends. *Double-extra-strong pipe* comes in sizes of 1/8″ to 8″ and is furnished in plain ends only. Table 14-3 shows the dimensions of standard-weight steel pipe.

Copper Water Tube

Copper water tube is widely used in water-distribution systems because it does not rust and is highly resistant to corrosion. Its smooth interior surface results in relatively low friction loss, which often permits the use of a smaller size. Since copper water tube is available in long lengths and is easily bent in most of the commonly used types and sizes, it eliminates the need for fitting and two joints at every change of direction.

Copper water tube is produced in three types in order to handle all installation conditions and types of application. Each type has a separate wall-thickness schedule and application scope, specific bending and flaring characteristics, and industry-approved identifying color markings. Sizes and applications of the three types are shown in Table 14-4. *Type K (heavy wall)*, identified by a 1/4-in. green stripe along the entire length of the pipe, is used primarily for underground services, plumbing, heating, and cooling

systems, snow-melting systems, and for steam, oil, air, oxygen, and hydraulic lines. *Type L (medium wall)*, identified by a blue stripe, is used for underground services, interior plumbing, heating and cooling systems, snow-melting systems, and steam, oil, and oxygen lines. *Type M (light wall)*, with a red stripe, is used for interior water distribution, heating and cooling systems, steam lines, interior waste lines, and drainage lines.

Copper water tube is available in both hard and soft tempers. The soft-tempered types are easily bent by hand or with a tube bender. Thus coiled, soft-tempered tube facilitates the installation of plumbing or heating risers in existing walls, where rigid piping would be difficult and costly to use. More rigid, hard-tempered copper tubing in straight lengths is used for exposed piping and horizontal runs, where neat appearance is important. With suitable bending tools hard-tempered copper tube can be bent to a limited radius without annealing. Spot annealing with a gas or blow torch can sometimes be used for slightly sharper bends.

A variety of fittings are available for joining copper tube. One method uses solder-type or brazing fittings, with the molten solder or brazing alloy drawn into the joint by capillary action. A second method involves a flared compression joint. Soft-soldered joints are by far the most widely used type for interior water systems. They are recommended for plumbing and heating applications where pressure requirements fall within the rated internal pressure of the tube, where operating temperatures are less than 250°F, and where vibration is not excessive. The fittings may be either wrought copper or cast bronze. Wrought-copper fittings have slightly better tinning characteristics and match the copper tube in color; cast-bronze fittings, because of their heavier wall thickness, have greater structural strength. Flared compression fittings are used on underground lines or where future disconnection may be necessary. Flared fittings are also recommended

Fig. 14-4 Typical bends and joints eliminated with copper tubing.

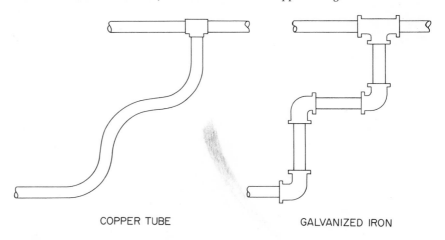

COPPER TUBE   GALVANIZED IRON

TABLE 14-4   Dimensions and capacities of copper water tube

type	applications, lengths, bending, joining Specifications: ASTM B88 Federal WW-T-799c	tube size nominal in.	tube size o.d. (actual) in.	wall thickness in.	I.D. in.	I.D. area sq. inch	pressure, allowable internal psi at 100° F.	capacity gal. per ft.* at 60°F.	weight lb. per ft.
HEAVY WALL K COLOR CODE GREEN	for: underground services, interior plumbing, heating and cooling systems — gas, oxygen, steam, oil lines, snow melting lengths— hard or soft temper: 20 ft. soft temper: ¼ thru 1½ in.: 60-ft. coils ½ thru 1 in.: 100-ft. coils 2 in.: 45-ft. coils bending— hard temper, ¼ thru ¾ in.: by machine soft temper, all sizes: by hand or machine joining—type of fitting hard temper— all sizes: solder-type ¼ thru 1 in.: compression soft temper — all sizes: solder-type, compression	¼	.375	.035	.305	.073	1060	.0038	.145
		⅜	.500	.049	.402	.127	1170	.0066	.269
		½	.625	.049	.527	.218	920	.0116	.344
		⅝	.750	.049	.652	.334	760	.0173	.418
		¾	.875	.065	.745	.436	880	.0227	.641
		1	1.125	.065	.995	.778	680	.0404	.839
		1¼	1.375	.065	1.245	1.22	550	.0632	1.04
		1½	1.625	.072	1.481	1.72	520	.0892	1.36
		2	2.125	.083	1.959	3.01	450	.1563	2.06
		2½	2.625	.095	2.435	4.66	420	.242	2.93
		3	3.125	.109	2.907	6.64	410	.344	4.00
		3½	3.625	.120	3.385	9.00	380	.468	5.12
		4	4.125	.134	3.857	11.7	370	.606	6.51
		5	5.125	.160	4.805	18.1	360	.940	9.67
		6	6.125	.192	5.741	25.9	370	1.350	13.9
		8	8.125	.271	7.583	45.2	390	2.35	25.9
MEDIUM WALL L COLOR CODE BLUE	for: underground services, interior plumbing, heating and cooling systems — gas, oxygen, steam, oil lines, snow melting lengths— hard or soft temper: 20 ft. soft temper: ¼ thru 1½ in.: 60-ft. coils ¼ thru 1 in.: 100-ft. coils bending— hard temper, ¼ thru ¾ in.: by machine soft temper, all sizes: by hand or machine joining—type of fitting hard temper— all sizes: solder-type ¼ thru 1 in.: compression soft temper — all sizes: solder-type, compression	¼	.375	.030	.315	.078	900	.0041	.126
		⅜	.500	.035	.430	.145	800	.0075	.198
		½	.625	.040	.545	.233	740	.0121	.285
		⅝	.750	.042	.666	.348	650	.0181	.362
		¾	.875	.045	.785	.484	590	.0253	.455
		1	1.125	.050	1.025	.825	510	.0428	.655
		1¼	1.375	.055	1.265	1.26	460	.0654	.884
		1½	1.625	.060	1.505	1.78	430	.0925	1.14
		2	2.125	.070	1.985	3.09	370	.1605	1.75
		2½	2.625	.080	2.465	4.77	350	.248	2.48
		3	3.125	.090	2.945	6.81	330	.354	3.33
		3½	3.625	.100	3.425	9.21	320	.478	4.29
		4	4.125	.110	3.905	12.0	300	.623	5.28
		5	5.125	.125	4.875	18.7	280	.973	7.61
		6	6.125	.140	5.845	26.8	260	1.395	10.2
		8	8.125	.200	7.725	46.9	280	2.43	19.3
LIGHT WALL M COLOR CODE RED	for: interior plumbing applications, hot water heating systems, chilled water lines, interior waste and drainage piping lengths— hard temper (only): 20 ft. (all sizes) bending— ⅜ and ½ in.: by machine joining—type of fitting solder-type only	¼	.375	.025	.325	.049	810	.0025	.106
		⅜	.500	.025	.450	.159	560	.0083	.145
		½	.625	.028	.569	.254	510	.0132	.204
		¾	.875	.032	.811	.517	420	.0269	.328
		1	1.125	.035	1.055	.874	340	.0455	.465
		1¼	1.375	.042	1.291	1.31	340	.0680	.682
		1½	1.625	.049	1.527	1.83	340	.0949	.940
		2	2.125	.058	2.009	3.17	300	.1650	1.46
		2½	2.625	.065	2.495	4.89	280	.254	2.03
		3	3.125	.072	2.981	6.98	260	.363	2.68
		3½	3.625	.083	3.459	9.40	260	.490	3.58
		4	4.125	.095	3.935	12.2	260	.637	4.66
		5	5.125	.109	4.907	18.9	240	.984	6.66
		6	6.125	.122	5.881	27.2	230	1.420	8.92
		8	8.125	.170	7.785	47.6	240	2.47	16.5

By permission of Revere Copper and Brass Incorporated.

where environmental conditions are unfavorable for soldering or where the flame of a soldering torch would present a fire hazard.

Copper, like most metals, expands when it is heated and contracts when cooled. Copper has a coefficient of expansion of 0.0000094 per degree up to 212°F. Consequently, a change of 100°F changes the length of a 100-ft copper pipe about 1¼ in. Expansion and contraction must be taken into consideration when copper tube is anchored at two ends. This may be done by means of expansion loops or pipe offsets.

Copper tubing should not be used in hot-water systems where the operating temperatures exceed 140°F, and it should not be embedded in concrete slabs, masonry walls, or footings. Tube may be buried in fill below the slab, provided straight runs are limited to 20 ft and contain no fittings. Some plumbing codes permit brazed fittings of wrought copper under slabs. Tube risers through the slab should be provided with a watertight sleeve of sufficient size to allow for adequate movement of the riser.

Brass Pipe

Where the water is known to be exceptionally corrosive, it may be necessary to use brass pipe with screwed fittings. Brass pipe is manufactured with standard pipe threads. In coastal areas, where salt water is used for cooling, baths, pools, or marine applications, brass pipe has given good service.

Lead Pipe

Lead pipe is sometimes used for water-supply systems. However, where the water is corrosive to lead, it may render the water unsafe for consumption. Local health offices generally have adequate information on the characteristics of local water supplies in this respect. The presence of lead in amounts greater than 0.1 part per million is considered sufficient to warrant rejection of the water supply.

Plastic Pipe

Rigid plastic pipe is characterized by light weight, outstanding chemical resistance, high impact and pressure strength, and ease of joining. As a result, it can provide important economies. Several types of plastic pipe and fittings have been used successfully to supplement cast-iron and steel pipe systems. Plastic pipe has proved exceptionally well suited for water-transmission systems, piping of potable water, sprinkling systems, and drainage and sewage systems for residences. The most common types are acrylonitrile butadiene styrene (ABS), polyvinyl chloride (PVC), and polyethylene. Local codes must be carefully checked for approval of specific types. Plastic pipe has an expansion rate several times that of steel or copper. ABS pipe will expand over 5 in. per 100 ft with a temperature change of 100°F. This must be compensated

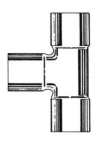

COMPRESSION FITTINGS   SOLDER-TYPE FITTINGS

Fig. 14-5 Compression and solder-type fittings. Compression fittings are recommended for underground piping or on lines where disassembly of the joint may be necessary. Solder-type fittings are recommended for interior plumbing and heating lines. They are less expensive than compression fittings and less space is required. (*By permission of Revere Copper and Brass, Inc.*)

Fig. 14-6 Forming an expansion loop in copper tubing. (*By permission of Revere Copper and Brass, Inc.*)

for in the design of the piping system. Information on such systems is available from the ABS Institute.

A wide variety of fittings are available for plastic pipe. The heavier types are suitable for threaded fittings similar to those used on steel pipe. Special adapters are produced for plastic-to-metal joints. The most commonly used fittings are made for solvent-welded joints. A sleeve fits over

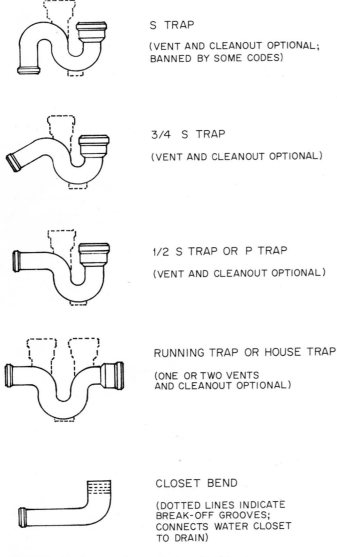

S TRAP

(VENT AND CLEANOUT OPTIONAL;
BANNED BY SOME CODES)

3/4 S TRAP

(VENT AND CLEANOUT OPTIONAL)

1/2 S TRAP OR P TRAP

(VENT AND CLEANOUT OPTIONAL)

RUNNING TRAP OR HOUSE TRAP

(ONE OR TWO VENTS
AND CLEANOUT OPTIONAL)

CLOSET BEND

(DOTTED LINES INDICATE
BREAK-OFF GROOVES;
CONNECTS WATER CLOSET
TO DRAIN)

Fig. 14-7 Typical cast-iron soil-pipe plumbing traps.

the pipe, and a solvent or cement, manufactured for that particular type of plastic, is used to hold the joint in place and form a watertight seal. Some types of plastic require the application of heat by a special tool.

DRAINAGE SYSTEMS

Each plumbing fixture in a system is served with a soil or waste stack, a vent system, and a trap. The vertical waste stack conveys both solid and liquid wastes to a building drain, located at the lowest point of the drainage system in a wall, basement space, or crawl space under the building. The building drain carries the waste to a point 2 ft from the perimeter of the building, where it is connected

with the building sewer. The building sewer carries the wastes to a public sewer, a private sewer, or an individual sewage-disposal system.

Vents and Traps

Vertical or horizontal vent stacks provide air circulation throughout a drainage system to dissipate sewer gas or pressure into the open air above the roof. A vent system consists of horizontal branch vents joined to a common vertical vent, to allow air circulation within the system and to protect trap seals from siphonage and back pressure. Horizontal runs of vent piping must slope up from the fixture to the vertical vent stack $\frac{1}{4}$ in. per foot of run.

A trap provides a water seal at each fixture to prevent the back passage of air. Under certain conditions one trap may serve several fixtures. The "Uniform Plumbing Code" allows three single-compartment sinks or lavatories to be served by one trap if it is located at the center fixture and the lavatories are not over 30 in. apart. Traps may be of cast iron, brass, or other approved material. An exposed trap on a residential fixture may be of brass tubing if it is accessible. Such traps are usually joined with slip joints and compression-type fittings.

The vertical distance between the fixture and the trap should be as short as possible. Most codes limit the vertical distance to 24 in. The allowed horizontal distance of the trap arms varies with local code requirements and the size of the pipe. Table 14-5, taken from the "Uniform Plumbing Code," gives the maximum horizontal distances allowed for trap arms, except those for water closets and similar fixtures.

TABLE 14-5 Horizontal distance of trap arms

SIZE OF TRAP ARM, IN.	DISTANCE TO VENT, FT
$1\frac{1}{4}$	$2\frac{1}{2}$
$1\frac{1}{2}$	$3\frac{1}{2}$
2	5
3	6
4 and larger	10

By permission of the International Association of Plumbing and Mechanical Officials.

Sometimes a *house trap* or a *running trap* is required between the building drain and the building sewer. This trap may or may not be equipped with a vent extending to the outside air. Some codes require a vent from the house trap extending through the roof.

Indirect Waste Piping

Indirect waste piping does not connect directly with the drainage system, but discharges liquid wastes into some other fixture or receptacle which is connected to the drainage system. Indirect waste systems are required for fixtures and appliances such as dishwashers, washing machines, air-conditioning-condensate drains, and swimming pools. The wastes are discharged through an air gap into an open floor sink or approved receptor that is properly connected to the drainage system. Fixtures such as island sinks, which cannot be vented in the usual manner because of their location, may discharge into an open floor sink. Properly trapped stand pipes framed flush into stud walls are used as indirect wastes. Vents for indirect wastes usually cannot be connected directly with any sewer-connected vent, but must be carried separately to the outside air.

Cleanouts

Each horizontal drainage pipe (or one not more than 45° from horizontal) must be provided at its upper terminal with a threaded, plugged opening for cleanout. Cleanouts are usually required at each change of direction of the horizontal piping. Some codes allow one change of direction or changes of not over 22½° without a cleanout. They must be accessible from the outside of the house or under the house, or covered with a removable plate.

Interceptors

Interceptors are used to keep undesirable materials out of the drainage system and permit normal waste or sewage to flow into the sewer outlet by gravity. Interceptors may be designed to separate grease, oil, sand, or flammable liquids. Grease interceptors are used in restaurant kitchens, garages, and other installations where the amount of grease or oil discharged is sufficient to clog the waste piping or interfere with the disposal of sewage. Interceptors are provided with large, easy-to-reach cleanouts for periodic cleaning.

Fig. 14-8   A residential drainage system.

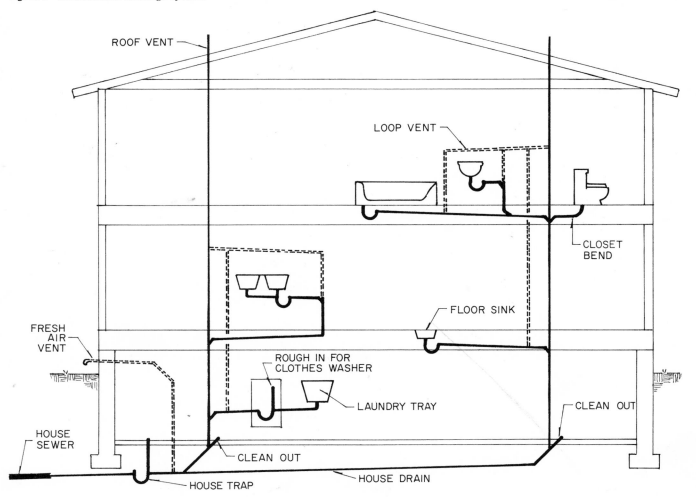

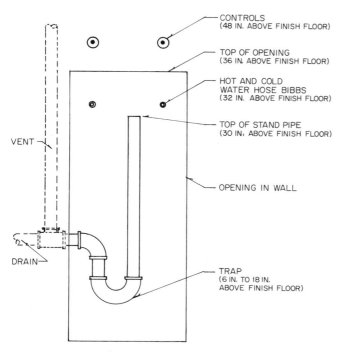

CONTROLS
(48 IN. ABOVE FINISH FLOOR)

TOP OF OPENING
(36 IN. ABOVE FINISH FLOOR)

HOT AND COLD
WATER HOSE BIBBS
(32 IN. ABOVE FINISH FLOOR)

TOP OF STAND PIPE
(30 IN. ABOVE FINISH FLOOR)

OPENING IN WALL

VENT

DRAIN

TRAP
(6 IN. TO 18 IN.
ABOVE FINISH FLOOR)

Fig. 14-9 Indirect-waste system for automatic clothes washer.

TABLE 14-6 Unit equivalent value of residential plumbing fixtures

FIXTURE	FIXTURE UNITS	MIN. TRAP SIZE, IN.
Bathtubs	2	1½
Bidets	2	1½
Drinking fountains	1	1¼
Laundry tube or clothes washers	2	2
Showers	2	2
Sinks, bar (private)	1	1½
Sinks, kitchen, and/or dishwashers	2	1½
Wash basins, single	1	1½
Wash basins, double	2	1½
Water closets	6	3

Drainage Piping

The minimum size of vertical and horizontal piping is governed by local codes, which establish the number of fixture units that may be attached to each size of waste and vent pipe. Tables 14-6 and 14-7 show the unit equivalent values of residential plumbing fixtures according to the "Uniform Plumbing Code."

Storm Drains

Metal gutters and leaders or downspouts outside the building are not usually included in the mechanical work. However, if they conduct rainwater down through the walls or inside the building, they are considered as plumbing. It may or may not be permissible, depending on the size of the building, location, and local codes, to connect rainwater drainage systems to the building drain. When separate rainwater drains are required, the house drains for sewage and waste water are called *sanitary drains* to differentiate them from *storm drains*.

If the roof drainage is connected to a combination storm and sanitary drain, traps should be used to seal off sewer gas that may escape through a roof drain. Each leader must be equipped with a separate trap and should have a cleanout at the bottom. When storm drains cannot be connected to a sanitary sewer, the water must be disposed of in a lawful manner.

Interior storm drains may be constructed of cast-iron, galvanized-iron, copper, or plastic pipe, depending on local plumbing codes. The size of the roof drains and leaders are based on the roof area to be drained. The roof area is usually calculated as the *projected roof area*, which includes the roof overhang. The slope of the roof has no bearing. Tables 14-8 and 14-9 show the approximate size of vertical and horizontal piping necessary to drain a given roof area. Permissible sizes depend on the local plumbing code.

DRAIN PIPE AND FITTINGS

The most common piping materials for domestic and commercial systems where corrosive wastes are not expected are galvanized steel and cast iron. Copper tubing and newly developed plastic pipe increase in use because of their light weight and ease of handling and joining. Brass and lead pipes are used where wastes are corrosive.

Cast-iron Soil Pipe

Cast-iron pipe is produced as either pressure pipe or soil pipe. Pressure pipe carries fluids under pressure, whereas soil pipe carries liquids, both waste and solid, only under gravity flow. An extensive cast-iron soil-pipe and water-distribution system was installed at Versailles, France, in 1664. A cast-iron water main 15 miles long was constructed to carry water to the thousands of fountains in Louis XIV's palace. This system is still functioning after 300 years.

Cast-iron soil pipe is made of grey iron containing large flakes of graphite, which helps protect the iron from corrosion. A bituminous coating is used on both the inside and the outside of the pipe for further protection against acid or alkaline soils. Types and specifications of cast-iron soil pipes and fittings are given in the "Cast Iron Soil Pipe and Fitting Handbook," published by the Cast Iron Soil Pipe Institute.

Galvanized, wrought-iron, or steel screwed pipe and fittings may be used for drainage lines or vents, except underground. Galvanized iron or steel must be kept a minimum of 6 in. above the ground at all times.

TABLE 14-7 Maximum unit loading and maximum length of drainage and vent piping based on a slope of ¼ in./ft

PIPE SIZE, IN.	MAX. UNITS[a]		MAX. LENGTH, FT		VENT PIPING, VERT. AND HORIZ.	
	VERT. DRAIN	HORIZ. DRAIN	VERT. DRAIN	HORIZ. DRAIN	MAX. UNITS	MAX. LENGTH, FT
1¼	0	0	0	unlimited	1[e]	45[e]
1½	2[b]	1	65	unlimited	8[c]	60
2	16[c]	8[c]	85	unlimited	24	120
3	48[d]	35[d]	212	unlimited	84	212
4	256	180	300	unlimited	256	400
5	600	356	390	unlimited	600	390

[a]Excluding trap arms.
[b]Except sinks and urinals.
[c]Except six-unit traps or fixtures.
[d]Only two six-unit traps or fixtures allowed.
[e]Vertical only.

Soil-pipe Joints

The traditional soil-pipe joint is made with oakum or jute and lead. *Oakum* consists of untwisted fibers of hemp. *Jute* consists of the untwisted fibers of the East Indian jute plant. A lower-cost compression joint is made with rubber gaskets in place of the lead and oakum. The most recently developed joint for cast-iron soil-pipe is the *no-hub joint*, which uses a one-piece Neoprene gasket and a stainless-steel shield with a stainless-steel retaining clamp.

LEAD-AND-OAKUM JOINTS   Lead-and-oakum joints are made of *hub-and-spigot pipe*. This consists of 5- or 10-ft lengths of cast-iron soil pipe with a hub, socket, or bell at one end and a plain end or spigot at the other, sometimes with a slight bead. The spigot is inserted into the hub end of the next length of pipe, and oakum is placed in the joint and driven in with a *yarning iron*. The oakum is then packed solidly into the joint with a *packing iron* and hammer. Additional strands are packed into the joint until it forms a uniform surface 1 in. from the top of the hub. Lead is then

TABLE 14-8   Sizing of vertical rain-water piping

DIAMETER OF LEADER, IN.	MAX. PROJECTED ROOF AREA, SQ FT
2	960
3	2,900
4	6,100
5	11,500
6	18,000
8	39,000

TABLE 14-9   Sizing of horizontal storm drains

DIAMETER OF DRAIN, IN.	MAX. PROJECTED ROOF AREA FOR DRAIN SLOPE		
	⅛ IN./FT	¼ IN./FT	½ IN./FT
3	2,000	1,500	2,300
4	2,500	3,500	5,000
5	4,400	6,300	9,000
6	7,000	10,000	13,700
8	15,300	21,700	30,600
10	27,600	38,900	55,200

Fig. 14-10   Joints in cast-iron soil pipe.

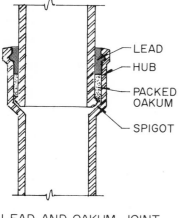

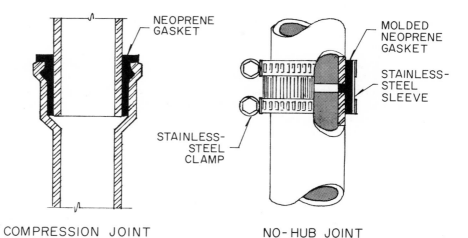

LEAD AND OAKUM JOINT   COMPRESSION JOINT   NO-HUB JOINT

poured into the joint until it is slightly above the hub, and the joint is caulked with a *caulking iron* until it is tight.

When lead-and-oakum joints are properly caulked, they are strong, flexible, and root proof. The difficulty in making proper lead-and-oakum joints on horizontal runs and in confined areas has led to increased use of Neoprene-gasket no-hub joints.

COMPRESSION JOINTS Hub-and-spigot pipe is also used for compression fittings, but the spigot end is plain, with no ridge or bead. A one-piece gasket is inserted into the hub, a lubricant is applied to the spigot and the gasket, and the spigot is driven into the gasketed hub or drawn in with a special pulling tool. The resulting joint is leakproof, absorbs vibration, and can be deflected up to 5° without damage.

NO-HUB JOINTS The no-hub joint provides a more compact joint than either of the other two methods, with no sacrifice in quality and permanency. The joint is simply and quickly put together. A Neoprene gasket is placed on one end of a plain pipe section and the stainless-steel shield-and-clamp assembly is placed on the end of the next section. The two ends are fitted snugly against the integrally molded shoulder inside the gasket, the shield and clamps are slid into position, and the clamps are tightened. The stainless-steel clamp compresses the Neoprene gasket to make a watertight and gastight joint that is strong and flexible. One of the advantages of this system is that joints can be made in limited space areas. The 2″ and 3″ sizes of cast-iron pipe with no-hub joints will fit into 2 × 4 stud walls without the need for furring.

Copper Drainage Tube

Copper drainage tube has been steadily increasing in popularity. Most copper drainage lines are fabricated from tubing designated as DWV—drainage, waste, and vent. This rigid copper tubing has thinner walls than the L or M tubings and comes in 20-ft lengths, although some codes require type-L tube for vents and underground installations. The substantial savings in time and material as a result of the lightweight walls and the need for fewer joints offset the higher cost of copper. The interior of the tubing is drawn smooth and totally free of obstructions. A 3-in. copper soil or vent stack can be installed in a 2 × 4 partition. Copper drainage tube is usually joined with solder-type wrought-copper or cast-bronze fittings, either by soldering or by brazing. Care must be taken in the design of copper drainage systems to compensate for the greater coefficient of expansion of copper over steel. Copper tubing must be joined to cast-iron or other drainage and vent piping through adapters.

Lead Drainage Pipe

Lead pipe and fittings are usually confined to drainage systems for chemical laboratories. Lead has greater resis-

tance to corrosion by a greater variety of chemicals than any other common metal. It is easy to install under even the most difficult conditions with a minimum of joints, since it can readily be bent for changes of direction. Joints in lead pipe are usually welded, or burned. The two sections are lapped, and the lead is fused together to form a uniform weld at least as thick as the pipe itself. Lead pipe is joined at cast-iron pipe by means of a *caulking ferrule* or a *soldering nipple*.

Plastic Drainage Pipe

Several types of plastic pipe have been accepted by some codes as drainage plumbing. Plastic pipe is significantly faster to install than most other materials, and the anti-fouling characteristics of the pipe interiors and integrity of the chemically welded joint make it a most efficient material where it is allowed. When plastic pipe is joined by chemical welding, the weld becomes the stongest part of the pipe, assuring leakproof connections.

Horizontal runs of plastic pipe should be continuously supported by a shelf or light channel. In designing plastic-pipe installations, the linear coefficient of thermal expansion must be considered. PVC, one of the most commonly used plastic pipes, has an expansion coefficient of 0.001 per degree of temperature change. This means that a 100-ft run of this pipe would increase or decrease 10 in. in length with a temperature change of 100°F.

Clay Sewer Pipe

Clay is used extensively for sewer lines outside of buildings but is banned by many codes for interior installations. The building sewer line is usually considered to start 2 ft from the perimeter of the building. It should slope a minimum of 3 in. and a maximum of 4 in. per foot.

The clay used for sewer pipe is similar to that used in burned brick. The clay pipe must be dense enough to withstand most acids and alkalis and root infiltration. *Vitreous clay pipe* is given a salt glaze which makes it particularly resistant to corrosive wastes. Most clay sewer pipe is of the hub-and-spigot type and is produced in diameters of 4″ to 36″, in 2-in. increments, and lengths of 24″, 30″, 36″, 48″, and 54″. Clay fittings are available in a large variety of sizes and shapes.

Clay sewer pipe is usually joined with a hot-poured compound. Approximately 25 percent of the joint area is packed with jute or hemp, a pouring collar is wrapped around the joint, and the hot compound (usually a bituminous product) is poured into the joint in one operation until the joint is full. The joint is ready for testing after 1 hour.

FUEL-GAS PIPING

Gas piping and fixtures, like other plumbing systems, are governed by local codes. These regulations cover the installation of all fuel-gas piping within the property lines of any premises. The gas may be natural gas, liquified-petroleum gas, coke-oven gas, carburated-water gas, commercial propane, or commercial butane. Each of these gases has a particular heating value, expressed in Btu per cubic foot of gas (one Btu is the amount of heat required to raise the temperature of one pound of water one degree Fahrenheit). Table 14-10 lists typical heating values of commercial gas. Local gas companies or gas suppliers must be consulted for exact values.

TABLE 14-10 Approximate heating values of commercial gases

GAS	NET HEATING VALUE, BTU/CU FT
Natural gas	970–1100
Coke-oven gas	515
Carburated-water gas	510
Propane	2400
Butane	2900

To determine the size of piping needed for gas-consuming appliances in a residence or commercial building, the manufacturer's rating of each appliance, in Btus per hour, figure must be divided by the heating value of the gas to be used. Table 14-11 lists the minimum demand of typical appliances for one type of gas.

TABLE 14-11 Minimum demand of typical residential gas appliances for natural gas at 1100 Btu/cu ft

APPLIANCE	DEMAND, CU FT/HR (CFH)
Standard gas range	75
Built-in range top	50
Built-in oven	25
40-gal water heater	45
Clothes drier	20
Fireplace loglighter	25
Barbecue	50
100,000-Btu forced-air furnace	82
180,000-Btu forced-air furnace	163

When the gas consumption of a system has been calculated, the supply piping must be sized for this flow as required by local building codes. The piping must be large enough in diameter to provide gas without excessive pressure loss as a result of the friction in the pipe. The length of piping must also be taken into consideration.

The most common material used for gas piping is standard-weight wrought iron or steel (galvanized or black), yellow brass, or internally tinned or treated copper. Copper tubing is corroded by most gases and is consequently banned by most codes. Fittings for gas pipe are usually malleable iron or yellow brass. The joints are usually screwed with standard pipe threads. Where unions are necessary, right- and left-hand nipples and couplings are used. Shutoff valves are required on each appliance. Flexible metal connectors, not over a specified length, may be allowed between the shutoff valve and the appliance.

PLUMBING FIXTURES

Plumbing fixtures must be constructed of dense, durable, nonabsorbent materials with smooth impervious surfaces. Table 14-12 lists the various materials used in plumbing fixtures.

TABLE 14-12 Materials used in plumbing fixtures

MATERIAL	CHARACTERISTICS
Vitreous china	A high-gloss easily shaped material; tends to warp, and dimensions vary; will not stand shock, crazes
Vitreous glazed earthenware	Better shock resistance than china, not affected by heat, cold, or acids, will not craze; widely used in hospitals and institutions
Porcelain-enameled cast iron	$\frac{1}{8}$-in.-thick glazed surface over a rigid cast-iron body; will withstand more shock than china or earthenware, acid resistant
Porcelain-enameled steel	A lightweight, inexpensive material; flexibility of steel shell tends to crack porcelain-enamel coating
Stainless steel	A high-cost material impervious to water; good wear, some types acid resistant
Plastics	Inexpensive, soft surface, low gloss
Cast concrete	Usually limited to inexpensive laundry trays or shower receptors; not allowed by some codes
Soapstone, lead, copper-based alloys, nickel-copper alloys, corrosion-resistant steel	Limited to special fixtures

Water Closets

Several types of water closets are available for residential or commercial installations. Most are constructed of vitreous china and may be either *floor set* or *wall hung*. Most commercial installations use a *flushmeter valve* to force a given quantity of water through the bowl. Water pressure of 15 psi is required for operation of flushmeter valves. Although this type of water closet is efficient, it tends to be noisy. Residential types use a flushing tank, either attached to the bowl or cast in one piece with the bowl.

Water closets are classified according to the method used to flush the water out of the bowl. In the *siphon-vortex* type, water from the rim creates a swirling action, or vortex, which washes the walls and causes the water to be discharged by siphon action. Operation is very quiet and efficient. In the *siphon jet* type water from the rim washes down the sides and is discharged by action of a jet in the upleg of the outlet, and siphoning action in the downleg. Operation is sanitary and relatively quiet. A *reverse-trap* water closet is similar to the siphon-jet type but has a

Fig. 14-11 One-piece low-tank water closet with elongated siphon-vortex bowl and matching bidet. (*By permission of American Standard.*)

Fig. 14-12 Two-piece water closet with regular siphon-jet bowl. (*American Standard.*)

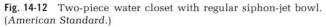

Fig. 14-13 Wall-hung water closet with close-coupled tank and elongated siphon bowl. (*American Standard.*)

Fig. 14-14 Exposed-flush-valve water closet with siphon-jet bowl. (*American Standard.*)

smaller bowl. In the *washdown* type, pressure of water in the bowl causes the water to overflow, creating a discharge siphon. This is an inexpensive, simple design, but is noisy. The *blowout* type, used only with a flushmeter valve, is efficient in water use, but noisy.

Lavatories

There are many types and sizes of lavatories, or basins, produced in vitreous china or porcelain-enameled cast iron. It is important to select the proper size if the lavatory is to be installed in a counter. They are obtainable from 12 to 20 in. front to back. *Counter-type lavatories* may be self-rimmed, to fit on top of the counter surface, or designed to fit flush with the countertop and be held in place with a stainless-steel or chrome-plated rim. Special types are produced to fit on the underside of a marble top. If the lavatory is not pierced to receive fixtures, additional space must be allowed in the countertop for surface-mounted fittings. Some manufacturers produce preassembled lavatories and counters. These may have a vitreous china lavatory or an integrally formed synthetic top and lavatory.

Fig. 14-16   Self-rimming lavatory. (*American Standard.*)

Fig. 14-15   Concealed-flush-valve wall-hung water closet with siphon-jet bowl. (*American Standard.*)

Fig. 14-17   Flush lavatory with stainless-steel rim. (*American Standard.*)

Wall-hung lavatories are supported by special hangers attached to the wall. They may be a slab type or a ledge type. Some wall-hung lavatories have provision for attaching a single vitreous-china or porcelain-enameled leg or pedestal under the center of the bowl or chrome legs at the corners. In some cases chrome towel bars are attached to the chrome legs.

Fig. 14-18 Lavatory for undercounter installation. (*American Standard.*)

Fig. 14-19 Wall-hung lavatory with chrome legs and towel bars. (*American Standard.*)

Bathtubs

Bathtubs are available in porcelain-enameled steel or porcelain-enameled cast iron. Some are produced in vitreous glazed earthenware. Tubs may have a pattern etched or raised in the bottom to make them nonslip when used with a shower.

Bathtubs must be ordered as either right-hand or left-hand tubs. A left-hand tub is one with the outlet on the left when viewed from the room. Tubs are produced as free-standing, corner, recessed, and roman-style units.

Showers

The fittings for showers over tubs are usually combined with those for both the tub and the shower. They may have separate handles for the hot and cold water or a simple mixing valve to control the water temperature. Pressure-activated mixing valves keep the water temperature constant when other fixtures are in operation. The most expensive type is thermostatically controlled to maintain constant water temperature. Most codes require that the walls above a tub shower be constructed of a material that is impervious to water for a height of 6 ft above the floor.

Stall showers may be built at the job site or delivered as prefabricated metal or plastic units. The bottom of a shower may be built-up on the job or installed as a prefabricated receptor. Prefabricated shower receptors and enclosures come in standard sizes. Selection depends on the design of the bathroom. Some codes specify a minimum dimension of 30 in., although 36 in. is the recommended minimum.

Sinks

Kitchen sinks for residential installation are produced of porcelain-enameled cast iron or stainless steel as one-, two-, or three-compartment units. Special shapes are produced to fit diagonally across a corner. Units with more than one compartment may have individual sinks the same depth or one sink 8 in. deep and the other 4½ in. deep. The width of double-sink units ranges from 32″ to 42″. Three-sink units may be as wide as 48″. Sinks must be specified as self-rimmed, for installation on top of the drainboard surface; flush, for installation with a stainless-steel rim; or to fit under the drainboard top. At least one side of a two-compartment sink should have a large opening to allow for the installation of a garbage-disposal unit.

There are a number of sink types for commercial or other residential applications. Laundry trays may be free-standing units on cast-iron legs or be built into cabinets. They may be of soapstone, cast iron, or concrete. The better types are usually cast iron with a porcelain-enamel interior. *Service sinks*, used in commercial and institutional installations, are usually of cast-iron construction similar to laundry trays. *Floor sinks* are cast-iron receptacles installed flush with the finish floor and usually covered with a cast-iron grille, either unfinished or porcelain

Fig. 14-22 Combination corner tub and shower receptor (38″ × 39″, 12″ high). (*American Standard.*)

Fig. 14-20 Corner tub. (*American Standard.*)

Fig. 14-23 Roman tub. (*American Standard.*)

Fig. 14-21 Recess tub. (*American Standard.*)

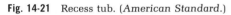

enameled. Floor sinks are used as waste receptors under island sinks, as emergency floor drains in laundry areas, and as condensate receptors for air-conditioning equipment or similar appliances.

HEATING SYSTEMS

The design and installation of a heating system for a building is based on the proper distribution of heat to the various rooms or zones. In determining the size and type of heating equipment, the first consideration is the design indoor and outdoor temperature. To maintain a constant temperature of 72°F on the inside while the outdoor temperature is zero, the inside must be heated at the rate that heat is lost through the floors, ceilings, and walls. The amount of heat loss, measured in Btu's, depends on the type of construction and insulation (see Chapter 9). The amount of warm air delivered to a room, measured in *cubic feet per minute*, depends on the size of the carrying ducts and the capacity of the furnace.

The capacity of the furnace is rated in two ways: as input rating in Btu's per hour and as bonnet capacity in Btu's per hour. The input rating is used in determining the fuel consumption and the bonnet capacity is a measure of the heat available at the output end of the furnace. The difference between the two figures indicates the *efficiency of the furnace.*

Warm-air Furnaces

A warm-air furnace is any device that warms air and circulates it to the locations needed. The gravity warm-air furnace is a direct-fired furnace which transfers heat by simple convection. As the denser cold air sinks, the less dense hot air rises. Thus air circulated through the furnace rises through large ducts to the areas to be heated, and the colder room air descends to the furnace to be reheated. This type of furnace requires basement installation and many large unsightly ducts. Another form of the gravity warm-air furnace is the *residential wall heater,*

Fig. 14-24   Tile-lined shower receptor. (*By permission of the Ceramic Tile Institute.*)

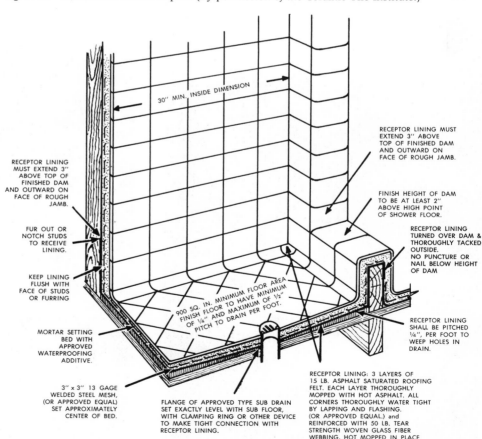

which draws in cold air near the floor, passes it over the heating unit, and exhausts warm air near the top.

The gravity furnace has been replaced largely by the *forced-air furnace* in which the air is circulated through relatively small ducts by means of a squirrel-cage fan. There are several possible arrangements of the elements that make up this type of furnace. The smaller furnaces, used in residences and smaller commercial applications consist of a burner, a heat exchanger, an outer casing, a filter, automatic controls, and sometimes a humidifier.

The operation of the forced-air furnace is quite simple. An oil or gas burner heats the steel fins of a heat exchanger. The flame is fed by air either taken from the space around the furnace or brought to the furnace by ducts called *combustion air*. The gas fumes are exhausted through a vent to the outside air. Air is passed over the heat exchanger and is then forced by the fan through supply ducts to the various areas to be heated. Return ducts return the air to the furnace for reheating. Outside air may be added to the

Fig. 14-25 Direct-drive upflow forced-air furnace. (*By permission of Lennox Industries, Inc.*)

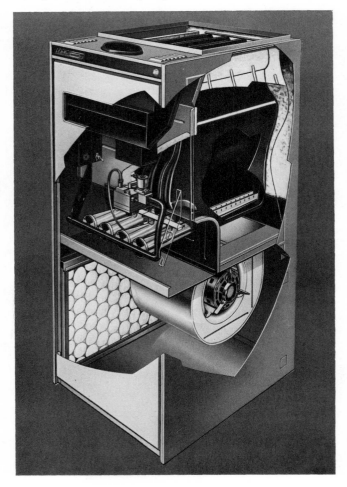

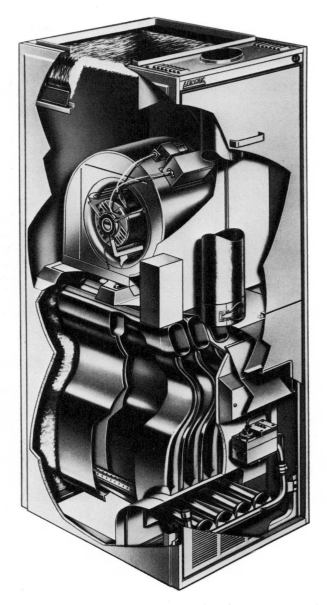

Fig. 14-26 Direct-drive downflow forced-air furnace. (*By permission of Lennox Industries, Inc.*)

return air to assure a continual supply of fresh air. The amount of outside air added may be controlled by a temperature-sensing device outside the house, which opens or closes dampers in the fresh-air duct as outside temperatures vary.

Most forced-air furnaces have removable filters in the return line just before the centrifugal blower, to eliminate any solid particles in the air before it is heated. They may also have humidifiers on the output side of the furnace, to replace moisture that has been removed from the heated air.

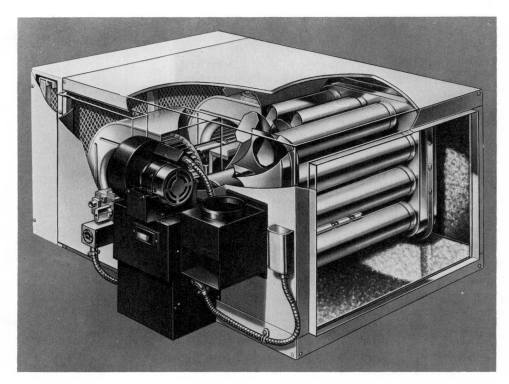

Fig. 14-27 Direct-drive horizontal forced-air furnace. (*By permission of Lennox Industries, Inc.*)

Fig. 14-28 Double-deflection register with opposed blade damper, series 880 O.B.D. (*Lear Siegler, Inc., Krueger Division.*)

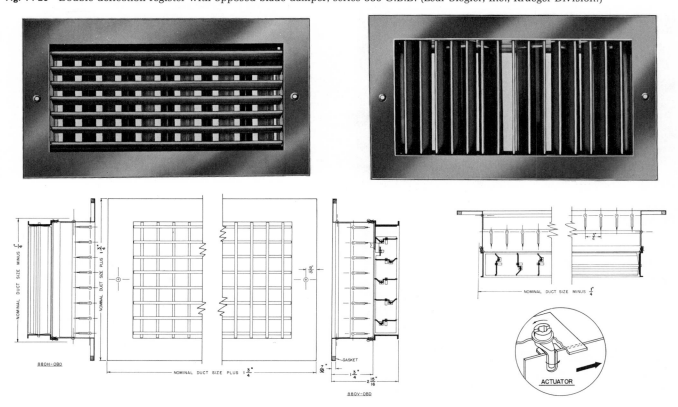

The furnace is controlled by two thermostats: a room thermostat and a thermostat in the bonnet on the output side of the heat exchanger. When room temperature drops below the level to which the room thermostat is set, the burner in the furnace turns on. As heat is generated in the heat exchanger, the bonnet temperature rises rapidly, since the blower is not operating. When the bonnet temperature has risen to a predetermined point (usually 110°F), the bonnet thermostat turns on the blower, which starts air circulation through the supply ducts. When the room temperature reaches the desired value, the room thermostat cuts off the furnace burner. The blower continues to operate until the bonnet temperature drops to a predetermined point (usually 80°F), when the fan is shut down. The cycle is repeated whenever the room temperature drops. As a safety factor, the bonnet thermostat automatically turns off the burner when the bonnet temperature exceeds 180°F.

Forced-air furnaces are classified according to the direction of air flow through the furnace. If the air flows downward through the furnace, it is called a *downflow furnace;* if the return air enters the bottom of the furnace and flows upward, it is classed as an *upflow furnace.* One type of upflow furnace, called a *lowboy,* has the blower adjacent to the heat exchanger to reduce the height of the unit; a furnace with a vertical arrangement is called a *highboy.* In a *horizontal furnace* the elements are arranged so that the air passes horizontally over the heat exchanger and is discharged from the side of the unit. This type of furnace can be used in areas with limited headroom, such as attics or the crawl space under wood floors. The furnace may be hung from the floor joists or be set on a concrete foundation on the ground.

Ducts and Outlets

The conditioned air from the forced-air furnace is carried through a system of ducts to supply outlets. A *plenum* is an air-compartment or chamber to which one or more ducts are connected, either as part of the distribution system or as part of the return system. A plenum may be a large duct, or it may be an enclosed area above a furred ceiling or in a wall. In some cases, depending on location and use, this space is lined with insulation or fireproofing material.

Ducts may be round, square, or rectangular and made of tin-plated steel, galvanized steel, or an approved type of flexible plastic. Tin-plated steel ducts are usually satisfactory if only heated air is to pass through them; however, moisture condensing out of cooled air tends to corrode tin-plated steel. If cooled air is to be carried through the same ducts as heated air, or there is the possibility of an air-conditioning installation at a future date, galvanized steel or plastic should be used. Ducts carrying heated or cooled air should be insulated. The most commonly used insulation consists of fiberglass or rock-wool blankets wrapped around the ducts. The insulation may be from ½ to 2 in. thick, depending on the location and the length of the run. Ducts through an unvented crawl space or basement usually are not insulated; those through vented crawl spaces and vented attics usually are. Most codes prohibit the installation of metal ducts in contact with the earth. For installations under a concrete slab the ducts, plenums, and fittings are usually constructed of asbestos-cement, concrete, clay, or ceramic materials.

Supply and return outlets in the area to be heated may be located in walls, ceilings, or floors. The cover may be a decorative grille, which merely conceals the duct opening, or a *register,* a grille that can be adjusted to vary or cut off the flow of air. A *diffuser,* either adjustable or nonadjustable, may be used to direct the flow of air. Some diffusers also include a register.

The type and location of supply outlets is usually the result of a compromise. Outlets supplying only hot air are most effective when they are located on or near the floor. The heated air from floor or low-wall outlets is then introduced into the coldest part of the room, and cold air is returned through high-wall registers or grilles. When cooled air is to be introduced into the area, it is more efficient to introduce the air from high-wall registers or ceiling diffusers and return it through low-wall or floor grilles. Smaller residences may have a single return-air grille located in a central hall. When this type of return-air system is used, doors leading to the hall are usually cut to clear the floor by 1 or 2 in.

The conditioned air may be carried to the supply outlets through ducts that radiate directly from the central furnace or by means of an *extended-plenum system.* In the extended-plenum system a large duct or furred area is extended the length of the house, and small ducts leading off from the plenum carry the air to individual areas. In a *perimeter system* outlets are located in the floor or baseboard under all windows and in front of doors. This system spreads a curtain of either warm or cooled air around the perimeter of the house and over outside openings, where the most heat gain or loss takes place.

Water Heating Systems

A water heating system, also termed a *hydronic system,* consists of a boiler, water-circulating piping, a water-circulating pump, and radiators. Older types of systems were similar to the gravity-type hot-air system; the hot water rose to the radiators, and the colder water returned to the boiler by gravity. With a circulating pump, the water is forced to the radiators and back to the boiler.

Three types of piping systems are used for water heating. *One-pipe systems* consist of a single supply loop from which the individual radiators take hot water and return cooled water in succession. Thus each successive radiator receives water at a lower temperature. The size of piping or the orifice at the radiator must be balanced to overcome the difference in temperature.

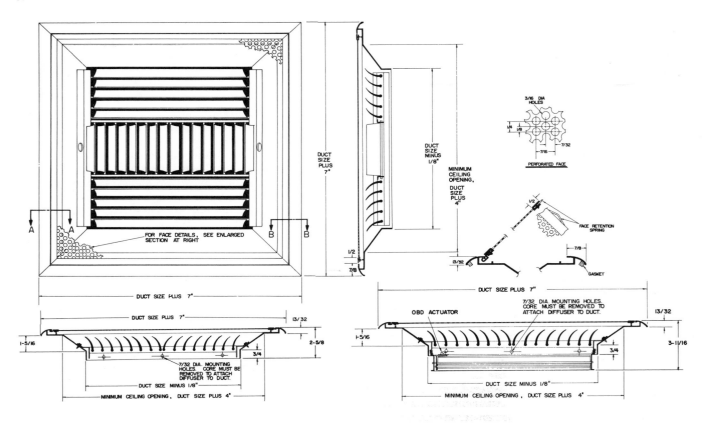

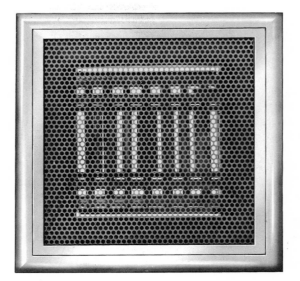

In *two-pipe systems* the water is returned from each radiator to a separate return portion of the supply loop. Thus each radiator receives water at the same temperature. However, the last radiator receives less water because the greater distance of flow increases the amount of resistance in the pipe. The size of the supply piping must be increased as the distance increases. *Two-pipe reversed-return systems* provide water at the same temperature to each radiator and have supply and return lines of the same length.

Steam Heating Systems

Steam heating systems are similar to water heating systems. They consist of a boiler, a piping system, and radiators or convectors. The boiler is fired by gas, electricity, oil, or coal. The heat source is controlled to keep a constant head of steam in the boiler to meet any demands that may be made on it. The boiler has a steam-release safety valve and a control that automatically shut off the heat source if the boiler water gets low. A hot-water supply can be produced by coils adjacent to or submerged in the boiler.

Fig. 14-29 Surface-mounted diffuser, series 1100. (*Lear Siegler, Inc., Krueger Division.*)

The simplest type of piping is a one-pipe system that uses the same pipe to convey the steam to the radiator and return the condensate to the boiler. When the unit is started, the steam must push the air out of the system. The air is allowed to escape at the radiators through thermostatically controlled air valves. When the air has been expelled from the system and steam reaches the valve, it closes automatically. As the steam gives up heat through the radiators, it condenses and the water runs back through the bottom of the supply piping. The supply mains must be large enough and sloped to allow the condensate to flow backward through the pipe without interfering with the flow of steam.

In a *two-pipe system* the steam flows into one end of the radiator and out the opposite end through a thermostatically controlled *drip trap*. The drip trap is set to open when the temperature drops below 180°F. Thus, when enough condensate accumulates in the radiator to cool it, the drip trap opens and allows the condensate to flow into the return lines and to a collecting tank. There are many variations and combinations of one- and two-pipe systems utilizing vacuum devices and pumps to return the condensate to the boiler for reheating.

Radiators and Convectors

The heat from a hot-water or steam system is released into the space to be warmed by both radiation and convection. The radiator in such systems usually consists of a series of interconnected cast-iron sections. As the hot water or steam flows through these vertical loops, the surface of the sections radiates heat to the surrounding walls and objects. Heat is also radiated to the surrounding air, causing it to rise, and the moving air sets up convection currents which transfer the heat throughout the room. Radiators may be freestanding units or attached to or recessed into walls.

Convectors transfer heat chiefly by the passage of air over the surface of the unit. They usually consist of iron or copper pipes surrounded by metal fins, which place a larger amount of heated surface in contact with the moving air. The units are usually placed near the floor, with openings at the bottom and top for air circulation. Relatively small units may be placed around the base of the wall; they are then termed *baseboard heaters*.

Unit Heaters

Large open areas can best be heated with unit heaters. Unit heaters, consisting either of coils which circulate hot water or steam or of gas-fired units, are usually hung from the ceiling. A fan behind the coils or units circulates the heated air throughout the area. Unit heaters are useful in garages, factories, or other large areas where appearance is not the primary factor.

A newer type of space heater, sometimes called an *infrared heater,* operates on the principle that radiant heat

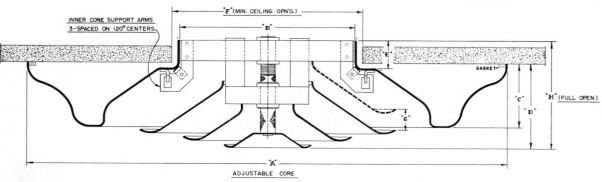

Fig. 14-30 Adjustable round ceiling diffuser, series RA-4. (*Lear Siegler, Inc., Krueger Division.*)

rays travel in a straight line and are not deflected by air. These units are used for high-ceilinged spaces that are difficult to heat. They can also be used in outdoor areas such as loading docks, golf driving ranges, outdoor restaurants, and patios. The units are gas fired and may be obtained either vented or unvented. The gas flame passes through slotted ceramic tiles, which emit the infrared rays.

Radiant Heating Systems

A radiant or panel heating system compensates for the heat loss in an area by creating warm surfaces that lessen the loss of body heat. The sensation of chill in a cold room is caused by loss of body heat to surrounding surfaces rather than by the temperature of the air. Thus if the surrounding surfaces are such that body heat is not lost to them, an enclosed area will be comfortable at a much lower air temperature.

The choice of conventional warm-air heating or radiant-panel heating should be based on several factors. Generally the installation cost of a radiant heating system is higher than that of a forced-air system, but operating costs may be considerably reduced with lower room temperatures.

Temperatures throughout the room are also more even; with conventional warm-air heating systems there may be as much as a 15°F temperature difference between a cold floor and the ceiling. In parts of the country where quick heating is needed only in the morning and evening, radiant heating may be unsatisfactory, as a radiant concrete

slab may take as long as 12 hours to come up to heat and 8 hours to cool down.

Radiant floors, walls, and ceilings may be developed by running hot water through copper or wrought-iron pipes embedded in concrete slabs, plaster walls, or ceilings. Because of the difficulty in finding and repairing leaks in a hot-water system embedded in concrete, all joints in copper pipe should be soldered or brazed and all ferrous pipes should be welded.

There is little difference in heating quality between a good hot-water radiant heating system and an electrical radiant heating system. Economic factors influencing the choice vary from area to area throughout the country. Electricity is usually more expensive than gas or oil; however, electrical systems are less expensive to install. Other advantages of electrical systems are the elimination of boilers, fuel-storage facilities, flues, and chimneys, and better control of heat supplied to individual rooms (individual rooms are seldom controlled separately in hot-water systems).

Electrical radiant-heating panels are produced by embedding factory-assembled units that consist of coils of insulated resistance wire attached to nonheating leads. The heating coils are made in standard lengths and are seldom cut or spliced. The resistance wire is attached to the gypsum lath on the ceiling with cloth tape or special staples that will not damage the insulation. Most building codes do not allow electrical panel heating in the walls. When the heating coils are installed in concrete slabs, they may be embedded in the structural slab or on top of the structural slab under a 1½ in. topping. The coils must be

Fig. 14-31   Gas-fired space heaters. (*Solaronics, Inc.*)

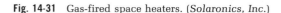

surrounded by at least 1½ in. of dense concrete. Special types of heating cable have been developed for use in exterior slabs for snow melting. These cables are copper sheathed to protect them from water that may penetrate the slab.

AIR CONDITIONING

Air conditioning, perhaps more properly termed comfort conditioning, refers to the maintenance of those atmospheric factors that affect human comfort. Specifically, it includes the maintenance of proper temperature; a balanced humidity; fresh air, free of odors; clean air, free of dust, dirt, and lint particles; and a uniform pattern of air motion.

Controlling the temperature of the air in a room is not enough to establish a comfortable environment. Comfort also depends on the humidity, the amount of moisture in the air. Cold air entering a house expands when it is heated, but the amount of moisture it contains remains the same. As a result, its *relative humidity*, the percentage of moisture it presently holds in relation to the amount it could hold, falls below the normal level required for comfort. When the humidity has dropped to 10 percent, air must be heated to 76°F before it feels comfortable. If it is *humidified* during the heating cycle to raise the relative humidity to 30 percent, the comfort zone is reached at a temperature of 72°F.

Conversely, as air is cooled it condenses, and so it must be *dehumidified*. If the temperature is lowered to 68°F, the humidity must be adjusted to 50 percent for comfort. It is the proper balancing of heat and humidity that makes for comfort conditioning. The recommended balance of temperature and humidity for the inside of a home is a temperature of 72°F and a relative humidity of 30 percent.

Filtration is necessary to purify the air. Outside air is seldom clean enough to be used directly. The addition of outside air to the conditioning system helps to dilute odors and to freshen the air. Filters help to remove odors, dust, dirt, pollens, and lint particles.

The smaller residential air-conditioning systems usually have either disposable or cleanable filters consisting of ½- to 4-in.-thick glass-fiber blankets in light perforated metal frames, which fit into standard filter racks located at the return-air side or fresh-air intake of the unit. Large commercial air-conditioning units may have electrostatic filters, which consist of electrically charged plates that remove and hold foreign particles. Even the smallest particles can be removed by this type of filter; however, *afterfilters* are usually needed to remove larger particles that may fall from the filter.

The movement of air through an area must be controlled. Moving air can cause loss of body heat by convection, resulting in discomfort even at temperatures that should be comfortable. Air must be introduced and exhausted from a room in such a way that the loss of body heat does not cause discomfort.

Fig. 14-32 Copper snow-melting system in place. (*Revere Copper and Brass, Inc.*)

Fig. 14-33 Copper snow-melting system in operation. (*Revere Copper and Brass, Inc.*)

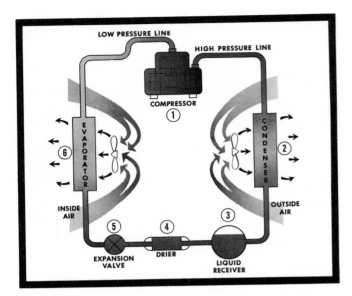

Fig. 14-34 Diagram of compression cooling system. (*Arkla Air Conditioning Company.*)

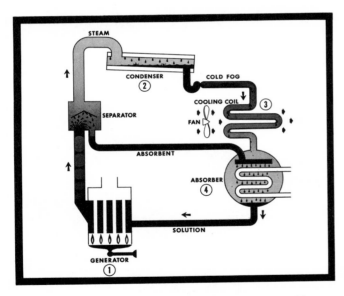

Fig. 14-35 Diagram of absorption cooling system. (*Arkla Air Conditioning Company.*)

Cooling Systems

There are several methods of cooling air. The two most commonly used in residential air conditioning are the compression system and the absorption system. Air cooling is nothing more than the transfer of indoor heat to the outside. Both systems accomplish the cooling by the expansion of a liquid to a vapor.

COMPRESSION COOLING A *compressor* is the heart of the compression air-conditioning system. The compressor takes low-pressure refrigerant gas (70 psi) and forces it through a high-pressure line at 300 psi. The gas is forced into a series of coils called a *condenser*. The condenser faces the outside air, and when a fan passes air over the coils, the refrigerant gas loses heat and condenses to a liquid. The liquid is then forced into a *liquid receiver*, or reservoir. From there it passes through an *expansion valve*, which regulates flow to the *evaporator*. In the evaporator the liquid changes to a gas at a low temperature. Water is chilled by the refrigerant and circulated by the *chilled-water pump* to coils located in or near the spaces to be cooled. The low-pressure gas is then drawn back into the compressor through the low-pressure line. See Fig. 14-34.

ABSORPTION COOLING The cooling cycle begins in the *generator*, where a solution of water and lithium bromide (similar to ordinary table salt) is heated to boiling point by a gas flame. The solution is carried up to the *separator*, which separates the lithium bromide from the water vapor and returns it to the *absorber*. The steam continues on to the *condenser*, where it is condensed back to water, which then flows down to the *evaporator*. The absorbing action of the lithium bromide causes a high vacuum in the evaporator, allowing the water to expand to a cold water vapor. The cold water vapor is then pumped to coils at the location to be cooled and continues on to the absorber, where it is reunited with the lithium bromide. The solution is returned to the generator, and the cycle is repeated. See Fig. 14-35.

WATER-COOLED SYSTEMS There are a number of variations of these two systems. In the compression system, instead of air, blown by a fan, cold water may be run over the coils in the condenser. The water may be reused after it has been cooled in an *atmospheric cooling tower*. The water is sprayed at the top of the tower, and as it falls through the air inside the redwood louvers, it is cooled by the air. This type of tower may be made more efficient by the use of large blowers to force air through the falling water.

AIR-TO-AIR SYSTEMS Package units have been produced to meet the demand for inexpensive air-conditioning installations in existing buildings. These units are usually placed in a window or framed into exterior walls. They consist of an extremely compact compression cooling system. The condenser faces the outside air, and a fan removes the heat from the high-pressure hot gas. The evaporator faces the room, and a fan draws outside air over the cold evaporator coils, cooling the room. The two fans are usually operated by the same motor, on standard 120-volt or 240-volt electric circuits. A variation of this type of unit is the *heat pump*. If the flow of refrigerant is reversed, with the condenser used as an evaporator and the evaporator used as a condenser, the unit will draw and heat air from the outside and expel cold inside air, thus acting as a heating rather than a cooling device.

Cooling Coils

The cooling unit for residential and small commercial summer air conditioning is usually located in any convenient place outside the building. It may be placed beside or behind a residence or on the roof of a commercial building. The chilled water produced by the unit is circulated through cooling coils near the air-conditioned space, and water which has absorbed the heat is returned to the unit. Most forced-air residential heating furnaces are designed for the addition of a cooling coil, added to the furnace when it is installed or at a later date. The heating coil is placed on the output side of the furnace and utilizes the forced-air-furnace blower to circulate the air over the coils. A dehumidifier and a condensate drain are also added to reduce the moisture in the air and carry condensate outside the building.

LOW-VELOCITY SINGLE-DUCT SYSTEMS   Most units in residences and small commercial buildings utilize a low-velocity single-duct system. If an upflow furnace or horizontal unit is located in the attic space or on top of the building, the ducts are usually run in the attic. For a downflow furnace or a unit located under the floor joists, the ducts are run in the crawl space or under a concrete slab. When underfloor systems are used, the conditioned air is usually carried up the wall to high-wall registers. With attic units the individual runs are made to high-wall registers or ceiling diffusers. Return air is handled in the same manner as forced-air heating systems.

The size of the ducts and the amount of air that must be delivered to the spaces to be conditioned depends not only on the amount of heat that is transferred through the building structure, but on the moisture brought in by humid outside air or given off by occupants, appliances, and use.

Most units are controlled by a thermostat connected with the compressor motor of the cooling unit. A single-duct system may be equipped for zone control. Where areas to be conditioned have widely different heat loads, at a given time, it may be necessary to install heating or cooling coils in the ducts for specific areas. These heating or cooling devices are connected with individual thermostats to modify the air supplied to the area outlets.

FAN-COIL UNITS   Fan-coil units contain a fan, coil, filter, condensate pan and drain, and possibly an outside-air inlet. A central unit furnishes conditioned air to the unit at a given velocity, and the duct coils heat or cool this air. The fan increases the flow of air over the coils. The amount of outside air introduced into the system, the temperature of the coil, and the amount of conditioned air forced over the coils may be controlled manually or thermostatically from

each room. This type of system is widely used in schools, motels, and apartment houses.

A three- or four-pipe system furnishes both hot and chilled water to a fan-coil unit in each area, with either a common return line (three-pipe system) or a separate return for each unit (four-pipe system). A special valve, connected to a thermostat, meters the right amount of hot and cold water through the coils. Outside air is furnished to the unit, or an auxiliary fresh air louver is used at some other location.

A double-duct system furnishes cooled air and warm air to each unit terminal. These terminals mix air automatically to maintain proper temperatures, as well as proper volume and air patterns.

QUESTIONS

1. List the major items that would be included in a plumbing section of the specifications for a residence.

2. What is a cross connection in a plumbing system?

3. What is an air gap, and where is it needed?

4. What are the advantages of water softeners?

5. What is the function of a check valve on a residential water heater?

6. What causes water hammer, and how is it avoided?

7. What are some of the advantages of copper water tubing in a water-supply system?

8. What is the difference between copper water tubing and copper pipe?

9. What are some of the advantages and disadvantages of plastic plumbing pipe?

10. What is a plumbing trap, and why is it needed?

11. Describe three methods of forming joints in cast-iron soil pipe.

12. Describe three types of joints used for copper pipe.

13. What information is needed to determine the sizes of piping for the various gas appliances in a residence?

14. What are the four most common materials used for plumbing fixtures, and what are their characteristics?

15. Describe three methods of installing a counter-type lavatory.

16. Describe three types of shower valves.

17. What is the design temperature?

18. How is the capacity of a forced-air furnace rated?

19. Diagram a forced-air gas-fired furnace, showing the principal parts.

20. Describe the controls of a forced-air furnace.

21. What is a plenum?

22. Describe three types of water heating systems.

23. How does a steam system differ from a water heating system?

24. What are the advantages and disadvantages of radiant-panel heating?

25. Why must humidity be adjusted in heating and cooling systems?

26. Diagram a compression-type air-conditioning system.

27. What is the function of a water tower in an air-conditioning system?

28. What is the major feature of an absorption cooling system?

29. What is an air-to-air comfort-conditioning system?

30. Describe the operation of a fan-coil unit.

REFERENCES FOR FURTHER STUDY

ABS Institute, Inc.: Pan American Building, 200 Park Avenue, New York, N.Y., 10017. "Plastic Pipe Manual," 1962. "3,000,000 Homes Can't Be Wrong: The Story of ABS Pipe Fittings," 1962.

American Brass Company: Waterbury, Conn., 06701. "Pipe Tube and Fittings."

American Iron and Steel Institute, Committee of Steel Pipe Producers: 101 Park Avenue, New York, N.Y., 10017. "Comparative Installed Costs of Galvanized Steel vs. Copper Plumbing Systems," 1968. *Steel Pipe News,* a periodical.

American Standard, Plumbing and Heating Group: 40 West 40th Street, New York, N.Y., 10018. "Plumbing Fixtures, Plumbing Fittings," Catalog PT69, 1969. "Air Conditioning Systems," 1970.

Callender, John Hancock: "Time-saver Standards," 4th ed., McGraw-Hill, New York, 1966.

Cast Iron Soil Pipe Institute: 2029 K Street, N.W., Washington, D.C., 20006. "Cast Iron Soil Pipe and Fittings Handbook," 1969.

Construction Specifications Institute: Suite 300, 1150 17th Street, N.W., Washington, D.C., 20036. "Specifying Irrigation Systems; Underground Sprinkler," 1968; "Specifying Metal Louvers, Stationary," 1967; "Specifying Duct: Sheet Metal, Low Pressure, Air-transmission," 1967. "Specifying Testing, Adjusting and Balancing of Mechanical Systems," 1969.

International Association of Plumbing and Mechanical Officials: 5032 Alhambra Avenue, Los Angeles, Calif., "Uniform Plumbing Code," 1970.

International Association of Plumbing and Mechanical Officials and International Conference of Building Officials: 50 South Los Robles Avenue, Pasadena, Calif., 91101. "Uniform Mechanical Code," 1970.

Merritt, Frederick S.: "Building Construction Handbook," McGraw-Hill, New York, 1958.

National Lumber Manufacturers' Association: 1619 Massachusetts Avenue, N.W. Washington, D.C., 20036. "Heating and Air Conditioning Study of a Wood-frame and a Masonry Structure," 1961.

Plumbing and Drainage Institute: 1018 North Austin Boulevard, Oak Park, Ill., 60302. "Testing and Rating Procedure for Grease Interceptors," 1968. "Water Hammer Arrestors," 1965.

Revere Copper and Brass, Incorporated: 230 Park Avenue, New York, N.Y., 10017. "The Application of Revere Copper Tube and Pipe," 1968.

Stoecker, W. F.: "Refrigeration and Air Conditioning," McGraw-Hill, New York, 1958.

ELECTRICAL ENERGY

Energy can be generated by forcing electrons (the most elementary electric charge) to move in a path or circuit. A *circuit* consists of a closed loop of *conductors*, through which electrons move outward from a generating device and back to the generator. The force that causes electrons to move through a circuit is called the *electromotive force* (emf) and is measured in *volts*.

The flow of electrons through a circuit is called *electric current* and is measured in *amperes* (amps). This current is governed by two factors: the amount of force, or voltage, generated and the resistance of the circuit to the current that passes through it. The amount of force depends on the input from the generating device. The amount of resistance in a particular circuit, however, depends on the elements of the circuit itself. One important factor is the size of the conductor. The smaller the diameter of the conductor and the greater its length, the greater the resistance. Another factor is the material from which the conductor is made. Each material has a different resistance to the flow of electricity, and this resistance

may either increase or decrease as the temperature rises, depending on the material. The power-consuming device being served by the circuit is also a factor, since it forms part of the closed circuit and contributes its own resistance.

Ohm's Law

There is a direct relationship between electromotive force (denoted as E), electric current (denoted as I), and resistance (denoted as R), as expressed by *Ohm's law*. This law states the relationship of, voltage, current, and resistance algebraically as

$$E = IR \qquad \text{or} \qquad \frac{E}{I} = R \qquad \text{or} \qquad \frac{E}{R} = I$$

where E = electromotive force, measured in *volts*
I = electric current, measured in *amps*
R = circuit resistance, measured in *ohms*

If we know any two of these factors, we can calculate the third. Current that always flows in the same direction through a circuit is said to be *direct current*. If we apply Ohm's law to direct current it is apparent that the greater the emf (volts), the more current (amps) will flow through a circuit of given resistance (ohms).

Electric Current

Direct current (dc) is produced by batteries and other devices. The current is said to flow from the *positive terminal* (marked +) to the *negative terminal* (marked −). *Alternating current* (ac) is supplied by most utility companies. Alternating current flows through a circuit in one direction and then alternates to flow in the other direction. A buildup of emf causing current to flow in one direction is followed by another buildup in emf that causes it to flow in the opposite direction. A complete set of these positive and negative values constitutes a *cycle,* and the number of cycles per second is the *frequency,* measured in *Hertz* (Hz). A frequency of 60 Hz has been accepted as a standard throughout most of the United States, although 25- and 50-Hz power is still furnished in some locations.

Electric Power

The rate at which electricity does work is called *electric power* and is measured in *watts*; a thousand watts is one *kilowatt.* When the energy is expended for a period of one hour, one *kilowatthour* of power has been used. Electric

power, in watts, is the product of electromotive force in volts and current in amps. Thus

$$P = EI \qquad \text{or} \qquad \text{watts} = \text{volts} \times \text{amps}$$

Note that voltage is not the same as power. Power can also be expressed as the product of the circuit resistance, in ohms, and the square of the current:

$$P = I^2R$$

Generators and power-consuming devices are sometimes rated in *kilovolt-amps* (kVA). However, the power in an ac circuit is seldom exactly equal to the product of volts times amps, but must be modified by a power factor. The *power factor* represents the ratio between the true power and the apparent power.

If the power furnished consists of a voltage and a current that vary at the same frequency, the current is said to be *single phase.* This type of current is usually furnished to residences, and, the power formula as shown above can be used. If the voltage and current vary three times during each cycle, the current is called *three phase.* Three-phase current is widely used for commercial and industrial installations, where heavy-duty three-phase motors are used.

POWER GENERATION

Most electric power is produced by a generator. An electromotive force is generated when a coil of wire is rotated within or through a magnetic field or a magnet is rotated

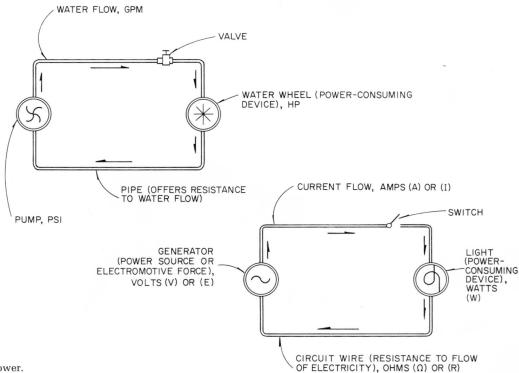

Fig. 15-1 Water and electric power.

within a coil of wire. The motive power for a generator may be a simple fan belt or a giant turbine located at a hydroelectric installation in connection with a dam. Steam plants fueled with natural gas, oil, coal, or nuclear reactors are also used to generate electric power.

Emergency-standby Electric Generators

Self-contained generators powered by diesel, gas, or gasoline engines are installed in hospitals, auditoriums, schools, office buildings, and other buildings where an interruption of electric service would cause danger or hardship. They are usually equipped with automatic starting devices that are actuated when normal power fails. The standby equipment automatically shuts down when service is resumed. Such generators usually have enough capacity to operate emergency corridor and stair lighting, emergency pumps for fire-fighting or fire-sprinkler systems, and at least one elevator that stops at each floor.

Transformers

A *transformer* is a device for changing the voltage and amperage of an ac system. Transformers permit the transmission of electric power over long distances at high voltages with low amperage and transform this energy to a low voltage for the user. Since power is the product of the circuit resistance and the square of the current, $P = I^2R$, the more we can reduce the amount of current, I, the more efficient our system will be.

In its simplest form a transformer consists of a primary coil, a secondary coil, and an iron core. The primary coil is connected to the power source, and the secondary coil delivers power to the load as shown in Fig. 15-2. E_1 represents the voltage delivered to the primary coil and E_2 represents the voltage output from the secondary coil. The voltage will be stepped up or stepped down in direct proportion to the number of turns in the primary and secondary coils. This is expressed by the formula:

$$E_2 = \frac{n_2}{n_1} E_1$$

where n_1 represents the number of turns in the primary coil and n_2 represents the number of turns in the secondary coil.

As an example, consider a transformer in which the primary voltage E_1, delivered into the transformer, is 480 volts. If the primary and secondary windings are $n_1 = 1000$ turns and $n_2 = 500$ turns, then the voltage that is output by the transformer, E_2, will be

$$E_2 = \frac{n_2}{n_1} E_1$$

$$= \frac{500}{1000} \times 480 = 240 \text{ volts}$$

If the secondary coil of a single-phase transformer is tapped at the midpoint and connected to the ground, two

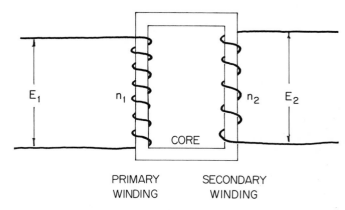

Fig. 15-2 Simplified diagram of a transformer.

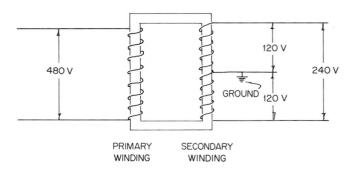

Fig. 15-3 Center-tapped single-phase transformer forming 120-volt lighting and appliance circuits and 240-volt power circuits.

secondary circuits are developed, each of which is one-half of E_2, or 120 volts. The center leg of the three-wire circuit is said to be the *neutral* or *ground* wire, and the two outer wires are said to be the *hot wires*.

The usual three-wire service furnished to residences includes two 115-volt services for lighting and small motors and a 230-volt service for electric heating and cooking appliances and larger motors. This is usually designated as 115/230V service.

Three-phase transformers have three interconnected secondary coils, connected in either *wye* or *delta* form. Delta connections are usually employed when the load is mainly power, and the wye, or star, connection is usually employed when the load is mainly lighting.

Power Distribution

By means of a transformer, the voltage can be increased and the amperage lowered. Electric power may have to be distributed hundreds of miles from hydroelectric plants to the user. This power is carried at an extremely high

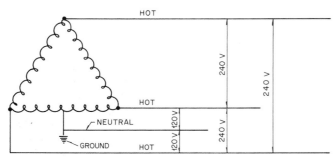

DELTA–CONNECTED TRANSFORMER

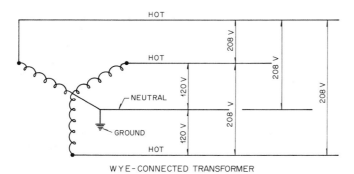

WYE–CONNECTED TRANSFORMER

Fig. 15-4 Three-phase transformer connections.

voltage (as high as 600,000 volts, depending on the distance and other factors). Approximately 90% of the high-voltage or *high-tension* wires consist of a steel cable surrounded by aluminum conductors. The steel imparts strength and the aluminum acts as the conductor. On a pound-for-pound basis, aluminum is one of the most efficient conductors known.

Near populated areas where the power will be distributed, the high-voltage lines from the power plant feed into a *substation*, an assembly of transformers and equipment which lower the voltage and convert it to the desired form for local distribution. A substation may also function as a switching station which can call on reserve sources of power from other power stations or systems in the event the prime source of power fails. In the summer of 1970 when two major generating plants failed in New York City, electric power was brought from as far as Tennessee to relieve the power shortage at peak hours of demand.

Different localities distribute electric power at different voltages. In New York City power is distributed directly into large buildings at 13,200 volts. Overhead or underground lines carry this power throughout the city to substations or transformers on power poles, where it is reduced to safe voltages for use in residences, offices, and small industrial plants. The service may be 480/960V, 240/480V, or 120/240V, depending on the requirements. Most residences are supplied with 120/240V power. It may be as low as 110/220V in some areas and in others it may

vary as the load in the area is increased. The National Electrical Code uses 115/230V for its calculations.

Where power is brought into a building at higher voltages, it usually is run underground to a transformer vault. Transformers used to reduce 13,000 volts to 480 or 240 volts are usually filled with flammable insulating oil. Oil-filled transformers must be installed in concrete vaults with locked doors.

SERVICES AND SERVICE EQUIPMENT

A *service* consists of the conductors and equipment necessary for delivering electric power from a public utility or private distribution system to the wiring system of the premises served. A *service cable* is the two or more conductors made up into a cable. A *service drop* consists of the overhead service conductors that carry the current from the power poles, or the terminals of a pole-mounted transformer, to the *service-entrance* conductors. The service-entrance conductors are spliced to the service drop and enter a metal conduit called a *service raceway* through a watertight weatherhead or gooseneck fitting. The service-entrance conductors continue to the terminals of the *service equipment*, which includes the necessary metering devices, fuses, circuit breakers, and accessories located near the service entrance.

Service drops

The "National Electrical Code," published by the National Fire Protection Association, recommends that a minimum of a 100-amp three-wire service be provided for all individual residences. This would require a minimum of three 2-gauge wires. For larger, all-electric residences a 200-amp three-wire service may be needed. The size of wire allowed can be determined from tables in the code. Where the voltage does not exceed 300 volts, a bare

TABLE 15-1 Minimum clearances of service drops

LOCATION	CLEARANCE
Above roofs	8 ft above the highest point of any roof; *except* 3 ft where the slope of the roof is not less than 4:12 or 18 in. where drops over not more than 4 ft of overhang
Above porches, balconies, or walks	10 ft above finished grade
Above private driveways or parking lots	12 ft
Above commercial areas, parking lots, or areas subject to truck travel	15 ft
Above public streets, alleys, and drives	18 ft

grounded conductor may be used as one wire of the three-wire system. The hot wires must have an approved type of insulation and must be kept a reasonable distance from people who stand, walk, or drive under them. Minimum clearances established to prevent mechanical damage and accidental contact with service drops are shown in Table 15-1.

Many new housing developments have power lines installed underground. The service is then brought into the building underground. If the house has a basement, it terminates there; otherwise it is carried up the outside of the house or within the walls. Underground services from overhead power lines are carried down the power pole and underground in metal conduit. The underground service, including the riser on the pole, is called a *service lateral*.

Service Equipment

METERS The meter, properly called a *kilowatthour meter*, measures the power consumed. The meter is installed outside the building between the service conductors and the main power panel of the building, in a location where it will be readily accessible to both the owner and the power company.

FUSES AND CIRCUIT BREAKERS If excessive current is permitted to flow in a wire, the wire will heat and may cause the insulation to burn. Failure of the insulation between conductors will result in a short circuit, with consequent loss of power. It can also present a shock hazard to persons touching the wire itself or metal objects in contact with the wire. In order to keep the current in the wires to a safe level, each circuit is provided with a fuse or a circuit breaker as current protection. A *fuse* is a device containing a low-melting-point metal insert through which the current is conducted. When current above the rated amperage passes through it, the insert melts and breaks the circuit. Fuses may be of the cartridge type or plug type. Cartridge-type fuses are widely used for high-current and high-voltage commercial installations. Plug fuses, which screw into a socket like an incandescent light bulb have largely been replaced in residences by circuit breakers. A *circuit breaker* contains a tripping mechanism which operates either magnetically or by thermal expansion to open a switch when the current exceeds the rated capacity. When the overload on the circuit has been removed, the circuit breaker can be reset. The main advantage of a circuit breaker over a fuse is that it need not be replaced after an overload. The circuit breaker may also act as a switch that can be controlled manually.

SERVICE PANELS The service panel, distribution box, or main switchboard is the termination of the service equipment and is the heart of the electrical system of a building. It is located in a metal box after the meter or, in large installations, in a special room where both the front and

back of the switchboard is accessible. In a residence the metal box may be mounted on the exterior wall surface or built into the wall on either the outside or the inside of the building. The equipment, which may be in more than one box, consists of a main disconnect switch and fuses or breakers. The distribution panel contains circuit breakers or fused switches which protect the feeder conductors to each circuit in the building. Each hot wire of a circuit is protected by a fuse or breaker, sized for the capacity of that circuit. The neutral ground wire of a circuit is never fused.

The three service conductors are connected to three vertical copper *busbars*, square or rectangular bars or strips. The center bar is connected to the neutral conductor of the service, in front of the service disconnect switch, and to the panel box. The metal panel box must then be grounded. The best ground is to a metallic water-piping system, at least 10 ft of which is underground. If such a system is not available, an electrode must be driven into the ground. Special *ground clamps* are manufactured for connecting the ground cable to the electrode or water pipe. If the ground is to be connected to copper water pipe, a copper clamp is used; if it is to a galvanized iron pipe, a galvanized iron clamp should be used. Special plated clamps are used for connections to aluminum pipe, so designed to avoid damage to the pipe.

Fig. 15-5 A residential service.

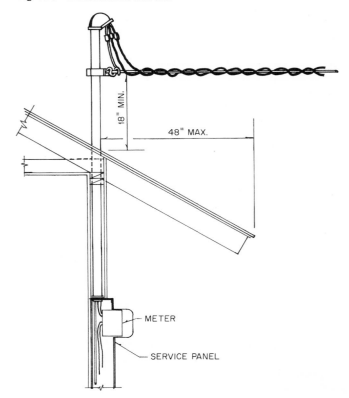

Fig. 15-6 Residential service panel.

Branch Circuits

The size of the service panel depends on the total demand of the branch circuits. For dwellings the "National Electrical Code" requires that 3 watts of power per square ft of area be supplied for general lighting. The outside dimensions of the building are used in figuring the area. The code further recommends a separate circuit for each 500 sq ft of area. The circuits used for general lighting, and convenience receptacles, are considered *general-purpose circuits*. They serve lights and convenience outlets throughout the house, except for those in kitchens, pantries, family rooms, and breakfast rooms. The general-purpose load for a 2667 sq ft residence would be

3 watts/sq ft × 2667 sq ft = 8001 watts

At least two additional 20-amp *light-appliance circuits* are required to serve the areas excluded from the general-purpose circuits. The load for these circuits is

2 × (20 amps × 120 volts) = 4800 watts

For fixed appliances such as garbage-disposal units, dishwashers, ranges and oven, clothes washers and driers, and heating and air-conditioning units, a separate *fixed-appliance circuit* is required. The load on this circuit is based on the rating for each appliance. These ratings are usually designated in volts and amps—for example, 115V-10A—, which must be converted to power in watts: 115 volts × 10 amps = 1150 watts. Table 15-2 shows average ratings of residential appliances.

TABLE 15-2 Average power demands of residential appliances

APPLIANCE	RATING	LOAD, WATTS
Counter-mounted cooking unit	230V-30A	6900
Wall-mounted oven	230V-25A	5750
Air conditioner	230V-20A	4600
Water heater	230V-11A	2500
Clothes drier	230V-20A	4600
Clothes washer	115V-10A	1150
Kitchen disposal unit	115V-8A	920
Kitchen fan (¼ hp)	115V-4.6A	529

In a residence with all the appliances in Table 15-2 the total load would be 26,979 watts. However, since all fixed appliances are not likely to be in operation at the same time, the total load on the fixed-appliance circuit can be reduced by 25 percent to 20,235 watts.

Thus the total power requirement for the residence under discussion is

General-purpose circuit	8,001 watts
Small-appliance circuits	4,800 watts
Fixed-appliance circuit	20,235 watts
Total	33,036 watts

From the power formula $P = EI$ we have

$$I = \frac{P}{E} = \frac{30,460 \text{ watts}}{230 \text{ volts}} = 131.4 \text{ amps}$$

With a current requirement of 131.4 amps, it would be wise to use a 150-amp service to take care of future demands. Space would be provided in the service panel for the installation of additional breakers. No more than 42 fuses or circuit breakers can be installed in a single panel box.

Both 120-volt and 240-volt circuits can be taken from the service panel. A circuit taken off the neutral bar and one of the side bars will be a 120-volt circuit. If the two side bars are used, 240 volts will be available. When 240-volt circuits are used, a neutral wire must be run to the appliance. This is called a *ground wire*. If metallic sheathed cable or rigid metal conduit is used, this may serve as the ground wire.

WIRING MATERIALS AND METHODS

Several factors must be considered in selecting the materials for the distribution of electric power within a building. Wires must be large enough to carry the required current. The thinner the wire, the greater its resistance and the more electrical energy it dissipates as heat. Thus an underdesigned wire results in inefficient operation and can also become a fire hazard. Each wire must be covered with the proper type of insulation to prevent contact with other wires, metal, the ground, or people. Wires must be further protected from mechanical damage by heavy protective coverings or metal raceways. Various devices are needed for securing wiring in place, making joints, and providing a solid base to which fixtures may be attached.

Conductors

Most conductors in buildings are copper, although the use of aluminum is increasing. As discussed in Chapter 7, wire sizes are designated by gauge numbers based on the diameter of the wire. Table 7-7 lists American Wire Gauge sizes and other pertinent data. Note that the smaller the gauge number, the larger the wire.

The amount of current a wire will carry without excessive heating or voltage loss depends on the *circular mils* of cross-sectional area, the type of metal, and the temperature of the conductor. Table 15-3 shows the allowable current-carrying capacity for wires used in branch circuits where the temperature is not above 86°F. Where wire is to be used at higher temperatures, the amperage must be reduced. The smallest wire allowed in branch circuits is 14 gauge.

TABLE 15-3 Current-carrying capacity for copper and aluminum wire

AMPERE*	COPPER (AWG)	ALUMINUM (AWG)
15	14	12
20	12	10
25	10	8
30	10	8
35	8	6
40	8	6
45	6	4
50	6	4
60	4	4
70	4	3
80	3	2
90	2	1
100	1	0
110	0	2/0
125	0	3/0
150	2/0	4/0
175	3/0	250 MCM† = 0.5″
200	4/0	300 MCM† = 0.55″

* Based on a demand factor of 80 percent or less, six or fewer cables in raceway.
†MCM = 1000 circular mils of area

Insulation

Both copper and aluminum conductors are protected from short circuits and damage by various types of coverings. Single conductors for general wiring are protected by rubber or thermoplastic coatings. The type and thickness of the coating or covering depends on the maximum volt-

age (wire for general wiring must be rated at 600 volts), the temperatures to which the wire will be exposed, whether it will be installed in a dry or wet location, and whether it will be buried in the ground, encased in concrete, or subjected to corrosive atmospheres or materials. Two or more single conductors may be encased in a flexible covering of cloth, plastic, or metal as a cable. Table 15-4 describes the properties of the most commonly used insulation and cables for general-circuit wiring. (All approved types are described in the National Electrical Code.) All cables are marked or tagged to indicate the maximum voltage, the manufacturer's name or trademark, the month and year of manufacture, the gauge or circular mils of the conductors, and the type of insulation or protection.

Open Wiring

Insulated conductors may be installed as open wiring on knobs or cleats where it is not concealed in the building structure. This type of installation is usually confined to high-tension wiring in transformer vaults and substations or to temporary wiring. The conductors are held away from contact with each other and with any object other than

Fig. 15-7 Diagram of residential service panel.

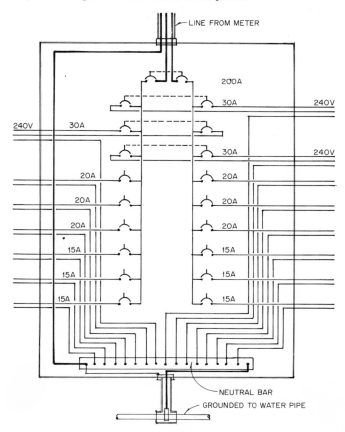

their insulating supports. They are held away from the surface over which they pass by porcelain, glass, or composition cleats or split knobs. For voltages of 300 or less the conductors must be kept 2½ in. apart and ½ in. from the surface of the structure. For voltages between 301 and 600 they must be separated 4 in. and must clear the surface by 1 in. When the conductors pass through timbers, partitions, ceilings, or floors, they are separated from the structure by tubes of porcelain, glass, or other material impervious to moisture.

Concealed Knob-and-tube Wiring

One of the oldest methods of supporting electrical conductors is with knob-and-tube wiring similar to that used in open wiring. The National Electrical Code describes the methods and materials to be used; however, many local codes ban this type of installation. Where it is allowed, it is usually confined to residences of wood-frame construction.

The method consists of installing individual conductors on nonabsorptive knobs and insulating tubes within concealed spaces in walls and ceilings. The conductors are separated by at least 3 in. and held away from the surface at least 1 in. Where they pass through wood framing members, such as studs, ceiling joists, or rafters, they must be protected by porcelain or flexible-insulation tubes sometimes called *loom*. When knob-and-tube wiring is used in an attic space that is accessible by means of permanent steps or ladders, the conductors must be run through the rafters and ceiling joists and protected by a *runningboard*. They may also be placed on the sides of the joists or rafters.

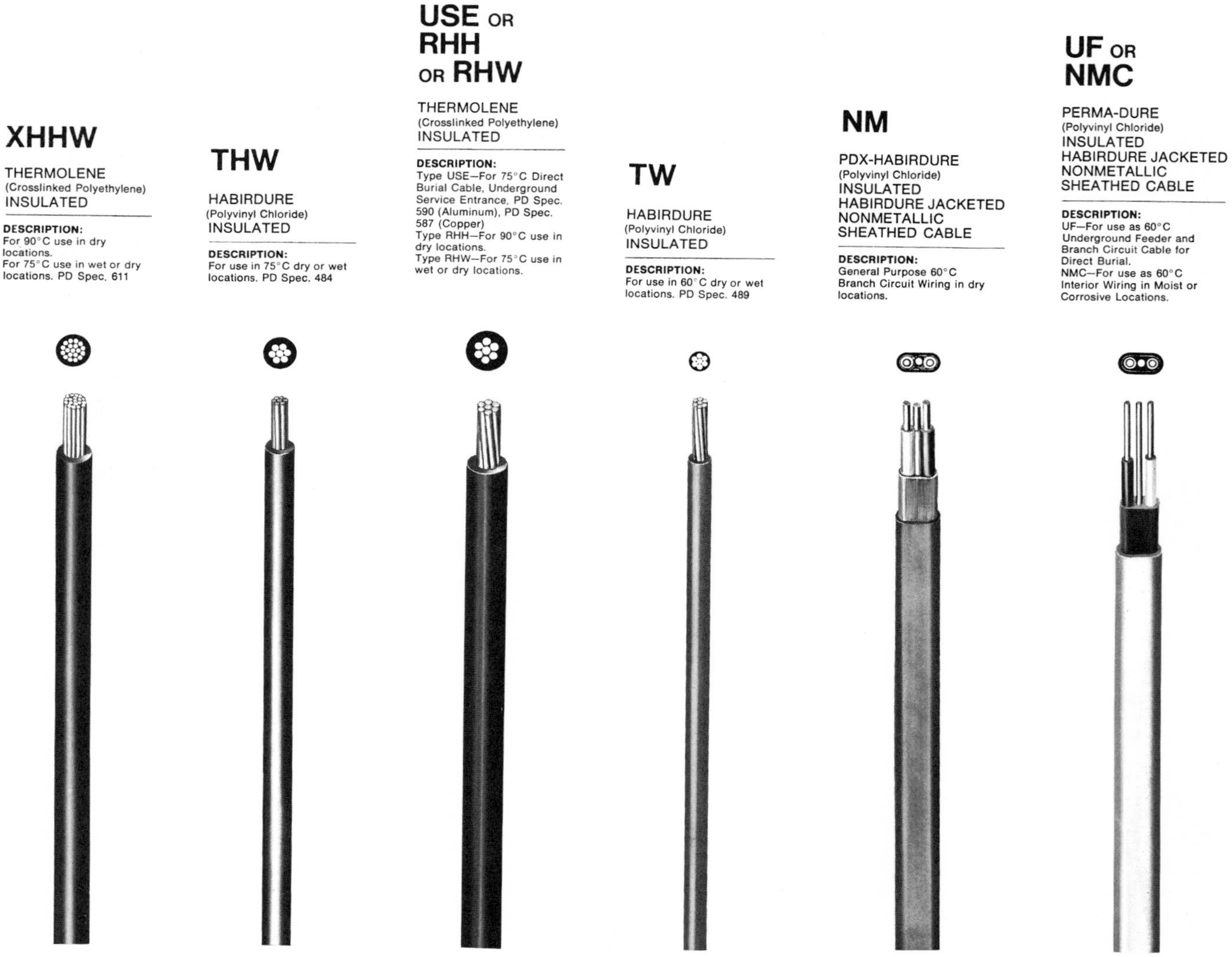

Fig. 15-8 Metal and nonmetallic sheathed cable. (*Phelps Dodge Cable and Wire Company.*)

XHHW

THERMOLENE
(Crosslinked Polyethylene)
INSULATED

DESCRIPTION:
For 90°C use in dry locations.
For 75°C use in wet or dry locations. PD Spec. 611

THW

HABIRDURE
(Polyvinyl Chloride)
INSULATED

DESCRIPTION:
For use in 75°C dry or wet locations. PD Spec. 484

USE OR **RHH** OR **RHW**

THERMOLENE
(Crosslinked Polyethylene)
INSULATED

DESCRIPTION:
Type USE—For 75°C Direct Burial Cable, Underground Service Entrance. PD Spec. 590 (Aluminum), PD Spec. 587 (Copper)
Type RHH—For 90°C use in dry locations.
Type RHW—For 75°C use in wet or dry locations.

TW

HABIRDURE
(Polyvinyl Chloride)
INSULATED

DESCRIPTION:
For use in 60°C dry or wet locations. PD Spec. 489

NM

PDX-HABIRDURE
(Polyvinyl Chloride)
INSULATED
HABIRDURE JACKETED
NONMETALLIC
SHEATHED CABLE

DESCRIPTION:
General Purpose 60°C
Branch Circuit Wiring in dry locations.

UF OR **NMC**

PERMA-DURE
(Polyvinyl Chloride)
INSULATED
HABIRDURE JACKETED
NONMETALLIC
SHEATHED CABLE

DESCRIPTION:
UF—For use as 60°C Underground Feeder and Branch Circuit Cable for Direct Burial.
NMC—For use as 60°C Interior Wiring in Moist or Corrosive Locations.

UD

THERMOLENE
(Crosslinked Polyethylene)
INSULATED
UNDERGROUND
DISTRIBUTION CABLE

DESCRIPTION:
Concentric neutral cable
for single and three phase
primary distribution, direct
burial or duct, rated at
90°C, to 46000 volts.
PD Spec. 581

SECONDARY UD

THERMOLENE
(Crosslinked Polyethylene)
INSULATED
SECONDARY OR
SERVICE UD
CABLE

DESCRIPTION:
Two phase conductors
of black Thermolene cabled
with yellow Thermolene
insulated neutral. 600 volts.
Rated at 90°C.

SECONDARY SD

THERMOLENE
(Crosslinked Polyethylene)
OR HABIRLENE
(Polyethylene)
Covered

DESCRIPTION:
Neutral Supported
Secondary and Service Drop
Cable: Aluminum and
ACSR Conductors.

MC

THERMOLENE
(Crosslinked Polyethylene)
INSULATED
METAL CLAD CABLE
GALVANIZED STEEL
INTERLOCKED
ARMORED

DESCRIPTION:
Type RHH insulated for
90°C dry locations. Type
RHW insulated for 75°C
wet or dry locations. For use
in aerial installations, metal
racks, trays, troughs, or
continuous rigid cable
supports. PD Spec. 588 and
612 with XHHW Conductors.

HIGH VOLTAGE

THERMOLENE
(Crosslinked Polyethylene)
INSULATED
THERMOPLASTIC
JACKETED

DESCRIPTION:
Rated at 90°C for 600—
15000 Volt Power Cable use
in aerial, direct burial,
conduit, open tray and
underground duct installations. PD Spec. 550

ARMO-LOK HIGH VOLTAGE

THERMOLENE
(Crosslinked Polyethylene)
INSULATED ARMO-LOK CABLE
GALVANIZED STEEL
OR ALUMINUM
INTERLOCKED ARMOR

DESCRIPTION:
Rated at 90°C for 600—
15000 Volt Power Cable use
in aerial, open tray, and rack
installations. PD Spec. 572

Fig. 15-8 (Continued)

Conduit

RIGID METAL CONDUIT   Most rigid metal conduit is of steel. The material is similar to water pipe, but somewhat softer for ease of bending. Steel conduit may be galvanized or enameled for protection. Enameled steel conduit is allowed only in interior installations. Rigid metal conduit is suitable for all but a few very special installations. In exposed locations it offers the greatest protection from physical abuse, and it is the standard protection for concealed wiring in concrete or masonry.

Conduit is produced in 10-ft lengths and is joined by fittings with standard tapered pipe threads or by threadless compression fittings. Where two lengths of rigid conduit cannot be coupled with a standard threaded fitting, a standard pipe union is used. Rigid conduit may be bent in the plant with power machinery or on the job with a *hickey*. The minimum radius of the bend depends on the size of the conduit and the type of wire it is to carry. Bends must be made in such a manner that the conduit is not injured and the internal diameter is not effectively reduced. Conduit should be installed with as few bends as possible so that conductors can be pulled in without injuring the insulation. No length of conduit should have more than four right-angle bends. The conduit is secured to pull boxes, junction boxes, or fixture boxes with threaded bushings.

TABLE 15-4 Conductor insulation and cable types

DESIGNATION	DESCRIPTION
RH	Single conductor, rubber insulation. General wiring for dry locations, 167°F maximum temperature.
RHH	Single conductor, rubber insulation, heat resistant. General wiring for dry locations, approved for areas with higher temperatures, 194°F maximum.
RHW	Single conductor, rubber insulation, heat and moisture resistant. For use underground, in concrete and masonry, and in raceways where moisture is likely to be present, 167°F maximum temperature.
RUH	Single conductor, latex-rubber insulation, heat resistant. General wiring for dry locations, 167°F maximum temperature.
RUW	Single conductor, latex-rubber insulation, moisture resistant. For use in dry or wet locations, can be used underground, embedded in concrete or masonry, 140°F maximum temperature.
T	Single conductor, thermoplastic insulation. General wiring for dry locations, 140°F maximum temperature.
TW	Single conductor, thermoplastic insulation, moisture and heat resistant. For use in dry or wet locations, can be used underground, embedded in concrete slabs or masonry, 140°F maximum temperature.
THW	Single conductor, thermoplastic insulation, moisture and heat resistant. Same as type TW, except approved for higher temperatures, 167°F maximum temperature.
MI	Mineral-insulated rigid, metal-sheathed cable. One or more conductors held in place and insulated by dense refractory mineral insulation, enclosed in a gastight and airtight rigid metal tube. For use in dry or wet hazardous locations with special fittings.
MC	Metal-clad, flexible shield enclosing insulated conductors. Two or more insulated conductors of a minimum 4-gauge copper or 2-gauge aluminum, covered with a spirally wound flexible steel shield. Used for power cables (in damp locations the metal shield must be impervious to moisture).

TABLE 15-4 Conductor insulation and cable types *(Continued)*

DESIGNATION	DESCRIPTION
AC	Metal-clad, flexible shield, enclosing insulated conductors. Rubber- or thermoplastic-insulated conductors enclosed in a spirally wound and interlocked flexible steel shield, with a continuous grounding strip under the shield, sometimes called *armored cable* or BX cable. May be embedded in plaster finish when not exposed to excessive moisture.
ACL	Metal-clad, flexible shield with a lead sheath over insulated conductors. Same as AC type, except that there is a lead sheath over the insulated conductors. May be used in dry or wet locations, underground, or embedded in concrete.
NM	Nonmetallic-sheathed cable. Two or more insulated conductors covered by a nonmetallic moisture-resistant, flame-retardant sheath; sometimes called Romex, a proprietary product. General concealed or exposed wiring in dry areas; may have a grounding wire inside sheath.
NMC	Nonmetallic-sheathed cable, corrosion resistant type. Same construction as type NM cable, except that the nonmetallic sheath is flame retardant, moisture resistant, fungus resistant, and corrosion resistant. May be installed in dry, wet, or corrosive locations and in masonry walls, but not be embedded in concrete.
SE	Service-entrance cable. Two insulated conductors with an insulated or uninsulated conductor wound spirally around them and covered by a metal or nonmetallic sheath that is flame retardant and moisture resistant. Used for overhead services or branch-service feeders.
USE	Service-entrance cable, underground type. Two rubber- or thermoplastic-insulated cables and one insulated or uninsulated conductor, usually with a spirally wound steel armor, covered with a saturated braid as protection against moisture. Used for underground service.
UF	Underground feeder cable, one or more insulated conductors enclosed in a covering that is flame retardant, moisture resistant, fungus resistant, and corrosion resistant. Suitable for direct burial in the earth; used for underground feeder or branch circuits, but not as service-entrance cables or exposed to sunlight.

The actual inside dimension of rigid conduit is larger than the nominal size designation, called the *electrical-trade size*. The interior dimension of $\frac{1}{2}''$ trade size is 0.622 in.; $\frac{3}{4}''$ is 0.824 in.; $1''$ is 1.049 in.

ELECTRICAL METALLIC TUBING Electrical metallic tubing (EMT), or thin-wall conduit, is similar to rigid metal conduit, except for the thickness of the walls. It is formed, resistance

welded, and galvanized or similarly finished. EMT is used for exposed or concealed work where it will not be subjected to severe mechanical damage. It may be buried in concrete slabs or built into masonry.

Pipe threads cannot be cut in tubing. Joints are made with a special threadless coupling. Where the tubing is to be buried in concrete, special concretetight fittings are used. When it is installed in wet locations, raintight fittings are required. Bronze tubing and fittings are available for use in corrosive atmospheres.

Both rigid metal conduit and electrical metallic tubing have identical inside dimensions. However, the thinner wall of EMT sometimes makes it possible to install the next larger size at the same cost as the normal size for threaded conduit. EMT can be obtained up to electrical-trade sizes of 4″.

RIGID NONMETALLIC CONDUIT   Nonmetallic materials with suitable characteristics for use as rigid conduit include asbestos cement, polyvinyl chloride (PVC), and polyethylene. For underground use the material must be resistant to moisture and corrosive agents and must be able to withstand continued loading likely to be encountered after installation. Rigid nonmetallic tubing may be installed underground provided that any portion of the tubing less than 18 in. below the surface is encased with 2 in. of concrete. It may be embedded in concrete or masonry. If it is installed in wet locations, the joints, boxes, and fittings must be watertight. Nonmetallic tubing is produced in standard electrical-trade sizes. The thickness of the walls will vary with the material. Where outlets must be grounded, a separate ground wire must be run inside the tubing.

FLEXIBLE METAL CONDUIT   A strong, flexible tubing of spirally wound, interlocking steel strip, sometimes called *flex*, has

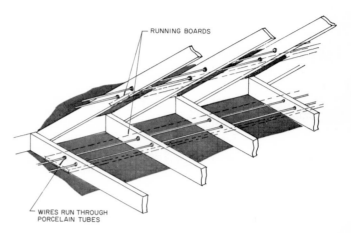

Fig. 15-10   Concealed knob-and-tube wiring.

Fig. 15-11   Installing rigid metal conduit on cellular steel decking. (*H. H. Robertson Company.*)

Fig. 15-9   Split knobs and cleats used in open wiring.

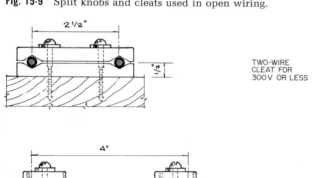

TWO-WIRE CLEAT FOR 300V OR LESS

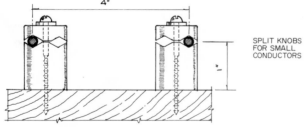

SPLIT KNOBS FOR SMALL CONDUCTORS

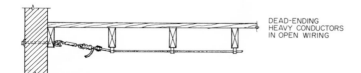

DEAD-ENDING HEAVY CONDUCTORS IN OPEN WIRING

been developed for use in dry areas. The tubing is usually galvanized, but it cannot be used in moist areas unless the conductors are lead sheathed. It cannot be used in hazardous locations or where rubber-insulated conductors may be exposed to gasoline, oil, or other materials that will affect rubber. Most flexible metal conduit cannot be considered as a means of grounding, and a separate grounding wire must be included inside the conduit.

Flexible steel conduit is available for general wiring purposes in electrical-trade sizes of ½″ to 3″. It must be secured by approved types of fasteners at regular intervals not to exceed 4½ ft and within 12 in. of all outlet boxes or

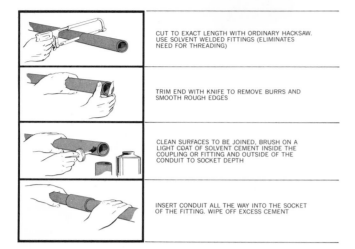

CUT TO EXACT LENGTH WITH ORDINARY HACKSAW. USE SOLVENT WELDED FITTINGS (ELIMINATES NEED FOR THREADING)

TRIM END WITH KNIFE TO REMOVE BURRS AND SMOOTH ROUGH EDGES

CLEAN SURFACES TO BE JOINED, BRUSH ON A LIGHT COAT OF SOLVENT CEMENT INSIDE THE COUPLING OR FITTING AND OUTSIDE OF THE CONDUIT TO SOCKET DEPTH

INSERT CONDUIT ALL THE WAY INTO THE SOCKET OF THE FITTING. WIPE OFF EXCESS CEMENT

Fig. 15-12   Joining rigid nonmetallic PVC conduit.

Fig. 15-13   Flexible-metal-conduit installation.

fittings. It is particularly important that bends be securely held, so the conduit will not be displaced when the wires are pulled.

A special type of flexible metal conduit, termed *liquid-tight flexible metal conduit*, consists of flexible steel or brass covered with an outer sheath of thermoplastic material. This is not intended for general wiring. It is used in wiring machine tools where it will not be exposed to gasoline or other substances that would damage the thermoplastic sheathing.

Conduit Installation

Conduit is installed with all the necessary pull boxes, junction boxes, and outlet boxes before the finish surfacing materials are applied to the construction. Each type of conduit must be securely fastened to the structural frame with fasteners approved for that type of conduit. After the finishing materials have been applied, wires are pulled through the conduit. Conductors must be fed through the conduit in continuous runs. Splices and joints may only be made in junction boxes.

Surface Raceways

Conductors may also be run through surface raceways, formed metal or plastic channels with snap-on covers. They may be installed only in dry locations where the voltage is 330 or less and where they will not be subject to severe physical damage or corrosive vapors. Surface raceways may be used in place of surface-mounted conduit. They may be extended through walls, floors, or ceilings if they are carried through the construction in unbroken lengths. They are particularly valuable for remodeling work.

As in all types of wiring inside a metal or plastic raceway, each box, fitting, or raceway must provide a continuous path of low resistance to the ground. In metal surface raceways the sections are mechanically and electrically connected to provide this path. In nonmetal raceways a grounding wire must be connected to each metal box or fixture inside the raceway.

MULTIOUTLET ASSEMBLIES   These assemblies, sometimes called *plug-in* or *plug strips*, are prewired surface raceways for installation in dry areas. They have outlets spaced at regular intervals along the face to provide flexible electrical service in homes, offices, laboratories, or wherever additional outlets are needed. Although the units are designed to be surface mounted, the metal type may be surrounded by building finish such as plaster as long as the removable cover can be removed. They may extend through dry partitions or floors if there is no outlet within the partition and some means is provided to remove the cover without removing the entire unit.

Underfloor Raceways

Raceways to be installed under concrete or other flooring are constructed of either steel or plastic. They provide a practical means of carrying electric power and telephone lines to desks in office buildings or showcases in stores. They may be installed within the structural slab or concrete topping ¾ to 1½ in. below the surface. Covered junction boxes or markers are provided at regular intervals, so

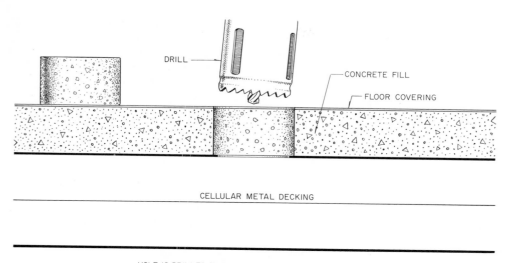

DRILL

CONCRETE FILL

FLOOR COVERING

CELLULAR METAL DECKING

HOLE IS DRILLED THROUGH FLOOR FINISH, FILL, AND TOP
OF CELLULAR METAL DECKING.

(a)

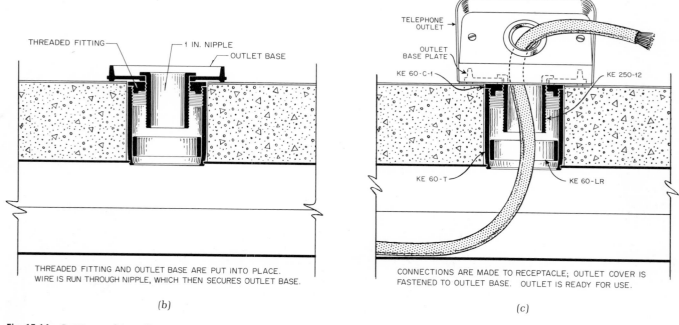

THREADED FITTING

1 IN. NIPPLE

OUTLET BASE

THREADED FITTING AND OUTLET BASE ARE PUT INTO PLACE.
WIRE IS RUN THROUGH NIPPLE, WHICH THEN SECURES OUTLET BASE.

(b)

TELEPHONE
OUTLET

OUTLET
BASE PLATE

KE 60-C-1

KE 250-12

KE 60-T

KE 60-LR

CONNECTIONS ARE MADE TO RECEPTACLE; OUTLET COVER IS
FASTENED TO OUTLET BASE. OUTLET IS READY FOR USE.

(c)

Fig. 15-14 Cutting and installing raised outlet to underfloor raceway. (*H. H. Robertson Company.*)

that the electric circuit may be tapped where needed. Approved underfloor raceways may be laid flush with the concrete floor and underwood or resilient flooring. The junction boxes used with underfloor raceways are installed flush with the floor grade and sealed against the entry of water.

Raceways installed flush with the floor may be used for modernizing existing buildings. The existing floor is trenched to provide a duct for the raceway, and flooring material is then laid over the top of the duct. Convenience receptacles are usually installed in raised outlet boxes.

Cellular-metal-floor Raceways

The hollow cells in cellular steel decking may be used as electrical raceways. Metal raceways, or *headers*, are placed on top of the metal deck, perpendicular to the cells of the

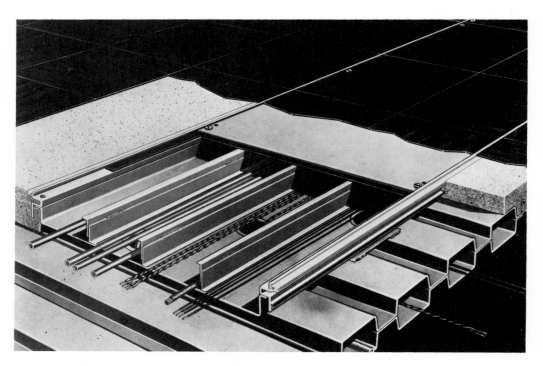

Fig. 15-15   Cellular metal deck and headers. (*H. H. Robertson Company.*)

Fig. 15-16   Cast zinc-alloy inserts to be incorporated in underfloor electrical raceways. (*American Die Casting Institute.*)

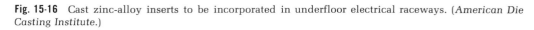

decking, for access to predetermined cells of the cellular deck. Junction boxes are installed at intervals along the headers and are covered with plates either flush with the finish floor or immediately under resilient flooring.

The headers and junction boxes are installed before the floor fill is placed. Some types have permanent screens and adjusting screws to assure that the junction boxes are flush with the finish floor. Suitable systems of markers, such as flat-headed brass machine screws, are screwed into the header to identify various circuits. Outlets may be located almost anywhere in the room after the finish flooring has been installed. A hole is drilled in the flooring, through the floor fill, and into the header or deck cell, and a special tool is used to install a ring that is clamped in place. Wires may then be pulled through the cells and headers to furnish power to the outlet. Special raised boxes are available to hold power receptacles or interconnecting telephone services. When a receptacle is disconnected and removed, the wires must be pulled from the raceways.

Cellular-concrete-floor Raceways

Cellular concrete floors are designed for use with skeletal steel framing, concrete framing, or wall-bearing masonry framing. The structural floor consists of precast concrete units that span between structural beams. The floor members are cast with hollow cells which lighten the structure and serve as raceways for electrical and signal wiring. When the concrete units are in place, parallel raceways are formed that span the width of the building. Metal header ducts are placed on top of the precast concrete units transverse to the concrete cells, and metal junction boxes are leveled to the top of the concrete floor fill and sealed against the entrance of water. Wires are pulled through the hollow concrete cells and the headers. Outlets may be located at any point in the headers.

JUNCTION BOXES, OUTLETS, AND SWITCHES

A junction or fixture box is required at every point at which conductors are brought out for splicing or connection to switches or fixtures. In wood frame construction junction boxes are usually the first part of the electrical system to be installed. When armored cable or nonmetallic sheathed cable is used, it must be installed before the finish is applied. In concrete construction the boxes and connecting conduit must be in place before concrete is poured. In masonry construction conduit and related boxes are installed as the masonry work progresses. Wires

Fig. 15-17 Installing a cellular concrete floor. *(Spancrete of California; photo by Harry H. Adams.)*

Fig. 15-18   Outlet boxes and box connectors.

are not pulled into conduit until the interior of the building has been protected from weather, and all finish work that might damage the conductors, such as plastering, has been completed.

In wood frame construction the boxes are nailed to the sides of studs through holes in a bracket that extends out from the side of the box and over the face of the stud. If the outlet is to be located between the studs, a special steel strap or hanger is used, bent in such a manner that it can be nailed to the face of the stud and attached to the back of the box with machine screws.

Junction Boxes

Junction boxes are made square, rectangular, or octagonal in trade sizes designed to hold a specific number of conductors and switches or receptacles. They are usually 1½ in. deep, called *deep boxes*, although ½ in. *shallow boxes* may be used where a structural member would have to be cut for a deeper box.

Boxes deeper than 1½ in. are called *device boxes* and may be up to 3½ in. deep to accommodate a device and its conductors. Those designed for more than one device are called *gang boxes*. When a single receptacle or switch is to be installed in an octagonal or square box, a *plaster ring* is used as a cover. The plaster ring reduces the opening to fit the single switch or receptacle and extends the box out flush with the surface of the plaster.

Fig. 15-19   Waterproof outlet boxes.

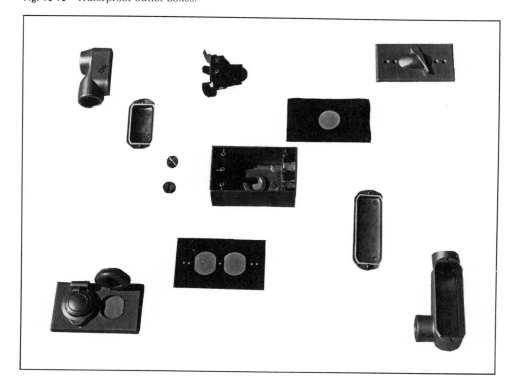

Both metal and nonmetal boxes are made with *knock-outs*, partially cut out round plugs that can be removed with a screwdriver or punch, leaving holes for the installation of standard fittings to hold conductors or conduit in place. Only those knockouts are removed to take care of the number of conductors entering the box. Single conductors, nonmetallic cables, and armored cable must be securely attached to the box with an approved type of box connector. Metal and plastic conduit is held in place with bushings and lock nuts.

In damp or wet locations a watertight or weathertight box called a *condulet* must be used. This is a cast-iron or cast-aluminum box with a cover fitted over a rubber or cork gasket. A weathertight box is one that will keep out rain and snow but will not necessarily exclude moisture. A weatherhead on a service raceway and an angle fixture to carry service conductors through a building wall would utilize this type of fitting. Boxes to support exterior floodlights, garden lighting, and similar applications must be watertight. Watertight boxes are cast with standard pipe threads and are connected to rigid metal conduit with tapered threads.

Fixture Outlet Boxes

Outlet boxes used to support lighting fixtures are usually hung from fixture bars or straps and bolted to the outlet box. The simplest type of lamp holder consists of a porcelain cover with a screw shell to receive a single incandescent bulb. A pull chain to operate a switch may be incorporated in the porcelain plate. If the fixture is one that does not completely cover the outlet box, a *fixture canopy* or *rosette* must be used. Rosettes are needed with *pennant fixtures*, hung from a flexible rubber or thermoplastic cord, and *swag fixtures*, hung from a chain. The chain is attached to the rosette, and a smooth bushing in the rosette allows passage of the flexible fixture wire.

Flush fixtures are installed in large galvanized fixture boxes designed for each type of fixture. The box and fixture must be ordered at the same time. The box is installed before the ceiling finish is applied, and the fixture is installed afterward. Most flush fixtures have an attached junction box for wire connections. Many are prewired, with all necessary fixture wires in place for final connection.

Convenience Receptacles

A convenience receptacle, slotted to receive the prongs of plugs, offers a safe means of connecting portable electrical units into the circuit. Receptacles for general-purpose circuits may be rated at either 15 amps or 20 amps and designed for flush mounting, surface mounting, or mounting in special boxes. Special receptacles are produced for 220-volt appliances. These receptacles are so slotted that a standard 120-volt appliance plug will not enter.

For years the standard 120-volt appliance plug consisted of two parallel blades; however, the "National

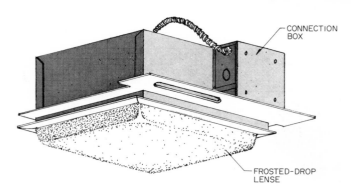

Fig. 15-20 Flush fixture.

Electrical Code" now specifies three-prong grounded receptacles at all convenience outlets. This is to assure that all appliances which require grounding can be grounded by simply attaching them to the convenience outlet. If one receptacle is mounted in an outlet box or device box, it is called a *single receptacle*. *Duplex receptacles* are integrally molded units having two sets of slots. They may be connected in such a way that one receptacle is connected to the circuit at all times and the other is connected to a switch. This system is widely used in residences where the major lighting in a room is by means of floor lamps or table lamps. A *triplex receptacle* consists of three sets of slots. Convenience outlets should be located along all walls in such a manner that a 6-ft cord will reach a receptacle without crossing a wall opening.

Special receptacles are produced for particular applications. *Clock receptacles* are recessed into a device box so that a plug can be inserted into the receptacle, and a clock, picture, sign, or similar unit can be hung flush to the wall with no cord showing. Weather-proof receptacles are used in wet or damp locations. The cover plate has a rubber or neoprene seal to help prevent moisture from entering the box. A hinged metal cover closes over the receptacle when it is not in use. All exterior receptacles should have weatherproof plates, even though they are installed on covered terraces or porches. A receptacle installed in the floor should have a gasketed cover plate that forms a watertight seal when the receptacle is not in use.

Cover plates for receptacles and switches may be made of plastic or metal to match the finish of the receptacle. Plastic cover plates are regularly produced in white, cream, brown, and black. Metal cover plates are produced in many colors and finishes to match any decor. Special combination plates are available to cover one or more switches and one or more outlets installed in a single gang box.

Switches

A switch is the mechanism used to make, break, or change connections in an electric circuit. The simplest type of switch is the *knife switch*, which consists of a copper blade that makes connection through forked contact jaws. This type of switch is used for large switchboards, and if it is to handle large voltages or high amperages, it is usually enclosed in a metal box with the handle on the outside. *Butt-contact switches* consist of platinum or silver points held in contact through an electromagnetic relay or by springs. This type of switch may be operated by a low-voltage remote-control switch. Tumbler, toggle, or push-button *snap switches* are used to control branch lighting circuits. The handle or toggle moves up and down, back and forth, or in and out, causing contact points to open and close. The contacts are snapped open or shut and held in place by phosphor-bronze springs. *Mercury switches* utilize mercury to make the contact. In the better type of mercury switches, two pools of mercury flow together through a hole in a ceramic separator to make or break the circuit as the handle is raised or lowered.

Switches may be single throw or double throw. A *single-throw switch* opens or closes a single wire in a circuit. A *double-throw switch* can be placed in one of three positions to open a circuit or to connect a single wire to either of two other wires. Switches may also be single pole, double pole, or triple pole. A *single-pole switch* has only one set of contacts. A *double-pole switch* opens two wires of a circuit simultaneously, and a *triple-pole switch* opens three wires.

Switches controlling general-lighting and appliance circuits are attached in the hot line of a circuit; the grounded line is never opened. They may be single-throw single-pole switches if only one switch is to control one or more fixtures or outlets. If one or more fixtures are to be controlled from two points, two *three-way switches* are needed. If they are to be controlled from three points, a four-way switch and two three-way switches are used. Three- and four-way switches are used where lights in a long hall are to be controlled from two or three places. They are also used at the top and bottom of staircases. Where there are two doors to a room it is wise to place a three-way switch at each door.

Some toggle switches are made with a tiny long-life neon glow lamp inside the handle. The neon lamp inside the translucent toggle emits a soft glow when the switch is in the off position and gives just enough light to locate the switch in the dark. A similar type of switch has a *pilot light* in a transparent toggle that lights up when the light is on. This type of switch is used for lights that are not in general view, such as exterior floods and garage or outbuilding lights and circuits. Special switches are produced for damp, moist, and wet locations. These switches must be

Fig. 15-21   Assorted receptacles.

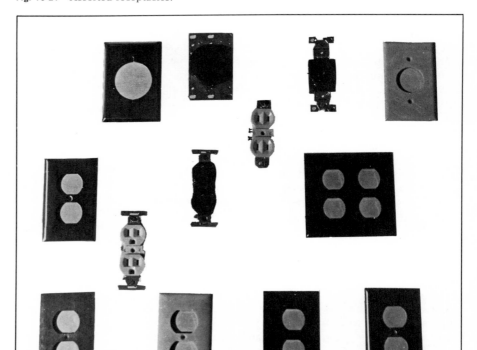

installed in weatherproof or waterproof outlet boxes. Special *explosion-type switches* are produced for use where a spark by the opening or closing of the contacts could cause a fire or explosion.

Dimmer switches vary the voltage supplied to a fixture. The voltage may be lowered by a variable resistor, transformer, or transistor. Most dimmers used for general lighting, either incandescent or fluorescent, are of the transistor type and usually include a switch to completely break the circuit. They are made to fit into a standard device box used for other types of switches. *Delayed-action switches* remain closed for one minute after they are turned off. *Time switches* are attached to a clockwork mechanism that turns off and on at preset times. These are widely used for swimming-pool filters and sprinkling systems and in homes that are frequently unoccupied in the evening.

Circuits may be controlled by *low-voltage switches*. In the low-voltage switching system, wall switches are connected to a central distribution box by low-voltage wiring (6 to 24 volts), usually inexpensive light bell wiring. This wiring does not have to be run in conduit, and there is no danger of shock at the switch. The low-voltage switch actuates a relay in the central distribution box which magnetically closes and opens the high-voltage circuit. Any or all

Fig. 15-22 Switching diagrams.

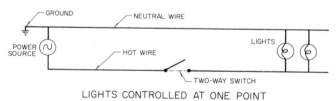

LIGHTS CONTROLLED AT ONE POINT

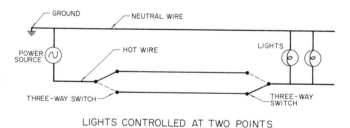

LIGHTS CONTROLLED AT TWO POINTS

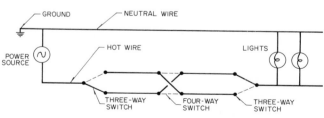

LIGHTS CONTROLLED AT THREE POINTS

Fig. 15-23 Relays for low-voltage switching.

lights can be controlled from any number of individual switches, or they can all be controlled individually or collectively from a central station.

LIGHTING

The amount of light needed to see comfortably is greater than that needed merely to discern surroundings. Different tasks require different amounts of illumination for ease and efficiency of performance. However, proper illumination entails more than the amount of light spotted on the work area. The eye does not adjust readily to extreme contrasts of light and darkness, and so the general illumination of areas surrounding the work surface must also be considered. Glare from any source in the visual field reduces visibility and causes discomfort. Glare may be produced by light reflected back into the eyes from work surfaces, reflective walls, or unshaded windows.

The designer of a lighting system must consider the purpose of the lighting, the source and type of light, its location in relation to both the work surface and the user, and the reflectivity of both the room and work surfaces.

TABLE 15-5 Recommended illumination levels

TYPE OF WORK	FOOTCANDLES ON TASK
Residential	
Living room, dining room, bedrooms, entrances, hallways, stairways, and family rooms	10
Kitchen, laundry, bathroom	30
Kitchen work surfaces and range	50
Shaving and makeup mirrors	50
Sink, workshop, reading fine print	70
Sewing	100
Office	
Corridors, elevators, stairways	20
Interviewing rooms, reception rooms, washrooms	30
Reading or writing	70
General office work, typing, filing	100
Accounting, auditing, bookkeeping	150
Detailed drafting	200

The lighting may be direct, indirect, or a combination of these two. Table 15-5 shows some of the recommended illumination levels for different living and work areas.

Measuring Illumination

Illumination is measured in *footcandles* of light at the work plane. One candlepower is approximately equal to the light emitted from one plumbers' candle, and a footcandle is the amount of light produced by this candle on one square foot of a spherical surface one foot from the light source. As the distance from the source is increased, light diffuses and its intensity, measured in *lumens*, decreases. The density of lumens reaching a given surface is measured with a *footcandle meter* laid on the work surface.

CALCULATING FOOTCANDLES In general the intensity of light varies inversely as the square of the distance from a light source. The light intensity of the source itself can be modified by reflectors or lenses that focus the light rays. How-

Fig. 15-24 Types of lighting.

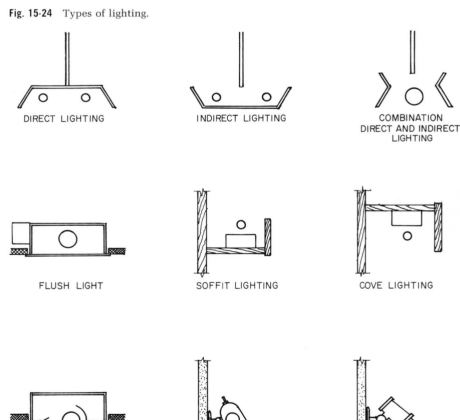

DIRECT LIGHTING   INDIRECT LIGHTING   COMBINATION DIRECT AND INDIRECT LIGHTING

FLUSH LIGHT   SOFFIT LIGHTING   COVE LIGHTING

BULLSEYE SPOT   WALL BRACKET   EXTERIOR FLOOD

ever, the illumination from a direct-lighting fixture, such as a bank of fluorescent lights, depends on the distance of the fixture from the work surface. Lowering such a fixture increases the illumination. With indirect lighting, which is reflected from a ceiling, the intensity of light reaching the work plane varies with the ceiling height. Thus lowering an indirect-lighting fixture does not increase the intensity of illumination on a desk, since the distance from the ceiling to the desk is unaffected.

When indirect-lighting fixtures or fixtures with an indirect component are used, the reflectivity of the ceiling is an important factor. A small room requires more wattage per square foot than a larger room, because of the absorption of light by the walls. Maintenance is also a factor. There is a loss in illumination with aging of the lamp and the accumulation of dirt on fixtures, walls, and ceilings. If the lamps are regularly changed before they burn out and the fixtures are kept clean, the lighting system will maintain approximately 50 to 70 percent of its efficiency—65 percent is considered the average maintenance factor.

Footcandles of illumination can be calculated by either the lumen method or the point-by-point method. The *point-by-point-method* consists of a detailed study of the candlepower at a great number of points on the working surface in terms of the output in lumens of each fixture. This method is very time consuming unless a computer is used. The *lumen method* is usually used to calculate the general lumination of a room. The first step is to determine the total output of the *luminaire*, the complete lighting unit, consisting of lamps, reflectors, and lenses. Manufacturers list the lumen output of each unit for each type of lamp that it can carry. The *coefficient of utilization* must also be determined. This depends on the ceiling or mounting height, the room size and shape, the reflectivity of the walls and ceiling, and the efficiency of the fixture. Finally, the calculation must include the maintenance factor.

For example, suppose a given room is 20 ft by 20 ft and has four 500-watt lamps rated at 9900 lumens each. If the coefficient of utilization is 30 percent and the maintenance factor is 65 percent, then

$$\text{Footcandles} = \frac{\text{no. of lamps} \times \text{lumens per lamp} \times \text{coefficient of utilization} \times \text{maintenance factor}}{\text{area}}$$

$$= \frac{4 \times 9900 \times 0.30 \times 0.65}{20 \times 20} = 19.3$$

LIGHT DISTRIBUTION CURVES A bare lamp or light source will distribute its output or candlepower uniformly in all directions. If a reflector is combined with it to form a luminaire, or fixture, the distribution of light will be altered. The nature and shape of the reflector surface have a marked effect on the output of the fixture. The more reflective the surface of the reflector, the more nearby light is reflected according to the geometry of the surface. Etched, matte, or painted surfaces diffuse light, and it becomes less intense.

Manufacturers of electrical fixtures publish candlepower distribution curves for each fixture they produce. These curves show the candlepower distribution of a particular fixture at a given angle. Thus it is possible to determine the spacing of fixtures needed to provide uniform light intensity over the work surface.

Direct and Indirect Lighting

Direct lighting is light focused directly onto the working plane. *Indirect lighting* is light directed to the ceiling or a wall and reflected onto the work plane. Indirect lighting gives a better, more uniform quality of light and is preferable for schools, offices, and other large areas where reading is done. Either fluorescent or incandescent lamps may by used for indirect lighting.

The light from recessed ceiling fixtures is always direct; it is not possible to direct light upward from a fixture that is above the level of the ceiling. Direct lighting is preferable for stores because it makes brighter reflections from the glossy surfaces of merchandise. Indirect lighting is more expensive and requires more electric power than direct lighting for the same level of illumination, since part of the light is absorbed by the surface to which it is directed.

Incandescent Lamps

An incandescent lamp, or light bulb, consists of a filament, a base, and a globe. The *filament* is a coiled tungsten wire which gives off light when it is heated by the flow of electricity. The *base* is an insulated brass shell which holds the lamp together. This shell is formed with threads to screw into the threaded brass receptor. The glass *globe* is used to protect the filament from damage and oxidation. The globe contains either a vacuum, an inert gas composed of argon, nitrogen, or other gases. It may be clear glass or frosted on either the inside or the outside. Frosted globes give a softer light than unfrosted ones.

Incandescent bulbs are rated by the number of watts of power they consume. Those for general illumination are produced in wattages from 15 to 300. Some provide three levels of brightness, for use with three-way fixtures. Special-purpose lamps up to 1500 watts are produced for outdoor or high-intensity lighting. However, these have been largely replaced with high-voltage electric-discharge lights.

Incandescent lamps are made in five standard socket sizes. The three smaller sizes are rated in volts rather than watts. *Miniature*, the smallest socket, is for lamps under 25 volts; some Christmas-tree lights fall into this classification. *Intermediate* sockets are used for lamps up to 125 volts; outdoor decorative lighting and some chandeliers use this type of light. *Candelabra* sockets, up to 125 volts, are used for outdoor decorative lighting, electrified candelabra, and some chandeliers and may be obtained in types that flicker like a candle. *Medium* is the standard size for general lighting, 15 to 300 watts. *Mogul* is for large-based lamps of 300 to 1500 watts, used mostly as outdoor floods.

A new development in incandescent lighting is the *parabolic aluminized reflector* (PAR). This lamp has a built-in reflector made with a multilayer metallic coating that is reflective to light but transparent to infrared radiation. This allows two-thirds of the heat of the lamp to be transmitted out the back. Air drawn through ventilated fixtures not only reduces the heat radiated into the room, but affords a supply of heated air that can be used to supplement the building heating system.

One of the latest developments is the *tungsten-halogen lamp,* sometimes referred to as the *quartz-iodine cycle lamp.* This incandescent lamp uses a tungsten filament surrounded by halogen gas and is an extremely compact unit. The elements for a 250-watt tungsten-halogen lamp can be put into the same size globe as those for a 150-watt PAR lamp, and its life is double that of the standard incandescent bulb.

Electric Discharge Lamps

Electric discharge lamps, also called *gaseous discharge lamps,* operate on a different principle from the incandescent lamp. Instead of passing current through a tungsten wire until it becomes white hot and gives off light, an electric discharge lamp passes current through a gas, such as neon, mercury vapor, or sodium vapor, until the gas glows. A high voltage (1000 volts or more), is needed to force the current to jump from a cathode at one end of the tube, through the gas, to the other end of the tube. Less voltage is required is the cathode is preheated. Hence there are two types of electric discharge lamps, hot cathode and cold cathode.

Neon, sodium-vapor, and mercury-vapor lamps are of the cold-cathode type. Neon lights are widely used for outline signs. The brilliant colors are not in the gas, but are developed by applying various substances to the walls of

Fig. 15-25 Diagram of a fluorescent lamp. When the switch is closed, the bimetallic strip expands and makes contact with stationary electrode to provide starting voltage for initial heating of the cathode. When the lamp is operating, the metal cools and the contact is broken.

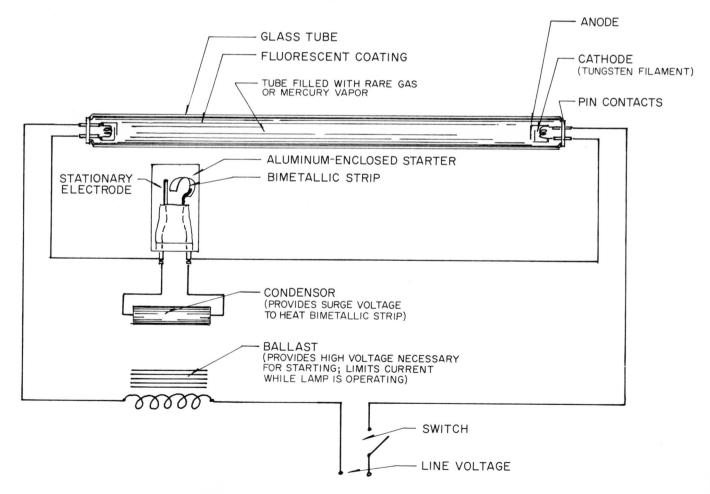

the tube. Mercury-vapor and sodium-vapor lights are used for outdoor and street lighting and in factories and commercial buildings where an efficient high-intensity light is needed. New high-intensity discharge lamps developed for interior use include a white-phosphor-coated mercury-vapor light, which contains metallic iodide vapor in addition to the mercury vapor and is called a *metal-halide lamp.*

FLUORESCENT LAMPS   A fluorescent lamp is a hot-cathode type of gaseous discharge lamp with the inside of the tube coated with phosphorus. This inside coating absorbs radiant energy of short wavelengths and reradiates it at longer wavelengths. Fluorescent lamps come in various lengths; the wattage varies with the length of tubing. Table 15-6 indicates the wattage for each length. The tubes may be straight or formed into a circle to fit into a recessed fixture.

TABLE 15-6   Wattage of fluorescent lamps

TUBE LENGTH, IN.	WATTAGE
9	6
12	8
21	13
15	14
18	15
24	20
36	30
48	40
60	100

The circuit of a fluorescent lamp consists of a *ballast* and a *starter* and the necessary wiring. If two lamps are used in the fixture, a ballast and a starter are needed for each lamp, and a capacitor is added to make one lamp lead the other. This reduces the flicker, or *stroboscopic effect,*

Fig. 15-26   Integrated ceiling. (*H. H. Robertson Company.*)

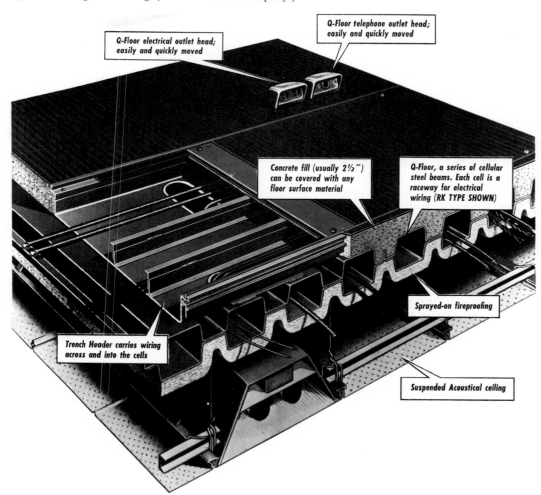

Q-Floor telephone outlet head; easily and quickly moved

Q-Floor electrical outlet head; easily and quickly moved

Concrete fill (usually 2½") can be covered with any floor surface material

Q-Floor, a series of cellular steel beams. Each cell is a raceway for electrical wiring (RK TYPE SHOWN)

Sprayed-on fireproofing

Trench Header carries wiring across and into the cells

Suspended Acoustical ceiling

caused by the fact that each lamp turns on and off twice during each cycle.

Fluorescent lamps are frequently used where a high light intensity is needed, as they create less heat than incandescent lamps of comparable wattage. They also put out more light for a given amperage and so are more efficient. Many fluorescent lights have a purplish cast that causes a slight color distortion in interior installations. However, newly developed coatings result in a light that is closer to daylighting; such lights are designated variously as warm white, cool white, daylight, or soft white. *Regular-start lamps* must warm up before they will produce light. *Quick-start lamps* will light immediately. Special fluorescent lamps for commercial applications are produced to operate at 600 volts and at 400 Hz. The service life of regular-start fluorescent tubes is about 7,500 hours, and that of the rapid-start type is about 4,000 hours. The life depends more on the number of starts than on the total time operated. In some office buildings it has been found more efficient to leave fluorescent fixtures on 24 hours a day than to turn them off whenever they are not needed. The savings in tube replacements offset the additional electricity used.

SLIMLINE LAMPS　Slimline lamps are a single-pin, instant-start, fluorescent lamp. They are superior to ordinary fluorescent lamps in that they do not flicker, have better color, and can be obtained with a low surface brightness. Like standard fluorescent lamps, they require less wiring, generate less heat, and cost less to operate than incandescent lamps. The starting voltage necessary for multiple operation of slimline lamps is between 450 and 700 volts.

Integrated-ceiling Units

An *integrated ceiling* is a suspended ceiling that includes all the necessary fixtures for sound control, lighting, heating, cooling, and ventilation for the room. Each part is specifically designed as a component of a system. The heat of lighting fixtures may be removed by water tubes incorporated in the fixture reflector. The heat picked up by the water may be dissipated by circulation through a cooling tower in summer or utilized to supplement the heating system in winter. Slots or perforations in the ceiling tile or supporting framework can be used to distribute conditioned air to heat or cool the room.

QUESTIONS

1. What determines the resistance to the flow of electric current in a circuit?

2. What causes electricity to flow through a circuit?

3. What is Ohm's law, and how is it used?

4. How many amperes of current must a circuit carry to supply a 2200-watt appliance at 110 volts?

5. If electric power costs 6 cents/kwh, how much would it cost to run a 150-watt lamp for 24 hours?

6. Explain the difference between ac and dc power.

7. Why is it economical to use high voltages for long-distance transmission lines?

8. How is the high voltage from transmission lines reduced to lower voltages for use by the consumer?

9. What is a service drop?

10. What is a circuit breaker, and how does it work?

11. Calculate the size of a service panel for a 4000-sq-ft residence with all electric appliances.

12. What four factors must be considered in selecting the type of insulation to be used on conductors?

13. Describe the properties of conductors designated as RH, RHW, and THW.

14. What is concealed knob-and-tube wiring, and where is it used?

15. What is the purpose of conduit?

16. Describe three types of conduit.

17. What is a surface raceway, and where is it used?

18. Describe three types of underfloor raceways.

19. Where is a device box used?

20. How is a device box attached in wood frame construction?

21. Describe a fixture outlet box.

22. Name five types of switches, and explain how they work.

23. What is a footcandle?

24. What determines the amount of illumination that reaches a surface from a light source?

25. Explain the lumen method of calculating footcandles.

26. What is the difference between direct and indirect lighting?

27. Describe an incandescent lamp and give its advantages and limitations.

28. What are the advantages and disadvantages of fluorescent tubes?

REFERENCES FOR FURTHER STUDY

Callender, John Hancock: "Time-saver Standards," 4th ed., McGraw-Hill, New York, 1966.

Croft, T., rev. by C. Carr: "American Electrician's Handbook," 8th ed., McGraw-Hill, New York, 1961.

Fink, Donald G., and John M. Carroll (eds.), "Standard Handbook for Electrical Engineers," 10th ed., McGraw-Hill, New York, 1968.

Hart, Charles J.: The NECA Standard of Installation, *The Construction Specifier*, November 1969, p. 73.

Henderson, Weldon W.: Lighting and Electrical Specifications, *The Construction Specifier*, April 1970, p. 36.

National Electrical Contractors' Association: 1730 Rhode Island Avenue, N.W., Washington, D.C., 20036. "NECA Standard of Installation," 1970. "Electrical Design Library," 1969.

Stetka, Frank: "NFPA Handbook of the National Electrical Code," McGraw-Hill, New York, 1969.

Underwriters' Laboratories, Inc.: 207 East Ohio Street, Chicago, Ill., 60611. "Electrical Appliance and Utilization Equipment List," 1970. "Electrical Construction Materials List," 1970.

APPENDIX

TRADE ASSOCIATIONS IN THE CONSTRUCTION INDUSTRY

ABS Institute, Inc., Pan American Building, 200 Park Avenue, New York, N.Y., 10017.

Access Floor Manufacturers' Association, 724 York Road, Baltimore, Md., 21204.

Acoustical Society of America, 335 East 45th Street, New York, N.Y., 10017.

Adhesive and Sealant Council, 159 North Dearborn Street, Chicago, Ill., 60601.

A.E.C. Western Catalog and Reference File, 5909 West Third Street, Los Angeles, Calif., 90036.

Air Conditioning and Refrigeration Institute, 1815 North Fort Myer Drive, Arlington, Va., 22209.

Air Pollution Control Association, 4400 Fifth Avenue, Pittsburgh, Penn., 15213.

The Aluminum Association, 420 Lexington Avenue, New York, N.Y., 10017.

American Arbitration Association, 140 West 51st Street, New York, N.Y., 10020.

American Association of Cost Engineers, P.O. Box 5199, University of Alabama, University, Ala., 35486.

American Concrete Institute, P.O. Box 4754 Bedford Station, Detroit, Mich., 48217.

American Concrete Paving Association, 1211 West 22d Street, Suite 727, Oakbrook, Ill., 60523.

American Concrete Pipe Association, 1501 Wilson Boulevard, Arlington, Va., 22209.

American Forest Products Industries Association, 1816 N Street, N.W., Washington, D.C., 20036.

American Hardboard Association, Suite 1452, 20 North Wacker Drive, Chicago, Ill., 60601.

American Hot Dip Galvanizers' Association, 1000 Vermont Avenue, N.W., Washington, D.C., 20005.

American Institute of Architects, 1785 Massachusetts Avenue, N.W., Washington, D.C., 20006.

American Institute of Steel Construction, 101 Park Avenue, New York, N.Y., 10017.

American Institute of Timber Construction, 1657 K Street, N.W., Washington, D.C., 20006.

American Insurance Association, 85 John Street, New York, N.Y., 10038.

American Iron and Steel Institute, 150 East 42d Street, New York, N.Y., 10017.

American National Standards Institute, Inc., 1430 Broadway, New York, N.Y., 10018.

American Parquet Association, Inc., 1750 Tower Building, Little Rock, Ark., 72201.

American Pipe Fittings Association, 60 East 42d Street, New York, N.Y., 10017.

American Plywood Association, 1119 A Street, Tacoma, Wash., 98401.

American Public Works Association, 1313 East 60th Street, Chicago, Ill., 60637.

American Road Builders' Association, ARBA Building, 525 School Street, S.W., Washington, D.C., 20024.

American Society of Architectural Hardware Consultants, P.O. Box 599, Mill Valley, Calif., 94941.

American Society of Civil Engineers, 345 East 47th Street, New York, N.Y., 10017.

American Society of Concrete Constructors, 2510 Dempster Street, Des Plaines, Ill., 60016.

American Society of Heating, Refrigeration and Air Conditioning Engineers, 345 East 47th Street, New York, N.Y., 10017.

American Society of Landscape Architects, 2013 Eye Street, N.W., Washington, D.C., 20006.

American Society of Mechanical Engineers, 345 East 47th Street, New York, N.Y., 10017.

American Society of Metals, Metals Park, Ohio, 44073.

American Society of Planning Officials, 1313 East 60th Street, Chicago, Ill., 60637.

American Society of Safety Engineers, 850 Busse Highway, Park Ridge, Ill., 60068.

American Society of Sanitary Engineering, 228 Standard Building, Cleveland, Ohio, 44113.

American Society for Testing and Materials, 1916 Race Street, Philadelphia, Penn., 19103.

American Waterworks Association, 2 Park Avenue, New York, N.Y., 10016.

American Welding Society, 345 East 47th Street, New York, N.Y., 10017.

American Wood Council, Suite 1625, 5454 Wisconsin Avenue, Chevy Chase, Md., 20018.

American Wood Preservers' Institute, 2600 Virginia Avenue, N.W., Washington, D.C., 20037.

American Zinc Institute, Inc., 292 Madison Avenue, New York, N.Y., 10017.

Architectural Aluminum Manufacturers' Association, 35 East Wacker Drive, Chicago, Ill., 60601.

Architectural Precast Concrete Association, 2201 East 46th Street, Indianapolis, Ind., 46205.

Architectural Woodwork Institute, Suite A, Chesterfield House, 5055 South Chesterfield Road, Arlington, Va., 22206.

Asphalt and Vinyl Asbestos Tile Institute, 101 Park Avenue, New York, N.Y., 10017.

The Asphalt Institute, Asphalt Institute Building, University of Maryland, College Park, Md., 20740.

Asphalt Roofing Manufacturers' Association, 757 Third Avenue, New York, N.Y., 10017.

Associated General Contractors of America, Inc., 1957 E Street, N.W., Washington, D.C., 20006.

Association Air Balance Council, 2146 Sunset Boulevard, Los Angeles, Calif., 90026.

Builders' Hardware Manufacturers' Association, 60 East 42d Street, New York, N.Y., 10017.

Building Materials Research Institute, Inc., 60 East 42d Street, New York, N.Y., 10017.

Building Officials' Conference of America, Inc., 1313 East 60th Street, Chicago, Ill., 60637.

Building Research Advisory Board, Dept. U.S.G., c/o National Academy of Sciences, 2101 Constitution Avenue, N.W., Washington, D.C., 20418.

Building Research Institute, 2101 Constitution Avenue, N.W., Washington, D.C., 20418.

Building Stone Institute, 420 Lexington Avenue, New York, N.Y., 10017.

Bureau of Reclamation Library, Building 67, Denver Federal Center, Denver, Colo., 80225.

Cabinet and Fixture Manufacturers' Guild, Suite 625, 1255 Post Street, San Francisco, Calif., 94109.

Calcium Chloride Institute, 909 Ring Building, Washington, D.C., 20036.

California Drywall Contractors' Association, Suite 305, 1830 West Eighth Street, Los Angeles, Calif., 90057.

California Lathing and Plastering Contractors' Association, 3558 West Eighth St., Los Angeles, Calif., 90005.

California Redwood Association, 617 Montgomery Street, San Francisco, Calif., 94111.

Canadian Prestressed Concrete Institute, 120 Eglington Avenue, East Toronto 12, Ontario, Canada.

Cast Iron Pipe Research Association, Suite 3440, Prudential Plaza, Chicago, Ill., 60601.

Cast Iron Soil Pipe Foundation, P.O. Box 5353, Metropolitan Station, Los Angeles, Calif., 90055.

Cast Iron Soil Pipe Institute, 2029 K Street, N.W., Washington, D.C., 20006.

Ceiling and Interior Systems Contractors' Association, 1201 Waukegan Road, Glenview, Ill., 60025.

Cellular Concrete Association, 755 Boylston Street, Boston, Mass., 02116.

Cement and Concrete Association of Australia, 147 Walker Street, North Sydney N.S.W. 2060, Australia.

Cement and Concrete Association (Great Britain), 52 Grosvenor Gardens, London SW1, England.

Ceramic Tile Institute, 3415 West Eighth Street, Los Angeles, Calif., 90005.

Chain Link Fence Manufacturers' Institute, 60 East 42d Street, New York, N.Y., 10017.

Clay Flue Lining Institute, Elephant Road M.R.-1, Perkasie, Pa., 18944.

Clay Products Association, P.O. Box 172, Barrington, Ill., 60010.

Clearinghouse for Federal Scientific and Technical Information, Springfield, Va., 22151.

Committee of Galvanized Sheet Producers, American Iron and Steel Institute, 150 East 42d Street, New York, N.Y., 10017.

Committee of Stainless Steel Producers, American Iron and Steel Institute, 150 East 42d Street, New York, N.Y., 10017.

Committee on Environmental Improvement, 1155 16th Street, N.W., Washington, D.C., 20036.

Concrete Joint Institute, Room 1604, 228 North La Salle Street, Chicago, Ill., 60601.

Concrete Reinforcing Steel Institute, 228 North La Salle Street, Chicago, Ill., 60601.

The Concrete Society Limited, Terminal House, Grosvenor Gardens, London SW1, England.

Construction Specifications Institute, Suite 300, 1150 17th Street, N.W., Washington, D.C., 20036.

Consulting Engineers' Council, 1155 15th Street, N.W., Washington, D.C., 20005.

Contracting Plasterers' and Lathers' International Association, 1343 H Street, N.W., Washington, D.C., 20006.

Copper Development Association, Inc., 405 Lexington Avenue, New York, N.Y., 10017.

Copper Institute, 50 Broadway, New York, N.Y., 10004.

Desco International Association, P.O. Box 74, Buffalo, N.Y., 14240.

Drywall Industry Trust Fund, Suite 712, 9800 South Sepulveda Boulevard, Los Angeles, Calif., 90045.

Edison Electric Institute, 750 Third Avenue, New York, N.Y., 10017.

Electric Heating Association, 437 Madison Avenue, New York, N.Y., 10022.

Expanded Shale, Clay and Shale Institute, 1041 National Press Building, N.W., Washington, D.C., 20004.

Facing Tile Institute, 333 North Michigan Avenue, Chicago, Ill., 60601.

Federation of Societies for Paint Technology, 121 South Broad Street, Philadelphia, Penn., 19107.

Fine Hardwoods Association, 666 North Lake Shore Drive, Chicago, Ill., 60611.

Flat Glass Jobbers' Association, 6210 West 10th Street, Topeka, Kan., 66615.

Flexcore Manufacturers' Association, 6739 West Belmont Avenue, Chicago, Ill., 60634.

Furring and Lathing Bureau, 5437 Laurel Canyon Boulevard, North Hollywood, Calif., 91607.

Gas Appliance Manufacturers' Association, Inc., 60 East 42d Street, New York, N.Y., 10017.

Guild for Religious Architecture, 1346 Connecticut Avenue, N.W., Washington, D.C., 20036.

Gypsum Association, 201 North Wells Street, Chicago, Ill., 60606.

Hardwood Association, 205 West Wacker Drive, Chicago, Ill., 60606.

Hardwood Plywood Institute, 2310 South Walter Reed Drive, Arlington, Va., 22206.

Hardwood Plywood Manufacturers' Association, 2310 South Walter Reed Drive, Arlington, Va., 22206.

Highway Research Board, 2101 Constitution Avenue, N.W., Washington, D.C., 20418.

Illuminating Engineering Society, 345 East 47th Street, New York, N.Y., 10017.

Indiana Limestone Institute, Inc., 702 H Street, N.W., Washington, D.C., 20001.

Insect Wire Screening Bureau, 441 Lexington Avenue, New York, N.Y., 10017.

Institute of Boiler and Radiator Manufacturers, 393 Seventh Avenue, New York, N.Y., 10001.

Institute of Electrical and Electronics Engineering, 345 East 47th Street, New York, N.Y., 10017.

Institute of Heating and Air Conditioning Industries, Inc., 5107 West First Street, Los Angeles, Calif., 90004.

Institute of Traffic Engineers, 2029 K Street, N.W., Washington, D.C., 20006.

Instrument Society of America, 530 William Penn Place, Pittsburgh, Penn., 15219.

Insulation Board Institute, 111 West Washington Street, Chicago, Ill., 60602.

International Association of Electrical Inspectors, Room 300, 201 East Eire Street, Chicago, Ill., 60611.

International Association of Plumbing and Mechanical Officials, 5032 Alhambra Avenue, Los Angeles, Calif., 90032.

Lead Industries Association, 292 Madison Avenue, New York, N.Y., 10017.

Lighting Protection Institute, 2 North Riverside Place, Chicago, Ill., 60606.

The Linen Supply Association of America, P.O. Box 2427, Arthur Godfrey Road, Miami Beach, Fla., 33140.

Lightweight Aggregate Producers' Association, 546 Hamilton Street, Allentown, Penn., 18101.

Lumber Association of Southern California, 2351 West Third Street, Los Angeles, Calif., 90057.

Manufacturers' Standardization Society of the Valve and Fittings Industry, 420 Lexington Avenue, New York, N.Y., 10017.

Maple Flooring Manufacturers' Association, Suite 104, 424 Washington Avenue, Oshkosh, Wisc., 54901.

Marble Institute of America, Inc., Pennsylvania Building, Washington, D.C., 20005.

Mason Contractors' Association of America, 208 South La Salle Street, Chicago, Ill., 60604.

Masonry Research, 2550 Beverly Boulevard, Los Angeles, Calif., 90057.

Metal Lathing and Furring Contractors' Association, Inc., 5437 Laurel Canyon Boulevard, North Hollywood, Calif., 91607.

Metal Roof Deck Technical Institute, 53 West Jackson Boulevard, Chicago, Ill., 60603.

Mo-Sai Institute, Inc., 110 Social Hall Avenue, Salt Lake City, Utah, 84111.

National Ash Association, Inc., 1819 H Street, N.W., Washington, D.C., 20006.

National Association of Architectural Metal Manufacturers, 228 North La Salle Street, Chicago, Ill., 60601.

National Association of Corrosion Engineers, 2400 West Loop South, Houston, Tex., 77027.

National Association of Home Builders, 1625 L Street, N.W., Washington, D.C., 20036.

National Association of Elevator Contractors, Shirlington Trust Building, 2772 South Randolf Street, Arlington, Va., 22206.

National Association of Power Engineers, Inc., 176 West Adams Street, Chicago, Ill., 60603.

National Builders' Hardware Association, 1290 Avenue of the Americas, New York, N.Y., 10019.

National Building Granite Quarries Association, Inc., P.O. Box 444, Concord, N.H., 03302.

National Cinder Concrete Products Association, Box 67, Primrose, Pa., 19019.

National Clay Pipe Institute, 1028 Connecticut Avenue, N.W., Washington, D.C., 20036.

National Concrete Masonry Association, P.O. Box 9185, Rosslyn Station, Arlington, Va., 22209.

National Council of Acoustical Consultants, 80 Danbury Road, Wilton, Conn., 06897.

National Crushed Stone Association, 1415 Elliot Place, Washington, D.C., 20007.

National Electrical Contractors' Association, 1730 Rhode Island Avenue, N.W., Washington, D.C., 20036.

National Electrical Manufacturers' Association, 155 East 44th Street, New York, N.Y., 10017.

National Fire Protection Association, 60 Batterymarch Street, Boston, Mass., 02110.

National Flaxseed Processors' Association, 6132 North Forest Glen, Chicago, Ill., 60646.

National Hardwood Manufacturers' Association, Inc., 400 West Madison Street, Chicago, Ill., 60606.

National Lime Association, 5010 Wisconsin Avenue, N.W., Washington, D.C., 20016.

National Limestone Institute, Inc., 1315 16th Street, N.W., Washington, D.C., 20036.

National LP-Gas Association, 79 West Monroe Street, Chicago, Ill., 60603.

National Lumber Manufacturers' Association, 1619 Massachusetts Avenue, N.W., Washington, D.C., 20036.

National Oak Flooring Manufacturers' Association, 814 Stereck Building, Memphis, Tenn., 38103.

National Paint, Varnish and Lacquer Association, Inc., 1500 Rhode Island Ave., N.W., Washington, D.C., 20005.

National Particleboard Association, 711 14th Street, N.W., Washington, D.C., 20005.

National Precast Concrete Association, 2201 East 46th Street, Indianapolis, Ind., 46205.

National Ready Mixed Concrete Association, 900 Spring Street, Silver Spring, Md., 20910.

National Sand and Gravel Association, 900 Spring Street, Silver Spring, Md., 20910.

National Slag Association, 300 South Washington Street, Alexandria, Va., 22314.

National Slate Association, 455 West 23d Street, New York, N.Y., 10011.

National Society of Professional Engineers, 2029 K Street, N.W., Washington, D.C., 20006.

National Terrazzo and Mosaic Association, Inc., 716 Church Street, Arlington, Va., 22314.

National Woodwork Manufacturers' Association, 400 West Madison Street, Chicago, Ill., 60606.

Northeastern Woodwork Manufacturers' Association, Inc., 271 Madison Avenue, New York, N.Y., 10016.

Northern Hemlock and Hardwood Manufacturers' Association, Washington Building, Oshkosh, Wisc., 54901.

N.Z. Portland Cement Association, P.O. Box 2792, Securities House, 126 The Terrace, Wellington, C.I., New Zealand.

Painting and Decorating Contractors of America, 2625 West Peterson Avenue, Chicago, Ill., 60645.

Parking and Highway Improvement Contractors' Association, Inc., 5107 West First Street, Los Angeles, Calif., 90004.

Pavement Safety Corporation, 542 Old Orchard Road, Skokie, Ill., 60076.

Pennsylvania Slate Producers' Guild, P.O. Box 98, Pen Argyl, Penn., 18072.

Perlite Institute, 45 West 45th Street, New York, N.Y., 10036.

Piping Promotion Trust, 742 Ponce de Leon Place, Atlanta, Ga., 30306.

Plastering Information Bureau, 11520 San Vicente Boulevard, Los Angeles, Calif., 90049.

Plumbing Brass Institute, 221 North La Salle Street, Chicago, Ill., 60601.

Plumbing and Drainage Institute, 1018 North Austin Boulevard, Oak Park, Ill., 60302.

Plywood Fabricator Service, Inc., 1119 A Street, Tacoma, Wash. 98401.

Plywood Research Foundation, 620 East 26th Street, Tacoma, Wash., 98402.

Porcelain Enamel Institute, Inc., 1900 L Street, N.W., Washington, D.C., 20036.

Portland Cement Association, 33 West Grand Avenue, Chicago, Ill., 60610.

Portland Cement Research and Development Laboratories, 5420 Old Orchard Road, Skokie, Ill., 60076.

Prestressed Concrete Institute, 205 West Wacker Drive, Chicago, Ill., 60606.

The Producers' Council, 1717 Massachusetts Avenue, N.W., Washington, D.C., 20036.

Red Cedar Shingle and Handsplit Shake Bureau, 5510 White Building, Seattle, Wash., 98101.

Roofing Industry Trust, 520 South Virgil Avenue, Los Angleles, Calif., 90005.

Scaffolding and Shoring Institute, 2130 Keith Building, Cleveland, Ohio, 44115.

Sealed Insulating Glass Manufacturers' Association, 2217 Tribune Tower, Chicago, Ill., 60611.

Sheet Metal and Air Conditioning Contractors' National Association, Suite 200, 1611 North Kent Street, Arlington, Va., 22209.

Sheet Metal Industry Fund of Los Angeles, Suite 114, 1830 West Eighth Street, Los Angeles, Calif., 90057.

Society of Fire Protection Engineers, 60 Batterymarch Street, Boston, Mass., 02110.

Society of Plastic Engineers, 65 Prospect Street, Stamford, Conn., 06902.

Southern Building Code Congress, 1116 Brown-Manx Building, Birmingham, Ala., 35203.

Southern California Plastering Institute, Inc., 11520 San Vicente Boulevard, Los Angeles, Calif., 90049.

Southern Cypress Manufacturers' Association, 1640 West Road, Jacksonville, Fla., 32216.

Southern Forest Products Association, P.O. Box 52468, New Orleans, La., 70150.

Southern Pine Association, P.O. Box 52468, New Orleans, La., 70150.

Southern Pine Inspection Bureau, P.O. Box 52468, New Orleans, La., 70150.

Steel Bar Mills Association, 188 West Randolph Street, Chicago, Ill., 60601.

Steel Deck Institute, 9836 West Roosevelt Road, Westchester, Ill., 60153.

Steel Door Institute, 2130 Keith Building, Cleveland, Ohio, 44115.

Steel Joist Institute, 2001 Jefferson Davis Highway, Arlington, Va., 22202.

Steel Kitchen Cabinet Manufacturers' Association, 1120 Chester Avenue, Clevelend, Ohio, 44114.

Steel Structures Painting Council, 4400 Fifth Avenue, Pittsburgh, Penn., 15213.

Steel Window Institute, 18445 Harvest Lane, Brookfield, Wisc., 53005.

Structural Clay Products Institute, 1520 28th Street, N.W., Washington, D.C., 20036.

Stucco Manufacturers' Association, 15926 Kittridge, Van Nuys, Calif., 91406.

Tile Council of America, Inc., 360 Lexington Avenue, New York, N.Y., 10017.

Tufted Textile Manufacturers' Association, P.O. Box 8, Dalton, Ga., 30720.

Underwriters' Laboratories, Inc., 207 East Ohio Street, Chicago, Ill., 60611.

U.S. Department of Commerce, Business and Defense Services Administration, Office of Technical Services, Commodity Standards Division, Washington, D.C., 20025.

United States Shellac Importers' Association, Inc., 425 Park Avenue, New York, N.Y., 10022.

Vermiculite Institute, Room 1785, 141 West Jackson Boulevard, Chicago, Ill., 60604.

Vinyl Fabrics Institute, 60 East 42d Street, New York, N.Y., 10017.

Water Pollution Control Federation, 3900 Wisconsin Avenue, N.W., Washington, D.C., 20016.

West Coast Lumber Inspection Bureau, 1410 Southwest Morrison Street, Portland, Ore., 97250.

Western Red Cedar Lumber Association, Yeon Building, Portland, Ore., 97204.

Western Wood Moulding Producers, Yeon Building, Portland, Ore., 97204.

Western Wood Products Association, Yeon Building, Portland, Ore., 97204.

Wire Reinforcement Institute, 5034 Wisconsin Avenue, N.E., Washington, D.C., 20016.

Wood Flooring Institute of America, 201 North Wells Street, Chicago, Ill., 60606.

Woodwork Institute of California, 1833 Broadway, Fresno, Calif., 93721.